# THE BIOLOGICAL BASIS OF HUMAN BEHAVIOR: A CRITICAL REVIEW

*Second Edition*

Robert W. Sussman

*Washington University, St. Louis*

*Advances in Human Evolution Series*

Prentice Hall, Upper Saddle River, New Jersey 07458

**Library of Congress Cataloging-in-Publication Data**

The biological basis of human behavior : a critical review / [edited
  by] Robert W. Sussman.
        p.   cm.
     Includes bibliographical references and index.
     ISBN 0-13-799735-3
     1. Sociobiology. 2. Psychobiology. 3. Genetic psychology.
  I. Sussman, Robert W.   (date).
  GN635.9.B532   1999
  304.5—dc21                                              98-25995
                                                             CIP

Editorial Director: *Charlyce Jones Owen*
Editor-in-Chief: *Nancy Roberts*
Director of Manufacturing and Production: *Barbara Kittle*
Managing Editor: *Sharon Chambliss*
Production Liaison: *Fran Russello*
Project Manager: *Marianne Hutchinson (Pine Tree Composition)*
Prepress and Manufacturing Buyer: *Lynn Pearlman*
Cover Director: *Jane Conte*
Cover Designer: *Bruce Kenselaar*
Cover Images: *Shaidar Skull–Eric Trinkaus; Children photo–Michelle Souther; Lemur photo–R.*
Marketing Manager: *Christopher DeJohn*

*For permission to use copyrighted material, grateful acknowledgment
is made to the copyright holders on pages xii–xiv, which are hereby
made part of this copyright page.*

This book was set in 10/12 Minion by Pine Tree Composition
and was printed and bound by Banta Company.
The cover was printed by Phoenix Color Corp.

©1999 by Prentice-Hall, Inc.
Upper Saddle River, New Jersey 07458

Printed in the United States of America

10   9   8   7   6   5   4   3

ISBN 0-13-799735-3

Prentice-Hall International (UK) Limited, *London*
Prentice-Hall of Australia Pty. Limited, *Sydney*
Prentice-Hall Canada Inc., *Toronto*
Prentice-Hall Hispanoamericana, S. A., *Mexico*
Prentice-Hall of India Private Limited, *New Delhi*
Prentice-Hall of Japan, Inc., *Tokyo*
Prentice-Hall Asia Pte. Ltd., *Singapore*
Editora Prentice-Hall do Brasil, Ltda., *Rio de Janeiro*

*I dedicate this book to Linda Sussman, and to my
two daughters, Katya and Diana, who are the wonderful
products of genes, environment, and chance.*

# ADVANCES IN HUMAN EVOLUTION
A Prentice Hall College Division Series of Texts and Monographs

**Advances in Human Evolution** is devoted to the timely publication of texts, monographs, and major edited works on all aspects of human evolution from the origin and diversification of the ape and human families to the appearance and differentiation of modern *Homo sapiens*. An interdisciplinary approach will be followed in this series emphasizing new avenues of research in human evolution through genetics, bimolecular and DNA studies, human biological studies, paleoecological and paleobehavioral studies, advanced methods of absolute dating, and seminal comparative anatomical, archaeological, and paleontological analyses. Many books in the series will be targeted for use in colleges and universities either as texts or as supplemental readings at the undergraduate and graduate levels.

### Series Editor: Prof. Russell L. Ciochon, The University of Iowa

## Now available:

**The Human Evolution Source Book** (©1993), Russell L. Ciochon and John G. Fleagle (Editors).

**Integrative Paths to the Past: Paleoanthropological Advances in Honor of E. Clark Howell** (©1994), Robert S. Corruccini and Russell L. Ciochon (Editors).

**The Biological Basis of Human Behavior: A Critical Review, 2/E**(©1999) Robert W. Sussman (Editor).

**The New Physical Anthropology**(©1999) Shirley C. Strum, Donald G. Lindburg, and David Hamburg (Editors).

Proposals for new books should be sent to the series editor who will begin the review process.

# Contents

## Part III.   The Biological Basis of Race and Racism   178

## Part IV.   The New Biological Determinism   253

# Part V.  The Brain, Hormones,
# and Human Behavior  331

# Introduction

Why do we behave the way we do? Surely humans have been occupied with this question ever since they were first able to formulate it. With advances in our understanding of genetics, hormones, and neuropsychology, our accumulation of hominid fossils, and our growing knowledge of animal and especially primate behavior, there is a feeling by many that we now better understand the biological basis of human behavior. Furthermore, there is a tendency for many to emphasize and popularize the underlying biological factors that may determine this behavior. For example, titles of recent popular books and magazine articles have read: "Infidelity: It may be in our genes"; "The biology of violence"; "Race, genes and I.Q."; "Human nature: why do we do what we do?; "Demonic males: Apes and the origins of human violence." In this reader, I include articles in which the authors examine some of the current scientific evidence available on these subjects.

This book was developed for an undergraduate anthropology course entitled "The Biological Basis of Human Behavior." Since the popular media, as well as scientific books and articles on this subject, constantly bombard students, it is necessary for them to be able to evaluate this literature. Questions on human nature and the biological basis of human behavior, at least for the past century or so, have been the subject matter of anthropology. Yet, there are few anthropology courses at present that directly address this subject, a subject that is not new but has been resurfacing for generations. The biological basis of human nature and the ways in which human variation affects this nature (and vice versa) were topics of controversy over a hundred years ago when Charles Darwin wrote *The Decent of Man* and when Thomas Huxley wrote *Man's Place in Nature*.

The influence of environment versus biology over behavior has been hotly debated ever since. In fact, many of the "new" theories and explanations mirror theories and explanations that have come and gone over the past century. Explanations of behavioral differences between the races, such as those detailed recently by Murray and Herrnstein in "The Bell Curve" and by Rushton (see Chapters 29 and 31), are similar to those espoused by Hernstein, Jensen, and Shockley in the 1970s and by the eugenics movement of the first forty years of this century. The "new" fields of evolutionary psychology, Darwinian anthropology, and behavioral ecology have their roots directly in "sociobiology" of the 1970s, and before that in Social Darwinism of the turn of the century.

The subject matter of anthropology is human behavior and evolution. As anthropologists, we attempt to study the fossil record of humans; we also study the evolution and behavior of our nearest living relatives, the nonhuman primates; and anthropologists study human behavior and society in its broadest sense. Our studies are not confined to one culture, but instead, we try to learn about all aspects of human behavior in all cultures and subcultures.

Therefore, anthropologists are often in an excellent position to evaluate theories about human nature and so-called human universals, as well as the proposed biological bases of human behavior. But the extremely broad base that anthropology offers is not always appreciated by anthropologists, and anthropologists are not alone in understanding the problems that hound many of these theories. As many of the articles in this book will illustrate, scientists from many different disciplines are aware of the environmental and cultural influences on behavior in humans and other animals.

My hope is that after you read this book you will be able to give intelligent answers to questions like the following: Is infidelity programmed into our genes? Do males use infanticide as a strategy to enhance reproductive success? Are men biologically driven to hunt giraffes? Do women and blacks have lower average intelligence than white males? Is it natural for men to be violent? Are class and economic status biologically determined? Do inner-city gangs have their natural roots in marauding all-male monkey groups? Is sexual harassment by some men just the natural outcome of economic success or high social status? If after reading this book, "NO" is not your answer to these questions, read the book again, and more carefully this time. I hope that the book serves as an antidote to such recent books as Robert Wright's *The Moral Animal: Why We Are the Way We Are,* Laura Betzig's *Human Nature: Why Do We Do What We Do?,* and Wrangham and Peterson's *Demonic Males.*

The book is divided into five sections. Part I, "Introductory Material: Evolution, Humans, and Primates," includes articles that review some of the subjects that might be covered in an introductory anthropology class. These include: the importance of genetic variation as one of the "functions" of sexual reproduction; the way in which one gene may affect many traits and one trait may be affected by many genes; human evolution and primate evolution and taxonomy. In Part II, "The Evolution of Human Behavior," I have included articles that focus on various interpretations of the early evolution of human behavior and hypotheses related to how this may have led to current human nature and human universals. Part III, "The Biological Basis of Race and Racism," deals with the new attempts to relate human physical variation to behavioral differences between peoples. As you will see, new racism is as easy to rebut scientifically as it was in the past, and many of the arguments and rebuttals have not changed. In Part IV, "The New Biological Determinism," the articles delve into the modern field of evolutionary psychology: How "biologically" fixed is our behavior? Did our genes really make us do it? Did evolution force us into fixed action patterns? How much free will do we really have? Well, don't give up yet, you may still have some free will! The final part, "The Brain, Hormones, and Human Behavior," focuses on the influences of hormones and the brain on behavior. Ultimately, is this the area from which answers about human nature and human universals will come?

At this point, I should emphasize that I do believe there is a biological basis to human behavior and there is something we can call "human nature." After all, humans generally behave more like each other than they do like gorillas or chimpanzees. And, for that matter, chimpanzees behave more like other chimps than they do like gorillas or humans. But at what level do these differences in nature take place? Different species seem to be playing different games on the same board (like playing checkers and chess on a checkerboard). Describing individual moves of the game may not help us a great deal in understanding the differences until we know the rules of the game. But where do we find these rules? Have we looked in the right places? I hope these readings will stimulate students to think about these age-old questions and to read, with a critical eye, those writers who believe that

they have found simple and simplistic answers to these very complex problems.

I would like to acknowledge the assistance of the many students and teaching assistants who have assisted me in compiling this book. They have improved it greatly. I also would like to thank those authors who have contributed original work or substantial revisions to already published pieces, especially Garland Allen, Betsy Schumann, Zuleyma Tang-Martinez, Ian Tattersall, and Alan Templeton. Thad Bartlett, Jane Phillips-Conroy, Milt and Sondra Schlesinger, and Linda Sussman suggested articles that appear in the book. I appreciate the assistance of Terry Gleason in organizing and assembling the final collection of articles. Finally, Terry Brennan, Nancy Roberts, Marianne Hutchinson, and the people at Simon & Schuster and Pine Tree Composition, Inc., have been extremely helpful and efficient in getting this book into final form.

The following is an outline of the course for which this reader was developed.

## THE BIOLOGICAL BASIS OF HUMAN BEHAVIOR

Part I. Introduction: Variability, Natural Selection, and Human Behavior.
    A. What is anthropology?
        1. Cultural, Linguistics, and archeology
        2. Physical anthropology
    B. Variability and evolutionary forces
        1. Hardy-Weinberg Equilibrium
        2. Mutation, selection, gene drive and gene flow
        3. Selection and modern humans
Part II. Evolutionary History: Vertebrates to the Primates: What Did We Inherit from Our Ancestors?
    A. Taxonomy and vertebrate evolution
        1. Taxonomy and systematics
        2. A brief review of the evolution of the vertebrates
    B. Primates taxonomy, evolution, and behavior
        1. What is a primate?
        2. Why did primates evolve?
        3. Some definitions
Part III. Evolutionary History: Evolution of Human Behavior
    A. Protohominid Behavior
        1. Overview of human evolution
        2. Australopithecines: Morphology and theories
        3. Why did we become bipedal?
        4. Man the hunter or man the dancer?
        5. Primate analogies for human behavior: Are we talking monkeys?
    B. Origins of modern humans
        1. Early modern types and dispersal
        2. Deception, self-awareness, and self-deception
        3. What is culture?

**Chapter 1** "Basic Concepts of Evolutionary Biology" from *Evolution and the Diversity of Life* by Ernst Mayr. Reprinted by permission of the publisher from *Evolution and the Diversity of Life* by Ernst Mayr, Cambridge, Mass.: Harvard University Press, Copyright © 1976 by the President and Fellows of Harvard College.

**Chapter 2** "The Evolution of Living Systems" from *Evolution and the Diversity of Life* by Ernst Mayr. Reprinted by permission of the publisher from *Evolution and the Diversity of Life* by Ernst Mayr, Cambridge, Mass.: Harvard University Press, Copyright © 1976 by the President and Fellows of Harvard College.

**Chapter 3** "Mitosis, Meiosis, and Genetic Variability" from *Human Evolution: An Introduction to the New Physical Anthropology*, Third Edition, by Joseph B. Birdsell. Copyright © 1981. Reprinted by permission of Addison Wesley Educational Publishing, Inc.

**Chapter 4** "Understanding the Genetic Construction of Behavior" by Ralph J. Greenspan (excluding all artwork). From *Scientific American*, Vol. 272, No. 4. © 1995. Reprinted with permission. Copyright © 1995 by Scientific American, Inc. All rights reserved.

**Chapter 5** Figure depicting the Auditory Bulla in mammals from *Living New World Monkeys* by Hershkovitz. Copyright © 1977 by the University of Chicago. Reprinted by permission.

**Chapter 7** "The Major Features of Human Evolution" by Ian Tattersall. Reprinted by permission of Ian Tattersall.

**Chapter 8** "Evolution of Humans May at Last be Faltering" by William K. Stevens. From *New York Times*, March 14, 1995. Copyright © 1995 by The New York Times. Reprinted by permission.

**Chapter 9** Excerpt titled "Selection in Modern Populations" from *Human Evolution: An Introduction to the New Physical Anthropology*, Third Edition, by Joseph B. Birdsell. Copyright © 1981. Reprinted by permission of Addison Wesley Education Publishing, Inc.

**Chapter 10** "Ghetto Legacy" by Stephen J. O'Brien. From *Current Biology*, Volume 1, No. 4, 1991. Reprinted by permission from Current Biology Ltd. and the author.

**Chapter 11** "The Evolution of Hunting" by Sherwood L. Washburn and C. S. Lancaster. From *Man the Hunter* edited by R. B. Lee and I. DeVore. © 1968 by Aldine de Gruyter. Reprinted with permission of the authors in Lee, Richard B. and deVore, Irven (eds.) *Man the Hunter.* (New York: Aldine de Gruyter). Copyright © 1968 by the Wenner-Gren Foundation for Anthropological Research, Inc.

**Chapter 12** "Gingrich: Men Love the Muck" as reprinted in the *Chicago Tribune* on January 19, 1995. Copyright © 1995 by the Associated Press. Reprinted with permission.

**Chapter 13** "Sociobiology: A New Approach to Understanding the Basis of Human Nature" by Edward O. Wilson. From *New Scientist*, Volume 70, 1976. Reprinted by permission from New Scientist.

**Chapter 14** "The New Synthesis Is an Old Story" by Science as Ideology Group of the British Society for Social Responsibility in Science. From *New Scientist*, Volume 70, 1976. Reprinted by permission from New Scientist.

**Chapter 15** "Sociobiology: The Art of Storytelling" by Stephen Jay Gould. From *New Scientist*, Volume 80, 1978. Reprinted by permission from New Scientist.

**Chapter 16** "Why Did Lucy Walk Erect?" by Donald C. Johanson and Maitland A. Edey. Reprinted with the permission of Simon & Schuster from *Lucy: The Beginnings of Human Kind* by Donald C. Johanson and Maitland A. Edey. Copyright © 1981 by Donald C. Johanson and Maitland A. Edey.

**Chapter 17** "Flesh & Bone" by Ellen Ruppel Shell. From *Discover*, December 1991 issue. Ellen Ruppel Shell © 1991. Reprinted with permission of Discover Magazine.

**Chapter 18** "Ape Cultures and Missing Links" by Richard Wrangham. From *Symbols*, published by Harvard University's Anthropology Department. Reprinted by permission from the author.

**Chapter 19** "Bonobo Sex and Society" by Frans B. M. de Waal (excluding all artwork). From *Scientific American*, Vol. 272, No. 3, March 1995. Reprinted with permission. Copyright © 1995 by Scientific American, Inc. All rights reserved.

**Chapter 21** "Reconstructions of Early Hominid Socioecology: A Critique of Primate Models" by Richard Potts, from *The Evolution of Human Behavior: Primates Models*, edited by Warren G. Kinzey. © 1987 by the State University of New York Press. Reprinted by permission of the State University of New York Press, from *The Evolution of Human Behavior* by Warren Kinzey © 1987, State University of New York. All rights reserved.

**Chapter 22** "Species-Specific Dietary Patterns in Primates and Human Dietary Adaptations" by Robert W. Sussman, from *The Evolution of Human Behavior: Primate Models,* edited by Warren G. Kinzey. © 1987 by the State University of New York Press. Reprinted by permission of the State University of New York Press. All rights reserved.

**Chapter 23** "Ancient Odysseys" by Michael D. Lemonick. From *Time,* February 13, 1995. © 1995 Time Inc. Reprinted by permission.

**Chapter 24** "Time, Temporal Envelopes and the Middle and Upper Paleolithic Transition" by B. A. Schumann and P. B. Petitt. From *Archaeological Review from Cambridge*, Volume 12, No. 2. 1995.

**Chapter 25** "Deception Among Primates" by Robert W. Sussman and Thad Q. Bartlett. Adapted from a paper presented at the AAAS meetings, Washington DC, February 16, 1991. Reprinted by permission of the American Association for the Advancement of Science.

**Chapter 26** Excerpted version of "Human Races: A Genetic And Evolutionary Perspective" by Alan R. Templeton. Reproduced by permission of the American Anthropological Association from *American Anthropologist* 100:3, September 1998. Not for further reproduction.

**Chapter 27** "Three Is Not Enough" by Sharon Begley. From *Newsweek,* February 13, 1995. © 1995, Newsweek, Inc. All rights reserved. Reprinted by permission.

**Chapter 28** "Why Psychologists Should Learn Some Anthropology" by Jefferson M. Fish. From *American Psychologist*, January 1995. Copyright © 1995 by the American Psychological Association. Reprinted with permission.

**Chapter 29** "Toward a Theory of Human Multiple Birthing: Sociobiology and r/K Reproductive Strategies" by J. Philippe Rushton. From *Acta Geneticae Medicae et Gemelloligiae,* Volume 36, 1987. Copyright © 1987 by Istituto di Genetica Medica e Gemellologia, Italy. Reprinted by permission of the publisher.

**Chapter 30** "Differential K. Theory and Racial Hierarchies" by Frederic Weizmann, Neil I. Wiener, David L. Wiesenthal, and Michael Ziegler. From *Canadian Psychology,* Volume 31, No. 1, 1990. Copyright 1990. Canadian Psychological Association. Reprinted with permission.

**Chapter 31** "Race, Genes, and IQ—An Apologia" by Charles Murray and Richard J. Herrnstein. From *The New Republic,* October 31, 1994. Reprinted by permission from Charles Murray. Richard J. Hernstein held the Edgar Pierce Chair in psychology at Harvard until his death in 1994. Charles Murray is the Bradley Fellow at the American Enterprise Institute in Washington, D.C.

**Chapter 32** "The Poor Person's Guide to the Bell Curve." From *Scientific American,* Volume 272, No. 4, April 1995. Reprinted with permission. Copyright © 1995 by Scientific American, Inc. All rights reserved.

**Chapter 33** "Critique of The Bell Curve," from *The Mismeasure of Man,* Revised and Expanded Edition by Stephen Jay Gould. Copyright © 1996, 1981 by Stephen Jay Gould. Reprinted by permission of W. W. Norton & Company, Inc.

**Chapter 34** "What Color Is Black?" by Tom Morganthau. From *Newsweek,* February 13, 1995. © 1995, Newsweek, Inc. All rights reserved. Reprinted by permission.

**Chapter 36** "New Vital Statistics Confirm Worsening of Black Health" from *Ethnicity and Disease,* Volume 2, 1992. Copyright © 1992 by the International Society on Hypertension in Blacks. Reprinted with permission.

**Chapter 37** "Black, White, Other" by Johathan Marks. With permission from *Natural History* (December 1994). Copyright the American Museum of Natural History 1994.

**Chapter 38** "Brave New Right" by Michael Lind. From *The New Republic,* October 31, 1994. Reprinted by permission of *The New Republic,* © 1994, *The New Republic,* Inc.

**Chapter 39** "The Nature of Human Universals" by Robert W. Sussman. From *Reviews in Anthropology,* Volume 24, 1995. Reprinted by permission from Gordon and Breach Publishers.

# Part I

# INTRODUCTORY MATERIAL: EVOLUTION, HUMANS, AND PRIMATES

In this section, I include articles that give the reader a background in some of the terms used throughout the remainder of the book. To some students this will be a review; to others, the material will be new. I have attempted to choose articles that are interesting and useful in either case.

The first two chapters are essays by Ernst Mayr written in the 1960s. Mayr, one of the most respected biologists and philosophers of biology of our time, provides a clear explanation of evolutionary theory and some of the questions that still remain in evolutionary biology. Chapter 3 is excerpted from a classic physical anthropology textbook by the late J. B. Birdsell, a human geneticist and ecologist who conducted field research on Australian aborigines. He outlines differences between asexual reproduction (mitosis) and sexual reproduction (meiosis) and explains how the latter leads to maximizing genetic variability. This variability is the raw material for evolution.

The article by Ralph Greenspan (Chapter 4), a professor of biology and neural science at New York University, is from a recent issue of *Scientific American*. Greenspan illustrates how, in most cases, genes do not stand alone. One gene may affect many behavioral or morphological traits (pleiotropism), and many genes may affect one trait (polygenic traits), even in fruit flies. This complexity of genetic interactions is a factor to keep in mind as you read through this book, and one that will be stressed in many of the articles throughout the volume.

In Chapter 5, I attempt to answer the question "What is a primate?" I approach this question in three ways: (1) taxonomically—how do humans and other primates fit into the general zoological classification system developed by Linneaus in the sixteenth century, and what animals are included in the primates? (2) morphologically—what morphological traits do primates share in common? (3) evolutionarily—what major adaptive

shift led to primates? Why did they originally evolve? What evolutionary and ecological factors led to the origins of our earliest ancestors?

In answering these questions, we might better understand why primates are different from other mammals and what initially put them on their particular evolutionary path. Each evolutionary lineage represents a package of morphological and behavioral traits. By tracing the origins of these "packages" we begin to learn something about why each package or lineage evolved, why certain ones were better able to persist, and how they differed from competing lineages. In this book, I am especially interested in the origins of three packages—the primate package, the first human-like creature, and the first modern human (*Homo sapiens*). The more we learn about the behavior, morphology, and ecology of these original populations, the more we will understand about the biological basis of modern human behavior.

In Chapter 7, Ian Tattersall, Curator of Anthropology at the American Museum of Natural History in New York, outlines the major features of human evolution. Chapters 8 and 9, the former a popular press article and the latter by J. B. Birdsell, ask the question "Are humans still evolving?" In the former, the answer is "no" and in the latter it is "yes." Certainly there are factors of everyday modern life affecting survival of certain individuals as explained by Birdsell. For example, some people are more susceptible than others to certain types of cancer given environmental stresses, and some differences in susceptibility are genetically determined. Thus, modern humans are under the influence of natural selection and ultimately evolutionary forces. This should not be confused with speciation—the process, over time, of evolution and genetic isolation of two populations of the same species. We are certainly not speciating but we most likely are evolving (e.g., changing gene frequencies over time), and most certainly we are still under the influence of natural selection. The final chapter in this section, by Stephen O'Brien of the National Cancer Institute, gives an excellent example of natural selection on modern populations.

There are three general trends in evolution that are worth keeping in mind as you read this book. (1) Genetic variability in individuals has increased since life first evolved. Whereas mitotic, asexual reproduction produces organisms that are identical, meiosis or sexual reproduction maximizes genetic variability and leads to an almost infinite variety of individual organisms. This variability appears to have been highly adaptive. (2) Throughout evolutionary history there seems to have been a trend from producing many offspring with little parental care to one of producing fewer offspring and giving each more care. (3) Finally, there is a general trend from animals depending mainly on innately programmed behaviors to those depending more on learning and having a greater ability to modify their behavior given different environmental circumstances.

We shall see in the later sections of this book that some modern biologists and anthropologists have virtually turned these trends upside down. They seem to be proposing that (1) genes try to replicate themselves and

that this is a major factor in behavior and evolution—this trend, if successful, would lead to less genetic variability (more genetic homozygosity), and in fact, under these conditions, wouldn't asexual reproduction be the ideal system? (2) Some propose that an individual's success in evolutionary terms is equivalent to "maximizing" reproduction, which, in turn, often translates into mating more and producing the most offspring. But much of the behavior of vertebrates is focused on ensuring the survival of fewer offspring. Thus, the behavior of the individual and long-term survival of his or her progeny is not directly related to individual mating success or maximizing reproduction *per se.* Finally, biological reductionists constantly try to describe more and more complex behaviors as being genetically inherited traits. Thus, we have scenarios describing the genes for alcoholism, petty criminality, infanticide, the propensity for violence, and so on.

As stated above, there has been a tendency to increase genetic variability, decrease the number of offspring, and to increase behavioral flexibility at the expense of genetically programmed behavioral patterns. All three of the above simplistic explanations of behavior actually run counter to these general evolutionary trends.

# Chapter 1

# *Basic Concepts of Evolutionary Biology*

## Ernst Mayr

That evolution is a fact and that the astonishing diversity of animals and plants evolved gradually was accepted quite universally soon after 1859. But how this evolution proceeded, particularly the nature of its moving force, has been a source of controversy from the very beginning.

Among specialists, almost complete agreement has been reached in recent decades. Whether they are botanists or zoologists, paleontologists or geneticists, all of them interpret the results of the evolutionary process in the same manner and find the same causal connections. With the nonspecialists the situation is different; whether biologists or not, they often remain unconvinced. Again and again some colleague has told me: "The story you present sounds quite logical and irrefutable, but I still can't get rid of the feeling that something isn't quite right." When I insist on being told what it is that is not right, it turns out that the doubter either has an altogether insufficient knowledge of basic facts or suffers from certain conceptual misunderstandings. In order to preclude this possibility, I shall begin by (1) stating the essential aspects of the modern interpretation of the causality of evolution in a few simple sentences; and then (2) attempt to explain the conceptual, indeed the philosophical, foundations of the evolutionary theory as it is now generally accepted.

## THE MODERN THEORY OF EVOLUTION

How does the modern biologist see the process of evolution? Most of the earlier theories of evolution based their explanation on a single factor, such as mutation, environment, or isolation; it was Darwin's genius to have proposed a two-factor explanation. The first factor, genetic variability, is entirely a matter of chance, whether it is produced by mutation, recombination, or by whatever other mechanism. Precisely the opposite is true of the second factor, natural selection, which is decidedly an "anti-chance" factor. Among the millions of individuals that are produced in every generation, selection always favors certain ones, whose advantageous attributes are due to specific genetic combinations. It must be emphasized once more that the most important component of Darwin's achievement was pointing out the duality of the evolutionary process. It is precisely this combination of chance and anti-chance that gives evolution both its great flexibility and its goal-directedness (Mayr 1963).

Darwin's explanation of evolution, in a sense, is dualistic. Dualism, however, is a word that has a bad reputation among biologists because for centuries they have suffered under the dualism of body and mind that Descartes brought back into philosophy. Biologists reject this dualism quite emphatically for reasons Bernhard Rensch has perceptively presented (Rensch 1968). Admittedly, there are quite a number of dualisms in biology, but they usually are not "either-or" dualisms but rather "first-then" dualisms, which we perhaps could designate as tandem dualisms. Mutation-selection is such a tandem dualism. Another dualism equally important for the understanding of evolution is the dualism of genotype-phenotype. We must fully understand this particular dualism before we can hope to understand the process of evolution.

The genotype is the totality of the genetic endowment that an individual received from his or her parents at conception (formation of the original zygote). The phenotype is the totality of the characteristics (the appearance) of an individual resulting from the interaction of the genotype (genetic program) with the environment during ontogeny.

But why is this duality of genotype and phenotype so important for the evolutionist? Embryologists have al-

From *Evolution and the Diversity of Life*. Belknap Press, Harvard University Press. Cambridge, Massachusetts. 1976.

ways silently assumed that the fertilized egg cell, including its nucleus, participates completely and directly in the development of the embryo. The only one who, for theoretical reasons, did not agree with this assumption was August Weismann, who was ahead of his time by several decades in this as in so many other ways. Weismann's solution, a separation of soma and germ line, was not validated. But his basic idea was nevertheless right. The ultimate solution of Weismann's problem was provided only recently by molecular genetics: The genetic material (DNA) does not participate itself in the development of the embryo but functions only as a blueprint. The instructions of the DNA are translated (with the help of RNA) into polypeptides and proteins, and it is only these that participate directly in the development of the embryo. The genetic material itself, the DNA, remains unchanged during this entire process.

I will not discuss further the highly interesting consequences for embryonic development that result from this functional separation of the DNA and the proteins. Instead, I want to point out the importance of this separation for certain evolutionary problems. First of all, it is now perfectly evident why a direct influence of the environment on the genetic material is impossible, an influence postulated by the majority of the Lamarckians. The way from the DNA (via the RNA) to the proteins is a one-way street. The environment can influence the developmental process but it cannot affect the blueprint that controls it. Changes in the proteins cannot be translated back into nucleic acids.

The second consequence is perhaps equally important. The complete separation of the DNA genotype from the protein phenotype has the result that much of the potential of the genotype of a given individual is not translated into the phenotype at all and thus is not exposed to selection. This is shown by the great number of recessive genes in diploid organisms and by the suppressor genes in epistatic systems. Such potentials can be mobilized in later generations through recombination. This method of reacting to fluctuations in the environment is clearly superior to a process of direct environmental induction as postulated by many Lamarckians. For instance, suppose we submit a cold-adapted experimental stock to increasingly higher temperatures over five generations and then suddenly expose it to cold temperatures. If this stock had been uniformly induced to great heat tolerance during the preceding five generations, it would surely be exterminated by the sudden cold shock. On the other hand, if the phenotype is not the direct product of the environment, then recombination can develop a whole population of new reaction norms in every generation, some of which—with great probability—will be preadapted to highly aberrant environmental conditions. The rapidity with which insects have developed DDT-resistant populations is evidence for the type of preadaptation that is stored in the blueprint of the DNA. In the ensuing discussion I shall return to the enormous importance of this difference in the roles of the genotype and the phenotype.

## PHILOSOPHICAL CONSIDERATIONS

Darwinism has a well-defined philosophical basis, an understanding of which is a prerequisite for the understanding of the evolutionary process. It has long been a puzzle for the historian of biology why the key to the solution of the problem of evolution was found in England rather than on the European continent. No other country in the world had such a shining galaxy of famous biologists in the middle of the last century as the Germany of Rudolphi, Ehrenberg, Karl E. von Baer, Schleiden, Leuckart, Siebold, Koelliker, Johannes Müller, Virchow, and Leydig, and yet the solution to the problem of evolution was found by two English amateurs, Darwin and Wallace, neither of whom had had thorough zoological training. How can one explain this? My answer is that philosophical thinking on the continent was dominated at the time by essentialism. This philosophy, as was shown by Reiser (1958), is quite incompatible with the assumption of gradual evolution. Essentialism had its roots in Plato's concept of the *eidos*. We all know Plato's famous allegory, according to which we see reality only indirectly like shadows on a cave wall, while the real nature of things, the *essence* of the scholastics, can be inferred only indirectly. Owing to the central importance of *essence* for this school of philosophy, it has been designated essentialism by Karl Popper (1950). By contrast, a very different kind of thinking, strongly supported by empiricism, had developed in England: the so-called population thinking, for which gradual evolution poses no difficulties. Population thinking is based on assumptions opposite to those of essentialism. It claims that only individual phenomena have reality and that every endeavor to infer from them an essence is a process of abstraction. Population thinking thus turns the dogma of essentialism upside down. The replacement of typological (essentialistic) thinking by population thinking was perhaps the most important conceptual revolution in the history of biology.

It is possible to make the philosophical problems even clearer by discussing some of the objections that are frequently raised against the Darwinian interpretation. I have heard, for instance, the statement "I cannot believe that so perfect an organ as the eye could have been produced by accidental mutations." The evolutionist entirely agrees with this. Accidental mutations alone, quite obviously, could not have done this. All a mutation does is to enrich the genetic variability of the gene pool. Mutation has nothing to do with adaptation. Selection is what achieves that. It is therefore also a misrepresentation of the situation to say that this or that product of evolution was the result of mutation pressure. There is no such thing as mutation pressure. Unfortunately, there are still some authors who have not yet abandoned the entirely misleading ideas on mutation advanced by de Vries and other mutationists of the first decade of this century. These early geneticists saw in mutation a process that could produce in a single step a new type, be it a new species or even a higher taxon. These mutationists' essentialism forced them to assume that all evolutionary change had to proceed by saltations. We now know that this idea conflicts with the factual evidence. Each error in the replication of DNA is a mutation. Since every higher animal has enough DNA in its genome for about 5 million genes, and since each gene has on the average a thousand mutable base pairs, it is quite possible that each individual differs from every other individual by at least one new mutation of the 5 billion base pairs. If a mutation does not lead to the immediate death of the cell in which it arises, it may change the cell's physiology so slightly that extremely sensitive methods are required to determine that a mutation has occurred. The essential characteristics of the process of mutation are therefore: (1) mutation enriches the gene pool with genetic variation, (2) mutation is a relatively frequent process, and (3) most mutations in higher organisms are cryptic. Each of these three conclusions conflicts with the beliefs of the early mutationists.

The misunderstandings concerning the nature of selection were equally large. There is, for instance, the ever-repeated claim that Darwin's explanation of evolution is a tautology. The Darwinian argument is misrepresented in the following manner: First question: "Who survives?"; answer: "He who is fittest." Second question: "Who is fittest?"; answer: "He who survives." This formulation totally misrepresents Darwin's position. Darwin says: "Any variation . . . if it be in any degree profitable to an individual of any species, in its infinitely complex relations to other organic beings and to external nature, will tend to the preservation of that individual." What Darwin says, and I agree, is that it is the possession of certain characteristics that determines evolutionary success and that such characteristics have, at least in part, a genetic basis. An individual that has these genetic properties will survive and reproduce with a much greater probability than another that lacks them. It is obvious that this correct formulation is not at all tautological.

Another matter is often misunderstood and thus requires clarification. Selection does not deal with single genes because its target is the phenotype of the entire individual. To assume that a given gene has a fixed selective value is an error because the contribution a gene makes to the fitness of an individual depends to a considerable extent on the composition of the genotype, that is, of the interaction of this gene with other genes. At best, one can calculate a statistical mean value for the fitness of a gene. Population geneticists were rather surprised when they found that certain genes with above-average fitness in some combinations became lethal in other combinations.

One should never ignore the difference between genotype and phenotype. In particular, one must always remember that a given component of the phenotype is rarely or never directly determined by a single gene. The influence of a gene is usually rather indirect. Neglect of this consideration has led to such assertions as "Natural selection cannot explain why all mammals have seven cervical vertebrae." A characteristic like the number of cervical vertebrae is the product of a large part of the genotype, and the greater the phylogenetic age of a character, the more extensively it is built into the blueprint of the DNA, and the more resistant it becomes to change. What is decisive is the selective value of the total genotype.

Molecular genetics has demonstrated how complicated the realization of a character is, even in such relatively simple organisms as bacteria. Each gene has its repressors and inducers and a complicated regulatory system. A great deal of imagination is not required to understand how many billions or trillions of mutual interactions of genes are possible in multicellular organisms and how few of these are actually realized. It would be easy to cite from the literature hundreds of objections to selection, all of which rest on the erroneous assumption that genotype and phenotype are one and the same phenomenon and that each component of the phenotype is directly and immediately controlled by a specific gene. The typical objection is well represented in this statement by a well-known biologist: "The appearance of teeth in the embryos of animals which, like the baleen whales, are toothless as adults, or of the splint bones in the foot of the horse, cannot in the slightest be explained in terms of natural selection." To be sure, we still lack an understanding of the details of the process of differentiation responsible for the long retention of these features in embryonic development, but no difficulty in principle exists. We now know that each gene participates, or can participate, in many developmental processes, and that the manifold interactions among genes impart, so to speak, a holistic stamp to the totality of embryonic development. Provided the development of a young baleen whale as a whole is harmonious, selection will erode the genetic basis for the tooth anlage only very gradually. To eliminate it too rapidly could possibly lead to drastic disturbances in the developmental process and would not be tolerated by selection.

Behavior plays an important role in evolution. It does not, of course, have a direct influence on the genotype, as was believed by Lamarck, but it sets up new selection pressures and may facilitate the invasion of new adaptive zones.

## UNSOLVED PROBLEMS

In conclusion, I would like to raise the question of the future of evolutionary biology. If the current theoretical framework of this field, as it was developed in the 1930s and 1940s, is truly able to counter all objections successfully, does this not mean that evolutionary biology has become a dead science? If evolutionary biology had the theoretical framework of physics, the answer to this question might indeed be yes. The goal of the physicist is to establish general laws and to reduce all phenomena to a minimal number of such laws. General laws, however, play a much smaller role in biology. Just about everything in biology is unique: every animal and plant community, fauna or flora, species or individual. The strategy of research in biology must, for this reason, be quite different from the strategy of the physicist. In this respect, biology may be nearer to such sciences as archeology and linguistics. As interesting and important as the general laws of linguistics are, they by no means diminish the importance of studying individual languages. However important the laws derived from a comparison of cultures, they by no means constitute a reason for abandoning the study of individual cultures. Indeed, a study of specific phenomena is an indispensable prerequisite for all comparative studies. It is the comparison of different languages, different cultures, different faunas, or different groups of animals and plants that leads to the most interesting generalizations.

In this respect we are still very much at the beginning in evolutionary biology. We are still utterly unable to answer questions such as these: Why have certain blue-green algae (*Cyanophycea*) hardly changed in 1 ½ billion years? Why have the faunas of certain geological periods been exposed to great catastrophes and why have these catastrophes occurred sometimes simultaneously in the ocean and on land and at other times in one or the other? Or: What were the special conditions that permitted only a single phyletic line to become man among probably more than a billion phyletic lines that existed on earth? Such questions indicate some of the problems that currently preoccupy the evolutionary biologist.

Molecular biology has posed some highly interesting new questions. I shall mention merely the riddle posed for us by the amount of DNA in each nucleus. We have been wondering for a good many years why there is evidence for only 5000 to 50,000 genes among higher animals, even though there is enough DNA for 5 million genes. More recently, it has been found that DNA can be rather heterogeneous, but that only some of it, perhaps not more than 25 percent, is clearly repetitive. As yet, we have no idea what the physiological and evolutionary significance of this heterogeneity is. I suspect that we are in for some major surprises.

The structure of the chromosomes in the eucaryotes likewise poses many puzzles. Why is the number of chromosomes relatively constant in many groups of animals and variable in others? Why is the number of chromosomes high in certain groups of animals and plants and low in others? Why are nearly all chromosomes approximately the same size in some groups of animals, whereas in others there is an enormous range of sizes? Even though

we are convinced that all these phenomena are controlled by natural selection, we must nevertheless admit that we still lack clues to the reasons for all these difficulties.

The problem of the rate of evolution is another package of unknowns. I have mentioned already the evolutionary stability of certain blue-green algae that have not changed visibly in more than a billion years, as compared with the enormous rapidity of evolution in freshwater fishes, which seem capable of generating new species in less than 5000 years. Is this great difference entirely a matter of recombination and selection, or are there actually differences in mutability? And if the latter, what chemistry regulates rates of mutation?

Unsolved puzzles exist at every level of integration. The mutation process itself is not yet entirely explained. The phylogenetic rate of change in macromolecules is a highly controversial subject and uncertainties exist at every succeeding level of organization, up to animal and plant communities. It is now possible even to take a new look at the problems of phylogeny. The new findings of chemical taxonomy provide clues to relationship that were hitherto unavailable. Concurrently, functional morphology has provided insights that were not accessible to the typologist in his *Bauplan* studies. It is evident that this is an area in which we can expect all sorts of new findings in the course of coming years. Curiously, none of this has weakened the basic Darwinian thesis. To the contrary, the new findings again and again have fully confirmed Darwin's brilliant vision.

Every biological phenomenon, every structure, every function, indeed everything in biology, has a history. And the study of this history, the reconstruction of the selection pressures that have been responsible for the biological world of today, is as much a part of the causal explanation of the world of organisms as physiological or embryological explanations. A purely physiological-ontogenetic explanation that omits the historical side is only half an explanation. It is not sufficient to know how the DNA program is translated into the phenotype if one wants to acquire a correct view of the phenomena of life: One must also attempt to explain the historical origin of the DNA program. Only evolutionary biology can make that contribution; thus the study of evolution remains an important branch of biology.

## REFERENCES

Mayr, E. (1963) *Animal species and evolution.* Cambridge, MA: Belknap Press of Harvard University Press.

Popper, K. R. (1950) "The open society and its enemies." In *The spell of Plato,* vol. 1. London: Routledge and Kegan Paul.

Reiser, O. L. (1958) In R. Buchsbaum (ed.), *A book that shook the world* (p. 68). Pittsburgh: University of Pittsburgh Press.

Rensch, B. (1968) *Biophilosophie auf erkenntnistheoretischer Grundlage.* Stuttgart: G. Fischer.

# Chapter 2

# *The Evolution of Living Systems*

## Ernst Mayr

The number, kind, and diversity of living systems is overwhelmingly great, and each system, in its particular way, is unique. So different indeed are the kinds of organisms that it would be futile to try to understand evolution as a whole by describing the evolution of viruses and fungi, whales and sequoias, or elephants and hummingbirds. Perhaps we can arrive at valid generalizations by approaching the task in a rather unorthodox way. Living systems evolve in order to meet the challenge of the environment. We can ask, therefore, what *are* the particular demands that organisms have to meet?

The first challenge is to cope with a continuously changing and immensely diversified environment, the resources of which, however, are not inexhaustible. Mutation, the production of genetic variation, is the recognized means of coping with the diversity of the environment in space and time. Let us go back to the beginning of life. A primeval organism in need of a particular complex molecule in the primordial "soup" in which it lived gained a special advantage by mutating in such a way that, after having exhausted this resource in its environment, it was able to synthesize the needed molecule from simpler molecules that were abundantly available. Simple organisms such as bacteria or viruses, with a new generation every 10 or 20 minutes and with enormous populations consisting of millions and billions of individuals, may well be able to adjust to the diversity and to the changes of the environment by mutation alone. Indeed, a capacity for mutation is perhaps the most important evolutionary characteristic of the simplest organisms. Furthermore, their system of phenotypic adaptation is remarkably flexible, permitting a rapid adjustment to changes of the environment.

More complex organisms, those with much longer generation times, much smaller population size, and particularly with a delicately balanced coadapted genotype, would find it hazardous to rely so greatly on mutation to cope with changes in the environment. The chances that the appropriate mutation would occur at the right time so that mutation alone could supply appropriate genetic variability for sudden changes in the environment of such organisms are virtually nil. What, then, is the prerequisite for the development of more complex living systems? It is the ability of different organisms to exchange "genetic information" with each other, the process the geneticist calls recombination, more popularly known as sex. The selective advantage of sex is so direct and so great that we can assume it arose at a very early stage in the history of life. Let us illustrate this advantage by a single example. A primitive organism able to synthesize amino acid A, but dependent on the primordial soup for amino acid B, and another organism able to synthesize amino acid B, but dependent on the primordial soup for amino acid A, would be able by genetic recombination to produce offspring with the ability to synthesize both amino acids and thus the ability to live in an environment deficient in both of them. Genetic recombination can speed up evolutionary change enormously and assist in emancipation from the environment.

Numerous mechanisms evolved in due time to make recombination increasingly precise in every respect. The result was the evolution of elaborately constructed chromosomes; of diploidy through two homologous chromosome sets, one derived from the father, the other from the mother; of an elaborate process of meiosis during which homologous chromosomes exchange pieces so that the chromosomes of father and mother are transmitted to the grandchildren not intact, but as newly reconstituted chromosomes with a novel assortment of genes. These mechanisms regulate genetic recombination among individuals, by far the major source of genotypic variability in higher organisms.

From *Evolution and the Diversity of Life*. Belknap Press, Harvard University Press. Cambridge, Massachusetts 1976.

The amount of genetic diversity within a single interbreeding population is regulated by a balance between mechanisms that favor inbreeding and those that favor outbreeding. The extremes in this respect are much greater among plants and lower animals than among higher animals. Extreme inbreeding (self-fertilization) and extreme outbreeding (regular hybridization with other species) are rare in higher animals. Outbreeders and inbreeders are drastically different living systems in which numerous adaptations are correlated in a harmonious manner.

The result of sexuality is that ever-new combinations of genes can be tested by the environment in every generation. The enormous power of the process of genetic recombination by sexual reproduction becomes evident if we remember that in sexually reproducing species no two individuals are genetically identical. We must admit, sex is wonderful!

However, even sex has its drawbacks. To make this clear, let me set up for you the model of a universe consisting entirely of genetically different individuals that are *not* organized into species. Any individual may engage in genetic recombination with any other individual in this model. Occasionally, as a result of chance, new gene complexes will be built up that have unique adaptive advantages. Yet, because in this particular evolutionary system there is no guarantee that such an exceptional individual will engage in genetic recombination *only* with individuals having a similarly adaptive genotype, it is inevitable that this exceptionally favorable genotype will eventually be destroyed by recombination during reproduction.

How can such a calamity be avoided? There are two possible means, and nature has adopted both. One method is to abandon sexual reproduction. Indeed, we find all through the animal kingdom, and even more often among plants, a tendency to give up sexuality temporarily or permanently in order to give a successful genotype the opportunity to replicate itself unchanged, generation after generation, taking advantage of its unique superiority. The history of the organic world makes it clear, however, that such an evolutionary opportunist reaches the end of its rope sooner or later. Any sudden change of the environment will convert its genetic advantage into a handicap and, not having the ability to generate new genetic variability through recombination, it will inevitably become extinct.

The other solution is the "invention," if I may be pardoned for using this anthropomorphic term, of the biological species. The species is a protective system guaranteeing that only such individuals interbreed and exchange genes as have largely the same genotypes. In this system there is no danger that breakdown of genotypes will result from genetic recombination, because all the genes present in the gene pool of a species have been previously tested, through many generations, for their

ability to recombine harmoniously. This does not preclude considerable variability within a species. Indeed, all our studies make us realize increasingly how vast is the genetic variability within even comparatively uniform species. Nevertheless, the basic developmental and homeostatic systems are the same, in principle, in all members of a species.

By simply explaining the biological meaning of species, I have deliberately avoided the tedious question of how to define a species. Let me add that the species can fulfill its function of protecting well-integrated, harmonious genotypes only by having some mechanisms (called "isolating mechanisms") by which interbreeding with individuals of other species is prevented.

In our design of a perfect living system, we have now arrived at a system that can cope with the diversity of its environment and that has the means to protect its coadapted, harmonious genotype. As described, this well-balanced system seems so conservative as to offer no opportunity for the origin of additional new systems. This conclusion, if true, would bring us into a real conflict with the evolutionary history of the world. The paleontologists tell us that new species have originated continuously during geological time and that the multiplication of species, in order to compensate for the extinction of species, must occur at a prodigious rate. If the species is as well balanced, well protected, and as delicate as we have described it, how can one species be divided into two? This serious problem puzzled Darwin greatly, and evolutionists have argued about it for more than a hundred years.

Eventually it was shown that there are two possible solutions, or perhaps I should say two normally occurring solutions. The first mode occurs very frequently in plants, but is rare in the animal kingdom. It consists in the doubling of the chromosome set so that the new individual is no longer a diploid with two sets of homologous chromosomes, but, let us say, a tetraploid with four sets of chromosomes or, if the process continues, a higher polyploid with an even higher chromosome number. The production of a polyploid constitutes instantaneous speciation; it produces an incompatibility between the parental and the daughter species in a single step.

The other mode of speciation is simplicity itself. Up to now, we have spoken of the species as something rigid, uniform, and monolithic. Actually, natural species, particularly those that are widespread, consist like the human species of numerous local populations and races, all of them differing more or less from each other in their genetic composition. Some of these populations, particularly those at the periphery of the species range, are completely isolated from each other and from the main body of the species. Let us assume that one of these populations is prevented for a long time from exchanging genes with the rest of the species, because the isolating barrier—be it a mountain range, a desert, or a waterway—is impassable. Through the normal processes of mutation, recombination, and selection, the gene pool of the isolated population becomes more and more different from that of the rest of the species, finally reaching a level of distinctness that normally characterizes a different species. This process, called "geographic speciation," is by far the most widespread mode of speciation in the animal kingdom and quite likely the major pathway of speciation also in plants.

Before such an incipient species can qualify as a genuine new species, it must have acquired two properties during its genetic rebuilding. First, it must have acquired isolating mechanisms that prevent it from interbreeding with the parental species when the two come again into contact. Second, it must also have changed sufficiently in its demands on the environment, in its niche utilization (as the ecologist would say), so that it can live side by side with mother and sister species without succumbing to competition.

## KINDS OF LIVING SYSTEMS

In our discussion of the evolution of living systems, I have concentrated, up to now, on major unit processes or phenomena, such as the role of mutation, of genetic recombination and sex, of the biological species, and of the process of speciation. These processes give us the mechanisms that make diversification of the living world possible, but they do not explain why there should be such an enormous variety of life on earth. There are surely more than 3 million species of animals and plants living on this earth, perhaps more than 5 million. What principle permits the coexistence of such a wealth of different kinds? This question troubled Darwin, and he found an answer for it that has stood the test of time. Two species, in order to coexist, must differ in their utilization of the resources of the environment in a way that reduces competition. During speciation there is a strong selective premium on becoming different from preexisting species by trying out new ecological niches. This experimentation in new adaptations and new specializations is the principal evolutionary significance of the process of speciation. Once in a long while one of these new species finds the door to a whole new adaptive kingdom. Such a species, for instance, was the original ancestor of the most successful of all groups of organisms, the insects, now numbering more than a million species. The birds, the bony fishes, the flowering plants, and all other kinds of animals and plants all originated ultimately from a single ancestral species. Once a species discovers an empty adaptive zone, it can speciate and radiate until this zone is filled by its descendants.

To avoid competition, organisms can diverge in numerous ways, for instance in size. Even though there is a general trend toward large size in evolution, some species and genera, often in the same lines as large species and genera, have evolved toward decreased size. Small size is by no means always a primitive trait.

Specialization for a very narrow niche is perhaps the most common evolutionary trend. This is the characteristic approach of the parasites. Literally thousands of parasites are restricted to a single host, indeed restricted to a small part of the body of the host. There are, for instance, three species of mites that live on different parts of the honeybee. Such extreme specialization is rare if not absent in the higher plants, but is characteristic in insects and explains their prodigious rate of speciation. The deep sea, lightless caves, and the interstices between sand grains along the seashore are habitats leading to specialization.

The counterpart of the specialist is the generalist. Individuals of such species have a broad tolerance to all sorts of variations of climate, habitat, and food. It seems difficult to become a successful generalist, but the very few species that can be thus classified are widespread and abundant. Man is the generalist par excellence, with his ability to live in all latitudes and altitudes, in deserts and in forest, and to subsist on the pure meat diet of the Eskimos or on an almost pure vegetable diet. There are indications that generalists have unusually diversified gene pools and, as a result, produce rather high numbers of inferior genotypes by genetic recombination. Widespread and successful species of *Drosophila* seem to have more lethals than rare or restricted species. It is not certain that this observation can be applied to man, but this much is certain, that populations of man display much genetic variation. In man we do not have the sharply contrasting types ("morphs") that occur in many polymorphic populations of animals and plants. Instead, we find rather complete intergradation of mental, artistic, manual, and physical capacities (and their absence). Yet, whether continuous or discontinuous, genetic variation has long been recognized as a useful device by which a species can broaden its tolerance and enlarge its niche. That the same is true for man is frequently forgotten. Our educators, for instance, have for far too long tended to ignore man's genetic diversity and have tried to force identical educational schedules on highly diverse talents. Only within recent years have we begun to realize that equal opportunity calls for differences in education. Genetically different individuals do not have equal opportunities unless the environment is diversified.

Every increase in the diversity of the environment during the history of the world has resulted in a veritable burst of speciation. This is particularly easily demonstrated for changes in the biotic environment. The rise of the vertebrates was followed by a spectacular development of trematodes, cestodes, and other vertebrate parasites. The insects, whose history goes back to the Paleozoic nearly 400 million years ago, did not really become a great success until the flowering plants (angiosperms) evolved some 150 million years ago. These plants provided such an abundance of new adaptive zones and niches that the insects entered a truly explosive stage in their evolution. By now three-quarters of the known species of animals are insects, and their total number (including undiscovered species) is estimated to be as high as 2 or 3 million.

## Parental Care

Let me discuss just one additional aspect of the diversity of living systems, care of the offspring. At one extreme we have the oysters, which do nothing whatsoever for their offspring. They cast literally millions of eggs and male gametes into the sea, providing the opportunity for the eggs to be fertilized. Some of the fertilized eggs will settle in a favorable place and produce new oysters. The statistical probability that this will happen is small, owing to the adversity of the environment, and although a single full-grown oyster may produce more than 100 million eggs per breeding season, it will have on the average only two descendants. That numerous species of marine organisms practice this type of reproduction, many of them enormously abundant and many of them with an evolutionary history going back several hundred million years, indicates that this shotgun method of thrusting offspring into the world is surprisingly successful.

How different is reproduction in species with parental care! This always requires a drastic reduction in the number of offspring, and it usually means greatly enlarged yolk-rich eggs, it means the development of brood pouches, nests, or even internal placentae, and it often means the formation of a pair bond to secure the participation of the male in the raising of the young. The ultimate development along this line of specialization is unquestionably humans, with their enormous prolongation of childhood.

Behavioral characteristics are an important component of parental care, and our treatment of the evolution of living systems would be incomplete if we were to omit reference to behavior and to the central nervous system. The germ plasm of a fertilized egg contains in its DNA a coded genetic program that guides the development of the young organism and its reactions to the environment. However, there are drastic differences among species concerning the precision of the inherited information and the extent to which the individual can benefit from experience. The young in some species appear to be born with a genetic program containing an almost complete set of ready-made, predictable responses to the stimuli of the environment. We say of such an organism that its behavior is unlearned, innate, instinctive, that its behavior *program* is *closed*. The other extreme is provided by organisms that have a great capacity to benefit from experience, to learn how to react to the environment, to continue adding "information" to their behavior program, which consequently is an *open program.*

Let us look a little more closely at open and closed programs and their evolutionary potential. We are all familiar with the famous story of how Konrad Lorenz imprinted goslings on himself. Young geese or ducklings just hatched from the egg will adopt as parent any moving object (but preferably one producing appropriate sounds). If hatched in an incubator, they will follow their human caretaker and not only consider him or her their parent but consider themselves as belonging to the human species. For instance, upon reaching sexual maturity they may tend to display to and court a human individual rather than another goose or duck. The reason for this seemingly absurd behavior is that the hatching bird does not have an inborn knowledge of the Gestalt of its parent; all it has is a readiness to *fill in* this Gestalt. Its genetically coded program is open; it provides for a readiness to adopt as parent the first moving object seen after hatching. In nature, of course, this is invariably the parent.

Let us contrast this open program with the completely closed one of another bird, the parasitic cowbird. The mother cowbird, like the European cuckoo, lays her eggs in the nests of various kinds of songbirds, such as yellow warblers, vireos, or song sparrows, and then abandons them completely. The young cowbird is raised by its foster parents, and yet, as soon as it is fledged, it seeks other young cowbirds and gathers into large flocks with them. For the rest of its life, it associates with members of its own species. The Gestalt of its own species is firmly imbedded in the genetic program with which the cowbird is endowed from the very beginning. It is—at least in respect to species recognition—a completely closed program. In other respects, much of the behavioral program of the cowbird is open, that is, ready to incorporate experiences by learning. Indeed, there is probably no species of animals, not even among the protozoans, that does not, at least to some extent, derive benefit from learning processes. On the whole, and certainly among the higher vertebrates, there has been a tendency to replace rigidly closed programs by open ones or, as the student of animal behavior would say, to replace rigidly instinctive behavior by learned behavior. This change is not a change in an isolated character. It is part of a whole chain reaction of biological changes. Since man is the culmination of this particular evolutionary trend, we naturally have a special interest in it. Capacity for learning can best be utilized if the young are associated with someone from whom to learn, most conveniently their parents. Consequently, there is strong selection pressure in favor of extending the period of childhood. And since parents can take care of only a limited number of young, there is selection in favor of reducing the number of offspring. We have here the paradoxical situation that parents with a smaller number of young may nevertheless have a greater number of grandchildren, because the mortality among well-cared-for and well-prepared young may be reduced even more drastically than the birth rate.

The sequence of events I have just outlined describes one of the dominating evolutionary trends in the primates, a trend that reaches its extreme in man. A broad capacity for learning is an indispensable prerequisite for the development of culture, of ethics, of religion. But the oyster proves that there are avenues to biological success other than parental care and the ability to learn.

One final point: How can we explain the harmony of living systems? Attributes of an organism are not independent variables but interdependent components of a single system. Large brain size, the ability to learn, long childhood, and many other attributes of man all belong together; they are parts of a single harmoniously functioning system. And so it is with all animals and plants. The modern population geneticist stresses the same point. The genes of a gene pool have been brought together for harmonious cooperation; they are coadapted. This harmony and perfection of nature (to which the Greeks referred in the word *kosmos*) has impressed philosophers from the very beginning. Yet there seems to be an unresolved conflict between this harmony of nature and the apparent randomness of evolutionary processes, beginning with mutation and including also much of reproduction and mortality. Opponents of the Darwinian theory of evolution have claimed that the conflict between the harmony of nature and the apparent haphazardness of evolutionary processes *cannot* be resolved.

The evolutionist, however, points out that this objection is valid only if evolution is a one-step process. In reality, every evolutionary change involves two steps. The first is the production of new genetic diversity through mutation, recombination, and related processes. On this level randomness is indeed predominant. The second step, however—selection of those individuals that are to make up the breeding population of the next generation—is largely determined by genetically controlled adaptive properties. This is what natural selection means; only that which maintains or increases the harmony of the system will be selected for.

The concept of natural selection, the heart of the evolutionary theory, is still widely misunderstood. Natural selection says no more and no less than that certain genotypes have a greater than average statistical chance to survive and reproduce under given conditions. Two aspects of this concept need emphasis. The first is that selection is not a theory but a straightforward fact. Thousands of experiments have proved that the probability that an individual will survive and reproduce is not a matter of accident, but a consequence of its genetic endowment. The second point is that selective superiority gives only a statistical advantage. It increases the probability of survival and reproduction, other things being equal.

Natural selection is measured in terms of the contribution a genotype makes to the genetic composition of the next generation. Reproductive success of a wild organism is controlled by the sum of the adaptive properties possessed by the individual, including its resistance to weather and its ability to escape enemies and find food. General superiority in these and other properties permits an individual to reach the age of reproduction.

In civilized humans these two components of selective value, adaptive superiority and reproductive success, no longer coincide. The individuals with above-average genetic endowment do not necessarily make an above-average contribution to the gene pool of the next generation. Indeed, shiftless, improvident individuals who have a child every year are certain to add more genes to the gene pool of the next generation than those who carefully plan the size of their families. Natural selection has no answer to this predicament. The separation in the modern human society of mere reproductive success from genuine adaptedness poses a serious problem for man's future.

# Chapter 3

# *Mitosis, Meiosis, and the Origins of Genetic Variability*

## J. B. Birdsell

### MITOSIS IS THE BASIC FORM OF CELL DIVISION

Two types of cell division take place in sexually reproducing animals. The basic type is called *mitosis*. This occurs in all the body cells and produces growth, maintains function, and repairs damage. The other type of cell division is called *meiosis* and occurs only in the gonads (testicles of males and the ovaries of females). Meiosis produces *gametes,* or matured sex cells, necessary for reproduction.

The genetic code is carried in the nucleus of *every* cell, both in body cells and sex cells alike. The two types of cell division are similar in most of their elements. Mitosis is the basic process, and meiosis has come into being through a few simple evolutionary modifications of the mitosis. The two types of division are distinguished by their products. Mitosis produces body cells that are *identical* to each other and to all other body cells, barring accidents. This pattern has been altered in meiosis, which produces an *almost infinite variability* of cells. That is, all gametes differ from each other. *Sperm* are the gametes produced by males. *Ova* are the gametic products of females. When a sperm fertilizes an ovum, a *zygote,* or one-celled stage of a new individual, results from the union.

Mitotic division goes through a series of stages, each of which has been given a technical name in cellular biology. For our purposes, all but one can be eliminated, the *interphase.* This is the stage prior to the beginning of division during which the chromosomes duplicate themselves, and it occurs again after division is complete. It is called the "resting phase" since the cell does not divide at this time. But in fact each cell is proceeding with all of its normal functions during interphase and is then a very *active* miniature biochemical factory, rather than a quiet island.

In Figure 3–1, the process of mitosis is diagrammed through eight consecutive stages. Beginning with interphase (a), the cell in its resting stage is bounded by its membrane, contains a nucleus in its center, and nearby the *centriole.* In step (b) some change is shown on the surface of the nuclear membrane where long twisted black lines have now become visible and in time slowly shorten to become rodlike, as shown in stage (c). The centriole has in stage c divided into two portions, each of which is moving toward what will become the cell poles. The centriole parts will establish the cell's axis, which will be used during its division.

In our diagram there are four chromosomes (two pairs), each shown in their duplicated condition. (Chromosomal reduplication occurred during the last stages of interphase, and so does not enter into this diagram.) Reduplicated chromosomes remain attached until the mechanical process of cell division is well under way. In this form, they are referred to as *chromatids.* For the purposes of clarity we have a long pair and a short pair of chromosomes. The cross-hatched pairs, long $As$ and short $Bs$, were originally derived from the father of the individual in whose body this division is occurring. The white pairs of chromosomes $A_m$ and $B_m$ came from the individual's mother. The chromosomes always occur in pairs in higher organisms, and human beings have 23 pairs. Each pair of chromosomes contains differing genes, that is, sections of the genetic code with different sets of instructions. The members of a single pair of chromosomes usually have the same set of genes, but each individual chromosome of that pair may contain slightly different variations of some genes, called *alleles.* Such a chromosome pair is called an *homologous pair.*

From *Human Evolution: An Introduction to the New Physical Anthropology,* Third Edition. Houghton Mifflin Company. Boston, Massachusetts. 1981.

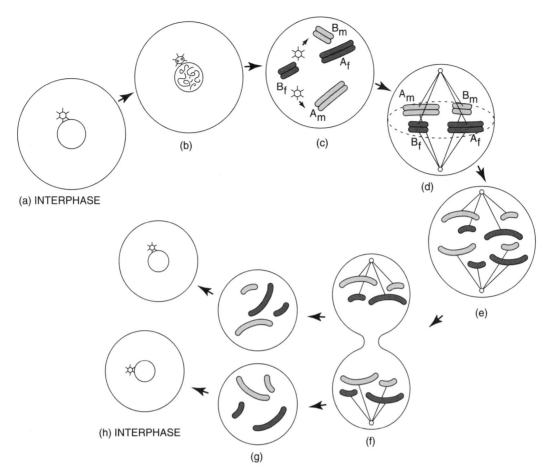

**Figure 3–1** A diagrammatic model of the process of mitosis.

Human females have 23 homologous pairs, while males have 22 and one nonhomologous pair, the sex chromosomes.

After a short period in which the chromosomes move haphazardly in the protoplasm, they come to rest as indicated in (d). The centrioles have at this point moved to establish a true polar axis. Perpendicular to this axis, the chromosomes have come to rest on an imaginary equatorial plane. The positions they take are by chance and bear no real relation to each other.

Note that, from each polar centriole, thin lines connect the centriole to the midpoint of each of the chromatids. These *spindle threads* are physically real and can exert pull. In stage (e) the spindle threads have shortened and begun to pull the individual chromatids to which they are attached. As the chromatids are pulled through the sticky protoplasm, they are literally bent from the resistance it offers.

Proceeding to stage (f), the spindle threads continue to shorten until the chromosomes have completely cleared the equatorial region. Then the equator of the cell constricts as it begins its division and separation. In the next to the last stage (g), the constriction is completed and the mitotic division has produced two descendant, or daughter, cells. Each contains the complete identical genetical code found in the original mother cell.

In the final stage (h), the nuclear membrane is reformed and again hides the chromosomes. Each centriole nestles against its nucleus. Through the absorption of body fluids of one kind or another, the two new cells slowly grow to the proper size characteristic of that cell. The time taken in mitotic division varies, but it ranges from about a half an hour to several hours, depending upon cell type. So, by fission, mitotic division produces two cells from one, each of which are identical in size and in the content of their genetic code. All the chromosomes in our body cells come in pairs; this is referred to as the *diploid number*. In our own cells, we have 23 pairs of chromosomes, making the diploid number 46.

There are a great many aspects of mitosis in which the mechanics are not well understood. The changes can be described, but the *forces* involved have not been identified. While a doubling process may not seem dramatic at first sight, when it is continued through many divisions the results are astronomic. In the course of twenty years, an individual being grows from one original cell, a zygote, to an estimated 10 trillion cells through, as we have said, only 46 consecutive divisions.

## Some Modifications in the Process of Mitosis

Mitotic division arose in evolution as a reproductive process by which one cell divided into two descendant cells and so on, to produce the lineages of asexual reproduction that we know as *clones*. The production of clonal descendants by single cells differs somewhat from the production of cells in more complex creatures. Both represent a form of mitosis, but an unknown transformation has occurred in the complex forms.

We are not concerned with the important but poorly understood problem of the origin of *multicellular* life. There is no doubt that original living forms appeared as simple molecules that, over a very long period of time, became elaborated into single cell life. Today all of the highest animals and plants are multicellular, meaning their bodies are comprised of many cells. If the process of mitotic division had simply been altered so that two daughter cells resulting from its division adhered to each other instead of separating, then the origin of multicellular life could be rather simply explained. A number of theorists believe that this is the way in which many-celled animals actually originated. Since the development of a body with many cells opens vast new avenues of evolution in terms of size, complexity, and differentiation of structure, this was a most important event.

In man and most other multicellular animals, mitosis continues to be the process by which growth is achieved and cellular replacements are obtained. But bisexual reproduction required a new type of cell division to be developed. For if the sex glands were to go through ordinary mitotic division, they would produce *sperm* in the male animal and *ova* in the female, each of which would contain the full number of 46 chromosomes characteristic of the species. When a sperm penetrates the membrane of an ovum to produce a new individual, this *zygote* would be characterized by 92 chromosomes, or 46 pairs. With each new generation this system would involve a doubling of chromosome numbers so that it would quickly become astronomical, and so biologically unimaginable. To avoid the doubling of chromosomes in each generation of reproduction, it is obvious that the functional sex cells, the sperm and the ovum, must have no more than one-half of the ordinary number, but that this complement should contain a complete DNA code of instructions. This is called the *haploid* condition, as opposed to the *diploid* condition, which exists both in normal body cells and in zygotes. We can therefore specify that cellular division in the sex cells must somehow be arranged so that only one chromosome in each pair is allotted to the maturing sperm and ovum. Evidently the program for mitotic division must be changed in order to achieve this end.

### Evolution of Bisexual Reproduction

With the great clarity that comes with hindsight, we can say that the evolution of bisexual reproduction arose to answer the need for greater variability in natural populations. This idea rests in part upon the fact that as the life cycles of most single-celled animals are examined, it is found that their reproduction is generally through simple mitotic fission. Many instances occur, however, in which two of the little creatures will adhere to each other, that is, *conjugate*, and exchange portions of their DNA. Such a jumbling of their code of life clearly introduces variability, and in a very crude way simulates the effects of bisexual reproduction. If we remember that reproduction by fission produces clones of single-celled plants and animals, among which each individual is genetically identical to the original progenitor of the lineage, then the reason for the sexual phases becomes clear. For barring mutational accident, all clonal species would consist of individuals in which the genetic code is identical. Owing to the fact that mutations do occur, a given species will contain a variety of clones that differ slightly genetically. These compete with each other and survival goes to the fittest cell type under a given environmental circumstance. Thus, generally single-celled animals evolve through competition between clones. These types of populations have limited variability and consequently evolve slowly in terms of their length of generation; but their rate of fission is usually so rapid that their evolutionary change in absolute time may also be rapid.

Bisexual reproduction produces such variability among offspring as to overwhelm the imagination. The meiotic division of cells in the sex glands must be arranged not only to produce functional gametes without any increase in the chromosomal numbers of the species, but also it must operate so as to maximize variations in the genetic code. The ways in which the basic mitotic process has been transformed to produce meiosis are astonishingly simple, considering the great consequences of the changes.

### The Process of Meiotic Division

Ongoing evolution requires a constant store of variability to work upon. Simple plants and animals reproduce asexually by mitotic division, and the result is a colony of identical individuals known as clones, but the evolutionary possibilities with this type of reproduction are relatively limited. To provide the means for the immense variability evolution requires, bisexuality seems to have evolved. Bisexual reproduction came into being as a result of the few basic changes in mitosis that became the *meiotic* process of division. Meiosis consists of two divisions, one occurring right after the other. As a result, the final gametes have only one half the chromosome number, one of each pair. This is the *haploid* condition, or haploid number.

The process of meiosis in *males* is diagrammed in Figure 3–2. All the cell structures not concerned with the production of matured sex cells again do not come into play and are ignored. In stage (a), interphase, the cell is seen at rest. In the next step (b), the long wiry chromosomes again begin to appear on the membrane of the nucleus. They have already undergone their duplication. Coming to stage (c), the nuclear membrane has dissolved, and the threadlike structures are shortening and thickening to become rodlike chromosomes. The two pairs of chromosomes move at random through the protoplasm of the cell. They are again labeled and shaded as in the preceding mitotic diagram, to show which of each pair comes from which parent. Genetic differences between the parents are involved, and these differences do become important later on. The centriole is divided in two, and its parts are now moving toward their future polar positions.

State (d), called *synapsis,* marks the first important change from the mitotic pattern. Here the members of each reduplicated pair of chromosomes fuse together or *synapse.* This is the first fundamental difference between mitosis and meiosis. When the spindle threads emerge from the polar-positioned centrioles, they are only half as numerous as they were in the earlier process. In meiosis, each centriole sends out two strands instead of the four observed in mitosis. Another important point is that the synapsed pairs of chromosomes line up on the equatorial plane in a purely chance fashion. This randomness affects all 23 pairs of chromosomes. It is this stage of random assortment that produces much of the enormous genetic variability of the sex cells.

Phase (e) represents the initial stages of the *first reduction division* in meiosis. The spindle threads have shortened, and the chromosomes separate from their synapsed position and now move as reduplicated pairs (two chromatids) toward their appropriate poles. Note this differs from mitosis, which only went through a single division. As the process of meiosis proceeds, the cen-

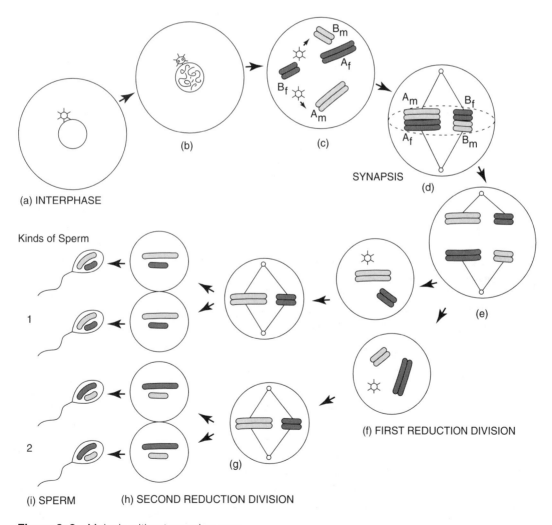

**Figure 3–2** Meiosis without crossing-over.

trioles divide again, establishing their polar positions for the *second reduction division.* In this division, the centrioles send out spindle threads to each of the chromatids as shown in stage (g). Without showing the constriction that precedes the actual division at the corresponding stage in mitosis, each of the daughter cells in meiosis now goes through the second reduction division. This time the spindle threads pull apart the chromatids so that, in the four immature sex cells, each original chromosome pair is represented by only a single strand. This is the *haploid* condition that characterizes gametes.

The matured male sex cells, or *sperm,* contain two chromosomes in single-strand condition, each one derived from a member of the original pair. Most of the cytoplasmic material is discarded on the second reduction division, consequently the sperm consists primarily of a head enclosing the nuclear material to which a small lashing tail is attached. This gives the cell the power of individual movement, for, in the process of fertilization, it must find its way to the immobile ovum in order to fertilize it.

Figure 3–2 shows that although there are four sperm produced from the original cell, the sperm are of only *two kinds* in terms of their chromosomal content. The top pair of sperm contains the large chromosome from the individual's mother and a small chromosome from his father. The bottom pair have the opposite combination. Turning to Figure 3–3, we can see that the second possible random arrangement produces four gametes of two types, both differing from those originally produced. Taken together, the two positions possible

through the random alignments of two pairs of chromosomes will produce *four different types of sperm.*

It can be calculated that the number of different kinds of sperm produced by any species is the basic number 2 raised to a power representing the pairs of chromosomes. Thus with three pairs of chromosomes, the number would be $2^3$ or 8. With four pairs of chromosomes it would be $2^4$ or 16. With 23 pairs of chromosomes, we can calculate 8,388,608 different kinds of sperm, each having a different genetic code. This calculation ignores *crossing-over,* which is the exchange of homologous blocks of DNA between strands of the same chromosome. We will discuss crossing-over in more detail later in this chapter.

Meiosis in the *female* is somewhat different from that in the male. The first reduction division gives one cell almost all the cytoplasm and the other almost none. Thus the yolk materials are concentrated in only one of the two daughter cells. Proceeding to the second reduction division, the fat cell divides again in the same way, concentrating virtually all of its cytoplasmic material in one cell which is to become the functional ovum. The other, known as a polar body, contains little or none. This type of division insures that the embryo resulting from the fertilization of the egg will have enough nutrients to keep it alive until it is finally implanted in the uterine wall. The impoverished cell resulting from the first division also divides again and produces two more underprivileged *polar bodies.* These seem to have no function and are lost in the oviduct of the woman. Chance alignment in synapsis in women is the same as in

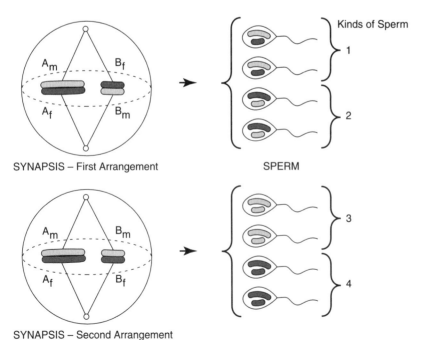

SYNAPSIS – First Arrangement

SPERM

SYNAPSIS – Second Arrangement

**Figure 3–3**   Random assortment increases gametic variety.

men; that is, the variations are equally numerous. And the single ovum, the only functional sex cell produced in women, still has the same *potential variability* as do the 300,000,000 sperm in men.

## SOME BASIC GENETIC TERMS

The concept of *locus* (or *loci* in the plural) is important for an understanding of genetics. A locus is simply a physical place on a chromosome where there is a single gene. If we assume for the moment that our species contains as many as 50,000 genes, then it is important for us to identify individual genes. A pair of homologous chromosomes is diagrammed in Figure 3–4. Look for a moment at locus 1000. Both chromosomes of this pair carry a gene at the same locus. Since one chromosome came from the individual's father and the other from its mother, each may well, and frequently does, contain slightly different versions of the gene. Variants in the genetic code that occur in the same place, like these, are called *alleles*. The alleles at a given locus on a homologous chromosomal pair both instruct the same *basic* message, but each *individual* message may differ slightly, and so produce somewhat different results. If a pair of chromosomes contains *identical* alleles at the same locus, the condition is called *homozygous*. But if locus number 1000 should contain slightly different messages, or two not quite similar alleles, the condition is called *heterozygous*.

We have already defined chromosomes, and we know humans have 23 pairs. The next step is to study the pair called the *sex chromosomes*. The sex chromosomes come in two forms, X and Y, and are responsible for determining the sex (male, female) of all individuals in our species. Women have two X chromosomes, men have an X and a Y. The X chromosomes contain a good many functional, or active genes, whereas no active genes are yet known to belong on the smaller Y chromosome. The female's sex chromosomes are homologous (XX), while the male's combination (XY) is nonhomologous. This situation almost suggests a genetic imbalance between men and women, but this is not really the case.

It has been hypothesized that in any one female cell only one X chromosome is active and functional. The other is represented by a small dark spot known as a *Barr body*. The X chromosome derived from the woman's father and that from her mother seem to be about equally often deactivated, or made into Barr bodies.

## THE VARIABILITY AVAILABLE IN A SINGLE HUMAN MATING

When we examine the variability available from a single human mating, we can really get a good sense of what variability means. A haploid sperm unites with a haploid ovum to produce a diploid zygote having the full chromosomal complement. The zygote has two chromosomes for each of the 23 chromosome types our species has. Meiosis without crossing-over produces about 8 million different arrangements in the genetic code of both the sperm of the human father and the ovum of the mother. Theoretically, one couple can produce approximately 70,000,000,000,000 (8 million × 8 million) different kinds of children! This fantastic number is almost too large to comprehend. It certainly is more than all the human beings who have ever lived until now—or perhaps who will ever live. If we then consider that the 2 billion adults presently living on this planet could mate at random, the resulting number of unique offspring would be astronomical. There is really no need to attempt to calculate it numerically; it is impressive enough that such vast amounts of variability could be released in a single generation of our species.

## THE CONSEQUENCE OF CROSSING-OVER

*Crossing-over* is the exchange of homologous blocks of genes between adjacent strands of *synapsed* chromosomes. Through processes that are not yet understood, pairs of strands break at identical places, or between the same loci. In some cases, the detached fragments of the strands later attach to *different* strands than those from which they broke. Figure 3–5 shows a recognizable crossing-over in which the broken portions of the chromosomes have healed in positions different from their original ones. Of the four sperm, two are unchanged and two are new. The new ones are products of crossing-over and contain portions of strands received from both parents. The cross is known as a *chiasma*. Crossing-over is not a rare occurrence; it regularly occurs at least once in every

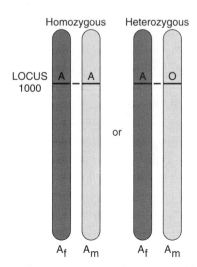

**Figure 3–4** On the nature of the locus.

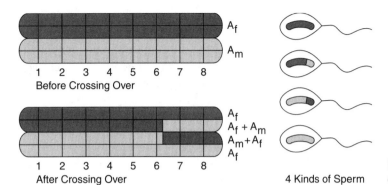

**Figure 3–5**  Crossing-over and its gametic consequences.

pair of synapsed chromosomes. Furthermore, crossing-over can simultaneously affect two, three, or four strands of synapsed chromosomes, thus producing a vast increase in variability. It is enough to say that the added amount of variability is literally incomprehensible. Roughly, in an individual human mating the man could potentially produce more than 70 *trillion* different kinds of sperm, and the woman could produce as many kinds of ova. This results in $4^{46}$ potentially different kinds of children from a single mating, a number large enough to thrill any mathematician.

## SUMMARY

The study of genetics formally began in the mid-nineteenth century with the research of an obscure Augustinian monk, Gregor Mendel. His careful studies of common garden plants allowed him to formulate the two rules of inheritance that form the basis of modern genetics, the Law of Segregation and the Law of Independent Assortment. Since 1900, when Mendel's work was rediscovered by DeVries, Tschermak, and Correns, the field of genetics has grown rapidly.

Some knowledge of genetics is essential for our understanding of evolution; it has to do with how humans actually become what they are. In this chapter, two basic processes of cell division have been described to illustrate important points. *Mitosis* is the process of division in body cells. It produces growth in the body's individual cells and in replacement cells needed in later life. Mitosis gives identity to those cells resulting from its divisions. The process is very important in the life cycle of all individuals from conception until death.

*Meiotic* division occurs only in the sex cells of mature individuals. It differs from body cell division because it has *two* reduction divisions rather than one. Also, the *synapsis* of homologous pairs of chromosomes preceding each division allows the random assortment of the chromosomal strands and provides some of the enormous variability found in the gametes of every individual. When combined with the *crossing-over* of homologous blocks of genes, variability in mature sex cells, which each individual is capable of producing, reaches astronomical figures. And this store of immediately available biological variability is of tremendous importance in evolution.

# Chapter 4

# *Understanding the Genetic Construction of Behavior*

## Ralph J. Greenspan

---

*Studies of courtship and mating in the fruit fly offer a window on the ways genes influence the execution of complex behaviors.*

Within the first fifteen years of this century, the newborn science of genetics had begun to give people their first glimpse of how heredity might work. Studies of such traits as flower color in plants and wing shape in fruit flies had confirmed Gregor Mendel's once obscure 1865 proposal that physical characteristics are passed from parents to progeny by discrete units of inherited material, or genes (the name these mysterious units was given in 1911). As commonly happens when a new discipline experiences its first flush of success, scientists and others soon began to apply the understandings of the budding field more broadly, and sometimes less carefully, to explain other phenomena—notably, the behavior of human beings. Often they claimed that complex behaviors were directed by single genes.

Yet even careful researchers have failed to link specific human behaviors convincingly to solitary genes or to small sets of genes. The reason could lie with methodology. When it comes to human behavior, there is virtually no way to disentangle unequivocally the influences of genes from those of culture and upbringing. On the other hand, if scientists could somehow manage to mask the effects of environment and focus solely on the genetic aspects of a behavior, they might still find the old assumptions flawed. Well-controlled investigations in simpler organisms suggest that a multitude of genes, some acting quite subtly, probably contribute to most behaviors.

From *Scientific American*, 272 (4) 1995.

## EARLY THINKING ON HUMANS

The question of whether human behavior is hereditary was initially asked more than a century ago. Francis Galton, a pioneer in the use of statistics, was among the first scientists to take up this issue. In the 1880s he analyzed various physical and behavioral traits in parents and their grown children. Using his newly invented "coefficient of correlation," he argued that behavioral traits are inherited. By comparing the distribution of traits in different generations, he concluded that each characteristic was the product of multiple donations from hereditary material.

A rather different view gained a following in the early 1900s on the heels of the rediscovery of Mendel's work, and it was embraced by such influential geneticists as Charles B. Davenport, a founder of Cold Spring Harbor Laboratory on Long Island. In the extreme, these researchers ascribed such ill-defined characteristics as musical ability, temperament, or "feeble-mindedness" to individual genes. In 1921, for instance, Davenport asserted that "it appears probable, from extensive pedigrees that have been analyzed, that feeble-mindedness of the middle and higher grades is inherited as a simple recessive [trait], or approximately so." (In spite of their divergent views on the mechanisms of inheritance, both men regrettably drew similar, dangerous conclusions from their observations. Galton, who coined the term "eugenics," became a strong advocate of improving the human race by selective breeding between people having desirable traits. Davenport ardently supported that practice as well.)

Some of the first experiments designed to assess the impact of genes on behavior were carried out in the 1920s on dogs. Those investigations examined, among other traits, pointing (indicating the locations of prey) and vocalizing during hunting.

Dog breeds are as distinctive in their behavior as they are in appearance. The early studies crossbred dogs that differed in some behavioral characteristics and then mated their offspring to one another. If one or just a few genes controlled a chosen behavioral trait, investigators would expect to find that the animals of the final generation divided into discrete groups in which one group closely resembled the mother, a second closely resembled the father and perhaps one or a few groups behaved in an intermediate manner. If many genes were involved, workers would expect to find no discrete classes and a broad range of behavior in the offspring. The results were consistent with the last pattern, indicating that many genes underlay the appearance of each trait. Similar conclusions came from studies of maze running by laboratory rats.

Such analyses were informative but had major limitations. Breeding experiments cannot meaningfully address the genetic basis of behaviors that are relatively invariant in all members of a species. To delve into that problem and others, scientists needed ways to identify the specific genes involved in behaviors. Unfortunately, they would not have those techniques until many years had passed.

By the 1960s, however, many of the technical obstacles to the genetic dissection of behavior in animals had begun to fall. The structure of DNA had been deciphered in 1953. Studies of microorganisms had revealed

that genes specify the makeup of proteins. When a gene is activated, it leads to the synthesis of the encoded protein. That protein, in turn, carries out some needed function in the body—such as helping to build and operate the nervous system (which itself ultimately shapes behavior). Such research had also clarified the steps by which genes give rise to proteins and had laid the foundation for development in the 1980s of many useful tools for isolating individual genes and determining the functions of their corresponding proteins.

Seymour Benzer of the California Institute of Technology was a leader in establishing that genes are linear segments of DNA. In the mid-1960s he also became one of the first investigators to go beyond linking genes to physical traits. Benzer began, in detailed studies of the fruit fly *Drosophila melanogaster,* to identify genes that affect behaviors. That effort is ongoing, particularly in the laboratory of Jeffrey C. Hall of Brandeis University, who was among the earliest researchers to work with Benzer in this new field. It also continues in my laboratory in New York University and elsewhere. I got involved in the mid-1970s, when I became Hall's first graduate student at Brandeis.

## SPOTLIGHT ON FRUIT FLIES

Among the behaviors receiving the most attention is the one the flies seem to do best: courting. This process consists of a series of actions, each of which is accompanied by the exchange of visual, auditory, and chemosensory signals between males and females. The male is the more active of the dancers in this intricate ballet and has therefore been the focus of much of the research.

The ritual begins with a step called orientation. The male, who needs no instruction in this process, stands facing the female, about 0.2 millimeter away. Then he taps her on the abdomen with a foreleg and follows her if she moves away. Next, he displays one wing and flutters it to execute his form of a "love song." Depending on the female's level of interest at this point, he may go back and repeat his actions. But if all is going well, he unfurls his proboscis (a tubular appendage carrying the mouthparts at the tip) and licks the female's genitals. He may then mount her and, if she is receptive, copulate with her. Fruit flies will not mate unless the males have gone through the entire routine and the female has become receptive. Rape is uncommon in the fruit-fly world.

As a first step to finding the genes that might participate in courtship, Hall, initially working in Benzer's laboratory, set out to identify the parts of the central nervous system that control each element in the courting routine. He did so by producing extraordinary flies, called genetic mosaics, that carried mixtures of male and female cells.

---

### Early Views of Human Behavior

In the first decades of this century the opinions of two men represented opposite poles of thinking on the question of whether single genes or many lie at the root of any given behavior. Beginning in the late 1800s Francis Galton, a pioneering statistician, argued that human traits, including behaviors, are controlled by a multitude of the hereditary units that later came to be called genes. Charles B. Davenport, a respected geneticist, subsequently asserted that single genes were in control. Studies of fruit flies and other animals indicate Galton's view was probably the more accurate of the two.

If the names of Galton and Davenport are familiar, it is because both are now notorious for their advocacy of eugenics, which in Galton's words involves checking "the birth-rate of the Unfit" and improving the human race by "furthering the productivity of the Fit." Galton introduced the term in the 1880s, and Davenport, who established a research center in human eugenics at Cold Spring Harbor Laboratory on Long Island, pushed the program forward.

The technique was based on an understanding of sexual development in fruit flies. In fly embryos, such development is controlled by the complement of X chromosomes within each cell. Cells that have one X chromosome give rise to male anatomical structures and behaviors in the fully formed fly; cells that have two X chromosomes lead to female anatomy and behavior. These differences arise because single-X (male) and double-X (female) cells activate separate, albeit overlapping, sets of so-called sex-determining genes. Hall knew that if a fly carried mainly female cells but harbored male cells in a particular site of the brain, any typically male courtship activities it displayed could be attributed to a male pattern of gene expression, or activation, in that site.

Once mosaics were produced, he monitored the animals' attempts at courtship. Then he froze the flies and painstakingly sliced the diminutive creatures (measuring just 1.5 millimeters long) into 20 thin sections, noting (with the help of a clever colorization technique) the distribution of male and female cells. The experiments were particularly nerve-racking in the 1970s because the method for creating mosaics had an inconvenient drawback: no two individuals ended up with exactly the same clusters of male and female cells. Each fly had to survive a battery of behavioral tests, and all 20 sections had to be analyzable. The uniqueness of each animal meant that the experimenter had no second chance.

After examining many of these mosaics, Hall concluded that initiation of courtship (orienting toward the female, tapping her abdomen, following, and extending a wing) required male cells in one side or the other of a relatively small region near the top and toward the back of the fly's brain. This region integrates signals from the fly's various sensory systems. In other words, male cells at that site somehow give rise to a trigger mechanism for courtship that is present in males but not in females. Later steps in courtship, especially those demanding precise motor coordination, require male tissue in additional parts of the nervous system. To perform a proper courtship song, for example, flies must have male cells in the "trigger" region as well as in parts of the thoracic ganglion, which is the fly's version of a spinal cord.

More recently my colleagues and I have also identified the region of the brain involved in determining sexual preference in fruit flies (Fig. 4–1). We did so almost inadvertently, after Jean-François Ferveur in my laboratory (now at the University of Paris in Orsay) created entire strains of mosaic flies that were mainly male but that had female cells in selected areas of the brain. Before studying the courting behavior of these insects, we wanted to see whether full-fledged males would mistake our mosaics for females. The mosaics were not per-

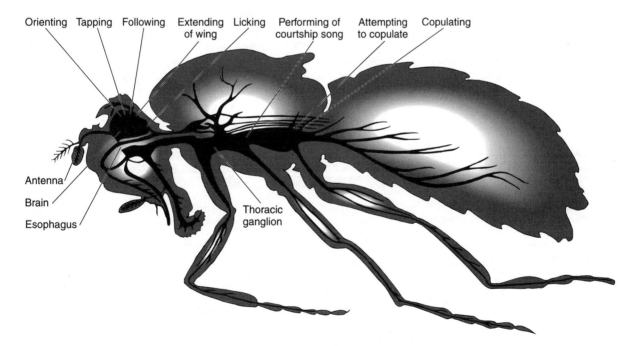

**Figure 4–1** Sites in the central nervous system that control the steps of courtship in male fruit flies have been mapped by studying flies that consist of a mixture of genetically male and female cells. To perform the initial steps of the mating routine (orienting, tapping, and wing extension) and to follow peripatetic females, flies must have male cells in a small trigger zone at the back of the brain. They also need male cells nearby to perform licking, in part of the thoracic ganglion to produce their song, and in many different sections of the thoracic ganglion to copulate. (Adapted from Jared Schneidman Design.)

ceived to be female. To our surprise, however, a few strains displayed an odd behavior of their own: They courted males as vigorously as they courted females.

Examination of the brains in these unusual insects, undertaken in conjunction with Klemens F. Störtkuhl and Reinhard F. Stocker of the University of Fribourg, revealed that sexual discernment was altered when either of two parts of the central nervous system was female: the antennal lobe or the mushroom body of the brain. Both these regions, the second of which lies close to the trigger site for courtship, participate in processing olfactory signals. If either or both of these centers for analyzing odors were female, the fly lost the ability to distinguish males from females and became equally interested in both.

## GENETIC INFLUENCES ON COURTSHIP

The discovery that so many different regions of the central nervous system are involved in male courtship suggests that a variety of genes also participate in the process. Indeed, more than a dozen have been discovered, mainly by Hall and his colleagues. For instance, the *fruitless* gene influences sexual preference. Mutation in this gene affects male flies in much the same way as having female cells in the antennal lobe or mushroom body does (Fig. 4–2): It causes males to court other males as avidly as they court females. The gene is also needed in the late stages of courtship; males carrying a mutant gene never attempt to copulate with females.

Hence, the picture beginning to emerge is more consistent with Galton's view than with Davenport's. Oddly enough, no one has yet identified any gene involved in courtship that is dedicated solely to that behav-

ior. Growing evidence suggests an explanation neither Galton nor Davenport would have predicted. It may be that most genes underlying courtship (and other behaviors) serve more than one function in the body. Identical genes may also be used for somewhat different purposes in males and females.

Consider, for example, one of the three genes known to participate in the male's courtship song. It is called *period* and has been studied most extensively by Hall and Charalambos P. Kyriacou of the University of Leicester.

Hall and Kyriacou decided to examine *period* when they discovered, in 1980, that the male song has a distinct rhythm to it. They already knew, from research done by Benzer's graduate student Ronald J. Konopka, that the gene affects the fly's circadian rhythms—the timed cycles, such as for waking and sleeping—that are characteristic of all living things. This property led them to wonder whether *period* might also affect the rhythm of the courtship song.

The song performed by fluttering the wing is not very musical to our ears, but it does have a detectable pattern. As the insect raises and lowers its wing once, the up-and-down motion produces a characteristic sound, or pulse, that can be picked up with a recording device. For approximately 27 seconds, the male gradually increases the interval between each successive pulse. Then, over another 27 or 28 seconds, he gradually decreases the interval, so that a plot of the intervals over time yields a smooth sinusoidal curve.

Hall and Kyriacou found that males carrying a normal *period* gene produce a normal song that makes females more receptive to their advances. In contrast, males carrying an inactive gene generate a song that lacks

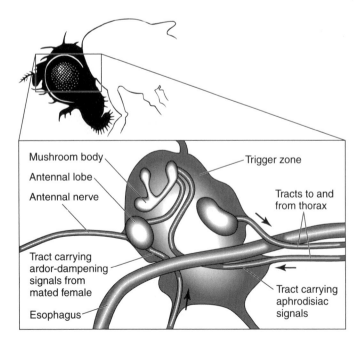

**Figure 4–2**  Seat of attraction to females resides in two sites in the male fruit fly's brain *(shown schematically)*. One is the antennal lobe; the other is the mushroom body, which lies close to the trigger zone responsible for initiating courtship. The importance of these regions was discovered when males engineered to contain female cells in either site began courting males as well as females. (Adapted from Jared Schneidman Design.)

the usual smooth rhythm and is apparently less effective at stimulating females: When computer-generated simulations of normal and rhythmless songs were played for lone females who were then paired with a male, the females exposed to the aberrant song proved less receptive to the male's advances. Similarly, less drastic mutations in the gene allow rhythmicity to be retained but stretch or shrink the sine curve; in the process, they reduce the song's power over a female.

The subtlety of *period*'s effects on the overall courtship routine, and on the song itself, adds credence to the notion that courtship—and other complex behavior—is regulated by multiple genes acting together. And the fact that the *period* gene participates in setting other clocks, and is also expressed in many parts of the central nervous system, supports the idea that any given gene may affect more than one behavior.

In a fascinating turn of events, Hall, Kyriacou, and Michael Rosbash, also at Brandeis, have recently pinpointed the exact part of the gene that controls song rhythm (Fig. 4–3). A small region in the middle is devoted to the song, and the balance of the gene controls other rhythms. That division of labor was deduced in part from the fact that a different species of fruit fly, *D. simulans,* has the same 24-hour cycle of activity and rest as is found in *D. melanogaster* but performs a song that differs in the intervals between pulses. The *period* gene in both species is similar, except for small differences in the

middle region. What is more, genetically engineered flies that carry a hybrid *period* gene made by replacing the middle region of the *D. melanogaster* gene with the corresponding segment of *D. simulans* will "sing" just like *D. simulans.*

Although sexual preference and courtship behavior are certainly programmed in fruit flies, males and females have the ability to modulate their activity in response to one another's reactions. In other words, they can learn. Just as the ability to carry out courtship is directed by genes, so, too, is the ability to learn during the experience. Studies of this phenomenon lend further support to the likelihood that behavior is regulated by a myriad of interacting genes, each of which handles diverse responsibilities in the body.

## LEARNING FROM EXPERIENCE

One thing a male can learn during courtship is not to waste time on a female who has already mated and who, consequently, will not be receptive. As Hall and Richard W. Siegel of the University of California at Los Angeles found, male flies will court virgin females tirelessly but will lose interest in mated females after about 30 minutes or an hour—when they finally become impressed by the inhibitory pheromone, or scent, emitted by mothers-to-be. Once males give up the chase, they become uninter-

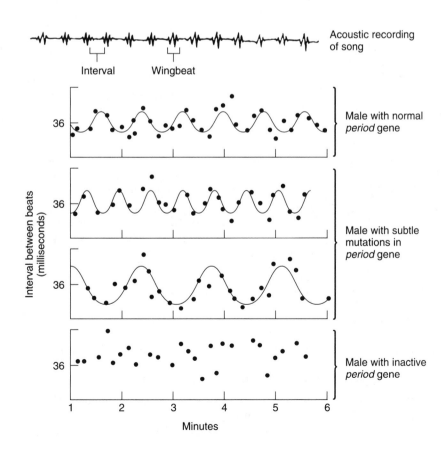

**Figure 4–3** Male fly extends a wing before vibrating it to produce his song. In the normal song the interval between each beat *(highlighted in an acoustic recording at top)* increases gradually over about 27 seconds and then decreases equally gradually; a plot of the intervals resembles a sine curve *(top curve).* This rhythmicity has been shown to be controlled by a gene called *period.* Flies carrying a healthy *period* gene display the usual song. But those with mildly defective genes produce abnormal rhythms *(middle curves),* and those harboring an inactive gene completely lose their ability to "carry a tune" *(bottom).* (Adapted from Jared Schneidman Design; Source: Charalambos P. Kyriacou and Jeffrey C. Hall.)

ested in all females, virgin or not, for a few hours. If there is discernible evolutionary logic to this behavior, it may be that the presence of a mated female in a group of females is a sign that most or all of them have already mated; hence, a male's efforts would be better spent elsewhere.

My explorations of the genetic underpinnings of this response began a few years ago and were undertaken with Leslie C. Griffith, who is now at Brandeis. We knew from the work of other investigators that an enzyme called calcium/calmodulin–dependent protein kinase II (CaMKII) can help record the effects of experience in neurons, in the process inducing molecular changes that are likely to be essential to learning. We therefore decided to see whether male fruit flies needed this protein—and thus the corresponding gene—in order to respond appropriately to mated females.

As a first step, Griffith engineered a strain of flies whose CaMKII protein could be quieted simply by increasing the body temperature of the flies. Sure enough, when the enzyme's activity was reduced even mildly, males of this strain behaved oddly. They were as avid as normal flies in their courtship of virgin females, and they lost interest in mated females after the usual hour or so, but they seemed to forget their rejection almost immediately. If they were placed with females soon after being with a mated one, they began their pursuit anew. When CaMKII was inhibited even more, the males did not learn at all: They pursued mated females unabated for hours. (Even in the world of fruit flies, it seems some men never learn.)

Once we knew that the *CaMKII* gene, through its enzyme product, did participate in learning during courtship, we naturally began to wonder how the enzyme itself helped to record experience. All protein kinases act by phosphorylating, or adding phosphate groups to, other molecules, thereby activating or inactivating the targets. But what was the kinase's target in neurons, and what happened after that target was phosphorylated? Such questions ultimately led us to demonstrate that a second gene expressed in neurons—*eag*—is instrumental in such learning as well.

## Another Learning Gene

The protein product of this gene is a component of certain membrane-spanning channels that regulate the flow of potassium ions out of neurons. Opening these channels helps to control excitability and the release of neurotransmitters, which carry messages from cell to cell. (The name derives from the fact, discovered in the 1960s, that when flies bearing mutated *eag* genes are anesthetized, their legs shake: In a sign of the times, the discoverers called the gene *ether-a-go-go*.)

On the basis of a number of clues from our own research, from that of our collaborators Jing Wang and Chun-Fang Wu of the University of Iowa and from others, Girth and I began to think the CaMKII enzyme might participate in learning by modifying the EAG protein in potassium channels. For instance, Eric R. Kandel and his colleagues at Columbia University had shown in the marine mollusk *Aplysia* that one kind of potassium channel is modified by a kinase during a simple form of learning. Moreover, we found that mutations of the EAG protein led to essentially the same "thickheadedness" in courting males as did inhibiting the activity of CaMKII. Such discoveries implied the two proteins might operate in the same cascade of molecular interactions and the CaMKII might act on the EAG protein.

To our delight, Girth confirmed that the enzyme could indeed modify the EAG protein, at least in the test tube. Based on these findings and on electrical recordings from synapses in mutant animals, we now speculate that males learn to give up on mated females through activation of the following sequence of molecular reactions.

First, exposure of males to antiaphrodisiac pheromones while they are courting mated females stimulates sensory systems that feed into the trigger region of the brain. As a result of this stimulation, calcium builds up locally in cells that normally promote sexual arousal during courtship. The buildup activates CaMKII, which phosphorylates the EAG protein in potassium channels carrying that protein. Such modifications causes the channels to open, allowing potassium ions to flow out of the neurons, thereby quieting the cells and reducing their ability to release neurotransmitters. As the cells become silent, the males lose interest in mating. Conversely, flies carrying defects in the genes for either protein presumably retain misplaced interest in mated females because the potassium channels remain closed in the critical cells, allowing the neurons to become hyperactive.

The *CaMKII* and *eag* genes turn out to be just two of several known to affect learning and memory in fruit flies. Some of the others also participate in courtship—a finding that meshes rather well with the view that behaviors arise from the interactions of vast networks of genes, most of which take part in many different aspects of an organisms's biology.

## Lessons for Humans?

Do the lessons from genetic studies of fruit-fly behavior bear any relevance to human beings? I think they do—within limits. There is every reason to believe that the genetic influences on behavior will be at least as complicated in people as they are in fruit flies. Hence, the notion of many, multipurpose genes making small contributions is likely to apply. And many of the gene products that function in the brains of flies will probably turn out to be important in the human brain. Human counterparts have already been discovered for a number of genes originally identified in the fly, such as *eag*. These findings should provide insights into the molecular interactions that enable the central nervous system to produce behavior.

New technologies hold promise for detecting the contributions of individual genes to human attributes. The techniques are already being applied to a variety of complex traits, including musical ability—though more carefully than in Davenport's day. Such work, and extrapolations from animal research, can probably help pinpoint some of the genes that contribute to specific human behaviors. But any research claiming to explain human activity in purely genetic terms must be viewed with caution. Society's well-founded unwillingness to rear human subjects in perfectly controlled environ-

ments makes it virtually impossible to prove the validity of such claims.

## FURTHER READINGS

Feveur, J. F. et al. (February 10, 1995). "Genetic feminization of brain structures and changed sexual orientation in male *Drosophila melanogaster.*" *Science, 267:* 902–905.

Girth, L. C. et al. (March 1993). "Inhibition of calcium/calmodulin-dependent protein kinase in *Drosophila* disrupts behavioral plasticity." *Neuron, 10,* (3) 501–509.

Girth, L. C. et al. (October, 1994). "Calcium/calmodulin–dependent protein kinase II and potassium channel subunit EAG similarly affect plasticity in *Drosophila.*" *Proceedings of the National Academy of Sciences, 91* (21): 10044–10048.

Hall, J. C. (March 25, 1994). "The mating of a fly." *Science, 264:* 1702–1714.

# Chapter 5

# *The Taxonomy and Evolution of Primates*

## Robert W. Sussman

### PRINCIPLES OF ANIMAL TAXONOMY

The necessity of aggregating things into classes is a general characteristic of all living things. The ability to classify is an absolute and minimal characteristic of being or staying alive. Even one-celled organisms must discriminate classes of objects. Animals group objects into classes but not necessarily the same objects into the same classes. For example, what may be dangerous, food, an enemy, a sleeping site, or a sex partner for one organism may not be so for another. The ways in which an ant, tick, bat, primate, and a human see the world and classify it are quite different (von Uexkull 1934, reprinted 1957), and are related to the senses of the particular organism, its learning experiences, and, at least in humans, their cultural background.

According to Simpson (1961:3), there are two major ways to order our perceptions: "association by contiguity" and "association by similarity."

> Association by contiguity (for our purposes) is a structural and functional relationship among things that, in a different psychological terminology, enter into a single Gestalt. The things involved may be quite dissimilar, or in any event the similarity is irrelevant. Such, for instance, is the relationship between a plant and the soil in which it grows, between a rabbit and the fox that pursues it, between the separate organs that compose an organism, among all the trees of a forest, or among all the descendants of a given population. Things in this relationship to each other belong both structurally and functionally to what may be defined in a broad but technical sense as a single system.

Objects associated by similarity, on the other hand, are classed together simply because they share one or more common characteristics.

> They may be all yellow, or all smooth, or all with wings, or all ten feet high. They may, for that matter, all be seats

with four legs and a back, in which case we call them chairs (Simpson 1961:4).

If there were no means of classification or of ordering nature, natural phenomena would appear chaotic. Indeed, the whole aim of theoretical science, it might be said, is to carry to the highest possible and conscious degree the perceptual reduction of chaos in natural phenomena (Simpson 1961). Is the order so achieved, however, an objective characteristic of the phenomena or an artifact constructed by the western scientist? In classifying potatoes, the western scientist would use only one term, *Solanum tuberosum*. The local Bolivian farmer has over 200 terms for potatoes. The botanist and the Bolivian farmer use different criteria in making their classifications. In fact, the usefulness of the classification depends upon the specific reasons or needs of the classifier.

The systematic study of biology, from the viewpoint of a western scientist, requires the construction of a formal system in which organisms are grouped into classes *(zoological classification)* and of names for these classes *(zoological nomenclature)* (Table 5–1). The present classificatory scheme used in biology is based on Linnaeus' *Systema Naturae* (10th edition, 1758). Since the mid-eighteenth century, however, the philosophy underlying biological classification has changed radically. Linnaeus based his scheme on the typological or archetypal concept, in which species are unchanging or immutable. The living animals in a class (or taxon) were considered to be imperfect copies of an ideal or perfect type which was created by God: Humans were considered the imperfect copy of God—western European man bearing the greatest likeness! Each class was considered to be fixed and distinct from all others. Thus, animals were classed into groups using association by similarity.

There have been two major changes in the philosophy of biology since the time of Linnaeus. The first grows from the discovery of evolutionary mechanisms and

## TABLE 5–1   Definitions

| | |
|---|---|
| Systematics | The scientific study of the kinds of diversity of organisms and any and all relationships among them. |
| Zoological Classification | The ordering of animals into groups (or sets) on the basis of their relationship. |
| Zoological nomenclature | The application of distinctive names to each of the groups recognized in any given zoological classification. |
| Taxonomy | The theoretical study of classification, including its basis, principles, procedures and rules. |
| Taxon | A group of real organisms recognized as a formal unit at any level of hierarchic classification. |
| Species | A population or group of populations of actually or potentially interbreeding animals that are reproductively isolated from other such groups. |
| Sympatric species | Two *non*-interbreeding populations living in the same environment. |
| Allochronic species | Two groups of animals in the same lineage but living in different time periods. |
| Allopatric species | Two groups of animals in the same or different species but isolated geographically. |

processes by Darwin, who demonstrated that species are not immutable and that they diverged from a single common ancestor. The second is typology as the basis for species has been replaced by the concept of breeding populations. Linnaeus classified animals by similarity. Modern biological systematists recognize the enormous variability that exists within breeding populations. In principle, animal classification in modern biology is based upon association by contiguity, that is, on genealogical relationships among organisms. In practice, however, much of biological classification is pragmatic and usually is still based on similarity, whatever the theory may be. For example, even modern DNA hybridization techniques gauge overall similarity in the genetic material.

Modern zoological classification, the basis for most zoological nomenclature, is referred to as the Linnaean hierarchy (though the scheme used by Linnaeus was not hierarchical). The major categories of this classificatory system are listed in Table 5–2. The customary indentation of subsequent categories indicates the decreasing inclusiveness of the various levels.

The basic unit of the Linnaean hierarchy is the *species*. As stated above, natural populations are not fixed, static qualities. Populations change through time and vary morphologically, genetically, and geographically. Naming them often involves creating discrete units out of continuous phenomena. Most biologists follow Mayr's (1963, Mayr and Ashlock 1991) definition of a species as *a population or group of populations of actually or potentially interbreeding animals that are reproductively isolated from other such groups.* It is considered to be a real, natural phenomenon and not an arbitrary analytical

category. Not all biologists agree with this definition (Raven et al. 1992, Templeton 1989). Problems arise when attempting to identify fossil species in an evolving lineage (see Rose and Bown 1986), and when comparing morphologically similar extant populations that are *allopatric* (geographically isolated) and, thus, have no chance to naturally express their potential for interbreeding. Another problem arises in the case of morphologically distinct populations in which hybridization occurs; how much genetic leakage should be tolerated before recognizing an independent species? This has led to considerable debate (e.g., see papers in Kimbel and Martin 1993, Otte and Endler 1989, Vrba 1985).

Recently, Templeton (1989, 1994) has introduced a new definition of species, the *cohesion concept of species*. Rather than looking at mechanisms that isolate populations, Templeton defines species by the mechanisms that maintain cohesion within a population and speciation is defined as the evolution of cohesive mechanisms. Using this definition, *species are groups of animals that share a suite of genetic, phenotypic, demographic, ecological, and behavioral characteristics or cohesive mechanisms that help maintain the group as a cohesive unit.* These characteristics allow what Templeton refers to as genetic and demographic exchangeability within the species. Similarly, Paterson (1985, see also Templeton 1987) defines sexually reproducing species as the most inclusive population of individual biparenting organisms that share a common fertilization system. In many animals, an important component of this system is the means by which the animals

## TABLE 5–2   Categories in the Current Classification (The Linnaen Hierarchy)

| | |
|---|---|
| Kingdom* | Animal |
| Phylum* | Chordate |
| Subphylum | |
| Superclass | |
| Class* | Mammalian |
| Infraclass | |
| Cohort | |
| Superorder | |
| Order* | Primates |
| Suborder | |
| Infraorder | |
| Superfamily | |
| Family* | Hominidae |
| Subfamily | |
| Tribe | |
| Subtribe | |
| Genus* | *Homo* |
| Subgenus | |
| Species* | *sapiens* |
| Subspecies | |

Adapted from Buettner-Janusch (1966)
*designates seven major categories of the Linnaen Hierarchy

attract and recognize each other, what Paterson calls the *specific-mate recognition system* (SMRS). By using Paterson's species recognition system, primatologists have tested the validity of current taxonomic divisions among the nocturnal galagos and a number of new species have been identified. In any case, as emphasized by Mayr (1963) and reiterated by Jolly (1993:104): "...taxonomic organization inevitably forces an oversimplified structure upon a complex evolutionarily dynamic situation."

Following the rules of nomenclature each species is scientifically referred to by its genus and species name (binomen). Thus the scientific name of humans is *Homo sapiens.* That of the rhesus monkey is *Macaca mulatta. Homo* and *Macaca* are names for the genera (plural of genus) and *H. sapiens* and *M. mulatta* are names for the species. There is only one living species in the genus *Homo;* the genus is monotypic. The genus *Macaca* is polytypic for it contains twelve species. The genus name is capitalized and italicized; the species name is italicized. Other conventions have been devised for the purpose of forming names of some of the higher categories in the Linnaean hierarchy. Some of these are found in Table 5–3.

The higher categories in zoological classification are those above the level of species. Groups of animals included in a higher taxon should be descended from a common ancestor, in which case the group is called *monophyletic.* Although it is not always possible, the classification of animals into higher categories should reflect valid phylogenetic entities. The criteria used to classify groups of species into genera, genera into families, families into orders, etc. are extremely complex and have been the subject of many books and articles (see, for example, Eldridge 1989, Hennig 1966, Kluge 1984, Martin 1990, Mayr 1969, Mayr and Ashlock 1991, Simpson 1945, 1961, 1975, Sneath and Sokal 1973). In a discussion of the origin of the Order Primates, to which I will return shortly, Cartmill (1972:97–98) summarizes these criteria as follows:

> Taxonomic boundaries are expected to correspond as much as possible to major adaptive shifts, represented in

the fossil record by phases of rapid morphological change that led to the fixation of some new complex of traits underlying a subsequent evolutionary radiation. Such a complex of traits can be used as a diagnosis of the derived higher taxon.... It is not always possible to identify a major adaptive shift accompanying the appearance of a new grade of organization.... In a situation like this—when, in Simpson's (1944) terms, there is no quantum evolution from one adaptive zone to another at the base of an adaptive radiation—placement of any taxonomic boundary between ancestral and descendent groups becomes largely a matter of caprice.

In Table 5–4, I present the classification of the Order Primates. Because of the difficulties of dividing a continuously evolving group into discrete units, and of other difficulties inherent in interpreting taxonomic relationships, there are still many debates concerning the classification of primates. For example, until the mid-1960s, tree shrews (Tupaiiformes) were considered to be primates, now it is generally agreed that they are not (Campbell 1974; Goodman 1966; Luckett 1980; Martin 1968, 1990; Van Valen 1965).

In addition, the Order Primates commonly is divided into two suborders, Prosimii (lemurs, lorises, and tarsiers) and Anthropoidea (monkeys, apes, and humans). The prosimians are the more primitive of the two suborders because they preserve many morphological characteristics similar to those of primates living in the Eocene epoch, 40 to 50 million years ago (Fleagle 1988). However, tarsiers apparently share some anatomical features with anthropoids, which suggests that anthropoids and tarsiers may be derived from a common ancestor (see relevant papers in Luckett and Szalay 1975 and Chivers and Joysey 1978; Aiello 1986; Fleagle and Kay 1994; Martin 1990).

For some taxonomists, who believe all higher taxa should be *holophyletic*—a strict form of monophyly in which not only must the members of a group share an ancestor but *all* the descendants of the ancestor must be classified in the taxon—the taxon Prosimii is invalid, even though it is monophyletic. For these classifiers, Primates

**TABLE 5–3** Names of Higher Categories

| Category | Suffix | Genus | Stem* | Name of higher category |
|---|---|---|---|---|
| Infraorder | -IFORMES | *Lemur* | LEMUR- | LEMURIFORMES |
| | | *Tarsius* | TARSI- | TARSIIFORMES |
| Superfamily | -OIDEA | *Lemur* | LEMUR- | LEMUROIDEA |
| | | *Cercopithecus* | CERCOPITHEC- | CERCOPITHECOIDEA |
| Family | -IDAE | *Lemur* | LEMUR- | LEMURIDAE |
| | | *Cercopithecus* | CERCOPITHEC- | CERCOPITHECIDAE |
| Subfamily | -INAE | *Lemur* | LEMUR- | LEMURINAE |
| | | *Alouatta* | ALOUATT- | ALOUATTINAE |

*The stem is usually taken from the name of a genus within the higher category.
Adapted from Buettner-Janusch (1966)

TABLE 5–4  Present Classification of the Order Primates

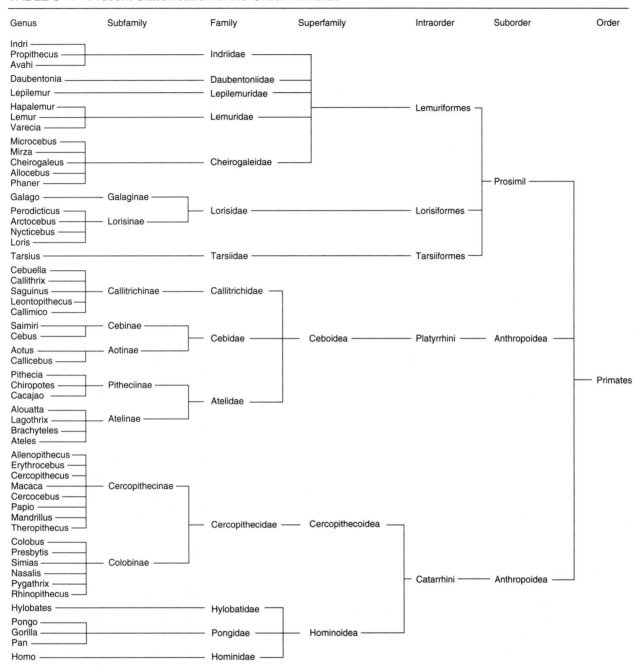

should be divided into the suborders Haplorhini (including tarsiers, monkeys, apes, and man) and the Strepsirhini (including lemurs and lorises), which are considered to be separate holophyletic assemblages. However, this classification is scientifically controversial and also impractical to apply to fossil primates (Rasmussen pers. comm.). A number of other taxonomic debates are currently in progress but are of little concern to this discussion. I mention these debates to make the reader aware of the fact that the names given to taxa by various authors may differ, even in cases when the phylogeny is agreed upon.

## WHAT IS A PRIMATE?

Using the terms discussed in the first section of this chapter, I can now say that the Order Primates is a monophyletic group of animals bound together by common ancestry. The question still remains, however, as to whether this group can be described by a complex of traits related to a major adaptive shift, which accompanied the origin of the order. This is an ecological, as well as a taxonomic, question and will be the focus of the remainder of this chapter.

One of the early definitions of primates, relied upon by numerous authors, was that of Mivart (1873):

Unguiculate, claviculate placental mammals, with orbits encircled by bone; three kinds of teeth, at least at one time of life; brain always with a posterior lobe and calcarine fissure, the innermost digits of at least one pair of extremities opposable; hallux with a flat nail or none; a well-developed caecum; penis pendulous; testes scrotal; always two pectoral mammae.

This definition was expanded by Le Gros Clark (1963), and the resultant list of anatomical characters and evolutionary trends (Table 5–5) is still used by most primatologists to define primates. Because these features, for the most part, involve the retention and elaboration of generalized mammalian features rather than a list of specialized anatomical traits, primates are often distinguished from other mammalian orders by their lack of specialization. As stated by Le Gros Clark (1963:42):

While many other mammalian orders can be defined by conspicuous specializations of a positive kind which readily mark them off from one another, the Primates as a whole have preserved rather a generalized anatomy and, if anything, are to be mainly distinguished from other orders by a negative feature—their lack of specialization.

This definition, however, does not clearly identify probably *derived* features of primates that would unambiguously prove their common ancestry. By including likely primitive features of placental mammals, it does not necessarily distinguish primates from other mammals. Furthermore, the trends included in this definition refer not to universally shared primate features, but to developments found only in some members of the group. Because of these problems, Martin (1968a, 1990) has devised a list of derived characters shared by primates that distinguish them from other mammals, and that should aid in any reconstruction of primate evolution.

Martin's resulting new definition of living primates, with some slight modifications, is as follows: Primates are (1) essentially *arboreal inhabitants of tropical/subtropical forest ecosystems.* This is related to a number of interrelated locomotor adaptations, including (2) extremities adapted for *prehension of branches* rather than clinging with claws. This is enhanced by possession of: (3) *flat nails and sensitive tactile pads* with cutaneous ridges (dermatoglyphs); (4) a widely divergent hallux allowing for a *powerful grasping action of the foot;* (5) locomotion is *hindlimb dominated;* and (6) the foot has a unique orientation at the point of thrust (*tarsifulcrumating* type of foot) and relative *elongation of the distal segment of the calcaneus* (heel bone).

There are also features of the sense organs and skull. (7) The *visual sense is greatly emphasized.* The (8) *eyes are relatively large* in relation to skull length, and the orbits possess a (9) *postorbital bar* (orbit completely enclosed with bone). Primates have a pronounced degree of (10) forward rotation of the orbits (viz. *orbital convergence*) that ensures a large degree of (11) *binocular vision.* (12) Ipsilateral and contralateral nerve *fibres passing to the optic tectum are approximately balanced* in primates, whereas in non-primates contralateral fibres predominate—this allows (13) effective *stereoscopic vision.* In primates, the bony enclosure of the middle ear cavity (the auditory bulla) is formed from the petrosal bone (14) (*petrosal bulla*). (15) *The brain is typically moderately enlarged in relation to body size,* and possesses a (16) true *Sylvian sulcus* and a (17) *triradiate calcarine sulcus.* Furthermore, (18) the *brain constitutes a significantly larger proportion of body weight at all stages of gestation.*

Unique reproductive features include: (19) *very early descent of the testes* into a postpenial scrotum; (20) *absence of a urogenital sinus* and (21) involvement of the *yolk-sac in placentation is suppressed.* Primates are also adapted for (22) *slow reproductive turnover:* They have (23) *long gestation periods* relative to maternal body size, (24) produce *small litters of precocial infants,* and (25) *fetal and postnatal growth are slow* in relation to maternal size. (26) *Sexual maturity is attained late* and (27) *life spans are long* relative to body size.

The (28) *dental formula exhibits a maximum of 2.1.4.3* (that is two incisors, one canine, four premolars, and three molars on both sides of the upper and lower jaws; a maximum of 40 teeth). The (29) *cheek teeth (molars and premolars) are typically relatively unspecialized,*

---

TABLE 5–5  Traits Often Used to Define Primates Developed from Le Gros Clark and Others

---

(1)  Preservation of a generalized limb structure with primitive pentadactyly—five fingers or toes on each of the extremities.

(2)  Enhancement of free mobility of the digits, especially the thumb (pollex) and big toe (hallux) (which are used for grasping).

(3)  Sharp, compressed claws are replaced by flattened nails, and this is associated with the development of highly sensitive tactile pads on the digits.

(4)  Reduction of olfaction and associated areas of the brain, and abbreviation of the snout.

(5)  Elaboration of the visual apparatus, with development of binocular vision.

(6)  The loss of certain elements of the primitive mammalian dentition, but the preservation of a simple cusp pattern of the molar teeth and the retention of teeth that are regionally differentiated in form (heterodonty).

(7)  Expansion and elaboration of the brain, especially the cerebral cortex.

(8)  Increase and elaboration of the development of the processes of gestation and of the uterine and placental membranes.

(30) *cusps are generally low and rounded,* and the lower molars possess a (31) *broad, grinding basin, or talonid.*

Another feature, not included in Martin's list but which is related to the unique reproductive features listed above, is (32) the tendency of primates to be highly social (see Chapter 6 on Socioecology). All diurnal primates live in relatively stable social groups, whereas the nocturnal prosimians generally are "solitary but social." In Table 5–6, I define the types of social structure found among extant primates.

Now I have gone one step further in answering the question "What is a primate?" A primate is a member of a monophyletic order of mammals. All primate taxa are believed to be descended from a common ancestral species, and share a number of traits in common. Can we learn more about the origin of primates by studying the adaptive significance of these traits, or by a study of the fossil record? Can we reconstruct the niche to which the ancestral primate was adapted? It is upon the morphological traits of this ancestral group of primates that all further adaptations have been built, but what was the initial impetus that brought about the adaptive radiation of the primates?

THE ORIGIN OF PRIMATES: THE ARBOREAL THEORY OF PRIMATE EVOLUTION

Traditionally, certain morphological traits of primates were thought to be related to the acquisition of an arboreal way of life by a pre-primate, primitive mammal of

the order Insectivora in the late Mesozoic (Table 5–7). Grafton Elliot Smith (1912), an English anatomist who specialized in comparative neurology, explained the reduction in the sense of smell and the elaboration of the senses of vision, touch, and hearing in early primates as adaptations to life amidst the branches of trees.

Wood Jones, an assistant to Smith, elaborated Smith's theories (Jones 1916). He focused on the postcranial features of the primate morphological pattern. Jones emphasized the adaptive significance of the use of the forelimbs for touch and climbing in the trees. This, Jones claimed, led to the "emancipation of the forelimbs" and improved eye-hand coordination. Since these early papers, this theory was elaborated upon and referred to as the "arboreal theory" of primate evolution (Clark 1963, Howells 1947).

Until the 1970s, this theory was generally accepted as the explanation for the adaptive significance of many unique primate morphological traits. These traits were considered to be adaptations of our earliest ancestors to the acquisition of an arboreal way of life. Le Gros Clark (1963:43) summarizes as follows:

The evolutionary trends associated with the relative lack of structural and functional specialization are a natural consequence of an arboreal habitat, a mode of life which among other things demands or encourages prehensile functions of the limbs, a high degree of visual acuity, and the accurate control and coordination of muscular activity by a well-developed brain.

## TABLE 5–6 Nonhuman Primate Social Groups

1. *Solitary but Social*—found in most nocturnal prosimians *plus* orangutans. Characteristics: Some individuals may sleep together in nesting groups, but forage separately—home ranges of females overlap; those of adult males usually do not. Adult males avoid each other. Each adult male interacts with more than one adult female. Adult females form *nesting groups* consisting of females and young. Male offspring forced out of group at puberty.

2. *One Male Group*—found in Black-and-White colobus monkeys (*Colobus guereza*), Patas monkeys (*Erythrocebus patas*), Gelada baboons (*Theropithecus gelada*), Hamadryas baboons (*papio hamadryas*), and most members of the genus *Cercopithecus*. Types of one-male groups can vary slightly, but the basic elements are the same: One adult male interacts with more than one adult female and immature offspring. Male offspring are forced to leave the group at puberty.

3. *Fission-Fusion*—characterized by the existence of a larger group that breaks into subgroups and reforms again over a period of time. Three types:
    (a) Spider monkeys (genus *Ateles*)—fairly small group breaks up into smaller subunits for feeding.
    (b) Gelada baboons (*Theropithecus gelada*) and Hamadryas (*Papio hamadryas*)—In this case the subunits are one-male units that remain constant from day to day. Composition of the larger group varies when different one male units come together.
    (c) Chimpanzees (genus *Pan*)—the large group, composed of up to 100 animals is called a regional population. Subgroups vary.

4. *Pair bonds* ("Family groups")—found in *Callicebus*, Hylobatidae, *Indri,* and other species that are characterized by exclusive use of space. One adult male and one adult female live together for life with their various *immature* offspring. Offspring of both sexes are forced out of the group at puberty.

5. *Cooperative polyandrous group* (communal breeding)—group composed of more than one unrelated male and female but only one female is reproductively active. Females, however, mate with more than one male and all animals (especially males) carry the young. Found only in the Callitrichidae.

6. *Multi-Male Group*—most common type of nonhuman primate social group—found widely throughout the order Primates, e.g.: most Cebidae, savanna baboons (except those above), diurnal lemurs, langurs (subfamily Colobinae), gorillas. Size varies from approximately 10 to more than 100 animals. Group consists of more than one adult male, more than one adult female, and offspring, of all ages. Larger groups sometimes called "troops."

TABLE 5–7   Recent Geologic Time Periods

| Eras | Duration of Periods (Millions of Years) | Periods | Epochs | (Millions of Years) |
|---|---|---|---|---|
| | 3 | Quarternary | Recent | 0.01 |
| | | | Pleistocene | 3 |
| CENOZOIC (65–70 million years duration) | 65 | Tertiary | Pliocene | 12–3 |
| | | | Miocene | 25–12 |
| | | | Oligocene | 34–25 |
| | | | Eocene | 58–34 |
| | | | Paleocene | 65–58 |
| MESOZOIC (130 million years duration) | 60 | CRETACEOUS | | |
| | 35 | JURASSIC | | |
| | 35 | TRIASSIC | | |
| PALEOZOIC (300 million years duration) | | | | |

## The Origin of Primates: A Paleontological Approach

The arboreal theory of primate evolution was developed by primate anatomists and behavioralists using traits that are found in taxa of living primates. Paleontologists have discovered late Cretaceous and early Paleocene mammals with some features that are unique and primate-like, and other features that are shared by a number of early mammalian groups. The best classification for these early primate-like mammals remains uncertain. Because they are working with forms close to the point of divergence between primates and other early Tertiary mammals, paleontologists often find it difficult to draw boundaries between higher taxonomic groups at this early stage. In fact, many students of the Primates claimed that no major adaptive shift occurred in the earliest stages of primate evolution (Clark 1963; McKenna 1966; Simpson 1955, 1961). These authors asserted that one would have to rely on specific "taxonomic traits," the adaptive significance of which is not necessarily recognized, to define the Order Primates. One such trait, the petrosal bulla, was thought by many to serve as a marker of the order (Covert 1986, Martin 1968, 1986a, McKenna 1966, Szalay and Delson 1979, Szalay et al. 1987, Van Valen 1965).

The early primate-like mammals are usually grouped into five or six families, the Paromomyidae, Picrodontidae, Plesiadapidae, Carpolestidae, Saxonellidae, and for some authors the Microsyopidae, all of which make up the suborder Plesiadapiformes (see reviews by Conroy 1990, Fleagle 1988, Gunnell 1989). The Plesiadapiformes, which may or may not fit in the Order Primates, stand in contrast to later certain primates of the Eocene, which are called *euprimates* (true primates) to avoid confusion with these archaic groups.

The plesiadapiforms are found in various Paleocene and Eocene deposits of Europe and North Amer-ica, and range in size from that of a mouse to a large domestic cat. They did not look like modern primates. They possessed long snouts, relatively small brains, a relatively large olfactory apparatus, minimally convergent orbits, and where postcranials have been discovered, clawed digits similar to those of a squirrel. However, the plesiadapoids (except for microsyopids) presumably possessed a petrosal bulla (Figure 5–1) (but see Kay et al. 1990 and MacPhee et al. 1983). Furthermore, some authors believed that they shared a number of dental characteristics with genera of Eocene euprimates (e.g. Gingerich 1986, Simpson 1935, Szalay 1968, 1969; but see Wible and Covert 1987, Martin 1990). Therefore, this group of Paleocene mammals has been classified by many as the earliest form of primate. Unlike many authors, however, Szalay (1968, 1972) proposed that these taxa were the result of an evolutionary shift from groups that were primarily insectivorous to those including more and more plant material in their diet.

> It is safe to presume that the various features of the early prosimian dentition reflect a rather important shift in the nature of the whole feeding mechanism. Sporadic finds of primate skulls in the early Tertiary confirm this shift as a change from an insectivorous diet (i.e., a carnivorous diet in a special sense) of the insectivore ancestry to a herbivorous one . . . it is only an increasing occupation of feeding on fruits, leaves, and other herbaceous matter that explains the first radiation of primates (Szalay 1968:32).

## The Origin of Primates: Terminal Branch Feeding Insectivores

Now I have presented three divergent points of view concerning primate origins and early adaptations: (1) primates are arboreally adapted mammals; (2) no recognizable major adaptive shift occurred at the primate-

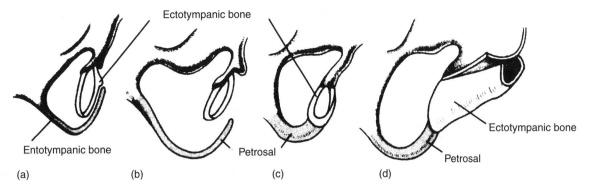

**Figure 5–1** The Auditory Bulla in Mammals. The main bone forming the bulla is the entotympanic in tree shrews (a) and the petrosal (part of the temporal bone) in primates: lemurs (b), lorises (c), and in tarsiers, Old World Monkeys, apes and humans (d). (From Conroy 1990).

insectivore border and ordinal traits (e.g., the petrosal bulla) must be used to distinguish early primates; and (3) dental features indicate that the insectivore-primate adaptive shift involved primarily a dietary shift from predominantly insect feeding to predominantly plant feeding animals. More recently, Cartmill (1972, 1974a, 1992) presented a fourth argument. He rejected the notion that the plesiadapoids are primates and did not agree with the arboreal theory of primate evolution.

Cartmill considered plesiadapoids to be close collateral relative to the earliest primates with whom they shared many traits (Cartmill 1974a, Kay and Cartmill 1977), but he rejected the view that the plesiadapoids shared a common adaptive trend with the primates. Cartmill argued that whereas some of these early mammals possess primatelike features, others do not display any significant adaptation that would justify including them in Primates. He argued further that an insectivore to plant-feeding shift does not define a boundary between insectivores and primates. In a detailed study of plesiadapoid dentitions, Kay and Cartmill (1977:31) stated:

> Early and Middle Paleocene plesiadapoids appear to have been insectivores. Specializations for eating plants do not appear among plesiadapoids until as much as 6 million years after the earliest known relatives of the group.

Cartmill asserted that a marked adaptive shift *can* be postulated to account for the evolution of primates. The earliest primates were those characterized by the traits described by Clark (1963) and Martin (1986a, 1990): e.g., prehensility of the hands and feet with flattened nails on the fingers and toes, orbital convergence and stereoscopic vision, and regression of the snout and olfactory senses. These "primates of modern aspect" (Simons 1972) or "euprimates" (Hoffstetter 1977) first appeared in the Eocene. The arboreal theory of primate evolution was usually used to explain the evolution of

these traits: i.e., they signify an adaptive trend in primate evolution towards an arboreal way of life. Cartmill argued otherwise:

> If the primate evolutionary trends have not been characteristic of other lineages of arboreal mammals, we may conclude that there is something wrong with the arboreal theory in its received form (Cartmill 1972:103).

Of the fourteen orders of terrestrial mammals, nine have arboreal forms. Many of these groups of animals have highly successful adaptations to life in the trees and do not have the characteristic traits developed by the Primates. For example, tree squirrels fill a specific set of niches in the forest canopy and these differ from those filled by primates. Unlike primates, tree squirrels normally range vertically using scansorial locomotion along large branches and tree trunks, and they are the primary and often sole consumers and dispersers of large hard fruits and nuts (Emmons 1980, Garber and Sussman 1984).

In an elegant use of the comparative method, Cartmill compared the function of specific traits shared by primates and other animals in an attempt to determine the precise niche that early primates might have filled. Cartmill (1972) found that

> grasping hands and feet are advantageous to animals that habitually forage in terminal branches, since they permit these animals to suspend themselves by their hind limbs (and tail, if prehensile) while using the forelimbs to reach and manipulate food items (107). . . . Prehensile hands and feet are universal among shrub layer insectivores and related herbivorous forms (108).

He also concluded that

> outside of primates, pronounced convergence of the optic axes is largely restricted to predators. Optic convergence is particularly marked in such animals as owls, hawks, and cats which depend on vision for the detection of prey (113).

Thus, Cartmill argued that the earliest primate adaptation involved nocturnal (because of their size), visually oriented predation on insects in the lower canopy and undergrowth of tropical forests.

> This implies that the last common ancestor of the extant primates, like many extant prosimians (for example, *Tarsius, Microcebus, Loris, Arctocebus,* and the smaller galagines), subsisted to an important extent on insects and other prey, which were visually located and manually captured in the insect-rich canopy and undergrowth of tropical forests (Cartmill 1974a:441; also Cartmill 1992:11).

### *Were the Earliest Primates Visually Oriented Predators?*

Although Cartmill's argument is indeed an elegant one, I now ask, "Is it correct?" There are two parts to this question. The first is whether the plesiadapoids are primates. The second, were the earliest primates visually oriented predators living in the terminal branches of the trees and shrubs? The first aspect of this question will not greatly concern me here. Whether plesiadapoids are considered to be primates often appears to revolve around one's nomenclatural philosophy (Gingerich 1986, Kay and Cartmill 1977, MacPhee et al. 1983, Martin 1986a, Schwartz et al. 1978, Szalay 1975, Szalay and Delson 1979, Tattersall 1986, Wible and Covert 1987).

At present, there is no direct phyletic link and no significant adaptive resemblance between the plesiadapoids and euprimates. In fact, recently discovered postcranials of the genus *Ignacius* have led to the hypothesis that one family of plesiadapoids, the paromomyids, are not related to primates but to the Southeast Asian gliding mammals, the dermopterans (Beard 1990), and the absence of a petrosal bulla in both *Plesiadapis* and *Ignacius* has prompted Kay et al. (1990) to propose that plesiadapoids actually represent the sister group of the Dermoptera (see also Beard 1989). However, the evidence for a specific link between plesiadapiforms and dermopterans also is open to question (Krause 1991, Martin 1993).

The more important aspect of my question, to an ecologist at least, is the second: Are the features shared by living primates the result of the adaptive shift to the role of visually oriented predator that searched for insects in the terminal branches? It is true that many small mammals, including primates, eat insects. However, since Cartmill first presented his theory, the diet of a number of prosimians has been studied in detail. Most small nocturnal primates feed mainly on crawling insects, many of which are captured on the ground (Charles-Dominique 1977; Charles-Dominique and Bearder 1979; Crompton and Andau 1986, Doyle 1974; Fogden 1974; MacKinnon and MacKinnon 1980, Martin 1972; Neimitz 1984, Oxnard et al. 1990).

Very few species of primates (i.e., the smaller galagos and lorises and the tarsiers) are known to have a diet including a greater proportion of insects than plant material and there is evidence that the primitive (i.e., ancestral) primate condition is omnivory. For example, the general anatomy of the digestive tract of primates (e.g., the presence of the caecum and the relative size of gut compartments) reflects adaptations for an omnivorous diet (Martin 1990, Martin et al. 1985), and the dietary pattern found among the vast majority of primates (over 95%) is omnivory (Harding 1981). Furthermore, according to Cartmill (1974a), the trend towards orbital convergence and approximation in primates culminates in the slow-moving lorises. Eight-five to 95 percent of the prey captured by the lorises are slow-moving and conspicuous. Lorises detect these insects with their highly developed sense of smell (Charles-Dominique 1977). Galagos and tarsiers seem mainly to use hearing in hunting prey.

> When a moving prey is present, bushbabies *(Galago demidovii)* direct their mobile ears in the appropriate direction, and . . . can localize perfectly sounds emitted by insects. Flying locusts and scurrying crickets can be localized on the other side of a plywood screen, and bushbabies will follow the movements of these insects with their heads, just as if they could actually see the prey (Charles-Dominique 1977:39).

Tarsiers, the primate most specialized for predation, also seem to use hearing to detect prey. The Bornean tarsiers "locate their prey primarily by sound and only secondarily by sight . . . *Tarsius bancanus* catch their prey with their eyes closed" (Neimitz 1979:642). In the larger Sulawesi tarsier, *Tarsius spectrum,* "cryptic or motionless prey are located by sight, moving prey are usually first detected by hearing, then fixated visually. The hunting tarsier's large papery ears are constantly twitching to the tiny sounds of the forest. Tarsiers pounce on insects on the ground or stretch and grab at insects in foliage" (MacKinnon and MacKinnon 1980:370). Almost identical observations of insect-foraging behavior have been described for *Galago senegalensis* (Doyle 1974, Oxnard et al. 1990) and *Microcebus murinus* (Martin 1972).

In a study of the role of vision in prosimian behavior, Pariente (1979:453) concludes:

> . . . in certain nocturnal prosimian species which are able to hunt mobile animal prey, there has been considerable development of the apparatus of hearing, particularly for the detection of high frequency sound. . . . In fact, the reduction of the sphere of vision imposed by very low light intensities renders nocturnal vision insufficient for this type of diet.

The visual anatomy of cats and primates are not very similar, and auditory stimuli are generally more compelling to carnivores than are visual stimuli (Raczkowski 1975). "It is well known that cats can catch mice in the dark or when they are hidden under fallen leaves in wood. . . . a blindfolded cat can locate a mouse on a table very quickly and, as soon as it touches with its vibrissae, grasps it with a precise nape bite at lightning speed." (Leyhausen 1979:71).

Finally, Rasmussen (1990) has shown that the arboreal marsupial *Caluromys* hunts for insects visually in the terminal branches of trees, and this species does not have marked orbital convergence. In fact, some animals that have these adaptations, such as sloths, koalas, and some phalangerid marsupials are strictly primary consumers. Many birds that do not have convergent eyes are highly insectivorous (see Cartmill 1992, Sussman 1995). The only mammals that possess a complex visual system similar to that of primates are the fruit bats (Megachiroptera) (Allman 1982, Pettigrew 1986). As stated by Martin (1986b:483):

> The fact that forward-facing eyes and primatelike organization of the retinotectal system should have evolved in fruit-eating megachiropteran bats, rather than in insect-eating microchiropteran bats, now provides support for the modified suggestion that the primate visual system evolved in connection with feeding on both fruits and arthropods in the "fine-branch niche" constituted by the terminal branches of trees.

It seems likely, therefore, that visual predation *per se* is not a sufficient explanation of the visual adaptations of the post-Paleocene primates.

### A New Theory of Primate Origins: Diffuse Coevolution with Angiosperms

The Paleocene-Eocene boundary was a period of rapid change that involved coincidental adaptive shifts in a number of plant and animal groups, including primates. It is in the context of the interrelationships between these groups that we might find an alternative hypothesis for the origin of primates (Sussman 1991, 1995).

I believe that the uniqueness of the earliest primates of modern aspect (the euprimates) involved a combination of the features described by both Cartmill and Szalay. I suggest that these early primates were *omnivores*, feeding on small-sized objects found in the terminal branches of trees. Thus the novel adaptive shift involved two aspects: (1) becoming well adapted to feed in the small branch milieu and (2) including a high proportion of plant material in the diet.

The evolution of birds and mammals is directly related to that of angiosperms and, in fact, vertebrate herbivores and dispersers have had a powerful influence on angiosperm evolution and vice versa. Herrera (1984) has termed this kind of broad evolutionary effect of one set of lineages upon another as "diffuse coevolution." Although the general outline of parallel evolutionary events has been traced between angiosperms and a number of tetropod herbivores (Collinson and Hooker 1987, Niklas et al. 1980, Tiffney 1984, Wing and Tiffney 1987a,b), this only recently has been done specifically for primates.

Angiosperms arose in the early Cretaceous, approximately 120 million years ago (MYA). The earliest flowering plants were pollinated by primitive insects, contained small seeds, and were wind or water dispersed with little or no specializations for animal dispersal (Behrensmeyer et al. 1992, Friis and Crepet 1987, Wing and Tiffney 1987b). They were low status shrubs and weeds located mainly in unstable environments. By the late Cretaceous, some larger arborescent individuals appeared but most flowering plants remained of low stature, occupying marginal habitats dominated by gymnosperms.

During the Cretaceous major coevolutionary events occurred between flowering plants and their insect pollinators. By the early Paleocene, floral biology had already reached modern form and most modern families of insects had appeared. Although advanced pollination systems were in place by the mid-Paleocene, most fruit seeds were still of small size and were dispersed abiotically.

In living plants, the size of the diaspore (propagative plant organ, e.g., fruit, seed, spore) is highly correlated with two classes of ecological traits: habit and habitat of the parent plant, and means of dispersal (van der Pijl 1982, Wing and Tiffney 1987b). Large, dominant forest trees and plants of late successional status tend to have large fruits and seeds, whereas herbaceous plants and early successionals usually have small propagules. The large seeds of large canopy trees reflect a higher need for stored nutrients in environments with low light levels. Furthermore, abiotically dispersed diaspores are small, while those that are dispersed by animals are generally larger and possess some reward or attractant, the nature of which depends upon the specific dispersal agent (Howe and Westley 1988, Janson 1983, van der Pijl 1982).

Only in the latest Cretaceous or early Tertiary did large diaspores begin to appear and did angiosperms evolve to include some physiognomically dominant trees of stable, climax forests (Figure 5–2). This is presumed to be related to a change from the dominance of abiotic dispersal mechanisms in the Cretaceous to an increase in the importance of biotic dispersal agents beginning in the Tertiary (Tiffney 1984). Although there appears to be no radical jump into new adaptive zones, the total diversity of angiosperms continued to increase across the Cretaceous–Tertiary boundary and into the early Tertiary (Friis et al. 1987, Niklas et al. 1980, Tiffney, 1981). This coincided with the extinction of the dinosaurs (Sussman 1995, Wing and Tiffney 1987a), and with a major radiation of birds (Olson 1985, Tiffney 1984) and mammals (Colbert 1969, Lillegraven et al. 1979).

**Figure 5–2** Artist's rendition of the latest Cretaceous. (Drawing by Laurie Schlueb).

This radiation included the origin and diversification of the plesiadapoids in Europe and North America during the Paleocene. A similar diversification of marsupials occurred at the same time in South America (Clemens 1968, Clemens et al. 1979). It included the invasion in more or less arboreal mixed feeding adaptive zones by some plesiadapoids (Figure 5–3) and other mammals (Beard 1990, Collinson and Hooker 1987, Kay and Cartmill 1977, Kay et al. 1990, Szalay and Dagosto 1980). As mentioned above, a number of these mammals have dental morphology that suggests convergent feeding adaptations (Szalay 1968).

This new feeding niche was the small branch milieu of the newly radiating angiosperms, which offered an array of previously unexploited resources, e.g., flowers, fruits, floral and leaf buds, gums, nectars, and also the insects that feed upon these items. Among the angiosperms, however, the Paleocene was a time of relative stability, during which plant species diversity continued to increase slightly but generally was maintained at a plateau level. Nothing seems to suggest that flowing plants were undergoing any major evolutionary change at this time (Hickey 1981, Niklas et al. 1980, Tiffney 1981, Tshudy 1977).

Not until the late Paleocene did large seeds with large endosperm reserves become common. Thus, fruits and seeds with clear adaptations, (thick walls, attractive flesh, etc.) for animal dispersal were not a major part of the flora until the end of the Paleocene (Wing and Tiffney 1987a,b). Furthermore, late Paleocene mammalian faunas contain few arboreal forms, few herbivores, and a large proportion of insectivores (Collinson and Hooker 1987). Few adaptations for mammalian plant-feeding had evolved, although the number of animals with adaptations for plant-feeding was undoubtedly continuing to increase throughout the Paleocene (Kay and Cartmill 1977, Beard 1990, Martin 1993).

If it is true that a major impetus for this diversification of mammals was the concurrent radiation of angiosperms and their occupation of new adaptive zones, then we would expect that certain groups of animals would evolve more efficient and competitive means of exploiting these resources. At the same time, angiosperms would evolve better means of protecting themselves from predation and efficient means of exploiting these animals as dispersal agents. These coevolutionary interactions appear to have reached a threshold

**Figure 5–3**   Artist's rendition of a plesiadapoid. (Drawing by Laurie Schlueb).

at the Paleocene–Eocene boundary. By the beginning of the Eocene angiosperms had evolved a range of diaspore sizes almost as great as modern floras. This dramatic increase in diaspore size is strong evidence for the increased importance of animal dispersal. It also implies that angiosperms would have had a greater ability to colonize and form closed canopy vegetation and, indeed, large angiosperm trunks do not become common until the Eocene (Figure 5–4) (Tiffney 1984, Wing and Tiffney 1987a,b, Upchurch and Wolfe 1987).

Thus, the apparent ecological stasis in angiosperm evolution is broken in the late Paleocene and early Eocene when there is a major rearrangement in the taxonomic composition of the angiosperm community across the entire Northern Hemisphere (Tiffney 1981). The Paleocene–Eocene boundary was the time of disappearance of many archaic taxa and of the appearance of a diverse array of modern families and genera of flowering plants. Modern evergreen tropical rainforests appear and become widespread during the Eocene (Niklas et al. 1980, Tiffney 1981, Upchurch and Wolfe 1987). As stated above, by this time a wide range of fruits and seeds adapted to animal dispersal were present (Tiffney 1984).

**Figure 5–4**   Artist's rendition of the Early Eocene. (Drawing by Laurie Schlueb).

Paralleling this modernization of the world's flora were major changes in the fauna of the Eocene. The fossil record of birds indicates a major radiation beginning in the latest Cretaceous. The number of modern families increased greatly in the Eocene and vegetarian birds first appear at that time. Furthermore, although the proportion of omnivorous birds remains steady, the proportion of vegetarian families continues to rise, while that of carnivorous families falls (Olsen 1985, Tiffney 1984). Among mammals, the earliest known fossils of the important Orders Rodentia, Lagomorpha (rabbits), Artiodacyla (even-toed ungulates), and Perissodactyla (odd-toed ungulates) appear at the base of the Eocene followed by dramatic evolutionary radiations. Bats also first appeared in the early Eocene. Although the earliest bats were most likely insectivorous, the morphological characters of bat-dispersed fruit and, likely, fruit bats evolved during this time period (Tiffney 1984). Along with these major changes, the first appearance and radiation of our first euprimate ancestors, the adapids and omomyids, occurred in the late Paleocene or early Eocene (for reviews, see Conroy 1990, Fleagle 1988, Martin 1993).

Thus, the establishment of biological interactions between angiosperms and their pollinators and dispersers is reflected in the rapid appearance of modern families and genera in the Eocene. The evolution of modern primates parallels that of other herbivorous mammals, of plant-eating birds, and of modern angiosperms; it also appears that many of these organisms were linked in a tight coevolutionary relationship. At present, frugivorous birds, bats, and primates are the most important seed dispersal agents in the tropics (Howe 1980, 1989, Stiles 1989, Terborgh 1986, 1992). As stated by Niklas et al. (1980:6), "plants and animals are not homologous evolutionary systems and . . . plants, by virtue of their inherent difference from animals will provide new insights into paleontological and evolutionary arguments."

The evolution of primates of modern aspect, therefore, as well as that of fruit bats and vegetarian birds, may be directly related to the evolution of improved means of exploiting flowering plants. Furthermore, the particular pattern of Paleocene extinctions of the plesiadapoids may be related to the rapid evolution and radiation of the primates, bats, and rodents and their improved ability to exploit insects, fruits, and flowers (see Maas et al. 1988, Sussman and Raven 1978).

Some plesiadapoids persisted into the Eocene, thereby overlapping in time with euprimates. We still do not know which mammalian lineage, if any of those known from the fossil record, gave rise to the primates of modern aspect sometime during the Paleocene. In contrast to the plesiadapoids, these euprimates possessed a divergent toe and thumb and flattened nails to produce effective grasping organs. It is generally agreed that these adaptations would have allowed Eocene prosimians far greater access to fruits and flowers, as well as plant-visiting insects, making them much more efficient at locomoting and foraging in the small terminal branches of bushes and trees than were the plesiadapoids (Cartmill 1972, 1992, Martin 1993, Sussman 1995).

This hypothesis does not explain the unique visual adaptations of primates and fruit bats, and this subject needs further study. However, these nocturnal animals were feeding on and manipulating items of very small size (e.g., fruits, flowers, *and* insects) at very close range and under low light conditions. This might require acute powers of discrimination and precise coordination. Tree squirrels cut large fruits or nuts from one set of branches and then move to a large horizontal support to feed. Primates do not transport food items from one support to another but usually consume a large number of items where they are acquired. They are able to venture out on very small support and then, maintaining a firm grasp with their hindlimbs, detach the food item with their forelimbs and/or mouth (Garber and Sussman 1984).

In summary, although they vary greatly in dietary preferences, most nocturnal primates are omnivorous, feeding mainly on plant material. The largest proportion of their prey are crawling insects, many of which are captured on the ground and detected by the senses of smell or hearing. It does not seem, therefore, that the visual adaptations of post-Paleocene primates can be explained by visually oriented predation. It is more likely that the explanation will be found in adaptations providing the fine discrimination needed to exploit the small food items available on the newly diversifying flowering plants. It is also likely that this improved, generalized ability to feed on a variety of items in the fine terminal branches was the most important impetus for the major adaptive shift seen in the Eocene primates. These first primates of modern aspect, the Eocene adapids and omomyids, were simply a more efficient version of the frugivorous-nectarivorous-insectivorous, i.e., omnivorous, plesiadapoids and other similar Paleocene mammals and they were a product of a diffuse coevolutionary interaction with the angiosperms.

Thus, I have answered the question "What is a primate?" in three ways. First, taxonomically, it is a monophyletic order of mammals containing two suborders, Prosimii and Anthropoidea, which derived from a common, yet unknown, ancestor. Second, morphologically, primates share a number of derived morphological traits, especially of the locomotor anatomy, skull morphology, dentition, and reproductive biology, that distinguish them from other mammals. Finally, these traits indicate that the adaptive shift accompanying the appearance of the primates was the occupation of new locomotor and feeding niches made available by the co-evolving angiosperm tropical rain forests. Although bats and birds can reach the terminal branches of large rain forest trees by flying to them, primates need their grasping appendages to obtain the same advantage (Figure 5–5). In

**Figure 5–5** Terminal branch feeding by a Malagasy primate, the sifaka.

fact, primates are the only major taxonomic groups of non-flying vertebrates to regularly exploit the terminal branch niche of the tropical forest.

## REFERENCES

Aiello, L. C. (1986) "The relationship of the Tarsiiformes: A review of the case for the Haplorhini." In *Major Topics in Primate and Human Evolution* (pp. 47–65). B. A. Wood; L. B. Martin; P. J. Andrews, eds. Cambridge: Cambridge University Press.

Allman, J. M. (1982) "Reconstructing the evolution of the brain in primates through the use of comparative neurophysiological and neuroanatomical data." In *Primate Brain Evolution* (pp. 13–28). E. Armstrong; D. Falk, eds. New York: Plenum.

Beard, K. C. (1989) *Postcranial Anatomy, Locomotor Adaptations, and Palaeoecology of Early Cenozoic Plesiadapidae, Paromomyidae, and Micromomyidae (Eutheria, Dermoptera).* PhD Thesis, Johns Hopkins University, Baltimore.

Beard, K. C. (1990) "Gliding behavior and palaeoecology of the alleged primate family Paromomyidae (Mammalia, Dermoptera)." *Nature* 345:340–341.

Behrensmeyer, A. K.; Damuth, J. D.; DiMichele, W. A.; Potts, R.; Sues, H. D.; Wing, S. L. (1992). *Terrestrial Ecosystems Through Time: Evolutionary Paleoecology of Terrestrial Plants and Animals.* Chicago: University of Chicago Press.

Buettner-Janusch, J. (1996) *Origins of Man.* New York: Wiley.

Campbell, C. B. G. (1974) "On the phyletic relationships of the tree shrews." *Mammal Rev.* 4:125–143.

Cartmill, M. (1972) "Arboreal adaptations and the origin of the order Primates." In *The Functional and Evolutionary Biology of Primates.* (pp. 97–122). R. Tuttle, ed. Chicago: Aldine.

Cartmill, M. (1974a) "Rethinking primate origins." *Science* 184:436–443.

Cartmill, M. (1992) "New views on primate origins." *Evol. Anthropol.* 1:105–111.

Charles-Dominique, P. (1977) *Ecology and Behavior of Nocturnal Primates.* New York: Columbia University Press.

Charles-Dominique, P.; Bearder, S. K. (1979) "Field studies of lorisid behavior: Methodological aspects." In *The Study of Prosimian Behavior* (pp. 567–629). G. A. Doyle; R. D. Martin, eds. New York: Academic.

Chivers, D. J.; Joysey, K. A., eds. (1978) *Recent Advances in Primatology: Vol. 3: Evolution.* New York: Academic.

Clark, W. E. Le Gros (1963) *The Antecedents of Man.* New York: Harper and Row.

Clemens Jr., W. A. (1968) "Origin and early evolution of marsupials." *Evolution* 22:1–18.

Clemens Jr., W. A.; Lillegraven, J. A.; Lindsay, E. H.; Simpson, G. G. (1979) "Where, when, and what—a survey of known Mesozoic mammal distribution. In *Mesozoic Mammals.* (pp. 7–58). J. A. Lillegraven, Z. Kielan-Jaworowska, W. A. Clemens, eds. Berkeley: University of California Press.

Colbert, E. H. (1969) *Evolution of the Vertebrates: A History of the Backboned Animals Through Time,* 2nd edition. New York: Wiley.

Collinson, M. E.; Hooker, J. J. (1987) "Vegetational and mammalian faunal changes in the Early Tertiary of southern England." In *The Origins of Angiosperms and Their Biological Consequences.* (pp. 259–304). E. M. Friis, W. G. Chaloner, P. R. Crane, eds. Cambridge: Cambridge University Press.

Conroy, G. C. (1990) *Primate Evolution.* New York: Norton.

Covert, H. H. (1986) "Biology of early Cenozoic primates." In *Comparative Primate Biology. Vol. 1: Systematics, Evolution, and Anatomy.* (pp. 335–359). D. R. Swindler; J. Erwin, eds. New York: Alan R. Liss.

Crompton, R. H.; Andau, P. M. (1986) "Locomotion and habitat utilization in free-ranging *Tarsius bancanus:* A preliminary report." *Primates* 27:337–355.

Doyle, G. A. (1974) "Behavior of prosimians." In *Behavior of Nonhuman Primates* (pp. 155–353). A. M. Schrier; F. Stollnitz, eds. New York: Academic.

Eldridge, N. (1989) *Macroevolutionary Systematics.* New York: McGraw-Hill.

Emmons, L. H. (1980) "Ecology and resource partitioning among nine species of African rain forest squirrels." *Ecol. Monogr.* 50:31–54.

Fleagle, J. G. (1988) *Primate Adaptation and Evolution.* New York: Academic Press.

Fleagle, J. G.; Kay, R. F., eds. (1994) *Anthropoid Origins.* New York: Plenum Press.

Fogden, M. (1974) "A preliminary study of the western tarsier, *Tarsius bancanus* Horsfield." In *Prosimian Biology* (pp. 151–165). R. D. Martin; G. A. Doyle; A. C. Walker, eds. London: Duckworth.

Friis, E. M.; Chaloner, W. G.; Crane, P. R. (1987) "Introduction to the angiosperms." In *The Origins of Angiosperms and*

*Their Biological Consequences* (pp. 1–15). E. M. Friis; W. G. Chaloner; P. R. Crane, eds. Cambridge: Cambridge University Press.

Friis, E. M.; Crepet, W. L. (1987) "Time of appearance of floral features." In *The Origins of Angiosperms and Their Biological Consequences* (pp. 259–304). E. M. Friss; W. G. Chaloner; P. R. Crane, eds. Cambridge: Cambridge University Press.

Garber, P. A.; Sussman, R. W. (1984) "Ecological distinctions between sympatric species of *Saguinus* and *Sciurus.*" *American Journal of Physical Anthropology* 65:135–146.

Gingerich, P. D. (1986) "*Plesiadapis* and the delineation of the order Primates." In *Major Topics in Primate and Human Evolution* (pp. 32–46). B. A. Wood; L. B. Martin; P. Andrews, eds. Cambridge: Cambridge University Press.

Goodman, M. (1966) "Phyletic position of tree shrews." *Science* 153:1550.

Gunnell, G. F. (1989) "Evolutionary history of Microsyopoidea and the relationship between Plesiadapiformes and Primates." *University of Michigan Papers in Paleontol.* 27:1–154.

Harding, R. S. O. (1981) "An order of omnivores: Nonhuman primates diets in the wild." In *Omnivorous Primates* (pp. 191–214). R. S. O. Harding, ed. York: Columbia University Press.

Hennig, W. (1966) *Phylogentic Systematics.* Urbana: University of Illinois Press.

Herrera, C. M. (1984) "Determinants of plant-animal coevolution: The case of mutualistic dispersal of seeds by vertebrates." *Oikos* 44:132–144.

Hickey, L. J. (1981) "Land plant evidence compatible with gradual, not catastrophic, change at the end of the Cretaceous." *Nature* 292:529–531.

Hoffsetter, R. (1977) "Phylogénie des Primates: Confrontation des résultats obtenus par les diverse voies d'approches de problème." *Bulletin Memoires Sociale Anthropologie,* Paris 4:327–346.

Howe, H. F. (1980) "Monkey dispersal and waste of a neotropical fruit." *Ecology* 61:944–959.

Howe, H. F. (1989) "Scatter- and clump-dispersal and seedling demography: Hypothesis and implications." *Oecologia* 79:417–426.

Howe, H. F.; Westley, L. C. (1988) *Ecological Relationships Between Plants and Animals.* Oxford: Oxford University Press.

Howells, W. W. (1947) *Mankind So Far.* Garden City: Doubleday.

Janson, C. H. (1983) "Adaptation of fruit morphology to dispersal agents in a neotropical forest." *Science* 219:187–189.

Jolly, C. J. (1993) "Species, subspecies, and baboon systematics." In *Species, Species Concepts, and Primate Evolution.* (pp. 67–107). W. H. Kimbel; L. B. Martin, eds. New York: Plenum.

Jones, F. W. (1916) *Arboreal Man.* London: Edward Arnold.

Kay, R. F.; Cartmill, M. (1977) "Cranial morphology and adaptations of *Palaecthon nacimienti* and other Parmomyidae (Plesiadapoidea,? Primates), with a description of a new genus and species." *Journal of Human Evolution* 6:19–53.

Kay, R. F.; Thorington, R. W.; Houde P. (1990) "Eocene plesiadapiform shows affinities with flying lemurs not primates." *Nature* 345:342–344.

Kimbel, W. H.; L. B. Martin, eds. (1993) *Species, Species Concepts, and Primate Evolution.* New York: Plenum.

Kluge, A. G. (1984) "The relevance of parsimony to phylogenetic inference." In *Cladistics* (pp. 24–38). T. Duncan; T. F. Stuessy, eds. New York: Columbia University Press.

Krause, D. W. (1991) "Were paromomyids gliders? Maybe, maybe not." *J. Hum. Evol.* 21:177–188.

Leyhausen, P. (1979) *Cat Behavior: The Predatory and Social Behavior of Domestic and Wild Cats.* New York: Garland.

Lillegraven, J. A.; Kielan-Jaworowska, Z.; Clemens, W. A. eds. (1979) *Mesozoic Mammals.* Berkeley: University of California Press.

Luckett, W. P. (1980) *Comparative Biology and Evolutionary Relationships of Tree Shrews.* New York: Plenum.

Luckett, W. P.; Szalay, F. S. eds. (1975) *Phylogeny of the Primates: A Multidisciplinary Approach.* New York: Plenum.

MacKinnon, J.; MacKinnon, K. (1980) "The behavior of wild spectral tarsiers." *International Journal of Primatology* 1:361–379.

MacPhee, R. D. E.; Cartmill, M.; Gingerich, P. D. (1983) "New Palaeogene primate basicrania and the definition of the order Primates." *Nature* 301:509–511.

Martin, R. D. (1986) "Towards a new definition of primates." *Man* 3:376–401.

Martin, R. D. (1972) "A preliminary field-study of the lesser mouse lemur (*Microcebus murinus,* J. F. Miller 1777)." *Zeitschrift Fur Tierpsychologie,* Beiheft 9:43–89.

Martin, R. D. (1986a) "Primates: A definition." In *Major Topics in Primate and Human Evolution* (pp. 1–31). B. A. Wood; L. B. Martin; P. Andrews, eds. Cambridge: Cambridge University Press.

Martin, R. D. (1986b) "Are fruit bats primates?" *Nature* 320:482–483.

Martin, R. D. (1990) *Primate Origins and Evolution: A Phylogenetic Reconstruction.* Princeton: Princeton University Press.

Martin, R. D. (1993) "Primate origins: plugging the gaps." *Nature* 363:223–234.

Martin, R. D.; Chivers, D. J.; MacLarnon, M. A.; Hladik, C. M. (1985) "Gastrointestinal allometry in primates and other mammals." In *Size and Scaling in Primate Biology* (pp. 61–89). W. L. Jungers, ed., New York: Plenum.

Mayr, E. (1963) *Animal Species and Evolution.* Cambridge: Belknap.

Mayr, E. (1969) *Principles of Systematic Zoology.* New York: McGraw-Hill.

Mayr, E.; Ashlock, P. D. (1991) *Principles of Systematic Zoology.* 2nd edition. New York: McGraw-Hill.

McKenna, M. C. (1966) "Paleontology and the origins of primates." *Folla Primatologica* 4:1–25.

Mivart, St. G. J. (1873) "On *Lepilemur* and *Cheirogaleus* and on the zoological rank of the Lemuroidea." *Proc. Zool. Soc. Lond.* 1873:484–510.

Neimitz, C. (1979) "Outline of the behavior of *Tarsius bancanus.*" In *The Study of Prosimian Behavior* (pp. 631–660). G. A. Doyle; R. D. Martin, eds. New York: Academic.

Neimitz, C. (1984) "Synecological relationships and feeding behavior of the genus *Tarsius.*" In *Biology of Tarsiers* (pp. 59–76). C. Neimitz, ed. Stuttgart: G. Fischer Verlag.

Niklas, K. J.; Tiffney, B. H.; Knoll, A. H. (1980) "Apparent changes in the diversity of fossil plants: A preliminary assessment." In *Evolutionary Biology, Vol. 12* (pp. 1–89). M. K. Hecht; W. C. Steere; B. Wallace, eds. New York: Plenum.

Olsen, S. L. (1985) "The fossil record of birds." In *Avion Biology, Vol. III* (pp. 79–237). D. Farner; J. King; J. K. Parkes, eds. New York: Academic Press.

Otte, D.; Endler, J. A. eds. (1989). *Speciation and Its Consequences.* Sunderland, MA: Sinauer.

Oxnard, C. E.; Crompton, R. H.; Lieberman, S. S. (1990) *Animal Lifestyles and Anatomies: The Case of the Prosimian Primates.* Seattle: University of Washington Press.

Pariente, G. (1979) "The role of vision in prosimian behavior." In *The Study of Prosimian Behavior* (pp. 411–459). G. A. Doyle; R. D. Martin, eds. New York: Academic.

Paterson, H. E. H. (1985) "The recognition concept of species." In *Species and Speciation* (pp. 21–29). E. S. Vrba, ed. Transvaal, Transvaal Museum.

Pettigrew, J. D. (1986) "Flying primates? Megabats have the advanced pathway from eye to midbrain." *Science* 231:1304–1306.

Pijl, L. van der (1982) *Principles of Dispersal in Higher Plants.* Berlin: Springer-Verlag.

Poirier, F. E.; Stini, W. A.; Wreden, K. B. (1994) *In Search of Ourselves,* 5th edition. Upper Saddle River, NJ: Prentice Hall.

Raczkowski, D. (1975) "Primate evolution: Were traits selected for arboreal locomotion or visually directed predation?" *Science* 187:455–456.

Rasmussen, D. T. (1990) "Primate origins: Lessons from a neotropical marsupial." *American Journal of Primatology* 22:263–277.

Raven, P. H.; Evert, R. F.; Curtis, H. (1992) *Biology of Plants,* 5th edition. New York: Worth.

Relethford, J. (1994) *The Human Species: An Introduction to Biology Anthropology,* 2nd edition. Mountain View, CA: Mayfield.

Rose, K. D.; Brown, T. M. (1986). "Gradual evolution and species discrimination in the fossil record." *Contrib. Geol. Univ. Wyoming* 3:119–130.

Schwartz, J. H.; Tattersall, I.; Eldredge, N. (1978) "Phylogeny and classification of the primates revisited." *Yearbook of Physical Anthropology* 21:95–133.

Simons, E. L. (1972) *Primate Evolution: An Introduction to Man's Place in Nature.* New York: Macmillan.

Simpson, G. G. (1935) "The Tiffany fauna, Upper Paleocene. 2. Structure and relationships of *Plesiadapis.*" *Am. Mus. Novit.* 816:1–30.

Simpson, G. G. (1944) *Tempo and Mode in Evolution.* New York: Columbia University Press.

Simpson, G. G. (1945) "The principles of classification and a classification of mammals." *Bull. Amer. Mus. Nat. Hist.* 85:1–350.

Simpson, G. G. (1955) "The Phenacolemuridae, new family of early Primates." *Bull. Amer. Mus. Nat. Hist.* 105:411–442.

Simpson, G. G. (1961) *Principles of Animal Taxonomy.* New York: Columbia University Press.

Simpson, G. G. (1975) "Recent advances in method of phylogenetic inference." In *Phylogeny of the Primates: A Multidisciplinary Approach* (pp. 3–19). W. P. Luckett; F. S. Szalay, eds. New York: Plenum.

Smith, G. E. (1912) "The evolution of man." *Smithsonian Institution Annual Report,* Washington DC: Smithsonian Institution.

Sneath, P. H. A.; Sokal, R. R. (1973) *Numerical Taxonomy: The Principles and Practice of Numerical Taxonomy.* San Fransisco: Freeman.

Stein, P. L.; Rowe, B. M. (1993) *Physical Anthropology,* 5th edition, New York: McGraw-Hill.

Sussman, R. W. (1991) "Primate origins and the evolution of angiosperms." *Am. J. Primatol.* 23:209–223.

Sussman, R. W. (1995) "How primates invented the rainforest and visa versa." In *Creatures of the Dark: The Nocturnal Prosimians.* L. Alterman; K. Izard; G. A. Doyle, eds. New York: Plenum.

Sussman, R. W.; Raven P. H. (1978) "Pollination by lemurs and marsupials: an archaic coevolutionary system." *Science* 200:731–736.

Stiles, E. W. (1989) "Fruits, seeds, and dispersal agents." In *Plant-Animal Interactions* (pp. 87–122). W. G. Abrahamson, ed. New York: McGraw-Hill.

Szalay, F. S. (1968) "The beginnings of primates." *Evolution* 22:19–36.

Szalay, F. S. (1969) "Mixodectidae, Microsyopidae, and the insectivore-primate transition." *Bull. Am. Mus. Nat. Hist.* 140:193–330.

Szalay, F. S. (1972) "Paleobiology of the earliest primates." In *The Functional and Evolutionary Biology of Primates* (pp. 3–35). R. Tuttle, ed. Chicago: Aldine.

Szalay, F. S. (1975) "Phylogeny of primate higher taxa: The basicranial evidence." In *Phylogeny of the Primates: A Multidisciplinary Approach* (pp. 91–125). W. P. Luckett; F. S. Szalay, eds. New York: Plenum.

Szalay, F. S.; Dagosto, M. (1980) "Locomotor adaptations as reflected on the humerous of Paleogene primates." *Folia Primatol.* 34:1–45.

Szalay, F. S.; Delson E. (1979) *Evolutionary History of the Primates.* New York: Academic Press.

Szalay, F. S.; Rosenberger, A. L.; Dagosto, M. (1987) "Diagnosis and differentiation of the order Primates." *Yearbook of Physical Anthropology* 30:75–105.

Tattersall, I. (1986) "Review of major topics in primate and human evolution." *Journal of Human Evolution* 15:313–321.

Templeton, A. R. (1987) "Species and speciation." *Evolution* 41:235–236.

Templeton, A. R. (1989) "The meaning of species and speciation: A genetic perspective." In *Speciation and Its Consequences* (pp. 3–27). D. Otte; J. A. Endler, eds. Sunderland, MA: Sinauer.

Templeton, A. R. (1994) "The role of molecular genetics in speciation studies." *Molecular Ecology and Evolution: Approaches and Applications.* B. Schierwater; J. A. Endler, eds. Basel: Birkhauser Verlag.

Terborgh, J. (1986) "Community aspects of frugivory in tropical forests." In *Frugivores and Seed Dispersal* (pp. 371–384). A. Estrada; T. H. Fleming, eds. Dordrecht: Dr. W. Junk.

Terborgh, J. (1992) *Diversity and the Tropical Rain Forest.* New York: Scientific American Library.

Tiffney, B. H. (1981) "Diversity and major events in the evolution of land plants." In *Paleobotany, Paleoecology, and Evolution, Vol. II* (pp. 193–230). K. J. Niklas, ed. New York: Praeger.

Tiffney, B. H. (1984) "Seed size, dispersal syndromes, and the rise of the angiosperms: Evidence and hypothesis." *Annals of the Missouri Botanical Garden* 71:551–576.

Tshudy, R. H. (1977) "Palynological evidence for change in continental floras at the Cretaceous–Tertiary boundary." *Journal of Paleontology* 51:29.

Uexkull, J. von (1957) "A stroll through the world of animals and men: A picturebook of invisible worlds." In *Instinctive Behavior: The Development of a Modern Concept* (pp. 5–80). C. H. Schiller, ed. New York: International Universities Press.

Upchurch Jr., G. R.; Wolfe, J. A. (1987) "Mid-Cretaceous to Early Tertiary vegetation and climate: Evidence from fossil leaves and woods." In *The Origins of Angiosperms and Their Biological Consequences* (pp. 75–105). E. M. Friis; W. G. Chaloner; P. R. Crane, eds. Cambridge: Cambridge University Press.

Van Valen, L. (1965) "Tree shrews, primates, and fossils." *Evolution* 19:137–151.

Vrba, E. S. ed. (1985) *Species and Speciation.* Transvaal, Transvaal Museum.

Wible, J. R.; Covert, H. H. (1987) "Primates: Cladistic diagnosis and relationships." *Journal of Human Evolution* 16:1–22.

Wing, S. L.; Tiffney, B. H. (1987a) "The reciprocal interaction of angiosperm evolution and tetrapod herbivory." *Review of Palaeobotany and Palynology* 50:179–210.

Wing, S. L.; Tiffney, B. H. (1987b) "Interactions of angiosperms and herbivorous tetrapods through time." In *The Origins of Angiosperms and Their Biological Consequences* (pp. 203–224). E. M. Friis; W. G. Chaloner; P. R. Crane, eds. Cambridge: Cambridge University Press.

# Chapter 6

# *Socioecology*

## Robert W. Sussman

The theory of *natural selection* predicts that evolution will act to increase the frequency of traits that improve an individual's ability to survive and to reproduce more successfully than other members of its species. Traits that confer survival and reproductive advantages upon an individual are referred to as *adaptive traits* or *adaptations.* There were, however, a number of characteristics that Darwin found difficult to explain when he developed the theory of natural selection. These included morphological and behavioral differences between the sexes that occur in many species, such as larger canines or body size, or greater aggressiveness in males than in females. In many cases it was not obvious how these secondary sexual characteristics gave any direct advantage to individuals in their attempt to obtain resources.

To explain these traits, Darwin (1874) formulated the theory of *sexual selection.* He proposed that many morphological and behavioral differences between the sexes evolved because they contributed directly to an individual's reproductive success, either by improving his competitive ability against members of the same sex, or by increasing attractiveness to the opposite sex. Some of the traits Darwin believed to be sexually selected were subsequently shown to proffer direct adaptive advantage to individuals. Indeed, he first developed this concept to explain racial differences in humans. However, sexual selection is an important mechanism in evolution.

A basic assumption of sexual selection theory is that there is a direct relationship between particular traits and genetics. If dominance in males is directly related to increased fitness, then males must be able to pass on this trait to their offspring. However, dominance is complex and involves a number of morphological and behavioral characteristics, as well as a social and ecological context. This is true of many other traits proposed to be sexually selected. It is often extremely difficult, if not impossible, to explain the genetics of these complex traits.

Another phenomenon scientists found difficult to explain was cooperative behavior. Why would animals cooperate if this did not increase their evolutionary fitness? If an animal avoids being eaten by a predator by joining forces with others, cooperation easily fits within the rubric of individual selection. However, there are many cooperative behaviors, especially among group-living animals, that appear to be of no benefit or are even dangerous to the individual. To explain these behaviors, the concepts of *kin selection* and *reciprocal altruism* were formulated.

Darwin was unaware of Mendelian genetics and thus genetic inheritance did not figure in his explanation of natural selection. Hamilton (1964) examined the potential genetic consequences of cooperative behavior and developed the theory of kin selection to explain altruistic behavior between related individuals. An individual's traits, and the genes responsible for them, are more likely to be shared by close relatives than by unrelated individuals. Thus, by sacrificing oneself for a number of one's kin, an individual may be ensuring the survival of genetically inherited traits. Since more closely related individuals are more likely to share copies of the same genes, altruism is expected to be selectively directed toward kin, and more close kin will accrue more costly altruism (Silk 1987).

However, many altruistic acts are performed by unrelated individuals. Trivers (1971) formulated the theory of reciprocal altruism to explain cooperation and assistance in these cases. He believed that altruistic acts would only occur between unrelated individuals if they were likely to reciprocate in the future and had the opportunity to do so, if the benefits to the recipient were greater than the costs to the altruist, and if there was little chance of cheating. Thus, both parties improve their individual fitness in the long term. In practice both types of altruistic interactions are often difficult to identify, and predictions derived from these theories are difficult to evaluate empirically (see Silk 1987 for an excellent review).

These concepts formed the basis of the subdiscipline of sociobiology (Wilson 1975), which was developed to explain the influences of biology on social behavior. Sociobiology was very controversial when first formulated because of the questionable genetic nature of many of the behaviors it attempted to explain. Were behaviors such as aggressiveness or dominance inherited or the result of a complex interaction between genetics and environment? However, many of the theories currently in vogue in socioecology also are based on sexual selection, kin selection, and reciprocal altruism. These include theories attempting to interpret variation in social structure, social organization, and social behavior in group-living primates, and the relationships between ecology and social systems. For example, one of the major theories attempting to relate individual spacing to that of resource distribution is based on sexual selection. In most vertebrates, females must invest a great deal of time and energy in successfully reproducing offspring whereas males invest a small amount. Because of this, the distribution of females in the environment is presumed to be more closely related to resources than is that of males. The distribution of males is related to the dynamics of male competition for females (Wrangham 1983, 1987). Thus, females compete for energy resources and males compete for females.

This may or may not be true. However, to date we still have not been able to relate patterns of resource distribution to patterns of social spacing among the primates. We know very little about the factors that underlie the enormous amount of variability in primate social systems. These theories so far have not led to a better understanding of the relationships that might exist between ecology and social structure.

## REFERENCES

Darwin, C. (1874) *The Descent of Man and Selection in Relation to Sex.* London: John Murray.

Hamilton, W. D. (1964) The genetical evolution of social behavior. *American Naturalist* 97:354–356.

Silk, J. B. (1987) Social behavior in evolutionary perspective. In *Primate Societies* (pp. 318–329). B. B. Smuts; D. L. Cheney; R. M. Seyfarth; R. W. Wrangham; T. T. Struhsaker, eds. Chicago: University of Chicago Press

Trivers, R. L. (1971) The evolution of reciprocal altruism. *Quarterly Review of Biology* 46:35–57.

Wilson, E. O. (1975) *Sociobiology: The New Synthesis.* Cambridge: Harvard University Press.

Wrangham, R. W. (1983) Social relationships in comparative perspective. In *Primate Social Relationships* pp. 325–334. R. A. Hinde ed. London: Oxford University Press.

R. W. Wrangham (1987) Evolution of social structure. In *Primate Societies* pp. 282–296. B. B. Smuts; D. L. Cheney; R. M. Seyfarth; R. W. Wrangham; T. T. Struhsaker, eds. Chicago: University of Chicago Press.

# Chapter 7

# *The Major Features of Human Evolution*

## Ian Tattersall

Over the last century or so, paleoanthropologists have toyed with many different notions of what it was that first set hominids on the road to humanity. Today we have large brains, small faces and dentitions, dextrous hands that we use to make tools, and a habitual upright posture and striding gait. Each of these has at one time or another been touted as the key "adaptation" that led ultimately to all the others. I use quotes around "adaptation," by the way, because the concept of adaptation has been widely abused by paleoanthropologists in the service of the notion that our biological history has been one of a slow, steady progress from primitiveness to perfection. Not only is this gradualist scenario of human evolution plainly wrong, as our fossil record shows, but it is equally erroneous to think of evolution as being somehow "driven" by adaptation. Any new characteristic has to arise within a population before it can serve an adaptive function, and it is only after a novelty has appeared that it can be favored (or not) by natural selection.

More importantly, natural selection is itself a here-and-now process that depends on fickle and ever-shifting environmental conditions. The evolutionary history of any lineage, not least our own, is thus subject to a healthy dose of chance, something that it is useful to bear in mind as we survey the major events that have marked the human evolutionary story. I belabor this at the very start of this chapter because there is something inherently and distortingly linear about looking backwards at our prehistory, as I shall necessarily be doing. Picking out the major events in the lineage that led ultimately to *Homo sapiens* tends inevitably to obscure the fact that the history of the family Hominidae has been one of frequent speciation and evolutionary experimentation, a process

that over a vast span of time gave rise to a vast branching bush of related forms. In pondering our history as human beings we should never forget that we are simply the sole surviving twig on this ramifying bush, rather than the products of a slow, steady, and single-minded process of perfection.

## THE EARLIEST HOMINIDS

There is some question as to the identity of the first known specifically human precursors. In 1994 researchers described various 4.4-million-year-old (4.4 myr-old) fragments from Aramis, in Ethiopia, as representing the early hominid genus and species *Ardipithecus ramidus.* The key character to which they pointed was a forwardly shifted foramen magnum (the hole through which the spinal cord exits the bottom of the skull), which in their view implied that the head was held erect, in turn suggesting that this creature had walked bipedally. If true, this was highly significant, since the fossil record had by that time amply confirmed that postural uprightness was the crucial behavioral/anatomical shift that got our lineage started. Other characteristics, such as the dentition, are, however, more arguable, and it is only with fossils from Kenya, dated in the 4.2 to 3.9 myr range, and assigned to the species *Australopithecus anamensis,* that we are securely in the hominid camp. Not only do leg bones of this form show unmistakable indications of uprightness, but the jaws and teeth of *A. anamensis* are quite similar to those of the later species *Australopithecus afarensis,* known from sites in Ethiopia and Tanzania dated between 3.8 and 3.0 myr ago (Fig. 7–1).

The best known representative of *A. afarensis* is "Lucy," a partial skeleton of a young adult who died about 3.2 myr ago. Lucy shows signs throughout the pre-

Reprinted by permission of Ian Tattersall.

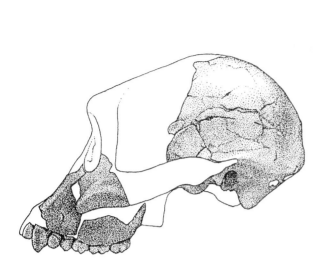
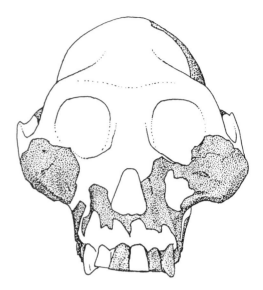

**Figure 7–1** Composite reconstruction of the cranium of *Australopithecus afarensis* from Hadar, Ethiopia. Ca. 3.4 myr old. From *The Fossil Trail: How We Know What We Think We Know About Human Evolution,* by Ian Tattersall (Oxford University Press, 1995).

served portions of her body of postural uprightness; but uprightness of a kind not familiar today. These early hominids walked erect, but at the same time preserved features that would have been very useful in the trees. These included narrow shoulders, relatively short hindlimbs, and longish feet that were better capable of grasping than ours are. That these small-bodied hominids (females stood only about 3½ feet tall, the considerably larger males about a foot taller) were capable of a striding gait on the ground is indisputable, as the famous 3.5 myr-old footprint trails found at Laetoli, in Tanzania, show; but at the same time they would have had considerable facility in the trees, which would have provided them with both food and shelter. A recently discovered foot and ankle from the South African site of Sterkfontein, perhaps as much as 3½ myr old, shows that although the ankle was relatively like ours, the long foot had a somewhat divergent big toe, with powerful grasping potential.

The environment in which these early bipeds lived matches these anatomical characteristics quite well. For long it had been thought that human bipedalism evolved in an open-country context, as a worldwide drying trend (particularly well documented in Africa, in which continent early hominids are exclusively known until about 2 myr ago) replaced forests by grasslands, evicting some groups of hominoids (members of the group to which humans and apes both belong) from their arboreal habitat and precipitating them on to the expanding savannas. Now, however, it seems that early hominids are often associated with quite densely wooded environments, where they may have mainly exploited the forest fringes but were nonetheless at home both in the more thickly forested and the more open areas of their ranges. The

reasons for their adoption of bipedalism are debated. It is still unclear whether moving on two legs was more energetically efficient than moving on four, and it has been pointed out that apes tend to move bipedally in the trees much more frequently than has been assumed. One intriguing possibility is that moving out of the shade of the trees exposed early hominids to much more intense solar radiation than they had been accustomed to, and that by standing upright they managed to minimize the amount of solar energy they absorbed. Keeping the brain cool is critical for any animal; and, lacking any specialized mechanisms for this, our hominoid ancestors may have benefited from the whole-body cooling promoted by upright posture. This posture also permits efficient cooling by the evaporation of sweat, which may be associated with the hairlessness that has very likely been characteristic of humans ever since.

Whatever the case, the early hominid have-your-cake-and-eat-it locomotor adaptation of early hominids was clearly successful, because this body form remained essentially stable for at least several million years, even as hominid species diversified, came, and went. In the 3 to 2 myr period, for example, there is evidence of more than one "gracile" (lightly built) species of australopith at sites in South Africa; and in a slightly later period fossils are found there of a "robust" australopith group, characterized by enormous grinding dentitions, whose origins can be traced to before about 2½ myr in East Africa, where the robust record persists to not much more than 1 myr ago. None of these early hominids had brains much bigger than those of today's apes, and there is no evidence that any of them made tools; there is, indeed, little to suggest that their cognitive capacities were vastly improved relative to those of modern apes, which is one reason why some paleoanthropologists have characterized this initial radiation of hominids as "bipedal chimpanzees."

## THE ORIGINS OF THE GENUS *HOMO*

When and how our own genus *Homo* emerged is a subject of some debate. Fragmentary fossils from sites in Ethiopia and Malawi dated to about 2½ myr ago suggest that by this time a dental pattern significantly different from those of the australopiths had emerged, and in the period around 2 myr ago, a very motley assemblage of fossils from eastern and southern Africa has been assigned to the species *Homo habilis.* Initially named from specimens about 1.8 myr old found at Tanzania's Olduvai Gorge, this species was placed in *Homo* principally because of its presumed association with crude stone artifacts found at the Gorge, and has since been augmented with fossils found in Kenya's East Turkana region and elsewhere. These include specimens with australopith-sized brains, and some with somewhat larger ones, notably the famous ER-1470 cranium from East Turkana. Associated postcranial elements are also hard to interpret, with some isolated leg bones from Turkana looking somewhat advanced while, for instance, the fragmentary partial skeleton OH-62 from Olduvai has been described as even more primitive in its proportions than Lucy. Clearly we have a mixture of species here and sorting the mess out is a major task for the future.

What is clear, however, is that hominids of some kind had begun making stone tools by possibly as much as 2½ myr ago. These were not necessarily, of course, the first human tools of any kind—after all, chimpanzees make tools of perishable substances such as twigs—but they are the first of which tangible evidence is preserved in the archaeological record, and there is plenty of evidence that these crude but sharp flakes, chipped off small nodules of fine-grained rock, were used in activities such as butchering the carcasses of dead animals. This doesn't mean, however, that these animals had been hunted; more likely, they were scavenged natural deaths or carnivore kills—resources that may have been particularly plentiful in the zone of intergradation between forest or woodland and savanna. Nonetheless, the mere existence of stone tools, however crude, marks a cognitive leap away from anything of which the great apes are capable. Figuring out how to hit one stone with another at the precise angle necessary to detach a sharp flake is a feat beyond the capacity of any ape, even one that has been intensively coached; and there is good evidence that these tools were not just ad hoc responses to immediate needs, but that planning and forethought (generally lacking in ape hunting behaviors) were involved. For example, suitable stones were carried distances of a couple of miles or more from their nearest natural sources and were then worked when the occasion demanded, as shown by the fact that archaeologists have been able to reconstruct entire cobbles from fragments found at butchery sites. A couple of decades ago much was made of the notion that many early sites at which, for example, an unexpectedly high proportion of ungulate limb bones were found, might have been "home bases," to which animal parts were habitually transported for sharing among the group—which in turn carried overtones of a complex social lifestyle and elaborate interindividual communication. It has since been realized, however, that such interpretations, depending as they do on the idea that if these creatures weren't apes, they must have been primitive forms of ourselves, lean excessively toward viewing these early hominids in our own image. More recent archaeological interpretations have been considerably more circumspect.

## EARLY HUMANS OF MODERN BODY FORM

If the degree of physical modernity of the earliest toolmakers is equivocal, there is no doubt about a new group of early humans whose remains are first known from the Turkana region in the period following about 1.8 myr ago. This is largely due to the discovery of the "Turkana Boy" in West Turkana in the mid-1980s (Fig. 7–2). The Boy consists of an astonishingly well-preserved skull and postcranial skeleton of an adolescent who died at the age of nine (though developmentally he is more advanced than modern nine-year-olds), some 1.6 myr ago. He is generally associated with slightly older adult specimens from East Turkana, which include a fairly complete cranium (ER-3733) and braincase (ER-3883), and are increasingly assigned to the species *Homo ergaster,* although some prefer to regard them as "early African *Homo erectus.*" Here is a form with a much more modern-looking skull and dentition than any australopith, and a brain well over half the size of our own (australopiths run about a third). The skull of *Homo ergaster* is nonetheless significantly less modern-looking than its body skeleton, as judged from the Boy (Fig. 7–3). Early hominids were rather small-bodied, but here we have an individual who was five feet three inches tall when he died, but would have stood a full six feet tall had he survived to adulthood. What's more, his body proportions were those typical of people who live today in hot, arid environments such as the one in which he lived—these early humans were clearly at home out on the savanna, far from forests—with long, slender arms, legs, and torso. There were differences from us, of course, but in essence here is an individual of modern body form.

Culturally, however, little had changed, at least at the start. The earliest *Homo ergaster* continued to make stone tools similar to those that had been made hundreds of thousands of years earlier. This may seem a little sur-

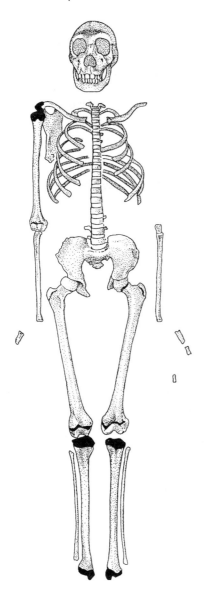

**Figure 7–2**   Skeleton of the "Turkana Boy" (KNM WT 15000) from West Turkana, Kenya. 1.6 myr old. From *The Fossil Trail: How We Know What We Think We Know About Human Evolution,* by Ian Tattersall (Oxford University Press, 1995).

prising, but a moment's thought will show that it's really what we should expect. There's no reason—or need—to expect technological innovation with the arrival of a new species, because there's really only one place where such innovations can occur, and that's within a species. Nonetheless, true technological innovation was not long in coming. A hundred thousand years or so after the Boy lived, we begin to find a radically new kind of stone tool in the archaeological record. This is the "Acheulean" handaxe and related implements. Unlike the early "Oldowan" tools, that were produced simply to obtain an attribute—a sharp cutting edge—handaxes were large, six to eight inches long and more, and consciously

shaped on both sides to a standard symmetrical form. These were general-purpose tools that were used for a variety of purposes such as cutting, scraping, and hacking, and their utility is attested to by the fact that they lingered in the archaeological record for well over a million years. How this new tool type reflected larger changes in lifestyle is not clear, but it is nonetheless evident that it embodies evidence of a significant cognitive advance.

It is in the period following about 2 myr ago that we first begin to find evidence for humans outside Africa. Very early dates for human presence in Asia (in the 1.8 to 1.5 myr range) are individually debated, but collectively suggest that humans exited Africa for the first time hard on the heels of their acquisition of modern body form, and the striding gait that came with it. Humans are walking machines, not fast but with incredible endurance, and they wasted no time in capitalizing on this ability. A very early departure from Africa also has the advantage of explaining why eastern Asia *Homo erectus* (physically not too dissimilar from *Homo ergaster,* as far as we can tell) never acquired Acheulean technology: Its emigrant ancestors left the continent of their birth before its invention.

## THE ICE AGES AND THE EARLIEST EUROPEANS

The emergence of *Homo ergaster* also more or less coincided with a period of unsettled climates and geography known as the "Ice Ages." For the last 1.8 myr or so, major cycles of cooling and warming have occurred worldwide with a frequency of about 100 thousand years (100 kyr). In cold times, the polar and montane ice caps expanded, "locking up" water, reducing sea levels, extending shorelines, and uniting continental islands with the mainland; in warmer periods the ice caps contracted, sea levels rose, and islands were once again cut off. Many fluctuations occurred within the major cycles, and the net result was to produce extremely propitious conditions for evolutionary innovation, by environmental change and even more importantly by the fragmentation of populations and the formation of isolates in which new features could mostly easily become fixed.

It was in this context that the first human populations invaded Europe, which from this point on will assume an ever-larger role in the human story if only because the record is incomparably better from this part of the Old World than from elsewhere. The earliest European human fossils known, just under 800 kyr old, come from the site of the Gran Dolina in the Atapuerca Hills of Spain, and consist of various fragments that have been very recently allocated to the new species *Homo antecessor.* It is unclear whether these specimens represent the precursors of later Europeans or whether they are the result of an initial, and ultimately unsuccessful, invasion of the region. The describers of the new species believe that

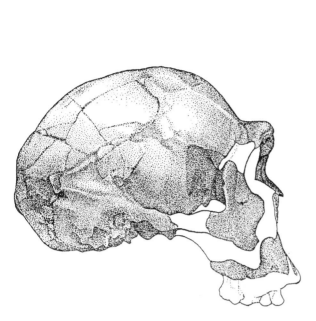

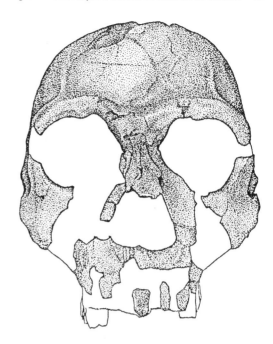

**Figure 7–3** Cranium of *Homo ergaster* (KNM ER 3733) from East Turkana, Kenya. Ca. 1.7 myr old. From *The Fossil Trail: How We Know What We Think We Know About Human Evolution,* by Ian Tattersall (Oxford University Press, 1995).

it represents the common ancestor of two lineages that led to *Homo sapiens* on the one hand, and, on the other, via a form known as *Homo heidelbergensis* (Fig. 7–4) to the Neanderthals, *Homo neanderthalensis*. I should probably note at this point that not all authorities agree on the existence of so many human species over the past 1 myr or so, and that some, indeed, would view all these forms (plus *Homo ergaster* and *Homo erectus*) as varieties of our own species *Homo sapiens* (Fig. 7–5). Such views are, however, unsustainable in light of what we know about interspecies variability in other speciose primate genera, and about the evolutionary process itself.

*Homo erectus* lingered on in eastern Asia into quite recent times while, in Africa, *Homo ergaster* gave rise at

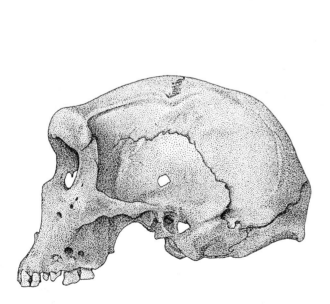

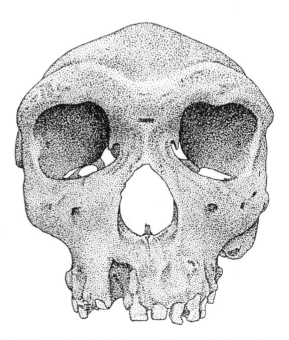

**Figure 7–4** Cranium of *Homo heidelbergensis* from Kabwe, Zambia ("Rhodesian Man"). Maybe 400 kyr old. From *The Fossil Trail: How We Know What We Think We Know About Human Evolution,* by Ian Tattersall (Oxford University Press, 1995).

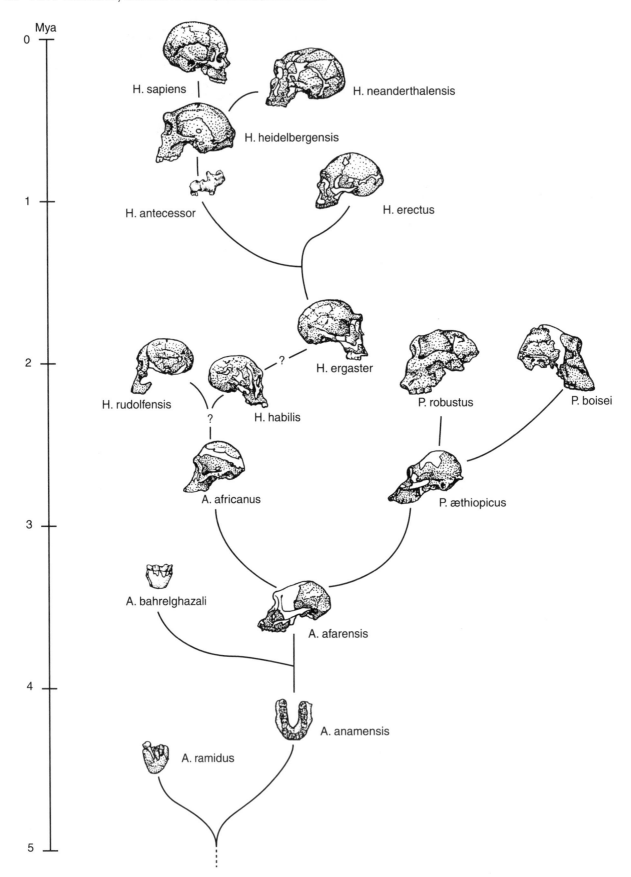

**Figure 7–5** One possible "family tree" of hominid species. From *The Fossil Trail: How We Know What We Think We Know About Human Evolution,* by Ian Tattersall (Oxford University Press, 1995).

some point over about 600 kyr ago to the species *Homo heidelbergensis,* representatives of which are also later on found in Europe. With *Homo heidelbergensis* we are approaching a more familiar skull form, with brain sizes up quite close to the modern average—although, in contract to *Homo sapiens,* in which a small facial skeleton is tucked beneath the front of a high, rounded cranial vault with a sharply rising forehead, these forms had relatively long and low braincases with forwardly positioned faces surmounted by distinct brow ridges. The archaeological record of *Homo heidelbergensis* is best in Europe, where several sites bear witness to the lifeways of these early humans and to several significant innovations. Although handaxes eventually reached Europe, the earlier stone tool assemblages wielded by *Homo heidelbergensis* there tend to be pretty unsophisticated; greater interest attaches, for example, to the fact that at the 400 kyr-old site of Terra Amata in southern France (which unfortunately lacks human fossils) has yielded the earliest traces of constructed shelters, in the form of saplings embedded in the ground in an oval arrangement, and bent inwards to come together over the center of the hut. Inside these structures animal bone refuse was haphazardly scattered around, although in one such hut there is a shallow, scooped-out hearth containing burned cobbles. Although there are traces of fire preserved at African sites as much as 1.5 myr old, Terra Amata provides us with the earliest substantial evidence of the domestication of fire, surely one of the most significant events in the history of human technology.

At the entrance to the cave of Arago, of similar age but several hundred miles to the west, fossils of *Homo heidelbergensis* have been found in a succession of "living floors" characterized by an abundance of stone tools and animal bones. It is still debated whether these bones or those found at Terra Amata testify to the hunting skills of *Homo heidelbergensis*—they might, after all, have been scavenged or accumulated by natural forces—but the recent discovery of miraculously preserved wooden throwing spears at a 400 kyr-old German site seems to tip the balance in favor of some active hunting, at least. What's more, the nature of sites such as Terra Amata and Arago offer the first plausible intimations of the "home base" of which recent studies have deprived earlier toolmakers. If this is correct, we are able to glimpse here the first glimmerings of some of those behavioral attributes we associate with our own kind. Yet, once more, specifics are elusive. Even the evidence of fire from Terra Amata is hard to interpret, since the control of fire in hearths only became a regular feature of the archaeological record subsequent to about 150 kyr ago. Particularly since the advantages of domesticating fire seem so evident, it's hard to know what to make of isolated instances such as this.

## THE NEANDERTHALS AND THEIR SUCCESSORS

Without any question, the best known of our extinct relatives is the species *Homo neanderthalensis,* known widely from sites in Europe and western Asia dated to between about 200 and 30 kyr ago. These distinctive humans had brains that were as large as our own, but that were housed in a long, low skull with a narrow and protruding face (Fig. 7–6). They also differed from us in var-

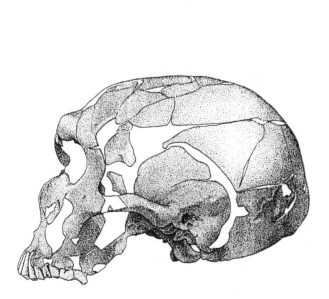
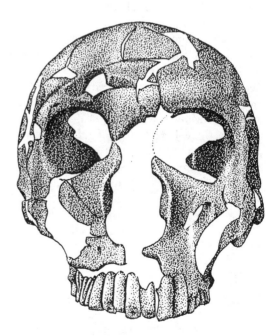

**Figure 7–6**   Cranium of *Homo neanderthalensis* from La Ferrassie, France. Probably ca. 50 kyr old. From *The Fossil Trail: How We Know What We Think We Know About Human Evolution,* by Ian Tattersall (Oxford University Press, 1995).

ious minor features of the postcranial skeleton, which is generally said to be highly robust, but is in some respects less so than is often claimed. The ultimate origins of the Neanderthals are unclear, although several European fossils in the 300 to 200 kyr range are said to show features that anticipate them. These include some exquisitely preserved crania from the "Pit of the Bones" in Spain's Atapuerca Hills, a slightly crushed cranium from Steinheim in Germany, and fossils from Reilingen, also in Germany, and Swanscombe, in England. Fuller analysis may show, however, that the Neanderthals are but one component of an endemic radiation of hominids in Europe, rather than the culmination of a single lineage of which these other fossils were earlier members. There is a growing consensus that the Neanderthals (and other subsequent humans) were ultimately derived from *Homo heidelbergensis*. However, certain features of the latter, such as an extreme development of the sinuses of the skull, may cast some doubt on this.

At some time before we have definitive evidence of *Homo neanderthalensis* (dating is vague) we find another significant technological innovation in the archaeological record. This involved preparing a nucleus of rock in such a way that a single blow would detach a flake that might serve as a finished tool or that could be modified for a number of purposes. In some cases a succession of blows would detach a series of flakes, each of which could be used in this way. This technique had the prime advantage of producing a single continuous cutting edge all around the periphery of the tool, rather than a succession of surfaces at various angles. It also provided greater economy of raw materials. Regardless of whoever invented this technique, however, it was taken to its highest pitch of perfection by the Neanderthals, whose "Mousterian" stoneworking tradition produced a wide variety of finely made tools, although attempts to categorize them have been confounded by the fact that many forms seem to result from a process of reduction, as blunted old tools were reworked to renew their edges. There was perhaps more regional variety than has generally been recognized, but Mousterian tools remained essentially uniform over the long tenure of the Neanderthals, and throughout the vast area of the world they inhabited. Nonetheless, the fact that Neanderthal toolmakers made a variety of different tools to patterns that they held in their minds bespeaks a degree of cognitive refinement relative to anything that went before.

Probably the major reason why the Neanderthals are so much better known biologically than earlier humans is that, at least occasionally, they buried their dead, a factor that favors preservation and contributes to the relatively large number of quasi-complete skeletons that have been found. More profoundly, however, this practice speaks to us as an intensely human type of behavior, although the motives of Neanderthals were not necessarily those that inspire humans to indulge in similar prac-

tices today. For, significantly, we have little evidence in a fairly abundant Neanderthal record of any other activities that we might regard as symbolic. This stands in dramatic contrast to the record left behind by the modern humans who entered Europe about 40 kyr ago and had entirely eliminated the Neanderthals from the region—how, exactly, is unclear, although it was certainly not by genetic absorption, as has often been claimed—by a little under 30 kyr ago. Not only did these *Homo sapiens* bury their dead with a variety of rich grave goods, but they left behind evidence of abundant symbolic activities of other kinds. Starting well over 30 kyr ago, we find notations on plaques of bone and stone; bone flutes with complex sound capabilities; elaborate symbolic systems on cave walls; and, in media ranging from engraving to bas-relief to monochrome drawings to sculpture and polychrome paintings, some of the finest art that has ever been created. What's more, it is clear that such activities were not oddities, but were integral parts of these people's daily lives and belief systems. These people were us.

In the technological realm the contrasts between *Homo neanderthalensis* and *Homo sapiens* were equally stark. While Neanderthals worked virtually exclusively in stone, the moderns showed mastery of diverse materials including bone and antler, even producing tiny-eyed needles from these materials by 26 kyr ago, thereby announcing the advent of tailored clothing. At the same time stoneworking was refined, with numerous long "blades" adaptable to multiple specific functions. Traditions of producing such tools diversified rapidly in different regions. Uses of fire became more complex; indeed, in one area of central Europe fire was used to heat kilns in which clay images were baked. The animal bones found at early modern human sites became more varied, coming to include fish and birds, for instance, and bearing witness to varied and sophisticated hunting techniques. The list of such contrasts could go on and on; but the essential point is that Neanderthals and moderns were creatures of a different order—in other words, that the Neanderthals did not simply do what we do, but not as well. Their approach to the world and life, like those of their predecessors, was radically different from ours. And, successful though the Neanderthals' way was for longer than *Homo sapiens* has been on the Earth, it eventually lost out to this new force on the landscape.

## THE ORIGIN OF MODERN HUMANS

Where did these extraordinary new creatures come from? I've noted that these people, identical physically to ourselves, first entered Europe, fully fledged, some 40 kyr ago (Fig. 7–7). But anatomically modern humans have been around much longer than that. There are hints in Africa of anatomically modern *Homo sapiens* as much as 120 kyr ago, or perhaps even a little more; but all of these

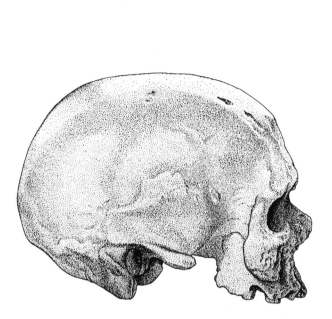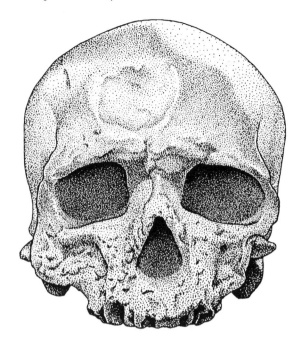

**Figure 7–7** Cranium of early European *Homo sapiens* from Cro-Magnon, France. Around 26 to 28 kyr old. From *The Fossil Trail: How We Know What We Think We Know About Human Evolution,* by Ian Tattersall (Oxford University Press, 1995).

remains are fragmentary or poorly dated, or both. Still, the notion of an African origin for our species is supported by studies of genetic diversity, and, more controversially, by mtDNA dating. What's more, the Levant, on the fringes of Africa and faunally part of the same province, has yielded good fossil evidence for anatomically modern humans in the period around 100 kyr ago, notably at the Israeli site of Jebel Qafzeh. The problem is, though, that anatomically modern humans somehow shared the Levant with Neanderthals from at least that time up to about 40 kyr ago—and that, throughout this long period, these two kinds of humans also shared virtually identical technologies—and, as far as we can tell, lifestyles, although a recent study suggests that Neanderthals and moderns may have had different approaches to exploiting the landscape.

What was going on? One suggestion is that the Neanderthals were "cold-adapted," and moved into the Levant from areas to the north in cooler periods, while the moderns retreated to the balmier climes of Africa. The reverse would have happened in warmer times. Maybe so; but this does not explain the virtual identity of the toolkits of the two forms. Clearly, humans can be modern in two distinct senses: anatomical and behavioral (no big surprise here; remember that I've already remarked that innovations of all kinds necessarily arise *within* species). Anatomical modernity almost certainly had its origins in Africa, though we don't yet understand the details of this because the record is poor there. Behavioral modernity may also have arisen in Africa,

though at a later time; for although the African record lacks the extravagance of symbol that we see in Europe, we have very early hints there of bone and blade tools, flint mining, and long-distance transport of materials—all things that are associated at a later date in Europe with art, music, notation, and all those other aspects of life that make it so easy to identify with the early Europeans as people like ourselves. Whatever the case, it is clear that *Homo sapiens* must have originated in a specific place, for all species do; and it was most likely born with a behavioral potential that was only later fully realized (again, nothing surprising; the history of life abounds with examples of capacities born in one context, and only later exploited in another).

What lies at the root of behavioral modernity? The complex and often unfathomable behaviors of people today are without a doubt a reflection of our capacity for symbolic thought, something the Neanderthals probably did not possess. And virtually synonymous with symbolic thought is language. For language is not simply a matter of stringing words together, but is rather a complex symbolic system in itself, that not only allows us to express associations we make in our minds but also allows certain kinds of association to be made. Those early Europeans who eliminated the Neanderthals certainly possessed language; while the Neanderthals, even though they may well have had a fairly complex system of interindividual communication, almost equally certainly did not. Studies of the cranial base, which forms the roof of the vocal tract, show that the ability to form the sounds associated with modern speech was beginning to develop in *Homo ergaster,* and that it was probably fully formed in *Homo heidelbergensis.*

The latent ability to produce speech thus goes back a long way, and we must hence conclude that the critical and much more recent leap to modernity was made in the brain, capitalizing on a pre-existing vocal potential. In which case, there was either a major biological change among humans subsequent to their acquisition of the skeletal modernity that we can detect in the fossil record—implausible on a variety of grounds; or the concealed potential for symbolic reasoning was born along with skeletal modernity, lying fallow for many millennia until it was kicked into action by some cultural stimulus, most plausibly the invention of language. This innovation was thus then able to spread rapidly by cultural contact among populations all having the latent ability to acquire it—a much more convincing scenario than the only alternative, which involves the wholesale replacement of populations Old World-wide in a relatively short period of time.

It is particularly frustrating that the event of events—the birth of our own unique species—is obscured by the apparent poverty of the available record. But actually this is a matter of perspective. If we knew as much about the remote process of the adoption of bipedalism by our earliest ancestors, or about the origin of the genus *Homo,* as we do about the much more recent origin of *Homo sapiens,* we would doubtless discern a much more complex situation than we are able to present and would feel an equal measure of frustration. The history of our lineage has been a long and complex one,

and increasing knowledge will only serve to emphasize this complexity. For every problem that is solved, several more will emerge as our fossil and archaeological records enlarge. And perhaps that is how it should be.

## FURTHER READINGS

Fuller discussion of matters both raised and neglected in this chapter will be found in the following recent books.

Eldredge, N. (1995) *Reinventing Darwin: The Great Debate at the High Table of Evolutionary Theory.* New York: John Wiley.

Johanson, D.; Edgar, B. (1996) *From Lucy to Language.* New York: Simon and Schuster.

Potts, R. (1996) *Humanity's Descent: The Consequences of Ecological Instability.* New York: William Morrow.

Schick, K. D.; Toth N. (1993) *Making Silent Stones Speak: Human Evolution and the Dawn of Technology.* New York: Simon and Schuster.

Stanley, S. M. (1996) *Children of the Ice Age: How a Global Catastrophe Allowed Humans to Evolve.* New York: Harmony Books.

Stringer, C.; McKie, R. (1996) *African Exodus: The Origins of Modern Humanity.* New York: Henry Holt.

Tattersall, I. (1995) *The Fossil Trail: How We Know What We Think We Know about Human Evolution.* New York: Oxford University Press.

Tattersall, I. (1995) *The Last Neanderthal: The Rise, Success and Mysterious Extinction of Our Nearest Human Relatives.* New York: Macmillan.

Tattersall, I. (1998) *Becoming Human: Evolution and Human Uniqueness.* New York: Harcourt Brace.

# Chapter 8

# *Evolution of Humans May at Last Be Faltering*

## William K. Stevens

Natural evolutionary forces are losing much of their power to shape the human species, scientists say, and the realization is raising tantalizing questions about where humanity will go from here.

Is human evolution ending, ushering in a long maturity in which *Homo sapiens* persists pretty much unchanged? Or will humankind, armed with the tools of molecular biology, seize control of its own evolution?

The questions have no immediate answers, but recent work by evolutionary biologists and others is bringing into focus some of the factors likely to influence humanity's fate.

A number of experts say that *Homo sapiens* is becoming increasingly disengaged from the forces of natural selection and speciation, the key processes that brought humankind into existence. Until quite recently on the evolutionary time scale, those processes bound humans to the confined and perilous existence of hunter-gatherers. But the explosion of human culture, already in full flower in the cave art of Europe some 35,000 years ago, has enabled the human species to liberate itself gradually from the harsh forces of natural selection.

"Natural selection has to some extent been repealed" in the case of humans, says Dr. Steve Jones, a geneticist at University College London. Most social changes "seem to be conspiring to slow down human evolution," he argues in a recent book, *The Language of Genes: Solving the Mysteries of Our Genetic Past, Present and Future* (Anchor Books, 1994).

Natural selection shapes species by choosing the fit over the unfit, generation after generation. Individuals born with advantageous genetic changes survive and have more progeny, while those who lose out in the genetic lottery may perish before breeding age.

From *The New York Times*, March 14, 1995.

The human line, until the relatively recent weakening of evolutionary pressures, evolved to exploit a life as hunters and gatherers. One major selective force on its emergence was climatic change. It was a global cooling around five million years ago, many paleontologists believe, that shrank the forests of Africa and induced the forebears of the human line—those genetically predisposed to do so—to walk upright and forage across the savanna.

Other environmental disruptions forced further adaptation, leading eventually to hunting, tool-making and language. Along the way, scientists believe, some populations became isolated by barriers of geography or habitat, and they evolved differently enough to split into new species. Many species probably arose as the human line evolved, but only one now remains.

*Homo sapiens,* the survivor, is departing from the script of natural selection in a number of ways, experts say, and evolutionary forces on humans consequently have weakened.

For instance, lions and leopards and sabre-toothed cats do not carry off the weak and unfit as they once did. "That's no longer there," notes Dr. Elisabeth S. Vrba, an evolutionist at Yale University.

Since most people now survive to reproductive age, according to one view, natural selection is being robbed of its most important raw material. If everyone survives and reproduces, no selection of the fittest can take place; in evolutionary terms, everyone is fit.

Humans, some evolutionists say, have wrapped themselves in such a snug cocoon, from clothing to central heating to hurricane warning systems, that populations are largely insulated from the environmental stresses that drive evolution. Technology and medicine also tend to cancel out inherited genetic defects.

Colonies, emigration, and travel have also blunted the shaping forces of evolution. When a population becomes isolated by geography from the rest of its species, it is most likely to evolve independently and eventually become a new species.

"*Homo sapiens* today is in a mode of intermixing rather than of differentiation, and the conditions for significant evolutionary change simply don't exist—and won't, short of some all-too-imaginable calamity," writes Dr. Ian Tattersall, a paleoanthropologist at the American Museum of Natural History in New York, in *The Fossil Trail* (Oxford University Press, 1995).

For Dr. Tattersall, the most striking factor in the relaxation of evolutionary pressures is the mobility of humans in the modern world. "What you have is a species that is spread over a huge variety of environments. There is no barrier that humans cannot cross now."

Humans are intermixing more than ever before, marrying people born in locations farther away and generally eliminating the isolation of populations that leads to speciation.

Dr. Stephen Jay Gould, an evolution expert at Harvard University, puts it this way. "We are not likely to speciate unless we send up some space colonies."

All this suggests to some scientists that human evolution is winding down and that humankind faces a long period of evolutionary stasis. "The biology of the future will not be very different from that of the past," Dr. Jones wrote. Humans, in his judgment, will never be superhuman; no X-ray vision, Superman strength, or ability to fly lies in the future.

Differences in fertility rates may have become an evolutionary factor relatively recently, Dr. Jones and others say. Among urban middle-class people, birth rates have dropped in the last two centuries, while they have remained high among many poorer groups, especially the more numerous rural people of the third world. Because the rural poor on average have more children per parent, and the children are more likely to survive than was the case not so long ago, they have become more successful than their middle-class urban compatriots in passing on their genes.

The evolutionary impact of these fertility factors is unclear, scientists say. One possibility, they say, is that if the global population doubles before stabilizing late in the next century as United Nations demographers predict, the more prolific groups will expand rapidly and genetically overwhelm the less prolific, who generally are more likely to be shielded from evolutionary pressures.

Another possibility is that after the population explosion has run its course, the majority of humanity will gradually be shielded from natural selection—albeit with an altered genetic profile.

The fertility factors may already be weakening. United Nations demographers say third-world birth rates are dropping so rapidly that on average, they will reach the "replacement level" of a little more than two births per woman of childbearing age in all countries within the next fifty years. If so, the evolutionary importance of fertility differences would be sharply reduced. However, they would not be eliminated if, as seems certain, some individuals continue to have more children than others.

Some evolutionary biologists believe humans will eventually take their future firmly into their own hands through genetic engineering. Once the 100,000 human genes are mapped in detail, "we will be in a position to choose our own course of evolution," said Dr. Edward O. Wilson of Harvard University.

Whether to intervene in that course deliberately is a political and moral issue, and Dr. Wilson says the decision may be to do nothing. If it is otherwise, "at that point, Darwinian natural selection will have ceased," he said, adding: "I don't think the human species will ever go extinct. I think we'll find the wisdom to put ourselves on the course of near-infinite tenancy of the earth."

All but 1 percent of all species that have ever lived are now extinct, but many, in Dr. Jones's words, "stayed unchanged as living fossils" for much of their species lifetimes. He said humans would probably also become living fossils, their evolution complete, "but fossils that redesign their own environment to stay alive."

While it may seem as if humans are indeed transcending natural selection, a longer view of evolution might take into account occasional but devastating events like ice ages, the movement of continents and the impacts of asteroids and comets.

Some scientists fear that human themselves may be creating a disaster of similar scale by destroying natural habitats worldwide and risking the onset of climate change set off by industrial pollutants. Natural or man-made calamities would have profound evolutionary implications for all life, including humans.

For now, Dr. Tattersall writes, given the absence of either a natural calamity or any sign that the human form is evolving further, "we shall have to learn to live with ourselves as we are. Fast."

# Chapter 9

# *Selection in Modern Populations*

## J. B. Birdsell

Selection is an evolutionary process of the utmost importance, for it has a major role in most genetic changes in time. It operates in a variety of ways whose total effect is expressed in terms of differential effective fertility (The ability to have offspring who themselves live to reproductive age). A variety of factors can contribute to differences in the way in which individuals hand on their genetic materials to the next generation. Early death, a refusal to marry or procreate, carelessness in the raising of children so they do not reach maturity, and a variety of other causes can all contribute to differences in effective fertility.

It is important to understand that no selection is operative unless differences in effective fertility are related to genetic differences in the people involved. Let us use a gruesome example to illustrate the point. Let us presume a small hydrogen bomb of five megatons is dropped upon the center of Manhattan Island. The so-called "lethal area" extends in a radius of four miles all around the point of impact. Within the 50 square miles represented by the "lethal area," presumably all of the individuals in the central portion will be killed, if not vaporized. This occurs irrespective of their genotype, and so selection is not acting upon them. They have merely been annihilated. Away from the center, an increasing number of survivors will be encountered. Most of these will have survived owing to the accident of their position at the time of the explosion. But as we reach the outer portion of the circle, survivorship becomes more common, and the possibility of selection now arises. If in the outer stretches of the devastated area, some people survive because they are genetically equipped to better withstand radiation and blast effects than are others, then se-

lection is going on. The point of this grisly example is that all deaths do not involve selection, only those in which genetic differences contribute to survivorship.

Crowded cities arose for the first time on this planet about 7000 years ago in the fertile valleys of Mesopotamia. Since that time cities have steadily increased in importance, and continue to do so today. What has been called "pathological togetherness" will no doubt increase as the world's population doubles in the next twenty-five to thirty years.

Aside from the inconveniences of city living, there are a number of hazards that certainly do contain the potential of acting as selective agents. Let us first consider smog. Medical research has not yet fully established the consequences of this type of atmospheric pollution. But in the city of Los Angeles it is said that an autopsy surgeon can closely estimate the length of time a person has lived in that city from the condition of the cadaver's lungs. Normal healthy lungs are a bright pink in color. Those of the citizenry of Los Angeles range from brown to black. Smog undoubtedly contains cancer-producing compounds, an effect confirmed by experiments with animals. Individual men and women differ considerably in their susceptibility to these cancer-producing agents. Without knowing any of the genetic differences involved, it is safe to say that smog is acting as a selective agent upon human populations living in cities. The smog also contains carbon monoxide (CO), a compound that limits the amount of oxygen that can be bonded to the red corpuscles and so distributed to the body. Slight amounts of carbon monoxide impair our perceptions and cause passing illness. In greater amounts it kills. People undoubtedly differ somewhat in their susceptibility to these effects. Finally, it has been shown that the asbestos incorporated in automobile brake linings fills the air around freeways with tiny fragmented fibers. These enter the lungs and in time can cause serious illness. Altogether it can be predicted that air pollutants of one or

From *Human Evolution: An Introduction to the New Physical Anthropology*, Third Edition. Houghton Mifflin Company. Boston, Massachusetts. 1981.

another kind in cities will so affect the lives of men as to select against those who do not have adequate genetic defenses. Since all known characters in man show genetic variability, it is extremely likely that people differ in their resistance and so in their responses. Selection surely operates in genetically significant terms in this sort of urban situation.

## DISEASE AS A SELECTIVE AGENT

Human beings, we know, have always died differentially as a consequence of diseases. Even today with modern medicine, diseases produce high mortality figures, affecting different individuals in very different ways. For example, infantile paralysis, or poliomyelitis, produces nothing more than a stiff neck in many individuals exposed to it while others suffer overall body paralysis. The difference lies in each person's immune system. Some people are well protected genetically against this particular disease, whereas others stand biochemically naked. The evolution of disease immunity of course involves genetic changes, showing selection in action.

Diseases as selective agents were revealed in dramatic fashion during the expansion of colonial Europeans into other continents. Europeans reaching the new continents of North and South America carried with them their own mild diseases. Yet measles and whooping cough became killers of native Americans who had no previous exposure to these diseases. The necessary evolutionary give-and-take came only after Amerindians had been through enough generations of exposure to the new parasites. Those individuals without immune systems that could handle these diseases died, but the survivors in time evolved proper genetic defenses through selective processes.

For many years after their discovery, the human blood groups were thought to be neutral in nature, or *not* subject to selective pressures. This naive view is now known to be incorrect. All of the variable blood group systems are maintained in a *balanced polymorphic state*. In recent years, medical researchers have uncovered a number of statistical associations between diseases and blood group types. These relationships suggest rather specific kinds of selective forces associated with the blood groups. No less than eight different studies conducted on large numbers of individuals in this country and in northwest Europe have shown that the individuals with the blood group O are slightly more susceptible to such diseases as gastric and duodenal ulcers than are individuals with the blood groups A, B, and AB. At the same time, it was revealed that individuals with the blood group A are slightly more prone to develop cancer of the stomach than are those with other types. Frank Livingstone has suggested that infectious diseases such as plague, smallpox, and cholera may have exerted different selective pressures on individual blood group types. Taking this a step further, this hypothesis would suggest that regional variations in blood group gene frequencies may in part have been molded by *diseases* as agencies of selection. Obviously investigations of selection in human populations have barely scratched the surface.

# Chapter 10

# *Ghetto Legacy*

## Stephen J. O'Brien

*Can the high incidence of Tay–Sachs disease in Ashkenazi Jews be linked to historic epidemics of tuberculosis in industrial European cities?*

In 1976, William McNeill, a noted historian from the University of Chicago, published a remarkable treatise (McNeill 1976) that persuasively argued that the single most important influence on human cultural development was the periodic occurrence of outbreaks of infectious disease. Earlier still, British geneticist J. B. S. Haldane had suggested that infectious pathogens have provided a key selective component in the struggle for survival of all species. Indeed, as the secrets of genomic organization begin to unravel through the methods and insight of molecular biology, we continue to encounter the molecular footprints of historic epidemics, notably vestigial endogenous retroviruses, mobile controlling elements, and convoluted gene rearrangements in complex cascades that mediate immune defenses. A fascinating new example of evolution's balancing act between host and parasite genetic adaptation has now emerged from an unexpected arena, namely the epidemiology of a devastating childhood hereditary syndrome, Tay–Sachs disease.

Of the thousands of inborn errors recognized today, Tay–Sachs disease must surely rank among the most horrific. Infants afflicted with the disease are born healthy, but within the first six months they develop neurological symptoms including seizures, rapid deterioration of cognitive ability, blindness and hypercephaly, which persist until their death usually between their third and fifth birthdays (Sandhoff et al. 1989). The defects stem from homozygosity for a recessive mutation in the *HEXA* gene, located on chromosome 15, that encodes the α-subunit of β-hexosaminidase. (*HEXB*, on chromosome 5, encodes the β-subunit.) This enzyme is one of over forty that are packaged in neuronal lysosomes and play important parts both in glycolipid hydrolysis and in the regulation of $G_{m2}$-ganglioside balance in the central nervous system. The neurological symptoms of Tay–Sachs disease result from the abnormal accumulation of $G_{m2}$-ganglioside in the brain and neural tissues.

The seminal discovery of the molecular basis of Tay–Sachs disease (Okada and O'Brien 1969), combined with the development of a histochemical test for both heterozygous carriers and affected fetuses *in utero* by amniocentesis (O'Brien et al. 1971) in the early 1970s led to a massive screening and genetic counseling program that has become a model for success in human genetics. In the past two decades, there has been a drop of nearly 90 percent in the incidence of affected births (Sandhoff et al., 1989).

Part of the success had been the result of cultural factors. The occurrence of Tay–Sachs disease is highly skewed in the United States with the great majority of cases occurring in marriages between descendants of Eastern European Jews, the Ashkenazim. The overall incidence of the disease in non-Jewish populations is 1 in 112,000, and the heterozygote carrier frequency is 1 in 167. Among Ashkenazi Jews identified in North American screens; the carrier frequency is five times higher (1 in 31) and the disease incidence is nearly thirty times greater (1 in 3900). A quick calculation reveals that 1 in 16 Ashkenazi Jewish couples (there are approximately 13 million Jews alive today and 75% of these are Ashkenazim) would be expected to have at least one Tay–Sachs gene. It is these daunting odds combined with a particu-

From *Current Biology*, 1 (4), 1991.

larly effective education campaign within the Jewish communities that have led to widespread screening of Jewish couples at risk for Tay–Sachs disease and the near elimination of new cases.

But why should the mutant gene frequency be so high in Ashkenazi Jews? A compelling case for heterozygote advantage (equivalent to selection against both homozygotes) has been offered by Jared Diamond, stimulated by a personal anxiety over the disease due to his own family's Ashkenazi ancestry (Diamond 1991). Diamond has revisited the early hypothesis that connects the widespread epidemic of pulmonary tuberculosis (TB) that afflicted urban European populations in the nineteenth century to Tay–Sachs disease and the Ashkenazi cultural background. The hypothesis suggests that TB provided an intense selective pressure that may have favored heterozygotes for the *HEXA* mutation, perhaps because they were somehow more resistant to tubercule bacillus infection and or TB progression than their relatives. The evidence, though correlative and epidemiological, is so evocative as to merit serious consideration.

Traditionally, increased gene frequencies of rare alleles in racial groups or isolated populations are thought to emerge from founder effects in small ancestral populations followed by genetic drift or sampling error. A useful analogy might be to consider a five card poker hand; the effect of sampling (the draw) is to change the frequencies of each card, initially $\frac{1}{52}$ to $\frac{1}{5}$ for each card in the hand and to zero for the other 47 cards. The founder effect hypothesis is a likely explanation for the existence of a Pennsylvania Dutch community of 383 people, 15 percent of whom carry a Tay–Sachs gene, that can trace its ancestry back to an eighteenth century couple. But the same hypothesis falls apart when applied to the high frequency in the Ashkenazi Jews. First, there is simply no evidence of an ancestral population contraction or bottleneck (a *sine qua non* for genetic drift) of the Ashkenazim over time or geography in the past few thousand years. Second Ashkenazi Jews are also afflicted with an elevated frequency of two other extremely rare genetic lysosomal storage diseases: Neimann–Pick disease, a sphingomyelinase deficiency, with a carrier frequency among Ashkenazim of 1 percent: and Gaucher's disease, caused by a defective glucocerebrosidase, with

Ashkenazi carrier frequency of 3 percent (Goodman and Motulsky 1979). That a single large outbred population would acquire three extremely rare glycolipid storage diseases by chance with no evidence of historic demographic contraction is highly unlikely. Third, if genetic drift were the primary explanation, one would expect that allele frequencies at other genetic loci would be shifted as well. However, genetic surveys that compared several loci unrelated to lysosomal enzymes revealed that the Ashkenazim are actually quite similar to other peoples from the Eastern Mediterranean (Goodman and Motulsky 1979). The failure of a founder effect or genetic drift to account for the disproportionate elevation in Ashkenazi Tay–Sachs disease was the first clue in the inference of a key role for natural selection.

Comparison of the molecular structure of the *HEXA* mutations found among Ashkenazi Jews and non-Jewish carriers proved to be particularly informative. Between 95 and 99 percent of the Tay–Sachs disease alleles in Ashkenazi Jews (Mahuran et al. 1990, Grebner and Tomczak 1991) can be accounted for by three distinct alleles, each with a specifically defined mutational defect in the *HEXA* gene (Table 10–1). These three variants constitute less than 20 percent of the alleles detected in non-Jewish heterozygous carriers sampled to date; the remaining alleles are uncharacterized. The fact that two of the three distinct alleles were found at far greater frequency in Ashkenazi Jews than in non-Jews is inconsistent with a chance effect of genetic drift. It is virtually impossible that three or even two mutant alleles that were so rare in the founding population could have co-occurred in a bottlenecked ancestral population by chance.

The case for selection of heterozygotes seems rather strong, but the selective agent needs to be identified. What agent might have put selective pressure on Ashkenazi Jews but not other Jews or non-Jews from Eurasia? Consider the history of the Ashkenazim. Between 1880 and 1920, the American Jewish population increased sixteen-fold, from 280,000 to 4,500,000, due to mass immigration from Eastern Europe. For centuries before then, Eastern European Jews were sequestered in urban environments, often crowded into ghettos because politics and prejudice precluded them from owning rural

## TABLE 10–1   *HEXA* Mutations and Their Frequencies

| | | | Carrier Frequencies | |
| --- | --- | --- | --- | --- |
| **Mutation** | **Location** | **Result** | Ashkenazim | Non-Jews |
| 4-base-pair insertion | Exon 11 | Chain termination | 73–79% | 14–16% |
| G → C | Exon 12 | Abnormal splicing | 15–18% | 0.63%* |
| G → A | Exon 7 | Gly269 → serine | 3–4% | 3–4% |
| Other alleles, not yet precisely defined | | | 1–5% | 81–82% |

*Not observed in 79 carriers

acreage. Historians remind us that crowded urban squalor was the focus of at least two major epidemics of TB, one in the seventeenth century and a second toward the end of the nineteenth century (McNeill 1976).

A clever epidemiological approach to the question of which agent might have produced heterozygote advantage reviewed the cause of death of 306 grandparents of American Tay–Sachs patients (Myrianthopoulos and Aronson 1972). In spite of the fact that the vast majority of these grandparents had lived in East European industrial centers at the height of the TB epidemic, when TB mortality among ill-fed and ill-housed urban dwellers of industrial Europe reached 20 percent, TB was listed as a cause of death in only one case. As at least half of these grandparents must have been heterozygous carriers, the correlative link between carrying one Tay–Sachs gene and resistance to TB was dramatic. Further, an extensive survey of geographic origins of Tay–Sachs disease carriers in North America (Peterson et al. 1983) revealed that the Tay–Sachs gene frequencies were up to three-fold greater (7–11%) in Austria, Hungary, and Czechoslovakia than in other regions of Ashkenazi origin (Figure 10–1). These countries are in precisely the regions of Europe where the TB epidemic was most intense from 1880 to 1920.

A fascinating addendum to these epidemiologic findings came from a look at the distribution of European origins among 1466 TB patients at a Jewish sanitorium in Denver in the early part of this century (Myrianthopoulos and Aronson 1972). Eligibility in this study required that the patients had been born outside the United States between 1860 and 1910 and had emigrated to the United States by 1920, before X-ray screening for pulmonary TB was introduced by immigration officials. Nearly twice as many of these patients as would be ex-

pected from control populations came from Austria, Hungary, and Czechoslovakia.

But doesn't the demographic clustering of elevated TB and Tay–Sachs disease in these areas actually contradict the expectations of the disease resistance hypothesis? If heterozygosity for the disease gene offers protection, would we not expect TB to occur at a lower frequency in areas with high disease? This is precisely the trap that many observers of the data fell into: The flaw in the logic being that the gene frequencies must be considered. Even with the relatively high frequency (1/31) of Tay–Sachs disease among Ashkenazi, the number of carriers would have little effect on TB incidence. Conversely, the high level of exposure to TB would have a noticeable effect on Tay–Sachs carriers and so drive up the gene frequencies. Stated differently, at low frequencies of the resistance gene, we actually expect to find the greatest relative gene frequency in areas where the epidemic is the most rampant. This is precisely the observation illustrated in Figure 10–1. A parallel situation with the sickle cell anemia gene, carriers of which are selectively favored by malaria, results in the highest incidence of the sickle cell gene in tropical Africa where the incidence of malaria is also the highest.

The case for TB as the force that selected the Tay–Sachs gene must remain unproven until a physiological mechanism is discovered. TB is a pulmonary infection whereas Tay–Sachs disease is a neurological disease. But the enzyme that mediates Tay–Sachs disease, β-hexosaminidase, is a "household" enzyme found in lysosomes of all cells. Could it be that moderate accumulation of glycolipids in membranes of pulmonary cells of Tay–Sachs heterozygotes somehow alters the dynamics or efficiency of infection by the tubercule bacillus? The answers to this and to other plausible alternatives must await empirical approaches. If affirmed, however, the relationship between Tay–Sachs disease and TB would be another cogent natural demonstration of the powerful selective role played by infectious agents, joining the familiar examples of sickle cell anemia and thalassemia, as well as the extreme balanced heterozygosity of the mammalian histocompatibility complex.

It may be significant that in each of these better known examples the selected genes are members of families of historically duplicated, functionally active, homologous genes (for example, HLA class I, A, B and C alleles; the β-globin complex). It is tempting to speculate that functional gene duplication provides an effective mechanism to fix the heterozygous state in every individual of a species and that the continued selective pressure of the pathogen has promoted some or all of these duplications in the distant past. Tay–Sachs disease would fit nicely in this scenario because the *HEXA* and *HEXB* genes that contribute subunits to both homodimeric and heterodimeric isozymes of β-hexosaminidase also arose from ancestral duplications to judge by their 60 percent

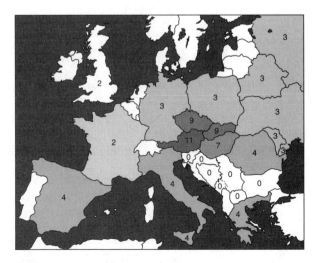

**Figure 10–1** Frequencies of U.S. Tay–Sachs gene carriers according to their European country of origin. (Adapted from Petersen et al. 1983)

DNA sequence homology (Proia 1988). That our four best candidates for pathogen-driven heterozygote advantage all involve homologous gene duplication may be another clue in our search for a rational basis for genome organization.

## REFERENCES

Diamond, J. (1991) "Curse and blessing of the ghetto." *Discover* 12:60–65.

Goodman, R. M.; Motulsky, A. G. (Eds.) (1979) *Genetic Diseases Among Ashkenazi Jews.* New York: Raven Press.

Grebner, E. E.; Tomczak, J. (1991) "Distribution of three α-chain β-hexosaminidase A mutations among Tay–Sachs carriers." *Am. J. Hum. Genet.* 48:604–607.

Mahuran, D. J.; Triggs-Raine, B. L.; Feigenbaum, A. J.; Gravel, R. A. (1990) "The molecular basis of Tay–Sachs disease: Mutation identification and diagnosis." *Clin. Biochem.* 23:409–415.

McNeill, W. H. (1976) *Plagues and Peoples.* New York: Anchor Press/Doubleday.

Myrianthopoulos, N. C.; Aronson, S. M. (1972) "Population dynamics of Tay–Sachs disease. II. What confers the selective advantage upon the Jewish heterozygote?" *Adv. J. Hum. Genet.* 35:1258–1269.

O'Brien, J. S.; Okada, S.; Fillerup, D. L.; Veath, M. L.; Adornato, B.; Brenner, P. H.; Leroy, J. G. (1971) "Tay–Sachs disease prenatal diagnosis" *Science* 172:61–64.

Okada, S.; O'Brien, J. S. (1969) "Tay–Sachs disease: Generalized absence of a β-D-N acetylhexosaminidase component." *Science* 165:698–700.

Petersen, G. M.; Rotter, J. L.; Cantor, R. M.; Field, L. L.; Greenwald, S.; Lim, J. S. T.; Roy, C.; Schoenfeld, V.; Lowden, J. A.; Kaback, M. M. (1983) "The Tay–Sachs disease gene in North American Jewish population: Geographic variations and origin." *Am. J. Hum. Genet.* 35:1258–1269.

Proia, R. L. (1988) "Gene encoding the human β-hexosaminidase β-chain: Extensive hormology of intron placement in the α- and β-chain genes." *Proc. Natl. Acad. Sci. USA* 85:1883–1887.

Sandhoff, K.; Conzelmann, E.; Kaback, M. M.; Suzuki, K. (1989) The $G_{m2}$ gangliosides." In *The Metabolic Basis of Inherited Disease* (pp. 1807–1842). C. R. Scriver; A. L. Beaudet; W. S. Sly; D. Valle, eds. New York: McGraw-Hill.

# Part II

# THE EVOLUTION OF HUMAN BEHAVIOR

Many anthropologists and biologists have theorized about the behavior of the earliest hominids and how this behavior might be related to the biological basis of modern human behavior. In the early years of the twentieth century, it was thought that the first humans would have large brains and primitive, ape-like bodies. This led to the relatively easy acceptance in 1912 of the Piltdown Man, with its human skull and ape-like jaw, as the "missing link" between humans and apes. This preconception of the characteristics of early humans also led to resistance in accepting as our earliest ancestor the first real early hominid, *Australopithecus africanus,* uncovered in Africa in 1924. However, in the early 1950s with the discovery that Piltdown was a fraud and with many more australopithecine fossils available, scientists realized that our earliest ancestors were more like non-human primates than like modern humans. This, in turn, led to a number of attempts to reconstruct the behavior of our earliest hominid ancestors, often using primate models.

It seems that each decade since the acceptance of the role of australopithecines in our evolutionary past, a recurrent theme has focused on the importance of hunting and its relationship to the propensity for human violence. This has led to many scenarios concerning the evolution of violence and its biological basis in modern humans.

In the 1960s, Washburn, who is considered one of the fathers of modern physical anthropology and of American field primatology, was among the first to develop a "Man the Hunter" theme of human evolution and behavior. In the 1970s, E. O. Wilson, one of the major founders of the subfield of biology referred to as sociobiology, explained much of human behavior as an outcome of our hunting past. (The sociobiological explanation has currently been adopted by evolutionary psychologists [see Part IV of this volume]. In the 1980s, with the discovery of earlier hominid fossils in Ethiopia, anatomist Owen Lovejoy and Donald Johanson, the paleontologist who discovered Lucy, explained many of the

features of hominid evolution with a modified version of male hunting and provisioning. The most recent version of this recurrent theme is that authored by Harvard professor and primatologist Richard Wrangham and science writer Dale Peterson in the their book, *Demonic Male.* In this theory, Wrangham links human hunting to an inherent propensity for violence shared by humans and common chimpanzees.

In the first eight chapters of this section (Chapters 11–18), these theories, and rebuttals to them, are presented. In chapter 19, I trace the origins and history of some of these theories and explain why I feel that the "Man the Hunter" theme is one of the myths of western Judeo-Christian culture. Chapter 19 illustrates how these myths can become part of the popular sociopolitical ideology. In Chapter 20, Richard Potts of the Smithsonian Institution provides a carefully thought-out approach to the way in which reconstructions of this sort should be done. In Chapter 21, I present an example of an alternative approach to constructing models of early human behavior using a traditional comparative methodology.

The final three chapters of this section focus on the origins of modern *Homo sapiens* and on some of the archeological remnants found in association with the earliest modern humans. Chapter 22 by Lemonick describes the rapid spread of artwork once it appears in the archeological record. Schumann and Pettitt, paleontologists specializing in the middle and upper Pleistocene, relate the artifacts and other vestiges of behavior of this period to modern human's conceptions of time. In the final chapter of this section, Bartlett and I hypothesize that many of the unique artifacts appearing around 40,000 years ago correspond with the acquisition of "culture" in these early *Homo sapiens.* We believe that this, in turn, relates to the evolution of deception in primates and of self-deception in humans. At about 40,000 years ago, what appears to separate many artifacts left by these early modern humans from all other fossil materials is the "gap" between the particular item and its immediate and direct use for subsistence. These modern humans seem to be creating an image or filter through which they see their world, with different groups of humans creating different images. We believe that this is the basis of human culture, which, in turn, is related to the way different people see the world differently. How does this relate to self-deception? Most people believe that their culturally determined way of seeing the world is the only way or, at least, the best way, and they can't all be right.

# Chapter 11

# *The Evolution of Hunting*

Sherwood L. Washburn
C. S. Lancaster

It is significant that the title of this symposium is Man the Hunter for, in contrast to carnivores, human hunting, if done by males, is based on a division of labor and is a social and technical adaptation quite different from that of other mammals.[1] Human hunting is made possible by tools, but it is far more than a technique or even a variety of techniques. It is a way of life, and the success of this adaptation (in its total social, technical, and psychological dimensions) has dominated the course of human evolution for hundreds of thousands of years. In a very real sense our intellect, interests, emotions, and basic social life—all are evolutionary products of the success of the hunting adaptation. When anthropologists speak of the unity of mankind, they are stating that the selection pressures of the hunting and gathering way of life were so similar and the result so successful that populations of *Home sapiens* are still fundamentally the same everywhere. In this essay we are concerned with the general characteristics of man that we believe can be attributed to the hunting way of life.

Perhaps the importance of the hunting way of life in producing man is best shown by the length of time hunting has dominated human history. The genus *Homo*[2] has existed for some 600,000 years, and agriculture has been important only during the last few thousand years. Even 6,000 years ago large parts of the world's population were nonagricultural, and the entire evolution of man from the earliest populations of *Homo erectus* to the existing races took place during the period in which man was a hunter. The common factors that dominated human evolution and produced *Homo sapiens* were preagricultural. Agricultural ways of life have dominated less than 1 percent of human history, and there is no evidence of

major biological changes during that period of time. The kind of minor biological changes that occurred and that are used to characterize modern races were not common to *Homo sapiens*. The origin of all common characteristics must be sought in preagricultural times. Probably all experts would agree that hunting was a part of the social adaptation of all populations of the genus *Homo*, and many would regard *Australopithecus*[3] as a still earlier hominid who was already a hunter, although possibly much less efficient than the later forms. If this is true and if the Pleistocene period had a duration of three million years, then pre-*Homo erectus* human tool using and hunting lasted for at least four times as long as the duration of the genus *Homo* (Lancaster, unpublished). No matter how the earlier times may ultimately be interpreted, the observation of more hunting among apes than was previously suspected (Goodall 1965) and increasing evidence for hunting by *Australopithecus* strengthens the position that less than 1 percent of human history has been dominated by agriculture. It is for this reason that the consideration of hunting is so important for the understanding of human evolution.

When hunting and the way of life of successive populations of the genus *Homo* are considered, it is important to remember that there must have been both technical and biological progress during this vast period of time. Although the locomotor system appears to have changed very little in the last 500,000 years, the brain did increase in size and the form of the face changed. But for present purposes it is particularly necessary to direct attention to the cultural changes that occurred in the last ten or fifteen thousand years before agriculture. There is no convenient term for this period of time, traditionally spoken of as the end of the Upper Paleolithic and the Mesolithic, but Binford and Binford (1966) have rightly emphasized its importance.

From *Man the Hunter*. R. B. Lee and I. DeVore (eds.) New York: Aldine de Gruyter.

During most of human history, water must have been a major physical and psychological barrier and the inability to cope with water is shown in the archeological record by the absence of remains of fish, shellfish, or any object that required going deeply into water or using boats. There is no evidence that the resources of river and sea were utilized until this late preagricultural period, and since the consumption of shellfish in particular leaves huge middens, the negative evidence is impressive. It is likely that the basic problem in utilization of resources from sea or river was that man cannot swim naturally but to do so must learn a difficult skill. In monkeys the normal quadrupedal running motions serve to keep them afloat and moving quite rapidly. A macaque, for example, does not have to learn any new motor habit in order to swim. But the locomotor patterns of gibbons and apes will not keep them above the water surface, and even a narrow, shallow stream is a barrier for the gorilla (Schaller 1963). For early man, water was a barrier and a danger, not a resource. (Obviously water was important for drinking, for richer vegetation along rivers and lakeshores, and for concentrating animal life. Here we are referring to water as a barrier prior to swimming and boats, and we stress that, judging from the behavior of contemporary apes, even a small stream may be a major barrier).

We think that the main conclusion, based on the archeological record, ecological considerations, and the ethnology of the surviving hunter-gatherers, will be sustained. In the last few thousand years before agriculture, both hunting and gathering became much more complex. This final adaptation, including the use of products of river and sea and the grinding and cooking of otherwise inedible seeds and nuts, was worldwide, laid the basis for the discovery of agriculture, and was much more effective and diversified than the previously existing hunting and gathering adaptations.

Hunting by members of the genus *Homo* throughout the 600,000 years that the genus has persisted has included the killing of large numbers of big animals. This implies the efficient use of tools, as Birdsell stressed at the symposium. The adaptive value of hunting large animals has been shown by Bourlière (1963), who demonstrated that 75 percent of the meat available to human hunters in the eastern Congo was in elephant, buffalo, and hippopotamus. It is some measure of the success of human hunting that when these large species are protected in game reserves (as in the Murchison Falls or Queen Elizabeth Parks in Uganda), they multiply rapidly and destroy the vegetation. Elephants alone can destroy trees more rapidly than they are replaced naturally, as they do in the Masai Amboseli Reserve in Kenya. Since the predators are also protected in reserves, it appears that human hunters have been killing enough large game to maintain the balance of nature for many thousands of years. It is tempting to think that man replaced the

saber-toothed tiger as the major predator of large game, both controlling the numbers of the game and causing the extinction of Old World saber-tooths. We think that hunting and butchering large animals put a maximum premium on cooperation among males, a behavior that is at an absolute minimum among the nonhuman primates. It is difficult to imagine the killing of creatures such as cave bears, mastodons, mammoths—or *Dinotherium* at a much earlier time—without highly coordinated, cooperative action among males. It may be that the origin of male-male associations lies in the necessities of cooperation in hunting, butchering, and war. Certainly butchering sites, such as described by F. Clark Howell in Spain, imply that the organization of the community for hunting large animals goes back for many, many thousands of years. From the biological point of view, the development of such organizations would have been paralleled by selection for an ability to plan and cooperate (or reduction of rage). Because females and juveniles may be involved in hunting small creatures, the social organization of big-game hunting would also lead to an intensification of a sexual division of labor.

It is important to stress, as noted before, that human hunting is a set of ways of life. It involves divisions of labor between male and female, sharing according to custom, cooperation among males, planning, knowledge of many species and large areas, and technical skill. Goldschmidt (1966, p. 87 ff.) has stressed the uniqueness and importance of human sharing, both in the family and in the wider society, and Lee (personal communication) emphasizes orderly sharing as fundamental to human hunting society. The importance of seeing human hunting as a whole social pattern is well illustrated by the old idea, recently revived, that the way of life of our ancestors was similar to that of wolves rather than that of apes or monkeys. But this completely misses the special nature of the human adaptation. Human females do not go out and hunt and then regurgitate to their young when they return. Human young do not stay in dens but are carried by mothers. Male wolves do not kill with tools, butcher, and share with females who have been gathering. In an evolutionary sense the whole human pattern is new, and it is the success of this particularly human way that dominated human evolution and determined the relation of biology and culture for thousands of years. Judging from the archeological record, it is probable that the major features of this human way, possibly even including the beginnings of language, had evolved by the time of *Homo erectus*.[4]

## THE WORLD VIEW OF THE HUNTER

Lévi-Strauss urged that we study the world view of hunters, and, perhaps surprisingly, some of the major aspects of world view can be traced from the archeological record. We have already mentioned that boats and the entire complex of fishing, hunting sea mammals, and using shellfish was late. With this new orientation, wide rivers and seas changed from barriers to pathways and sources of food, and the human attitude toward water must have changed completely. But many hundreds of thousands of years earlier, perhaps with *Australopithecus*, the relation of the hunters to the land must also have changed from an earlier relationship that may be inferred from studies of contemporary monkeys and apes. Social groups of nonhuman primates occupy exceedingly small areas, and the vast majority of animals probably spend their entire lives within less than four or five square miles. Even though they have excellent vision and can see for many miles, especially from tops of trees, they make no effort to explore more than a tiny fraction of the area they see. Even for gorillas the range is only about fifteen square miles (Schaller 1963), and it is of the same order of magnitude for savanna baboons (DeVore and Hall 1965). When Hall tried to drive a troop of baboons beyond the end of their range, they refused to be driven and doubled back into familiar territory, although they were easy to drive within the range. The known area is a psychological reality, clear in the minds of the animals. Only a small part of even this limited range is used, and exploration is confined to the canopy, lower branches, and bushes, or ground, depending on the biology of the particular species. Napier (1962) has discussed this highly differential use of a single area by several species.

In marked contrast, human hunters are familiar with very large areas. In the area studied by Lee (1965), eleven waterholes and 600 square miles supported 248 Bushmen, a figure less than the number of baboons supported by a single waterhole and a few square miles in the Amboseli Reserve in Kenya. The most minor hunting expedition covers an area larger than most nonhuman primates would cover in a lifetime. Interest in a large area is human. The small ranges of monkeys and apes restrict the opportunities for gathering, hunting, and meeting conspecifics, and limit the kind of predation and the number of diseases. In the wide area, hunters and gatherers can take advantage of seasonal foods, and only man among the primates can migrate long distances seasonally. In the small area, the population must be carried throughout the year on local resources, and natural selection favors biology and behavior that efficiently utilize these limited opportunities. But in the wide area, natural selection favors the knowledge that enables a group to utilize seasonal and occasional food sources. Gathering over a wide and diversified area implies a greater knowledge of flora and fauna, knowledge of the annual cycle, and a different attitude toward group movements. Clearly one of the great advantages of slow maturation is that learning covers a series of years, and the meaning of events in these years become a part of the individual's knowledge. With rapid maturation and no language, the chances that any member of the group will know the appropriate behavior for rare events is greatly reduced.

Moving over long distances creates problems of carrying food and water. Lee (1965, p. 124) has pointed out that the sharing of food even in one locality implies that food is carried, and there is no use in gathering quantities of fruit or nuts unless they can be moved. If women are to gather while men hunt, the results of the labors of both sexes must be carried back to some agreed upon location. Meat can be carried away easily, but the development of some sort of receptacles for carrying vegetable products may have been one of the most fundamental advances in human evolution. Without a means of carrying, the advantages of a large area are greatly reduced, and sharing implies that a person carries much more than one can use. However that may be, the whole human pattern of gathering and hunting to share—indeed, the whole complex of economic reciprocity that dominates so much of human life—is unique to man. In its small range, a monkey gathers only what it itself needs to eat at that moment. Wherever archeological evidence can suggest the beginnings of movement over large ranges, cooperation, and sharing, it is dating the origin of some of the most fundamental aspects of human behavior—the human world view. We believe that hunting large animals may demand all these aspects of human behavior that separate man so sharply from the other primates. If this is so, then the human way appears to be as old as *Homo erectus*.

The price that man pays for his high mobility is well illustrated by the problems of living in the African savanna. Man is not adapted to this environment in the same sense that baboons or vervet monkeys are. Man needs much more water, and without preparation and cooking he can only eat a limited number of the foods on which the local primates thrive. Unless there have been major physiological changes, the diet of our ancestors must have been far more like that of chimpanzees than like that of a savanna-adapted species. Further, man cannot survive the diseases of the African savanna without lying down and being cared for. Even when sick, the locally adapted animals are usually able to keep moving with their troop; and the importance to their survival of a home base has been stressed elsewhere (DeVore and Washburn 1963). Also man becomes liable to new diseases and parasites by eating meat, and it is of interest that the products of the sea, which we believe were the last class of foods added to human diet, are widely regarded as indigestible and carry diseases to which man is particularly susceptible. Although many humans die of disease and injury, those who do not, almost without exception, owe their lives to others who cared for them when they were unable to hunt or gather, and this uniquely human caring is one of the patterns that builds social bonds in the group and permits the species to occupy almost every environment in the world.

A large territory not only provides a much wider range of possible foods but also a greater variety of potentially useful materials. With tool use this variety takes on meaning, and even the earliest pebble tools show selection in size, form, and material. When wood ceases to be just something to climb on, hardness, texture, and form become important. Availability of materials is critical to the tool user, and early men must have had a very different interest in their environment from that of monkeys or apes. Thus, the presence of tools in the archeological record is not only an indication of technical progress but also an index of interest in inanimate objects and in a much larger part of the environment than is the case with nonhuman primates.

Hunting changed man's relations to other animals and his view of what is natural. The human notion that it is normal for animals to flee, the whole concept of animals being wild, is the result of man's habit of hunting. In game reserves many different kinds of animals soon learn not to fear man, and they no longer flee. James Woodburn took a Hadza into the Nairobi Park, and the Hadza was amazed and excited, because although he had hunted all his life, he had never seen such a quantity and variety of animals close at hand. His previous view of animals was the result of his having been their enemy, and they had reacted to him as the most destructive carnivore. In the park the Hadza hunter saw for the first time the peace of the herbivorous world. Prior to hunting, the relations of our ancestors to other animals must have been very much like those of the other noncarnivores. They could have moved close among the other species, fed beside them, and shared the same waterholes. But with the origin of human hunting, the peaceful relationship was destroyed, and for at least half a million years man has been the enemy of even the largest mammals. In this way the whole human view of what is normal and natural in the relation of man to animals is a product of hunting, and the world of flight and fear is the result of the efficiency of the hunters.

Behind this human view that the flight of animals from man is natural lie some aspects of human psychology. Men enjoy hunting and killing, and these activities are continued as sports even when they are no longer economically necessary. If a behavior is important to the survival of a species (as hunting was for man throughout most of human history), then it must be both easily learned and pleasurable (Hamburg 1963). Part of the motivation for hunting is the immediate pleasure it gives the hunter, and the human killer can no more afford to be sorry for the game than a cat can for its intended victim. Evolution builds a relation between biology, psychology, and behavior, and, therefore, the evolutionary success of hunting exerted a profound effect on human psychology. Perhaps, this is most easily shown by the extent of the efforts devoted to maintain killing as a sport. In former times royalty and nobility maintained parks where they could enjoy the sport of killing, and today the United States government spends many millions of dollars to supply game for hunters. Many people dislike the notion that man is naturally aggressive and that he naturally enjoys the destruction of other creatures. Yet we all know people who use the lightest fishing tackle to prolong the fish's futile struggle, in order to maximize the personal sense of mastery and skill. And until recently war was viewed in much the same way as hunting. Other human beings were simply the most dangerous game. War has been far too important in human history for it to be other than pleasurable for the males involved. It is only recently, with the entire change in the nature and conditions of war, that this institution has been challenged, that the wisdom of war as a normal part of national policy or as an approved road to personal social glory has been questioned.

Human killing differs from killing by carnivorous mammals in that the victims are frequently of the same species as the killer. In carnivores there are submission gestures or sounds that normally stop a fatal attack (Lorenz 1966). But in man there are no effective submission gestures. It was the Roman emperor who might raise his thumb; the victim could make no sound or gesture that might restrain the victor or move the crowd to pity. The lack of biological controls over killing conspecifics is a character of human killing that separates this behavior sharply from that of other carnivorous mammals. This difference may be interpreted in a variety of ways. It may be that human hunting is so recent from an evolutionary point of view that there was not enough time for controls to evolve. Or it may be that killing other humans was a part of the adaptation from the beginning, and our sharp separation of war from hunting is due to the recent development of these institutions. Or it may be simply that in most human behavior stimulus and response are not tightly bound. Whatever the origin of this behavior, it has had profound effects on human evolution, and almost every human society has regarded killing members of certain other human societies as desirable (D. Freeman 1964). Certainly this has been a major factor in man's view of the world, and every folklore contains tales of culture heroes whose fame is based on the human enemies they destroyed.

The extent to which the biological bases for killing have been incorporated into human psychology may be measured by the ease with which boys can be interested in hunting, fishing, fighting, and games of war. It is not that these behaviors are inevitable, but they are easily learned, satisfying, and have been socially rewarded in most cultures. The skills for killing and the pleasures of killing are normally developed in play, and the patterns of play prepare the children for their adult role. At the conference Woodburn's excellent motion pictures showed Hadza boys killing small mammals, and Laughlin described how Aleuts train boys from early childhood so that they would be able to throw harpoons with accuracy and power while seated in kayaks. The whole youth of the hunter is dominated by practice and appreciation of the skills of the adult males, and the pleasure of the games motivates the practice that is necessary to develop the skills of weaponry. Even in monkeys, rougher play and play fighting are largely the activities of the males, and the young females explore less and show a greater interest in infants at an early age. These basic biological differences are reinforced in man by a division of labor that makes adult sex roles differ far more in humans than they do in nonhuman primates. Again, hunting must be seen as a whole pattern of activities, a wide variety of ways of life, the psychobiological roots of which are reinforced by play and by a clear identification with adult roles. Hunting is more than a part of the economic system, and the animal bones in Choukoutien are evidence of the patterns of play and pleasure of our ancestors.

## THE SOCIAL ORGANIZATION OF HUMAN HUNTING

The success of the human hunting and gathering way of life lay in its adaptability. It permitted a single species to occupy most of the earth with a minimum of biological adaptation to local conditions. The occupation of Australia and the New World was probably late, but even so there is no evidence that any other primate species occupied more than a fraction of the area of *Homo erectus*. Obviously, this adaptability makes any detailed reconstruction impossible, and we are not looking for stages in the traditional evolutionary sense. However, using both the knowledge of the contemporary primates and the archeological record, certain important general conditions of our evolution may be reconstructed. For example, the extent of the distribution of the species noted above is remarkable and gives the strongest sort of indirect evidence for the adaptability of the way of life, even half a million years ago. Likewise all evidence suggests that the local group was small. Twenty to fifty individuals is suggested by Goldschmidt (1959, p. 187) Such a group size is common in nonhuman primates and so we can say with some assurance that the number did not increase greatly until after agriculture. This means that the number of adult males who might cooperate in hunting or war was very limited, and this sets limits to the kinds of social organizations that were possible. Probably one of the great adaptive advantages of language was that it permits the planning of cooperation between local groups, temporary division of groups, and the transmission of information over a much wider area than that occupied by any one group.

Within the group of the nonhuman primates, the mother and her young may form a subgroup that continues even after the young are fully grown (Sade 1965, 1966; Yamada 1963). This grouping affects dominance, grooming, and resting patterns, and, along with dominance, is one of the factors giving order to the social relations in the group. The group is not a horde in the nineteenth-century sense, but it is ordered by positive affectionate habits and by the strength of personal dominance. Both these principles continue into human society, and dominance based on personal achievement must have been particularly powerful in small groups living physically dangerous lives. The mother-young group certainly continued and the bonds must have been intensified by the prolongation of infancy. But in human society, economic reciprocity is added, and this created a wholly new set of interpersonal bonds.

When males hunt and females gather, the results are shared and given to the young, and the habitual sharing between a male, a female, and their offspring becomes the basis for the human family. According to this view, the human family is the result of the reciprocity of hunting, the addition of a male to the mother-plus-young social group of the monkeys and apes.

A clue to the adaptive advantage and evolutionary origin of our psychological taboo on incest is provided by this view of the family. Incest prohibitions are reported universally among humans and these always operate to limit sexual activity involving subadults within the nuclear family. Taking the nuclear family as the unit of account, incest prohibitions tend to keep the birth rate in line with economic productivity. If in creating what we call the family the addition of a male is important in economic terms, then the male who is added must be able to fulfill the role of a socially responsible provider. In the case of the hunter, this necessitates a degree of skill in hunting and a social maturity that is attained some years after puberty. As a young man grows up, this necessary delay in his assumption of the role of provider for a female and her young is paralleled by a taboo that prevents him from prematurely adding unsupported members to the family. Brother-sister mating could result in an infant while the brother was still years away from effective social maturity. Father-daughter incest could also produce a baby without adding a productive male to the family. This would be quite different from the taking of a second wife that, if permitted, occurs only when the male has shown he is already able to provide for and maintain more than one female.

To see how radically hunting changed the economic situation, it is necessary to remember that in monkeys and apes an individual simply eats what it needs. After an infant is weaned, it is on its own economically and is not dependent on adults. This means that adult males never have economic responsibility for any other animal, and adult females do only when they are nursing. In such a system, there is no economic gain in delaying any kind of social relationship. But when hunting makes females and young dependent on the success of male skills, there is a great gain to the family members in establishing behaviors that prevent the addition of infants, unless these can be supported.

These considerations in no way alter the importance of the incest taboo as a deterrent to role conflict in the family and as the necessary precondition to all other rules of exogamy. A set of behaviors is more likely to persist and be widespread if it serves many uses, and the rule of parsimony is completely wrong when applied to the explanation of social situations. However, these considerations do alter the emphasis and the conditions of the discussion of incest. In the first place, a mother-son sexual avoidance may be present in some species of monkeys (Sade 1966) and this extremely strong taboo among humans requires a different explanation than the one we have offered for brother-sister and father-daughter incest prohibitions. In this case, the role conflict argument may be paramount. Second, the central consideration is that incest produces pregnancies, and the most fundamental adaptive value of the taboo is the provision of situations in which infants are more likely to survive. In the reviews of the incest taboo by Aberle and others (1963) and Mair (1965), the biological advantages of the taboo in controlling the production of infants are not adequately considered, and we find the treatment by Service (1962) closest to our own. In a society in which the majority of males die young, but a few live on past forty, the probability of incest is increased. By stressing the average length of life rather than the age of the surviving few, Slater (1959) underestimated the probability of mating between close relatives. Vallois (1961, p. 222) has summarized the evidence on length of life in early man and shows that "few individuals passed forty years, and it is only quite exceptionally that any passed fifty."

That family organization may be attributed to the hunting way of life is supported by ethnography. Since the same economic and social problems as those under hunting continue under agriculture, the institution continued. The data on the behavior of contemporary monkeys and apes also show why this institution was not necessary in a society in which each individual gets its own food.[5] Obviously the origin of the custom cannot be dated, and we cannot prove *Homo erectus* had a family organized in the human way. But it can be shown that the conditions that make the family adaptive existed at the time of *Homo erectus*. The evidence of hunting is clear in the archeological record. A further suggestion that the human kind of family is old comes from physiology; the loss of estrus is essential to the human family organization, and it is unlikely that this physiology, which is universal in contemporary mankind, evolved recently.

If the local group is looked upon as a source of male-female pairs (an experienced hunter-provider and a female who gathers and who cares for the young), then it is apparent that a small group cannot produce pairs regularly, since chance determines whether a particular child is a male or female. If the number maturing in a given year or two is small, then there may be too many males or females (either males with no mates or females with no providers). The problem of excess females may not seem serious today or in agricultural societies, but among hunters it was recognized and was regarded as so severe that female infanticide was often practiced. How grave the problem of imbalance can become is shown by the following hypothetical example. In a society of approximately forty individuals there might be nine couples. With infants born at the rate of about one in three years, this would give three infants per year, but only approximately one of these three would survive to become fully adult. The net production in the example would be one child per year in a population of forty. And because the sex of the child is randomly determined, the odds that all the children would be male for a three-year period are 1 in 8. Likewise the odds for all surviving children being female for a three-year period are 1 in 8. In this example the chances of all surviving children being of one sex are 1 in 4, and smaller departures from a 50/50 sex ratio would be very common.

In monkeys, because the economic unit is the individual (not a pair), a surplus of females causes no problem. Surplus males may increase fighting in the group or males may migrate to other groups.

For humans, the problem of imbalance in sex ratios may be met by exogamy, which permits mates to be obtained from a much wider social field. The orderly pairing of hunter males with females requires a much larger group than can be supported locally by hunting and gathering, and this problem is solved by reciprocal relations among several local groups. It takes something on the order of 100 pairs to produce enough children so that the sex ratio is near enough to 50/50 for social life to proceed smoothly, and this requires a population of approximately 500 people. With smaller numbers there will be constant random fluctuations in the sex ratio large enough to cause social problems. This argument shows the importance of a sizable linguistic community, one large enough to cover an area in which many people may find suitable mates and make alliances of many kinds. It does not mean either that the large community or that exogamy does not have many other functions, as outlined by Mair (1965). As indicated earlier, the more factors that favor a custom, the more likely it is to be geographically widespread and long lasting. What the argument does stress is that the finding of mates and the production of babies under the particular conditions of human hunting and gathering favor both incest taboo and exogamy for basic demographic reasons.

Assumptions behind this argument are that social customs are adaptive, as Tax (1937) has argued, and that nothing is more crucial for evolutionary success than the orderly production of the number of infants that can be supported. This argument also presumes that, at least under extreme conditions, these necessities and reasons are obvious to the people involved, as infanticide attests. The impossibility of finding suitable mates must have been a common experience for hunters trying to exist in very small groups, and the initial advantages of exogamy, kinship, and alliance with other such groups may at first have amounted to no more than, as Whiting said at the conference, a mother suggesting to her son that he might find a suitable mate in the group where her brother was located.

If customs are adaptive and if humans are necessarily opportunistic, it might be expected that social rules would be particularly labile under the conditions of small hunting and gathering societies. At the conference, Murdock pointed out the high frequency of bilateral kinship systems among hunters, and the experts on Australia all seemed to believe that the Australian systems had been described in much too static terms. Under hunting conditions, systems that allow for exceptions and local adaptation make sense and surely political dominance and status must have been largely achieved.

## Conclusion

While stressing the success of the hunting and gathering way of life with its great diversity of local forms and while emphasizing the way it influenced human evolution, we must also take into account its limitations. There is no indication that this way of life could support large communities of more than a few million people in the whole world. To call the hunters "affluent" is to give a very special definition to the word. During much of the year, many monkeys can obtain enough food in only three or four hours of gathering each day, and under normal conditions baboons have plenty of time to build the Taj Mahal. The restriction on population, however, is the lean season or the atypical year, and, as Sahlins recognized, building by the hunters and the accumulation of gains was limited by motivation and technical knowledge, not by time. Where monkeys are fed, population rises, and Koford (1966) estimates the rate of increase on an island at 16 percent per year.

After agriculture, human populations increased dramatically in spite of disease, war, and slowly changing customs. Even with fully human (*Homo sapiens*) biology, language, technical sophistication, cooperation, art, the support of kinship, the control of custom and political power, and the solace of religion—in spite of this whole web of culture and biology—the local group in the Mesolithic was no larger than that of baboons. Regardless of statements made at the symposium on the ease with which hunters obtain food some of the time, it is still true that food was the primary factor in limiting early human populations, as is shown by the events subsequent to agriculture.

The agricultural revolution, continuing into the industrial and scientific revolutions, is now freeing man from the conditions and restraints of 99 percent of his history, but the biology of our species was created in that long gathering and hunting period. To assert the biological unity of mankind is to affirm the importance of the hunting way of life. It is to claim that, however much conditions and customs may have varied locally, the main selection pressures that forged the species were the same. The biology, psychology, and customs that separate us from the apes—all these we owe to the hunters of time past. And, although the record is incomplete and speculation looms larger than fact, for those who would understand the origin and nature of human behavior there is no choice but to try to understand "Man the Hunter."

## Endnotes

1. This paper is part of a program on primate behavior, supported by the United States Public Health Service (Grant No. 8623) and aided by a Research Professorship in the Miller Institute for Basic Research in Science at the University of California at Berkeley. We wish to thank Dr. Phyllis C. Jay for her helpful criticism and suggestions about this paper.
2. The term *Homo* includes Java, Pekin, Mauer, etc., and later forms.
3. Using the term to include both the small *A. africanus* and large *A. robustus* forms. Simpson (1966) briefly and clearly discusses the taxonomy of these forms and of the fragments called *Homo habilis*.
4. In speculations of this kind, it is well to keep the purpose of the speculation and the limitation of the evidence in mind. Our aim is to understand human evolution. What shaped the course of human evolution was a succession of successful adaptations, both biological and cultural. These may be inferred in part from the direct evidence of the archeological record. But the record is very incomplete. For example, Lee (personal communication) has described, for the Bushmen, how large game may be butchered where it falls and only meat brought back to camp. This kind of behavior means that analysis of bones around living sites is likely to underestimate both the amount and variety of game killed. If there is any evidence that large animals were killed, it is probable that far more were killed than the record shows. Just as the number of human bones gives no indication of the number of human beings, the number of animal bones, although it provides clues to the existence of hunting, gives no direct evidence of how many animals were killed. The Pleistocene way of life can only be known by inference and speculation. Obviously, speculations are based on much surer ground when the last few thousand years are under consideration. Ethnographic information is then directly relevant and the culture bearers are of our own species. As we go farther back in time, there is less evidence and the biological and cultural difference becomes progressively

greater. Yet it was in those remote times that the human way took shape, and it is only through speculation that we may gain some insights into what the life of our ancestors may have been.

5. The advantage of considering both the social group and the facilitating biology is shown by considering the "family" in the gibbon. The social group consists of an adult male, an adult female, and their young. But this group is maintained by extreme territorial behavior in which no adult male tolerates another, by aggressive females with large canine teeth, and by very low sex drive in the males. The male-female group is the whole society (Carpenter 1941, Ellefson 1966). The gibbon group is based on a different biology from that of the human family and has none of its reciprocal economic functions. Although the kind of social life seen in chimpanzees lacks a family organization, to change it into that of a man would require far less evolution than would be required in the case of the gibbon.

## REFERENCES

Aberle, D. F.; U. Bronfenbrenner; E. H. Hess; D. R. Miller; D. M. Schneider; J. N. Spuhler. (1963). "The incest taboo and the mating patterns of animals." *American Anthropologist* (n.s.), 65: 253–65.

Binford, L. R.; S. R. Binford. (1966) "The predatory revolution: a consideration of the evidence for a new subsistence level." *American Anthropoligist* (n.s.), 68(2), pt. 1: 508–512.

Bourlière, F. (1963) "Observations on the ecology of some large African mammals." In F. C. Howell and F. Bourlière (Eds.), *African ecology and human evolution* (pp. 43–54). Chicago: Aldine Publishing Company.

Carpenter, C. R. (1941) *A field study in Siam of the behavior and social relations of the Gibbon (Hylobates lar).* Baltimore: Johns Hopkins Press.

DeVore, I. and K. R. L. Hall. (1965) "Baboon ecology." In I. DeVore (Ed.), *Primate behavior.* (pp. 20–52). New York: Holt, Rinehart, and Winston.

DeVore, I.; S. L. Washburn (1963) Baboon ecology and human evolution. In F. C. Howell and F. Bourlière (Eds.), *African ecology and human evolution* (pp. 335–367). Chicago: Aldine Publishing Company.

Ellefson, J. O. (1966) *A natural history of gibbons in the Malay Peninsula.* Unpublished doctoral dissertation, University of California, Berkeley.

Freeman, D. (1964) "Human aggression in anthropological perspective." In J. D. Carthy and F. J. Ebling (Eds.), *The natural history of aggression* (pp. 109–220). New York: Academic Press.

Goldschmidt, W. R. (1959) *Man's way: a preface to the understanding of human society.* New York: Henry Holt.

Goldschmidt, W. R. (1966). *Comparative functionalism: an essay in anthropological theory.* Berkeley and Los Angeles: University of California Press.

Goodall, J. (1965) "Chimpanzees on the Gombe Stream reserve." In I. DeVore (Ed.), *Primate behavior* (pp. 425–473). New York: Holt, Rinehart and Winston.

Hamburg, D. A. (1963) "Emotions in the perspective of human evolution." In P. H. Knapp (Ed.), *Expression of the emotions in man* (pp. 300–317). New York: International Universities Press.

Koford, C. B. (1966) "Population changes in rhesus monkeys: Cayo Santiago, 1960–1964." *Tulane Studies in Zoology,* 13: 1–7.

Lee, R. B. (1965) *Subsistence ecology of !Kung Bushmen.* Unpublished doctoral dissertation, University of California, Berkeley.

Lorenz, K. Z. (1966) *On aggression.* Trans. by Marjorie K. Wilson. New York: Harcourt, Brace and World.

Mair, L. (1965) *An introduction to social anthropology.* Oxford: Clarendon Press.

Napier, J. R. (1962) "Monkeys and their habitats." *New Scientist,* 15: 88–92.

Sade, D. S. (1965) "Some aspects of parent-offspring and sibling relations in a group of rhesus monkeys, with a discussion of grooming." *American Journal of Physical Anthropology* (n.s.), 23(1): 1–17.

Sade, D. S. (1966) *Ontogeny of social relations in a group of free ranging Rhesus monkeys (Macaca mulatta Zimmerman).* Unpublished doctoral dissertation, University of California, Berkeley.

Schaller, G. B. (1963) *The mountain gorilla: ecology and behavior.* Chicago: University of Chicago Press.

Service, E. R. (1962) *Primitive social organization: an evolutionary perspective.* New York: Random House.

Simpson, G. G. (1966) "The biological nature of man." *Science,* 152(3721): 472–78.

Slater, M. K. (1959) "Ecological factors in the origin of incest." *American Anthropologist* (n.s.), 61: 1042–59.

Tax, S. (1937) "Some problems of social organization." In Fred Eggan (Ed.), *Social anthropology of North American tribes* (pp. 3–34). Chicago: University of Chicago Press.

Vallois, H. V. (1961) "The social life of early man: the evidence of skeletons." In S. L. Washburn (Ed.), *Social life of early man* (pp. 214–235). Chicago: Aldine Publishing Company.

Yamada, M. (1963) "A study of blood-relationship in the natural society of the Japanese macaque." *Primates (Journal of Primatology),* 4: 43–66.

# Chapter 12

# *Gingrich: Men Love the Muck*

Women aren't meant for traditional military combat since "females have biological problems staying in a ditch for 30 days." But they might outdo men at missile computers because males "are biologically driven to go out and hunt giraffes."

Newt Gingrich's college course is supposed to be about history, but the new House speaker digressed a bit recently to give his views on what separates the sexes.

The comments are from his first "Renewing American Civilization" lecture since the Georgia Republican took over as the House's top lawmaker.

Since the changing of the guard in Congress, Democrats and other Gingrich opponents have been hanging on every Gingrich word, not only looking for the direction Republicans will take but also for controversy.

So after obtaining a videotape of Gingrich's January 7 class, three days after he became speaker, a resourceful Gingrich critic made a script and distributed it to reporters.

Some nuggets:

"We know [what] personal strength meant in the neolithic: You carried a big club and you had a rock. What does personal strength mean in the age of the laptop? Which, by the way, is a major reason for the rise in the power of women. If upper body strength matters, men win. They are both biologically stronger and they don't get pregnant.

"Pregnancy is a period of male domination in traditional society. On the other hand, if what matters is the speed by which you can move the laptop, women are at least as fast and in some ways better. So you have a radical revolution based on technological change and you've got to think that through.

"If you talk about being in combat, what does combat mean?

"If combat means living in a ditch, females have biological problems staying in a ditch for 30 days because they get infections and they don't have upper body strength. I mean some do, but they're relatively rare.

"On the other hand, men are basically little piglets, you drop them in the ditch, they roll around in it, it doesn't matter, you know. These things are very real.

"On the other hand, if combat means being on an Aegis-class cruiser managing the computer, controls for twelve ships and their rockets, a female may again be dramatically better than a male who gets very, very frustrated sitting in a chair all the time because males are biologically driven to go out and hunt giraffes."

From the Associated Press reprinted from the Chicago Tribune Jan. 19, 1995.

# Chapter 13

# Sociobiology: A New Approach to Understanding the Basis of Human Nature

## Edward O. Wilson

*Through a new synthesis of a wide range of biological sciences, sociobiologists are attempting to explore the genetic contribution to patterns of human behaviour, some of which may be universals of humanity, while others may influence cultural diversity.*

Sociobiology is the systematic study of all forms of social behavior, in animals and humans. For many important reasons we may be particularly preoccupied with understanding human behavior, and to achieve that goal requires us to pay attention to our evolutionary history, both in the recent period as hominids (during the past 10 million years) and as part of the animal kingdom as a whole. Currently the study of human behavior is the domain of the sociologists. They are attempting to explain our behavior primarily by the empirical description of behavior patterns and without reference to evolutionary explanations in any true genetic sense. The role of sociobiology with reference to human beings, then, is to place the social sciences within a biological framework, a framework constructed from a synthesis of evolutionary studies, genetics, population biology, ecology, animal behavior, psychology and anthropology.

While being aware of the possible dangers of analogy, sociobiology puts heavy emphasis on the comparison of societies of different kinds of animals and of man. The aim is to construct and test theories about the underlying hereditary basis of social behavior. Sociobiologists are attempting to discover the way in which the rich arrays of social organization devised by the animal kingdom adapt the particular species to specific environmental niches. Turning more directly to man, I believe we can reject two extreme interpretations of man's behaviour proposed in recent years. We are not, as Konrad

From *New Scientist* Vol. 70, 1976.

Lorenz would have us believe, at the mercy of an aggressive instinct which must be relieved periodically either through war or football matches. Certainly, we are an aggressive species, but that behavior is finely adjusted to circumstances and capable of remaining dormant for long periods in the correct environment.

At the other extreme is the behaviourist school, exemplified by B. F. Skinner, which postulates that we are mere stimulus–response machines moulded by reward, punishment, and a few basic learning rules. That is also wrong. The truth is much more complicated than either of these two alternatives. Human behavior must fall somewhere in between, and finding out just where is what sociobiology is all about. I should like to illustrate this by discussing a number of behavioral activities in man and animals, starting from the basis of genetic evolution.

Natural selection is the key element in evolution that determines that certain genes are transmitted more favorably from one generation to the next. The forces in the environment that exert the selection pressures operate on the manifestation of those genes. For instance, a genetically determined increase in the efficiency of reproduction or in techniques of food gathering means that the individual having the genes will produce more offspring to carry the parental genetic endowment into the next generation. During natural selection, therefore, any device that helps to transmit a higher proportion of certain genes into subsequent generations will come to characterize the species.

For the most part species characteristics involve physical or behavioral properties that serve to increase the chances of each individual passing on its genes to the next generation. Fitness in Darwinian terms may therefore be viewed as particular individual's success in achieving this goal. However, with the emergence of complex social behavior—a manifestation of the genes' more sophisticated techniques for replicating themselves—selfish behavior becomes tempered by altruism, a form of activity that develops to exaggerated degrees in some species. This brings us to a central theoretical problem in sociobiology: How can altruism, which by its nature reduces individual fitness, possibly evolve by natural selection? The answer is kinship, the sharing of common genes by related individuals.

In a group of individuals it is quite possible that an altruistic act by a group member will increase the chances of survival or reproductive efficiency of other members, thus raising the Darwinian fitness of the population as a whole. If the group members are related genetically, it follows that an act of altruism by an individual will help to favor the transmission of its (shared) genes to subsequent generations. Natural selection will therefore select favorably for such altruistic acts, and thus for the genes that determine them. This has been described as group selection, but it is more accurately termed kin selection.

The animal kingdom abounds with examples of altruistic behaviors that are instantly understandable in human terms. For instance, certain small birds, such as robins, thrushes, and titmice, warn others of the approaching threat from a hawk. They crouch low and produce a distinctive thin reedy whistle. Because of its acoustic properties the source of the whistle is very difficult to locate. Nevertheless, by giving the warning signal an individual is drawing attention to itself in a dangerous situation and a more selfish act would be to keep quiet. Dolphins will often group round an injured individual to push it to the surface where it can breathe, rather than abandoning it. And in African wild dogs, the most social of all carnivorous mammals, one sees altruism in a social context. When there are young in the pack most adults go off on a hunting expedition leaving the pups to be cared for by an adult, usually but not always the mother. When the hunters return they regurgitate food for all the animals in the camp, which occasionally includes sick and crippled individuals, too.

## Food Sharing among Chimps

Chimpanzees, man's closest relative, display an interesting form of altruism when they temporarily abandon their normally vegetarian diet and indulge in meat eating. Adult chimps—usually the males—sometimes hunt and catch young monkeys, and through a system of elaborate begging gestures other members of the troop can share in the catch. Curiously, chimps do not share in this way when they are eating leaves and fruit.

We have to look to the social insects, however, to encounter altruistic suicide comparable with that sometimes displayed by man. A large percentage of ants, bees, and wasps are ready to defend their nests with insane charges against intruders. Such attacks may involve inevitable suicide through heads being ripped off (as in the social stingless bees of the tropics), viscera torn out (honeybee workers), or the whole body being blasted by "exploding" glands (an African termite). In all these cases the suicidal deterrent is inflicted by individuals who are sterile or have low reproductive potential. But by their sacrifice they are (in terms of Darwinian fitness) increasing the reproductive chances of their fertile relatives, thus ensuring that their (shared) genes are transmitted to future generations.

It is the unusual distribution of reproductive potential in the social insects that allows the emergence of exaggerated biological altruism. But, as we have seen, altruism appears to have been selected evolutionarily in higher animals too, mediated by kin selection. What can we say of man? If we look back into our immediate evolutionary past we see that almost certainly the social unit was the immediate family and a tight network of close relatives. Such social cohesion, combined with a detailed awareness of kinship made possible by high intelligence, is certainly very favorable for the operation of kin selection and may explain why this evolutionary force is stronger in humans than in monkeys and other animals.

An essential change of gear in the emergence of man, of course, was when cultural evolution became more important than biological evolution, a change that occurred perhaps about 100,000 years ago. As a result it seems clear that human social evolution is more cultural than genetic. Nevertheless, I consider that the underlying emotion of altruism, expressed powerfully in virtually all human societies, is the consequence of genetic endowment. The sociobiological hypothesis does not therefore account for differences between societies, but it could explain why human beings differ from other mammals and why, in one narrow aspect, we more closely resemble social insects. It is salutary to consider the possibility that, with the extreme family dispersal characteristic of advanced industrialised society, altruistic behaviors will decline through the loss of group selection, a process that could spread over perhaps two or three centuries.

On the opposite side of the coin to altruism is aggression, one of the most important and widespread organising techniques in the animal kingdom. Animals use it to stake out their territories and to establish and maintain their group hierarchies. Some people argue that humans share a general aggressive instinct with animals and that it must be relieved, if only through competitive sport. But if we look closely at a number of species we see that aggression occurs in a myriad of forms and is subject to rapid evolution—there is no general instinct. For instance, we commonly find one species of bird or mammal to be highly territorial, employing elaborate, aggressive displays and attacks, while a second, closely related, species shows no territorial behavior. If aggression were a deeply rooted instinct such differences would not arise.

The key to aggression is the environment. We see that, despite the fact that many kinds of animals are capable of a rich, graduated repertoire of aggressive actions, and despite the fact that aggression is important in their social organization, it is possible for individuals to go through a normal life, rearing offspring, with nothing more than occasional bouts of play-fighting and exchanges of lesser hostile displays. Aggression may increase under conditions of social stress, the result perhaps of crowding or limitations in food supplies. We can only conclude that the evidence from comparative studies of animal behavior cannot be used to justify extreme aggression, bloody drama, or violent competitive sports practiced by man.

This brings us to a crucial issue with which sociobiology has to grapple: What are the relative contributions to human behavior of genetic endowment and environmental experience? It seems to me that we are dealing with a genetically inherited array of possibilities, some of which are shared with other animals, some not, which are then expressed to different degrees depending on environment. Our overall social behavior most closely resembles that of the species of Old World monkeys and apes, which, on the basis of anatomy and biochemistry, are our closest relatives. This is just what one would expect if behavior is not based on experience alone but is the result of interplay between experience and the pattern of genetic possibilities. It is the evolution of this pattern that sociobiology seeks to analyze.

For at least a million years—probably more—man engaged in a hunting-gathering way of life, giving up the practice a mere 10,000 years ago. We can be sure that our innate social responses have been fashioned largely through this lifestyle. With caution, we can therefore, look at the dwindling number of contemporary hunter-gatherers and hope to learn something about our basic social organization. And we can compare the most widespread hunter-gatherer qualities with similar behavior displayed by some of the nonhuman primates that are closely related to man. Where the same pattern of traits occurs in man—and in most or all of those primates—we can conclude that it has been subject to little evolution. Variability in traits implies evolutionary plasticity.

The list of human patterns that emerges from this screening technique is intriguing: (1) The number of intimate group members is variable, but is normally 100 or less; (2) some degree of aggressive territorial behavior is basic, but its intensity is graduated and its particular forms cannot be predicted from one culture to the next; (3) adult males are more aggressive and are dominant over females; (4) the societies are largely organized around prolonged maternal care and extended relationships between mothers and children; and (5) play, including at least mild forms of contest and mock aggression, is keenly pursued and probably essential to normal development.

In addition to this list a number of unique human characteristics, so distinct they can be safely classified as genetically based can be added: the overwhelming drive to develop some form of true semantic language, the rigid avoidance of incest by taboo, and the weaker but still strong tendency for sexual division of labor. That this division of labor persists from hunter-gatherers through to agricultural and industrial societies is highly suggestive of a genetic origin. We do not know when this trait emerged in human evolution, nor how resistant it is to the continuing and justified pressures for women's rights.

At this point I should stress a constant danger in sociobiology, and that is the trap of the naturalistic fallacy of ethics that uncritically concludes that what is should be. The "what is" in human nature is the legacy of a long heritage as hunter-gatherers. Even when we can identify genetically determined behavior it cannot be used to justify a continuing practice in present and future societies. As we live in a radically new and changing environment of our own making, such a practice would invite disaster. For example, the tendency under certain conditions to indulge in warfare against competing groups may well be in our genes, having been advantageous to our Neolithic ancestors, but it would be global suicide now. And the drive to rear as many healthy children as possible, once the path to security, is now environmental disaster.

Sociobiology can help us understand the basics of human behavior and the fundamental rules that govern our potential. We will need to know how, genetically, certain types of behavior are linked to others. And we must understand the mechanism and the history of the human mind. The special insights made possible by sociobiology can join with the social sciences to create a new study of man, one by which we might hope to steer our species safely in the difficult journey ahead.

# Chapter 14

# *The New Synthesis Is an Old Story*

### Science as Ideology Group of the British Society for Social Responsibility in Science

*Sociobiology is merely a new form of Social Darwinism, according to critics of the proposed discipline. Dressed up in the garb of modern population genetics, it preaches what such theories have always preached: that the present social order is natural, inevitable, and unchangeable.*

The proposed new discipline of sociobiology is, in the words of its principal exponent, E. O. Wilson, "the systematic study of the biological basis of all social behavior," which will ultimately encompass all of human history since "sociology and the other social sciences as well as the humanities are the last branches of biology waiting to be included in the Modern Synthesis" (E. O. Wilson, *Sociobiology: The New Synthesis,* Cambridge: Harvard U. Press). The theory proposes to depict all of human society and its growth, development, present state, and future prospects in biological and genetic terms.

In the United States the new discipline is appearing in college curricula and a school text has been written in which students are required to give genetic evolutionary answers to such questions as "Why do children hate spinach while adults like it?", or rather less innocuously "Why don't females compete?", "Why aren't males choosy?", and "How did the pair bond become part of human nature?" (I. deVore, G. Goethals, R. Trivers, *Exploring Human Nature,* Unit 1: Educational Development Corporation, Cambridge, MA, 1973).

## ENTHUSIASTIC MEDIA RESPONSE

Despite disclaimers of political intent by sociobiologists and despite the similarity of sociobiology to other works of biological determinism such as Lorenz's instinctual theo-

From *New Scientist* Vol. 70, 1976.

ries and C. D. Darlington's genetic explanations of all of history (*The Evolution of Man and Society,* New York: Simon and Schuster, 1969), the media have responded quickly and enthusiastically to Wilson's book. The *New York Times* ran a front page piece (May 28, 1975) that stated "Sociobiology carries with it the revolutionary implications that much of *man's* behavior towards *his* fellows may be as much a product of evolution as the structure of the hand or the size of the brain" (our emphasis). A review in *New Society* (March 9, 1976), although critical, hailed the text as a "truly monumental book" and a "valuable and outstanding work of scholarship."

The potential implications of the new discipline have been analyzed by the Sociobiology Study Group of Science for the People in Boston. In a series of detailed criticisms (Science for the People, 16 Union Square, Somerville, Mass.) they have examined the new discipline for its scientific content and rigor, its ideological assumptions, and its political extrapolations. On all these aspects there is room for concern. Two major premises are embedded in its arguments about the continuity between human and animal social behavior: The first is that *all* human societies share certain specific human behaviors that constitute a universal "human nature." The second is that these behaviors are the expression of specific genetic structures and thus are a result of evolutionary adaptation through natural selection.

The specific human behaviors presumed by Wilson to be genetically coded include aggression, allegiance, altruism, conformity, ethics, genocide, indoctrinability, love, male dominance, the mother-child bond, military discipline, parent-child conflict, the sexual division of labor, spite, territoriality, and xenophobia. These elements are combined into a view of a presumed universal human economy based on scarcity and unequal distribution of resources and rewards (Wilson, p. 554).

One is inclined to dismiss this view of the universal human society as the vision of a person completely bound by a near-sighted cultural chauvinism. The image of society presented depicts today's European and American capitalist societies. It ignores ethnographic documentation that contradicts this conception of social organization. Societies exist that are *not* differentiated by role sectors, which are *not* differentiated by higher and lower strata, and which are *not* characterized by deprived access to social rewards (see M. Sahlins, *Stone Age Economics,* Chicago: Aldine-Atherton, 1972). Wilson (pp. 564, 574) is aware of exceptions to his presumed universals, but claims that the exceptions are "temporary" aberrations or deviations.

The major sociobiology argument, however, rests on a presumed genetic basis to human social traits and on presumed similarities between human societies and other animal societies. Specific genetic structures are postulated to exist for the social behaviors listed above. There is no direct evidence for the existence of such structures. Modern biology has not discovered any part of DNA that codes for any human behavior, let alone for such specific traits as altruism, conformity, domination, or spite. Specific genetic structures for particular traits are thus speculations woven into the argument only by assumption.

In Wilson's book the distinction between assumption and fact is often confused. For example, on page 554 he says, "Dahlberg (1947) showed that *if* a single gene appears that is responsible for success and upward-shift in status... Furthermore there are *many* Dahlberg genes..." (our emphasis). The effect of this confusion is to leave the reader with the idea that there is a firm basis for the existence of genetically coded traits while at the same time permitting Wilson and his defenders (for example, Robert May in *Nature,* April 1, 1976) to argue that in fact they are only speculating that such genes may exist.

In the absence of direct genetic evidence, the biological links between animals and humans must be established by observing similarities between human and animal behavior. Sociobiology, in common with a long biological tradition, uses metaphors from human societies to describe animal societies and in so doing posits behavioral similarities between humans and animals. The classic examples of this practice, which long antedate sociobiology, are the use of the terms "slavery" and "monarchy." Human slavery involves members of one's own species, the use of force, and the use of the slave as a commodity and as a producer of economic surplus.

"Slavery" in ants involves "slave-making" species of ants that capture immature members of "slave" species. When the captured ants hatch they perform housekeeping tasks with no compulsion as if they were members of this captive species. A more apt term for this might be "domestication" rather than "slavery." Human slavery has nothing to do with ants except by weak and spurious analogy. Similarly the so-called "queen" bee may be more a captive of the "workers," than their "ruler" since in many species she is only a laying machine bloated with eggs, forced by "workers" to remain in one place and to reproduce continually. Sociobiology uses metaphors from human social arrangements to find culture (Wilson, pp. 173, 559), division of labour (p. 299), aesthetics (p. 564), and role playing (p. 299) among animal societies. From there it is a short step to assert that magic, religion, ritual, and tribalism are evolutionary genetic adaptations in human societies (p. 560). Human institutions thus appear natural, universal, and genetically based.

## MULTIPLIER AND THRESHOLD FUDGE FACTORS

Two further more technical points are worth discussing. The first concerns specific tests of a genetic model of human cultural evolution. Population genetics is capable of making specific *quantitative* predictions about rates of change of characters in time and about the degree of differentiation between populations. In addition there exists hard data on genetic differentiation between populations for biochemical traits. Both the theoretical allowable rates of genetic change in time and the observed *genetic* differentiation between populations are too small to agree with the very rapid changes that have occurred in human *cultures* historically and the very large *cultural* differences observed between contemporaneous populations. Sociobiologists acknowledge this problem. But rather than evaluate the theory in hard terms, the problem is evaded through the introduction of a fudge factor, the "multiplier effect" (a phrase borrowed from Keynesian economics). The multiplier effect postulates that very small differences (Wilson, pp. 11 and 572) in genotypic frequencies can result in major cultural differences. To account for the fact that nonhuman animal societies do not show equally rapid evolution and equally dramatic interpopulation variation in social traits an additional effect, the threshold effect, is postulated. It argues that organisms must reach a certain (unspecified) level of social complexity before the multiplier effect will operate (p. 573). They serve to seal off the theory from tests against the real world of cultural change and diversity.

The second technical point concerns the question of altruism. A significant accomplishment of sociobiology, for the naturalist, has been to generate a coherent solution to the problem posed by the existence of self-sacrificing behaviors, bearing a superficial resemblance to human altruism, in certain species. Unfortunately, the word "altruism" has been appended to this, by a process similar to the use of words like "slavery." This animal "altruism" poses a problem for the neo-Darwinian theory of evolution, as it did for Darwin, because the theory is based absolutely upon competition between individual sets of genes (within individuals of a species) to drive evolution.

How then can altruism have evolved? Theoretical work of Wilson and others has shown how certain breeding systems could support such organic evolution. Wilson puts forward the supposition that human altruism, too, has a comparable genetic basis. Seen thus it would appear to be the resultant of a blind process of competition between individuals for *genetic* success, throughout pre-history.

Sociobiology represents yet another attempt to employ the methods and perspective of biology to deal with the problems of human society. This practice has had a long and frequently ugly history. Throughout the development of modern science, ideologues have dreamed of developing theories in the name of science that could legitimize the massive social inequity generated by Western capitalism.

Eight years before the publication of the *Origin of Species,* Herbert Spencer, the English social theorist, argued that the elimination of poverty was unnatural since "the poverty of the incapable, the distresses that come upon the imprudent, the starvations of the idle, . . . are the decrees of a large far-seeing benevolence . . . under the natural order of things society is constantly excreting its unhealthy, imbecile, slow, vacillating, faithless members. . . . " (*Social Statics,* 1883 New York: D. Appleton, p. 353).

In addition to grand biological determinist theories like Spencer's, the history of the last 100 years is replete with examples of specific theories devised to account for specific social ills. Pellagra, a dietary disease caused by niacin deficiency, was diagnosed as an hereditary disease of the poor with no treatment possible. In the U.S. South, slaves who repeatedly ran away were presumed to have drapetomania, a blood disease. Twenty-two U.S. states passed sterilization laws against the "feeble-minded" and the Nazi eugenic laws were in part indebted to American legislation from this period as well as to continental expressions of Social Darwinism in the work of Ernst Haeckel.

## CHALLENGES TO THE STATUS QUO

The past ten years have seen a reemergence of such particularized biological determinist explanations of social problems. This reemergence has coincided with the growth of a vocal women's movement that is challenging the traditional division of labor between the sexes, a growing struggle against racism and a steadily deteriorating economic situation accompanied by militant trades union activity at home while abroad there are increasingly successful Third World revolutionary movements with all the challenges they imply. Such a context provides fertile ground for the growth of biologically based theories to deny the legitimacy of these challenges to the status quo. The list is a long one. Genetics and IQ to deal with racism and unemployment, XYY—the criminal chromosome—to deal with crime, genetics and sex role differences to deal with sexism, drug "therapies" for "hyperactive" children, and leucotomies for enraged women and prisoners are among the wares plied by scientists of different disciplines offering explanations for the irrevocability of the ills of a society predicated upon divisions based on race, sex and class.

Wilson himself in an article in the *New York Times Magazine* (October 12, 1975) stated, concerning the division of labor between the sexes: "This strong bias persists in most agricultural and industrial societies and on that ground alone appears to have a genetic origin. . . . My own guess is that the genetic basis is intense enough to cause a substantial division of labor even in the most free and egalitarian of future societies. . . ."

It is important to recognize the continuity between the current theories and their less sophisticated antecedents—a continuity well illustrated by theories about women and education. Today we are told that women and men have different cognitive abilities. While women excel at verbal skills (or rather at the executive aspects of language: spelling, grammar and punctuation), men excel at spatial and analytical skills. It is suggested this reflects a biologically based division of labour. Men *need* spatial ability if they are to hunt and protect territory while women *need* verbal skills if they are to provide the child (whom it is presumed will spend most of its time with its mother) with the rich linguistic environment it needs in order to acquire language. These postulated inevitable differences are then used to "explain" the different educational achievements of women and men, and in particular the low representation of women in science. Biology is brought in as the mechanism of these supposed differences by appeals to different rates of brain lateralization in females and males, or the different impact of oestrogen and androgen, or to the existence of a sex-linked recessive gene for spatial ability. Thus an argument to keep women out of science and to deprive them of the opportunities for science education in a period of education cuts can easily be justified by reference to contemporary biology. These are but more scientifically sophisticated versions of the theories that were popular in the nineteenth century as to why women should not be allowed higher education.

Sociobiology is the modern successor to Spencer's Social Darwinism. Survival of the fittest is replaced by the theoretical framework of population genetics with the necessary postulates and fudge factors added to make the theory an untestable whole. Its ideological basis is clear. Yet in a society where there is a belief that science is a rational, objective, and value-free activity, there may be resistance to the idea that science or scientific theories have ideological content.

But there is no justification for treating scientific theories differently from others, or scientists as experts to be deferred to for social and political guidance. In order to uncover this ideological content, the theories must be located and analyzed against the contemporary social situation in which they are formulated. Sociobiology arrives at a time when wide-ranging challenges to the existing social order are being made. Unlike the more particularistic theories (such as race and IQ), it avoids specific charges of racism and sexism because its all-encompassing nature enables it to explain the foci of all these theories at once. It is, of course, racist, and sexist— and classist, imperialist, and authoritarian, too. By assuming that there are specific genetic structures that embody particular manifestations of human behavior, sociobiology neatly defuses these challenges by exposing their supposed biological hopelessness. And whether Wilson likes it or intends it, his work is part of this. *Sociobiology: The New Synthesis* will be used and indeed is already being used to justify the biological inevitability of the status quo. The trouble with sociobiology is not merely that it makes assumptions and extrapolations that are misleading. More importantly, it directs our gaze to evolutionary theory as the key to the limits of human nature and it implies in its long agenda for scientific research that a better social order must await the findings of scientists.

What is needed, and what sociobiology clearly cannot provide, is a clear understanding of the uniqueness of the human species. We are unique animals, who, while having a physical basis in organic life, transcend it. We alone possess the capacity for language, culture, and the ability consciously to transform our environment. It is to these capacities that the creative roots of a theory of our history and our social problems must look. The development of such autonomous cultural and social theory, taking as its basis those qualities unique to human life, is currently stultified in the Anglo-American world by a deep-rooted deference on the part of many social scientists towards biological knowledge. This deferential posture ensures a readiness on the part of the human sciences, and hence the community in general, to adopt biologically molded models into their own thought. It is maintained by the primacy of biology in school-level science education. But one is taught early on how organic life is distinguished from its component molecules by various emergent qualities and capacities, whilst recognising their material continuity with inorganic nature.

We would like to see those other emergent qualities that distinguish humanity equally profoundly from its organic material basis treated also as basic in our educational curricula. Genetics has as little to tell us about human societies as nuclear physics has to tell us about genetics. In the same way that we do not turn to physics in order to understand genetics, we should not turn to genetics in order to understand human history and culture.

# Chapter 15

# *Sociobiology: The Art of Storytelling*

## Stephen Jay Gould

*Too many sociobiological explanations of behavior come into the category of "Just So" stories: They may be plausible but are less than rigorously supported by solid evidence.*

Ludwig von Bertalanffy, a founder of general systems theory and a holdout against the neo-Darwinian tide, often argued that natural selection must fail as a comprehensive theory because it explains *too* much—a paradoxical, but perceptive statement. In 1969 he wrote:

> If selection is taken as an axiomatic and *a priori* principle, it is always possible to imagine auxiliary hypotheses—unproved and by nature unprovable—to make it work in any special case . . . Some adaptive value . . . can always be construed or imagined.
>
> I think the fact that a theory so vague, so insufficiently verifiable and so far from the criteria otherwise applied in "hard" science, has become a dogma, can only be explained on sociological grounds. Society and science have been so steeped in the ideas of mechanism, utilitarianism, and the economic concept of free competition, that instead of God, Selection was enthroned as ultimate reality.

Similarly, the arguments of Christian fundamentalism used to frustrate me until I realized that there are, in principle, no counter cases and that, on this ground alone, the theory is bankrupt.

The theory of natural selection is, fortunately, in much better straits. It could be invalidated as a general cause of evolutionary change. (If, for example, Lamarckian inheritance were true and general, then adaptation would arise so rapidly in the Lamarckian mode that natural selection would be powerless to create and would operate only to eliminate.) Moreover, its action and efficacy have been demonstrated experimentally by sixty years of manipulation within *Drosophila* bottles—not to

From *New Scientist* Vol. 80, 1978.

mention several thousand years of success by plant and animal breeders.

Yet in one area, unfortunately a very large part of evolutionary theory and practice, natural selection has operated like the fundamentalist's God—he who maketh all things. Rudyard Kipling asked how the leopard got its spots, the rhino its wrinkled skin. He called his answers "Just So Stories." When evolutionists study individual adaptations, when they try to explain form and behavior by reconstructing history and assessing current utility, they also tell just-so stories—and the agent is natural selection. Virtuosity in invention replaces testability as the criterion for acceptance. This is the procedure that inspired von Bertalanffy's complaint. It is also the procedure that has given evolutionary biology a bad name among many experimental scientists in other disciplines. We should heed their disquiet, not dismiss it with a claim that they understand neither natural selection nor the special procedures of historical science.

This style of storytelling might yield acceptable answers if we could be sure of two things: first, that all bits of morphology and behavior arise as direct results of natural selection, and secondly, that only one selective explanation exists for each bit. But, as Darwin insisted vociferously, and contrary to the mythology about him, there is much more to evolution than natural selection. (Darwin was a consistent pluralist who viewed natural selection as the most important agent of evolutionary change, but who accepted a range of other agents and specified the conditions of their presumed effectiveness. In Chapter Seven of the *Origin of Species* (sixth edition), for example, he attributed the cryptic coloration of a flatfish's upper surface to natural selection and the migration of its eyes to inheritance of acquired characters. He continually insisted that he wrote his two-volume *Variation of Animals and Plants Under Domestication* (1868), with its Lamarckian hypothesis of pangenesis, primarily to illustrate the effect of evolutionary factors other than natural selection. In a letter to *Nature* in 1880, he used the sharpest and most waspish language of his life to castigate Sir Wyville Thompson for caricaturing his theory by ascribing all evolutionary change to natural selection.)

Since all theories cite God in their support, and since Darwin comes close to this status among evolutionary biologists, the panselectionists of the modern synthesis tended to remake Darwin in their image. But we now reject this rigid version of natural selection and grant a major role to other evolutionary agents (genetic drift, fixation of neutral mutations, for example). We must also recognize that many features arise indirectly as developmental consequences of other features directly subject to natural selection. Moreover, and perhaps most importantly, there are a multitude of potential selective explanations for each feature. There is no such thing in nature as a self-evident and unambiguous story.

When we examine the history of favored stories for any particular adaptation, we do not trace a tale of increasing truth as one story replaces the last, but rather a chronicle of shifting fads and fashions. When Newtonian mechanical explanations were riding high, G. G. Simpson wrote (in 1961), "The problem of the pelycosaur dorsal fin . . . seems essentially solved by Romer's demonstration that the regression relationship of fin area to body volume is appropriate to the functioning of the fin as a temperature regulating mechanism." Simpson's firmness seems almost amusing since now—a mere fifteen years later with behavioral stories in vogue—most palaentologists feel equally sure that the sail was primarily a device for sexual display. (Yes, I know the litany: It might have performed both functions. But this too is a story.)

On the other side of the same shift in fashion, a recent article on functional endothermy in some large beetles had this to say about the why of it all: "It is possible that the increased power and speed of terrestrial locomotion associated with a modest elevation of body temperatures may offer reproductive advantages by increasing the effectiveness of intraspecific aggressive behavior, particularly between males." This conjecture reflects no evidence drawn from the beetles themselves, only the current fashion in selective stories. We may be confident that the same data, collected fifteen years ago, would have inspired a speculation about improved design and mechanical advantage.

Most work in sociobiology has been done in the mode of adaptive storytelling based on the optimizing character and pervasive power of natural selection. As such, its weaknesses of methodology are those that have plagued so much of evolutionary theory for more than a

century. Sociobiologists have anchored their stories in the basic Darwinian notion of selection as individual reproductive success.

Sociobiologists have broadened their range of selective stories by invoking concepts of inclusive fitness and kin selection to solve (successfully, I think) the vexatious problem of altruism—previously the greatest stumbling block to a Darwinian theory of social behavior. (Altruistic acts are the cement of stable societies. Until we could explain apparent acts of self-sacrifice as potentially beneficial to the genetic fitness of sacrificers themselves—propagation of genes through enhanced survival of kin, for example—the prevalence of altruism blocked any Darwinian theory of social behavior.)

Thus, kin selection has broadened the range of permissible stories, but it has not alleviated any methodological difficulties in the process of storytelling itself. Von Bertalanffy's objections still apply, if anything with greater force, because behavior is generally more plastic and more difficult to specify and homologize than morphology. Sociobiologists are still telling speculative stories, still hitching without evidence to one potential star among many, still using mere consistency with natural selection as a criterion of acceptance.

David Barash, for example, tells the following story about mountain bluebirds. (It is, by the way, a perfectly plausible story that may well be true. I only wish to criticize its assertion without evidence or test, using consistency with natural selection as the sole criterion for useful speculation.) He reasoned that a male bird might be more sensitive to intrusion of other males before eggs are laid than after (when he can be certain that his genes are inside). So Barash studied two nests, making three observations at 10-day intervals, the first before the eggs were laid, the last two after. For each period of observation, he mounted a stuffed male near the nest while the male occupant was out foraging. When the male returned, he counted aggressive encounters with both model and female. At time one, males in both nests were quite aggressive towards the model and less, but still substantially aggressive towards the female as well. At time two, after eggs had been laid, males were less aggressive to models and scarcely aggressive to females at all. At time three, males were still less aggressive towards models, and not aggressive at all toward females.

## Is Consistency Enough?

Barash concludes that he has established consistency with natural selection and need do no more: "These results are consistent with the expectations of evolutionary theory. Thus aggression toward an intruding male (the model) would clearly be especially advantageous early in the breeding season, when territories and nests are normally defended. . . . The initial, aggressive response to the mated female is also adaptive in that, given a situation suggesting a high probability of adultery (that is, the presence of the model near the female) and assuming that replacement females are available, obtaining a new mate would enhance the fitness of males. . . . The decline in male-female aggressiveness during incubation and fledgling stages could be attributed to the impossibility of being cuckolded after the eggs have been laid. . . . The results are consistent with an evolutionary interpretation. In addition, the term 'adultery' is unblushingly employed in this letter without quotation marks, as I believe it reflects a true analogy to the human concept, in the sense of Lorenz. It may also be prophesied that continued application of a similar evolutionary approach will eventually shed considerable light on various human foibles as well."

Consistent, yes. But what about the obvious alternative, dismissed without test in a line by Barash: male returns at times two and three, approaches the model a few times, encounters no reaction, mutters to himself the avian equivalent of "it's that damned stuffed bird again," and ceases to bother. And why not the evident test: Expose a male to the model for the *first* time *after* the eggs are laid?

We have been deluged in recent years with sociobiological stories. Some, like Barash's are plausible, if unsupported. For many others, I can only confess my intuition of extreme unlikeliness, to say the least—for adaptive and genetic arguments about why fellatio and cunnilingus are more common among the upper classes, or why male panhandlers are more successful with females and people who are eating than with males and people who are not eating.

Not all sociobiology proceeds in the mode of storytelling for individual cases. It rests on firmer methodological ground when it seeks broad correlations across taxonomic lines, as between reproductive strategy and distribution of resources, for example, or when it can make testable, quantitative predictions as in Bob Trivers and Hope Hare's work on haplodiploidy and eusociality in *Hymenoptera*. Here sociobiology has had and will continue to have success. And here I wish it well. For it represents an extension of basic Darwinism to a realm where it should apply.

Sociobiological explanations of human behavior encounter two special difficulties, suggesting that a Darwinian model may be generally inapplicable in this case.

- *First,* we have very little direct evidence about the genetics of behavior in humans; and we know no way to obtain it for the specific behaviors that figure most prominently in sociobiological speculation—aggression and conformity, for instance. With our long generations, it is very difficult to amass much data on heritability. More importantly, we cannot (ethically, that is) perform the kind of breeding experiments, in standardized environments, that would yield the

required information. Thus, in dealing with humans, sociobiologists rely even more heavily than usual on speculative storytelling.

At this point, the political debate engendered by sociobiology comes appropriately to the fore. For these speculative stories about human behavior have broad implications and proscriptions for social policy—and this is true quite apart from the intent or personal politics of the storyteller. Intent and usage are very different things; the latter marks political and social influence, the former is gossip or, at best sociology.

The common political character and effect of these stories lies in the direction historically taken by nativistic arguments about human behavior and capabilities—a defence of existing social arrangements as part of our biology.

In raising this point, I do not act to suppress truth for fear of its political consequences. Truth, as we understand it, must always be our primary criterion. We live, because we must, with all manner of unpleasant biological truths—death being the most pervasive and ineluctable. I complain because sociobiological stories are not truth, rather they are unsupported speculations with political clout (again, I must emphasize, quite apart from the intent of the storyteller). All science is embedded in cultural contexts, and the lower the ratio of data to social importance, the more science reflects the context.

In stating that there is politics in sociobiology, I do not criticize the scientists involved in it by claiming that an unconscious politics has intruded into a supposedly objective enterprise. For they are behaving like all good scientists—as human beings in a cultural context. I only ask for a more explicit recognition of the context—and, specifically, for more attention to the evident impact of speculative sociobiological stories. For example, when the *New York Times* runs a weeklong front page series on women and their rising achievements and expectations, spends the first four days documenting their progress towards social equality, devotes the last day to potential limits upon this progress, and advances sociobiological stories as the only argument for potential limits—then we know that these are stories with consequences: "Sociologists believe that women will continue for some years to achieve greater parity with men, both in the work place and in the home. But an uneasy sense of frustration and pessimism is growing among some advocates of full female equality in the face of mounting conservative opposition. Moreover, even some staunch feminists are reluctantly reaching the conclusion that women's aspirations may ultimately be limited by inherent biological differences that will forever leave men the dominant sex" (*New York Times*, November 30, 1977).

The article then quotes two social scientists, each with a story. First, "If you define dominance as who occupies formal roles of responsibility, then there is no society where males are not dominant. When something is so universal, the probability is—as reluctant as I am to say it—that there is some quality of the organism that leads to this condition." Secondly, "it may mean that there never will be full parity in jobs, that women will always predominate in the caring tasks like teaching and social work and in the life sciences, while men will prevail in those requiring more aggression—business and politics, for example—and in the 'dead' sciences like physics."

- *Second,* the standard foundation of Darwinian just-so stories does not apply to humans. That foundation is the implication: if adaptive, then genetic—for the inference of adaptation is usually the only basis of a selective story, and Darwinism is a theory of genetic change and variation in populations.

Much of human behavior is clearly adaptive, but the problem for sociobiology is that humans have developed an alternative, non-genetic system to support and transmit adaptive behavior—cultural evolution. (An adaptive behavior does not require genetic input and Darwinian selection for its origin and maintenance in humans; it may arise by trial and error in a few individuals who do not differ genetically from their groupmates in any way relevant to this behavior spread by learning and imitation, and stabilize across generations by value, custom, and tradition.) Moreover, cultural transmission is far more powerful in potential speed and spread than natural selection—for cultural evolution operates in the "Lamarckian" mode by inheritance through custom, writing, and technology of characteristics acquired by human activity in each generation.

Thus, the existence of adaptive behavior in humans says nothing about the probability of a genetic basis for it, or about the operation of natural selection. Take, for example, Trivers's concept of "reciprocal altruism." The phenomenon exists, to be sure, and it is clearly adaptive. In honest moments, we all acknowledge that many of our "altruistic" acts are performed in the hope and expectation of future reward. Can anyone imagine a stable society without bonds of reciprocal obligation? But structural necessities do not imply direct genetic coding. (All human behaviors are, of course, part of the potential range permitted by our genotype—but sociobiological speculations posit direct natural selection for specific behavioral traits.) As Benjamin Franklin said: "Either we hang together, or assuredly we will all hang separately."

The grandest goal—I do not say the only goal—of human sociobiology must fail in the face of these difficulties. That goal is no less than the reduction of the behavioral (indeed most of the social) sciences to Darwinian theory. Edward Wilson presents a vision of the human sciences shrinking in their independent domain, absorbed on one side by neurobiology and on the other by sociobiology.

But this vision cannot be fulfilled, for the reason cited above. Although we can identify adaptive behavior in humans, we cannot tell if it is genetically based (while much of it must arise by fairly pure cultural evolution). Yet the reduction of the human sciences to Darwinism requires the genetic argument, for Darwinism is a theory about genetic change in populations. All else is analogy and metaphor.

My crystal ball shows the human sociobiologists retreating to a fallback position—indeed it is happening already. They will argue that this fallback is as powerful as their original position, though it actually represents the unravelling of their fondest hopes. They will argue: Yes, indeed, we cannot tell whether an adaptive behavior is genetically coded or not. But it doesn't matter. The same adaptive constraints apply whether the behavior evolved by cultural or Darwinian routes, and biologists have identified and explicated the adaptive constraints. (Steve Emlen tells me, for example, that some Indian peoples gather food in accordance with predictions of optimal foraging strategy—a theory developed by ecologists.)

But it does matter. It makes all the difference in the world whether human behaviors develop and stabilize by cultural evolution or by direct Darwinian selection for genes influencing specific adaptive actions. It makes a great difference because cultural and Darwinian evolution differ profoundly in the three major areas that embody what evolution, at least as a quantitative science, is all about:

1. *Rate.* Cultural evolution, as a "Lamarckian" process, can proceed in orders of magnitude more rapidly than Darwinian evolution. Natural selection continues its work within *Homo sapiens,* probably at characteristic rates for change in large, fairly stable populations, but the power of cultural evolution has dwarfed its influence (alteration in frequency of the sickling gene versus changes in modes of communication and transportation). Consider what we have done in the past 3000 years, all without the slightest evidence for any change in the power of the human brain.
2. *Modifiability.* Complex traits of cultural evolution can be altered rapidly; Darwinian change is limited to much slower rates of spread of alleles by natural selection.
3. *Diffusability.* Since traits of cultural evolution can be transmitted by imitation and inculcation, evolutionary patterns include frequent and complex anastomosis among branches. Darwinian evolution is a process of continuous divergence and ramification.

I believe that the future will bring mutual illumination between two vigorous, independent disciplines—Darwinian theory and cultural history. This is a good thing, joyously to be welcomed. But there will be no reduction of the human sciences to Darwinian theory and the research program of human sociobiology will fail.

The name, of course, may survive. It is an irony of history that movements are judged successful if their label sticks, though the emerging content of a discipline may lie closer to what opponents originally advocated. Modern geology, for example, is an even blend of Lyell's strict uniformitarianism and the claims of catastrophists. But we call the hybrid doctrine by Lyell's name.

I welcome the coming failure of reductionistic hopes because it will lead us to recognize human complexity at its proper level. For consumption by *Time*'s millions, my colleague Bob Trivers maintained: "Sooner or later, political science, law, economics, psychology, psychiatry, and anthropology will all be branches of sociobiology" (*Time*, August 1, 1977, p. 54). It's one thing to conjecture, as I would allow, that common features among independently developed legal systems might reflect adaptive constraints and might be explicated usefully with some biological analogies. It is quite another to state, as Bob Trivers did, that the entire legal profession, among others, will be subsumed as mere epiphenomena of Darwinian processes.

I read Trivers's statement the day after I had sung in a full production of Berlioz's *Requiem*. And I remembered the visceral reaction I had experienced upon hearing the four brass choirs, finally amalgamated with the ten tympani in the massive din preceding the great *Tuba mirum*—the spine tingling and the involuntary tears that almost prevented me from singing. I tried to analyze it in the terms of Wilson's conjecture—reduction of behavior to neurobiology on the one hand and sociobiology on the other. And I realized that this conjecture might apply to my experience. My reaction had been physiological and, as a good mechanist, I do not doubt that its neurological foundation can be ascertained. I will also not be surprised to learn that the reaction has something to do with adaptation (emotional overwhelming to cement group coherence in the face of danger, to tell a story). But I also realized that these explanations, however "true," could never capture the meaning of that experience.

And I say this not to espouse mysticism or incomprehensibility, but merely to assert that the world of human behavior is too complex and multifarious to be unlocked by any simple key. I say this to maintain that this richness—if anything—is both our hope and our essence.

# Chapter 16

# *Why Did Lucy Walk Erect?*

Donald C. Johanson
Maitland A. Edey

---

## Is It a Matter of Sex?

*You don't gradually go from being a quadruped to being a biped. What would the intermediate stage be—a triped? I've never seen one of those.*

—Timothy White

*Man, to put it briefly, is continuously sexed; animals are discontinuously sexed. Man is prepared to mate at any time: animals are not. . . . If we try to imagine what a human society would be like in which the sexes were interested in each other only during the summer, as in songbirds, or, as in female dogs, experienced sexual desire only once every few months, or even only once in a lifetime, as in ants, we can realize what this peculiarity has meant.*

—Julian Huxley

*You might not think that erect walking has anything to do with sex, but it has, it has.*

—C. Owen Lovejoy

"For any quadruped to get up on its hind legs in order to run is an insane thing to do," said Owen Lovejoy, the locomotion expert. "From the standpoint of pure efficiency, bipedalism is a preposterous way of running." Lovejoy had dropped in at my laboratory early in 1980 to discuss locomotion with some of my students. I thought it would be a good idea for me to listen in.

"I mean, it's just plain ridiculous," he said. "Even the arguments for it are ridiculous:

"'Man moved out on the savanna and learned to stand up so that he could see over tall grass.' Poppycock. It may have helped him see over tall grass when he got there. But if he had to learn to do it after he got there, forget it. He never would have made it.

From *Lucy: The Beginnings of Human Kind.* Simon and Schuster, 1980.

"'Man was a tool user. He had to stand up in order to have his hands free to carry tools and weapons.' Ultimately, yes. But originally, rubbish. That idea never did make sense. Now it is exploded by the Laetoli and Hadar fossils. Those animals were bipedal, but that had nothing to do with tools. They were walking that way maybe a million years before their descendants began using tools.

"'Man proceeded through a knuckle-walking stage like a gorilla or a chimpanzee, and gradually worked himself up on his hind legs.' Balderdash. The idea that a chimp represents some sort of halfway stage leading to erect walking is idiocy. Knuckle walking is a specialized adaptation to a particular mode of living. It leads nowhere."

The way to think about locomotion, Lovejoy went on, was not in single cause-and-effect terms, but as part of an overall survival strategy. The paleontologist or the anatomist has a tendency to pick out one feature in an animal, and then identify that animal as a purveyor of that feature: It is a brachiator; it is a biped. That is simplistic. In reality, the animal's locomotor system or its reproductive system turns out to be part of a complex adaptation to a specific ecology. There must be a constellation of attributes working together. In short, one must look at a chimpanzee's total survival strategy before its locomotor system makes sense. Even before that is done, there must be some understanding of what arms and legs are like and how they function. To Lovejoy, the amount of ignorance about how legs work, even among people who teach locomotion, is staggering. He would go back to basics.

Looked at most simply, a body is a package of flesh lying on the ground or in the water. If it needs to move to get food, it must have fins or a tail to propel it through the water; on land (snakes excepted) it needs legs. If the only function of the legs is to shove the body ahead, then

**86**

**Figure 16–1** The legs of various land animals function differently (see text for details).

there will be considerable scraping, friction, and large energy loss every time it moves. That is why an animal that needs to walk or run must have legs that can give its body not only forward motion but upward force to hold if off the ground.

The legs of the earliest walking vertebrates—amphibians and reptiles, and even of newts and alligators that survive today—performed both those functions, but not very well. Their legs stuck out from the sides of their bodies—a poor design for running, as a front view of an alligator makes clear (Figure 16–1). The sheer effort of supporting a body on legs that stick out to the sides is considerable. It is comparable to what a man would experience if he lay on the floor and tried to do push-ups with his arms extended to the sides instead of under him. That is why an alligator can run neither fast nor far. It proceeds by moving the front left limb and the rear right limb together. It can do this slowly if it wants to walk, or faster if it wants to run, but that is all it can do.

For walking and running, a mammal's legs are a great improvement on the reptile model. They stick down instead of out to the sides, which is why a horse can support itself comfortably on its legs all day, whereas the same effort would exhaust an alligator very quickly. In addition to standing and walking, a horse can trot and gallop. A trotting alligator is an impossibility.

"Why are alligators so inefficient?" Lovejoy was asked.

"They're not."

"But you just said—"

"I said they were poor runners. That's a different thing. An alligator is very good at slithering unobtrusively off a mudbank. It is a superb underwater hunter. Go back to what I just said about an animal being a constellation of attributes working together. You have to look at *all* the evolutionary strategies of an animal to understand any of them. A horse is very good at its thing, but its thing is not underwater swimming. Its legs reflect that."

"Mammals' legs also reflect the process by which they achieved better running ability. A mammal's limbs not only have moved directly under the body but have also turned. The hind limb is rotated so that the knee faces forward. The forelimb is rotated so that the "elbow" faces backward. These new alignments make for a more efficient input of energy into running, and a more efficient consumption of it.

Lovejoy went on to explain that all running is a matter of putting in energy and consuming it. The energy is put in when the hind legs propel the animal forward, and consumed by the front legs as the animal lands. If an animal's body were suspended in space, and a force applied to it, it would accelerate until the top speed attainable by that force was reached. Then, if it were in a vacuum, it would coast forward forever. But real animals do not float in vacuums. When they run they must constantly touch the ground, and each time they do they lose much of the forward motion they have achieved. Therefore, to move the body forward another step, momentum must be put in again. But the body will fall to the ground if the forelimb is not thrust forward again and its muscles used to hold the body up—and so on: energy put in to move the body ahead, energy absorbed to hold it up.

To understand how energy is absorbed by the forelimb, one might regard it as a kind of shock absorber acting to cushion the impact of the body's landing on it at the completion of a step. As the limb joint begins to buckle under that descending force, its muscles act to resist it. That muscular resistance, the act of trying to straighten up the front limb as the weight of the body presses it down—negative energy, one might call it—is what absorbs the energy that was put in by the forward thrust of the hind limb.

To act like a proper shock absorber, the forelimb should not be fastened directly to the skeleton, and it is not. It is held in place only by muscles. If it were attached directly, there would be no way for a muscle to begin smoothly resisting the weight of the descending body, and there would be a horrible jolt as all the energy was absorbed in one crashing contact. By having its forelimb separated from its shoulder (rather than nestled in a bony socket, as the leg is), an animal is given an opportunity during each step in running to absorb energy smoothly.

A mammal's hind limb, by contrast, does not need to be a shock absorber. Its function is to put in energy, not absorb it. Consequently, the top of the thighbone can fit directly into the socket of the pelvis, and is held there by tendons and ligaments. Direct fits are stronger, and would be preferable for the forelimb too, were it not more important that it be an energy absorber. Football players know about the disadvantages of an indirect coupling. They are constantly suffering from shoulder separations when the muscles that hold their arms in place are torn. But the disadvantages of a direct coupling for a shock absorber are even greater. The reader need only jump stiff-legged from a one-foot step to discover that the impact will rattle every bone in the body. With the leg attached directly to the hip and the knee locked, there can be no absorption of energy; there is nowhere for it to go.

Given the preceding model of a typical quadrupedal mammal—limbs sticking straight down, rear ones rotated forward and front ones rotated backward; rear ones attached directly to the skeleton, front ones attached only by muscles—it becomes possible to understand why, when the model is converted to bipedality, it becomes less efficient. That is best shown by an examination of how the energy used in running is applied. If a great deal of it is put into forward motion and only a little absorbed by holding the body up, the result will be a high rate of speed. But if most of the energy put in is consumed by holding the body up, then high speed is impossible. That is what is wrong with bipedality: too much energy devoted to holding the body up.

That is demonstrated by a man walking (Figure 16–2). In the middle of a step, with one foot on the ground and the other swinging forward, there is some leftover momentum from the previous step that carries the body forward also. That momentum is added to (energy input) when the man uses his leg muscles to straighten out his leg at the knee and ankle, making it longer and thus pushing his body ahead. The body is now out of balance, and the other leg, swinging forward, must be planted to support it. That action eats up most of the forward energy. These components of forward motion and upward motion can be expressed as a vector—a combination of the two forces that shows the man's true forward motion, or speed.

If he wants to increase his speed, the man can tilt his body forward, giving a greater component forward and a smaller one upward. That also achieves the beginning of falling, because he has reduced the component that is holding his body up. Therefore, to keep from falling, a man must apply the upward force more frequently—work his legs more rapidly. That is what running is. When a man starts running he can lean way for-

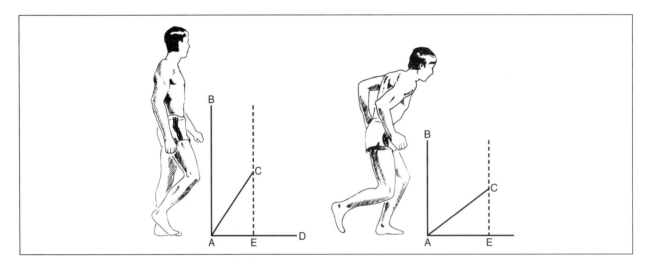

**Figure 16–2** A man walking expends more energy holding his body up (AB) than he does propelling it forward (AD). The combination of those two forces produces a vector (slanted line AC). The vector may be used to measure the man's true speed (AE). When he starts to run, the man leans his body forward and begins to work his legs faster. Less energy is put into holding the body up and more into propelling it forward. The resulting vector slants more in the direction of running, and the distance AE is greater—that is, more speed.

ward (like a sprinter in starting blocks), but as soon as his legs are going as fast as he can churn them, he must assume a nearly vertical position. He can lean forward again to gain more speed, but if his legs will not go any faster, he will simply fall down. Sprinters lunging at a tape do that. At the very end of a race they hurl themselves forward, and they often do fall after crossing the finish line.

A quadrupedal animal does not have that problem. Its body is already leaning so far forward that it is horizontal to the ground. Most of the energy supplied by the hind limbs is invested in forward motion, and very little of it consumed by the forelimbs to hold the body up. They are already out in front, ready to be planted as a kind of pivot on which the animal rests momentarily as its body comes forward and its hind limbs are gathered for another spring. The most highly developed quadrupedal running machine is the cheetah (Figure 16–3). It has long legs and a long, very supple backbone. When it starts a leap forward, its backbone is coiled. As it straightens out its hind legs with a tremendous push, it also straightens out its backbone, and its body is shot forward twenty feet or more in one bound, its forelimbs using only a small part of that energy as they touch down.

"What has all that got to do with the origins of bipedalism?" Lovejoy was asked. "You've made it clear why quadrupeds can run faster than bipeds. Why did any of them change?"

"To answer that question," said Lovejoy, "you must remember that our ancestors evolved in the trees, and then ask yourself what they were doing up there."

The earliest ancestors of the primates, he went on, were not tree dwellers. They were insect-eating quadrupeds about the shape of squirrels that lived and hunted on the ground. But as huge tracts of hardwood tropical forest developed, providing an excellent home for all sorts of arboreal insects, not to mention a great variety of slightly larger potential prey—small frogs, lizards and snakes—some of those early little ground predators were encouraged to climb into the trees after them. It was only a matter of time before the forest canopy was populated by large numbers of small clawed carnivores that spent all their time aloft.

It is one thing to hunt small prey on the ground. It is quite another to do it in a tree. Although some beetles and all caterpillars are so slow-moving that they may be plucked and eaten almost like berries, lizards are speedy and extremely elusive. One that is not caught at first pounce will dart to the underside of the branch and get away. The pouncer must be able to jump on it from a distance, grab it, hold it and—now being in a three-dimensional world—also be able to hang on itself. In short, a small hunter that expects to do its hunting in trees must become a leaper, a grabber, and a clinger. The earliest primate ancestors, which are believed to have resembled the insectivorous tree shrews of Asia, apparently began to develop longer and more prehensile digits on their forepaws as they began to aspire to larger prey like tree frogs and arboreal lizards. Their claws evolved into flat nails on the tops of their toes, and the toes themselves began to resemble fingers. The primate "hand" gradually appeared.

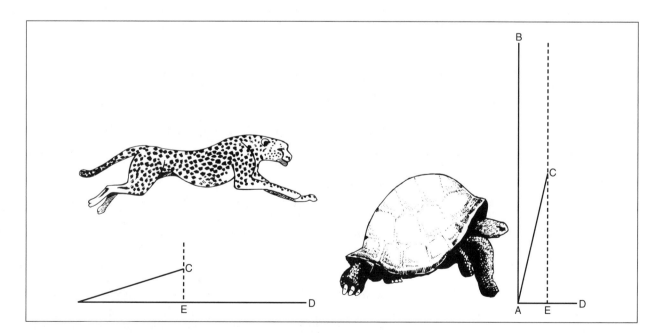

**Figure 16–3**  The cheetah's vector shows how the investment of only a little energy into upward motion and a great deal into forward motion can translate into speed, in its case seventy miles an hour. A Galápagos tortoise, by contrast, has to invest nearly all its energy in holding up its enormous shell. Its top speed is less than one mile an hour.

Its owner, instead of being primarily a runner, was now more of a clinger and jumper. In exchange for better catching ability it gave up some of its nimbleness in running about in the branches. No tarsier or bush baby—to mention a couple of small primates that still jump and cling in tropical forests—can scramble about in a tree nearly as fast as a squirrel can. A clawed animal is always better at that than a "handy" one. A squirrel can also run up and down the trunk of any tree, which is something that a primate cannot do. The clinging little ones stay aloft, coming to the ground only on the rare occasions when they have to change trees. Big ones, like chimpanzees, that do come to the ground regularly can shinny up medium-sized trees, but large trees defeat them; the trunks are too fat for them to get their arms around. To climb a really big tree, an animal must have claws.

That explains why squirrels never developed hands. Climbing and running have always been more important to them than catching. They eat nuts, pinecones and seeds, stationary things they can pick and nibble at their leisure. A primate, by contrast, is an animal that has managed to develop a way of being arboreal and at the same time preserve a way of being predatory.

Other specializations have gone with handedness. If one is going to jump and snatch, one had better be able to judge distances accurately. If not, one will come up empty-handed at best; at worst, one will miss the branch entirely and fall. The way to precise distance judgment is via binocular vision: focusing two eyes on an object to provide depth perception. That requires that the eyes be set in the front of the skull and facing forward, not on the sides of the head, as a squirrel's eyes are. Primate ancestors developed such vision. Their skulls became rounded to accommodate the new position of the eyes, and with that change in shape came an enlargement of the skull capacity and the opportunity to have a larger brain. At the same time, the jaw became smaller. With hands, an animal does not have to do all its foraging and hunting with its teeth. It can afford a shorter jaw and fewer teeth. Modern apes and monkeys—and humans—have sixteen teeth in each jaw. Their ancestors had as many as twenty-two.

Safe from ground predators, the emerging primates were extremely successful in the trees. Many of them became bigger-bodied and increasingly specialized as they found different ways of gaining a living aloft. Some of them turned more to fruits and berries for their diet. Some ended up eating nothing but leaves. They developed different ways of getting about in the branches. Some of the little ones, like tarsiers and bush babies, continued to jump and cling; they had rather short forelimbs and long hind limbs, and gave up running entirely. One large group, although it had a primate hand, and even a primate foot with a flat sole and prehensile digits, remained quadrupedal. These were the monkeys. They walked on branches in preference to clinging to them or swinging from them. Their backbones were rather long. They were preserving a way of running because many of them were returning to the ground, and they needed a good deal of speed to enable them to regain the safety of a tree in the face of danger. In retaining quadrupedalism, monkeys are distinct from apes.

Apes are designed more for swinging. Instead of walking along branches, they hang from them, sit on them, stand up in them, go up or down hand over hand. They have shorter spines than monkeys—three or four lumbar vertebrae instead of seven—and as a result they are not nearly as good runners. Some of them, in fact, can scarcely run at all.

There are five kinds of apes in the world today. Two of them—gibbons and siamangs—are true swingers. They move by brachiation, by swinging like pendulums from branch to branch. Their arms are exceedingly long, their hands and fingers elongated and specialized (Figure 16–4). Their bodies are short and light, their legs shrunken. With that design—a minimum of weight at the bottom of the pendulum—they can move remarkably rapidly through the trees, swinging from branch to branch with a sureness and smoothness that must be seen to be appreciated, often negotiating gaps of ten feet or more. When they come to the ground, which is almost never, gibbons stand erect, waddling along on their short, weak legs, holding out their long arms to either side for balance. A strolling gibbon reminds one of a tightrope walker.

The orangutan is just as arboreal as the gibbon but in an entirely different way. Its hip joint is close to being a universal joint. It can extend its leg down, backward, forward, straight out to the side, and almost straight up. All of its extremities are good at grasping. It is, in effect, an animal with four arms and four hands. Like a huge orange-brown spider, it spread-eagles itself in trees, holding on with any handy foot or hand and reaching out to grab food—mostly fruit—with any other. On the rare occasions when it comes to the ground, it goes on all fours, slowly and deliberately like an old man walking with a couple of canes (as Sarel Eimerl once said), proceeding on the soles of its feet and the knuckles of its hands, although it quite often balls up its hands into fists and walks on them. As a result, the orang might be called a partial knuckle walker.

The gorilla is a true knuckle walker. It is the one ape that has returned to the ground almost completely. All its food—coarse vegetable matter, roots, bamboo shoots, berries—is found there. It has given up running in favor of large size and enormous strength. Gorillas depend for survival on being big and powerful—up to four hundred pounds for an adult male—and by looking fierce. Young gorillas hang and play in trees, but adults are too large and lethargic for that. Sometimes they will squat in groups on very low, very broad branches, but they really prefer the ground. They are extremely sedentary, stay in the same places for long periods of time, and almost never run at all.

The chimpanzee, also a knuckle walker, is the most adaptable of the apes. It is a sort of all-purpose model that reflects its all-purpose approach to living. It eats a great deal of fruit, particularly figs, and is adept at climbing after them in the upper canopy. Its arms are long enough to enable it to shinny up and down all but the largest trees. Its legs, though short, are long enough to allow it to run surprisingly fast. A man chasing a chimpanzee would have little chance of catching it. So endowed, the chimpanzee spends a large part of its time on the ground, living on grubs, termites, berries, insects, buds, and roots when the figs are not ripe. It is also, in a small way, a cooperative hunter. Occasionally a group of male chimpanzees will corner a young baboon or other monkey in an isolated tree, catch it and eat it.

Despite their radically different lifestyles and markedly disparate bodily adaptations, all apes are potentially erect animals. They are all forest dwellers that make their living in ways that do not require running. By the beginning of the Miocene, about twenty million years ago, during a period when there was an immense band of forest stretching right around the earth in the tropical and subtropical regions, apes were numerous and successful. Monkeys, by contrast, were far less so. Today just the reverse is true. Though the decline of tropical forests at the end of the Miocene as a result of changes in climate certainly had something to do with the decline of apes, there were other, subtler forces at work. Lovejoy has attempted to analyze these and believes he has found an explanation for the origins of bipedalism in the interplay of those forces.

"Thank goodness we're getting back to bipedalism," muttered somebody. "I was getting bored with those apes."

"Bored or not, you have to understand their origins: Predators that went up into the trees and managed to find a way of being both predatory and arboreal by becoming semierect swingers with hands, short spines, binocular vision and large brains. Nothing like them had ever been seen before on earth. When some of the bigger ones, like gorillas and chimpanzees, came back to the

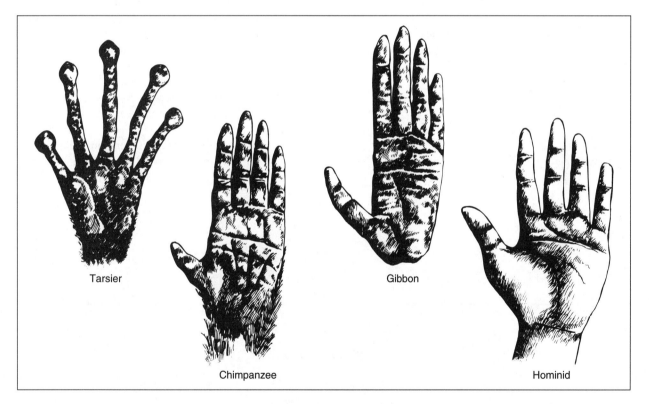

Tarsier

Gibbon

Chimpanzee

Hominid

**Figure 16–4**  All primates are dexterous, having flexible fingers with flat nails, but the different shapes of their hands reflect the different locomotion and survival strategies of their owners. The tarsier, a leaper and clinger, has extra-large finger pads for gripping branches. The gibbon's hand is almost all long, strong fingers, which it uses as hooks while brachiating. The chimpanzee, a partly arboreal, partly terrestrial animal, has excellent manual dexterity and can even manipulate crude implements. It has a fairly well developed opposable thumb, but it is stubby and meets the forefinger along its side, not at its tip. In the hominid hand, the thumb is much larger and is twisted so that it faces the forefinger. This is a logical concomitant to bipedalism and produces a great increase in dexterity. All hominids seem to have had this kind of hand—even *afarensis,* the oldest one now known. Its hand is scarcely distinguishable from a modern man's. (Reprinted by permission from the Cleveland Museum of Natural History.)

ground, they were able to carve out new ecological niches for themselves because of their radically new equipment."

"But they didn't become bipedal."

"Some did. The hominids—our own ancestors."

"We know that, but why?"

"Would you like to talk about sex?"

"I'd rather talk about bipedalism.

"Okay, we'll talk about sex."

Talking about sex is getting back to basics with a vengeance. It recalls the shrewd remark made nearly a century ago and attributed to Herbert Spencer: "A hen is an egg's way of getting another egg." Which is to say: Look at the survival of the species not from the point of view of the individual but from the lowly but all-important view of the gene. Consider that what counts in the long run is the preservation of genes, the getting of another individual like oneself.

Lovejoy, in this matter, thinks like Spencer. Every living individual of every species is nothing more than a protective envelope containing the seeds of propagation, skillfully packaged to maximize the likelihood that it will live long enough to produce more of its kind. To do that, it must eat. To eat, if it is a mammal, it must move around. Therefore, an animal's locomotor adaptation cannot be thoroughly understood unless its sexual strategy is also understood.

There are two fundamentally different ways in which an animal can function sexually. It can produce a great many eggs, with an investment of very little energy in any one egg. Or it can produce very few eggs, but put a large investment in each. These are known to science as the "r" strategy and the "K" strategy respectively (Figure 16–5).

An extreme example of "r" would be an oyster, which may produce as many as five hundred million eggs a year. The most extreme examples of "K" are the great apes—the gorilla, chimpanzee and orangutan—which produce only one infant every five or six years. In between is a bewildering mix of "r" and "K" among animals that have tried every blend of it. Both "r" and "K" work as long as they are not pushed to their limits. Conceivably, an oyster might be able to double its egg output to a billion, but if the energy it had to invest in eggs was fixed, the available energy per egg would be cut in half. That might shortchange all the eggs to a point at which, although there were more of them, even fewer of the very few that now survive would reach maturity. It is clear that pure "r" is an impossibility, and that it is now being exploited to its limit by such lowly creatures as oysters. Indeed, extreme "r" can be considered an inefficient way of reproduction. What is the value of producing half a billion eggs if only half a dozen will reach maturity?

The value to the oyster is that it has no other option. It has rudimentary sense organs, it has no brain, it cannot move. It is incapable of taking care of its eggs; it cannot even put them in a safe place. All it can do is pour them out—so it maximizes its survival chances as a species by pouring out as many as it *reasonably* can.

Although "r" works for oysters (they are still with us), it is obviously extravagant. As more highly developed animals evolved, other more frugal options began to be available. When creatures with backbones and brains came on the scene, the beginnings of crude parental care began to be possible. Certain fish make

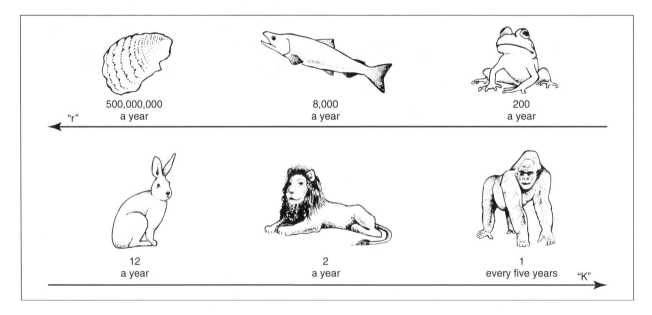

| "r" | | |
|---|---|---|
| 500,000,000 a year | 8,000 a year | 200 a year |
| 12 a year | 2 a year | 1 every five years "K" |

**Figure 16–5** Reproductive strategies in the animal world go all the way from extreme "r," the strategy that relies on maximum egg output and no parental care, to extreme "K," in which nearly all emphasis is on care and the birthrate is reduced to a minimum.

nests for their eggs. Others hold the eggs in their mouths until they hatch and can swim on their own. Some reptiles do even better. An alligator makes a large nest mound for its eggs, guards them during incubation, and when the babies hatch and begin squeaking, it hears them and helps them out by tearing the nest apart. But not many reptiles are that attentive, and none protect or teach their young as they grow. That would be left for the even more intelligent and even more "K"-oriented mammals that succeeded the reptiles.

What dinosaurs did as parents, no one knows, although some of them, on the evidence of clutches of fossil eggs found in the Gobi Desert, were certainly stingy egg producers; some "nests" contain only a dozen or two. Thus, if dinosaurs were no better parents than most other reptiles, they would have been losers in two ways: "r"-oriented in their probable inability to give their young intensive care, "K"-oriented in their tendency to lay small numbers of eggs. That could explain their extinction in a world that was beginning to fill up with "K"-oriented mammals that were better parents.

"You don't have to look for sunspots, climatic upheavals or any other weird explanation to account for the disappearance of the dinosaurs," said Lovejoy. "They did fine as long as they had the world to themselves, as long as there was no better reproductive strategy around. They lasted more than a hundred million years; humans should as well. But once a breakthrough adaptation was made, once dinosaurs were confronted by animals that could reproduce *successfully* three or four times as fast as they could, they were through."

"K" is obviously far more efficient than "r", but it too has its limits. Accidents, predation, seasonal food failure, illness—all take their toll of animals. Losing an infant to one of those hazards after an investment of five or six years is hideously costly compared with the loss of an egg by an oyster. Two or three such accidents in a row could mean extinction for a particular assortment of genes possessed by a particular ape mother, because her fertile years might then be over. For a whole population of apes—an entire gene pool—a slow reproduction rate is as dangerous as it is for an individual. A series of disasters could wipe it out forever.

Indeed, the level of "K" demonstrated by modern apes is already dangerously high, All of them exist today in perilously small numbers and only in the most favorable environments. Their extreme vulnerability to extinction has been obscured by the role humans have played in accelerating their disappearance in recent times. We are constantly being told that we are exterminating apes. That is true, but it is only the final flourish in what apes have been doing to themselves for some millions of years. Left alone, they probably would become extinct anyway. Monkeys, on the other hand, have prospered and multiplied. That difference in success is so dramatic that it is worth comparing the two to see if

there is any basic difference between them that might explain it.

It turns out that there are two such differences. Monkeys, as has been noted, are quadrupeds. Apes are potential bipeds. Monkeys also are less "K"-oriented than apes. They have infants every two years instead of every five or six. They are not quite as intelligent as apes, nor are they quite as good parents, but they are good enough to more than make up for that deficiency with their improved reproductive rate. The modern success of the more "r"-oriented monkey strongly suggests that the more "K"-oriented ape has pushed that strategy too far.

Why do something that is bad? This is the second time that question has come up. First it was Why become bipedal if it is inefficient? Now it is Why push "K" too far if it is dangerous? The two are interrelated, and must be considered together.

First, it should be clear from the preceding discussion of primate evolution that apes, living in forests and spending their time as climbers and swingers in trees or sitting and walking about under the trees, are not inefficient. They have no real need to be good runners. The short spines and semierect postures that they developed earlier in the trees proved to be no handicap to some of them later on the ground, as long as forests were extensive and productive of the kinds of food they ate.

The lesson to be learned from this is that quadrupedalism, although it is apparently advantageous, can be given up—indeed, *will* be given up—if other, more useful adaptations are available. To repeat what Lovejoy said at the start of this chapter: Good running ability seems so obviously efficient that to abandon it seems capriciously stupid. But when the total survival strategy of the creature is studied, that advantage disappears. That is what makes possible the appearance of potentially erect apes, on the ground, in Miocene forests. To understand why certain ones went all the way, we must study other needs and other strategies.

The next thing to consider is that all through the Cenozoic, from about 70 million years ago right up into the Miocene, there was among primates a growing trend toward "K" in their reproductive strategy. It continued to intensify because it worked. As ape mothers became more highly evolved and more capable of solicitous parental care, the survival rate of their infants vis-à-vis the infants of less solicitous mothers was bound to be better.

At this point, the mechanics of a complex feedback loop—in which several elements interact for mutual reinforcement—must be examined. If parental care is a good thing, it will be selected for by the likelihood that the better mothers will be more apt to bring up children, and thus intensify any genetic tendency that exists in the population toward being better mothers. But increased parental care requires other things along with it. It requires a greater IQ on the part of the mother; she cannot increase parental care if she is not intellectually up to it. That means brain development—not only for the mother, but for the infant daughter too, for someday she will become a mother. Bringing a large-brained child to term requires a great deal of oxygen and the passage of a considerable load of energy through the placenta—a large investment by the mother. That is because there can be no development outside the uterus of a large-brained child. There are various reasons for this, one being that the neurological system has to be pretty much adult at birth. One does not learn unless one has a good brain to start with; if one is born with too undeveloped a brain, there can be no catching up later on. Therefore, the mother has to be responsible for much of that development inside her own body. Since her ability to transfer energy to a fetus is always limited (just as the oyster's ability to invest in eggs is limited), the result of having a larger brain has to be fewer offspring.

To express this in reverse: If one is going to have fewer offspring, one had *better* have a larger brain to take better care of them. That is the feedback principle in action. Each tendency works with, depends on and reinforces the other.

In the case of primate evolution, the feedback is not just a simple A-B stimulus forward and backward between two poles. It is multipoled and circular, with many features to it instead of only two—all of them mutually reinforcing. For example, if an infant is to have a large brain, it must be given time to learn to use that brain before it has to face the world on its own. That means a long childhood. The best way to learn during childhood

is to play. That means playmates, which, in turn, means a group social system that provides them. But if one is to function in such a group, one must learn acceptable social behavior. One can learn that properly only if one is intelligent. Therefore, social behavior ends up being linked with IQ (a loop back), with extended childhood (another loop), and finally with the energy investment and the parental care system that provide a brain capable of that IQ, and the entire feedback loop is complete.

All parts of the feedback system are cross-connected. For example: If one is living in a group, the time spent finding food, being aware of predators, and finding a mate can all be reduced by the very fact that one is in a group. As a consequence, more time can be spent on parental care (one loop), on play (another), and on social activity (another), all of which enhance intelligence (another) and result ultimately in fewer offspring (still another). The complete loop shows all poles connected to all others (Figure 16–6).

"Look at it another way," said Lovejoy. "Imagine the feedback loop without one of its essentials, and see what you get. Imagine a baby chimp brought up in a laboratory incubator without any opportunity to learn by playing with his friends. Give him a few critical years in there and then let him out as an adolescent to join regular chimp society. He won't be able to join; he won't know what to do, how to behave. He won't be able to jump around and climb as well as the others. He won't know how to fight or how to avoid fights, how to be respectful to his elders. A young gorilla brought up in isolation doesn't even know how to mate. He has to be shown movies."

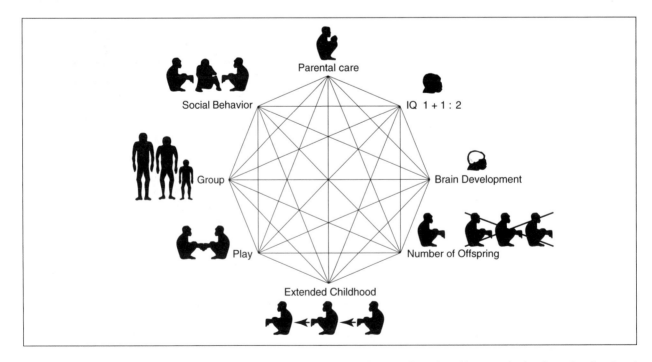

**Figure 16–6** Feedback loop relating number of offspring to other factors. (Reprinted by permission from Sterling Lord Literistics.)

So, Lovejoy continued, there were a number of very good reasons to explain how "K" could get rolling. It went hand in hand with the improvement and increasing specialization of vertebrates through time. Frogs are smarter than oysters. Alligators are smarter than frogs. Rabbits are smarter than alligators. Monkeys are smarter than rabbits. Apes are smarter than monkeys. More brains, fewer eggs, more "K."

"I won't go so far as to say that 'K' *produces* intelligence, but the two are certainly related. Since intelligence is obviously adaptive, it is not hard to see that under the right circumstances, it will be intensified. Those circumstances apparently were right for certain primates. By the Miocene, although we have only the indirect evidence of fossils, we can speculate that intelligence already had gone pretty far among apes. Those fossils give us a picture of animals that were not unlike modern chimpanzees. They were semierect, manually dexterous, and already had larger brains than monkeys. We can also speculate that they were strongly 'K'-oriented. It has taken us a while to get here, but we are now in a position to examine what it was in one line of apes that led it to become truly bipedal. In other words, what did 'K' have to do with erect walking?"

Bipedalism has plagued anthropologists for about a century. Not long after Dubois discovered the Java ape-man in 1891, he came up with a leg bone indicating that it walked erect. So little did people believe that such a primitive skull could be associated with erect walking that the general reaction was to deny the connection between the two fossil parts: The leg belonged to a later manlike creature and had gotten buried near the skull by accident; nothing as primitive as the Java ape-man could possibly have walked erect.

Accidental association or not, the reaction reflects a long and durable prejudice. It was stormily revived when Raymond Dart claimed erect walking for the Taung Baby. Even as late as the 1960s, long after the world had been forced to concede erect walking to australopithecines, it hung on—but in modified form: Anthropologists insisted that australopithecines were poor walkers, inefficient shufflers.

There grew up a general consensus that bipedalism, brain development, and tool use had arisen together. A feedback loop was constructed to explain this, each trait operating on the others to intensify them. Thus, an animal beginning to use tools, and with an enlarged brain capable of making them, would begin carrying them around more, and the incentive to do so would encourage erect walking. As erect walking freed the hand for carrying things, it would further increase the tendency toward tool use and brain development. About two million years ago, the idea went, all three tendencies had reached a semideveloped stage: The brain had grown larger but was still small; tools (on the evidence of those found at Olduvai) did exist, but were about as primitive as they could be while still deserving to be called tools; erect walking (if the pattern of hand-in-hand development with the other two emerging traits was to be followed) was also probably just emerging and was not yet perfected.

In the early 1960s, Sherwood Washburn of the University of California, in the midst of a long and eminent career as a student of primate evolution and behavior, hypothesized that a clue to erect walking could be found in the knuckle walking of chimpanzees and gorillas. He suggested that this could be an intermediate step on the road to true bipedalism, and pointed out that traces of it could still be found in human behavior: in the knuckles-down three-point stance of a football lineman, or in the way a man leans over a desk, supporting himself on his knuckles and his thumbs. The role of tools in the gradual elevation of knuckle walkers to true bipedalism, Washburn thought, was significant. "Locomotion and tool use were both cause and effect of each other," he wrote in 1974.

Other advantages were also hypothesized. When better knowledge of geology and climate suggested that australopithecines were probably open-country dwellers, it seemed sensible to derive another benefit from bipedalism: An erect posture that would make individuals taller and thus able to spot predators better in tall grass.

To Lovejoy, not long out of graduate school and already becoming interested in all aspects of locomotion, there was something unconvincing about all those ideas. He could not shake himself free of the conviction that no hominid could ever have ventured out on the savanna as a stumbling, imperfect walker and learned to do it better there. If it had been unfitted for erect strolling on the savanna, it would not have gone. If it had gone, it would not have survived the trip.

The conclusion he arrived at was that hominids *already* were erect walkers when they moved onto the savanna, and that they had perfected that odd gait for reasons that had nothing to do with savanna dwelling—and perhaps not with tool use either. How could tools have been a factor if, as he suspected, true bipedalism had been perfected before tools began to show up in the geological record?

Lovejoy's problem was that he could find no fossil evidence to support his ideas. He argued them on logical grounds with his peers, but without much success. He threw himself into an analysis of the mechanics of locomotion, and came away with a better understanding of it than most anatomists possess. But the "smoking gun," as he called it—hard fossils that would prove his contention—eluded him. The oldest well-dated australopithecine was only about two million years old, and it could already walk well. Or so he thought; others did not agree. It was utterly frustrating to Lovejoy that australopithecine leg and foot bones were not well enough represented in collections to nail that point down. So he was quite bowled over when I walked into his office early in 1974 with what I said was a three-million-year-old knee joint from Hadar.

Suddenly, erect walking was a million years older than it had been the day before.

"*Maybe* it was," Lovejoy said to the group in my lab. "There was just that one little knee joint. I told Don he would have to go back and find me a whole animal. He obliged by finding Lucy. I said, 'Okay, get me some variety,' and the next year he found the First Family. When I had a chance to study those bones, it became clear that they were excellent erect walkers. Now I had enough confidence to go ahead and try to figure out why. It couldn't be tools. Don's fossils were older than any known tools. I turned to reproductive strategy. That got me thinking about 'K.'"

Then he turned to one of the students. "All right," he said, "you're a species with too much 'K'; what are you going to do to try to improve that?"

"Well, reduce 'K' somehow. Monkeys are more successful; be more like them."

"You mean, go backwards?" said Lovejoy. "Return to quadrupedalism? Get a smaller brain?"

"Something like that."

"You can't do that. Not with that feedback loop you're in. Everything in it is pushing the other way."

"What, then?"

"How about aiming at the most obvious point in the loop: low birth rate? How about having more babies?"

"But," the student protested, "extreme 'K' prevents that. You said so yourself. You gave a very convincing feedback-loop argument."

"Okay, suppose we change one thing in a way that might let you have more babies."

"Like what?"

"Like becoming bipedal."

That quantum leap, that apparent non sequitur, so confounded the group that Lovejoy had to pause again for a review. He referred back to the Miocene, when apes were abundant and poised to explore various modes of living and locomotion. Out of those Miocene forebears came some that were brachiators, some that were "four-handed," some that were knuckle walkers, and some that were bipeds. All were well into "K," and all but the biped must be regarded today as failed evolutionary experiments.

If the biped succeeded, what did it do that was different? The answer: It managed to avoid a trap that the "K"-oriented others fell into—namely, primate birth spacing, the strategy that sentences all apes to a very low birth rate. Their habit is to bring up one infant at a time. However long that takes, however long the mother must devote herself to carrying the infant around, feeding it, looking out for it, that will be the time spent before she

can have another. A chimpanzee mother will not become sexually receptive until her baby is about five years old, the practical reason being that she has her hands full with the first one and cannot cope with a second. The biological reason is that nursing and infant care actually inhibit the onset of estrus.

"If you could find a way," said Lovejoy, "to speed up that rate so that the babies could overlap more, that would be a way out. How would you do that?"

"She'd have to toss out the first baby sooner."

"You don't get a toss-out," he said. "You get a mother taking care of two together. She divides her energy first among two, then three and four."

"How does she do that?"

"She moves around less. That way she uses up less energy." Also, he explained, the more infants are moved around, the more dangerous it is. There is more chance of their getting lost, of their falling out of trees and of their being caught by predators. If the mother is carrying an infant, either it is holding on to her or she is holding on to it. If she goes up into a tree after figs, and reaches for one, she may drop the infant. If she stays in one place on the ground, there is less chance that the infant will fall and less chance that it will be found by a predator, for both mother and infant have the protection of the group. They also have a better alarm system—thirty pairs of eyes instead of only one. They have other animals scouting around for food. When they find it, the mother can go directly to it with a minimum waste of time or exposure to predators. She spends her life in a small territory that she knows intimately. She knows where the climbable trees are. She knows the shortest distance to each in time of danger.

There was a simple rule for that, Lovejoy went on: "Less mobility is an adaptation. If you can achieve it, you may be able to have infants more often. There is always the tendency to have them more often anyway. The only thing that holds it back is the mother's inability to take proper care of them. She has to make sure she brings up one infant to the point where she knows it is going to make it on its own before she has a second. Staying in one place improves that chance and makes it possible for her to have a second a little sooner."

There was a flaw in Lovejoy's logic, and my group picked it up immediately: "Closer spacing raises a problem. The food requirement becomes greater—the mother has more mouths to feed—just when less mobility makes food harder to get."

"I was waiting for that," said Lovejoy. "What you're saying is that the mother must have more help. You're right. Somebody will have to bring food to her. People will tell you that can't happen. They point to baboons and say, 'They live on the savanna like hominids; they don't share food.' Or they point to chimps and say, 'They're like us, and they don't share food either.' Well, the proper way to look at that is to examine the reproductive strategies of all primates. They vary, and you also find a varying amount of sharing and caring. Among marmosets, a kind of New World monkey, the male is the primary parental caretaker. It's an ecological adaptation. Marmosets are small, active animals that have worked out a way of beating the primate birth-spacing problem by having twins. Because of their small size and their activity, they must eat a lot and eat often. With one infant, the mother might make it, but not with twins. So the father has to carry them around. The mother forages for herself and comes back to nurse them. It's the same with the owl monkeys and some others. Primates are exceptionally plastic in their behavior. You find that it runs the gamut from the father being the principal caretaker to the mother being the exclusive caretaker.

"So you inject some male behavior into the infant-rearing cycle," he continued. "But as soon as you do that, you get other problems. If the female has to have help, then there must be a good level of group cooperation. That's obvious. If a bunch of apes are going to live together as an intelligent, mutually supportive social unit with all the advantages we have already spoken of, then those animals are going to have to get along. There can't be a lot of fighting within the group. Unfortunately, when you mix up males and females—and you spell that S-E-X—that's when the fighting is most apt to start. In groups of lemurs, baboons—you name it—when a female comes in heat [into estrus], that's when the males are the most aggressive. It's natural. It's your job to get your genes into that female before some other fellow does."

There are ways of defusing that aggression, he explained. One is to lower the competition for sex. That can be done by the development of a pair-bonding system. If each male has its own female, its own private gene receptacle, it doesn't have to fight with other males for representation in succeeding generations.

"How do you get that started? One way would be to get rid of a free-for-all mating setup. Give up some of those sexy visual signals, the swellings and the exciting odors that say, 'I'm in heat,' because that's what drives all the males crazy. But if only half the males are excited by a certain female, then you reduce the potential for fighting by half right away. You can do that by making the sexual symbols more individualistic. Concentrate more and more in the individualization of sexual responses, and after a while you may find that a particular female is sexually exciting to only a few males, maybe only one. She's just not attractive to the others; they ignore her. The development of stimulating systems that are specific to individuals is called epigamic differentiation. I call it being in love.

"Baboons don't fall in love, they fall for sex—sex with any female displaying the signs of estrus. Among baboons all the girls, whenever they come in heat, appeal to all the boys. Baboon societies deal with that explosive situation by working out male-dominance hierarchies. The top, or alpha, male has gotten to the top by fighting

with other males, and he stays there by the threat of further fighting. He's the strongest and most intimidating in the crowd, and the one who gets the first crack at the females without any argument. The other males defer to him in a clear order of descending rank. The trouble with that system is that the alpha male's authority is enforced only by his presence. If he goes down to the river for a drink, he loses it. Some other watchful fellow is always hanging around. By the time the alpha male gets back, his chance for having any offspring may be gone."

It was becoming clear to the group that the level of social cooperation among animals whose sexual aggressiveness is high and whose sexual discrimination is low has to be limited. Introduce pair bonding into such a society, and social harmony can grow. Males can leave the group for short periods of time without forfeiting their chance for sexual representation in the next generation. Male parental care and food sharing become possible. As a result, the females can afford to become less mobile.

"You're now in another feedback loop," said Lovejoy. "We can look at it by starting with mobility (Figure 16–7). If you become less mobile, you can become more bipedal. Why? Because if you don't have to run much, you can afford to be less efficient at it in order to do other things that now begin to have more survival value—like holding and carrying the extra food you need as you increase the number of children you're nurturing. We've just spoken about pair bonding. If your mate is now walking upright, he's better equipped to carry food, and more likely to bring some to you. Meanwhile, you're better off too. As a quadruped you had only one free hand. You walked on one hand and carried with the other. Now you have two hands—one to provision yourself, the other to hold your baby. And it's getting more important that you do hold him because he's losing the ability to hold on to you. His foot is becoming a bipedal mechanism and losing the ability to grasp. A hominid baby can't hold on to his mother with his feet at all; they are no longer shaped for holding. In fact, he can scarcely hold on with his hands; he's too helpless as a small infant. A baby chimp is much better at that, but even it has to have a lot of holding by its mother. An Old World monkey, by contrast, can hold tight with its hands and feet. It has to; its mother doesn't hold it at all. If a baby monkey in a tree ever lets go, that's the end of it. Therefore, when I saw bipedality in Don's Hadar fossils I knew something about the social and reproductive strategies of those creatures. I knew the babies couldn't hold on. I knew the parents had to give their infants considerable care."

"That's all very well," said a member of the group, "but there's something not quite right about these feedback systems. If everything depends on everything else, what triggers it off?"

"There's no trigger," said Lovejoy. "Just a very gentle flow. You have a lot of time—maybe hundreds of

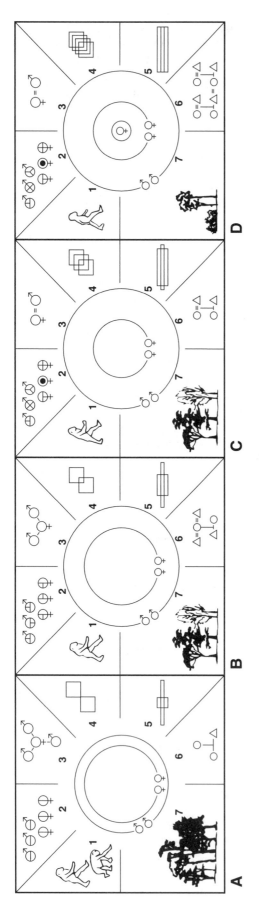

**Figure 16–7** These four diagrams, prepared by Owen Lovejoy, illustrate some of the conditions he believes acted in concert to produce a fully erect hominid. Section 1 of each diagram traces the probable progress of erectness itself. Section 2 refers to epigamic differentiation, the symbols for males and females becoming increasingly individualistic as time goes on, and leading to greater selectivity in sexual pairing. This is reflected in the mating patterns shown in Section 3, where males at first mate indiscriminately with females but later settle down as mated partners of specific females. Section 4 deals with the spacing of infants. In Diagram A there is no overlap, in Diagram B there is a little, and finally, in diagram D, there are families of three and four children.

These changes are accompanied by changes in sexual receptivity. In Diagram A, virtually all sexual activity takes place during estrus. In the subsequent diagrams the period of receptivity increasingly lengthens, eventuating, in Diagram D, in a condition of continuous sexual receptivity on the part of the female, entirely independent of her estrus cycle. Meanwhile, kinship relationships are changing (Section 6). In Diagram A, the only kinship bonds are between a mother and her children. In Diagram B there is a beginning of a male-female relationship, but no true bonding. In Diagram C the male is established as a parent, and a family group is formed. In Diagram D there are many such groups.

All these activities take place within (and probably under the influence of) a changing environment (Section 7), where the tropical forest in which quadrupedal apes casually mated and formed no families gradually changed to open woodland and savanna. The circles in the centers of the four diagrams have to do with foraging and movement. The inner circle marks the core area of the group, where females and infants spend their time. The larger circle represents the limit to which males forage. In Diagram A the two circles are nearly the same size, because the female is not being given any food by the male and must do all her own foraging. In diagram B the male ranges more widely to remove himself from the core area and leave more food for the female—which she must have because she is beginning to have more infants to feed. In Diagram C, this behavior intensifies. The male is now bringing food back to his mate. To do this he ranges still farther, and she can afford to move around less, thus exposing herself to less danger. Diagram D shows the establishment of a true home base, where the mother can leave her infants in the care of aunts or older siblings. Now she is free to range more widely herself. (Reprinted by permission from C. Owen Lovejoy.)

thousands of years. You have slightly different environments here and there, with slightly different emphases being put on different behaviors. You also have pretty smart animals. That's important. They can observe and imitate one another. They can try things. Not in the sense that they say to themselves, 'Wow, we're bipedal, we've got a free hand, let's take some lunch home to the little lady.' It's nothing like that. No animal is ever remotely conscious of the evolutionary processes it is undergoing. Those take place through tiny increments. Any slightest bulge anywhere in the loop, if it is adaptive, will have an effect on that part of the loop and, spreading out from there, to all the other parts."

There was still some dissatisfaction with this analysis. "Okay, but you've left out something important. Why *should* the male bring food to the female? If so much hinges on that, and if there is no sign that it is practiced by any other ape, how can you just assume it for this bipedal one?"

"I said we'd talk about sex."

"Right."

"Let's continue to talk about sex. This whole thing is a reproductive strategy. We're beginning to understand that you don't talk about locomotion just as a way of getting around; it's part of your entire species-survival mechanism, which involves mating and socializing just as much as it involves running and eating and child play. We have seen what pair bonding can do in decreasing aggression and improving the chances for male cooperation. What you're asking—and you betray that with your previous question—is: How does the male *get started* bringing food? Right?"

"Exactly."

"Maybe he likes the female."

"Now, wait a minute."

"I mean it. We spoke a minute ago about epigamic differentiation, about being in love. The only purpose of all the sexual signals that a female puts out when she is in estrus is to attract males, to generate a maximum amount of sexual activity so that the egg she is producing at that very moment will get fertilized. If she doesn't wave those flags pretty energetically, she may miss. If she misses, she will have to go until her next estrus before she has another chance. All mammals are efficient in advertising their sexual availability. That is what estrus is for: *to guarantee sexual activity*. If there is none, a female will ovulate in vain. For an ape that is perhaps too far into 'K' already, that would be a terrible extra strain on its already low rate of reproduction. The ape that comes into heat has got to be impregnated immediately for the good of all apes."

"But," said a student, "if you increase sexual discrimination, you decrease the number of males that are interested in that female, and you lower her chance of being impregnated."

"Not necessarily," said Lovejoy. "You may increase a particular male's interest in her. Even among chimps, although they regularly mate indiscriminately, you find an occasional honeymoon couple that goes off by itself for several days when the female is in heat. That's a little epigamic differentiation right there."

"Even so—"

"What if you extend the period of a female's sexual attractiveness to a given male? Suppose she flashes the sexual signals for a little longer. Suppose she gradually begins to switch from signals like odors and swellings that are part of the estrus cycle and begins to rely on some permanent features of her body—her hair, her skin, her shape. That's more like what humans do. Think about that for a moment. Human males and human females are sexually attractive to each other constantly, regardless of time or season. That has nothing to do with the estrus cycle. No other mammal is like that. Why are humans?"

No one had an answer.

"Come on. What have we just been talking about? A pair-bonding system was arising among those early hominids and prehominids as a way of keeping a male attracted to a female and ensuring that she be impregnated by him through the strategy of fairly continuous mating instead of a frenzy of it at the peak of her ovulatory cycle. You can't have a tremendous amount of fighting and indiscriminate copulating, *and* have pair bonding and food sharing. They just don't go together. So, what better substitute is there than a system that would bring the male back? And if he brought food, the selective value of that behavior would begin to show up pretty rapidly in the presence of a greater number of his genes in the gene pool."

"So there's no trigger," I said.

"None at all," said Lovejoy. "I think this is a gradual thing. We can speculate that it took a long time. It starts when a female continues to look sexy for a week or so at the end of her estrus cycle. Slowly that stretches out. Finally, the estrus flags don't count; she has permanent ones that keep her man—her hominid—interested in her all the time.

"And she'd better keep him interested, because she's fertile for only about three days. If she copulates once every two weeks, her chance of getting pregnant is pretty low. She can't afford that. It's her job to get pregnant quickly, as soon as she can handle the next infant."

"What you're saying," said a student, "is that bipedalism causes pair bonding, and that causes food sharing, and that causes more babies."

"I'm not talking cause," said Lovejoy. "That's the wrong word. You don't get cause in a feedback loop. You get reciprocal reinforcement. I'm saying that all these things happened and that each had an effect on all the others. I'm not saying which came first. I don't know which did. I doubt if anybody ever will know. I suspect there wasn't a first. But they did happen. We know that because you and I are sitting here talking about them.

We are the result. And if I list the principal behavior differences between apes and hominids, and ask you to find a better way to explain how we got where we are, I'd like to hear it." He started listing items on a piece of paper. "Look at these. They all happened more than two million years ago. They've got to be interrelated (see table below).

"What I'm trying to say," Lovejoy concluded, "is that you don't go off and adopt what seems to be a stupid way of walking for no reason. If you want to know why Lucy stood upright, you have to consider a lot more than just how she moved around. If you put it very crudely, you might say she stood up so that she could have babies more often. But that would be a direct cause, and we want to get away from that. If you want to put it more accurately, you'd say that in an animal with a complex of specializations that lead it too far into 'K,' bipedalism is a way out, a way of reducing 'K' again."

"Or," I said, "in a highly intelligent social animal that requires an extended childhood and long maternal care, an animal that already has the potential for upright posture, an animal that is so 'K'-oriented it can live only in the most favored environments, an animal that shares its food, that—"

"Yes, yes, all of that," said Lovejoy. "It's what I've been saying."

"I was just summarizing," I said, "because I think you left out one point."

"What's that?"

"You made the point that apes, because of their 'K' problems are practically extinct. But you left out that hominids, because they are more 'r'-oriented, are everywhere now."

"I'll accept that, but it's another ball game. It's a late thing. It gets us into the importance of tools and culture as encouragers of survival and population spread. Without them we'd still be stuck on the tropical savanna, somewhat better off than apes, but not all that much better. Our topic today was bipedal locomotion, something that happened to man *before* he became a man. Tools and culture have to do with him *after* he became a man.

"Let me summarize. I think that hominids learned to locomote bipedally in the forest, not out on the savanna, even though that's where you find them living

later. They went there as bipeds. They did it—and we learn this from your fossils, Don—close to four million years ago, maybe much earlier. They did it without the benefit of tools. I think the reason was primarily sexual and social. Once they had perfected upright walking, they were free to walk wherever they chose, because upright walking, in itself, is not inefficient. I can walk all day as well as a dog can. It's only when I try to run that the dog has it over me. So, if I don't have to run on the savanna, I can go there. And I probably go there because it's beginning to get crowded in the forest. I'm breeding pretty well now, and it's getting congested in there with those other apes. You know I did move out, because by one or two million years ago I'm spread all over the place.

"If I spread only twenty feet a year—that isn't much—in two million years I've spread four thousand miles. Tools probably helped that spread. Did I use tools to begin with? Probably no more than a chimpanzee does. But now I'm bipedal. Once you get me upright, you can expect something different. I've got a much better ability to hold and carry and throw things. There was a period somewhere between four million and, say, one and one-half million when tool using went from being wholly insignificant to being critical in hominid development. I didn't get my start by being a tool-using ape, as people have been telling you for so long. I was a socially and sexually innovative ape who became a biped and, as a result, managed to propagate my kind better than other apes. It was sheer luck that my ability to stand up and use my hands led to a later development of tools and a culture, and a still larger brain, and ultimately to four billion others like me. But all those things came as a byproduct of what it was really all about: a better reproductive strategy."

Lovejoy put on his coat. "You could say his 'r' innovations made man possible. Then it would be appropriate to say that tools refined him. Tools were responsible for *Homo erectus,* not for *Homo* himself."

After Lovejoy had gone, I was asked if I believed everything he had said.

"In general, I do," I said, "although Owen himself would not ask you to 'believe' it. That word is just as in-

| Hominid | Pongid (Ape) |
| --- | --- |
| Exclusively ground-dwelling. | Some predominantly in trees. Some predominantly on the ground. None exclusively terrestrial. |
| Bipedal. | Not bipedal. |
| Pair-bonded, leading to establishment of nuclear families. | Not pair-bonded. No nuclear families except in gibbons. |
| Increasing immobility of females and young. Possibility of a home base. | Females move to secure food and take infants with them. No home base. |
| Food sharing | No food sharing. |
| Beginnings of tool use and tool making. | Tool use absent or inconsequential. |
| Brain continues to enlarge. | Brain does not enlarge. |
| Continuous sexuality. | Sexuality only during estrus. |
| Multiple infant care. | Single infant care. |

appropriate as 'cause.' How can you believe something you can't prove? You accept it as probable if it satisfies the data and if it seems logical."

"But you believe in evolution."

"Yes, I do. That's because the theory has been kicked around for so long. It has withstood all that violent treatment, and yet it is *still* logical. In fact, the longer you look at it—the more you learn about it—the more logical it becomes. Give Owen's theory that same test of time; if it stands up, then I'll believe it. Right now I'll accept it as the best explanation of bipedalism yet formulated."

Tim White was asked his opinion.

"You know me. I don't believe anything I can't measure, and sexual behavior leaves no fossils. But in general I agree with Don; it's the best game in town. I think Owen's entirely right when he says that bipedalism

developed back in the forest. You don't get it lurching around on the savanna. Stand up to run away when you're just learning how to run that way? That's absurd."

"What did bring hominids out on the savanna?" I asked.

"As Owen said," said Tim. "It was getting crowded back there in the forest. Not only because there were more hominids, but because the forest was shrinking. By the Pliocene—by the time when all this may have been happening—that huge Miocene tropical forest had shrunk way down. What I don't entirely buy is that theory about bringing food back to females and young. You don't need it. I think that carrying objects, carrying children, carrying food was enough of an incentive for bipedalism."

"You'd leave out the estrus argument?" I said.

"Yes. I've never seen an estrus fossil."

# Chapter 17

# *Flesh & Bone*

## Ellen Ruppel Shell

A tour of Adrienne Zihlman's laboratories at the University of California at Santa Cruz is an exercise in the macabre. There's a hairy arm and ghostly white hand, the last vestiges of a chimp, poking over the rim of what looks like a stainless steel pasta pot. There's a pair of human cadavers laid out neatly under a sky-blue tarpaulin like slabs of bread dough beneath a towel. There's a sealed aquarium swarming with carnivorous beetles polishing off the last bits of flesh from a dog's skull. And then there are the bones.

"I collected most of these from road kills," Zihlman says, pulling out drawer after drawer of animal skeletons, zipped neatly in thick plastic bags. "We've got skeletons of possum, lynx, fox, raccoon, and coyote."

The bones are here because Zihlman, a paleoanthropologist, contrives and tests ideas about the origins of humankind by studying the remains of living things. The dog skull, for instance, will be used to highlight differences between primates like us and other mammals for her anatomy students. And the human cadavers will become part of the university's burgeoning collection of primate skeletons.

Such remnants and fragments of life allow Zihlman to wrestle with some of the most thorny and fundamental issues in human evolution. Not content to tinker at the periphery of her field, she's challenged colleagues to rethink long-standing ideas about how people came to be. One of these cherished notions is that the initiation of hunting by males made us what we are today: It spurred us to stand on two feet and freed up our hands for toolmaking. Most important, it forged the first social contract between males and females.

Zihlman has come up with evidence showing this is not necessarily the way things were. She has fashioned a convincing argument that activities pursued by females, such as food gathering and caring for infants,

were just as likely as hunting to be behind two-legged walking and more stable social relationships. The major reason that male hunting has been portrayed as a seminal event in human development, she says, is that men—male anthropologists in particular—were doing the portraying.

"Science has been characterized as a masculine activity," she says. "I think that is precisely the case."

Zihlman is firm in her belief that the evolutionary picture has been distorted by people who have yet to acknowledge their own biases. Much of this distortion occurs, she says, when researchers attempt to force the archeological and fossil record into the context of modern Western male-dominated culture.

For her views, Zihlman has endured more than a little criticism, ranging from thoughtless dismissals in academic journals to vilification at international meetings. Her ideas have caused her to clash with prominent researchers, such as Donald Johanson, famed as the discoverer of "Lucy," a 3-million-year-old ancestor and a cornerstone of the latest version of the male-hunting hypothesis. Although clearly shaken by these battles, Zihlman shows no signs of retreat. "I don't have ulcers," she says, alternating dainty bites of avocado and yogurt in a lunch break wedged between meetings. "I give them to other people."

The daughter of working-class parents who felt that their children should be "exposed to everything," Zihlman has fond memories of trips to the Field Museum in Chicago, where she grew up, and to her grandmother's farm in Iowa. "My grandmother gave me my first lesson in neuroanatomy," she says. "I learned that a chicken really does run around after it gets its head cut off." Zihlman attended Miami University in Ohio, where, after reading Margaret Mead's *Coming of Age in Samoa* for a class, she decided to major in anthropology. When she found that Miami University had no such department, she transferred to the University of Colorado

From *Discover* December, 1991.

in Boulder, which did. She completed her degree and, in 1962, went on to do graduate work at Berkeley, where she set herself to the task of finding out how our ancestors began to walk.

"In monkeys," she explains, "seventy percent of bones, muscle, and skin are devoted to moving around. And almost everything about what humans are is about being bipeds. I was always interested in the anatomical basis of behavior, and locomotion is the key thing—the origin of the human line can be traced to a change in locomotion. It was the first feature to definitely indicate a hominid."

As part of her doctoral research Zihlman traveled to the Transvaal Museum in Pretoria, South Africa, to measure, describe, and photograph the fossilized bones of our oldest preserved ancestors, the australopithecines. Her thesis compared chimpanzees with these hominids and detailed the changes in the angle of the hip sockets, the length and thickness of the thighbones, and other modifications that made bipedality possible for these creatures. And—ironically, in light of her current views—Zihlman included in her thesis a conjecture about the origins of the two-legged gait: It evolved, she wrote, to allow more efficient movement on long hunting trips through the African savanna. "Later I changed my mind about the hunting part," she says, smiling.

That Zihlman included hunting at all is a measure of the pervasive influence of the idea at the time. Hunting, in the 1960s, had become the standard by which most prehistoric artifacts were judged, and upon which most theories of early humans were built. The objects that supported the "man the hunter" theory were pieces of sharpened bone found in close proximity to antelope skeletons in some South African caves—caves inhabited by australopithecines 2 million years ago. Zihlman saw these bones herself during her travels; she also met the man who found them, the late anthropologist Raymond Dart. "At the time I met Dart I received my own personal demonstration of how the bones were used to kill animals, a sort of reenactment of the film *2001*," she recalls.

And it was the males—assumed by Dart and most other anthropologists, including Zihlman's adviser, Sherwood Washburn, to be larger, more powerful, and unencumbered by the care of young children—who did the hunting. Anthropologists went on to reconstruct a strictly sex-specific picture of early human social life: Males invented and built tools, hunted the food and dragged it home to hungry females, who were tied, helpless, to the hearth by demanding infants. Pair-bonds between males and females formed for the good of the species, monogamy giving a male more reason to defend his home and family.

But after completing her thesis in 1967, Zihlman got to thinking that there was something wrong with this picture of early human life. The reconstruction placed females at the mercy of the all-powerful male and gave

them no purpose other than to reproduce and serve. In 1970 she heard a paper delivered by anthropologist Sally Linton entitled "Woman the Gatherer: Male Bias in Anthropology" that seemed to crystallize her thoughts. Linton argued that men's control and dominance of women should be seen as a modern institution, not a natural fact arising from our animal past.

That same year some holes in the man-the-hunter hypothesis started to appear when paleontologist C. K. Brain of the Transvaal Museum examined some bite and gnaw marks on animal bones in australopithecine caves near Dart's celebrated sites. Brain concluded that the bones had been dragged in by leopards, not hunted and killed by hominids. Similar marks on the hominid bones themselves led Brain to suggest that Dart had the food chain going in the wrong direction: Australopithecines were more likely to be prey than predators.

"I was teaching a course in biology and the culture of sex roles at Santa Cruz at the time," Zihlman says, "and I had become alerted to the fact that women had essentially been invisible as far as evolutionary theory was concerned. The man-the-hunter theory has the male bringing home food to one female and to their offspring, and this pair-bond was key. But the data anthropologists were getting on the !Kung, a hunter-gatherer society in southern Africa, showed the women were pretty independent. They controlled the resources they collected."

!Kung women, according to studies by anthropologist Richard Lee, gathered the tubers, roots, and fruits that are the staples of the !Kung diet. No one was suggesting that the !Kung were living australopithecines, but they lived in a similar environment and had only rudimentary technology. So it was possible that early hominid female life resembled the life of !Kung women, who weren't tethered to a home base by child rearing. Instead they carried their young while walking miles across the savanna in search of food. And food gathering, Zihlman realized, was just as likely as hunting to have brought early hominids to their feet.

"A lot of the African vegetation went underground or grew thick coverings to protect itself through the dry season," she says. "Hominids needed tools to dig these fruits out or crack them open." Carrying these tools around, and using them to dig, required free hands. And that left only two feet for walking.

It also seemed less and less likely to Zihlman that the carnivorous, monogamous early hominids presumed by the hunting hypothesis would have evolved out of chimps or other apes who ate little meat and were rather fluid in their sexual relationships.

"I had done my dissertation on chimps," Zihlman says, "and I knew that chimps did not form stable pair-bonds and that the males came and went. Females and their offspring formed the core group within chimp societies. The whole idea of pair-bonding is completely overrated. It's a typical projection of the ideal American family life back in time. Gradually I was developing a view of human origins that took into consideration comparative anatomy, ape and human behavior, and the fossil record. And it firmly put women into the story of human evolution."

Zihlman began publishing a series of papers that drew these lines of evidence together to show gathering was an alternate route for human evolution to travel. "Woman the gatherer," in Zihlman's view, was not the absolute prehistoric truth. But it was a scenario at least as plausible as "man the hunter."

Many of Zihlman's arguments rested on her contention that current primate behavior, particularly that of chimpanzees, provided a rough analogue to early hominid behavior. This reasoning was supported by studies done in the mid-1960s, comparing chimp and human blood proteins. Biochemists Vincent Sarich and the late Allan Wilson of Berkeley had used similarities in these proteins to show that chimps are our closest living primate relatives, probably diverging from a common ancestor 5 million years ago.

Zihlman became particularly intrigued by Sarich's speculation that the common ancestor must have looked something like a small chimpanzee (since animals tend to evolve into larger forms). To Zihlman, this called to mind the pygmy chimp, a species native to the Zaire River basin in equatorial Africa. The notion that pygmy chimps were "living links" to man's earliest ancestor was first put forward by Harvard zoologist Harold J. Coolidge in 1933. But it was never substantiated, partly because not enough was known of this rare and elusive animal to take the theory beyond the realm of speculation.

"There just weren't that many pygmy chimps around to study," Zihlman says. So in 1973, along with Douglas Cramer, a graduate student at the University of Chicago who was studying pygmy chimp cranial features, Zihlman visited the African Museum in Belgium (Zaire was a Belgian colony until 1960) to study the museum's relatively extensive collection of pygmy and common chimp skeletons. Zihlman and Cramer found that pygmy chimps differ from common chimps in a number of ways—their trunks are smaller, their arms are shorter, and their legs are a little longer.

Zihlman then observed pygmy chimps in action at the Yerkes Primate Center in Atlanta. She noticed that they often assumed a two-legged position when climbing, jumping, and standing. In essence, though arboreal by nature, pygmy chimps seemed to her to be poised on the edge of bipedalism. At Yerkes, Zihlman also observed that pygmy chimps seemed more social and less aggressive—more "human"—than common chimps.

All the differences were in the human direction," Zihlman says. "Here, it seemed to me, was an even better prototype for the ancestral human than the common

chimpanzee. The pygmy chimp was a living ape that seemed to represent the 'transition' from quadrupedal to bipedal locomotion."

Zihlman went so far as to compare the pygmy chimpanzee with "Lucy," the hominid fossil skeleton found at Hadar in Ethiopia in 1974 by Donald Johanson, then at the Cleveland Museum of Natural History. The similarities between the two seemed striking. They were almost identical in brain and body size and stature, and the major differences, the hip and knee, could well be the outgrowth of Lucy's adaptation to bipedal walking. In an illustration Zihlman published in 1982 of Lucy's left side abutting the right side of a pygmy chimp, the two creatures looked almost like one image in a slightly cracked mirror.

One consequence of tying Lucy so tightly to pygmy chimp anatomy was that Zihlman theorized that males and females of Lucy's species were about the same size, as are male and female pygmy chimps. This innocuous-sounding conclusion unleashed a storm of controversy that's still raging today. For one of Johanson's cherished assertions about Lucy's kind is that males were much bigger than females.

Johanson and his colleague Tim White of Berkeley had taken Lucy's skeleton and similar bones from other hominids and put them into one species—the oldest one known, they claim, the ancestor to all other forms—called *Australopithecus afarensis.* Some of these individuals were much bigger than others, and Johanson and White accounted for this by saying that the big ones were males. "It was necessary for the females to be small," says Johanson, who is now president of the Institute of Human Origins in Berkeley. "If they were large, they wouldn't have been able to survive on the low quality food available to them and still nourish their fetus and their young. The males needed to be large in order to compete for the females and to protect the troop." Another of Johanson's colleagues, Owen Lovejoy of Kent State University, has proposed that these large males had begun to come down from the trees to hunt far and wide for food to bring up to their patiently waiting mates. So males invented walking, and man the hunter stalked again.

Zihlman, not surprisingly, doesn't buy this idea at all. No such extreme size difference between sexes has been noted before in other australopithecine species, she says, no such difference exists in chimps, and there is no convincing evidence that it exists in Johanson's fossils. It's entirely possible, Zihlman argues, that Johanson has taken two or more different species, including a big one and a small one, and lumped them together.

"Johanson is asserting, not demonstrating, that there is this extreme size difference in *Australopithecus afarensis,*" Zihlman says. "But he's never published a detailed argument with measurements to back this up. In modern humans, males and females can be distinguished most of the time by the pelvis, but in *Australopithecus afarensis,* with only one pelvis—Lucy's—there can be no comparisons. For all we know, Lucy might just as well have been a male as a female. As far as I'm concerned, it's a toss-up. All we know for sure is that Lucy was small."

Such statements infuriate Johanson and White, who have all but based their careers on the theory that *Australopithecus afarensis* is a single species. "What we are looking at in these samples is one geologic second in time," Johanson says. "And what we have found in that slice are some rather large and some rather small specimens of the same species." In the first place, he says scornfully, anatomical comparisons show the pygmy chimp is no more closely related to Lucy than it is to modern humans. He argues that the teeth of pygmy chimps are much smaller than those of early hominids. Turning Zihlman's argument back on itself, he notes that while male and female pygmy chimps differ very little in anatomy, the fossil record shows dramatic differences between male and female hominids.

"I don't put a lot of emphasis on this notion of a 'living link,'" Johanson scoffs. "But in any case, it is clear to me that the pygmy chimp does not appear to be it."

White goes even further, accusing Zihlman of distorting her science to fit her politics. "The bones that were found at Hadar don't have labels, so you can interpret them any way you want," White says. "You could also go to a cemetery, dig up the bones you find there, and say that each skeleton represents a different species. The question is whether the fossils show so much variation that we need to recognize them as two different species, and they don't. We've grounded our inference in the modern world. If Zihlman must accommodate the data of the real world to some politically correct manifesto, then she should write science fiction, not science."

Zihlman agrees that differences exist between the early hominids and the pygmy chimp, especially when it comes to their teeth. But the chimp is only a model of the early ancestor, one that probably shared both common and pygmy chimp characteristics. "I never meant to suggest that pygmy chimps were exactly like the apes that gave rise to humans," she says. "But in terms of their body proportions, the early hominids are more like the pygmy chimp than any other ape."

As for the rest of the dispute, Zihlman contends that she is willing to defend her view in an open forum, but that so far she has not been asked to sit on the same podium with Johanson and White to argue her case. Zihlman says she tried to take measurements of the fossils herself, but when she asked Johanson for permission to see the collection when it was under his care at the Cleveland Museum, he said she could do so only if she gave him the right to review any paper she wrote on the fossils before she sent it to a journal. "The implication was that he had to approve it," Zihlman says. She felt

that was a form of censorship and refused to work under those conditions. The collection has since been returned to Ethiopia.

Stalemates such as this, marked by displays of territoriality and possessiveness, have frustrated Zihlman to the point where this past year she decided to do something about it. With Mary Ellen Marbeck, an anthropologist at the University of Arizona, she organized a conference on female biology and evolution with the explicit purpose of encouraging free and open speech among the participants. To that end, the organizers invited only women researchers.

The move was immediately denounced as sexist by critics, both in her profession and in the press. However, Zihlman remains staunch in its defense, saying that what distinguished conference participants was not the possession of two X chromosomes but a supportive and cooperative attitude. "Studies in anthropology, sociolinguistics, and psychology document that men and women communicate differently," she says. "Men frequently use language to dominate. My goal at the meeting was that language be used to communicate. And as it turned out, that is what happened. People didn't compete with one another, they didn't interrupt one another, they actually listened. We got down to the nitty-gritty very fast and could really discuss the issues."

For Zihlman, one of the key issues was the effect females have on the evolution of their species. "Natural selection is operating at all stages of life, not just reproduction," she says. But most studies of the role of the individual in evolution focus on mating, she notes, on getting the genes into the next generation. "But mating is a male-dominated behavior," Zihlman says. "For females, that's just the beginning. They're involved with offspring for their whole lives."

This is particularly true for primates. "A primate lives a long life, with distinct stages of development," she says. "Chimps live twelve to thirteen years before they reproduce, and there are many things that happen during that time that can influence the health of their offspring. They can get sick or lose a parent or be injured. This is experiential, not genetic. To say genes are the be-all and end-all renders everything else—development, life experience, ecology—irrelevant. I don't think getting genes into the next generation is what it's all about. To reduce everything to genes is boring and simplistic, and I don't buy it for a minute. It might work for insects or birds—though I have my doubts—but it certainly does not work for primates." This is what Zihlman calls looking at the whole organism—and that, ultimately, is what she is interested in.

"I knew early on that if I was going to survive in this business, I was going to have to diversify," Zihlman says. "If I had committed myself to studying fossils and only fossils, I would have failed, because when it comes to looking at fossils, access is everything and I knew I wouldn't get it. But fossils and bones are not enough—

they just don't tell you all that much. For example, there's nothing in the bones of the goats in the Galápagos islands that says they should be able to climb trees and eat vegetation. But they do. The whole point is trying to conceptualize what was on the bones and what it allowed individuals to do."

To illustrate the limitations of trying to reconstruct the life of an animal from its fossil remains, Zihlman walks back to one of the tall wooden bone chests in her laboratory and pulls out drawers filled with plastic bags that hold the remains of common chimps brought to her by Jane Goodall from her research center at Gombe National Park in Tanzania. Goodall has followed these chimps for 30 years, sometimes from birth to death, and has kept detailed records on the events that shaped their lives. Zihlman and Morbeck examined and measured the bones and skulls of the Gombe chimps to determine the extent to which these events also shaped their bodies.

For example, the bones of one chimp, "Gilka," are small and asymmetrical. If Gilka were the only female skeleton available, this might lead researchers to speculate that females of her species are much smaller than males. In fact, Gilka was stunted by a bout of polio suffered early in life. She bore four infants, all of whom died. By contrast "Flo," who lived to be 43, had a larger skeleton than many Gombe males and gave birth to five infants, three of whom survived to adulthood.

"The variation among individuals regardless of sex is enormous," Zihlman says. "What the Gombe studies show is the importance of the individual in evolution, that it's reductionist to focus on a few bones. Animals don't go from gene to protein to bone, there's a life that is lived in between. Bone is one of the most mobile of tissues, it is constantly being turned over and remodeled— the bone you have today is not the same bone you had six years ago."

Zihlman says she and Morbeck plan to use the data they glean from the Gombe bones in concert with Goodall's field notes to provide a basis for reevaluating what has been written about the early hominid fossil record. "Here we have information on the skeleton and information on the whole animal," she says. "From this we have a holistic view, we can learn what bones really tell us, and what they do not. There's a good chance we might overturn a lot of what's been accepted about the fossil record. Right now it's only a work in progress, but of course, I hope it shakes things up."

It's likely to. Fossil hunters are often strongly wedded to their interpretations of their finds and are unlikely to accept criticism gracefully, particularly from an outsider who has not devoted her life to the dig. While not oblivious to the possibility of backlash, Zihlman is not concerned about it.

"In science, being outspoken and being a woman is an unforgivable combination," she says. "I've learned to live with the consequences. For me, there is no choice. I really don't know how to play the game even if I wanted to."

# Chapter 18

# *Ape Cultures and Missing Links*

## Richard Wrangham

It's a most wonderful honor to give the first Getty Lecture. Gordon Getty's leadership of the Leakey Foundation has galvanized our field with an unprecedented combination of philanthropy, intellect, engagement, and fun. As a result of all these, he now brings a positively professorial expertise as well. No one has done as much to encourage our field. To be speaking in a lecture named for him is a truly humbling experience.

In recognition of Gordon Getty's extraordinary reach, I'm going to address the three questions at the heart of the Leakey Foundation's mission. I'll frame those questions in a minute. But first, ladies and gentlemen, we've all had a long day, so please fill your glasses, sit back, and relax. And incidentally, as far as I'm concerned feel free to drink your wine with your fingers, or by dipping a napkin in it, or by sucking the tablecloth, or however you choose. I say this because I want to encourage you into the spirit of our ancestors . . . but, well, I'll come back to all that in a minute.

Last Saturday, six days ago, I was in Kibale Forest in western Uganda with a party of ten chimpanzees. About eight o'clock, we met a group of sixty red colobus monkeys. The high-ranking chimps stopped and stared. The younger adult males did the same. The colobus chirped in alarm. Some chimps started climbing. Others watched from the ground. Within minutes, chimps were hunting. Two drove a party of monkeys towards a third waiting in ambush fifty feet above the ground. The colobus did their best to file away through the tree-crowns, searching for an escape among the branches. But they found their path blocked. They turned, and tried another escape. The chimpanzees kept turning them back. The hunts went on for an hour and twenty minutes. At one point, thirty monkeys were trapped on a high branch, two chimps drove them higher, till one by one they jumped. There was a chimp waiting at the land-

From *Symbols* Spring, 1995.

ing point. The first three just escaped. The fourth was caught. The fracas went on. There were fourteen separate hunts in an hour and a half. By the end, three colobus were dead, three chimps had killed, and five human observers were enthralled.

How things have changed. In 1959, 100 years after *The Origin of the Species* was published, humans were the only primate known to prey on mammals. Last week's observation would have been a paper in *Science.* Today, thanks to grantees of the Leakey Foundation, it's almost routine. We know now that chimpanzees everywhere kill and eat their own prey; that to do so, they often use elaborate cooperative strategies; that the meat is held by males, who share it with friends and lovers in exchange for favors; and that they can hunt so well and so often as to kill 15 to 30 percent of their prey population per year, a higher proportion than any carnivore does.

So what does this sort of observation mean for our history? Does it suggest a cooperatively hunting killer-ape in our past? Some people think so. But why shouldn't we focus on other apes instead? For example, think about bonobos, the sister species to the chimpanzee. Bonobos live in similar forests with similar monkeys. They like to eat meat. But they don't cooperate in hunting monkeys. They don't even kill monkeys, even though they occasionally catch them and play with them like pets! And when they do eat meat (meat of small antelopes), it's the females, not males that hold the carcass. Should we think, because of bonobos, that our male ancestors disdained the hunt, and ceded meat to females?

I'm not going to focus on hunting this evening. I use hunting just as an example. The same issues apply to any behaviors we're interested in. Whether we're talking about hunting, or communicating, or tool-using, or anything else, we have to sort out what ape behavior today means for the human past.

In this lecture I'm going to argue that to be with chimpanzees in an African forest is to climb into a time machine . . . that by stepping into the world of these extraordinary apes we move back six million years, to glimpse where we have come from. The glimpse isn't a perfect picture, but it's amazingly good. That's the argument.

Let's begin by looking back 25 years. In those first years of the Leakey Foundation, I couldn't have made *any* suggestion about apes as time machines without sounding very silly. At that time, with genetic and fossil data still poor, apes and humans were thought to be distantly related, not only to each other but also to their common ancestors.

Apes were certainly *fascinating* to visionaries like Louis Leakey, but then to that extraordinary man, everything was interesting. Happily, he supported Jane Goodall. And he was thrilled when she found chimpanzees modifying tools (and hunting prey), because this meant that chimps were a sort of bridge between humans and other primates. This gave flesh to the idea of evolution. But because at that time, 25 years ago, the kinship between humans and chimpanzees was thought to have ended in the distant past, maybe 15 to 20 million years ago, no one was sure what these observations meant for our history. And anyway, the idea of chimps as a bridge was undermined by an apparent gulf between apes and humans in certain critical aspects of behavior.

Certainly there were *some* similarities. Mothers were strongly attached to their infants. Many gestures were strikingly similar. But the parallels evaporated at a critical point: There was no evidence of serious aggression. Chimpanzees were seen to live wonderfully peaceful lives. So human society was something apart. Reviewing the chimpanzee studies of the 1960s, Robert Ardrey decisively affirmed the human-ape divide. The life of chimpanzees was an "arcadian existence of primal innocence."

This became the conventional wisdom for other apes. George Schaller and Dian Fossey found gorillas to be a gentle giant. Their new picture rightly challenged the view that gorillas were natural aggressors towards people. In so doing, it left them unconnected with modern human behavior. So the prevailing view was that "human forms of social life were largely unique to human, created by us, subject to human manipulation according to our vision of human good."[1] Apes had nature; people had culture, and culture, it seemed, wasn't always so great.

In the first hundred years after Darwin, in every area of human thought, people were searching for new meanings of human existence . . . and this was a common conclusion. Paul Gauguin was one of the first artists to do what the Leakey Foundation does, to search in the primitive. This painting he considered his spiritual legacy. It looks to an imagined past, a primitive idyll where man and nature lived in harmony. It has on it, written in the top left-hand corner, the three questions of

the Leakey Foundation, questions that go back to Thomas Carlyle's *Sartor Resartus*. On the right is a newborn child, representing "Where do we come from?" The figure plucking fruit in the centre shows our day-to-day existence: ("What are we?"). On the left, an old woman facing death symbolizes concern for the future: "Where are we going?"

You might think that, like ourselves today, Gauguin would have been inspired by his exploration of the human past, present, and future. No; he was oppressed. Near the center, you can see by the tree of knowledge two sinister figures. Their sombre colors show the suffering that comes from leaving nature, pain that Gauguin felt acutely. For Gauguin, human history was a story of acquired sin.

The challenge of completing the painting kept him alive during a period of depression over his daughter's death, but its conclusions left him empty. As soon as he'd finished his masterpiece, he walked out into the mountains, took a massive dose of arsenic, and lay down to wait for death. Should we feel the same depression from looking into the past? Was Gauguin right to see humans as figures of tragedy, doomed by the very abilities of brains and culture that represent the best of our achievements? No. We have new, more confident answers now, coming not from an imaginary vision of primitive Tahiti but from the real world of living primates. The story of human evolution that emerges is different from Gauguin's, still discomfiting, but much richer and more inspiring. It's a story of unfinished challenges. I'm going to address them by taking Gauguin's, and our Foundation's, three questions in turn. Let's begin with the past. "Where do we come from?"

So what made a savannah-living, upright hominid out of a forest-living quadrupedal ape? And what was that ancestral species like in how it looked and how it behaved? I claimed just now that our prehominid ancestor looked like a chimpanzee. Let me explain why I think so.

First, it's obvious that the three African apes, chimpanzees, gorillas, and bonobos, are all very similar, much more like each other than they are like any other species. The genetic evidence unambiguously supports our intuitions. Let's look at these three species.

Genetic evidence from Phil Morin, Maryellen Ruvolo, and others show that West African chimps have been separate for about 1½ million years from chimpanzees in East Africa. But morphologically, there's very little difference in chimpanzees across the continent. Like all the great apes, this is a conservative species. Most gorillas are lowland gorillas. Recent Leakey Foundation studies are exciting because they are some of the first to watch lowland gorillas undisturbed. They are so similar to chimpanzees that people can find it hard to tell big chimpanzees and small gorillas apart.

Bonobos are the third African ape. They look so like chimpanzees that they weren't recognized to be different until 1933, when they were called "pygmy chimpanzees." But so-called pygmy chimpanzees are actually no smaller than some chimpanzees. Most people prefer to call them bonobos. They live south of the Zaïre River, where there are no gorillas or chimpanzees. Chimpanzees live north of the Zaïre River and share much of their range with gorillas.

The evolutionary relationship among these three apes is undisputed: Chimpanzees and bonobos split most recently around 2.5 mya, and their common ancestor split with gorillas much earlier, about 8 to 10 mya. So where do humans fit? Probably everyone here knows of the shocking genetic evidence now showing chimpanzees to be more closely related to humans than they are to gorillas. The last four years in particular give mounting confidence to this view, as every new nuclear or mitochondrial gene is looked at, currently more than 10 genes in detail as well as from DNA hybridization looking at the genome as a whole. This means that human ancestors are no sister group to the apes, but instead arose within the African ape tree. Our hominid ancestors apparently split from the chimp-bonobo line *after* the split from gorillas. Louis Leakey, a great iconoclast, would have loved it. Now, this surprise gives us an unexpected bonus. It implies that our ancestral 6 mya species is likely to have been very like a modern-day chimpanzee. We can see why by reconstructing our various common ancestors.

First, what was the common ancestor of chimpanzees and bonobos like? The answer depends on comparisons with gorillas, the first ape to split off. Which is more similar to gorillas? Is it chimpanzees? or bonobos? The answer is clear: In characteristics that differ between chimpanzees and bonobos, chimpanzees are consistently more like gorillas. This is true for things we can see, such as the body build, the shape of the head, or the structure of the genitals, as well as those we can't, such as chromosomes and blood groups. Chimpanzees are like small gorillas, whereas bonobos are like changed chimpanzees. So the common ancestor of chimpanzees and bonobos should have looked like a chimpanzee.

What about the common ancestor of chimpanzees and gorillas? Well, a gorilla is basically a big chimpanzee. The difference between chimpanzees and gorillas in morphology, as well as in feeding behavior, sexual anatomy, grouping patterns and, social relationships, can all be explained simply by gorillas being larger. These two species are so similar that they should be in the same genus. So the common ancestor of chimpanzees and gorillas was surely an animal built on their body plan, more chimpanzee-1ike if it was smaller, more gorilla-like if it was larger.

Finally, the early, ape-like australopithecine, *afarensis,* is sufficiently well-known for its body weight to be closely estimated. They were about the size of chimpanzees.

So our ape-like ancestor that gave rise to our hominid ancestors was presumably also the size of a chimpanzee and built on the body plan of a chimpanzee. And with *Australopithecus ramidus* suddenly presented to us, the earliest australopithecine is looking, as expected, more chimpanzee-like.

This is all very disturbing, and exciting. For years we were brought up to say that the living apes were interesting, but we mustn't think of them as our living ancestors. But now maybe one of them was!

So here's the scenario. At 8 to 10 mya a chimpanzee-like species gave rise to early gorillas; at 5 to 6 mya it calved off australopithecines; at 2 to 3 mya it gave rise to bonobos; and it's still going. You can still argue, and some people do, that gorillas and chimpanzees are similar from parallel evolution rather than common phylogeny. If so, this argument falls. But the great thing is . . . that this question will eventually be settled when the astonishing fossil gap is filled. (There are no known fossil ancestors of the African apes!—except perhaps the 10 mya *Ouranopithecus,* which in one extraordinary fossil shows an amazingly gorilla-like face staring out across 10 million years of fossilization—a potentially vivid support for the antiquity of the African ape clade). The most reasonable view for the moment, however, is that chimpanzees are a conservative species and an amazingly good model for the ancestor of hominids. So . . . "What do we come from?" Our ancestor was likely a black-haired, knuckle-walking, large-brained, deep-voiced, heavily built, big-mouthed, thin-enameled fruit-eating, fission-fusion, male-bonded species living at low population density in the forests of equatorial Africa.

If we know what our ancestor looked like, naturally we get clues about how it behaved . . . that is, like modern-day chimpanzees. This helps in some ways of course. But Gary Larson is right. We can't just talk about The Chimpanzee: We have to talk about particular chimpanzee cultures, because chimps invent lots of different signals and different ways to live. For instance, look at the ways chimpanzees drink. They can put their lips to water. But they often make leaf-sponges, which they dip into water and suck. Sometimes they make drinking-brushes, dipped into narrow-holes. One population uses natural water-bottles. Another uses a pestle and mortar to smash up the juicy parts of a palm. And one, as Denise Waydill has seen this year in Burundi, uses whole leaves as bowls to scoop up water. These different drinking styles come from Guinea and Zaïre and Uganda and Tanzania and Burundi. So you make the call: What did an Ethiopian australopithecine do?

I love this list of drinking styles because it makes two other points. First, it shows how dynamic this field is. The stem-sponges were first seen less than five years ago, the pestle-and-mortar was reported this year, the moss-sponges and water-bowls haven't yet been published. People are moving into new chimpanzee populations and seeing new traditions all the time, not just in drinking but in eating, body care, signaling, play, everything! Earlier this year, Rosalind Alp found chimpanzees in Sierra Leone using leafy branches like sandals: They do this when they climb along the thorn-studded branches of capok trees, holding their leafy sandals in their hands and feet to raise their soles and palms above the spines. So did Lucy sometimes wear shoes?

The inventiveness of chimpanzees is remarkable, and sometimes one can even see it directly. Last year, I watched a lonely boy chimpanzee, eight-year-old Kakama, playing for four hours with a log. He carried it on his back, on his belly, in his groin, on his shoulders. He took it with him every time he moved. He carried it up four trees, and down again. He lay in his nest and held it above him like a mother with her baby. And he made a special nest that he didn't use himself, except to put the log in. Three months later, he did it again, watched by two of my field assistants in Kibale Forest. They recovered the log, and pinned to it a description of the behavior. Their report was headed *'Kakama's toy baby.'* Imagination made wood.

As more chimpanzee populations are watched, each has its own culture. But the differences aren't understood. A tiny few can be attributed to simple ecological causes, but most appear arbitrary. The explanation of cultural differences is becoming an exciting challenge, and it involves explaining not only why traits are invented and passed on, but also why they go extinct. That's the first lesson of the drinking tools. And what it means for our big questions is both inspiring and annoying. It means that we can look to our past and see a cultural ape that could show a hundred or more inventions of tools and signs and ways to get food . . . but alas, an ape with so much invention that we can't easily predict where and what it did.

The second lesson is that some of the new observations are wonderfully suggestive about ape-hominid transitions. People have argued that hominids were seed-eaters, making dramatic the hammer-tools used by chimps in West Africa. The fat-rich seeds made available by smashing nuts provide much of the calories for the Taï chimps, at some times of year. Did australopithecines harvest palm nuts along the fringes of a Pliocene swamp draining Lake Turkana? Here is an adaptation they could easily have brought with them from the forests.

Others think that hominids were root-eaters, using, like root-eating pigs, the seasonal stores of diverse savannah tubers. This is reasonable because roots could supply the fallback food eaten when fruits were scarce. But could root-eating have started in the forest? Until the 1990s, there was no evidence of it, and it makes little sense . . . forests have few large storage organs, a tribute to their relatively even micro-climate. But now we have Annette Lanjouw's extraordinary observations of the root-eating chimpanzees of Tongo. The Tongo chimps,

in eastern Zaïre, live on a lava flow. All water drains quickly; there are no streams or pools. So these chimps use their moss-sponges, up to 20 minutes a day, but it's laborious. So, when they're lucky, they have another trick. Sometimes they find a stem that excites them. Pulling the lava boulders away, they dig deep into the soil, maybe up to their shoulders, and extract a root. The prize is prized indeed. Like a prey monkey, the root is guarded by the possessor while around him his companions scream and hug and charge in joy. The root may be divided and shared. It can be carried for a kilometer or more, while it's slowly finished. What's in the root that excites them so? It's saturated with water, according to Annette. She thinks it's a bottle.

So I like the idea of some strangely desiccated forest, on a lava flow, perhaps, or on an upland granite outcrop, leading an early Pliocene population of forest chimpanzees to become root-eaters—first for water, and only then for food . . . forest root-eating, precursor to savannah life.

And once on the savannah, can chimps help us imagine the past? In Chambura Gorge in western Uganda, Cathy Poppenwimer's work in the last two years has uncovered a forest-based group of chimpanzees that come into the open savannahs for figs. They can nest in these isolated fig trees. In the savannah grassland they chase the young antelope, the Uganda kob. Presumably they catch them sometimes. There are two lion dens in the gorge, but the chimps survive; leopards they chase in groups. And only two months ago, the first observations emerged of Ugandan chimpanzees using tools to fish for termites out on the savannah rim of the gorge.

Nut-smashing, root-eating, savannah-using chimpanzees, resembling our ancestors, and capable by the way of extensive bipedalism. Using ant-wands, and sandals, and bowls, meat-sharing, hunting cooperatively. Strange paradox . . . a species trembling on the verge of hominization, but so conservative that it has stayed on that edge, little changed for 6 million years or more. It's hard to imagine what more one could ask for as preadaptations to a savannah life. But the history of chimpanzee studies shows that our imagination is limited only by what we know. We're still a long way from defining the limits of what chimpanzees do, and therefore from imagining the range of our ape ancestor's feats. We have a good answer, however, to "Where do we come from?" For one thing, we come from an ape with enough brains to invent novel cultural adaptations in every new environment.

The second of Gauguin's questions, "What are we?," goes to the heart of his anxieties. The big issue was the source of evil . . . human aggression and pain and misery. Gauguin, as we saw, thought it unnatural, the result of the loss of nature . . . a widespread romantic view, from Rousseau to Ardrey. But others saw deep roots. Dostoyevsky grappled with the question for a lifetime and gave a stern answer in *The Brotbers Karamazov:* "In every man, a demon lies hidden—the demon of rage, the demon of lustful heat at the screams of the tortured victim, the demon of lawlessness let off the chain. . . ."[2] Who was right? Did humans get their demons after leaving nature, or have we inherited them from our ancient forest lives?

The last two decades allow, at last, a reasonably confident comparison of human and chimpanzee behavior. The first similarities we find in the social behavior of chimpanzees and humans are those attractive ones from the era of Louis Leakey. Wherever chimpanzees are studied they form long-lasting individual social relationships, based on exchanges of gestures and favors in remarkably human-like patterns.

But the dramatic discoveries, of course, of the last two decades, have been of the violence that occasionally erupts to destroy Ardrey's "arcadian existence of primal innocence." I'm sure most people here know of the gut-wrenching episodes of male raiding that culminated in at least ten lethal attacks at Gombe and the mortal elimination of seven males that had recently set themselves up as their own independent group. Much was horrifying about that so-called warfare. It involved males that knew each other well, associating as close companions before the split; victims were stalked and hunted like prey; the kills appeared the result of deliberate attempts to maim often with extreme cruelty, such as the tearing of skin up an arm, or the twisting of a limb to break it.

Does this mean chimpanzees are naturally violent? Ten years ago it wasn't clear. The warfare was in Gombe, where chimpanzees were fed bananas. Maybe other populations, unaffected by human provisioning, would be found to have escaped the horror of cooperative male violence? Alas, the evidence is mounting, and it all points the same way. Here from my study site in Kibale are the bones of the one of our chimpanzees killed by the neighboring group during a period of feeding competition . . . the first death known in an undisturbed population. In Mahale, border patrols, stalking, counter-chasing, and the extinction of the males of a community all suggest a comparable pattern of inter-group attacks. In Taï, reports of wounds from territorial encounters. In captivity, lethal gang attacks. In this cultural species, it may turn out that one of the least variable of all chimpanzee behaviors is the intense competition between males, the violent aggression they use against strangers, and their willingness to maim and kill those that frustrate their goals.

As the picture of chimpanzee society settles into focus, it now includes infanticide, rape, and regular battering of females by males. Some of these occur in other apes. If we leave Africa for a moment and go to Asia, we find that male orangutans rape regularly, so that perhaps half of their copulations involve force and patent resistance by the female. Orangutan rape has never been pho-

tographed in the wild, but something like it has been shown in captivity. And in the wild, adult male orangutans can't be together without violent aggression.

Back in Africa, the threat and practice of infanticide appears to lie at the heart of the mountain gorilla social system. Males fight violently for the control of groups, and can sometimes kill each other. The average female experiences infanticide at least once in her lifetime, and infanticide has been found responsible for 37 percent of infant deaths in these gentle giants. As in chimpanzees and orangutans, sexual coercion emerges readily in captivity. Males attack females, who copulate more willingly as a result.

There is a common theme to these relationships: male sexual aggression against females whose only defense is other males. The females of these species of ape live at risk of male brutality. The risk is not constant. For years on end a female gorilla may endure charmed days of relaxed relationships. But intermittent scenes of violence appear to pervade all their lives, so that all must be constantly on their guard.

What a change we see now from the 1968 view. Then, humans were an independent line, and the violence of our species represented novelty, perhaps arbitrary, perhaps random, perhaps a maladaptive trait, but at least without any evolutionary precedence.

Now, not merely do we see humans as descended from within the tightly related cluster of African apes, but the apes also show similar kinds of violence to ourselves. What makes this especially vivid is that these patterns of violence are generally uncommon in other primates and other animals. Deliberate raiding into neighbouring territories to ambush neighbors; sexual coercion, especially of females outside estrus . . . these are rare. The implication is that strong aspects of human violence have long evolutionary roots. "What are we?" In our aggressive urges we are not Gauguin's creatures of culture. We are apes of nature, cursed over 6 million years or more with a rare inheritance, a Dostoyevskyan demon.

It's a galling scenario. The implication is that for 6 million years or more, while we have been evolving from ape to australopithecine to human, through several foraging specializations, while abandoning the trees and committing ourselves to earth, while brains expanded and faces shrunk and hair became short and fine, while sexuality shifted from promiscuity towards bonding, throughout all this we clung to a suite of characters so rare that it's not confirmed in any other species, and so dangerous that it threatens the survival of our species. Through all these changes we retained intense rivalry between neighboring groups of males, lethal coalitionary behavior, and a systematic use of violent sexual coercion. On another day, we could discuss the reasons, which look consistent and visceral: unbalanced power corrupts and pays. There's much still waiting to be explained about the conditions that lead to male-bonding. But once male-bonding is present, lethal aggression follows easily. The coincidence of demonic aggression in ourselves and our closest kin bespeaks its antiquity.

If that's what we are, "Where *are* we going?" The big issue, in taking up the third question, is whether we can go beyond our past. Gauguin eventually did. His suicide failed: he threw up the arsenic. Eventually, he decided to send his picture to Paris, and it was his curiosity about the public response to it that dispelled his mood of morbid helplessness[3] and led to his painting a pastoral that was an optimistic counterpoint to the tragedy of his earlier fresco. The fourth ape gives us the equivalent to our Tahitian pastoral, our opportunity to be optimistic about controlling our natural demon.

Bonobos, as we saw, have apparently evolved from a chimpanzee ancestor. Yet, as we shall see, they have escaped the violence of chimpanzees. How has this happened?

Bonobos have been watched less than other apes, so generalizations are a little less secure. Still, from Kano's group in Wamba, the Stony Brook group in Lomako, and several studies in captivity, the overall pattern is clear. Bonobos have communities like chimpanzees, founded on a resident group of males and their sons. But the violence has died.

Male chimps commonly batter females. Male bonobos hardly ever attack females. And when they do, these occasional incidents suggest one main way that bonobos reduce male aggression. A female that is attacked screams, and what happens? Other females pour in on her side, and chase the offending male. Alliances among females keep males from getting out of hand. Kano saw them in Wamba. Amy Parish has been showing this very clearly in captivity, and just recently Barbara Fruth and Gottfried Hohmann have been seeing it in Lomako.

The extraordinary thing is that this doesn't happen in wild chimps. Why not? I mentioned that female chimps rarely travel together. So how can they help each other? But female bonobos are hardly ever apart: Small parties are made up of *females* with the occasional male, whereas small parties of chimps are *males* with the occasional female. Do female bonobos support each other simply because they can spend time together? Yes—just like chimps in captivity. They also have to trust each other. Female bonobos invest a lot of time in developing friendly relationships with each other, using the most exotic means. If they're going to spend a lot of time together, supportive relationships are invaluable.

Bonobos have much else to recommend them, such as their famous sexual gymnastics, but I want to focus just on this use of alliances among females to deter male aggression. What does it do for the species? It means that sexual coercion doesn't pay. So males compete for mates not by being brutal, but by being socially attractive. This, I believe, lies at the heart of the bonobo

changes from chimpanzees. Bonobos are neotenous, retaining a suite of juvenile characters into adulthood. They are slender, and their vocal repertoire is full of high-pitched, submissive-sounding calls. They have become sexy, friendly, mild. If only males assisted in parenting, they'd be a feminist's dream.

How did this change come about? The critical change, I believe, was the evolution of grouping patterns. Chimpanzee females travel together when fruits are abundant, but when fruits are scarce they split up. That clearly suggests they travel alone to feed well. But bonobo females travel together all the time. Is there something different about the foods of bonobos?

Several years ago a number of us suggested that the key difference was that bonobos eat more piths from the forest floor. Pith-eating is a good thing if you can do it. The piths of forest herbs, like sugar-cane, provide good alternatives to fruits. And there's often a lot of it, so there's no need for foraging parties to break up if they can find a field of piths. Gorillas eat a lot of piths. It's the fields of pith that appear to allow the groups of lowland gorillas to forage together as a group.

But do bonobos eat more piths? Recently Richard Malenky and I compared pith densities and the amount of pith taken by bonobos in Lomako and chimpanzees in Zaire. We found that bonobos passed much more pith than the chimps did over the year. They were consistently more focussed on the pith fields than chimps were. So they seem to have a good back-up food when fruits are few—and one that allows groups to stay together.

Let me, then, imagine one way that bonobos evolved from their chimp ancestors. Genetic evidence dates the split at 2 to 3 mya ago. We know from Liz Vrba and others that around 2.5 mya there was a major drying event. I suggest that south of the Zaïre River, gorillas and chimps, or ancestors very like them, lived together as they do now to the north of the river. Then the drying event, and what happened? Only chimps survived. As we see today, in the more seasonal areas north of the Zaïre River, gorillas give out and only chimps remain.

Then the moistness returned, and with it, the piths that gorillas like to eat, as recent studies have been finding in Gabon. But there were no gorillas. So the chimps expanded to occupy the empty niche, including gorilla-foods—in other words, the piths—alongside their previous chimp-foods—that is, the tree-fruits. And as they adapted to the new combination of gorilla foods and chimp foods, they changed. They were rarely forced to travel alone. Females lived together. They developed supportive relationships. They attacked aggressive males. Aggressive males were failures as mates. Males were juvenilized.

The details of the process can barely be guessed at the moment. Certainly, a major role was played by the prolonged sexuality of bonobos, maybe involving concealed ovulation. But the principle will surely remain that bonobos evolved from changed circumstance; and the way it happened was for a change in the environment to allow a political change. Bonobos weren't constrained by their chimpanzee past to keep their legacy of male violence. Social strategies have different pay-offs in different contexts. They can be easily changed when the contexts change. And a remarkable feature of the alliances among bonobo females is that they are developed among strangers. In other animals, alliances are linked to kinship. In bonobos, alliances are produced from recognition of common interest, a recognition that takes brains. The development of big brains and advanced cognition has brought with it the ability to escape from the constraints of biology, even in a species with little self-consciousness. Gauguin thought us tragic: the very skills that make us human, our intellect and emotions, also bring demons. But that romantic view is wrong, almost the reverse of history as we can see it now. Our demons come from our ape past, and we need our intellect and emotions to forge the alliances that can defeat the beast. It's common sense, supported by the evidence.

What does it do for us, then, to know the behavior of our closest relatives? Chimpanzees and bonobos are an extraordinary pair. One, I suggest, shows us some of the worst aspects of our past and our present; the other shows an escape from it. In thinking creatively about our future, I hope we honor our sister species, who by being different from ourselves, emphasize the unity of our humanity.

Let me return to the extraordinary achievements of the Leakey Foundation. In this talk I've referred to perhaps twenty field studies. All have input from the Leakey Foundation. I should be referring to each by name, and honoring the individual scientists that make a broad review possible. But let me honor, instead, the trustees and supporters of the Leakey Foundation, who have put their time, their money, and their spirit into helping us all.

In a mere quarter-century, this imaginative group has presided over the golden age of biological anthropology, stimulated a range of exciting discoveries, brought academics face to face with the public that supports them, and incidentally greatly benefited primate conservation efforts.

The knowledge so gained should help us, though some fear it. For Gauguin, "primitive" was good. Those who ate from the tree of knowledge suffered. For others today, "biology" (the primitive) is fearful. Many people reject the idea that we still follow rules that we can trace to the Pilocene. So we can pretend it's not true, but much good that may do us. Denial of our demons won't make them go away. But even if we're driven to accepting the evidence of a grisly past, we're not forced into thinking it condemns us to an unchanged future. There are many challenges.

For primatologists: to understand more precisely the conditions that favor male aggression, and the conditions that suppress it. Are there populations of chimpanzees that have evolved beyond violence? Are there bonobos that are violent like chimpanzees? We can ex-

pect some such local adaptations to special conditions—can we use them to explain the ill effects of testosterone poisoning in our own ape lineage?

For psychologists: What has the long legacy of aggression done to our psyche? Has it made men specially vulnerable to deindividuation—that mindless loss of self, and acceptance of gang wisdom; . . . or to dehumanization—the cruel emotional deafness to the cries of outsiders? If it prepared us for a career of obedience to authority, of heroism and impulsivity, of quick acceptance of group norms, how can our understanding of history create an enlightened world? The human future may depend on taming the demonic male. It may involve the growing political power of women. But it will not happen in quite the bonobo way. We must look to nature not to copy but to learn.

It may be tempting to condemn the aggressive apes and overly praise the bonobo. But of course apes are not humans, even though humans may be apes. Their failure to conform to a human morality is their problem, not ours, and they deserve sympathy, respect, and admiration, not disdain. Apes provide us both with a story of our ancestry and a glimpse of a better future. So let us celebrate their lives as instructive visions of other worlds. We still know little, but every population of apes teaches something new. Of course, those populations are disappearing fast. Even the vast forests of Zaïre, uncut though they may be, are being attacked: this year, when I was in Wamba, all mammals but the tabooed bonobo were gone; and the local population had already started killing and eating the bonobos. The same problems are everywhere. We have only a few decades to recover the extraordinary evidence waiting elusively in a hundred forests still unvisited by scientists. Future generations will think ill of us for letting them slide unknown into oblivion. But if we *can* get the observers into the field, and watch the apes in nature, we will surely continue to learn and to be inspired. In that way, the next version of this lecture (in 25 years' time) won't have to be retitled "Ape Links . . . and Missing Cultures"!

So ladies and gentlemen, for our sakes and theirs, the apes need all the support they can get. I ask you therefore to raise your glasses, or suck your tablecloths, in celebration of all that's been done, and will be done, by Gordon Getty and the Leakey Foundation!

ENDNOTES

1. Adapted from R. Ardrey (1967). *The Territorial Imperative*, p. 232, Fontana.

2. Dostoyevsky, Fyodor (1880). *The Brothers Karamazov.* Translated by Constance Garnett. Random House, New York (1950). Part I, Book V, Chapter IV: "Rebellion" (pp. 282–292), p. 287.

3. Thomson, B. (1987). *Gauguin.* London: Thames and Hudson.

# Chapter 19

# *Bonobo Sex and Society*

## Frans B. M. de Waal

*The behavior of a close relative challenges assumptions about male supremacy in human evolution.*

At a juncture in history during which women are seeking equality with men, science arrives with a belated gift to the feminist movement. Male-biased evolutionary scenarios—Man the Hunter, Man the Toolmaker, and so on—are being challenged by the discovery that females play a central, perhaps even dominant, role in the social life of one of our nearest relatives. In the past few years many strands of knowledge have come together concerning a relatively unknown ape with an unorthodox repertoire of behavior: the bonobo.

The bonobo is one of the last large mammals to be found by science. The creature was discovered in 1929 in a Belgian colonial museum, far from its lush African habitat. A German anatomist, Ernst Schwarz, was scrutinizing a skull that had been ascribed to a juvenile chimpanzee because of its small size, when he realized that it belonged to an adult. Schwarz declared that he had stumbled on a new subspecies of chimpanzee. But soon the animal was assigned the status of an entirely distinct species within the same genus as the chimpanzee, *Pan*.

The bonobo was officially classified as *Pan paniscus*, or the diminutive *Pan*. But I believe a different label might have been selected had the discoverers known then what we know now. The old taxonomic name of the chimpanzee, *P. satyrs*—which refers to the myth of apes as lustful satyrs—would have been perfect for the bonobo.

The species is best characterized as female-centered and egalitarian and as one that substitutes sex for aggression. Whereas in most other species sexual behavior is a fairly distinct category, in the bonobo it is part

and parcel of social relations—and not just between males and females. Bonobos engage in sex in virtually every partner combination (although such contact among close family members may be suppressed). And sexual interactions occur more often among bonobos than among other primates. Despite the frequency of sex, the bonobo's rate of reproduction in the wild is about the same as that of the chimpanzee. A female gives birth to a single infant at intervals of between five and six years. So bonobos share at least one very important characteristic with our own species, namely, a partial separation between sex and reproduction.

## A Near Relative

This finding commands attention because the bonobo shares more than 98 percent of our genetic profile, making it as close to a human as, say, a fox is to a dog. The split between the human line of ancestry and the line of the chimpanzee and the bonobo is believed to have occurred a mere 8 million years ago (Figure 19–1). The subsequent divergence of the chimpanzee and the bonobo lines came much later, perhaps prompted by the chimpanzee's need to adapt to relatively open dry habitats [see "East Side Story: The Origin of Humankind," by Yves Coppens; *Scientific American*, May 1994].

In contrast, bonobos probably never left the protection of the trees. Their present range lies in humid forests south of the Zaire River, where perhaps fewer than 10,000 bonobos survive. (Given the species' slow rate of reproduction, the rapid destruction of its tropical habitat, and the political instability of central Africa, there is reason for much concern about its future.)

From *Scientific American*, Vol. 272, No. 3, March 1995. Reprinted with permission. Copyright © 1995 by *Scientific American, Inc.* All rights reserved.

If this evolutionary scenario of ecological continuity is true, the bonobo may have undergone less transformation than either humans or chimpanzees. It could most closely resemble the common ancestor of all three modern species. Indeed, in the 1930s Harold J. Coolidge—the American anatomist who gave the bonobo its eventual taxonomic status—suggested that the animal might be most similar to the primogenitor, since its anatomy is less specialized than is the chimpanzee's. Bonobo body proportions have been compared with those of the australopithecines, a form of prehuman. When the apes stand or walk upright, they look as if they stepped straight out of an artist's impression of early hominids.

Not too long ago the savanna baboon was regarded as the best living model of the human ancestor. That primate is adapted to the kinds of ecological conditions that prehumans may have faced after descending from the trees. But in the late 1970s, chimpanzees, which are much more closely related to humans, became the model of choice. Traits that are observed in chimpanzees—including cooperative hunting, food sharing, tool use, power politics, and primitive warfare—were absent or not as developed in baboons. In the laboratory the apes have been able to learn sign language and to recognize themselves in a mirror, a sign of self-awareness not yet demonstrated in monkeys.

Although selecting the chimpanzee as the touchstone of hominid evolution represented a great improvement, at least one aspect of the former model did not need to be revised: Male superiority remained the natural state of affairs. In both baboons and chimpanzees, males are conspicuously dominant over females; they reign supremely and often brutally. It is highly unusual for a fully grown male chimpanzee to be dominated by any female.

Enter the bonobo. Despite their common name—the pygmy chimpanzee—bonobos cannot be distinguished from the chimpanzee by size. Adult males of the smallest subspecies of chimpanzee weigh some 43 kilograms (95 pounds) and females 33 kilograms (73 pounds), about the same as bonobos. Although female bonobos are much smaller than the males, they seem to rule.

## GRACEFUL APES

In physique, a bonobo is as different from a chimpanzee as a Concorde is from a Boeing 747. I do not wish to offend any chimpanzees, but bonobos have more style. The bonobo, with its long legs and small head atop narrow shoulders, has a more gracile build than does a chimpanzee. Bonobo lips are reddish in a black face, the ears small and the nostrils almost as wide as a gorilla's. These primates also have a flatter, more open face with a higher forehead than the chimpanzee's and—to top it all off—an attractive coiffure with long, fine, black hair neatly parted in the middle.

Like chimpanzees, female bonobos nurse and carry around their young for up to five years. By the age of 7 the offspring reach adolescence. Wild females give birth for the first time at 13 or 14 years of age, becoming full grown by about 15. A bonobo's longevity is unknown, but judging by the chimpanzee it may be older than 40 in the wild and close to 60 in captivity.

Fruit is central to the diets of both wild bonobos and chimpanzees. The former supplement with more pith from herbaceous plants, and the latter add meat. Although bonobos do eat invertebrates and occasionally capture and eat small vertebrates, including mammals, their diet seems to contain relatively little animal protein. Unlike chimpanzees, they have not been observed to hunt monkeys.

Whereas chimpanzees use a rich array of strategies to obtain foods—from cracking nuts with stone tools to fishing for ants and termites with sticks—tool use in wild bonobos seems undeveloped. (Captive bonobos use tools skillfully.) Apparently as intelligent as chimpanzees, bonobos have, however, a far more sensitive temperament. During World War II bombing of Hellabrun, Germany, the bonobos in a nearby zoo all died of fright from the noise; the chimpanzees were unaffected.

Bonobos are also imaginative in play. I have watched captive bonobos engage in "blindman's buff." A bonobo covers her eyes with a banana leaf or an arm or by sticking two fingers in her eyes. Thus handicapped, she stumbles around on a climbing frame, bumping into others or almost falling. She seems to be imposing a rule on herself: "I cannot look until I lose my balance." Other apes and monkeys also indulge in this game, but I have never seen it performed with such dedication and concentration as by bonobos.

Juvenile bonobos are incurably playful and like to make funny faces, sometimes in long solitary pantomimes and at other times while tickling one another. Bonobos are, however, more controlled in expressing their emotions—whether it be joy, sorrow, excitement, or anger—than are the extroverted chimpanzees. Male chimpanzees often engage in spectacular charging displays in which they show off their strength, throwing rocks, breaking branches, and uprooting small trees in the process. They keep up these noisy performances for many minutes, during which most other members of the group wisely stay out of their way. Male bonobos, on the other hand, usually limit displays to a brief run while dragging a few branches behind them.

Both primates signal emotions and intentions through facial expressions and hand gestures, many of which are also present in the nonverbal communication of humans. For example, bonobos will beg by stretching out an open hand (or, sometimes, a foot) to a possessor of food and will pout their lips and make whimpering sounds if the effort is unsuccessful. But bonobos make different sounds than chimpanzees do. The renowned low-pitched, extended "huuu-huuu" pant-hooting of the latter contrasts with the rather sharp, high-pitched barking sounds of the bonobo.

## LOVE, NOT WAR

My own interest in bonobos came not from an inherent fascination with their charms but from research on aggressive behavior in primates. I was particularly intrigued with the aftermath of conflict. After two chimpanzees have fought, for instance, they may come together for a hug and mouth-to-mouth kiss. Assuming that such reunions serve to restore peace and harmony, I labeled them reconciliations.

Any species that combines close bonds with a potential for conflict needs such conciliatory mechanisms. Thinking how much faster marriages would break up if people had no way of compensating for hurting each other, I set out to investigate such mechanisms in several primates, including bonobos. Although I expected to see peacemaking in these apes, too, I was little prepared for the form it would take.

For my study, which began in 1983, I chose the San Diego Zoo. At the time, it housed the world's largest captive bonobo colony—ten members divided into three groups. I spent entire days in front of the enclosure with a video camera, which was switched on at feeding time. As soon as a caretaker approached the enclosure with food, the males would develop erections. Even before the food was thrown into the area, the bonobos would be inviting each other for sex: males would invite females, and females would invite males and other females.

Sex, it turned out, is the key to the social life of the bonobo. The first suggestion that the sexual behavior of bonobos is different had come from observations at European zoos. Wrapping their findings in Latin, primatologists Eduard Tratz and Heinz Heck reported in 1954 that the chimpanzees at Hellabrun mated *more canum* (like dogs) and bonobos *more hominum* (like people). In those days, face-to-face copulation was considered uniquely human, a cultural innovation that needed to be taught to preliterate people (hence the term "missionary position"). These early studies, written in German, were ignored by the international scientific establishment. The bonobo's humanlike sexuality needed to be rediscovered in the 1970s before it became accepted as characteristic of the species.

Bonobos become sexually aroused remarkably easily, and they express this excitement in a variety of mounting positions and genital contacts. Although chimpanzees virtually never adopt face-to-face positions, bonobos do so in one out of three copulations in the wild. Furthermore, the frontal orientation of the bonobo vulva and clitoris strongly suggest that the female genitalia are adapted for this position.

Another similarity with humans is increased female sexual receptivity. The tumescent phase of the female's genitals, resulting in a pink swelling that signals willingness to mate, covers a much longer part of estrus in bonobos than in chimpanzees. Instead of a few days out of her cycle, the female bonobo is almost continuously sexually attractive and active [see Figure 19–3].

Perhaps the bonobo's most typical sexual pattern undocumented in any other primate, is genito-genital rubbing (or GG rubbing) between adult females. One female facing another clings with arms and legs to a partner that, standing on both hands and feet, lifts her off the

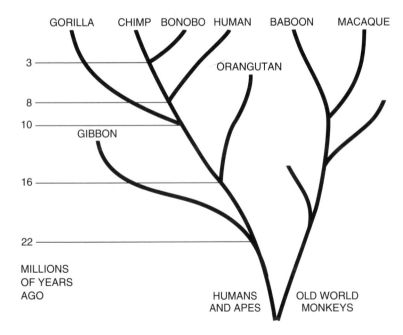

**Figure 19–1** Evolutionary tree of primates, based on DNA analysis, shows that humans diverged from bonobos and chimpanzees a mere eight million years ago. The three species share more than 98 percent of their genetic makeup.

BONOBO

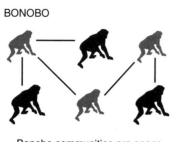

Bonobo communities are peace-loving and generally egalitarian. The strongest social bonds are those among females (gray), although females also bond with males. The status of a male (black) depends on the position of his mother, to whom he remains closely bonded for her entire life.

CHIMPANZEE

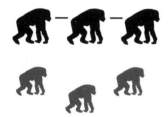

In chimpanzee groups the strongest bonds are established between the males in order to hunt and to protect their shared territory. The females live in overlapping home ranges within this territory but are not strongly bonded to other females or to any one male.

GIBBON

Gibbons establish monogamous, egalitarian relations, and one couple will maintain a territory to the exclusion of other pairs.

HUMAN

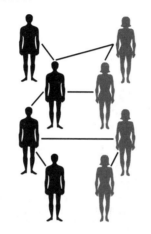

Human society is the most diverse among the primates. Males unite for cooperative ventures, whereas females also bond with those of their own sex. Monogamy, polygamy and polyandry are all in evidence.

GORILLA

The social organization of gorillas provides a clear example of polygamy. Usually a single male maintains a range for his family unit, which contains several females. The strongest bonds are those between the male and his females.

ORANGUTAN

Orangutans live solitary lives with little bonding in evidence. Male orangutans are intolerant of one another. In his prime, a single male establishes a large territory, within which live several females. Each female has her own, separate home range.

**Figure 19–2**   Social Organization among Various Primates

ground. The two females then rub their genital swellings laterally together emitting grins and squeals that probably reflect orgasmic experiences. (Laboratory experiments on stump-tailed macaques have demonstrated that women are not the only female primates capable of physiological orgasm.)

Male bonobos, too, may engage in pseudocopulation but generally perform a variation. Standing back to back one male briefly rubs his scrotum against the buttocks of another. They also practice so-called penis-fencing, in which two males hang face to face from a branch while rubbing their erect penises together.

The diversity of erotic contacts in bonobos includes sporadic oral sex, massage of another individual's genitals and intense tongue-kissing. Lest this leave the impression of a pathologically oversexed species, I must add, based on hundreds of hours of watching bonobos, that their sexual activity is rather casual and relaxed. It

appears to be a completely natural part of their group life. Like people, bonobos engage in sex only occasionally, not continuously. Furthermore, with the average copulation lasting 13 seconds, sexual contact in bonobos is rather quick by human standards.

That sex is connected to feeding, and even appears to make food sharing possible, has been observed not only in zoos but also in the wild. Nancy Thompson-Handler, then at the State University of New York at Stony Brook, saw bonobos in Zaïre's Lomako Forest engage in sex after they had entered trees loaded with ripe figs or when one among them had captured a prey animal, such as a small forest duiker. The flurry of sex contacts would last for five to 10 minutes, after which the apes would settle down to consume the food.

One explanation for the sexual activity at feeding time could be that excitement over food translates into sexual arousal. This idea may be partly true. Yet another

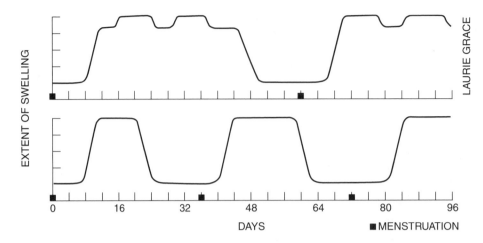

**Figure 19–3** Female receptivity for sex, manifested by swollen genitals, occupies a much larger proportion of the estrus cycle of bonobos *(top)* than of chimpanzees *(bottom).* The receptivity of bonobos continues through lactation. (In chimpanzees, it disappears.) This circumstance allows sex to play a large part in the social relations of bonobos. Adapted from a graph provided by Jeremy Dahl of the Yerkes Primate Center.

motivation is probably the real cause: competition. There are two reasons to believe sexual activity is the bonobo's answer to avoiding conflict.

First, anything, not just food, that arouses the interest of more than one bonobo at a time tends to result in sexual contact. If two bonobos approach a cardboard box thrown into their enclosure, they will briefly mount each other before playing with the box. Such situations lead to squabbles in most other species. But bonobos are quite tolerant, perhaps because they use sex to divert attention and to diffuse tension.

Second, bonobo sex often occurs in aggressive contexts totally unrelated to food. A jealous male might chase another away from a female, after which the two males reunite and engage in scrotal rubbing. Or after a female hits a juvenile, the latter's mother may lunge at the aggressor, an action that is immediately followed by genital rubbing between the two adults.

I once observed a young male, Kako, inadvertently blocking an older, female juvenile, Leslie, from moving along a branch. First, Leslie pushed him; Kako, who was not very confident in trees, tightened his grip, grinning nervously. Next, Leslie gnawed on one of his hands, presumably to loosen his grasp. Kako uttered a sharp peep and stayed put. Then Leslie rubbed her vulva against his shoulder. This gesture calmed Kako, and he moved along the branch. It seemed that Leslie had been very close to using force but instead had reassured both herself and Kako with sexual contact.

During reconciliations, bonobos use the same sexual repertoire as they do during feeding time. Based on an analysis of many such incidents, my study yielded the first solid evidence for sexual behavior as a mechanism to overcome aggression. Not that this function is absent in other animals—or in humans, for that matter—but the art of sexual reconciliation may well have reached its

evolutionary peak in the bonobo. For these animals, sexual behavior is indistinguishable from social behavior. Given its peacemaking and appeasement functions, it is not surprising that sex among bonobos occurs in so many different partner combinations, including between juveniles and adults. The need for peaceful coexistence is obviously not restricted to adult heterosexual pairs.

## FEMALE ALLIANCE

Apart from maintaining harmony, sex is also involved in creating the singular social structure of the bonobo (Figure 19–2). This use of sex becomes clear when studying bonobos in the wild. Field research on bonobos started only in the mid-1970s, more than a decade after the most important studies on wild chimpanzees had been initiated. In terms of continuity and invested (wo)manpower, the chimpanzee projects of Jane Goodall and Toshisada Nishida, both in Tanzania, are unparalleled. But bonobo research by Takayoshi Kano and others of Kyoto University is now two decades under way at Wamba in Zaïre and is beginning to show the same payoffs.

Both bonobos and chimpanzees live in so-called fission-fusion societies. The apes move alone or in small parties of a few individuals at a time, the composition of which changes constantly. Several bonobos traveling together in the morning might meet another group in the forest, whereupon one individual from the first group wanders off with others from the second group, while those left behind forage together. All associations, except the one between mother and dependent offspring, are of a temporary character.

Initially, this flexibility baffled investigators, making them wonder if these apes formed any social groups with stable membership. After years of documenting the travels of chimpanzees in the Mahale Mountains, Nishida first reported that they form large communities: All members of one community mix freely in ever-changing parties, but members of different communities never gather. Later, Goodall added territoriality to this picture. That is, not only do communities not mix, but mates of different chimpanzee communities engage in lethal battles.

In both bonobos and chimpanzees, males stay in their natal group, whereas females tend to migrate during adolescence. As a result, the senior males of a chimpanzee or bonobo group have known all junior males since birth and all junior males have grown up together. Females, on the other hand, transfer to an unfamiliar and often hostile group where they may know no one. A chief difference between chimpanzee and bonobo societies is the way in which young females integrate into their new community.

On arrival in another community, young bonobo females at Wamba single out one or two senior resident females for special attention using frequent GG rubbing and grooming to establish a relationship. If the residents reciprocate, close associations are set up, and the younger female gradually becomes accepted into the group. After producing her first offspring, the young female's position becomes more stable and central. Eventually the cycle repeats with younger immigrants, in turn, seeking a good relation with the now established female. Sex thus smooths the migrant's entrance into the community of females, which is much more close-knit in the bonobo than in the chimpanzee.

Bonobo males remain attached to their mothers all their lives, following them through the forest and being dependent on them for protection in aggressive encounters with other males. As a result, the highest-ranking males of a bonobo community tend to be sons of important females.

What a contrast with chimpanzees! Male chimpanzees fight their own battles, often relying on the support of other males. Furthermore, adult male chimpanzees travel together in same-sex parties, grooming each other frequently. Males form a distinct social hierarchy with high levels of both competition and association. Given the need to stick together against males of neighboring communities, their bonding is not surprising: Failure to form a united front might result in the loss of lives and territory. The danger of being male is reflected in the adult sex ratio of chimpanzee populations, with considerably fewer males than females.

Serious conflict between bonobo groups has been witnessed in the field, but it seems quite rare. On the contrary, reports exist of peaceable mingling, including mutual sex and grooming, between what appear to be different communities. If intergroup combat is indeed unusual, it may explain the lower rate of all-male associations. Rather than being male-bonded, bonobo society gives the impression of being female-bonded, with even

adult males relying on their mothers instead of on other males. No wonder Kano calls mothers the "core" of bonobo society.

The bonding among female bonobos violates a fairly general rule, outlined by Harvard University anthropologist Richard W. Wrangham, that the sex that stays in the natal group develops the strongest mutual bonds. Bonding among male chimpanzees follows naturally because they remain in the community of their birth. The same is true for female kinship bonding in Old World monkeys, such as macaques and baboons, where males are the migratory sex.

Bonobos are unique in that the migratory sex, females, strongly bond with same-sex strangers later in life. In setting up an artificial sisterhood, bonobos can be said to be secondarily bonded. (Kinship bonds are said to be primary.) Although we now know *how* this happens—through the use of sexual contact and grooming—we do not yet know *why* bonobos and chimpanzees differ in this respect. The answer may lie in the different ecological environments of bonobos and chimpanzees—such as the abundance and quality of food in the forest. But it uncertain if such explanations will suffice.

Bonobo society is, however, not only female-centered but also appears to be female-dominated. Bonobo specialists, while long suspecting such a reality, have been reluctant to make the controversial claim. But in 1992, at the 14th Congress of the International Primatological Society in Strasbourg, investigators of both captive and wild bonobos presented data that left little doubt about the issue.

Amy R. Parish of the University of California at Davis reported on food competition in identical groups (one adult male and two adult females) of chimpanzees and bonobos at the Stuttgart Zoo. Honey was provided in a "termite hill" from which it could be extracted by dipping sticks into a small hole. As soon as honey was made available, the male chimpanzee would make a charging display through the enclosure and claim everything for himself. Only when his appetite was satisfied would he let the females fish for honey.

In the bonobo group, it was the females that approached the honey first. After having engaged in some GG rubbing, they would feed together, taking turns with virtually no competition between them. The male might make as many charging displays as he wanted; the females were not intimidated and ignored the commotion.

Observers at the Belgian animal park of Planckendael, which currently has the most naturalistic bonobo colony, reported similar findings. If a male bonobo tried to harass a female, all females would band together to chase him off. Because females appeared more successful in dominating males when they were together than on their own, their close association and frequent genital rubbing may represent an alliance. Females may bond so as to outcompete members of the individually stronger sex.

The fact that they manage to do so not only in captivity is evident from zoologist Takeshi Furuichi's summary of the relation between the sexes at Wamba, where bonobos are enticed out of the forest with sugarcane. "Males usually appeared at the feeding site first, but they surrendered preferred positions when the females appeared. It seemed that males appeared first not because they were dominant, but because they had to feed before the arrival of females," Furuichi reported at Strasbourg.

## SEX FOR FOOD

Occasionally, the role of sex in relation to food is taken one step further, bringing bonobos very close to humans in their behavior. It has been speculated by anthropologists—including C. Owen Lovejoy of Kent State University and Helen Fisher of Rutgers University—that sex is partially separated from reproduction in our species because it serves to cement mutually profitable relationships between men and women. The human female's capacity to mate throughout her cycle and her strong sex drive allow her to exchange sex for male commitment and paternal care, thus giving rise to the nuclear family.

This arrangement is thought to be favored by natural selection because it allows women to raise more offspring than they could if they were on their own. Although bonobos clearly do not establish the exclusive heterosexual bonds characteristic of our species, their behavior does fit important elements of this model. A female bonobo shows extended receptivity and uses sex to obtain a male's favors when—usually because of youth—she is too low in social status to dominate him.

At the San Diego Zoo, I observed that if Loretta was in a sexually attractive state, she would not hesitate to approach the adult male, Vernon, if he had food. Presenting herself to Vernon, she would mate with him and make high-pitched food calls while taking over his entire bundle of branches and leaves. When Loretta had no genital swelling, she would wait until Vernon was ready to share. Primatologist Suehisa Kuroda reports similar exchanges at Wamba: "A young female approached a male, who was eating sugarcane. They copulated in short order, whereupon she took one of the two canes held by him and left."

Despite such quid pro quo between the sexes, there are no indications that bonobos form humanlike nuclear families. The burden of raising offspring appears to rest entirely on the female's shoulders. In fact, nuclear families are probably incompatible with the diverse use of sex found in bonobos. If our ancestors started out with a sex life similar to that of bonobos, the evolution of the family would have required dramatic change.

Human family life implies paternal investment, which is unlikely to develop unless males can be reasonably certain that they are caring for their own, not someone else's, offspring. Bonobo society lacks any such guarantee but humans protect the integrity of their family units through all kinds of moral restrictions and taboos. Thus, although our species is characterized by an extraordinary interest in sex, there are no societies in which people engage in it at the drop of a hat (or a cardboard box, as the case may be). A sense of shame and a desire for domestic privacy are typical human concepts related to the evolution and cultural bolstering of the family.

Yet no degree of moralizing can make sex disappear from every realm of human life that does not relate to the nuclear family. The bonobo's behavioral peculiarities may help us understand the role of sex and may have serious implications for models of human society.

Just imagine that we had never heard of chimpanzees or baboons and had known bonobos first. We would at present most likely believe that early hominids lived in female-centered societies, in which sex served important social functions and in which warfare was rare or absent. In the end, perhaps the most successful reconstruction of our past will be based not on chimpanzees or even on bonobos but on a three-way comparison of chimpanzees, bonobos, and humans.

## FURTHER READINGS

de Waal, F. B. M. (September 1988) "The communicative repertoire of captive bonobos *(Pan paniscus)* compared to that of chimpanzees." *Behaviour*, 106, (3–4), 183–251.

de Waal, F. B. M. (1989) *Peacemaking among Primates.* Cambridge, MA: Harvard University Press.

Heltne, P; Marquardt, L. A., Eds. (1989) *Understanding Chimpanzees.* Cambridge, MA: Harvard University Press.

Kano, T. (1992) *The Last Ape: Pygmy Chimpanzee Behavior and Ecology.* Stanford, CA: Stanford University Press.

Susman, R.L. Ed. (1984) *The Pymny Chimpanzee: Evolutionary Biology and Behavior.* New York: Plenum Press.

Wrangham, R.; McGrew, W.C.; de Waal, F. B. M.; Heltne, P. (1994) *Chimpanzee Cultures.* Cambridge, MA: Harvard University Press.

# Chapter 20

# *The Myth of Man the Hunter/Man the Killer and the Evolution of Human Morality*

Robert W. Sussman

## THE EARLIEST HOMINIDS AS HUNTERS

With the development of the theory of evolution, Darwin put humans in their place with the rest of the animal kingdom, subject to the same laws of nature. However, in so doing, even Darwin visualized a spiritual and intellectual gap between humans and their closest ancestors and relatives. As he stated: "There can be no doubt that the difference between the mind of the lowest man and that of the highest animal is immense" (Darwin 1874).

Late nineteenth century theorists took this gap to heart and looked for early human fossils that fit this expectation. Sir Arthur Keith (1949) went so far as to set up a brain volume threshold of 750 cc between man and the apes.

It is no wonder that the Piltdown Man, with its ape-like jaw and large cranium, was immediately accepted as the earliest hominid ancestor, while the small skulled, ape-like australopithecine discovered in 1924 by Raymond Dart was considered a pathological specimen or a mere ape. While Piltdown supporters were busy explaining the intellectual endowments of our large-brained ancestors, Dart was convinced his small-brained creature was the first ape-man, and he developed a theoretical picture of the behavior of this transitional form. At first, Dart (1926) believed that australopithecines were scavengers barely eking out an existence in the harsh savannah environment; a primate that did not live to kill large animals, but scavenged small animals in order to live.

Few cared what Dart believed, however, because few took his ape-man seriously. In fact, it was not until a quarter of a century later, with the unearthing of many more australopithecines and the discovery in 1953 that

Piltdown was a fraud, that students of human evolution realized our earliest ancestors indeed were more ape-like than they were like modern humans. This led to a great interest in using primates to understand human evolution and the evolutionary basis of human nature (Sussman in press). With these discoveries began a long list of theories attempting to recreate the behavior and often the basic morality of the earliest hominids.

By 1950, Dart developed a different view. Given the game animals with which they were associated and some dents and holes in the skulls of the australopithecines, Dart became convinced that the mammals had been killed, butchered, and eaten by the ape-men, and that these early hominids had even been killing one another. He stated:

> The ancestors of *Australopithecus* left their fellows in the trees of Central Africa through a spirit of adventure and the more attractive fleshy food that lay in the vast savannahs of the southern plains. (Dart and Craig 1959:195)

Rather than leaving the trees to search out a meager existence in the savannah, Dart now saw that hunting, and a carnivorous lust for blood, drew the man-apes out of the forest and was a main force in human evolution.

Dart's view of human evolution was not devoid of moral judgment. In fact, with their innovative subsistence pattern, Dart believed that the earliest hominids also created a new moral code. The hunting hypothesis, as it is referred to by Cartmill (1997:511) "was linked from the beginning with a bleak, pessimistic view of human beings and their ancestors as instinctively bloodthirsty and aggressive." Dart claimed the australopithecines were

> confirmed killers: carnivorous creatures that seized living quarries by violence, battered them to death, tore

This is a shortened version of a paper to appear in *Zygone, Journal of Religion & Science* (in press).

apart their broken bodies, (and) dismembered them limb from limb, greedily devouring livid writhing flesh.... The loathsome cruelty of mankind to man is explicable only in terms of man's carnivorous and cannibalistic origin.... this mark of Cain separates man dietetically from his anthropoidal relatives and allies him with the deadliest of carnivores. (1953:209)

Dart's vision of early human morality, however, is not new in Western myth, religion and philosophy. Cartmill (1993), in his recent book *A View to a Death in the Morning,* shows that it is reminiscent of the earlier Greek and Christian views of human morality. Dart himself began his 1953 paper with a quote from the seventeenth-century Calvinist divine Richard Baxter: "of all the beasts the man-beast is the worst, / to others and himself the cruellest foe." In 1773, James Burnet introduced the "Man the Hunter" theme, arguing "that when necessity forced man to hunt, the wild beast part of him became predominant, war succeeding hunting, and he became fiercer than any other animal—when not subdued by laws and manners" (quoted in Bock 1980:202). As Cartmill states, the early Christian philosophers believed that:

> We human beings are free ... to choose what is unnatural for us. It follows from this that only human beings have the capacity to be corrupted. Most ancient philosophers assumed that whatever is natural is good. Since animals always do what is natural for them but people do not, animals are better than people in this regard.... The idea that the other animals are by their nature better and saner than man is essentially a modern idea. It commingles classical animalitarianism with a distinctively Christian belief—the doctrine that in human beings nature herself has gone rotten. (1993:45)

This view of the depravity of human nature is related to the idea of man's fall from grace and of the Christian notion of original sin. As we shall see, these medieval myths still pervade many modern "scientific" interpretations of the evolution of human behavior and of human nature and morality.

Dart's evidence for Man the Hunter was not good and his particular vision of the human hunter/killer hypothesis did not have much staying power. Upon examination of the evidence, C. K. Brain (1981) noted that the bones associated with the man-apes were exactly like fragments left by leopards and hyenas. The round holes and dents in the fossil skulls matched perfectly with fangs of leopards and with impressions of rocks pressing against the buried fossils. It seems that the australopithecines were likely the hunted and not the hunters.

## MAN THE HUNTER OR MAN THE DANCER?

The next widely accepted version of this recurring Man the Hunter theme was presented in the late 1960s by Sherwood Washburn and his colleagues. They claimed that many of the features that define MEN as hunters again separated the earliest humans from their primate relatives.

> To assert the biological unity of mankind is to affirm the importance of the hunting way of life. It is to claim that, however much conditions and customs may have varied locally, the main selection pressures that forged the species were the same. The biology, psychology, and customs that separate us from the apes—all these we owe to the hunters of time past. And, for those who would understand the origin and nature of human behavior there is no choice but to try to understand "Man the Hunter." (Washburn and Lancaster 1968:303).

Like Dart, Washburn related human hunting to human morality, both of which had their biological basis in our evolutionary past.

> Man takes pleasure in hunting other animals. Unless careful training has hidden the natural drives, men enjoy the chase and the kill. In most cultures torture and suffering are made public spectacles for the enjoyment of all.... carnivorous curiosity and aggression have been added to the inquisitive and dominance striving of the ape. This carnivorous psychology may have had its beginnings in the depredations of the australopithecines. (Washburn and Avis 1958:433–434)

Again much like Dart before him, Washburn did not amass a large amount of evidence to support his theory. Rather, he relied upon a nineteenth century anthropological concept of cultural "survivals" (Tylor 1871); behaviors that are no longer useful in society but that persist and are pervasive are survivals from a time when they were adaptive.

> Men enjoy hunting and killing, and these activities are continued in sports even when they are no longer economically necessary. If a behavior is important to the survival of a species (as hunting was for man throughout most of human history), then it must be both easily learned and pleasurable. (Washburn and Lancaster 1968:299)

Using a similar logic, I have developed an alternative, but no less feasible, theory—Man the Dancer. After all, men *and* women love to dance, it is a behavior found in all cultures and has less obvious function in most cultures than does hunting.

Although it takes two to tango, a variety of forms of social systems could develop from various forms of dance: square dancing, line dancing, riverdance, or the funky chicken. The footsteps at Laetoli might not represent two individuals going out for a hunt, but the Afarensis shuffle, one of the earliest dances. In the movie 2001, it was wrong to depict the first tool as a weapon. It could easily have been a drumstick, and the first battle may not have involved killing at all but a battle of the bands. Other things such as face-to-face sex, cooperation, language and singing, and bipedalism (it's difficult to dance on all fours), even moving out of the trees and onto the ground might all be better explained by our propensity to dance than by our desire to hunt. Although I am being facetious, using the cultural survival approach, the evidence for dancing is certainly as good as that for hunting.

Between 1961 and 1976, the playwright Robert Ardrey popularized the then current version of the Man the Hunter/Man the Killer myth with a number of popular books. He believed that it was the competitive spirit, as acted out in warfare, that made humans what they are today ". . . the mentality of the single Germanic tribe under Hitler differed in no way from that of early man or late baboon"(Ardrey 1961:171). Because of a lack of a competitive, territorial instinct, Ardrey believed, gorillas had lost the will to live and with it the drive for sex. He argued that gorillas defend no territory and copulate rarely. And their story "will end, one day, not with a bang but with a whimper" (p. 325). To Ardrey, it is war and the instinct for territory that led to the great accomplishments of Western Man.

> How can we get along without war? It is the only question pertaining to the future that bears the faintest reality in our times; for if we fail to get along without war, then our future will be as remarkably lacking in human problems as it will be remarkably lacking in men. . . . Do you care about freedom? Dreams may have inspired it, and wishes promoted it, but only war and weapons have made it yours. (Ardrey 1961:324)

Although more spectacular than the claims of contemporary scientists, Ardrey's views of human nature did not differ greatly from them, nor from the ancient Christian beliefs of man's fall from grace and original sin. To Ardrey (1961), however, sin is good.

> We are Cain's children. The union of the enlarging brain and the carnivorous way produced man as a genetic possibility (315). . . . Man is a predator whose natural instinct is to kill with a weapon (316). . . . If man is unique, and his soul some special creation, and his future is to be determined by his innate goodness, nobility, and wisdom, then he is finished. But if man is not unique, and a proud creature bearing in his genes the scars of the ages, then man has a future beyond the stormiest contradiction (326).

## THE HUNTER MYTH AND SOCIOBIOLOGY

This might be considered the beginning of what has been called evolutionary ethics (Ruse 1994), which was developed with the next major scientific statement on the importance of hunting in the formulation of human nature. This theory was introduced in the mid 1970s by E. O. Wilson and the proponents of sociobiology. Wilson (1975) describes a number of behavioral traits that he

claims are found in humans generally and are genetically based human universals. These include: territoriality, aggressive dominance hierarchies, permanent male-female bonds, male dominance over females, extended maternal care, and matrilineality.

The argument Wilson uses to support his idea that these traits are biologically fixed, genetically based characteristics is their relative constancy among our primate relatives and their persistence throughout human evolution and in human societies, generally. Elsewhere, I have provided evidence that these behavioral characteristics are neither general primate traits nor human universals (Sussman 1995, reprinted in this volume). Again, these traits were believed to be a product of our hunting past.

> For at least a million years—probably more—Man engaged in a hunting-gathering way of life, giving up the practice a mere 10,000 years ago. We can be sure that our innate social responses have been fashioned largely through this lifestyle. (Wilson 1976; reprinted in Sussman 1997:65–66).

Social Darwinism proclaimed that human morality should be based on the evolutionary process of the survival of the fittest (Ruse and Wilson 1985). Individuals, ethnic groups, races, or societies that were most fit would survive and those that were weak would be eliminated, and this was good! Competition, especially winning in competition, was the basis of human ethics and morality. Herbert Spencer, the father of Social Darwinism, argued that we should cherish the evolutionary process so that the fittest would be able to survive and the inadequate would be rigorously eliminated. This, of course, is reminiscent of Ardrey's proclamations.

Sociobiologists do not find fault with the fact that Social Darwinists linked evolution to ethics but simply that, when this theory was popular, the mechanisms of evolution were poorly understood. As stated by Ruse and Wilson (1985:50): "Recent advances in evolutionary theory have cast a new light on the matter, giving substance to the dreams of the old theorists."

Given sociobiological tenets, the claim was that we now can proceed from "known facts," rather than mere theory, to ethics. These facts are basically: (1) The goal of living organisms is to pass on one's own genes at the expense of all others; (2) an organism should only cooperate with others if (a) they carry some of his or her own genes (kin selection), or (b) if at some later date the "others" might aid you (reciprocal altruism). However, since animals cannot make these calculations, evolution has endowed our genes with a moral ethic to reciprocate because, ultimately, this may help us perpetuate and multiply our own genes. As explained by Ruse and Wilson:

> It used to be thought, in the bad old days of Social Darwinism when evolution was poorly understood, that life

is an uninterrupted struggle—"nature red in tooth and claw." But this is only one side of natural selection, the same process also leads to altruism and reciprocity. Morality is merely an adaptation put in place to further our reproductive ends. . . . Ethical codes work because they drive us to go against our selfish day-to-day impulses in favor of long-term *group survival* . . . and thus, over our lifetimes, the multiplication of our genes many times. [emphasis mine] (1985:50–52)

Following this logic, evolutionary morality ultimately has allowed us to build group cohesion *in order to* successfully compete with strangers, and thus pass on our genes. We should not look down upon our warlike, cruel nature but rather understand that it has led to success, in an evolutionary sense, when coupled with "making nice" with some, but not with other individuals or groups of individuals. The "making nice" part is genetically driven and the basis of human morality. As Wilson (1975) states:

> Throughout recorded history the conduct of war has been common (572) . . . some of the "noblest" traits of mankind, including team play, altruism, patriotism, bravery on the field of battle, and so forth, are the genetic product of warfare (573) . . . If the planned society were to deliberately steer its members past those stresses and conflicts that once gave the destructive phenotypes their Darwinian edge, the other phenotypes might dwindle with them. In this, the ultimate genetic sense, social control would rob man of his humanity (575).

Or as more recently stated by Ruse:

> Where kin selection fails, reciprocal altruism provides a back-up. But as one grows more distant in one's social relationship, one would expect the feeling to decline . . . it is silly to pretend that our dealings across countries are going to be intimate or driven by much beyond self-interest. . . . Jesus did not suggest that the Samaritan was in the general business of charity to strangers. (1994:102)

This sounds very much like the claims of Dart and Ardrey, and the Social Darwinists before them. Furthermore, the scientific evidence for human universal traits or for the sociobiological tenets is just as weak as was the evidence provided by Ardrey and Dart to support their theories of human morality.

And how do these theories relate to the western European, Christian system and views of morality? Ruse explains:

> If you complain to me that this all starts to sound like warmed-over Christianity, I shall agree again, "Love your neighbor as yourself" sounds like a pretty good guide to life to me, and I gather it also does to many other people in non-Christian cultures. . . . a major reason why Christianity was such a raging success. (1994:100–101)

But we must always ask: Are the Christian morals professed generated by the scientific evidence for biologically based morality, or do we think they are biological universals *because* they happen to fit our own Christian ethics? Ruse (1995:106) states: "I am not much of a relativist. I condemn as strongly as anyone the rapes in Yugoslavia and the atrocities of Hitler . . ." But morality is usually in the eyes of the beholder, and I am sure that Ruse's code of ethics is not the same as that of the Yugoslavs and of Hitler's troops (mainly Christians) who committed these offenses.

## CHIMPANZEE AND HUMAN MALES AS DEMONIC KILLERS

The newest claim of the importance of killing and the biological basis of morality is that of Richard Wrangham and Dale Peterson in their new book, *Demonic Males*. They argue that, twenty to twenty five years ago, we thought human aggression was unique. Research on the great apes had revealed that they were basically unaggressive, gentle creatures and also that the separation of humans from our ape ancestors occurred 15 to 20 mya.

Although earlier theorists proposed that hunting, killing, and extreme aggressive behavior were biological traits inherited from our earliest hunting, hominid ancestors, many anthropologists still believed that patterns of aggression were environmentally and culturally determined, learned behaviors. Our sins were thought by most to be acquired and not inherited characteristics. They were not original (our sins, that is). Wrangham and Peterson argue that new evidence indicates that killer instincts are not unique to humans—we share this characteristic with our nearest relative, the common chimpanzee. In fact, it is this inherited propensity for killing that allows hominids and chimps to be such good hunters.

Wrangham's and Peterson's theory is as follows: The split between humans and common chimpanzees is much more recent than was once believed, only 6 to 8 mya. Furthermore, humans may have split from the chimpanzee-bonobo line after gorillas, with bonobos (or pygmy chimpanzees) separating from chimps only 2.5 mya. Because chimpanzees may be the common ancestor of all these forms, and because the earliest australopithecine was quite chimpanzee-like, Wrangham (in the previous article) speculates that: "The most reasonable view for the moment is that chimpanzees are a conservative species and an amazingly good model for the ancestor of hominids. . . . (and) If we know what our ancestor looked like, naturally we get clues about how it behaved . . . that is, like modern-day chimpanzees"(Wrangham 1995:5). Finally, if modern chimpanzees and modern humans share certain behavioral traits, these traits have "long evolutionary roots" and are likely to be fixed, biologically inherited components of our nature and not culturally determined.

Wrangham (1995:6) goes on by illustrating a number of traits shared by early hominids and chimpanzees, and states that this is a "strange paradox: a species trembling on the verge of hominization, but so conservative that it has stayed on that edge." Chimpanzees even have different "cultural" traditions in different populations. However, it is not these traits that are of the most interest, rather it is presumed shared patterns of aggression. Wrangham and Peterson (1996:24) claim that only two animal species, chimpanzees and humans, live in patrilineal, male-bonded communities "with intense, male-initiated territorial aggression, including lethal raiding into neighboring communities in search of vulnerable enemies to attack and kill." Wrangham asks:

> Does this mean chimpanzees are naturally violent? Ten years ago it wasn't clear . . . In this cultural species, it may turn out that one of the least variable of all chimpanzee behaviors is the intense competition between males, the violent aggression they use against strangers, and their willingness to maim and kill those that frustrate their goals. . . . As the picture of chimpanzee society settles into focus, it now includes infanticide, rape, and regular battering of females by males. (1995: 7)

Since humans and chimpanzees share these violent urges, Wrangham believes that we also share an inborn morality.

> The implication is that strong aspects of human violence have long evolutionary roots. "What are we?" In our aggressive urges we are not Gauguin's creatures of culture. We are apes of nature, cursed over six million years or more with a rare inheritance, a Dostoyevskyan demon . . . The coincidence of demonic aggression in ourselves and our closest kin bespeaks its antiquity. (Wrangham 1995:7)

Like Dart, Washburn, and Wilson before them, Wrangham and Peterson theorize that killing and violence are inherited from our ancient relatives. However, they argue this is not a trait unique to hominids nor is it a by-product of hunting. In fact, it is just this violent nature and a natural "blood lust" that makes both humans and chimpanzees such good hunters. Bonobos help Wrangham and Peterson come to this conclusion. Since, they claim, bonobos have lost the desire to kill, they also have lost the desire to hunt.

> . . . do bonobos tell us that the suppression of personal violence carried with it the suppression of predatory aggression? The strongest hypothesis at the moment is that bonobos came from a chimpanzee-like ancestor that hunted monkeys and hunted one another. As they evolved into bonobos, males lost their demonism, becoming less aggressive to each other. In so doing they lost their lust for hunting. . . . Murder and hunting may be more closely tied together than we are used to thinking. (Wrangham and Peterson 1996:219)

Wrangham believes that blood lust ties killing and hunting tightly together, but in his scenerio it is the desire to kill that drives the ability to hunt. Like other sociobiologists, Wrangham and Peterson believe this lust to kill is based upon the selfish gene. They argue:

> The new theory, elegantly popularized in Dawkins's *The Selfish Gene,* is now the conventional wisdom in biological science because it explains animal behavior so well. . . . the general principle that behavior evolves to serve selfish ends has been widely accepted; and the idea that humans might have been favored by natural selection to hate and to kill their enemies has become entirely, if tragically, reasonable. (Wrangham and Peterson 1996:23)

Of course, the selfish gene theory is also used to explain why bonobos don't kill their enemies. This level of generality has about the same explanatory power as that of the late eighteenth century biologist Jeremy Bentham's "moral philosophy," which claimed that human behavior is governed by pleasure and pain. Bentham believed that all behavior is dictated by seeking to enhance pleasure and to minimize the likelihood of pain. In fact, both of these philosophies attempt to explain everything and, therefore, explain very little. But that is for another essay.

## PROBLEMS WITH THESE THEORIES

As with many of the new sociobiological theories, I find problems with both the theory itself and with the evidence used to support it. According to Wrangham and Peterson, humans and chimpanzees might share biologically fixed behaviors because: (1) They are more closely related to each other than chimpanzees are to gorillas, and (2) chimps are a good model for our earliest ancestor and retain conservative traits shared by both. The first of these statements is still hotly debated because the chimps, gorillas, and humans are so close that it is difficult to tell exact divergence times or patterns between the three (Marks et al. 1988, Marks 1991, Templeton personal communication 1997).

The second statement is just not true. Chimpanzees have been evolving for as long as humans and gorillas, and there is no reason to believe that ancestral chimps were similar to present-day chimps. The fossil evidence is extremely sparse, and it is likely that many forms of apes have become extinct. Furthermore, even if chimpanzees were a good model for the ancestral hominoid and a conservative representative of this phylogenetic group, this would not mean that humans would necessarily share specific behavioral traits. As Wrangham and Peterson emphasize, chimps, gorillas, and bonobos are all very different from one another in their behavior and in their willingness to kill conspecifics. Because of these differences, in fact, Wrangham and Peterson agree that evolutionary inertia alone cannot explain behavioral similarities or differences.

Thus, the proof of Wrangham's and Peterson's theory does not rest on theoretical grounds but relies solely on the evidence that violence and killing in chimpanzees and in humans are behaviors that are similar in pattern, have ancient shared evolutionary roots, and are inherited.

Wrangham and Peterson (1996:68) state: "That chimpanzees and humans kill members of neighboring groups of their own species is . . . a startling exception to the normal rule for animals." They go on to point out that this is especially true of adults killing adults. "Fighting adults of almost all species normally stop at winning: They don't go on to kill" (p. 155). However, as Wrangham points out, there are exceptions, such as lions, wolves, spotted hyenas, and, I would add, a number of other predators. In fact, most species do not have the weapons to kill one another as adults. Agonism between adults of many species is common in various circumstances (see Small 1997), but certainly it would take two adult squirrels, rabbits, or aardvarks much more energy than it is worth to kill their opponent than to drive it away. They just don't have the tools. Chimpanzees and humans do, although the tools they use are radically different.

## CHIMPANZEE AGGRESSION

Just *how common* is conspecific killing in chimpanzees? This is where the real controversy may lie. During the first fourteen years of study at Gombe (1960–1974), chimpanzees were described as a peaceful, unaggressive species. In fact, during a year of concentrated study, Goodall observed 284 agonistic encounters: Of these 66 percent were due to competition for introduced bananas, and only 34 percent "could be regarded as attacks occurring in 'normal' aggressive contexts"(Goodall 1968:278). Furthermore:

> Only 10 percent of the 284 attacks were classified as "violent," and even attacks that appeared punishing to me often resulted in no discernable injury . . . Other attacks consisted merely of brief pounding or hitting after which the aggressor often touched or embraced the other immediately. (Goodall 1968:277)

Chimpanzee aggression before 1974 was considered no different from patterns of aggression seen in many primate species. In fact, Goodall (1986:3) explains that in her monograph *The Chimpanzees of Gombe* she uses data mainly from after 1975 because the earlier years present a "very different picture of the Gombe chimpanzees" as being "far more peaceable than humans." Other early naturalist's descriptions of chimpanzee behavior were consistent with those of Goodall and confirmed her first

fourteen years of observation. Even different communities were observed to come together with peaceful, ritualized displays of greeting (Ghighiari 1984; Goodall 1965, 1968; Reynolds and Reynolds 1965; Sugiyama 1972).

However, between 1974 and 1977, five adult males from one subgroup were attacked and disappeared from the area, presumably dead. Why after fourteen years did the patterns of aggression change?

Was it because the stronger group saw the weakness of the other and decided to improve its genetic fitness? Surely there were stronger and weaker animals and subgroups before this time. We can look to Goodall's own observations for an answer. In 1965, Goodall began to provide "restrictive human-controlled feeding." A few years later she realized that:

> the constant feeding was having a marked effect on the behavior of the chimps. They were beginning to move about in large groups more often than they had ever done in the old days. They were sleeping near camp and arriving in noisy hordes early in the morning. Worst of all, the adult males were becoming increasingly aggressive. When we first offered the chimps bananas, the males seldom fought over their food; . . . (now) not only was there a great deal more fighting than ever before, but many of the chimps were hanging around camp for hours and hours every day. (Goodall 1971:143)

By this time the social behavior and ranging patterns of the animals was already disrupted, and the increasing aggression eventually created so many problems that observation was almost ended at Gombe (see Wrangham 1974:85).

The possibility that human interference was a main cause of the unusual behavior of the Gombe chimps was the subject of an excellent book by Margaret Power (1991). Wrangham and Peterson essentially ignore this book, stating that yes, this might have been unnatural behavior if it weren't for new evidence of similar behavior occurring since 1977 and "elsewhere in Africa" (Wrangham and Peterson 1996:19). What is this evidence? Wrangham and Peterson provide four examples:

**1.** Between 1979 and 1982, the Gombe group extended its range to the south and conflict with a southern group, Kalande, was suspected. One day in 1982, a "raiding" party of males reached Goodall's camp. Wrangham and Peterson (1996:19) state: "Some of these raids may have been lethal." However, Goodall (1986:516) describes the *only reported* "raid" as follows: One female "was chased by a Kalande male and mildly attacked. Her four-year-old son . . . encountered a second male—but was only sniffed." Although Wrangham and Peterson imply that these encounters were similar to those at Gombe, in this single observed raid, no violence was ever witnessed. However, Wrangham and Peterson report that in 1981 an adult male, Humphrey, was found dead near the home range border. They *fail* to mention that Humphrey was approximately 35 years old, and wild chimps rarely live past 33 years (Goodall 1986).

**2.** From 1970 to 1982, six adult males from one community in the Japanese study site of Mahale disappeared, one by one, over this twelve-year period. None of these animals were ever observed being attacked or killed, and one was sighted later roaming as a solitary male. Nishida et al. (1985:287) state: "Why the adult males disappeared in succession remains a puzzle." They go on to speculate that at least some of these males may have been killed by chimpanzees from another group. However, the rationale for this assumption is that "at Gombe adult males of the main group exterminated those of the branch group" (Nishida et al. 1985:289).

**3.** In another site in West Africa, Wrangham and Peterson (1996:20) report that researchers Boesch and Boesch believe "that violent aggression among the chimpanzees is as important as it is in Gombe." However, in the paper referred to, the authors simply state that encounters by neighboring chimpanzee communities are more common in their site than in Gombe and that this may lead to larger, more cohesive group structure, and a "higher involvement of the males in social life" (Boesch and Boesch 1989:567). There is no mention whatsoever of violence or killing during these encounters.

**4.** Finally, at a site that Wrangham began studying in 1984, an adult male was found dead in 1991. Wrangham and Peterson (1996:20) state: "In the second week of August, Ruizoni was killed. No human saw the big fight. . . . the day before he went missing, our males had been travelling together near the border exchanging calls with the males of another community, evidently afraid to meet them. Four days after he was last seen, our team found his disintegrating body hunched at the bottom of a little slope." However, there is no other mention of violence at this site during the seven years before, or the six years following this event.

In fact, this is the total amount of evidence of male-male killing among chimpanzees after thirty-seven years of research by an army of researchers! The data for infanticide and rape among chimpanzees are even less impressive. In fact, data are so sparse for these behaviors among chimps that Wrangham is forced to use examples from the other great apes, gorillas and orangutans. However, just as for adult killing among chimpanzees, both the evidence and the interpretations of infanticide and rape are suspect and controversial (see, for example, Bartlett et al. 1993, Galdikas 1995).

This is not to say that obtaining meat may not have been significant in human evolutionary history. There is still some debate concerning the importance of hunting, scavenging, and gathering during various stages of human evolution (as was emphasized mainly by feminist anthropologists in the alternative "woman the gatherer"

scenerio of human evolution. See Dahlberg 1981, Linton 1975, for example). This continues to be an important subject of empirical investigation (i.e., Rose and Marshall 1996). However, even if hunting does turn out to be a common subsistence technique among early hominids, this does not necessitate aggressiveness in human interactions. It seems that the neurophysiology of interspecies predation is quite different from the spontaneous violence linked to intraspecific aggression of humans. This was the subject of initial rebuttal by Konrad Lorenz (1963) of early "hunter-killer" scenerios, and more recently by Archer (1988). Thus, I am not saying that chimpanzees or humans are not violent under certain circumstances, as we all know, but simply that the claims of inherent demonism might be greatly exaggerated, just as were earlier claims of Rousseauian paradise.

## REALITY OR MYTH?

So far, you could say that I have been a devil's advocate, or adversary, depending on your point of view. But, you might ask, what if Wrangham is correct and we and our chimp cousins are inherently sinners? Are we doomed to be violent forever because this pattern is genetically coded? Is original sin an inborn, fixed action pattern that will ultimately destroy us, or as asked by Wrangham, can we go beyond our past?—get out of our genes, so to speak. In Christianity, presumably it is faith in Christ that will lead us out of our sinful ways. Wrangham and Peterson believe that we can look to the bonobo as our potential saviors.

Bonobos, although even more closely related to the common chimpanzee than humans, have become a peace-loving, love-making alternative to chimpanzee-human violence. How did this happen? In chimpanzees and humans, females of the species select partners that are violent. As Wrangham and Peterson (1996:239) say: "While men have evolved to be demonic males, it seems likely that women have evolved to prefer demonic males. . . . as long as demonic males are the most successful reproducers, any female who mates with them is provided with sons who themselves will likely be good reproducers." However, among pygmy chimpanzees females form alliances, reduce male power, and have chosen to mate with less aggressive males. So, after all, it is not violent males that have caused humans and chimpanzees to be their inborn, immoral selves. It is, rather, poor choices by human and chimpanzee females.

In any case, now, after 5 million years of human evolution, is there a way to rid ourselves of our inborn evils? Wrangham believes so.

What does it do for us, then, to know the behavior of our closest relatives? Chimpanzees and bonobos are an extraordinary pair. One, I suggest shows us some of the worst aspects of our past and our present; the other shows an escape from it. . . . Denial of our demons won't make them go away. But even if we're driven to accepting the evidence of a grisly past, we're not forced into thinking it condemns us to an unchanged future. (1995:9)

In other words, we can learn how to behave by watching bonobos. But, if we can change our inherited behavior so simply, why haven't we been able to do this before Wrangham and Peterson enlightened us? Surely, there are variations in the amounts of violence in different human cultures and individuals. If we have the capacity to change by learning from example, then our behavior is determined by socialization practices and by our cultural histories and not solely by our nature! This is true whether the examples come from benevolent bonobos or conscientious objectors. As stated by Kenneth Bock (1980:76):

> Surely there can be no disputing the fact that humans are able to be aggressive, and there is little guidance in that observation when we are already aware from historical evidence of warfare and other forms of violence in human experience. . . . to observe merely that there has been natural selection for capacities to carry on a social or cultural activity is of limited significance as long as the variations on which selection works occur in a genetic base that is so general as to serve a great variety of such activities. Then the range of possible cultural results is not explicable by natural selection.

Thus, the theory presented by Wrangham and Peterson, although it includes chimpanzees as our murdering cousins, is very similar to "Man the Hunter/Killer" theories proposed in the past. Further, it does not differ greatly from early Euro-Christian beliefs about human ethics and morality. We are forced to ask: Are these theories generated by good scientific fact, or are they just "good to think" *because* they reflect, reinforce, and reiterate our traditional cultural beliefs? Are the scientific facts being interpreted in such a way as to reinforce our traditional Euro-Christian myths of morality and ethics? Is the theory generated by the data, or are the data manipulated to fit preconceived notions of human morality and ethics? Since data supporting these theories are extremely weak, and yet the stories continue to repeat themselves, I am forced to believe that "Man the Hunter" is a myth, and that the myth will continue in Western European views on human nature long into the future.

## REFERENCES

Archer, J. (1988) *The Behavioral Biology of Aggression.* Cambridge: Cambridge University Press.

Ardrey, R. (1961) *African Genesis: A Personal Investigation into Animal Origins and Nature of Man.* New York: Atheneum.

Bartlett, T. Q.; Sussman, R. W.; Cheverud, J. M. (1993) "Infant killing in primates: A review of observed cases with specific reference to the sexual selection hypothesis." *American Anthropologist* 95:958–990.

Bock, K. (1980) *Human Nature and History: A Response to Sociobiology.* New York: Columbia University Press.

Boesch, C.; Boesch, H. (1989) "Hunting behavior of wild chimpanzees in the Taï National Park." *American Journal of Physical Anthropology* 78:547–573.

Brian, C. K. (1981) *The Hunted or the Hunter? An Introduction to African Cave Taphonomy.* Chicago: University of Chicago Press.

Cartmill, M. (1993) *A View to a Death in the Morning: Hunting and Nature Through History.* Cambridge: Harvard University Press.

Cartmill, M. (1997) "Hunting hypothesis of human origins." In *History of Physical Anthropology: An Encyclopedia* (pp. 508–512), F. Spencer, ed. New York: Garland.

Dahlberg, F. (1981) *Woman the Gatherer.* New Haven: Yale University Press.

Dart, R. (1926) "Taung and its significance." *Natural History* 115:875.

Dart, R. (1953) "The predatory transition from ape to man." *International Anthropological and Linguistic Review* 1:201–217.

Dart, R.; Craig, D. (1959) *Adventures with the Missing Link.* New York: Harper.

Darwin, C. (1874) *The Descent of Man and Selection in Relation to Sex.* Chicago: The Henneberry Company (Second Edition).

Galdikas, B. M. F. (1995) *Reflections of Eden: My Years with the Orangutans of Borneo.* New York: Little, Brown.

Ghiglieri, M. P. (1984) *The Chimpanzees of Kibale Forest: A Field Study of Ecology and Social Structure.* New York: Columbia University Press.

Goodall, J. (1965) "Chimpanzees of the Gombe Stream Reserve." In *Primate Behavior: Field Studies of Monkeys and Apes* (pp. 425–473). I. DeVore, ed. New York: Holt, Rinehart and Winston.

Goodall, J. (1968) "The Behaviour of free-living chimpanzees in the Gombe Stream Reserve." *Animal Behaviour Monographs* 1:165–311.

Goodall, J. (1971) *In the Shadow of Man.* Boston: Houghton Mifflin.

Goodall, J. (1986) *The Chimpanzees of Gombe: Patterns of Behavior.* Cambridge: Belknap Press.

Keith, A. (1949) *A New Theory of Human Evolution.* New York: Philosophical Library.

Linton, S. (1975) "Woman the gatherer: Male bias in anthropology." In *Women in Cross-Cultural Perspective: A Preliminary Sourcebook* (pp. 9–21). S. E. Jacob, ed. Champaign: University of Illinois.

Lorenz, K. (1963) *On Aggression.* New York: Harcourt, Brace and World.

Marks, J. (1991) "What's old and new in molecular phylogenetics." *Am. J. Phys. Anthropol.* 84:207–219.

Marks, J.; Schmid, C.W.; Sarich, V.M. (1988) "DNA hybridization as a guide to phylogeny: Relations of the Hominoidea." *J. Human Evol.* 17:769–786.

Nishida T.; Hiraiwa-Hasegawa, M.; Takahata, Y. (1985) "Group extinction and female transfer in wild chimpanzees in the Mahali National Park, Tanzania." *Zeitschrift für Tierpsychologie* 67:281–301.

Power, M. (1991) *The Egalitarians Human and Chimpanzee: An Anthropological View of Social Organization.* Cambridge: Cambridge University Press.

Rose, L.; Marshall, F. (1996) "Meat eating, hominid sociality, and home bases revisited." *Current Anthropology* 37:307–338.

Reynolds V.; Reynolds, F. (1965) "Chimpanzees of Budongo Forest." In *Primate Behavior: Field Studies of Monkeys and Apes* (pp. 368–424). I. DeVore, ed. New York: Holt, Rinehart and Winston.

Ruse, M. (1994) "Evolution and ethics: The sociobiological approach." pp. 91–109. In Environmental Ethics: Readings in Theory and Application. L. A. Pojman, ed. Boston: Jones and Bartlett.

Ruse, M.; Wilson, E. O. (1985) "The evolution of ethics." *New Scientist* 108:50–52.

Small, M. F. (1997) "The good, the bad, and the ugly." *Evolutionary Anthropology* 5:143–147.

Sugiyama, Y. (1972) "Social characteristics and socialization of wild chimpanzees." In *Primate Socialization* (pp. 145–163). F. E. Poirier, ed. New York: Random House.

Sussman, R. W. (1995) "The nature of human universals." *Reviews in Anthropology* 24:1–11.

Sussman, R. W., ed. (1997) *The Biological Basis of Human Behavior.* Boston: Simon and Schuster.

Sussman, R. W. (in press). "Piltdown Man: The father of American field primatology." In *Changing Images of Primate Societies: The Role of Theory, Method, and Gender.* S. Strum; L. Fedigan, eds. Chicago: University of Chicago Press.

Tylor, E. B. (1871) *Primitive Culture.* London: John Murray.

Washburn, S. L., Lancaster, C. K. (1968). "The evolution of Hunting." In *Man the Hunter* (pp. 293–303). R. B. Lee,; I. DeVore, eds. Chicago: Aldine.

Washburn, S. L.; Avis, V. (1958) "Evolution of human behavior." In *Behavior and Evolution* (pp. 421–436). A. Roe; G. G. Simpson, eds. New Haven: Yale University Press.

Wilson, E. O. (1975) *Sociobiology: The New Synthesis.* Cambridge, MA: Harvard University Press.

Wilson, E.O. (1976) "Sociobiology: A new approach to understanding the basis of human nature." *New Scientist* 70:342–345. (reprinted In R. W. Sussman (1997) *The Biological Basis of Human Behavior,* pp. 63–66).

Wrangham, R. W. (1974) "Artificial feeding of chimpanzees and baboons in their natural habitat." *Animal Behaviour* 22:83–93.

Wrangham, R. W. (1995) "Ape culture and missing links." *Symbols* (Spring 1995):2–9, 20.

Wrangham, R.; Peterson, D. (1996) *Demonic Males: Apes and the Origins of Human Violence.* Boston: Houghton Mifflin.

# Chapter 21

# *Reconstructions of Early Hominid Socioecology:*
# *A Critique of Primate Models*

## Richard Potts

## INTRODUCTION

Information about the behavior of living primates has increased enormously over the past twenty years. During this time the data base about early hominids and their habitats has also grown rapidly. Paleoanthropologists attempt to use data from actual traces of hominids and their environmental settings to reconstruct hominid behavior and ecology. New methods of analysis have enabled inferences about early hominid locomotion, diet, tool use, and other aspects of behavior and ecology. Recent findings and changing assumptions in paleoanthropology suggest that there are important limitations in using living primates to reconstruct the behavior and socioecology of early hominids. This chapter will discuss (1) the kinds of fossil evidence for early hominid behavior; (2) whether there is a method for choosing accurate primate models for hominid behaviors that cannot be inferred directly from the fossil record; (3) the problem of possibly unique behaviors among early hominids, as suggested by archeological evidence; and (4) the importance of primate behavior research for the study of early hominid adaptations.

## PALEOANTHROPOLOGICAL INFERENCES

This section provides a brief overview of the kinds of prehistoric data that help to reconstruct early hominid behavior and ecology. This overview will serve to indicate gaps in our knowledge about early hominid behavior and, thus, where living primate models might be most welcome.

From *The Evolution of Human Behavior: Primate Models.* Warren G. Kinzey (ed.) State University of New York Press, Albany. 1987.

Certain aspects of hominid behavior and ecology can be more readily inferred, or directly tested, with evidence from the geological record. The evidence falls into three major categories: hominid fossils, paleoenvironmental data, and archeological data. Use of this evidence to reconstruct hominid adaptations requires inferential principles or analogies established from modern animals and environments. Often living primates contribute importantly to uniformitarian and analogical bases for reconstruction. Each of the three categories of evidence will be considered below.

### Hominid Fossils

Hominid fossils provide data on skeletal morphology and its modification during an individual's lifetime (growth, biomechanical alterations, and changes due to diet and pathology). When arranged chronologically, fossils provide information that helps to test ideas about phylogeny. Paleoanthropologists have also used fossils to assess important behavioral and ecological characteristics of early hominids. Some examples are body size (Steudel 1980), sexual dimorphism (Trinkaus 1980, Wolpoff 1976), locomotion (Lovejoy et al. 1973, Preuschoft 1971, Stern and Susman 1983), hand function (Napier 1962, Susman and Creel 1979), and diet (Grine 1981, 1984, Kay 1981, Walker 1981). Inferences about behavior and body size depend on how well observable anatomical traits correlate with inferred characteristics. For instance, accurate body weight estimates require high correlations (with low standard errors) between body weight and measurable traits—e.g., femur length (Steudel 1981) or skull length (Wood 1979). That is, any given value measured from a fossil should correspond to a narrow range of body sizes.

Modern primates are important for testing correlations between morphological variables, on the one hand, and body size or anatomical functions, on the other. However, inferences about early hominids are extrapolations beyond known primate species. This often leads to disagreements among paleoanthropologists about those inferences. Body size estimates of hominids again provide an example of the problems involved. Many researchers consider it inappropriate to use regression formulas across different populations of *Homo sapiens.* If so, then the application of a body weight regression across species (from living to extinct species) is difficult to justify. Furthermore, interspecific regressions and correlations between body size and metric variables are affected by differences in locomotor and other behavioral characteristics. This may partially explain why interspecific and intraspecific body size regressions sometimes differ (Steudel 1981, 1982a, 1982b). Thus, an estimate of hominid body size must take into account postural/locomotor equivalence between early hominids and the reference sample on which the estimate (regression) is based (Wolpoff 1983). It is probably unjustified to base body weight estimates for bipedal hominids on regressions for quadrupedal primates.

A similar problem occurs in functional interpretations of fossils. Modern *Homo sapiens* is the only biped on which to base behavioral inferences from early hominid fossils. Bipedalism in modern humans is usually treated as a functionally uniform pattern of locomotion, though considerable anatomical variation is involved. Yet the overall postcranial anatomy of Plio–Pleistocene hominids appears to lie outside the range of modern human variation (Lovejoy et al. 1973, Oxnard 1975, Stern and Susman 1983, Walker 1973, Zihlman 1978). Some researchers contend that a functionally modern pattern of bipedalism also occurred in these hominids (Lovejoy 1978, Lovejoy et al. 1973, Robinson 1972). Others disagree; unique morphological patterns and morphological similarities to arboreal primates are thought to be functionally significant, indicating a behaviorally different pattern of bipedalism from that in modern humans (Jungers 1982, Preuschoft 1971, Robinson 1972, Stern and Susman 1983, Susman and Stern 1982). Judgments about early hominid locomotion, of course, are limited in that no living primate shows the same combination of postcranial features observed in the fossils. Nonetheless, further biomechanical studies of living primates potentially offer a way to assess alternative behavioral interpretations of fossils. (See Wood 1978 for a detailed treatment of methods of functional analysis of fossils.)

This brief discussion of behavioral and body size interpretations from hominid fossils brings up the issue of unique adaptations among extinct hominids and the difficulty of recognizing them. This is a problem that will be explored later with regard to archeological reconstructions of hominid activities.

*Paleoenvironmental Evidence*

Inferences about paleoenvironment and ancient geomorphology are possible from fossil and geological evidence. An ecological context for early hominid behavior is provided by reconstructions of paleoenvironments. Accordingly, paleoenvironmental data help in building and testing adaptive scenarios for hominid evolution (e.g., Laporte and Zihlman 1983). Some techniques of paleoenvironmental analysis (e.g., oxygen isotopes) concern broad, even worldwide, climatic events. Others apply to sediments within small areas, such as single paleontological sites or sedimentary basins. These latter methods (e.g., lithofacies and pollen analyses) yield more detailed information about local habitats where hominids lived. Yet even localized paleoenvironmental reconstructions often may not provide the kind of resolution (e.g., seasonality) necessary to make some important ecological inferences about early hominids.

Paleoenvironmental interpretations are obtained from four major areas of research. First, sedimentological studies aim to identify different sediment types (lithofacies) based on particle size, mineralogy, and sedimentary structures. This information permits reconstruction of depositional environments and ancient geomorphological settings, such as the distribution of lake, lake margin, deltaic, and riverine zones (e.g., Hay 1976). Second, geochemical studies, such as those on oxygen isotope ratios, provide evidence for climatic fluctuations, including glacial cycles and changes in rainfall (Cerling et al. 1977, Shackleton 1967).

A third source of paleoenvironmental data is fossil plants. Pollen, in particular, has been used in reconstructions of early hominid environments (Bonnefille 1979). Since many plants do not leave a pollen record, fossil pollen samples give a biased picture of local and regional vegetation. Detailed reconstructions of vegetation from pollen analysis are problematic, especially when mosaics of vegetation are involved that may lack modern analogues, such as suggested for the Asian Miocene (Pilbeam et al. 1979). Thus, fossil pollens, especially the frequency of montane forest species, have been used mainly to infer ancient rainfall patterns rather than detailed, local vegetation.

Faunal remains are a fourth source of information about ancient environments. Inferences from faunal assemblages about ecological communities depend on taphonomic studies of bone preservation and time averaging (Behrensmeyer 1982, Behrensmeyer and Hill 1980, Shipman 1981). Some species are more sensitive to ecological conditions than others. Microfauna (e.g., rodents, insectivores, small birds) tend to be better indicators than large animals of climatic/ecological changes. But at present taphonomic biases seem to be less clearly understood for small animals than for large mammals. Due to small size, microfauna are affected greatly by taphonomic processes that destroy bones or remove them from their original habitat (Dodson 1973). Large animals are also subject to important, and better studied, taphonomic biases. Large mammals, in particular, have been used to reconstruct broad climatic and vegetation patterns where hominids lived (Vrba 1980, Potts 1982).

### Archeological Evidence

Compared with the kind of information available from living species, inferences made from archeological evidence about early hominid behavior and ecology are very limited. Behavioral inferences include the use of stone tools, techniques of their manufacture, and functions of some artifacts (Isaac 1976, Keeley and Toth 1981, Toth 1982). The outcrop sources of stone tool materials can sometimes be identified (e.g., Hay 1976). Accordingly, direct inferences can be made about the minimum distances over which hominids ranged to get and transport those materials. The existence of archeological sites relatively undisturbed by water action implies that early hominids carried stone to certain, delimited areas and discarded artifacts over the landscape. The transport of parts of animal carcasses to archeological sites also can be shown from study of faunal remains (e.g., Potts 1982, 1984a). The means of acquiring animal tissues (i.e., various modes of hunting and scavenging) can be assessed from data on skeletal age of animals and skeletal part (Binford 1981, Klein 1982, Potts 1983, Vrba 1980). Identification of stone tool cutmarks on faunal remains (Bunn 1981, Potts and Shipman 1981) shows that early hominids used animal tissues. The fact that hominids were involved with the animal bones on early archeological sites implies that Plio–Pleistocene hominids ate more meat than do nonhuman primates (Bunn 1981, Isaac 1978a). Yet it is unclear how often meat was consumed or what percentage contribution meat made to early hominid diets (Isaac and Crader 1981, Potts 1984a). Further levels of interpretation attempt to explain in adaptive terms why hominids produced clusters of stone artifacts and animal bones and to reconstruct the ranging patterns and socioecology of early hominids (Isaac 1976, 1978, 1980). Some of these interpretations (e.g., the existence of home bases) will be discussed later.

This brief overview of paleobehavioral/ecological information from the fossil record indicates crucial gaps in our knowledge about early hominids. Although the living primates offer an important context in which to view reconstructions of hominid diet or locomotion, the fossil record potentially provides the only adequate tests of what particular hominids ate and how they moved. On the other hand, early hominid social behavior, social organization, and most demographic and life history characteristics are difficult, at best, to infer directly from the fossil evidence. The issue here is how living primates can help in this regard.

I will focus on two problems concerning the use of living primates to reconstruct hominid social and demographic characteristics. The first is whether there are adequate criteria for choosing specific primate models for particular periods of hominid evolution. The second problem is whether reconstructions based on living primates take into account possibly unique behaviors in early hominids. Since particular species of living primates may exhibit behaviors and socioecological features not seen in other species, it is possible that the behavior and socioecology of early hominids also were not like those observed in any modern primate. Although extant species provide a wealth of models of early hominid socioecology, even these may be too limited to reconstruct the unique trajectory of hominid behavioral evolution.

## PRIMATE MODELS

One goal of field primatology has been to explain variations in primate social organization. Relationships between ecological and social variables have been especially important in developing a theory on this (Clutton-Brock and Harvey 1977, Crook and Gartlan 1966, Eisenberg et al. 1972, Jolly 1972, Richard 1985). Yet few researchers seem to recognize that "the problem of the emergence of hominid social organization would be one test of the explanatory power of such a theory" (Reynolds 1976:74). Rather, interpretive leaps about early hominid social life, guided by the characteristics of living species, are often considered necessary in the study of hominid evolution (Isaac 1976a, Lancaster 1968). Since the fossil evidence provides few clues about behavior, modern species are used as analogues for early hominids. Living animals facilitate reconstructions of early hominid adaptations (e.g., Brace 1979).

The problem is that living species offer a variety of plausible models for early hominid adaptations. The earliest hominids inhabited areas characterized by a mosaic of habitats including open plains, woodland, and gallery forest (Van Couvering 1980). Thus, behavioral and ecological analogues for early hominids can be chosen from species that inhabit a wide range of ecological zones. Those who believe that hominids originated under very specific selection pressures may choose from many specific adaptive models to characterize early hominids (e.g., hunting models, gathering models, baboon models). Others point out that because behavioral flexibility and variability typify all higher primates, hominids also have always been able to adapt to a wide variety of conditions. An emphasis on omnivorous diets rather than on a narrow range of foods, such as meat or nuts, is an example of this line of reasoning (Harding and Teleki, 1981).

Is there a method for selecting one plausible model over another? Is there a sound rationale to infer that early hominid social systems, group size and composition, or life history characteristics were like those of one living species but not another? Further, do living species necessarily provide good models for early hominid socioecology?

Interpretations of early hominid behavior are typically based on (1) analogies with living animals, and (2) adaptive reasoning to account for behavioral differences between modern humans and other primates. The major goal is to bridge the behavioral gap between humans and other primates. Direct analogies emphasize the behavioral continuities. The best behavioral reconstructions also account for major adaptive differences (e.g., regular tool use in humans). To incorporate distinctive human traits into an evolutionary scenario, judgments must be made about the ecological conditions under which such traits were beneficial to hominids. Adaptive reasoning plays this judgmental role.

An example of this latter aspect of behavioral reconstruction comes from Brace (1979). Early hominids were adapted to savannas as are modern baboons; yet humans are tool users whereas baboons are not. It is reasoned that use of a simple digging stick by early hominids would have greatly increased their available food supply. Thus, digging sticks were probably used by the earliest hominids.

As is typical of adaptationist reasoning, the reconstruction is plausible, but there is no clear reason provided by Brace to choose it over other plausible adaptive models that do not mention digging sticks. Further, it is unclear whether the use of a digging stick might have occurred first at 2.5 million years rather than 4 or 5 million years ago. That is, the timing of this behavioral novelty cannot be specified.

Analogies, or species-specific models, are derived from animals that are either phylogenetically close to humans or species believed to be adapted to ecological conditions that also prevailed where early hominids lived (e.g., terrestrial baboons; a historical summary of the baboon as a model for early hominids is provided by Strum and Mitchell 1987). Many researchers contend that living chimpanzees are the best model for the last common ancestor of hominids and the African apes (e.g., Tanner 1981, Tanner and Zihlman 1976, Zihlman et al. 1978). Accordingly, the earliest hominid is considered chimplike. As a result, an ape-human dichotomy is created. Early hominid adaptations are on a continuum between ape-like and human-like. For example: "Living chimpanzees represent the kind of population from which we evolved. Contemporary gathering-hunting peoples provide data on evolved patterns. We can then look at the two ends of the continuum and try to fill in the missing parts" (Tanner and Zihlman 1976: 587–588).

The problem with placing early hominids along a chimp-human continuum is that it precludes considering unique adaptations off that continuum. Information from the hominid fossil record suggests that such unique adaptations did occur. For example, the cheek teeth of *Australopithecus* were larger and capped with thicker enamel than in either living chimpanzees or humans. Thus, in this aspect of dental anatomy *Australopithecus* did not fall on the proposed continuum. Other features of early hominid crania (e.g., supraorbital torus) and postcranial anatomy (e.g., skeletal robusticity) indicate that early *Homo* also did not fall on a chimp-human continuum in certain features. While it is easy to see whether early hominid morphology fits on the continuum, it is less easy to judge whether a simple ape-human dichotomy portrays adequately the behavioral and ecological characteristics of *Australopithecus* and early *Homo*.

Many researchers, in fact, do not ascribe strictly to this continuum. For instance, analogues for early hominids are often based on tropical, open country monkeys (*Papio, Erythrocebus, Theropithecus*). These analogues suggest adaptive changes that occurred when hominid ancestors shifted from a closed vegetation habitat to savannas sometime between 14 and 2 mya. Large mammalian carnivores are also a popular source for analogies. A standard interpretation of the earliest archeological evidence 1.8 to 2.5 mya is that a shift to meat-eating and hunting characterized early *Homo*. Although this interpretation has been questioned (Binford 1981, Potts 1984a, Shipman 1983, Zihlman 1981), some researchers replace a chimp or baboon model with a carnivore model, emphasizing social cooperation and food sharing, to describe the adaptation of early Pleistocene hominids (King 1975, Schaller and Lowther 1969, Thompson 1975, 1976). As an alternative, human hunter-gatherers also join the pool of possible living analogues for tool-making hominids that lived during the Plio-Pleistocene.

Each modern analogue has its proponents. The reasons for choosing a particular analogue often conflict, as do the resulting models of early hominid behavior. A brief comparison between two models illustrates this point. A recent reconstruction by Brace (1979) suggests that large game hunting is the basis of human adaptation. Many others have also proposed this idea (e.g., Ardrey 1976, Dart 1953, Washburn and Lancaster 1968). In contrast, Tanner (1981, Tanner and Zihlman 1976, Zihlman 1983) maintains that the initial and most important innovation in human evolution was the gathering of plant foods and specifically not the hunting of animals. Both scenarios are plausible and consistent with the fossil evidence. Brace and Tanner provide the rationales underlying their reconstructions. In Tanner's model, comparisons between apes and humans help to determine ancestral behavior patterns. The predominance of plant foods in the diets of modern chimpanzees and hunter-gatherers is emphasized. Thus, Tanner focuses on an important change within the herbivorous pattern of chimps and humans, i.e., the gathering of plant foods. In contrast, Brace's model is more concerned with adaptive analogues off the chimp-human continuum. He considers how the adaptations of animals to open savannas would have modified an initial ape-like ancestral condition. Hunting behavior is considered by Brace to be one of those adaptations.

The problem in choosing the right analogue might appear to be circumvented if it is acknowledged that many animals provide useful models for reconstructing early hominid adaptations. In fact, some paleoanthropologists have adopted this viewpoint. For example, Campbell (1979) points out that there are close similarities in social organization between monkeys, apes, human hunter-gatherers, and social carnivores. Given these similarities, Campbell maintains that "we do not need to postulate any major development in social organization during hominid evolution" (Campbell 1979: 301–302). This compromise viewpoint shows the problem of accepting or rejecting plausible analogies, whether based on animals phylogenetically close to early hominids or ostensibly similar in behavior. Monkeys, apes, modern humans, and large carnivores may show general similarities in sociality, but different species vary widely in socioecological characteristics. We are still left with the problem of trying to choose the most accurate analogy or combination of analogies for early hominids. As is made clear by Campbell's comment, all models seem appropriate when superficial similarities are emphasized; this eliminates the important question—the unique trajectory of hominid behavioral evolution.

## Problem of Behavioral Uniqueness

The accuracy of behavioral or socioecological models depends in part on how well they allow for behavioral uniqueness among extinct hominids. Field primatologists document and try to account for variations in social systems in living species. Ecological variables are thought to be especially important in determining the social, demographic, and life history characteristics of species (Hinde 1983, Jolly 1972, Krebs and Davies 1978, Richard 1985). By adopting this orientation toward socioecology, paleoanthropologists should also consider (1) possible ecological differences between early hominids and living primates, including modern humans, and (2) the difficulties of explaining or predicting social characteristics from ecological features. Early hominid socioecology can be evaluated if ecological factors known to influence social characteristics can be studied in the fossil record. This section will illustrate how socioecological factors can be inferred for tool-making hominids from the Plio–Pleistocene. Problems for socioecological models based on living primate species will be considered.

Attempts to reconstruct the behavior of Plio–Pleistocene hominids, 2.5 to 1.5 mya, are faced with the pos-

sibility of unique adaptations, i.e., unlike those of modern humans or other primates. Plio–Pleistocene hominids lived 2 to 6 million years after the divergence of hominids from African apes, according to most recent estimates; and they preceded modern *Homo sapiens* by about 1.5 to 2.0 million years. As noted previously, these hominids show some features found in no modern hominoids (e.g., cheek tooth morphology). Further, the presence of more than one contemporaneous hominid species provided an adaptive context that differed from that during both earlier and later periods of hominid evolution. Therefore, Plio–Pleistocene hominids do not have a particularly close temporal connection with either modern humans or the last common ancestor, and there is reason to believe that adaptive differences occurred.

The earliest archeological sites, nonetheless, seem to provide evidence of a Plio–Pleistocene behavior pattern for which there is a good modern analogue, i.e., human hunter-gatherers. However, socioecological reconstructions of the hominids that made these early sites illustrate the problems with analogies based on modern species. A modern analogue (tropical hunter-gatherers) is the traditional source of interpretation of the earliest archeological sites. Yet paleoecological inferences from archeological data conflict with important aspects of this analogy. These inferences provide an alternative to a traditional analogical viewpoint for discussing the socioecology of early hominids.

The earliest archeological sites come from the period 2.5 to 1.5 mya. Sites over 2.0 million years old are rare and have not yet been studied fully (Harris and Johanson 1983). In contrast, sites in the 2.0 to 1.5 million year period have been studied in detail from taphonomical, paleoecological, and behavioral viewpoints. The archeological sites from Bed I at Olduvai Gorge are perhaps the best known sites from this period (Leakey 1971). They are discussed in this section. Description of the sites and detailed data analyses are contained in other sources (Potts 1982, 1984a, 1984b). A brief description and summary of analyses pertinent to hominid ecology will serve here.

Most of the archeological sites from Bed I Olduvai have several features in common, as originally described by Leakey (1971). A concentration of stone artifacts and animal bones, 10 to 20 meters in diameter, defines each site. These are called "type C" sites by Isaac (1978, Isaac and Crader 1981). The animal bones are broken and represent a variety of species, particularly mammals ranging in size from small gazelle to elephant. Stone artifacts consist of a variety of tools, cores, waste flakes, and unmodified raw material. A variety of raw materials were used. Some of the sources were approximately 2 to 3 kilometers from the excavated sites (Hay 1976, Potts 1982). Taphonomic studies indicate that hominids transported both animal bones and stone artifacts to well-delimited spots on the ancient landscape, though other agents besides hominids were also important in the formation of these archeological sites (Bunn 1982, Potts 1982, Potts and Shipman 1981).

The dominant interpretation of the Olduvai sites is that they were home bases—i.e., spatial nodes of social activity and food sharing among early hominids (Campbell 1982, Fagan 1983, Isaac 1976, 1978a). It has been assumed that early archeological clusters of bones and stone artifacts are indistinguishable from hunter-gatherer campsites; thus, "they seem to indicate that the movements of Plio–Pleistocene hominids were organized around a home base" (Isaac 1976a: 500). One implication of the home base hypothesis is that modern, tropical hunter-gatherers constitute a reasonable model of the foraging behavior and social group characteristics of Plio–Pleistocene hominids. As a result, a wide range of distinctively human characteristics are also implied in the home base interpretation. These include daily use of tools, regular eating of meat, division of labor, language, and delayed reciprocity in social feeding (Isaac 1976, 1978a, Potts 1984b).

Behavioral comparisons between humans and nonhuman primates have helped to identify two salient features of human home bases (Table 21–1). These features are safety and food sharing. First, Washburn and DeVore (1961) characterized hominid home bases as safe places where injured, sick, elderly, or young members of the social group could stay while others foraged. They point out, in contrast, that in Old World monkeys and apes, all group members move from their sleeping locations during the day. Second, Isaac (1978, 1980, 1983) has pointed out that in nonhuman primates, individuals feed themselves as they forage, whereas humans often exhibit an additional feeding pattern—the transport of food to a home base for sharing with other foragers.

The early archeological sites from Olduvai are often believed to be the best evidence for early hominid home bases, characterized by both safety and food sharing. However, the home base interpretation has been questioned recently by Isaac (1983) and others (Binford 1981, Potts 1982, 1984b). Detailed study of the earliest Olduvai sites shows some contradictions to a model based on tropical hunter-gatherer socioecology (Potts 1982, 1984b). First, taphonomic analysis indicates that

animal bones were brought to these sites by hominids probably over periods of at least several years. This period of bone accumulation is much longer than the period over which modern, tropical hunter-gatherers reoccupy their campsites. Second, patterns of bone modification indicate that carnivores, such as hyaenids and felids, had visited these sites during the entire period of bone accumulation. They damaged the bones, possibly as extensively as hominids did, and had access to complete bones rich in meat and marrow. Damage inflicted by carnivore teeth and by hominid stone tools to the bones within each site assemblage, and sometimes to the same bone, suggests that hominids and carnivores had competed at least in an indirect way over animal tissues carried to these sites. Finally, the animal bones from Olduvai are not modified as intensively as are bones processed for meat and marrow at modern campsites. For example, 9 percent of the total number of major limb bone specimens from Olduvai sites are complete. This contrasts with only 1.2 percent complete limb bones from a sample of sixteen !Kung San campsites (Yellen 1977). Relative inefficiency in bone/meat processing by Olduvai hominids may explain why carnivores were attracted repeatedly to these sites of bone accumulation (Potts 1982, 1984b, Potts and Shipman 1981).

It is difficult to reconcile a home base interpretation to these findings about the processing of animal tissues and site utilization by Olduvai hominids. The hunter-gatherer analogy is based primarily on the fact that Olduvai hominids accumulated artifacts and animal bones, as do modern hunter-gatherers. This general similarity begins to fade in the light of taphonomic findings and paleoecological inferences from the archeological sites. In particular, the presumed safety of the home base seems violated by evidence for high potential, and actual, competition between early hominids and carnivores over animal tissues at these sites. The removal of bones from carcasses by hominids probably reduced the chances of direct interaction with predators. However, repeated transport of animal tissues to sites probably resulted in costs from carnivore competition that differed from those incurred by modern hunter-gatherers. The latter have a variety of means to deal with potential predators and carnivore competitors. These include fire, more

TABLE 21–1  The Characteristics of the home base concept

| Characteristics | Primates | Humans | Ref. |
|---|---|---|---|
| Safety | All group members move during daily round. | Some members (injured, sick, elderly, young) stay at home base. | Washburn and DeVore, 1961 |
| Food sharing | Individuals feed-as-you-go. | Delayed food consumption; food taken to home base. | Isaac 1978a, 1983 |

complete or efficient bone/meat processing activities, and possibly more effective weapons than possessed by Olduvai hominids. Moreover, evidence for repeated attraction of carnivores to these sites suggests that hominids had to adapt their movements and their use of sites and animal tissues to the activities of large carnivores in a way unknown among recent hunter-gatherers. Hominid use of these sites as refuges of safety and, therefore, as central areas for social activity appears doubtful. This implies that social activities were not focused at the primary locations where stone and animal food resources were transported.

These behavioral and ecological inferences from archeological data have implications for socioecological reconstruction. Resource acquisition and predator pressure are considered to be major determinants of primate social adaptations (Bernstein and Smith 1979, Jolly 1972, Richard 1981, Wrangham 1983a, 1983b). If, as suggested here, Olduvai hominids differed from modern hunter-gatherers in these traits, it is possible that they also differed in their social organization and demographic characteristics. A generalized interpretation of the earliest sites at Olduvai is needed that relies less on socioecological analogies to modern hunter-gatherers. It is clear that early hominids transported at least two kinds of resources to these sites—stone tool material and animal bones. Although resource transport by tropical hunter-gatherers involves a socioecology focused around transient home bases, the carrying of resources to sites by early hominids need not imply similar social or demographic characteristics to those found in their modern counterparts.

To show alternatives to the hunter-gatherer home base model exist, I have suggested previously a "stone cache" interpretation for the early Olduvai sites (Potts 1984b). This idea takes into account faunal assemblage features noted previously to conflict with the home base analogy. These include long periods of bone accumulation by hominids at sites, modification of the bones by carnivores over the period of bone accumulation, and relatively inefficient processing of bones at these sites. Further, the stone cache idea is based on the general notion that hominids transported stone artifacts and food resources requiring stone tool use to the same places.

According to the stone cache interpretation, sites were established throughout the hominid foraging range. Figure 21–1 shows one scenario where six sites were produced around a central source of stone raw material. The sites are situated in the various vegetation and sedimentary zones known to have existed 1.8 mya at Olduvai (Hay 1976, Potts 1982). Sites were produced by carrying stone raw material from outcrops to delimited locations in the foraging area. The stone material was useful for making cores and tools that were reused over the long term. Hominids located animal tissues already detached from the skeleton, or they cut portions from carcasses with tools carried from caches of stone. Bones were transported to a nearby cache, and the tissues were processed quickly and incompletely. The site was then abandoned. Carnivores were attracted repeatedly to the bone assemblages at each cache and to some of the same bones modified by hominids. This scenario does not specify how frequently hominids visited caches or where they went after leaving a cache, since no archeological evidence at present seems to bear on these questions. The existence of social bases away from the caches (and bone accumulations) or sleeping areas similar to those of nonhuman primates seems likely.

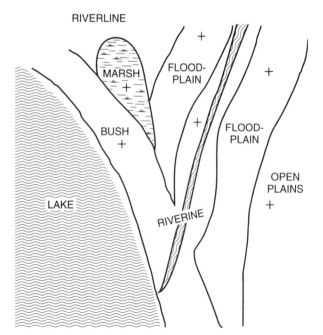

**Figure 21–1** Reconstruction of six stone caches produced around a central stone raw material source (+). The caches occur in a variety of sedimentary and vegetation zones known to have existed at ancient Olduvai.

This brief scenario illustrates an alternative interpretation to the home base model. Whether or not the stone cache idea is correct in detail, a general resource transport interpretation of the Olduvai sites does not imply a socioecology centered around home bases, as in human hunter-gatherers.

Furthermore, important differences from nonhuman primates can be noted. Hominid foraging at Olduvai must have incurred competition with predators unlike that faced by other higher primates, especially since the latter do not exploit large mammals. Stone and food resources were transported in a manner unknown among nonhuman primates. The archeological sites do bear some resemblance to chimpanzee nut-cracking sites, which also contain tools and food refuse (Sugiyama and Koman 1979). But the similarity is superficial. Foraging by Olduvai hominids differed in that it involved transport of foods (at least animal tissues) to their sites, whereas chimpanzee nut-cracking sites occur at the source of the food itself. As for hunter-gatherers, modern nonhuman primates appear to differ from Olduvai hominids in aspects of foraging ecology and predator avoidance.

It is important to note that living primates still offer numerous plausible models of Olduvai hominid socioecology. For example, did early hominids at Olduvai move in social groups resembling those of hunter-gatherers—i.e., changeable in composition but composed of several family units that consistently reunited at a social base to which artifacts and bones were not taken? Were they like common chimpanzees, living in communities of males and females that ranged independently throughout an area and formed short-lived parties (Goodall 1975, Harcourt and Stewart 1983)? Were they like pygmy chimps, which form more stable parties of males and females than do common chimps (Kuroda 1979)? Or do multiple male-female groups (as in common baboons) or "family units" (hamadryas baboon) that shift as a cohesive unit while foraging best portray the social groups of Olduvai hominids?

There is no specific paleoecological inference for ancient Olduvai that suggests at present that one of these analogues is more appropriate than the others. In fact, each of the analogues seems consistent with a general resource transport interpretation of the Olduvai sites. On the other hand, differences in foraging and predator avoidance suggest that Olduvai hominids may have had social strategies found in none of these modern species. Archeologists assume that concentrations of stone artifacts and animal bones specify important aspects of hominid social and economic organization. This assumption is correct only if a hunter-gatherer model is applicable. In contrast, other mammals which accumulate resources or leave debris (e.g., porcupines, hyenas, chimps at nut-cracking sites) seem to provide no general model of sociality, group size, composition, or organization.

Olduvai provides excellent data about ancient ecological settings and hominid activities. Yet this information does not direct us to a particular living primate model to reconstruct hominid socioecology. Wrangham (1983) suggests that it is not possible to reconstruct a model of this from living forms because of behavioral variability in the African apes. In response, some might remark that the fossil record has left us with yet another mystery (cf., Reynolds 1976: 73). However, the study of human behavioral evolution is possibly furthered by knowing that long-persisting species of extinct hominids thrived with adaptations for which there is no modern parallel.

## Value of Primate Studies

This chapter has focused on problems of applying socioecological analogies from living primates to early hominids. Analogies are often based on assumed or superficial resemblances. In contrast, analysis of the prehistoric record suggests that early hominids may have differed from living primates in ecological features that influence species' social and demographic characteristics. The differences implied in socioecology would be masked by analogies adopted from living species. This analysis exemplifies the shortcomings of static models of adaptation based on particular modern primates. Despite this critique, primate studies continue to be a valuable source of ideas and information pertinent to hominid evolution. Primate behavior research is valuable to the study of early hominid adaptation for several reasons.

First, testable hypotheses about hominid evolution can result from comparisons between living nonhuman primates and particular species of early hominids. An example is Jolly's seed-eating hypothesis, developed in part from anatomical comparisons between terrestrial monkeys and extinct hominoids (Jolly 1970, 1973). In response to this hypothesis, dietary analyses of early hominid teeth have shown that while a grass-eating adaptation can be dismissed, small, hard objects were probably a part of the diet of early hominids (Walker 1981, Kay 1981). In order to test hypotheses based on comparisons with living primates, such hypotheses must identify the species or period of hominid evolution to which they pertain. Furthermore, they should specify aspects of hominid anatomy, diet, behavior, or ecological setting that can be evaluated ultimately with data from the geological record.

Second, the idea of human behavioral evolution is founded on comparisons between humans and nonhuman primates (Isaac 1976a, Jay 1968, Lancaster 1968). These comparisons help to define the endpoints of the trajectory of hominid behavioral evolution. However, knowing the differences and similarities between humans and other primates does not make the evolutionary trajectory straightforward. In particular, neither behavioral comparisons nor living primate models inform us about the rate of behavioral evolution or help to identify unique hominid behaviors for which there is no appropriate primate analogue.

Finally, studies of modern primates can explore processes of behavioral variation and change. Research oriented toward adaptive processes can show the conditions (e.g., ecological, social) under which certain behavioral variations resembling human behaviors occur (e.g., Reynolds 1976, Strum 1981). A distinction between *results* and *processes* is an important one (Richard 1981). Field studies of primates not only describe the static results of adaptation but also show *how* primates adapt and *how* behavioral variations arise. It is the application of static primate models to early hominids that yields the methodological difficulties and conflicting reconstructions discussed earlier.

For example, the fact that chimpanzees hunt does not necessarily mean that hunting was practiced by protohominids or by *Australopithecus*. However, it is useful to know the ecological and social conditions under which higher primate hunting is practiced and becomes more frequent (Strum 1981, Strum and Mitchell 1987). If evidence for these conditions can be recognized in the hominid fossil record, then the process of hominid behavioral evolution, in this case the development of hunting, can be studied. As another example, the fact that chimpanzees make tools does not mean that all species of early hominids made tools, even though this is plausible. Yet behavioral traditions, including patterns of tool use and food preparation, have been documented in chim-

panzees (Boesch and Boesch 1984, McGrew et al. 1979, Tanner this volume) and macaques (Frisch 1968; Kummer 1971). Transmission of behavior patterns across generations in these species indicates that modern human cultural processes (e.g., language) are not the only means to explain traditions. This has implications for how traditions of early hominid stone tool manufacture are interpreted.

If the goal of studying hominid behavioral evolution is to understand the unique events that led to modern humans, then primate studies may contribute greatly to this end by showing how unique aspects of socioecology and behavior arise in primates. The emphasis here is on process, not static analogies. Problems in understanding modern primate adaptations (Richard 1981) can inform us about some of the difficulties in reconstructing early hominid socioecology. The problem of unique hominid adaptations can be illustrated by living species. Assuming that only the anatomy and geographic distribution of a living species is known, misleading models of its behavior and social organization result from analogies with other modern primates.

As an example, would we be able to reconstruct the socioecology of *Papio hamadryas* from its anatomy, inferences about diet, and knowing that it occupied cliffs in dry habitats? Table 21–2 presents some of the salient features of hamadryas social groups and compares them with the social systems of related monkeys. The baboon morphology of *P. hamadryas* might suggest that a general baboon model would provide the best socioecological reconstruction. However, the social and demographic characteristics of hamadryas contrast greatly with what occurs in other

TABLE 21–2  Some distinctive socioecological characteristics of *Papio hamadryas* and comparisons with other *Papio* species, gelada (*Theropithecus*), and patas (*Erythrocebus*). Information from Dunbar and Dunbar (1975), Dunbar (1983), Kummer (1971), and Richard (1985).

| Socioecological Feature | Appearance of Feature in Hamadryas Baboons | Comparisons with Other Primate Species |
|---|---|---|
| Social grouping | 1-male reproductive units aggregate into bands. | Unlike all other *Papio,* but similar kind of social grouping to geladas. Patas have 1-male units but lack large band aggregates. |
| Band foraging movements | Highly coordinated; strongly controlled by males, who keep individual 1-male units from dispersing. | Unlike geladas; males do not maintain tight control over group movements. |
| Social relationships | Weak social bonds among females. | Unlike geladas; reproductive unit is maintained by strong female bonds. |
| | Srong female relationship to harem male. | A different kind of alliance occurs in geladas. Unlike patas; no herding/defense of females by male. |
| | Strong social bonds among males. | Unlike geladas; 1-male units unite with and disperse from the band easily. Unlike patas; hostile male interactions. |

*Papio* baboons (Dunbar 1983). A savanna baboon model would miss unique aspects of hamadryas socioecology and would preclude an evolutionary study of what made *P. hamadryas* a distinct species. The social systems of geladas and hamadryas baboons are superficially similar. But important differences do exist (Table 21–2). The similarities appear to have evolved for rather different ecological reasons, and the contrasts reflect important differences in social behavior (Dunbar 1983). Social grouping in hamadryas appears to be an adaptive response to foraging under conditions of scarce food resources. However, some aspects of hamadryas social organization have perhaps their closest parallels in gorillas, which live in a very different kind of habitat. Strong social bonds occur between hamadryas females and the leading male, whereas relatively weak relationships occur among females. This situation is similar to social group relationships in gorillas, where females tolerate one another but have strong bonds to the leading male (Harcourt 1979a, 1979b). Yet due to phylogenetic distance and differences in ecological setting, it is doubtful that gorillas would be considered as a model for hamadryas social relationships. Even so, the behavioral/ecological reasons for this pattern of social relationships are different in the two cases (Harcourt and Stewart 1983).

The point of this exercise is that unique and evolutionarily important aspects of primate socioecology—whether in the past or present—may be masked by supposedly plausible reconstructions based on other primates. Furthermore, accurate analogies might be overlooked because of taxonomic and broad ecological dissimilarities. The usual rationales for selecting modern primate analogues for the behavior of other primates, including early hominids, are not reliable.

Returning to early hominids, paleoanthropology aims to document and explain how humans evolved. Yet attention should also be paid to anatomical and behavioral variations within the hominid clade, including differences from modern humans. Rather than using modern primate analogies to make interpretive leaps about early hominid behavior, this latter aspect of paleoanthropology adopts the theoretical goals and interpretive issues of modern primatology. Inferences about early hominid socioecology are subject to at least the same difficulties faced by primatologists in accounting for socioecological variations in modern primates. Accordingly, unique behaviors and adaptive variations among the hominids are important to discover; and they imply variations in socioecology, as they do among modern primates. Consequently, one of the significant tasks of paleoanthropology is to ascertain how modern human adaptations emerged from a more variable set of behavioral possibilities that existed among early hominids.

Unifying paleoanthropology and behavioral primatology in this way makes the reconstruction of early hominid socioecology extremely difficult. To make this possible, primatologists must work toward a better understanding of socioecological determinants in primates. From this, paleoanthropologists can try to develop methods to infer those ecological features that best predict social characteristics. This dialectic between paleoanthropologists and primatologists is based on an optimistic view, namely, that primate socioecology, in fact, can be understood and the development of inferential methods in paleoanthropology and paleoecology has only begun.

## Summary

Does an adequate method exist for choosing primate models to reconstruct early hominid socioecology? Conflicting models, based especially on chimpanzees and baboons, have been advocated previously without much concern for testing those models with evidence from the geological record or without considering possibly unique adaptations among early hominids. The issue of uniqueness is discussed for Plio–Pleistocene hominids from Olduvai. Reevaluation of the earliest archeological sites at Olduvai suggests that (1) Olduvai hominids interacted with the carnivore community and had to deal with predators in ways not usually faced by nonhuman primates or hunter-gatherers; and (2) hominids foraged in a manner unlike nonhuman primates or human hunter-gatherers (namely, they transported resources but not to home bases having the same social functions as modern campsites).

Variations in foraging and in predator avoidance strategies are deemed important determinants of socioecological variation in living primates. Evidence for different hominid adaptations from those known among living primates suggest that there is no single primate species that serves as an appropriate socioecological analogue. Thus, the use of *particular* species either as models or to create a simple evolutionary continuum (chimp to human) is questionable. If paleoanthropology concerns behavioral variation and uniqueness in hominids, its goals become much more closely allied with those of behavioral primatology. Documentation and explanation of species' differences in behavior and socioecology are important in the study of living primates. A similar approach can be adopted in the study of hominid adaptations. In this approach superficial similarities between early hominids and living primates are deemphasized. Instead, behavioral differences and the emergence of modern human adaptations from a more varied set of early hominid behaviors and socioecological adaptations are emphasized.

## References

Ardrey, R. (1976) *The Hunting Hypothesis.* New York: Bantam.

Berhrensmeyer, A. K. (1982) "Time resolution in fluvial vertebrate assemblages." *Paleobiology,* 8: 211–227.

Behrensmeyer, A. K.; Hill, A., eds. (1980) *Fossils in the Making.* Chicago: University of Chicago Press.

Bernstein, I.; Smith, E., eds. (1979) *Primate Ecology and Human Origins.* New York: Garland.

Binford, L. R. (1981) *Bones: Ancient Men and Modern Myths.* New York: Academic Press.

Boesch, C. and Boesch, H. (1984) "Possible causes of sex differences in the use of natural hammers by wild chimpanzees." *J. Human Evolution* 13: 415–440.

Bonnefille, R. (1979) "Method palynologique et reconstitutions paleoclimatique au Cenozoique dans le Rift Est Africain." *Bull. Soc. Geol. France,* 12: 331–342.

Brace, C. L. (1979) "Biological parameters and Pleistocene hominid life-ways." In *Primate Ecology and Human Origins* (pp. 263–289). I Bernstein; E. Smith, eds. New York: Garland.

Bunn, H. T. (1981) "Archaeological evidence for meat-eating by Plio-Pleistocene hominids from Koobi Fora and Olduvai Gorge." *Nature,* 291: 574–577.

Bunn, H. T. (1982) *Meat-eating and human evolution.* Ph.D. dissertation, University of California-Berkeley.

Campbell, B. G. (1979) "Ecological factors and social organization in human evolution." In *Primate Ecology and Human Origins* (pp. 263–289). I. Bernstein and E. Smith, eds. New York: Garland.

Campbell, B. G. (1982) *Humankind Emerging.* Boston: Little/Brown.

Cerling, T. E.; Hay, R.; O'Neil, J. R. (1977) "Isotopic evidence for dramatic climatic changes in East Africa during the Pleistocene." *Nature,* 267: 137–138.

Clutton-Brock, T.; Harvey, P. (1977) "Primate ecology and social organization." *J. Zool. London,* 183: 1–39.

Crook, J. H.; Gartlan, J. S. (1966) "Evolution and primate societies." *Nature,* 210: 1200–1203.

Dart, R. A. (1953) "The predatory transition from ape to man." *Intern. Anthro. Ling. Rev.* 1: 202–213.

Dodson, P. (1973) "The significance of small bones in paleoecological interpretation." *Cont. Geol.,* 12: 15–19.

Dunbar, R. (1983) "Relationships and social structure in gelada and hamadryas baboons." In *Primate Social Relationships* (pp. 299–307). R. Hinde, ed. Sunderland, MA; Sinauer.

Dunbar, R.; Dunbar, E. (1975) *Social Dynamics of Gelada Baboons.* Basel: Karger.

Eisenberg, J.; Muchenhirn, N.; Rudran, R. (1972) "The relation between ecology and social structure in primates. *Science,* 176: 863–874.

Fagan, B. (1983) *People of the Earth.* Boston: Little/Brown.

Frisch, J. E. (1968) "Individual behavior and interroop variability in Japanese macaques." In *Primates* (pp. 243–252). F. Jay, ed. New York: Holt, Rinehart and Winston.

Goodall, J. van Lawick. (1975) "The behavior of the chimpanzee." In *Hominisation und Verhalten.* G. Kurth and I Eibl-Eibesfeldt, eds. Stuttgart: Gustav Fischer Verlag.

Grine, F. (1981) "Trophic differences between 'gracile' and 'robust' australopichecines." *South African Journal of Science,* 77: 203–230.

Grine, F. (1984) "Deciduous molar microwear of South African Australopithecines." In *Food Acquisition and Processing in Primates,* pp. 525–534. D. J. Chivers; B. Wood; A. Bilsborough, eds. New York: Plenum.

Harcourt, A. H. (1979a) Social relations among adult female mountain gorillas." *Animal Behavior,* 27: 251–261.

Harcourt, A. H. (1979b) "Social relationships between adult male and female mountain gorillas in the wild." *Animal Behavior,* 27: 325–342.

Harcourt, A. H., Stewart, K. (1983) "Interactions, relationships and social structure: the great apes." In *Primate Social Relationships* (pp. 307–314). R. Hinde, ed. Sunderland, MA: Sinauer.

Harding, R.; Teleki, G., eds. (1981) *Ominvorous Primates.* New York: Columbia University Press.

Harris, J. W. K. (1983) "Cultural beginnings: Plio-Pleistocene archaeological occurrences from Afar, Ethiopia." *African Archaeological Review,* 1: 3–31.

Harris, J. W. K., and Johanson, D. C. (1983) "Cultural beginnings: Plio-Pleistocene archaeological occurrences from the Afar, Ethiopia." *African Archaeological Review.* 1: 3–31.

Hay, R. (1976) *Geology of the Olduvai Gorge.* Berkeley: University of California Press.

Hinde, R. A., ed. (1983) *Primate Social Relationships.* Sunderland, MA: Sinauer.

Isaac, G. (1976) "The activities of early African hominids." In *Human Origins* (pp. 483–514). G. Isaac; E. McCown, eds. Menlo Park, CA: Benjamin/Cummings.

Isaac, G. (1978) "The food-sharing behavior of protohuman hominoids." *Scientific American,* 238 (4): 90–108.

Isaac, G. (1980) "Casting the net wide: A review of archaeological evidence for early hominid land-use and ecological relations." In *Current Argument on Early Man* (pp. 227–251). L.-K. Konigsson, ed. New York: Pergamon Press.

Isaac, G., (1983) "Bones in contention: Competing explanations for the juxtaposition of early Pleistocene artifacts and faunal remains." In *Animals and Archaeology,* vol 1 (pp. 3–19). J. Clutton-Brock; C. Grigson, eds. London: British Archaeology Reports.

Isaac, G. Crader, D. (1981) "To what extent were early hominids carnivorous?" In *Omnivorous Primates* (pp. 37–103), R. Harding; G. Teleki, eds. New York: Columbia University Press.

Jay, P., (1968) "Primate field studies and human evolution." In *Primates.* P. Jay, ed. New York: Holt Rinehart and Winston.

Jolly, A. (1972) *The Evolution of Primate Behavior.* New York: Macmillan.

Jolly, C. (1970) "The seed eaters: A new model of hominid differentiation based on baboon ecology." *Man,* 5: 6–26.

Jolly, C. J. (1973) Changing views of hominid origins. *Yearbook of Physical Anthropology* 16: 1–17.

Jungers, W. L. (1982) "Lucy's limbs: Skeletal allometry and locomotion in *Australopithecus afarensis.*" *Nature,* 297: 676–678.

Kay, R. F. (1981) "The nut-crackers: A new theory of the adaptations of the ramapithecines." *American Journal of Physical Anthropology,* 55: 141–152.

King, G. (1975) "Socioterritorial units among carnivores and early hominids." *Journal of Anthropological Research,* 31: 69–87.

Keeley, L.; Toth, N. (1981) "Microwear polishes on early stone tools from Koobi Fora, Kenya." *Nature,* 293: 464–465.

Klein, R. (1982) "Age (mortality) profiles as a means of distinguishing hunted species from scavenged ones in Stone Age archaeological sites." *Paleobiology*, 8: 151–158.

Krebs, J.; Davies, N. (1978) *Behavioral Ecology*. Sunderland, MA: Sinauer.

Kummer, H. (1971) *Primate Societies*. Chicago: Aldine-Atherton.

Kuroda, S. (1979) "Grouping of the pygmy chimpanzees." *Primates*, 20: 161–183.

Lancaster, J. (1968) "On the evolution of tool-using behavior." *American Anthropologist* 70: 56–66.

Laporte, L. F.; Zihlman, A. L. (1983) "Plates, climate and hominid evolution." *South African Journal of Science*, 79: 96–110.

Leakey, M. D. (1971) *Olduvai Gorge, vol. 3*. London: Cambridge University Press.

Lovejoy, C. O. (1978) "A biomechanical review of the locomotor diversity of early hominids." In *Early Hominids of Africa* (pp. 403–429). C. Jolly, ed. New York: St. Martin's Press.

Lovejoy, C. O.; Heiple, K.; Burnstein, A. (1973) "The gait of *Australopithecus*." *American Journal of Physical Anthropology*, 38: 757–780.

McGrew, W.; Tutin, C.; Baldwin, P. (1979) "Chimpanzees, tools, and termites: Cross-cultural comparisons of Senegal, Tanzania, and Rio Muni." *Man*, 14: 185–214.

Napier, J. (1962) "Fossil hand bones from Olduvai Gorge." *Nature*, 196: 409–411.

Oxnard, C. (1975) *Uniqueness and Diversity in Human Evolution*. Chicago: Chicago University Press.

Pilbeam, D.; Behrensmeyer, A. K.; Barry, J.; Shah, S. Ibrahim (1979) "Miocene sediments and faunas in Pakistan.: *Postilla*, 179: 1–45.

Potts, R. (1982) *Lower Pleistocene Site Formation and Hominid Activities at Olduvai Gorge, Tanzania*. Ph.D. dissertation, Harvard University.

Potts, R. (1983) "Foraging for faunal resources by early hominids at Olduvai Gorge, Tanzania." In *Animals and Archaeology*, vol. 1 (pp. 51–62). J. Clutton-Brock and C. Grigson eds. London: Brit. Arch. Rep.

Potts, R. (1984a) "Hominid hunters: Problems of identifying the earliest hunter-gatherers." In *Community Ecology and Human Adaptation in the Pleistocene*. R. Foley, ed. London: Academic Press.

Potts, R. (1984b) "Home bases and early hominids." *American Scientist*, 72: 338–347.

Potts, R.; Shipman, P. (1981) "Cutmarks made by stone tools on bones from Olduvai Gorge, Tanzania." *Nature*, 291: 577–580.

Preuschoft, H. (1971) "Body posture and mode of locomotion in early Pleistocene hominids." *Folia Primatologica*, 14: 209–240.

Reynolds, P. C. (1976) "The emergence of early hominid social organization: I. The attachment systems." *Yearbook of Physical Anthropology*, 20: 73–95.

Richard, A. (1981) "Changing assumptions in primate ecology." *American Anthropologist*, 83: 517–533.

Richard, A. (1985) *Primates in Nature*. San Francisco: Freeman.

Robinson, J. (1972) *Early Hominid Postures and Locomotion*. Chicago: University of Chicago Press.

Schaller, G.; Lowther, G. (1969) "The relevance of carnivore behavior to the study of early hominids." *Southwest Journal of Anthropological Research*, 25: 307–341.

Shackleton, N. (1967) "Oxygen isotope analyses and Pleistocene temperatures re-assessed." *Nature*, 215: 15–17.

Shipman, P. (1981) *Life History of a Fossil*. Cambridge, MA: Harvard University Press.

Shipman, P. (1983) "Early hominid lifestyle: Hunting and gathering for foraging and scavenging." In *Animals and Archaeology*, vol. 1 (pp. 31–49). J. Clutton-Brock; C. Grigson, eds. Brit. Arch. Rep.

Stern, J.; Susman, R. (1983) "The locomotor anatomy of *Australopithecus afarensis*." *American Journal of Physical Anthropology*, 60: 279–317.

Steudel, K. (1980) "New estimates of early hominid body size." *American Journal of Physical Anthropology*, 52: 63–70.

Steudel, K. (1981) "Body size estimators in primate skeletal material." *International Journal of Primatology*, 2: 81–90.

Steudel, K. (1982a) "Patterns of intraspecific and interspecific allometry in Old World primates." *American Journal of Physical Anthropology*, 59: 419–430.

Steudel, K. (1982b) "Allometry and adaptation in the catarrhine postcranial skeleton." *American Journal of Physical Anthropology*, 59: 419–430.

Strum, S; Mitchell, W. (1987) "Baboons: Baboon models and muddles." In *The Evolution of Human Behavior: Primate Models* (pp. 87–104). W. G. Kinzey, ed. Albany: S.U.N.Y. Press.

Strum, S. (1981) "Processes and products of change: Baboon predatory behavior at Gilgil, Kenya." In *Omnivorous Primates* (pp. 255–302), R. Harding; G. Teleki, eds. New York: Columbia University Press.

Sugiyama, Y.; Koman, J. (1979) "Tool using and making behavior in wild chimpanzees at Boussou, Guinea." *Primates*, 20: 513–524.

Susman, R.; Creel, N. (1979) "Functional and morphological affinities of the subadult hand (OH 7) from Olduvai Gorge." *American Journal of Physical Anthropology*, 51: 311–332.

Susman, R.; Stern, J. (1982) "Functional morphology of *Homo habilis*." *Science*, 217: 931–933.

Tanner, N. (1981) *On Becoming Human*. Cambridge, England: Cambridge University Press.

Tanner, N.; Zihlman, A. (1976) "Women in evolution. Part 1: Innovation and selection in human origins." *Signs*, 1: 585–608.

Thompson, P. R. (1975) "A cross-species analysis of carnivore, primate and hominid behavior." *Journal of Human Evolution*, 5: 547–558.

Thompson, P. R. (1976) "A behavioral model for *Australopithecus africanus*." *Journal of Human Evolution*, 4:113–124.

Toth, N. (1982) *The Stone Technologies of Early Hominids at Koobi Fora, Kenya*. Ph.D. dissertation, University of California, Berkeley.

Trinkaus, E. (1980) "Sexual differences in Neanderthal limb bones." *Journal of Human Evolution*, 9: 377–399.

Van Couvering, J. A. H. (1980) "Community evolution in East Africa during the late Cenozoic." In *Fossils in the Making* (pp. 272–298). A. K. Behrensmeyer; A. Hill, eds. Chicago: University of Chicago Press.

Vrba, E. (1980) "The significance of bovid remains as indicators of environment and predation patterns." In *Fossils in the Making* (pp. 247–271). A. K. Behrensmeyer; A. Hill, eds. Chicago: University of Chicago Press.

Walker, A. (1973) "New *Australopithecus* femora from East Rudolf, Kenya." *Journal of Human Evolution,* 2: 529–536.

Walker, A. (1981) "Dietary hypotheses and human evolution." In *The Emergence of Man* (pp. 57–64). London: Royal Society and British Academy.

Washburn, S.; DeVore, I. (1961) "Social behavior of baboons and early man." In *Social Life of Early Man* (pp. 91–105). S. Washburn, ed. Chicago: Aldine.

Washburn, S.; Lancaster, C. (1968) "The evolution of hunting." In *Man the Hunter* (pp. 293–303). R. Lee and I. DeVore, eds. Chicago: Aldine.

Wolpoff, M. (1976) "Some aspects of the evolution of early hominid sexual dimorphism." *Current Anthropology,* 17: 579–606.

Wolpoff, M. (1983) "Lucy's little legs." *Journal of Human Evolution,* 12: 443–453.

Wood, B. (1978) "An analysis of early hominid fossil postcranial material: Principles and methods." In *Early Hominids in Africa* (pp. 347–360). New York: St. Martin's Press.

Wood, B. (1979) "Relationship between body size and long bone lengths in *Pan* and *Gorilla.*" *American Journal of Physical Anthropology,* 50: 23–26.

Wrangham, R. (1983a) "Ultimate factors determining social structure." In *Primate Social Relationships* (pp. 255–261). R. Hinde, ed. Sunderland, MA: Sinauer.

Wrangham, R. (1983b) "Social relationships in comparative perspective." In *Primate Social Relationships* (pp. 325–333). R. Hinde, ed. Sunderland, MA: Sinauer.

Yellen, J. (1977) *Archaeological Approaches to the Present.* New York: Academic Press.

Zihlman, A. (1978) "Interpretations of early hominid locomotion." In *Early Hominids of Africa* (pp. 361–377). C. Jolly, ed. New York: St. Martin's Press.

Zihlman, A. (1981) "Women as shapers of the human adaptation." In *Woman the Gatherer* (pp. 75–119). F. Dahlberg, ed. New Haven: Yale University Press.

Zihlman, A. (1983) "A behavioral reconstruction of *Australopithecus.*" In *Hominid Origins* (pp. 207–238). K. J. Reichs, ed. Washington DC: University Press of America.

Zihlman, A.; Cronin, J.; Cramer, D.; Sarich, V. (1978) "Pygmy chimpanzee as a possible prototype for the common ancestor of humans, chimpanzees, and gorillas." *Nature,* 275: 744–746.

# Chapter 22

# Species-Specific Dietary Patterns in Primates and Human Dietary Adaptations

## Robert W. Sussman

Throughout most of human evolution, subsistence was based on a gathering and hunting economy. It is only within the last 9 to 10,000 years that humans have cultivated their own food. We must assume that *Homo sapiens* developed certain dietary preferences that correlated with adaptations of the gastrointestinal tract during the long period of evolution of the genus. Do human gastrointestinal and dental adaptations reflect any of this past evolutionary history?

Research into this question revolves around a number of questions related to both recently adapted and phylogenetically conservative features. For example, is there something we might call a "natural" diet of man? As a result of their evolutionary history, are humans adapted for a specific type of diet? Are there correlations between digestive tract adaptations and dietary patterns in primates? If so, do any of these adaptations occur in humans? Can we find differences in digestive tract adaptations in human populations with different types of diets? Has the use of fire or cultivated crops greatly altered digestive tract adaptations? Finally, will studies of this sort lead to a better understanding of the evolution of human dietary patterns?

In this chapter, I will describe the concept of "species-specific dietary pattern." I will then describe two field studies (Sussman 1974, 1977, and Sussman and Tattersall 1981), as well as a number of other studies of primates, to illustrate this concept. Third, I will review some of the dietary patterns found among primates generally and compare these to patterns found among human hunting and gathering groups. Finally, I will describe some of the possible relationships between these dietary patterns and morphophysiological adaptations.

From *The Evolution of Human Behavior: Primate Models.* Warren G. Kinzey (ed.) State University of New York Press, Albany. 1987.

## SPECIES-SPECIFIC DIETARY PATTERNS

In recent years through numerous detailed studies of primate diets (see below), investigators have shown that two populations of the same species living in different areas will often feed on: (1) the same proportion of particular food items (e.g., fruits, flowers, leaves, insects, etc.); and (2) a similar number and proportion of plant species, even though the particular plant species may be entirely different. I have referred to these as *species-specific dietary patterns* (Sussman 1978). In other words, I hypothesize that each primate species is relatively fixed in certain features of its dietary preferences; although plant and or animal species eaten may differ in different localities, the types of items eaten and the degree of diversity of the diet remain quite constant. These dietary patterns are ultimately dependent upon the morphological and physiological adaptations of the species that, in turn, determine taste preferences, foraging patterns, and the ability to process and digest potential foods. Parameters used to measure dietary patterns are, for example: the percentage of different plant parts and animal prey in the diet; the total number of species eaten in a given time period; the percentage of the most-consumed species; the percentage of the five most frequently consumed species in the diet; and the percentage of the ten most frequently consumed species in the diet.

When comparing species-specific dietary patterns between different primate species, we often find that these patterns are not dependent upon taxonomic relationships. Closely related species often have very different diets, whereas many unrelated species have convergent dietary patterns. However, at some level, we would assume that there is a relationship between dietary patterns, foraging patterns, and anatomical and physiologi-

143

cal adaptations. Unfortunately, in the examples that follow, comparable data have not always been collected. Therefore, I will necessarily be using different types of measures in an attempt to illustrate the usefulness of the concept of species-specific dietary patterns.

## Two Lemurs and a Macaque: Examples of Species-Specific Dietary Patterns

I first began to think of species-specific dietary patterns during a study of two closely related species of lemur in Madagascar: the ringtailed lemur *(Lemur catta)* and the brown lemur *(Lemur fulvus)* (Figure 22–1). This study was carried out in three separate forests (Figure 22–2): Antserananomby, where the two species coexisted; Tongobato, where the brown lemur was found alone; and Berenty, where the ringtailed lemur lived alone. Observations at Antserananomby were conducted during the dry season, whereas those at the other two forests took place during the wet season. This study has been described in detail elsewhere (Sussman 1974, 1977) and only certain aspects of feeding behavior will be discussed here.

Quantitative data were collected on the diet and feeding behavior of these two species and their diets were found to be radically different. The brown lemur had a very limited diet, feeding on a very narrow range of food items; the ringtailed lemur had a relatively diverse diet. The brown lemur ate only 8 plant species at Tongobato and 11 at Antserananomby, eating a total of 13 species in both forests combined. The ringtailed lemur fed on 24 plant species at each forest. Only three of these plant species were eaten by *L. catta* in both forests; they therefore fed on a total of 45 different plant species combined. Neither lemur was observed feeding on animal prey.

The diet of the brown lemur was further limited by the fact that a few species of plant made up a large portion of the diet and the leaves of *Tamarindus indica* (the dominant tree species in all three forests) were the main staple. At Antserananomby, three species of plant constituted 85 percent of the diet: *Acacia rovumae, Ficus soroceoides,* and *Tamarindus indica.* At Tongobato, *Flacourtia ramontchi, Tamarindus indica,* and *Terminalia mantaly* accounted for over 80 percent of the diet. Tamarind leaves accounted for over 40 percent of the diet at Tongobato and over 75 percent during the dry season at Antserananomby.

The diet of the ringtailed lemur was more diverse than that of the brown lemur. Eight species of plant made up over 70 percent of the diet at Antserananomby. At Berenty, eight species of plant accounted for 80 percent of the diet. The tamarind tree provided 23 to 24 percent of the diet in the two forests, with tamarind pods and leaves providing approximately equal proportions regardless of season.

The parts of the plants eaten and the seasonal variation in diet were related to the foraging patterns of these two prosimians. Brown lemur groups had very small day ranges (125 to 150 meters) and home ranges (about one hectare). They stayed mainly in the canopy of the trees and rarely came to the ground. The ringtailed lemur moved 1000 or more meters daily and had relatively large home ranges, averaging around 9 hectares. Ringtailed groups constantly surveyed their home range, covering the whole area every 7 to 10 days. Although this species fed in all forest strata, most group travel and almost one third of its feeding took place on the ground.

**Figure 22–1** (a) Ring tailed lemur *(Lemur catta).* (b) Brown lemur *(Lemur fulvus).*

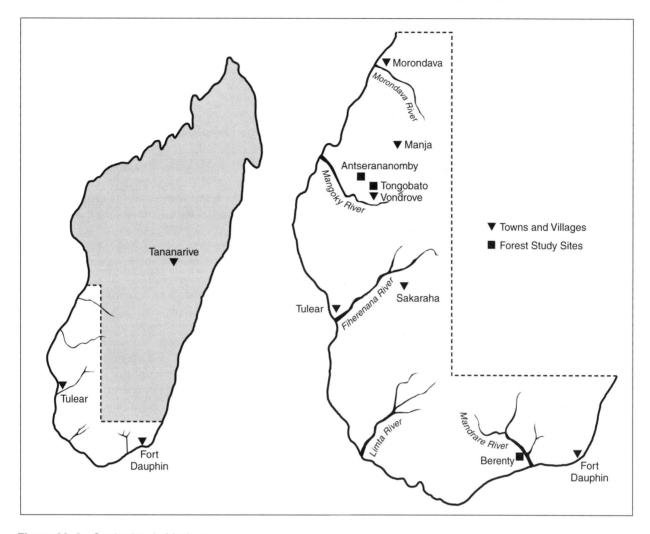

**Figure 22–2**   Study sites in Madagascar.

Both lemur species ate fruit, shoots, leaves, flowers, bark, and sap. However, the restricted ranging pattern of the brown lemur corresponded to a dependence on the tamarind tree and a highly folivorous diet. In the dry season at Antserananomby, this lemur was able to subsist almost entirely on mature leaves, mainly from tamarind. In the wet season (Tongobato), it supplemented its mainly folivorous diet with readily available fruit (42%) and flowers (5%), though tamarind leaves still accounted for 42 percent of the diet. The pattern of plant part utilization by the ringtailed lemur did not change a great deal seasonally. Because the ringtails constantly surveyed their home range and fed in all forest levels, they were able to exploit a number of different resources over a wide area. Their constant movement was not related to any noticeable depletion of resources. Even during the dry season at Berenty, ringtailed lemurs were able to find and exploit many species of plant that were in fruit and flower.

The second study I wish to summarize was conducted on a group of long-tailed macaques *(Macaca fas-cicularis)* in Mauritius (Figure 22–3). These monkeys are not endemic to Mauritius but were brought to this small island from Java about 450 years ago (Sussman and Tattersall 1981). Mauritian macaque males weigh about 7 kg and females weigh about 4.5 kg. The monkeys found in the Mauritian savannah live in large groups of between 70 to 90 individuals. One of the long-term foci of this study was to compare dietary patterns and foraging behavior of populations living in degraded, savannah habitats with those inhabiting the undisturbed endemic, evergreen forest of Mauritius and, eventually, with the parent population in Indonesia. Given the extreme differences in plant species composition and distribution in these three areas, I hoped to determine whether a predictable, species-specific dietary pattern could be found among these long-tailed macaque populations.

Before going to Mauritius, I attempted to predict what the dietary pattern might be, given previous research on the morphology and behavior of *Macaca fascicularis.* From studies of molar morphology, Kay (1978) infers that the dietary adaptations of macaques range

**Figure 22–3** Mauritian long-tailed macaque *(Macaca fascicularis).*

from highly folivorous to extremely frugivorous. *M. fascicularis* is intermediate in this range, having a molar morphology that suggests a diet consisting predominantly of fruit with some leaves and insects. From studies of gut morphology, Chivers and Hladik (1980) also indicate that these monkeys should be frugivores, tending towards folivory. Preliminary field studies in Malaysia support these predictions. MacKinnon and MacKinnon (1980) found *M. fascicularis* in Malaysia to have a diet made up of 72.5 percent fruit and flowers, 24 percent leaves and 4.7 percent animal prey. In a separate study, Aldrich-Blake (1980) found the diet to be composed of 70 percent fruit and flowers, 25 percent leaves, and 5 percent animal prey. These authors report that Malaysian long-tailed macaques are very eclectic feeders with a high level of short-term selectivity. They concentrate on a few food sources at any one time, but change this concentration as different resources become available.

Results from different seasons in 1977 and 1979 reveal a pattern very similar to that described for the Malaysian long-tailed macaques. In June to July 1977 a total of 21 plant species were eaten in 125 hours and from September to December 1979, 31 species were eaten in 200 hours. In both seasons, however, only 14 plant species were eaten over 1 percent of the time and only 6 of these species were fed upon in both years. Furthermore, fruit from two species accounted for over 50 percent of the diet and five species accounted for between 65 and 75 percent of the diet (Table 22–1). In both years, the proportions of plant parts eaten were extremely similar to those reported for the Malaysian long-tailed monkeys (Table 22–2). Thus, as in Malaysia, the diet of the Mauritian macaque is mainly frugivorous but includes a relatively high proportion (almost 30%) of leaves and insects. As predicted, these monkeys feed on a large number of plant species but the major portion of their diet consists of a few species at any one time.

TABLE 22–1  Mean Percentage Item and Species Composition of Diet of Long-tailed Macaques in Two Separate Years in Mauritius

| A. % of Species Eaten—1977 | | | | |
|---|---|---|---|---|
| Species | Part | % | | |
| *Tamarindus indica* | pod | 33 | } 55% | |
| *Ficus* | fruit | 22 | | } 74% |
| *Saccarum officianarum* | stem | 8 | | |
| *Acacia eburnea* | pod | 6 | | |
| *Leucaena leucocephela* | pod | 5 | | |

| B. % of Species Eaten—1979 | | | | |
|---|---|---|---|---|
| Species | Part | % | | |
| *Tamarindus indica* | pod | 28 | } 51% | |
| *Mango* | fruit | 23 | | |
| *Albizzia* | flowers, stems, new leaves | 7 | | } 69% |
| *Eleocharis (grass)* | stem | 5 | | |
| *Acacia concinna* | leaves | 3 | | |
| *Ficus* | fruit | 3 | | |

TABLE 22–2   Mean Percentage Item Composition of Diet of Long-tailed Macaques in Malaysia and Mauritius

|  | **Malaysia** | | | |
| --- | --- | --- | --- | --- |
|  | MacKinnon 1980 | Aldrich-Blake 1980 | Mauritius 1977 | Mauritius 1979 |
| Fruit & flowers | 72.5 | 70 | 71 | 66 |
| Leaves & stems | 24 | 25 | 22 | 22 |
| Invertebrates | 4.4 | 5 | 5 | 4 |
| ? |  |  | 2 | 7 |

## FURTHER EXAMPLES OF SPECIES-SPECIFIC DIETARY PATTERNS

Although data have often been collected using different methods and emphasizing different aspects of the diet, species-specific dietary patterns have been found in a number of species. I will only give a few examples here. Pollock (1977) observed two adjacent groups of indri (*Indri indri*) in Madagascar. He found that the percentages of plants making up the greatest part of the diet and the proportion of the different plant parts eaten by both groups was essentially the same (Table 22–3). From patterns of food choice each day, Pollock has the impression that the indris had an organized variability in their diet and "that a precise control of dietetic variety existed" (1977:54). This, further, was related to a highly organized strategy of feeding and ranging.

Milton (1980) studied two groups of howler monkeys (*Alouatta palliata*) in different areas of Barro Colorado. One of the forests (Lutz Ravine) was largely composed of secondary forest and the second (referred to as Old Forest) was undisturbed, mature forest. She found that the *number* of food species eaten in both forests was exactly the same, 73 plant species, but 75 percent of the particular *species* eaten were different (Table 22–4). The *number* of species of plants used for each of the three major dietary categories was also strikingly similar although the species used for these plant parts were mainly different. Milton states:

TABLE 22–3   Percentage Composition of Diet of Indri (*Indri indri*) in Two Study Sites in Madagascar (from Pollock 1977)

|  | Group P | Group V |
| --- | --- | --- |
| Top Ranked | 14% | 19% |
| Top Five | 50% | 50% |
| Young Leaves & Shoots | 36.1% | 32.2% |
| Fruit | 26.4% | 23.8% |
| Flowers | 2.3% | 0.0% |
| Mature Leaves | 0.9% | 0.2% |
| Unidentified | 34.3% | 43.8% |

When examined separately, both study areas showed the same pattern in the number of food species used during the same period ... Thus despite the differences in the forest between the two areas, both troops diversified the species used as food sources to the same extent (1980: 59–60).

The differences in plant species used by the two howler groups were mainly the result of differences in plant composition in the two study areas.

Struhsaker (1975, 1978) and Clutton-Brock (1972) studied different groups of red colobus (*Colobus badius*) in Uganda and Tanzania, respectively. Again the patterns of the diets of the two populations were strikingly similar, though the number of shared plant species was very small (Table 22–5). Struhsaker (1978) also found the diet of red colobus to be stable over a five year period (1970–1975), even though species composition changed somewhat over time.

The examples discussed so far are from highly folivorous primates, but more generalized, omnivorous primates show species-specific dietary patterns as well. Kavanaugh (1978), for example, studied vervet monkeys (*Cercopithecus aethiops*) in two different forests for four months each. Although he found differences in the proportions of food items and of different food species in the diet of the two populations, certain aspects of the diversity of the diets were very similar. The range of species eaten during any monthly sample varied from 9 to 17 at one forest, and from 8 to 18 at the other. Furthermore, the top five species accounted for monthly minima of 52 percent in both forests and maxima of 83 percent and 81 percent at the forests. Kavanaugh (1978) states:

> The diet varied seasonally within habitats and few species were common to more than one study site, but the total ranges of foodparts showed little variation between habitats ... (60) Interhabitat differences in the particular species eaten reflect differences in the availability of those species (57).

Homewood (1978) studied mangabeys (*Cercocebus galeritus*) in two sites, Mchelelo and Mnazini, along the Tana River in Kenya. Despite major differences in vegetation and species composition, the percentage contribution of different food items was very similar for the monkeys in

TABLE 22–4   Number of Different Species Eaten by Howlers (*Alouatta palliata*) in Two Studies in Barro Colorado Island (from Milton 1980)

|  | Old Forest | Lutz Ravine | In Common | Total Different |
|---|---|---|---|---|
| Total | 73 | 73 | 37 | 109 |
| Leaves | 59 | 59 | 31 | 87 |
| Fruit | 25 | 23 | 12 | 36 |
| Flowers | 13 | 16 | 4 | 25 |

[data from samples over 9 month period in both study sites at B.C.I.]

the two areas (Figure 22–4). The mangabeys at both forests concentrated on a few prolific species at any one time; the top five species for each month accounted for a median of 78 percent of the diet at Mnazini and 83 percent in Mchelelo. Comparing her study with a study by Quris (1975) in Gabon, Homewood found mangabeys from West and East Africa to have very similar diets. As with the ringtailed lemur, *C. galeritus* did not greatly alter the food item portion of its diet seasonally or in different areas. Homewood emphasizes that the versatility and adaptability of the mangabey foraging, locomotor, and social behavior "ensures relative dietary constancy (in terms of composition by item) despite environmental change" (1978:389)

In a study comparing three adjacent groups of savannah baboons (*Papio cynocephalus*) at Amboseli, Stacey (1986) found the amount of overlap in the individual plant species and plant parts eaten by the three groups to be "surprisingly low." However, compared on the basis of general food types, the percentage of time spent feeding on each category was almost identical (Table 22–6). The groups fed upon the same types of foods in very similar proportions, but the actual species utilized by each group were frequently different.

Finally, the diet of orangutans has been studied in two forests in Borneo (MacKinnon 1974, Rodman 1977) and in a Sumatran forest (Rijksen 1978). In all three forests, the main food categories eaten were fruits, leaves, bark, and insects. The proportion of fruit and leaves eaten by the orangutan populations was similar (Figure

22–5). The amount of time eating insects by the Sumatran orangs was higher than that by the Bornean apes and the proportion of bark eating was lower. However, Rijken included the amount of time spent actually searching for and collecting insect food, rather than the actual feeding time. Given the different methods used in collecting feeding data, at this level, the dietary patterns in the three populations, representing two subspecies, are remarkably similar.

## DIETARY PATTERNS AMONG PRIMATES

In the species discussed above there is an interrelationship among foraging pattern, diversity of diet, and seasonal variation in diet. Feeding patterns, as defined by types of food items eaten and relative diversity of the diet, appear to be species-specific and determined by the ecology, distribution, and evolutionary history of the primates concerned. The foraging and dietary patterns of these species are not unique among primates. As can be seen in Table 22–7), there are convergent patterns among unrelated species. As with the brown lemur, a high proportion of the diets of the purple-faced langur and of the black-and-white colobus are made up of leaves. During certain seasons, these species are able to exist almost exclusively on mature leaves. Other species with similar dietary adaptations include the sportive lemur (*Lepilemur*) and gelada baboons (*Theropithecus*). The gray langur, red colobus, and ring-tailed lemur have more diverse

TABLE 22–5   Number of Plant Species and Percentage Composition of Top Ranked Species Eaten by Red Colobus (*Colobus badius*) in Two Study Sites in East Africa—Kibale (Struhsaker 1975); Gombe (Clutton-Brock 1972)

|  | Gombe (9 months) | Kibale (12 months) |
|---|---|---|
| Total # of Species | 60 | 68 (5 in common) |
| % of top 5 ssp. | 55% | 55.9% |
| % of top 10 ssp. | 78.4% | 75% |
| Top species | 15.4% (*Newtonia*) | 15.4% (*Celtis africana*) |
| Index of Dietary Diversity (H) | 2.65 | 2.96 |

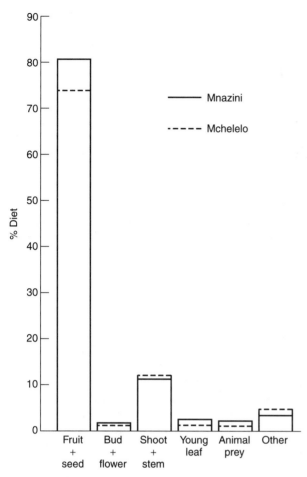

**Figure 22–4** Median percentage item composition of diet in mangabeys *(Cercocebus galeritus)* at two study sites in Kenya (from Homewood 1978).

diets and although they consume a fair proportion of leaf material, presumably they cannot subsist on diets composed exclusively of mature leaves.

Long-tailed macaques, vervet monkeys, mangabeys, baboons, and orangutans include some animal matter in their diets and, along with many other primate species, are omnivores. In fact, most species of primate are omnivorous (see Harding 1981) and omnivory should be considered an evolutionarily conservative and generalized trait among primates. It is very likely that the earliest primates became distinct from insectivores by taking advantage of the food resources offered by newly diversifying flowering plants (see Sussman, Chapter 5). The earliest "primates of modern aspect" were small, nocturnal prosimians much like some of the extant lemurs and lorisids. The majority of these animals are primarily frugivorous but obtain most of their protein from insects. Among primates, the proportion of animal material included in the diet is related to body size. Small primates are able to obtain most of their protein needs from insects whereas larger forms must utilize leaves or other plant sources to fulfill some or all of their protein requirements. Because of the difficulty in obtaining a sufficient amount of insect prey, omnivorous mammals over 2 to 3 kg in weight must rely heavily on social insects or on small vertebrates for protein (Charles-Dominique 1975, Kay 1975, Hladik 1981, Terborgh 1983). The ability to subsist without animal protein and to obtain all protein requirements from folivory is a more specialized, derived feeding adaptation among primates. Figure 22–6 is a hypothetical scheme of the evolution of general primate feeding adaptations.

Thus, omnivorous primates are mainly frugivorous and, depending upon body size, obtain most of their protein from insects or leaves. In all large, omnivorous, nonhuman primates, animal protein is a very small but presumably necessary component of the diet. Ani-

**TABLE 22–6** Percentage Item Composition and Dietary Indices of Three Groups of Baboons *(Papio cynocephalus)* in Amboseli National Park, Kenya (from Stacey 1986)

| Food type | Percentage of Total Feeding Time | | | |
|---|---|---|---|---|
| | Limp's Group | Hook's Group | Alto's Group | All Groups |
| Grasses | 38 | 40 | 43 | 41 |
| Fruits | 33 | 22 | 31 | 28 |
| Seeds | 12 | 27 | 12 | 18 |
| Sap | 10 | 7 | 7 | 8 |
| Flowers | 2 | 2 | 6 | 3 |
| Leaves | 2 | 1 | 1 | 1 |
| Animal Matter | 0 | 2 | 0 | 1 |
| Miscellaneous | 2 | 0 | 1 | 1 |
| Index of Dietary Diversity ($I_D$) | 13.37 | 13.93 | 14.14 | |
| Index of Dietary Similarity ($I_C$) | *L&H* | *L&A* | *H&A* | |
| Plant Species | 0.476 | 0.507 | 0.588 (very low) | |
| General Food Types | 0.935 | 0.990 | 0.945 (almost identical) | |

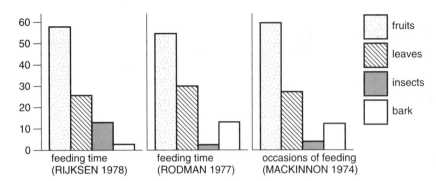

**Figure 22–5** Percentage item composition of diet of orangutans *(Pongo pygmaeus)* at three study sites in Sumatra and Borneo.

mals falling into this category usually have the largest home ranges and day ranges and the most diverse diets of all primates. Although there has been a great deal of publicity given to the fact that some large primates, such as baboons and chimpanzees, include animal prey and especially small vertebrates in their diets, given the evolutionary history and dietary patterns of primates generally, this is not at all surprising. Table 22–7 lists the dietary patterns of some omnivorous primates.

For the purpose of comparison, Table 22–7 includes data on a human hunting and gathering group, the ≠Kadi San Bushman of the Kalahari. The study of this group (Tanaka 1976, 1980) is one of the most detailed to date on the diet of modern hunters and gatherers. Because of the methods employed, the estimates shown are comparable to those obtained for nonhuman primates. At this level of comparison, the ≠Kadi San Bushman diet is very similar to that of nonhuman primate omnivores and most similar to that of the chimpanzee. It is probably not surprising to anyone that human and chimpanzee dietary patterns are generally similar, but it might be somewhat of a surprise that so little animal prey is eaten by these hunters and gatherers. However, this probably is not unusual. A number of estimates of the diets in these societies have also shown that most "hunters" subsist mainly by gathering, with 65 percent to over 80 percent of the diet being made up of plant material (Lee 1968, 1969, Tanno 1981, Woodburn 1968). Given these behavioral data, the body size of early hominids, and their general dental and gut tract anatomy (see below), we may hypothesize that the earliest relatives of *Homo* were mainly frugivorous omnivores with a dietary pattern similar to that of modern chimpanzees, though the specific plant species and food items utilized are likely to have been quite different.

Table 22–8 presents a very preliminary and simplified classification of some of the major categories of feeding types found among primates. The classification is preliminary because of the paucity of comparative data on the diets of most nonhuman primates and simplified because it is likely that more classes and subclasses will be found as more data are gathered. Furthermore, even within the general categories, there is a great deal of variability possible at the species level. What is defined by these categories is not a specific set of diets, but groups of primates with relatively similar dietary patterns. Each species of primate is predicted to have a species-specific dietary pattern and those species filling similar ecological roles in different communities may have convergent dietary patterns. In this way, we may eventually be able to define specific feeding guilds among primates. These patterns probably exist in conjunction with certain limits in the range and proportion of food items that would constitute an acceptable diet for a given species. We assume that to some extent these dietary patterns and limitations are physiologically based.

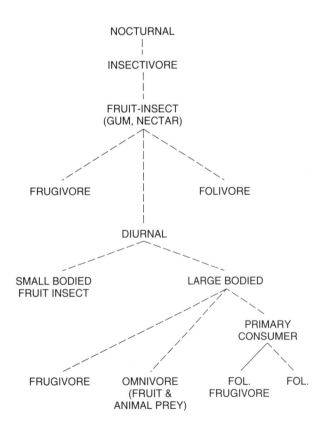

**Figure 22–6** Hypothetical scheme of the evolution of primate feeding adaptations.

TABLE 22–7  Dietary Patterns among Some Diurnal, Large-bodied Primates

| Species | Species of plants | | | Parts of plants and animal prey | | | References |
|---|---|---|---|---|---|---|---|
| | No. of plant species eaten | % of most utilized species | No. of plant species comprising majority of diet | % of mature leaves | % of other plant material (fruit) | % of animal prey | |
| 1) Specialized folivores | | | | | | | |
| Brown lemur (Lemur fulvus) | 8, 11 | >60 | 3 (85%) | ≅70 | 30 (24) | 0 | Sussman (1977) |
| Purple-faced langur (Presbytis senex) | 12 (>90%) | 41 | 3 (70%) | 60 | 40 (28) | 0 | Hladik (1977) |
| Black-and-white colobus (Colobus guereza) | 6, 8 | >70 | 3 (90%) | ≅60 | 40 | 0 | Clutton-Brock (1975) |
| 2) Folivore-frugivores | | | | | | | |
| Ring-tailed lemur (Lemur catta) | 24 | 23 | 8 (70%) | 34 (young & mature) | 66 (46) | 0 | Sussman (1977) |
| Gray langur (Presbytis entellus) | 25 (>90%) | ≅10 | 10 (70%) | 21 | 79 (45) | 0 | Hladik (1977) |
| Red colobus (Colobus badius) | 20 (>90%) | 11 | 9 (70%) | 20 | 80 | 0 | Clutton-Brock (1975) |
| 3) Omnivores | | | | | | | |
| Cebus monkey (Cebus capucinus) | 54 | Unspecified | 36 (60%) | Small | 80 (65) | 20 | Hladik and Hladik (1969), Oppenheimer (1968) |
| Toque macaque (Macaca sinica) | >40 | Unspecified | 22 | Small | 96 (77) | 4 | Hladik and Hladik (1972); Dittus (1974) |
| Vervet monkey (Cercopithecus sabaeus) | >65 | 7.2 | 12 (50%) | Small | 87 (50) | 13 | Harrison (1984) |
| Chimpanzee (Pan troglodytes) | 78 | Unspecified | 18 (80%) | Small | 96 (68) | 4 | Suzuki (1969, 1975) |
| 4) Human hunter/gatherers | | | | | | | |
| ≠Kadi San Bushman | 79 | Unspecified | 13 | Small | 96.4 | 3.6 | Tanaka (1976) |

Data represent yearly averages (Adapted from Sussman 1978)

151

TABLE 22–8   Primate Feeding Types

| Size | Classification | Diet |
|---|---|---|
| | *Nocturnal primates* | |
| Small bodied (to ≅ 500 g) | Insectivores | ≅70% animal prey |
| | Insectivore–frugivores | 50% animal prey |
| Large bodied (1–2 kg) | Frugivores | Mainly fruit, little or no animal prey |
| | Folivores | Mainly leaves, little or no animal prey |
| | *Diurnal primates* | |
| Small bodied (to ≅ 500 g) | Insectivore–frugivores | 30–50% insects |
| Large bodied (over 1 kg) | Omnivores | Mainly fruit w/some animal prey |
| | Specialized frugivores | Very high % fruit |
| | Folivore–frugivores | Little or no animal prey |
| | Specialized folivores | Mature leaves, no animal prey |

## RELATIONSHIPS BETWEEN MORPHOPHYSIOLOGY AND DIETARY PATTERNS IN PRIMATES

In Figure 22–7, I present a model depicting how morphophysiology might mediate foraging and feeding behavior. In this model, I assume that the feeding niche of a species (and the morphological, physiological, and, therefore, behavioral adaptations directly related to food exploitation) is evolutionarily conservative. Over long-term evolutionary history, behaviors, such as food preferences and the ability to find and exploit certain food items, are dependent upon morphophysiological adaptations that are phylogenetically conservative. Species-specific dietary patterns are the result of these conservative feeding adaptations, and the food selected from what is potentially available in any given habitat is determined to a large extent by phylogenetic adaptations. This would explain why sympatric species choose different resources, with potentially the same resources available, and why populations of the same species search for similar types of resources in different habitats. (It also gives us some insight into why models of optimal foraging strategy, which use resource distribution as an independent variable and do not take into account phylogenetic feeding

adaptations, have proven to be relatively unfruitful.) Given this model, short term, population-specific foraging behaviors will depend upon specific patterns of food distribution and availability. At some level, perturbations and stresses caused by difficulty of access or the absence of certain foods will lead to changes in the normal patterns of food acquisition behavior and possibly to changes and selection at the morphophysiological level. However, behavior, and subsequently morphology, will only vary if the phylogenetically conservative species-specific patterns cannot be achieved.

Thus, we assume there is a relationship between certain morphophysiological characteristics and feeding and foraging behavior. Although variation occurs in the diet of a primate species, this variation is constrained by morphological and physiological adaptations. The diet is related, first, to specific morphological and physiological adaptations of the digestive tract of the species and, secondly, to environmental variables. Furthermore, the specific patterns of different species may be variable in different ways and a study of the types of *patterns* that exist among primates should be quite informative. The assumption that dietary patterns are conservative and may constrain changes in other variables underlies many ar-

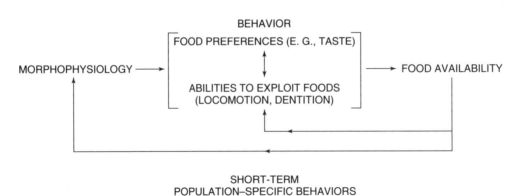

Figure 22–7   Model representing relationships between morphophysiology, feeding behavior, and food availability.

guments concerning the relationships between ecology and social structure (e.g., Altmann 1974, Crook 1970, Denham 1971, Jarmon 1974, Lack 1968), although it is rarely made explicit (see, however, Clutton-Brock and Harvey 1977, Hladik 1977, 1981).

The above discussion assumes that certain feeding adaptations are quite conservative and may allow us to predict dietary patterns. Recent research on primate dental and intestinal tract morphology indicates that this is so. For example, a number of investigators have been able to determine relationships between dental morphology and dietary propensity in a variety of primate taxa (Hylander 1975, Kay 1975, 1978, 1981, Kay and Hylander 1978, Kay et al. 1978, Kinzey 1978, Rosenberger and Kinzey 1976). Kay (1975) showed that species that eat different proportions of fruit, leaves, and insects have different molar structure. Taking allometric adjustments into account, primates with folivorous or insectivorous diets tend to have proportionately larger molars with relatively longer shearing blades and higher crowns than do frugivorous species. Molars with thick enamel and poorly developed shearing crests correspond with a diet made up mainly of fruit and especially hard nuts, seed, and tough pods (Kay 1981). Kay and Hylander (1978:174) state:

> . . . any dietary interpretation based on morphology may be slightly out of phase with the present behavior. But if an animal's morphology were too far out of step with its environment, extinction would result. It is not surprising then that . . . minor dental variations correspond remarkably well with what is known of dietary preferences of species in the wild.

Dietetic differences among primates are also related to variation in digestive tract anatomy and physiology (Amerasinghe et al. 1971, Chivers and Hladik 1980, 1984, Hladik 1967, Hladik et al. 1971, Martin et al. 1985). In general mammals subsisting mainly on animal matter have a simple stomach and colon and a long small intestine. Those feeding on leaves have a complex stomach or an enlarged caecum and colon. Mammals that are mainly frugivorous have an intermediate morphology but tend towards one direction or the other depending upon the tendency to supplement their diet with animal matter or leaves.

In general, the alimentary tract of primates is relatively generalized with few extreme specializations (Chivers and Hladik 1980, 1984, Hill 1972, Martin et al. 1985). This is true of both the stomach, which generally remains a simple globular sac, and the small intestine, which varies somewhat in proportionate length but is fairly uniform in form and distribution throughout the primates. Only in the more specialized leaf-eating primates is some major gastric specialization encountered. This, again, indicates that the common ancestral primate was most likely an omnivore (i.e., fed on both plant and animal matter).

Given the fact that the proportions of different compartments of the intestinal tract are generally related to the proportion of foliage, animal matter, and fruit in the diet of mammals, Chivers and Hladik (1980, 1984) made interspecific comparisons of 78 mammals, including 48 primate species, in an attempt to describe and predict these relationships. By taking the ratio of surface area of the small intestine plus one-half that of the stomach, caecum, and colon ("potential area for absorption") in relation to body length, they could predict whether a species was mainly folivorous, frugivorous, or faunivorous at an 85 percent confidence level (except in the smallest sized animals) (Figure 22–8). Furthermore, among frugivores, the propensity to supplement the diet with leaves or animal protein could be predicted. Martin et al. (1985), using many of the same specimens as Chivers and Hladik, scaled gastrointestinal compartments in relation to metabolic requirements and body weight. Although mammals (primates as well as nonprimates) with specializations for folivory separated out with multivariate clustering techniques, there was a "considerable lability among mammal species exhibiting less specialized guts." Both Chivers and Hladik (1980) and Martin et al. (1985) found that measurements of gastrointestinal compartments varied in captive and wild specimens of the same species.

Thus, at least at a general level, relationships exist between dietary patterns, dental morphology, and alimentary tract adaptations, and we may ask the question: Can relationships be found between morphology and diet in humans, and do these dental and gastrointestinal adaptations reflect past dietary patterns? As discussed above, Kay (1981, pers. comm.) found an inverse relationship between relative shearing capabilities of the molars and relative enamel thickness, with the latter adaptation being related to a greater proportion of fruit, seeds, and hard objects in the diet versus foliage or animal matter. Human dentition, both modern and fossil, is characterized by having thick enamel.

In their comparative studies, Chivers and Hladik (1980, 1984) compared "coefficients of gut differentiation" (surface area of stomach + caecum + colon)/(surface area of small intestine) between faunivores, frugivore, and folivores. The values for faunivores fell between 0.08 and about 0.55; for frugivores between approximately 0.33 and 2.0; the coefficient for folivores was between 1.0 and 6.0. In a preliminary study of modern human intestinal tracts from dissection specimens in an urban U.S. medical school, using the same methods as Chivers and Hladik, we found a coefficient of 0.62 (N=6, range 0.37–1.15). Thus, in this measurement of proportionate lengths of gastrointestinal compartments, the modern humans we measured fall within the middle of the frugivorous range, but slightly in the direction of faunivores. However, when we compare the relationship between potential area for absorption (surface area of small

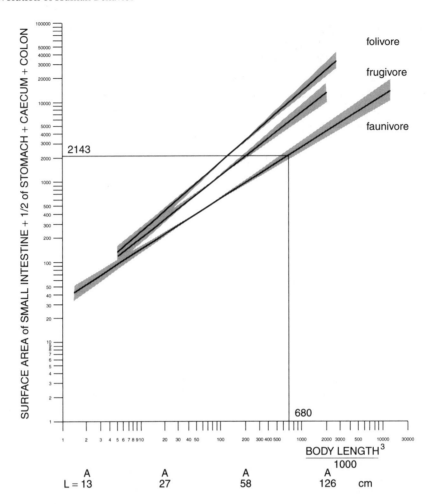

**Figure 22–8** The relationship, determined by Chivers and Hladik (1980), between potential area for absorption (surface area of small intestine and half the combined areas of stomach, caecum, and colon) and body length in faunivores, frugivores, and folivores in the form of regressions derived from individual data. The stippled areas demarcate the 95 percent confidence limits for the slopes; the three dietary groups are quite distinct at the 85 percent limit. Human data collected at Washington University (area for absorption = 2143; body length[3] = 680) fall within the faunivore range. (Adapted from Chivers and Hladik 1980).

intestine and half the combined areas of stomach, caecum, and colon) and body length in a number of mammals (as per Chivers and Hladik 1980), our measurements predict a faunivorous diet for this human population (Figure 22–8). Martin et al. (1985) also measured six human gut tracts and found that humans clustered with faunivorous mammals.

Do these results suggest that the "natural diet" of *Homo sapiens* is highly faunivorous? How can we reconcile interpretations from the general patterns of the gastrointestinal tract, the dentition, and modern hunters and gatherers' diets with allometrically corrected gut tract morphology? Are these measurements valid for interpretations of early human dietary adaptations and present dietary propensities? Unfortunately, I think that relative proportions of gastrointestinal compartments of modern humans will not help us understand the evolu-

tion of human dietary patterns—at least not until we know more about the physiology of digestion. There are too many unanswered questions. For example:

**1.** Gut tract compartmental dimensions appear to be quite malleable. Mammals, including primates, maintained in captivity exhibit different dimensions from wild-living conspecifics (Chivers and Hladik 1980, Hladik 1967, Martin et al. 1985), and presumably intraspecific variation might occur in wild populations with vastly different diets. How much of the morphology of humans in our samples is related to the high proportion of animal protein in the diet of modern Western industrialized populations? What would these dimensions look like in hunters and gatherers or highly vegetarian populations?

**2.** How have intestinal dimensions kept pace with the increase in body size over the past few generations? It is difficult to assess the effect of these rapid secular trends in height and weight on intestinal tract proportions.

**3.** Finally, and perhaps most importantly, how has cooking affected gastrointestinal adaptations over the past half million or so years? Just as the physical properties of foliage and insect chitin similarly affect the morphology of dentition (Kay 1984, Kay and Hylander 1978), cooked foods may require less extensive digestion than raw plant foods. Thus the use of cooked foods may have resulted in a morphology in humans similar to that in mammals with highly faunivorous diets.

Further comparative studies of the histology of the gut tract of primates in conjunction with detailed and quantitative studies of the food habits of natural populations are needed to determine if more precise dietary/digestive tract relationships exist. Studies of this type should lead to a better understanding of digestive physiology. However, whether we can ever determine the "natural diet" of man by such comparisons still remains an unanswered question.

## Summary

In this chapter I have attempted to make the following points:

1. There are a variety of foraging and dietary patterns among primates; different species have generally obligate food habits in that the types of food items eaten and the degree of dietary diversity are relatively fixed.
2. There are a number of convergent dietary patterns among primates that are not taxonomically dependent; closely related species may have different food habits, while the diets of unrelated forms may be quite similar.
3. At least at a general level, in naturally occurring animals, relationships exist between dietary patterns and alimentary tract adaptations.
4. Studies of the dimensions of intestinal tract compartments in humans have not led to a greater understanding of the evolution of the human diet because the human diet has changed so rapidly and the intestinal tract is quite malleable.
5. The further study of species-specific dietary patterns among primates may lead to a better understanding of the role of primates in ecological communities and to the definition of primate feeding guilds.
6. Early hominids were relatively large animals, mainly terrestrial, and lived in edge or savannah habitats. There is no indication that they were dietary specialists. Most primates living in similar environments are mainly frugivorous and feed on a small proportion of animal protein, depending upon body size. Furthermore, these species have quite diverse diets (i.e., they eat a large number of food items and plant species), though some have seasonal specialties. Comparing dietary patterns of other primates living under these conditions, I suspect that early ho-

minids were mainly frugivorous omnivores that consumed a relatively minor proportion of animal matter. Dental adaptations further indicate that they ate relatively small hard foods, or foods containing gritty material, at least some proportion of the time. These latter foods could have been nuts, seeds (or fruit with hard seeds), hard pods, or possibly soiled roots.

## Acknowledgements

I would like to thank Jerry Purvis, Betty Bacandreas and Jeff McKee for their assistance in preparation and analysis of the data from human intestinal tracts. I would also like to thank Steven Ward for making these specimens available. I appreciate the helpful comments made on various aspects of this paper by Richard Kay, Warren Kinzey, Tom Przybeck, and Linda Sussman. This research was supported in part by Research Fellowship MH 46268-01 of the National Institute of Mental Health, United States Public Health Service, Research Grant BNS-7916561 of the National Science Foundation, and by a research grant from the National Geographic Society of Washington, DC.

## References

Aldrich-Blake, F. P. G. (1980) "Long-tailed macaques." In D. J. Chivers (ed.), *Malayan Forest Primates: Ten Years' Study in Tropical Rain Forest* (pp. 147–165). New York: Plenum Press.

Altmann, S. A. (1974) "Baboons, space, time and energy." *Am. Zool.,* 14: 221–248.

Amerasinghe, F. P.; Van Cuylenberg, B. W. B.; Hladik, C. M. (1971) "Comparative histology of the alimentary tract of Ceylon primates in correlation with diet." *Ceylon J. Sci. Biol. Sci.,* 9:75–87.

Charles-Dominique, P. (1975) "Nocturnality and diurnality: An ecological interpretation of these two modes of life by an analysis of the higher vertebrate fauna in tropical forest ecosystems." In W. P. Luckett and F. S. Szalay (eds.), *Phylogeny of the Primates: A Multidisciplinary Approach* (pp. 69–88). New York: Plenum Press.

Chivers, D. J.; Hladik, C. M. (1980) "Morphology of the gastrointestinal tract in primates: Comparisons with other mammals in relation to diet." *J. Morphology,* 166: 337–386.

Chivers, D. J.; Hladik, C. M. (1984) "Diet and gut morphology in primates." In *Food Acquisition and Processing in Primates,* (pp. 213–230). D. J. Chivers, B. A. Wood and A. Bilsborough, eds. New York: Plenum Press.

Clutton-Brock, T. H. (1972) *Feeding and Ranging Behavior in the Red Colobus Monkey.* Ph. D. thesis, Cambridge University, England.

Clutton-Brock, T. H. (1975) "Feeding behaviour of red colobus and black and white colobus in East Africa." *Folia primatol,* 23:165–207.

Clutton-Brock, T. H.; Harvey, P. H. (1977) "Species differences and ranging behaviour in primates." In T. H. Clutton-

Brock (ed.), *Primate Ecology: Studies in Feeding and Ranging Behaviour in Lemurs, Monkeys and Apes* (pp. 559–584). London: Academic Press.

Crook, J. H. (1970) "The socio-ecology of primates." In J. H. Crook (ed.), *Social Behaviour in Birds and Mammals*. London: Academic Press.

Denham, W. W. (1971) "Energy relations and some basic properties of primate social organization." *Am. Anthropol.,* 73: 77–95.

Dittus, W. P. J. (1974) *The Ecology and Behavior of the Toque Monkey, Macaca sinica.* Ph. D. Thesis, University of Maryland, College Park.

Harding, R. S. O. (1981) "An order of omnivores: Nonhuman primate diets in the wild." In *Omnivorous Primates: Gathering and Hunting in Human Evolution* (pp. 191–214). R. S. O. Harding and G. Teleki, eds. New York: Columbia U. Press.

Harrison, M. J. S. (1984) "Optimal foraging strategies in the diet of the green monkey, *Cercopithecus sabaeus,* at Mt. Assirik, Senegal." *I. J. Primatol.,* 5:435–471.

Hill, W. C. O. (1972) *Evolutionary Biology of Primates.* New York: Academic Press.

Hladik, A.; Hladik, C. M. (1969) "Rapports trophiques entre vegetation et primates dans la foret de Barro Colorado (Panama)." *Terre Vie,* 23:25–117.

Hladik, C. M. (1967) "Surface relative au tractus digestif de quelques primates. Morphologie des villosites intestinales et correlations avec le regime alimentaire." *Mammalia,* 31:120–147.

Hladik, C. M. (1977) "A comparative study of the feeding strategies of two sympatric species of leaf monkeys: *Presbytis senex* and *Presbytis entellus.*" In *Primate Ecology: Studies of Feeding and Ranging Behaviour in Lemurs, Monkeys, and Apes* (pp. 323–353). T. H. Clutton-Brock, ed. London: Academic Press.

Hladik, C. M. (1981) "Diet and the evolution of feeding strategies among forest primates." In *Omnivorous Primates: Gathering and Hunting in Human Evolution* (pp. 215–254). R. S. O. Harding; G. Teleki, eds. New York: Columbia U. Press.

Hladik, C. M.; Hladik, A. (1972) "Disponibilites alimentaires et domaines vitaux des primates a Ceylan." *Terre Vie,* 26:149–215.

Hladik, C. M.; Charles-Dominique, P.; Valdebouze, P.; Delort-Laval, J.; Flanzy, J. (1971) "La caecotrophie chez un primate phyllophage du genre *Lepilemur* et les correlations avec les particularites de son appareil digestif." *C. R. Acad. Sci.,* Paris 272:3191–3194.

Homewood, K. (1978) "Feeding strategy of the Tana mangabey *(Cercocebus galeritus galeritus)* (Mammalia: Primates)." *J. Zool.,* London 186:375–391.

Hylander, W. L. (1975) "Incisor size and diet in anthropoids with special reference to Cercopithecidae." *Science,* 189:1095–1098.

Jarmon, P. J. (1974) "The social organization of antelope in relation to their ecology." *Behaviour,* 48: 215–267.

Kavanagh, M. (1978) "The diet and feeding behaviour of *Cercopithecus aethiops tantalus.*" *Folia Primatol.,* 30:30–63.

Kay, R. F. (1975) "The functional adaptations of primate molar teeth." *Am. J. Phys. Anthropol.,* 43:195–216.

Kay, R. F. (1978) "Molar structure and diet in extant Cercopithecidae." In *Development, Function and Evolution of Teeth* (pp. 309–339). P. M. Butler and K. A. Joysey, eds. New York: Academic Press.

Kay, R. F. (1981). "The nutcracker—a new theory of the adaptations of the Ramapithecinae." *Am. J. Phys. Anthropol.,* 55:141–151.

Kay, R. F. (1984) "On the use of anatomical features to infer foraging behavior in extinct primates." In *Adaptations for foraging in Nonhuman Primates* (pp. 21–53). P. S. Rodman and G. H. Cant, eds. New York: Columbia Univ. Press.

Kay, R. F.; Hylander, W. L. (1978) "The dental structure of arboreal folivores with special reference to primates and Philangeroidea (Marsipialia)." In *The Ecology of Arboreal Folivores* (pp. 173–191). G. G. Montgomery, ed. Washington, DC: Smithsonian Institution Press.

Kay, R. F.; Sussman, R. W.; Tattersall, I. (1978) "Dietary and dental variations in the genus *Lemur,* with comments concerning dietary-dental correlations among Malagasy primates." *Am. J. Phys. Anthropol.,* 49:119–127.

Kinzey, W. G. (1978) "Feeding behaviour and molar features in two species of titi monkey." In *Recent Advances in Primatology,* Vol. 1, *Behaviour* (pp. 373–385). D. J. Chivers and J. Herbert, eds. London: Academic Press.

Lack, D. (1968) *Ecological Adaptations for Breeding in Birds.* London: Methuen.

Lee, R. B. (1968) "What hunters do for a living, or how to make out on scarce resources." In *Man the Hunter* (pp. 30–48). R. B. Lee and I. DeVore, eds. Chicago: Aldine.

Lee, R. B. (1969) "!Kung bushman subsistence: An input-output analysis." In *Environment and Cultural Behavior* (pp. 47–79). A. P. Vayda, ed., New York: Natural History Press.

MacKinnon, J. R. (1974) "The behaviour and ecology of wild orangutans *(Pongo pygmaeus)." Anim. Behav.* 22:3–74.

Martin, R. D.; Chivers, D. J.; MacLarnon, A. M.; Hladik, C. M. (1985) "Gastrointestinal allometry in primates and other mammals." In *Size and Scaling in Primate Biology* (pp. 61–90). W. L. Jungers, ed. New York: Plenum Press.

Milton, K. (1980) *The Foraging Strategy of Howler Monkeys: A Study in Primate Economics.* New York: Columbia Univ. Press.

Oppenheimer, J. R. (1968) "Behavior and ecology of the white-faced monkey, *Cebus capucinus,* on Barro Co, C. Z." Ph. D. thesis, Univ. of Illinois, Urbana.

Pollock, J. I. (1977) "The ecology and sociology of feeding in *Indri indri.*" In *Primate Ecology: Studies of Feeding and Ranging Behaviour in Lemurs, Monkeys and Apes* (pp. 38–69). T. H. Clutton-Brock, ed. London: Academic Press.

Quiris, R. (1975) "Ecologie et organisation sociale de *Cercopithecus galeritus agilis* dans le Nord-est du Gabon." *Terre Vie,* 29:337–398.

Rijksen, H. D. (1978) *A Field Study on Sumatran Orang Utans (Pongo pygmaeus abelii* Lesson 1827). Wageningen: H. Veenman and Zonan B. V.

Rodman, P. S. (1977) "Feeding behaviour of orang-utans of the Kutai Reserve." In *Primate Ecology: Studies of Feeding and Ranging Behaviour in Lemurs, Monkeys and Apes.* T. H. Clutton-Brock, ed. London: Academic Press.

Rosenberger, A. L.; Kinzey, W. G. (1976) Functional patterns of molar occlusion in platyrrhine primates. Am J. Phys. Anthropol. *45* (2):281–298.

Rotenberry, J. T. (1980) "Dietary relationships among shrub-steppe passerine birds: Competition or opportunism in a variable environment?" *Ecological Monographs,* 50: 93–110.

Stacey, P. (1986) "Group size and foraging efficiency in yellow baboons." *Bali Ecol. Sociobio.,* 18:175–187.

Struhsaker, T. T. (1975) *The Red Colobus Monkey.* Chicago: Univ. of Chicago Press.

Struhsaker, T. T. (1978) "Food habits of five monkey species in the Kibale Forest, Uganda." In *Recent Advances in Primatology.* Vol. 1. *Behaviour.* D. J. Chivers and J. Herbert, eds. London: Academic Press.

Sussman, R. W. (1974) "Ecological distinctions in sympatric species of *Lemur.*" In *Prosimian Biology,* R. D. Martin, G. A. Doyle, and A. C. Walker, eds. London: Duckworth.

Sussman, R. W. (1977) "Feeding behaviour in *Lemur catta* and *Lemur fulvus.*" In *Primate Ecology: Studies in Feeding and Ranging Behaviour in Lemurs, Monkeys and Apes.* T. H. Clutton-Brock, ed. London: Academic Press.

Sussman, R. W. (1978) "Foraging patterns of nonhuman primates and the nature of food preferences in man." *Fed. Proc., Fed. Amer. Soc. Exp. Biol.,* 37:55–60.

Sussman, R. W.; Raven, P. H. (1978) "Pollination by lemurs and marsupials: An archaic coevolutionary system." *Science,* 200:731–736.

Sussman, R. W.; Tattersall, I. (1981) "The ecology and behavior of *Macaca fascicularis* in Mauritius." *Primates,* 22:192–205.

Suzuki, A. (1969) "An ecological study of chimpanzees in a savanna woodland." *Primates,* 10:103–148.

Suzuki, A. (1975) "The origin of hominid hunting: A primatological perspective." In *Socio-ecology and Psychology of Primates* (pp. 259–278). R. H. Tuttle, ed. The Hague: Mouton.

Tanaka, J. (1976) "Subsistence ecology of Central Kalahari San." In *Kalahari Hunter-Gatherers: Studies of the !Kung San and Their Neighbors* (pp. 98–119). R. B. Lee and I. DeVore, eds. Cambridge, Ma: Harvard U. Press.

Tanaka, J. (1980) *The San Hunters-Gatherers of the Kalahari: A Study in Ecological Anthropology.* Tokyo: U. of Tokyo Press.

Tanno, T. (1981) "Plant utilization of the Mbuti Pygmies—with special reference to their material culture and use of wild vegetable foods." *African Study Monographs.* Vol. 1.

Terborgh, J. (1983) *Five New World Primates: A Study in Comparative Ecology.* Princeton: Princeton Univ. Press.

Woodburn, J. (1968) "An introduction to Hadza ecology." In *Man the Hunter* (pp. 49–55). R. B. Lee and I. DeVore, eds. Chicago: Aldine.

# Chapter 23

# *Ancient Odysseys*

## Michael D. Lemonick

*As early humans migrated around the globe, image making spread rapidly.*

The human mind can't easily comprehend huge expanses of time. Once the years run into the tens of thousands, our brain lumps them together into an undifferentiated mass. The catchall term prehistoric art works perfectly with this sort of thinking. It sounds like just another episode in art history—modern art, Renaissance art, Byzantine art, prehistoric art.

In reality, the artworks created before history began—prior, say, to about 10,000 B.P. (Before the Present)—cover a much longer time span than what has come afterward. Southwestern European cave painting, only the most familiar expression of ancient creativity, was done over a period of at least 10,000 years. And when Paleolithic people first crawled into the Chauvet cave to daub the walls with images of rhinos and bears, nearly half of all art history was already over with.

When art first appeared, presumably around 40,000 B.P., it spread quickly. Within a mere 5000 years—barely the blink of an eye on paleontological time scales—the work of early artists popped up in several corners of the globe. Archaeologists have found more than 10,000 sculpted and engraved objects in hundreds of locations across Europe, southern Africa, northern Asia, and Australia. The styles range from realistic to abstract, and the materials include stone, bone, antler, ivory, wood, paint, teeth, claws, shells, and clay that have been carved, sculpted, and painted to represent animals, plants, geometric forms, landscape features, and human beings—virtually every medium and every kind of subject that artists would return to thousands of years later.

From *Time* Feb. 13, 1995.

This creative explosion is best documented in Europe, largely because that is where most of the excavations have taken place. Early body decoration, for example, was found in the 1950s by Soviet archaeologists at Sungir, near the Russian city of Vladimir. From graves dating back to 28,000 B.P., they unearthed the remains of a 10-year-old-girl, a 12-year-old boy and a 60-year-old man. The three are festooned with beads, more than 14,000 all told. But each is adorned in a different way, evidence that body decoration was used to emphasize gender and age distinctions in social groups. In addition to the beads, the girl has delicate snowflake-like carvings around her head and torso. The boy has no snowflakes but wears a belt made from 240 fox canine teeth. And the man is wearing a single pendant made of stone in the middle of his chest. Another distinction: The beads on the children's bodies are approximately two-thirds the size of those the man is wearing.

At about the same time that the three were being buried—give or take a few millenniums—a new sort of artifact begins to appear in the prehistorical record. Archaeologists working at sites all across Europe and well into Russia have found dozens of so-called Venus figurines: miniature sculptures of big-breasted, broad-hipped women. The statuettes, which may have been used in fertility rites or even religious ceremonies, suggest a worshipful attitude toward fertility and reproduction.

By 22,000 B.P., archaeologists have found, the first evidence of the cave paintings that appeal so strongly to modern eyes began to appear. The paintings, some of them realistic portraits of animals, others depicting half-human, half-animal figures or abstract symbols, soon became the dominant form of prehistoric European art. They remained important until 10,000 B.P., when, along with the glaciers of the last Ice Age, they seem to have melted away from human consciousness.

Those are the broad outlines, at least of early art history. The details are much messier: It's not as though one phase gave way smoothly to another. Beadwork and statuette carving didn't stop just because cave painting began—and the presence of caves didn't automatically inspire people to cover them with images. Says Jean Clottes, one of France's pre-eminent authorities on prehistoric art: "There are a lot of caves in Yugoslavia, for example, but no paintings in them." Moreover, there is an enormous regional variation in what sorts of art were produced at what times.

The story is even less straightforward in other parts of the world. Not only have extensive explorations been less common outside Europe, but also what's been found has proved difficult to date. Nonetheless, it is clear that artists were at work in Australia and southern Africa, at least, at roughly the same time as their European cousins.

The Australian continent abounds in Aboriginal rock art, both paintings and engravings. Much of it lies in a 1500-mile-long, boomerang-shaped area across the country's north coast. Archaeologist Darrel Lewis of the Australian National University estimates that there are at least 10,000 rock-art sites on the Arnhem Land plateau alone, in the Northern Territory. "Each of these sites," he says, "can have several hundred paintings." But unlike early inhabitants of Europe, who frequently decorated caves over a short period and then abandoned them, the Australian Aborigines would return over and over to the same sites—a practice that still goes on today. Unraveling the history of a single site can thus be extremely complicated.

How old is Australia's art? Some archaeologists insist that certain paintings of human hands and life-size crocodiles and kangaroos were done 50,000 years ago, but these experts may be overconfident of their dating techniques. Another controversial assertion is the claim by anthropologist Alan Thorne of the Australian National University that a small piece of red ochre (a kind of clay), dated to 50,000 B.P., was worn down on one side like a piece of chalk by humans. "Whether it was ground to paint a shelter or a person or part of a wall, I don't think anyone would disagree that it is evidence of art," says Thorne. Even if Australia's art is not as ancient as Thorne thinks, there is strong evidence that at least two rock carvings found in the Bimbowrie Hills are more than 40,000 years old, and that scores of others in the area fall between 30,000 and 20,000 B.P.

Southern Africa's artistic record is much sparser. Scientists have unearthed a pendant made from a seashell that may be more than 40,000 years old, carved bones and beads made from ostrich eggshells that probably date from around 27,000 B.P., and paintings on slabs of rock in a Namibian cave that may be nearly as old. But like Australia's Aborigines, southern Africa's indigenous people carried on their rock-art tradition into modern times, confusing anthropologists' tasks considerably.

And in the rest of the world . . . nothing. Not in the Middle East, not in Southeast Asia, not in China or Japan or Korea, and not in North Africa before 15,000 B.P. at the very earliest—although there is ample evidence of an ancient human presence in all these areas. This may mean the people there weren't interested in art, or it may simply be that they painted or carved on wood or animal skins, which have long since rotted away.

Nobody can do more than speculate about the answer. That uncertainty, along with the spottiness of the archaeological record—even in an intensively studied area like southern France—makes it hard to know whether art, once invented, was a universal practice. Probably not, argues archaeologist Olga Soffer, of the University of Illinois at Urbana-Champaign: "Art is a social phenomenon that appears and disappears and, in some places, may not arise at all." But many anthropologists counter that the term art is usually defined too narrowly. What paleolithic humans really invented, they say, is symbolic representation, and by that definition art may well appear in every culture—though it might not be easy for us to recognize.

It's also difficult to say whether art originated in a specific part of the world. By the time of humanity's great artistic awakening, *Homo sapiens* had probably already traveled from its African homeland through most of Europe and Asia. The urge to make art could have arisen in any of these places and spread throughout the world, or it could have happened in many areas independently.

There are problems with either scenario however. "The pattern is puzzling," observes anthropologist Randall White. "One of the most common forms of body adornment in Western Europe during this early period is canine teeth from carnivores, drilled with holes and worn as dangling ornamentation. And damned if in Australia, some 35,000 to 40,000 years ago, this isn't exactly what they're doing too." It might seem like an unremarkable coincidence—after all, carnivores must have loomed large in every culture. But anthropologists have learned that such coincidences are actually quite rare. If art did spread around the world, it moved with astonishing speed (on a paleontological time scale, that is), and, says White, "it's a long way from southern France to Australia."

One possible explanation: Art was percolating along for tens of thousands of years before most of the known examples show up. Perhaps the original *Homo sapiens* populations in Africa invented art and carried it to other regions. The reasons nothing much has been found dating before 40,000 B.P., goes the argument, are that scientists haven't looked hard enough and most of the evidence has perished. As appealing as it may seem though, this art-is-older-than-we-think theory has attracted little support; the demarcation line at 40,000 B.P., is just too sharp.

New discoveries like the one at the Chauvet cave, and more intensive study of existing sites, are constantly giving archaeologists more information to work with. Also, dating techniques are becoming more refined. It used to be that scientists needed to test a large sample of paint to pinpoint its age. And, says anthropologist Margaret Conkey, "no one was willing to scrape a bison's rump off the wall." Now it takes only a tiny sample. French prehistory expert Arlette Leroi-Gourhan estimates dates by using pollen particles preserved on cave floors.

The results of all these studies, while always enlightening, don't necessarily simplify things for scientists.

A new analysis of the Cosquer cave on the French Riviera, for example, has shown that painted hand prints on the walls date to 27,000 B.P., while images of horses and other animals came 9,000 years later. Rather than being decorated in a single prolonged burst of creativity, the cavern was painted over scores of centuries, quite possibly by artists who had no connection of any kind with one another, unlike Aborigines, whose culture has direct links to the distant past.

Prehistoric art was created over so long a period by so many different humans in so many parts of the world, and presumably for so many different reasons that it may never fit into a tidy catalog. These ancient masterpieces are telling us that our prehistoric forebears had modes of expression more varied than we once imagined—and also that we'll never truly understand just how rich their lives must have been.

# Chapter 24

# Time, Temporal Envelopes and the Middle to Upper Paleolithic Transition

## B. A. Schumann and P. B. Pettit[1]

*It would, I think, be easy to show that, since past and future are part of the same time-span, interest in the past and interest in the future are interconnected. The line of demarcation between prehistoric and historical times is crossed when people cease to live only in the present, and become consciously interested both in their past and in their future.*

—E. H. Carr (1967) *What Is History?*

## INTRODUCTION

The current research interest in the origins of anatomically modern humans has generated much discussion of the symbolic activity of palaeolithic societies, with the notion of a major cognitive restructuring occurring with the origin of modern humans and the concomitant Upper Paleolithic revolution (Mellars 1990, Mellars and Stringer 1989, Whallon 1989). While some suggest that this cognitive change could relate to the appearance of language (Mellars 1991), such notions have remained vague, largely due to the coarse grain of the archaeological record for this time period and the questionable relevance of the available data for answering cognitive questions. One objective of this paper is to suggest that notions of such a cognitive change need to be defined in more specific terms if the data base is to be used at all successfully to test such models of behavioral advance. One major aspect of cognitive organization—the way we conceptualize time—is examined within the context of the archaeological record of the Middle and Upper Pale-olithic of Europe for any signs that a major restructuring of time concepts occurred around this transition. This follows the stimulus of Bailey (1983) and Clark (1992) who noted that concepts of time may have evolved significantly throughout human evolution and that they should therefore be central to any investigation of past behavior. While many areas of the data are ambiguous or open to alternative interpretation, it is suggested here that the cognitive process underlying many behavioral changes in this period can be related to concepts of time, based on the assumption that such concepts will affect the way that behavior is organized and therefore contribute towards the patterning of the archaeological record. We suggest that this process, evident in anatomically modern populations *some time prior* to the Early Upper Paleolithic of Europe, evolved through to the late Upper Paleolithic and can explain many aspects of the "human revolution."

## CONCEPTS OF TIME

The "sense" of time is an intellectual construction; the recognition that humans create the time scales within which they live and communicate (Clarke 1992) goes back to Aristotle and was elaborated by St. Augustine

This paper is a revised version of Falling into History: Hominid Conceptions of Time at the Middle to Upper Paleolithic Transition by P. B. Pettitt and B. A. Schumann (1993). *Archaeological Review from Cambridge*, 12:25–50.

(Whitrow 1980). In his seminal analysis of the role of time in Quaternary prehistory, Bailey (1983) noted how an expanded temporal horizon is by common consensus a distinguishing feature of human behavior. Paleoanthropologists often work within a constricted notion of time—linear and gradual: the capitalist concept of time according to Shanks and Tilley (1987). This singular conception of time persists despite the Quaternary period encompassing different "definitions" of time (e.g., geological and archaeological, within an overall cosmological framework—Bailey 1983). One has only to go back to the seventeenth century to see how different concepts of time are used in different social contexts (Sinclair 1987). Time is more plastic than we tend to suppose. The ethnographic record abounds with variable concepts of time. These concepts are often far different from those of the western world, although frequently sharing a similar theme of *cyclical* time (Zimmerman 1987). Whatever the actual conception of time, animals, including humans, can be characterized by their *temporal envelopes* (Bailey 1983), which can be defined as the conceptual distance to which organisms can stretch back into the past (memory) and toward the future (expectation/prediction). This cognitive threshold will have major effects on the ability of any community to formulate and integrate *signal* (that is information in transit either as energy or material culture) both *inter* and *intra* specifically. Furthermore, it is this expansion in the hominid temporal envelope which will lead to better information exchange, donation and acquisition (see King 1994).

Whitrow (1980) has noted how the idea of space developed before the idea of time, as a result of spatial movements in three dimensions in response to natural desires. Accordingly, concepts of time arose later and were dependent upon a reproductive imagination or the ability of representation. These might in turn have been connected to memory and possibly to the use of descriptive speech. In any case, time is intimately connected to language; rhythm and repetition are important to conceptualizing time, and to speech (Whitrow ibid.). The notion of events in temporal order relies on the ability to represent ideas; we have no hard evidence for a representational capacity until the Upper Paleolithic. Bailey (1983) notes how cyclical conceptions of time may have been replaced by linear. With such a development of the temporal envelope in a linear sense comes the recognition of the 'self' in an historical sense. Whallon (1989) has noted how reference to the past is crucial in order to make predictions about the future, as these require generalisations from past experiences. Group memory, he argues, is created through the sharing of individual memories and the ability to refer to them. The result of this is the increase in the time-depth of available information (a higher frequency of signal) significantly beyond the lifespans of individuals. For Whallon (ibid.),

this has important adaptive advantages in that it allows cycles of occupation at a larger scale than the individual life and of areas otherwise closed to occupation. It will also enhance information exchange within a broader temporal and spatial framework.

There is clearly a difference between the signal integration of modern humans and other extant hominoids expressed in terms of temporal envelopes: Wagener (1987) notes how non-human primates can only extend conceptually into the past and future in a very general way. This paper raises the notion that the Neanderthal/Middle Paleolithic archaeological record can be characterized by a restricted temporal horizon. As the evolution of temporal awareness probably occurred later than that of spatial awareness, it is suggested that the behavioural record of Neanderthals can be explained in terms of a highly developed sense of *space* and that we need not invoke explanatory scenarios that involve heightened perceptions of time. A dramatic increase in temporal perception may have occurred within anatomically modern groups during (and probably throughout) the Upper Paleolithic. Given that planned hunting, the use of language and cognition may have evolved in close interaction (Passingham 1982), it would not be surprising that the temporal envelope expanded *throughout* the course of the Upper Paleolithic as a result of further social integration.

This paper examines the archaeological records of the Middle and Upper Paleolithic for evidence of an extension of the human perception of time. We are *not* suggesting that Neanderthals were completely incapable of this expanded temporal awareness, but merely discussing the available cultural record during these two periods in order to assess the potential of this concept. Through an analysis of lithic technology, hunting and settlement patterns, burials and the use of art and symbol, two premises emerge: first, that there are significant differences between the Middle and Upper Paleolithic behavioural records and that secondly, the modern human ability to distinguish between the past (memory) and the future (expectation/foresight), that is to 'plan' in time, is clear from these facets of the material record of the European Upper Paleolithic.

## TOOLS

Middle Paleolithic technology is flake-based, with a variety of Levallois or non-Levallois *chaînes opératoires* (Table 24–1) (Boeda et al. 1990, Bordes 1953, Bordes and Bourgon 1951). There is a repetitive aspect to the dominant tool forms; scrapers, points, bifaces, and denticulates/notches vary in space and time and have been used to define major industrial variants (Bordes 1961). Most Middle Paleolithic technology, from France to Russia, uses local raw material, especially the Quina Mousterian

TABLE 24–1   Diagnostic Artifacts during Different Periods of Human Evolution

| Pleistocene Periods | | Hominid Species | Archaeological Industry | Diagnostic Artifacts |
|---|---|---|---|---|
| Middle Pleistocene | | Archaic *Homo sapiens* | Lower Paleolithic Acheulean | Bifaces |
| | 180,000 | Neanderthals | MIDDLE PALEOLITHIC Mousterian | flake, core, chopping tools |
| | 130,000 | | | flake based technology with Levallois and non-Levallois chaines operatoires |
| Late Pleistocene | 45,000 | | UPPER PALEOLITHIC Aurignacian | general blade technology; endscrapers, carinate scrapers; split based bone points; animal carvings, figurines, beads, pendants |
| | 30,000 | Anatomically modern *Homo sapiens* | Gravettian Perigordian | Gravette points, noailles burins, font robert points; female figurines |
| | 18,000 10,000 | | Magdalenian and other Late Upper Paleolithic industries | Bone harpoon points, microlithic elements, blade and bladelets |

(Soffer 1989, Turq 1992), although fine quality material can be transported up to 100 km in western Europe (Geneste 1985, 1989, Roebroeks et al. 1988) and 300 km in central and eastern Europe (Féblot-Augustins 1993), but accounts for only around 1 to 2 percent of any given assemblage (Geneste 1985, 1989). Technological activity is, on the other hand, highly situational, occurring presumably as an *ad hoc* response to needs as they arise in the landscape. Overall, Middle Paleolithic technology is fairly unstructured (Otte 1992) and has an archaic and monotonous appearance. After the appearance of Levallois technology (and probably the associated production of points) by 250 kyr, there are no innovations in Middle Paleolithic technology.

In contrast to this long period of low levels of innovation and cyclical, repetitive change, Upper Paleolithic technology is characterized by increasingly rapid diffusions of newly invented techniques and tool types (Isaac 1972). Design complexity accelerated and cultural differentiation escalated. While during the Middle Paleolithic, bone, antler, and ivory were worked in the same manner as stone, during the Upper Paleolithic, the shaping of these materials was accomplished through various carving and polishing techniques.

With the onset of the Aurignacian, the archaeological record suggests the development of a high degree of production standardization. Unlike the preceding Mousterian assemblages, tool types during the Upper Paleolithic assume a certain conformity to a strict, morphological norm rather than a general edge morphology. During the Upper Paleolithic, Mellars (1991) states that there is clear evidence of a "greater degree of investment" in tool manufacture, including various retouch and reduction processes so as to achieve a highly repetitive final form. It is these characteristics, "form" and "structure," which Mellars (1991:64) believes to be indicative of a "more structured and formalized pattern of thinking."

The highly structured, standardized, and complex lithic assemblages of the Upper Paleolithic are probably indicative of some degree of long-term planning of tool manufacture (and therefore a more formalized pattern of thought). It is the production of such diverse and standardized tool assemblages that requires "time budgeting" (Torrence 1983). The budgeting of time in turn requires (1) a predetermination of the structure of an assemblage and (2) a scheduling of the procurement, manufacture, and maintenance activities. This "time budgeting" and expection/prediction capabilities may relate to the expansion of the modern human temporal envelope into the future. The existence of large workshop sites (Chirica 1989) and the mass production of stone tools renders further support to the notion that tools were being produced for some future rather than immediate use (i.e., time budgeting). Workshop sites indicate that some level of planning for future needs was an integral component to the lithic production and hunting/subsistence practices of these groups.

## HUNTING, SUBSISTENCE, AND SETTLEMENT PRACTICES

The organization of hominid groups in the landscape is potentially the most informative avenue of this inquiry. While organization may simply relate to spatial cognition, an increase in subsistence planning may indicate a broadening of the temporal envelope. Following Whallon's observation of the critical role of the past in predictive behavior, it is probable that Upper Paleolithic subsistence behavior operated with increasing time-depths.

Middle Paleolithic faunal assemblages are usually very generalized from western Europe to Russia, but often dominated by one or two herbivore species, varying regionally (Chase 1988). Some specialized hunting may be indicated by the dominance of one particular species—for example, ibex at Hortus, bison at La Borde and bovids at Mauran (Farizy et al. 1994, Jaubert et al. 1990)—but this may relate to opportunistic hunting of resources as they are encountered in a relatively eclectic manner (Chase 1988). The generalized faunal evidence from many Middle Paleolithic sites may indicate that Neanderthals exploited species as they were found, rather than in a systematic, methodical fashion.

The introduction of multi-seasonal, semi-permanent settlements and improved storage facilities during the Upper Paleolithic is evidence for dramatic shifts in hunting, settlement, and subsistence practices (Conkey 1980, Hahn 1987, Kozlowski 1972). These changes were abetted by expansive raw material procurement and a superior lithic technology, both in terms of quantity and quality. With the increase in use of exotic raw materials, which often required travel over distances of several hundred kilometers (Mellars 1989, Svoboda 1994), for example, in the Early Upper Paleolithic of Russia (Soffer 1989) and 700 km in the Polish Magdalenian (Kozlowski 1991), there evolved a more systematic exploitation of certain geographical regions (hence, for example, the workshop sites). In turn, this perhaps led to greater regional specialization and possibly a social subdivision of labor (Kozlowski 1972, Jelinek personal communication, Whallon 1989). As a result of the changes in economic and social organization of modern human groups (Mellars 1991), it seems probable that there ensued a greater specialization in the pattern of animal exploitation

through the employment of more systematic hunting practices.[2]

Specific patterns of animal exploitation and the diversification of subsistence practices based on systematic hunting in conjunction with deteriorating climate led to greater dietary specialization (Mellars 1991). Unlike the generalized faunal assemblages of the Middle Paleolithic, the majority of Upper Paleolithic sites have yielded much more specialized faunal assemblages, with a concentration usually on one megafaunal species. This may be indicative of greater subsistence scheduling (perhaps including the ability to anticipate animal migrations and to predict the movements and cycles of herd numbers [Gamble 1986, Whallon 1989]) as well as economic diversification. The extreme dependence on one or two animal species (usually reindeer) suggests that the hunters of this period were specialized (Gamble 1978, 1979; but cf. Chase 1989), which in turn may reflect cooperative hunting strategies, for example, with the aggregation of dispersed bands to accumulate enough adult males who were available to hunt large, migratory herd animals (S. Binford 1968a). Furthermore, Binford (1985) notes striking differences in the faunal remains of Middle and Upper Paleolithic sites and suggests that these differences indicate an absence (in the Middle Paleolithic) of long-term planning and cooperation. While Binford's opinion that Middle Paleolithic peoples were unable to hunt large game and had to rely on scavenging appears to be unfounded, he is implying that there were significant cognitive changes. These include a social and intellectual restructuring and the development of foresight.

While it has been recognized that the hunters of the Upper Paleolithic did specialize in the hunting of one main species, they also diversified and expanded their exploitation of prey, supplementing their diets with other food sources (Mellars 1973), including marine animals, with more active, sophisticated, and thorough subsistence strategies (Bahn 1977, 1984, Clark and Straus 1983, Dolukhanov 1979, Soffer 1987, Straus and Heller 1988). Furthermore, the presence of bone and antler harpoons and artistic manifestations of fish (e.g., Abri du Poisson in the Dordogne) in conjunction with carbon/strontium analyses have indicated an increase in the reliance on and consumption of marine resources. This evidence for the expansion of resource exploitation in turn may have allowed for larger and more sedentary settlements. The large river valley settlements such as Laugerie-Haute in the Dordogne and the Kostenki-Avdeevo aggregation along the Dneistr River (among others) may be a result of such an expanded resource base (Grigor'ev 1993).

---

[2]Please note that some authors (see, for example, Delpech 1983) feel that systematic, specialized hunting, as evidenced in the shift in patterns of faunal exploitation, did not occur until the middle Magdalenian in southwest France.

Hunter-gatherer mobility strategies, residential and logistic, refer to the seasonal movements of groups across the landscape in relation to resource availability (Kelly 1983). It is the increased mobility of groups and the extension of territories that account for the so called "aggregation sites," maximum bands comprised of loosely interlocking networks of minimum bands (several families that share a settlement) maintained possibly through ritual communication and exchange (Bahn 1982). The frequently cited evidence from the Pyrenees, sites such as Isturitz, Mas d'Azil, Altamira, and Cueto de la Mina (Bahn 1982, Conkey 1980, Hayden 1981), and other large, sedentary settlements and aggregation sites may indicate that a restructuring of human relations was occurring, perhaps even as a result of changes in hunting and subsistence strategies. With the advent of logistical economic strategies and sophisticated social networks, it is likely that such aggregations of otherwise dispersed groups would exist. The extension of these seasonal movements and increased mobility (Kozlowski 1990; Soffer 1993), especially during the colder periods, in conjunction with changes in the habitat and natural resources (i.e., mammoth availability) may have caused shifts (and most likely west to east) in core residential areas and annual territories throughout this 4000 year period (Grigor'ev 1993, Soffer 1993).

The changes in both social and economic organization of human groups, the appearance of better quality/exotic raw materials and the reliance on one megafaunal species undoubtedly affected the settlement practices of the first modern humans in Europe. During the Upper Paleolithic, there appeared more structured forms of human settlement associated with systematic hunting, a specialized pattern of animal exploitation, an apparent increase in the density of human populations, as well as an apparent increase in the maximum size of residential groups (Mellars 1991). These changes in human settlement and subsistence practices at the end of the Pleistocene indicate changing relations between not only people and the environment but between otherwise isolated groups of individuals. Relationships between such individual groups, through various modes of contact and exchange, demonstrate a social restructuring of societies and an expansion of individual and group awareness within the landscape.

## BURIALS

There is no *a priori* reason why burial, with or without associated ritual or grave goods, should be indicative of hierarchical social ties and an expanded temporal envelope. Simple inhumation may be associated with emotion and need not be symbolic (Dibble and Chase 1993). When burial can be clearly associated with elaborate body ornamentation or grave goods, there may be a possible relationship to social ties, which in turn may be contingent upon temporal awareness.

Despite a recent attempt to question Neanderthal burial data (Gargett 1989), there is clear evidence of intentional inhumation in the Middle Paleolithic. Conservative estimates place the total number of burials from western Europe to Uzbekistan at around 30 (Harrold 1980) while more inclusive estimates indicate around 59 (Smirnoff 1989). While this establishes that the act of burial was present from around 70 kyr (Defleur 1993), there are no clear associations with grave goods, with the exception of Skhul and Qafzeh, which although associated with a Middle Paleolithic technology, are both anatomically modern humans. As Middle Paleolithic burials are, without exception, associated with relatively rich occupation floors, they include cultural material from the horizon that they cut and in no case can a Neanderthal burial be shown to be in unequivocally direct association with any cultural items. As Mellars (1996) notes, while the case for Middle Paleolithic burial is clear, that for associated ritual is very weak.

Neanderthal burials are relatively rare compared to amounts of skeletal remains. Although there are problems with the dating of some Middle Paleolithic burials, examples seem to date from 70 to 35 kyr (Defleur 1993). With the exception of La Ferrassie and Qafzeh, burials are isolated (Defleur 1993). They are usually single burials; examples of double or multiple inhumations (Spy and Shanidar) are most likely fortuitous. burials are often associated with pits and positions vary considerably. For the Middle Paleolithic period then, including areas outside of Europe, at least 80 kyr in duration at a conservative estimate, we have up to 59 single inhumations, generally isolated, with no unequivocal evidence of accompanying ritual.

This paucity of clear information patterning has not deterred some authors from inferring Neanderthal conceptual capacities specifically from the burial data. Smirnoff (1989) notes the presence of burial as indicating that social ties had, by the Middle Paleolithic, extended enough to apply to the dead. Although Botscharow (1989) notes that Middle Paleolithic burials do not seem to represent social organization, power, or rank, they do show a clear conceptual distinction between the living and the dead, relating to a conceptual quandary that the unburied dead are ambiguous. There is nothing in the record to imply any form of social persona, *sensu* Binford (1971), which is being "worked off" by the act of burial in the Middle Paleolithic. Although some differences in disposal practices may relate to broader social factors—for example at Kebara (Bar-Yosef 1988) two babies were "dumped" in a rubbish zone, while an adult was interred at the center where the interstratification of hearths was most intensive—there is no evidence for the use of burial in a social sense.

By contrast, the evidence for systematic internments during the Upper Paleolithic is both vast and varied. There are approximately seventy-five clearly identified burials throughout the Upper Paleolithic of Europe, spanning a period of 25 kyr. Upper Paleolithic burials are very diverse, including single, double, triple, and multiple inhumations. There are also significant differences in body position (placement of the arms, hands, and lower limbs, and direction [north, south, east, west] in which the bodies are placed) (Binant 1991). Many of the burials contain varying amounts of grave goods (the Barma Grande triple burial contains pierced shells and teeth, ivory and bone pendants, and fish vertebrae; the burial from Brno [individual 2] only contains a head piece [coiffe] of pierced shells while some contain none (Cap Blanc, Predmosti, Chancelade [Vallois 1972], and Maritza [Grifoni and Radmilli 1964]). The extensive personal ornamentation (Sungir 2, Arene Candide 1), the extensive use of colorants (Arene Candide, Kostenki, Paviland), and the exotic and often unusual grave goods (for example, the extremely long blades found in the triple burial of Barma Grande) as well as sophisticated mobiliary art (Bruniquel, Arene Candide, and Dolni Vestonice [Svoboda and Vlcek 1991]) all suggest a heightened sense of the self, expressed through personal ornamentation. We suggest that all of these individuals had acquired a social persona that was extended into the future through the act of burial. In this sense, at least certain individuals existed in history. They all had a past that warranted them an extension into the future, through burial. Furthermore, this lack of homogeneity may reflect multiple status distinctions in addition to regional variability (Harrold 1980).

The evidence for a sense of self-awareness implied through burial and other potential aspects of developed ritual practices lends support to the notion of a temporal restructuring. The burial of certain individuals invokes an expansion of the temporal envelope both into the past and future. While interpretation in cognitive terms may be problematic, there is a general feeling that such burials reflect status acquired in the here and now. While status may simply be acquired throughout an individual's lifetime, the act of burial and associated ritual may imply a "forward" extension of the individual in a temporal sense.

We feel that burial and its associated ritual indicates a temporal restructuring, placing some degree of significance in the past and revealing an ability to distinguish individuals (a sense of otherness) based on that past. At the act of burial, temporal awareness expands in both directions: to the past in defining the deceased individual's persona and to the future by extending that persona through ritual. Burials and their association with the explosion of personal ornamentation in the beginning of the Upper Paleolithic may be a reflection of the ability to define the self in an extrasomatic sense

(through material objects) and of the development of greater social complexity (White 1989). Therefore, it is this sense of awareness beyond one's own body and situation that can be linked directly to time, through an individual's age or experience, and can be seen as a major component of the temporal expansion occurring during the Upper Paleolithic. While the act of burial itself need not reveal much in itself, it is the combination of this with the ornamented body that, we suggest, is indicative of extension of the persona in a temporal sense.

## ART AND SYMBOL[3]

Symbolism and the ability to symbol imply expanded concepts of time. Symbols derive from past human experiences and their existence acts to bridge the division of time between past and future. Furthermore, they are inevitably contingent upon the mental ability to conceptualize distance in temporal terms. The appearance of style, through media of "art" and "symbol" (which includes beads, pendants, engravings, paintings, and statuettes), is therefore closely related to cognitive evolution (Conkey 1978), and may relate to expanded temporal facilities. Symbolism may serve as a means of demarcating individuals and groups from each other and maintaining boundaries, as well as a bearer of information and a mechanism for communication (ie the transmission of signal). While symbolism *per se* need not reveal anything about cognition (the thousands of beads found in the burial of the young boy at Sungir, for example), it may simply represent personal ornamentation alone (Bednarik 1992). More specific works of "art" or "symbol" in conjunction with other aspects of behavior, however, might be taken to imply certain conceptual horizons.

There have been numerous claims for a variety of Middle Paleolithic symbols (Hayden 1993, Marshack 1976, Simek 1992). The central problem is the rarity of such examples in the Middle Paleolithic; the contrast with the Upper Paleolithic is dramatic (Chase and Dibble 1987, Mellars 1996). If there is any defining characteristic of such items in the Middle Paleolithic, it has to be their absolute rarity (Bar-Yosef 1988). A typical category of supposed examples of symbolic activity in the Middle Paleolithic are "worked" and/or "engraved" bone fragments. The problem with this category is that no rigor-

---

[3]In this section, specific examples of art and symbol, such as the [possible] pudentorial motifs, beads, and pendants found during the Aurignacian, the Venus figurines of the Gravettian or the cave art of the Magdalenian, will not be discussed here as there are numerous studies of "art" from the Upper Paleolithic. Subsequently, this section discusses art and symbol, and symbolic behavior in general, in a way so as to support a notion of cognitive evolution, in the form of both temporal expansion and social restructuring. For a general review of Upper Paleolithic art and symbol see Bahn 1986 and 1994, Marshack 1991, White 1989 and 1993, Hahn 1971, Lindley and Clark 1990, and Conkey et al. 1997.

ous methodology has been applied to the database (d'Errico personal communication). Many of the supposed items may have been created by natural causes, such as ungulate gnawing (Justus and Turner 1990), by the chemical deposition of bone under mechanical stress (d'Errico 1993), by blood vessels (Bordes 1969, Freeman 1983, Gonzalez-Echegary 1988), or by carnivore activity (d'Errico 1991). Until exact criteria for the identification for worked bone have been developed (d'Errico 1991), we must first consider that such pieces are produced naturally by adopting a refutationalist strategy (Bednarik 1992). The point to make, however, is that there is an absence of the concept that bone is a plastic material that can be shaped by means other than percussion, for instance, by carving. Even if one accepts some Middle Paleolithic pieces as "art," they are still extremely rare and need say nothing about cognitive ability: There is no convincing evidence of notation, depiction, or symbol. Such a lack of evidence is consistent with a lack of developed language (Mellars 1996).

The contrast between the Middle and Upper Paleolithic is clear. An explosion of artistic activity in which a variety of materials are worked to depict and symbol occur from the early Upper Paleolithic onwards, for example, at Isturitz and Parpallo in southwest Europe (Straus 1990). Very early examples of such art are extremely sophisticated, such as the ivory carvings of southwest Germany (Vogelherd, Geissenkosterle, and Hohlenstein Stadel) and the "dancing Venus" of Galgenberg, Austria (Bahn 1994). Differences in symbolic behavior between the synchronous Châtelperronian and Aurignacian of southwest France may be "related to complexity of social or cognitive organization, and perhaps even cognitive abilities" of anatomically modern *Homo sapiens* (Harrold 1988:177). The increasing dependence on and participation in symbolic behavior throughout the Upper Paleolithic is evidenced through the escalation in quantity and greater differentiation of stylistic types and does suggest an expanded temporal awareness.

This "symbolic" explosion suggests that there was an expansion in scale and complexity of encoded information (symbol) being communicated between groups. The portable carved and engraved bone and antler implements found throughout Europe during the Upper Paleolithic may very well have served to convey information between spatially distant groups (Gamble 1986, Jelinek 1990, Mithen 1988, Sieveking 1991). It is important to consider (1) that a large amount of carved antler and bone has no obvious specific physical function and (2) that not all antler and bone objects are engraved. One might suppose, therefore, that those that are engraved may be a possible medium for the flow and exchange of information. Through an interregional comparison of designs and forms, the occurrence of rather similar yet unusual pieces of carved bone found at Laugerie Basse in

the Dordogne and in the Bruniquel region of Tarn et Garonne (Sieveking 1991) may be suggestive of information exchange between these two regions, that is, spatially extensive signal transmission.

The exchange of information has assumed an important role in interpretations of Upper Paleolithic art (Gamble 1986). While the identification of systems of notation is often problematic (d'Errico 1993), certain notational systems do appear, as reflected in engraved bone and antler (Marshack 1976). Communication through the medium of engraved/carved bone may also be supported by the "map" from Dolni Vestonice that was engraved into ivory (Jelinek 1990). Such notational systems, if taken at face value, imply an expanded temporal envelope; indeed, this would be an important factor if these objects are to have any use in conveying information. Notational systems *by their very nature* render time usable by displaying the symbols in a spatial context. Although many supposed examples of notation are dubious and can be explained by other factors, the clearest tangible examples that do exist are perhaps the best example of expanded temporal awareness throughout the Upper Paleolithic.

Although the diachronic patterning of Upper Paleolithic art is not as clear-cut as has been supposed (Bahn 1994), it does display certain temporal and geographic styles (in terms of tool form and mobiliary art). There can be local and individual variation in style while at the same time a widespread dispersal of similar forms (e.g., Marshack's [1991] "time-factored" explanation of the use of female imagery). Regional stylistic differences are frequently as strong as temporal ones (Hahn 1971). It is these regional differences in style that can be seen as a means for establishing social consciousness and group identity. For example, during the Aurignacian, there are clear distinctions between the artistic manifestations (i.e., form) found in France and central Europe. In France we find human representations that have been interpreted as vulva (Delluc and Delluc 1978; for a different interpretation, see Bahn 1986 and Mithen 1988) while in the latter region there is no known "vulvic" imagery (Hahn 1971). Additionally, White (1989) notes striking differences in the technological production and the form of beads between these two regions during the Aurignacian. Yet with the onset of the Gravettian there is less regionalization of form (the widespread distribution of "Venus" figurines and certain tool forms such as Gravette and Font-Robert points), which may be indicative of a restructuring of social groups (i.e., increased contact and exchange, larger territorial ranges, greater mobility). While style can operate as a mechanism for internal cohesion and external differentiation among and between identity-conscious groups (Conkey 1978, David 1966) it is probable that the explosion of art and symbol and the acceleration of stylistic variation during the Upper Paleolithic were used to enhance ethnic boundaries.

## Concluding Remarks

From this survey of the European Paleolithic record, we can see that with the appearance of anatomically modern *Homo sapiens* in Europe and the transition from the Middle to Upper Paleolithic a significant and rather dramatic shift in the composition (both qualitative and quantitative) of the archaeological record, which we interpret in terms of an increased scale, in both time and space, of signal integration in hominid societies. We suggest that this relates to an expanded temporal envelope. Strengthened signals of longer and larger scales accompanied by increasingly complex and communicative messages (in the form of meaningfully constituted action and symbolic behavior) are indicative of some degree of a cognitive restructuring or reordering of the *scale* of temporal awareness. It is this restructuring that may have resulted in a greater conceptualization of directional time (inclusive of an awareness of the future and the past). It is the striking differences of the archaeological records of these two periods that indicate an expansion of "present" time into past and future time. Behavioral change at this transition indicates an increase and sophistication of the quality of information flow between and within groups. Material culture (*signals*) from the Upper Paleolithic became a means of bearing complex and communicative information between and within modern human groups over larger geographical areas.

With this expansion of the temporal envelope during the Middle to Upper Paleolithic transition, we witness a restructuring of social relations within (i.e., burials) and between (i.e., contact, exchange, and aggregation sites) groups. According to White (1982:176), "a total restructuring of social relations across the Middle/Upper Paleolithic boundary [occurred] in the course of which corporate and individual identity became important and were enhanced by stylistic improvements. . . ." Additionally, S. Binford (1968b:148) notes that there was "a new form of social organisation, one in which greater corporate awareness and increased status differentiation played a role." These conclusions draw support from all of the aforementioned evidence: improvements in the working of stone, antler, and bone, burials, the procurement of exotic raw materials and the aggregation of otherwise dispersed groups. Yet perhaps the greatest body of evidence emanates from varying aspects of art and symbol found in the archaeological record, in the projection of style and form. The new sociocultural structures evident in the Upper Paleolithic may have emanated from technological improvements and a modified relationship between man and the environment, but it is not without the development of enriched "fundamental human capacities for conceptualization and communication" that these structures evolved (Whallon 1989). We suggest that this extension of *signal* and *scale* and the expansion of the modern human tempo-ral envelope is a critical component of this cognitive restructuring occurring across the transition from the Middle to Upper Paleolithic in Europe. For us, this is a major aspect of the human revolution.

## References

Bahn, P. (1977) "Seasonal migration in south-west France during the late glacial period." *Journal of Archaeological Science*, 4, 245–257.

Bahn, P. (1982) "Inter-site and inter-regional links during the Upper Paleolithic: The Pyrenean evidence." *Oxford Journal of Archaeology*, 1, 247–268.

Bahn, P. (1984) *Pyrenean Prehistory*. Warminster, England: Aris & Phillips Ltd.

Bahn, P. (1986) "No sex, please, we're Aurignacians." *Rock Art Research*, 3(2), 99–120.

Bahn, P. (1994) "New advances in the field of Ice Age art." In *Origins of Anatomically Modern Humans* (pp. 121–132). M. H. Nitecki and D. V. Nitecki, eds. New York: Plenum Press.

Bailey, G. N. (1983) "Concepts of time in quaternary prehistory." *Annual Review of Anthropology*, 12, 165–192.

Bar-Yosef, O. (1988) "Evidence for Middle Paleolithic symbolic behavior: A cautionary note." In *L'Homme de Neanderthal*, volume 5. Liège: ERAUL.

Bednarik, R. G. (1992) "Palaeoart and archaeological myths." *Cambridge Archaeological Journal*, 2, 27–57.

Binant, P. (1991) *Les Sepultures du Paleolithique*. Paris: Editions Errance.

Binford, L. (1971) "Mortuary practices: Their study and their potential." In *Approaches to the Social Dimensions of Mortuary Practices* (pp. 6–20). J.A. Brown, ed. Memoires of the Society for American Archeology, 25.

Binford, L. (1985) "Human ancestors: Changing views of their behavior." *Journal of Anthropological Archaeology*, 4, 292–327.

Binford, S. (1968a) "Early Upper Pleistocene adaptations in the Levant." *American Anthropologist*, 70, 707–717.

Binford, S. (1986b) "A structural comparison of disposal of the dead in the Mousterian and the Upper Palaeolithic." *Southwestern Journal of Anthropology*, 24, 139–154.

Boeda, E., Geneste, J.-M.; Meignen, L. (1990) "Identification de chaines operatoires lithiques du Paleolithique ancien et moyen." *Paleo*, 2, 43–79.

Bordes, F. (1953) "Essai de classification des industries 'Mousteriennes'." *Bulletin de la Societe Prehistoire Francaise*, 50, 457–466.

Bordes, F. (1961) "Typologie du Paleolithique ancien et moyen." *Publications de l'Institute de Prehistoire de l'Universite de Bordeaux*, Memoire I.

Bordes, F. (1969) "Os Perce Mousterien et Os Grave Acheulean du Pech de l'Aze II." *Quaternaria*, 11, 1–6.

Bordes, F.; Bourgon, M. (1951). "Le complexe Mousterien: Mousteriens, Levalloisien et Tayacien." *L'Anthropologie*, 55, 1–23.

Botscharow, L. J. (1989) "Sites as texts: An exploration of Mousterian traces." In I. Hodder (ed.) *The Meaning of Things*. New York: Routledge, Chapman and Hall.

Carr, E. H. (1967) *What is History?* New York: Random House.

Chase, P. G. (1988) "Scavenging and hunting in the Middle Palaeolithic: The evidence from Europe." In *Upper Pleistocene Prehistory of Western Eurasia* (pp. 161–180). H. Dibble and A. Monet-White, eds. Philadelphia: University of Pennsylvania Press.

Chase, P. G. (1989) "How different was Middle Palaeolithic subsistence? A zooarchaeological perspective on the Middle to Upper Palaeolithic transition." In *The Human Revolution* (pp. 321–337). P. Mellars and C.B. Stringer, eds. Edinburgh: Edinburgh University Press.

Chase, P. G.; Dibble, H. (1987) "Middle Palaeolithic symbolism: A review of current evidence and interpretations." *Journal of Anthropological Archaeology,* 6, 263–296.

Chirica, V. (1989) *The Gravettian in the East of the Romanian Carpathians.* Jassy: Al. I. Cuza.

Clark, G. A.; Straus, L. G. (1983) "Late Pleistocene hunter-gatherer adaptations in Cantabrian Spain." In *Hunter-Gatherer Economy in Prehistory* (pp. 131–148). G. Bailey (ed.) Cambridge: Cambridge University Press.

Clark, G. (1992) *Space, Time and Man.* Cambridge: Cambridge University Press.

Conkey, M. (1978) "Style and information in cultural evolution: Toward a predictive model for the Paleolithic." In *Social Archaeology: Beyond Subsistence and Dating* (pp. 61–85). C. Redman et al., eds. New York: Academic Press.

Conkey, M. (1980) "The identification of prehistoric hunter-gatherer aggregation sites: The case of Altamira." *Current Anthropology,* 21, 609–630.

Conkey, M.; Soffer, O.; Stratmann, D.; Jablonski, N. (eds.) (1997) *Beyond Art: Pleistocene Image and Symbol.* San Francisco: Memoirs of the California Academy of Sciences, number 23.

d'Errico, F. (1991) "Carnivore traces or Mousterian skiffle?" *Rock Art Research,* 8, 12–132.

d'Errico, F. (1993) "Criteria for identifying utilised bone: The case of the Cantabrian 'Tensors'." *Current Anthropology,* 34, 58–62.

David, N. C. (1966) "Perigordian V regional facies: An attempt to define Upper Palaeolithic ethnic groups." *VII Congres International des Sciences Prehistoriques et Protohistoriques.* Prague.

Defleur, A. (1993) *Les Sepultures Mousteriennes.* Paris: CNRS.

Delluc, B; Delluc, G. (1978). "Les manifestations graphiques Aurignaciennes sur support rocheux des environs des Eyzies (Dordogne)." *Gallia Prehistoire,* 21, 213–438.

Delpech, F. (1983) *Les faunes de Paleolithique superieur dans le sud-ouest de la France.* Paris: CNRS.

Dibble, H; Chase, P. (1993) "On Mousterian and Natufian burialism in the Levant." *Current Anthropology,* 34, 170–176.

Dolukhanov, M. (1979) "Evolution des systemes eco-sociaux en Europe durant le pleistocene recent et le debut de l'holocene." In *La Fin des Temps Glaciares en Europe* (pp. 869–876). D. de Sonneville-Bordes, ed. Paris: CNRS.

Farizy, C.; David, F.; Jaubert, J. (1994) "Hommes et bisons du Paleolithique moyen a Mouran (Haute Garonne)." *Gallia Prehistoire,* 30th supplement.

Féblot-Augustins, J. (1993) "Mobility strategies in the late Middle Palaeolithic of Central Europe and Western Europe: Elements of stability and variability." *Journal of Anthropological Archaeology,* 12, 211–265.

Freeman, L. G. (1983) "More on the Mousterian: Flaked bones from Cueva Morin." *Current Anthropology,* 24, 366–377.

Gamble, C. (1978) "Resource exploitation and the spatial patterning of hunter-gatherers: A case study." In *Social Organisation and Settlement* (pp. 153–185). D. Green, C. Haselgrove, and M. Spriggs, eds. Oxford: BAR International Series, 47.

Gamble, C. (1979) "Hunting strategies in the Central European Palaeolithic." *Proceedings of the Prehistoric Society,* 45, 35–52.

Gamble, C. (1986) *The Palaeolithic Settlement of Europe.* Cambridge: Cambridge University Press.

Gargett, R. H. (1989) "Grave shortcomings: The evidence for Neanderthal burial." *Current Anthropology,* 157–190.

Geneste, J-M. (1985) *Analyse lithique d'industrie Mousteriennes du Perigord. Une approche technologique du comportament des groupes humaines au Paleolithique moyen.* Doctoral Thesis, Universite de Bordeaux.

Geneste, J.-M. (1989) "Economie des resources lithiques dans le Mousterien du sud-ouest de la France." In *L'Homme de Neanderthal, La Subsistence, vol. 6* (pp. 75–97). M. Otte, ed. Liège: ERAUL.

Gonzalez-Echegary, J. (1988) "Decorative patterns in the Mousterian of Cueva Morin." In *L'Homme de Neanderthal,* volume 5. Liège: ERAUL.

Grifoni, R.; Radmilli, A. M. (1964) "La Grotta Maritza e il Fucini Prima dell'eta Romana." *Rivista di scienze preistoriche,* 19, 53–127.

Grigor'ev, G. P. (1993) "The Kostenki-Avdeevo archaeological culture and the Willendorf-Pavlov-Kostenki-Avdeevo cultural unity." In *From Kostenki to Clovis: Upper Paleolithic-Paleo-Indian Adaptations* (pp. 51–65). O. Soffer and N.D. Praslov, eds. New York: Plenum Press.

Hahn, J. (1971) "Aurignacian signs, pendants and art objects in Central and Eastern Europe." *World Archaeology,* 3(1), 252–266.

Hahn, J. (1987) "Aurignacian and Gravettian settlement patterns in Central and Eastern Europe." In *The Pleistocene Old World: Regional Perspectives* (pp. 251–261). O. Soffer, ed. New York: Plenum Press.

Harrold, F. B. (1980) "A comparative analysis of Eurasian Palaeolithic burials." *World Archaeology,* 12, 195–211.

Harrold, F. B. (1988) "The Chatelperronian and the Early Aurignacian in France." In *The Early Upper Paleolithic: Evidence from Europe and the Near East* (pp. 157–192). J. Hoffecker and C. A. Wolf, eds. Oxford: BAR International Series 437.

Hayden, B. (1981) "Research and development in the Stone Age: Technological transitions among hunter-gatherers." *Current Anthropology,* 22, 519–548.

Hayden, B. (1993) "The cultural capacities of Neanderthals: A review and re-evaluation." *Journal of Human Evolution,* 24, 113–146.

Isaac, G. (1972) "Chronology and the tempo of cultural change during the Pleistocene." In *A Calibration of Hominid Evolution* (pp. 381–430). W. W. Bishop and J. A. Miller, eds. Edinburgh: Scottish Academic Press.

Jaubert, J.; Lorblanche, M.; Laville, H.; Slott-Moller, R.; Turq, A.; Brugal, J-P. (1990) "Les chasseurs d'aurochs de la borde. Un site du Paleolithique moyen (Livernon, Lot). *Documents d'Archeologie Francais,* volume 27.

Jelinek, J. (1990) *Umeni v zrcadle veku.* Brno: Anthropos.

Justus, A.; Turner, E. (1990) "A forked bone from Middle Palaeolithic levels in the Wannen Volcano (Rhineland Palatinate)." *Cranium,* 7, 58–62.

Kelly, R. L. (1983) "Hunter-gatherer mobility strategies." *Journal of Anthropological Research,* 39, 277–306.

King, B. J. (1994) *The Information Continuum.* Santa Fe: SAR Press.

Kozlowski, J. (1972) "The origin of lithic raw material used in the Palaeolithic of the Carpathian countries." *Acta Archaeologica carpathica,* 13, 5–19.

Kozlowski, J. (1990) "Northern Central Europe ca. 18,000 BP." In *The World at 18,000 BP, Northern Latitudes* (pp. 204–227). O. Soffer and C. Gamble, eds. London: Unwin Hyman.

Kozlowski, J. (1991) "Le Paleolithique superieur en Pologne." In *Le Palaeolithique Superieur Europeen* (pp. 45–51). M. Otte, ed. Liege: ERAUL.

Lindley, J. M.; Clark, G. A. (1990) "Symbolism and modern human origins." *Current Anthropology,* 31, 233–261.

Marshack, A. (1976) "Some implications of the Palaeolithic symbolic evidence for the origins of language." *Current Anthropology,* 17, 274–282.

Marshack, A. (1991) "The female image: A 'time-factored' symbol. A study in style and aspects of image use in the Upper Palaeolithic." *Proceedings of the Prehistoric Society,* 57, 17–31.

Mellars, P. (1973) "The character of the middle-upper palaeolithic transition in southwest France." In *The Explanation of Cultural Change* (pp. 255–276). C. Renfrew, ed. London: Duckworth.

Mellars, P. (1989) "Major issues in the emergence of modern humans." *Current Anthropology,* 30, 349–385.

Mellars, P. (1990) *The Emergence of Modern Humans.* Edinburgh: Edinburgh University Press.

Mellars, P. (1991) "Cognitive changes and the emergence of modern humans." *Cambridge Archaeological Journal,* 1(1), 63–76.

Mellars, P. (1996) *The Neanderthal Legacy: A Case Study of Middle Palaeolithic Behaviour in Western Europe.* Princeton: Princeton University Press.

Mellars, P.; Stringer, C. B. (1989) *The Human Revolution.* Edinburgh; Edinburgh University Press.

Mithen, S. J. (1988) "Looking and learning: Upper Palaeolithic art and information patterning." *World Archaeology,* 19, 297–327.

Otte, M. (1992) "The significance of variability in the European Mousterian." In *The Middle Palaeolithic: Adaptation, Behaviour and Variability* (pp. 45–52). H. Dibble and P. Mellars, eds. Philadelphia: Museum Publications.

Passingham, R. P. (1982) *The Human Primate.* New York: Freeman.

Peyrony, D. (1933) "Les industries 'aurignaciennes' dans le bassin de la Vezere: Aurignacien et Perigordien." *Bulletin de la Societe Prehistorique Francaise,* 38, 181–228.

Roebrooks, W.; Kolen, J.; Rensink, E. (1988) "Planning depth, anticipation and the organisation of Middle Palaeolithic technology: The 'archaic natives' meet Eve's descendants." *Helenium,* 28, 17–34.

Shanks, M.; Tilley, C. (1987) "Abstract and substantial time." *Archaeological Review from Cambridge,* 6, 32–41.

Sieveking, A. (1991) "Palaeolithic art and archaeology: The mobiliary evidence." *Proceedings of the Prehistoric Society,* 57, 33–50.

Simek, J. (1992) "Neanderthal cognition and the Middle to Upper Palaeolithic transition." In *Continuity or Replacement: Controversies in* Homo sapiens *Evolution* (pp. 231–246). G. Brauer and F. Smith, eds. Rotterdam: A.A. Balkema.

Sinclair, A. (1987) "Time and class: Some aspects of time in seventeenth and eighteenth century England." *Archaeological Review from Cambridge,* 6, 62–74.

Smirnoff, Y. (1989) "International human burial: Middle Palaeolithic (late Glaciation) beginnings." *Journal of World Prehistory,* 3, 199–233.

Soffer, O. (1987) "Upper Paleolithic connubia, refugia and the archaeological record." In *The Pleistocene Old World: Regional Perspectives* (pp. 333–348). O. Soffer, ed. New York: Plenum Press.

Soffer, O. (1989) "The Middle to Upper Palaeolithic transition on the Russian Plain." In *The Human Revolution* (pp. 714–742). P. Mellars and C. B. Stringer, eds. Edinburgh: Edinburgh University Press.

Soffer, O. (1993) "Upper Paleolithic adaptations in Central and Eastern Europe and man-mammoth interactions." In *From Kostenki to Clovis: Upper Paleolithic-Paleo-Indian Adaptations* (pp. 31–49). O. Soffer and N. D. Praslov, eds. New York: Plenum Press.

Straus, L. G. (1990) "The Early Upper Palaeolithic of Southern Europe: Cro-Magnon adaptations in the Iberian Peripheries, 40,000–20,000 BP." In *The Emergence of Modern Humans* (pp. 276–302). P. Mellars, ed. Edinburgh: Edinburgh University Press.

Straus, L. G.; Heller, C. (1988) "Explorations of the twilight zone: The Early Upper Palaeolithic of Vasco-Cantabrian Spain and Gascony." In *The Early Upper Palaeolithic: Evidence from Europe and the Near East* (pp. 97–133). J. Hoffecker and C. A. Wolf, eds. Oxford: BAR International Series 437.

Svoboda, J. (1994) "The Pavlov Site, Czech Republic: Lithic evidence from the Upper Paleolithic." *Journal of Field Archaeology,* 21, 69–81.

Svoboda, J.; Vlcek, E. (1991) "La nouvelle sepulture de Dolni Vestonice (DVXVI) Tchecoslovaquie." *L'Anthropologie,* 95, 323–328.

Torrence, R. (1983) "Time budgeting and hunter-gatherer technology." In *Hunter-Gatherer Economy in Prehistory* (pp. 11–22). G. Bailey, ed. Cambridge: Cambridge University Press.

Turq, A. (1992) "Raw material and technological studies of the Quina Mousterian in Perigord." In *The Middle Palaeolithic: Adaptation, Behaviour and Variability* (pp. 74–85). H. Dibble and P. Mellars, eds. Philadelphia: Museum Publications.

Vallois, H. (1972) "Le gisement et le squelette de Saint-Germain-La-Riviere." *Archives de l'Institut de Paleontologie Humaine,* memoire 34.

Wagener, J. S. (1987) "The evolution of man's sense of time." *Human Evolution* 2, 121–133.

Whallon, R. (1989) "Elements of cultural change in the Later Palaeolithic." In *The Human Revolution* (pp. 433–454).

P. Mellars and C. B. Stringer, eds. Edinburgh: Edinburgh University Press.

White, R. (1982) "Rethinking the Middle/Upper Palaeolithic transition." *Current Anthropology,* 23, 169–192.

White, R. (1989) "Production complexity and standardization in early Aurignacian bead and pendant manufacture: Evolutionary implications." In *The Human Revolution* (pp. 366–390). P. Mellars and C. Stringer, eds. Edinburgh: Edinburgh University Press.

White, R. (1993) "The dawn of adornment." *Natural History* 5:60–67.

Whitrow, G. J. (1980) *The Natural Philosophy of Time.* Oxford: Oxford University Press.

Zimmerman, L. J. (1987) "The impact of the concepts of time and past in the concepts of archaeology: Some lessons from the reburial issue." *Archaeological Review from Cambridge,* 6, 42–50.

# Chapter 25

# *Deception among Primates*

## Robert W. Sussman and Thad Q. Bartlett

Recently the issue of deception in nonhuman primates has gained considerable attention, particularly in relation to the study of the evolution of human intelligence. Because of this focus, morphological modes of deception among primates have been largely neglected. Deception in primates is a very broad biological phenomenon including a wide array of morphological and behavioral traits. Here we provide a brief review of deceit among primates, using the definition of deception provided by Goodenough (1991). In considering the forms of deception displayed by primates two distinctions must be made, that between morphological and behavioral mechanisms and that between inter- and intraspecific deception. The selective mechanisms involved in deception may operate in significantly different ways depending upon whether the deceiver and target are members of the same species.

## MORPHOLOGICAL DECEPTION

Like other animals, primates exhibit visually deceptive morphological traits that generally function as predator avoidance mechanisms. The most common form of visual deception is camouflage. Among New World primates, marmosets and tamarins, which are typically active in dense foliage, are vulnerable when harvesting exudates on exposed tree trunks. Some species have developed cryptic coat coloration in response to predator pressure. The patchy coat color is difficult to distinguish from the visual pattern of the tree trunk (Figure 25–1) (Garber 1980).

In addition, tamarins often sleep in huddled groups in dense vegetation. This may also be a visually deceptive strategy. Upon first seeing a tamarin group

huddled together at a sleeping site, Dawson (1976) thought it was a termite nest and believed this might be an example of crypsis or protective mimicry.

The highly terrestrial patas monkey (*Erythrocebus patas*) also shows cryptic coloration. Its tan coat serves as effective camouflage in dry savannah-grass and the white underside may be an example of countershading. Countershading enhances the effect of cryptic coloration by dissolving the shadow and obscuring the outline of the body. This phenomenon is quite common in birds, fish, and small mammals (Owen 1982).

Another form of visual deception in primates is exhibited by the aye aye (*Daubentonia madagascariensis*). Aye ayes have two large white eye-spots (Figure 25–2). The function of these spots is not clear, but they are likely defensive markings. Many animals use eye-spots to

**Figure 25–1** A tamarin feeding on a large branch. (Photo by Paul Garber).

Adapted from a paper presented at the American Association for the Advancement of Science meetings, Washington D.C., February 16, 1991.

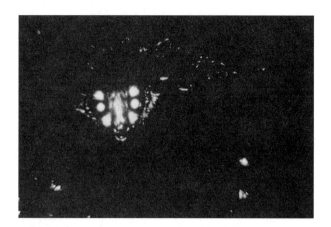

**Figure 25–2** Eye spots of the aye aye. These serve as defensive markers in this nocturnal primate. (Photo by Jean-Jacques Petter).

frighten or confuse potential predators. While this does not seem to be the case in the aye aye, it is possible that the white eye patches make the animal appear larger to potential predators and thus may discourage attack.

Another way animals may cause themselves to appear larger is by pilo-erection. This is a familiar behavior in household cats and the phenomenon is presumably similar in primates. A number of primatologists have noted this trait in chimpanzees. For example, Goodall (1971) offered the following description: "Flow rushed out of Figan's way when he careened toward her, dragging a branch and with his hair on end looking twice his normal size," and de Waal (1986) gives another example: "the two males approach each other, their hair on end, making themselves look as big as possible."

Hair-raising in chimpanzees occurs (though perhaps not exclusively) in an intraspecific context and may play a role in sexual competition. Another type of morphological deception in primates that is used intraspecifically is self-mimicry, or automimesis (Wickler 1967, 1968). Automimesis is the phenomenon whereby one part of an animal's morphology mimics another. For example, the tail of the leaf-tailed gecko resembles its head. In the gecko automimesis acts to confuse potential predators as to where to strike (Keeton 1980).

In primates, automimesis appears to facilitate social interactions. For example, according to Wickler (1968), the red anogenital coloration of the male hamadryas baboon mimics the conspicuous estrous swellings of the female. The appearance of the swollen, red rump in males, he argues, inhibits aggressive attacks by dominant animals. Wickler (1968) asserts that "since the males also greet and subdue one another with presentation gestures they must imitate these swellings of the female if their presentation is to be as effective" (p. 231). Furthermore, while presentation in hamadryas baboons has a different function in males than in females, he believes that the signal "has passed through a mimetic

phase at which time it would have been taken for something else." (p. 231–232).

## BEHAVIORAL DECEPTION

It is common to divide the discussion of animal behavior into voluntary and involuntary acts. However, behavior does not always neatly fall into such categories. *Voluntary* and *involuntary* behaviors must be recognized as ends of a continuum. In fact, very few primate behaviors can be considered strictly involuntary. However, among primates there are at least two examples of predator avoidance behaviors that appear to be wholly involuntary.

Roughly 75 percent of living prosimians are nocturnal. Predator avoidance is almost certainly an important factor in nocturnal small-bodied prosimians. In addition to being nocturnal, lorises use a pattern of cryptic locomotion to deceive potential predators. Lorises move in slow motion, like chameleons. This physiologically enforced crypticism presumably aids in escaping detection. Because it is unable to flee potential predators, the potto is also equipped with structural defenses. When discovered it tucks its head under its body exposing spine-like vertebrae and sensitive vibrissae to the predator. If this defense proves ineffective, the animal will release its grip, fall to the ground and hide (Charles-Dominique 1977). In this case the crypsis, which acts to withhold information from potential predators, is clearly part of an evolved adaptive complex, subject to a great deal of genetic control.

A number of other primates deceive predators much more actively. Rather than withholding information they provide misinformation. Male patas monkeys draw potential predators away from the group (Hall 1965). Patas males are vigilant, typically climbing into small trees or scanning for predators. When a male patas observes a predator approaching its group, he performs a noisy display, shaking the branches and overtly calling attention to himself. Once seen, the animal will often run towards the predator and draw it into a high-speed chase while the rest of the group hides in the grass.

This behavior can be compared to the distraction display described for birds. Ideally, the predator pursues the male and leaves the family group alone. The success of this strategy is no doubt related to the fact that the patas monkey is the fastest primate, capable of speeds up to 55 km per hour. However, similar patterns of predator defense have been described for a number of arboreal primates (Raemaekers and Chivers 1980, Tilson and Tenaza 1976).

It would be difficult to argue that such behaviors are completely involuntary or genetically fixed. Certainly given the plasticity of behavior exhibited by primates such responses must entail some degree of voluntary control. On the other hand, because of the profound influence that predation has had on the evolution of primate behavior, distraction displays and invitations to pursuit presumably entail some genetic control.

Most examples of deception occur between animals of different species. Generally, intraspecific deception is quite rare (Dawkins and Krebs 1978). Among some primates, however, successful intraspecific deceit is common and occurs in a social context. Given the remarkable plasticity of social behavior among primates, the argument for strict genetic control in intraspecific deception is less tenable. Rather, skeptics of tactical deception in primates typically regard candidates for such behavior as the result of conditioning or opportunism (Quiatt 1984, Whiten and Byrne 1988).

## TACTICAL DECEPTION

To this point the features we have discussed contain a significant genetic component and are clearly adaptive to the species as a whole. Such adaptations have been described as phylogenetic deception (Wickler 1968). We now wish to consider deception, which occurs predominantly within a social context. Byrne and Whiten (1985) label this kind of behavior "tactical deception," which they define as:

> acts from the normal repertoire of an individual, used at low frequency and in contexts different from those in which it uses the high frequency (honest) version of the act, such that another familiar individual is likely to misinterpret what the acts signify, to the advantage of the actor (p. 672).

We assume that they consider these acts to be conscious and intentional.

The authors draw a number of examples from their own work with chacma baboons. For instance, on more than one occasion, Byrne and Whiten (1985) witnessed a juvenile animal emit an unprovoked alarm call while seated near a feeding adult. The alarm summoned in one case the juvenile's mother, and in another, a dominant male who chased away the feeding adult, leaving the juvenile to feed unmolested on the vacated food patch. In another instance, an individual was able to halt the pursuit of aggressors by engaging in vigilant behavior. The fleeing animal stopped abruptly, stood on its hind legs, and scanned the horizon. Seeing this, his pursuers also stopped and looked in the indicated direction. There was no predator or other baboon troop in sight.

Motivated by their own findings, Whiten and Byrne (1988) distributed a questionnaire to 115 primatologists asking for examples of tactical deception. From the responses, they identified a total of five types (including numerous sub-types) of tactical deception exhibited by monkeys and apes. These were: *concealment, distraction, creating an image, manipulation of target using social tool,* and *deflection of target to fall guy.*

According to Whiten and Byrne, the most common forms of deception involve the manipulation of the attention of other animals, especially through concealment or distraction. An example of distraction was given above in the case of feigned vigilance in chacma baboons.

Concealment can take one of two forms, concealment of all or part of one's self, or concealment of an object. Kummer offers the following example of partial concealment in hamadryas baboons (Whiten and Byrne 1988: 215) (Figure 25–3).

> An adult female spent 20 minutes gradually shifting her position over a distance of 2 meters to a place behind a rock where she began to groom the subadult follower of the unit—an interaction not tolerated by the adult male . . . the adult male leader could, from his resting position, see the tail, back and crown of the female's head, but not her front, arms and face; the subadult male sat in a bent position . . . and was also invisible to the leader.

It is assumed that what makes this behavior different from simple hiding is the ability of the female to accurately represent the dominant male's view of the situation. Numerous examples of this type of behavior also exist for chimpanzees. De Waal (1986) has observed many instances of subordinate males concealing their erections in a way that the erect penis is visible to a specific female, but not to a nearby dominant male.

Both of these examples of concealment fit into Whiten and Byrne's sub-class *hiding from view.* Another

**Figure 25–3** Partial concealment in a hamadryas baboon, illustrating one form of tactical deception. (From Byrne and Whiten, *Machiavellian Intelligence,* reprinted by permission of Oxford University Press.)

common form of concealment is *inhibition of attention.* The following example from Goodall (1971) is probably the earliest and most widely cited instance for deception occurring in wild primates:

> One day sometime after the group had been fed, Figan spotted a banana that had been overlooked—but Goliath [a dominant male] was resting directly underneath it. After no more than a quick glance from the fruit to Goliath, Figan moved away and sat on the other side of the tent so that he could no longer see the fruit. Fifteen minutes later, when Goliath got up and left, Figan without a moment's hesitation went over and collected the banana (pp. 96–97).

Deception of this form appears inherently more complex than simple hiding from view. In this case the animal shows an awareness of his own ability to inadvertently yield information about the location of the food source. Responding accordingly, Figan removed himself from the precarious situation. Goodall also reports that Figan learned to lead the group away from the feeding site before the food had been depleted. Later he would double-back and get more food for himself. Similar behaviors have also been reported for gorillas.

Interestingly, however, the sub-classes of deception exemplified above, *inhibition of attention* and *distract by leading away* are not widely reported in monkeys. Whiten and Byrne (1988) indicate that this may point to a phylogenetic difference between monkeys and apes in their capacity for deception. "It is possible," they suggest, "that monkeys inhibit attention to others whom they wish to avoid, whereas only apes inhibit attention to resources they want" (p. 222). Furthermore, they argue, that "in the chimpanzee cases of *distract by leading away,* the repeated and skillful use of the tactic implies that the agent is indeed pursuing the goal of distracting the target."

The issue of goal-directed behavior remains a controversial subject. Laboratory experiments designed to investigate the capacity for intentional behavior in chimpanzees yields the best evidence for intentional deception. Perhaps not incidentally the categories involved included *inhibition of attention* and *distraction by leading away.*

Menzel (1974) conducted an experiment in which he showed a lone juvenile female chimpanzee the location of a hidden food item within a large enclosure. After a period of delay the female along with several other group members was allowed to enter the enclosure. During the first trial, the female excitedly ran to the site of the hidden food. Because her behavior gave away the source of her excitement the other animals followed and the food was taken from her by dominant group members. After several trials the female changed her behavior. Instead of running to the actual hiding place she ran in a false direction. When other animals followed, she held

back until they had passed and then went immediately to the true hiding place and retrieved the food.

Woodruff and Premack (1979) (see also Premack and Premack 1982), imposed greater experimental control and showed that chimpanzees could learn to "lie" to unfriendly human trainers (Figure 25–4). The subjects were shown the hiding place of a food item but separated from it by a wire mesh. The chimpanzee was then confronted by either a friendly or an unfriendly trainer. If the friendly trainer could determine the location of the food item from the animal's behavior, he would share the food with the subject. An unfriendly trainer, on the other hand, would keep the food for himself. Over the course of the experiment, all four subjects learned to suppress behaviors that would give away the location of a food item to an unfriendly trainer. Two subjects learned to consistently misdirect the unfriendly trainer by motioning toward the incorrect box.

These studies suggest that chimpanzees have the capacity for conscious, intentional deceptive behavior, and that they can predict its consequences. Furthermore, they can imagine a series of events that are yet to take place. In fact, it can be argued that, in instances in which a chimpanzee leads another away from a food site, it is creating an imaginary goal.

Byrne and Whiten further claim that the ability of primates to deceive is linked in large part to their ability to represent the attentional states of others. They believe that, unlike other animals, primates are able to accurately judge what another individual is capable of seeing,

**Figure 25–4**  Unfriendly trainer in chimpanzee experiments. (Adapted from Woodruff and Premack 1979).

and based on that information, consciously redirect the other animal's attention.

## DECEPTION, SELF-DECEPTION, AND THE EVOLUTION OF HUMAN INTELLIGENCE

Perhaps among of the most interesting findings of the survey conducted by Byrne and Whiten are the phylogenetic differences in tactical deception. There have been no reports of tactical deception among prosimians, and this type of behavior is much more prevalent and complex among the great apes, especially chimpanzees, than among monkeys. Of course few would argue that lying and deception are common behaviors among humans.

In the previous sections, we have shown that deception in primates is a widely used adaptive strategy. As conscious, intraspecific deception became more common in social situations among primates, one would expect deceptive signals to become more subtle and that a spiral of complex deceptive–counter-deceptive strategies could develop. Conscious, intentional deception among higher primates is a common social strategy and it seems to have evolved along with what we consider higher intelligence. However, what does the study of tactical deception tell us about thought patterns and the evolution of intelligence in humans? The relationship between tactical deception in chimpanzees and lying in humans is as obscure as that between chimpanzee communication and human language, and the study of language in chimpanzees has not added a great deal to our knowledge of the evolution of human intelligence.

However, if we are allowed to speculate a bit, there is one area related to deception that has not been studied in great detail, that is *self-deception*. The study of self-deception might give us some insight into differences between ape and human intelligence. As Trivers (1985) has stated: "With powers to deceive and to spot deception being improved by natural selection, a new kind of deception may be favored: self-deception." In our opinion, *sustained* self-deception is not found in any other species of animal, including non-human primates, but pervades all of human existence. This does not mean that all human beliefs are the result of self-deception. Some can be tested against natural phenomena and, as far as we can tell given our perceptual abilities, can be shown to be true. However, the evidence for self-deception actually separates *Homo sapiens* from apes and earlier hominids in the fossil record.

Burials first appear around 80,000 years ago, along with the earliest modern *Homo sapiens*, and burial goods, cave paintings, effigies, and amulets appear more recently, around 40,000 years ago (see two preceding chapters). These artifacts suggest that early humans, unlike any animals before them, created imaginary worlds and myths about life after death. In order to have a myth of

Professor Feldman, traveling back in time, gradually succumbs to the early stages of nonculture shock.

**Figure 25–5** *The Far Side* by Gary Larson. (The Far Side © 1988 Farworks, Inc. Used by permission of Universal Press Syndicate. All rights reserved.)

life after death, one must go against physical evidence and empirical reality. After all there is nothing "heavenly" about a human corpse.

Only humans have religion and each human sees the world through the filter of his own culture. As Clifford Geertz (1973) has said "Man is an animal suspended in webs of significance he himself has spun." No two religions and no two cultures imagine the world in precisely the same manner. Thus, religion and culture must be seen as the result of human self-deception. Humans cannot exist without this filter of culture. As Geertz (1973) states; "without men, no culture, certainly; but equally, and more significantly, without culture, no men" (p. 49). In the past, we have defined *Homo sapiens* as the "wise" or "thinking" being. We would suggest that a more accurate definition might be the "self-deceiving" being. This is one trait that we believe does separate us qualitatively from our closest relatives (Figure 25–5).

## REFERENCES

Bryne, R. W.; Whiten A. (1985) "Tactical deception of familiar individuals in baboons." *Animal Behavior*, 33: 669–673.

Charles-Dominique, P. (1977) *Ecology and Behavior of Nocturnal Prosimians*. London: Duckworth.

Dawkins, R.; Krebs, J. R. (1978) "Animal signals: Information or manipulation." In *Behavioral Ecology: An Evolutionary Approach.* J. R. Krebs and N. B. Davies, eds. Oxford: Blackwell.

Dawson, G. A. (1976) *Behavioral ecology of the Panamanian tamarin, Saguinus oedipus (Callitrichidae: Primates).* Unpublished Ph.D. dissertation, Michigan State University.

de Waal, F. (1986) "Deception in the natural communication of chimpanzees." In *Deception: Perspectives on Human and Non-human Deceit* (pp. 221–244). R. W. Mitchell and N. S. Thompson, eds. Albany: State University of New York Press.

Garber, P. A. (1980) "Locomotor behavior and feeding ecology of the Panamanian tamarin (*Saguinus oedipus geoffroyi*, Callitrichidas, Primates)." *International Journal of Primatology* 1:185–201.

Geertz, C. (1973) *The Interpretation of Cultures.* New York: Basic Books.

Goodall, J. (1971) *In the Shadow of Man.* Boston: Houghton Mifflin.

Goodenough, U. (1991) *Molecular Deception.* Paper presented at the annual meetings of the American Association for the Advancement of Science.

Hall, K. R. L. (1965) "Behavior and ecology of the wild patas monkey, *Erythrocebus patas*, in Uganda." *The Journal of Zoology*, 148:15–87.

Keeton, W. T. (1980) *Biological Science*, 3rd ed. New York: W. W. Norton and Co.

Menzel, E. W. (1974) "A group of young chimpanzees in a one-acre field." In *Behavior of Non-human Primates*, vol. 5.

A. M. Schrier and F. Stollnitz, eds. New York: Academic Press.

Owen, D. (1982) *Camouflage and Mimicry.* Chicago: The University of Chicago Press.

Premack, D.; Premack, A. 1982. *The Mind of an Ape.* New York: Norton.

Quiatt, D. (1984) "Devious intentions of monkeys and apes?" In *The Meaning of Primate Signals* (pp. 9–40). R. Harre and V. Reynolds, eds. Cambridge: Cambridge University Press.

Raemaekers, J. J.; Chivers, D. J. (1980) "Socio-ecology of Malayan forest primates." In *Malayan Forest Primates.* D. J. Chivers, ed. New York: Plenum Press.

See: Open Peer Commentary to: Whiten A.; Byrne, R. W. 1988. Tactical deception in primates. *Behavioral and Brain Sciences*, 11:233–273.

Tilson, R. L.; Tenaza, R. R. (1976) "Monogamy and duetting in an Old World monkey." *Nature* 263: 320–321.

Trivers, R. 1985. *Social Evolution.* Benjamin Cummings.

Whiten, A.; Bryne R. W. (1988) "The manipulation of attention in primate tactical deception." In *Machiavellian Intelligence* (pp. 211–223). R. Byrne and A. Whiten, eds. New York: Oxford University Press.

Wickler, W. (1967) "Socio-sexual signals and their intraspecific imitation among primates." In *Primate Ethology.* D. Morris, ed. Chicago: Aldine.

Wickler, W. (1968) *Mimicry in Plants and Animals.* New York: McGraw-Hill.

Woodruff, G.; Premack, D. (1979) "Intentional communication in the chimpanzee: The development of deception." *Cognition*, 7:333–362.

# Part III

# THE BIOLOGICAL BASIS OF RACE AND RACISM

Shortly after modern humans evolved, they began to disperse to all regions of the earth. The patterns of dispersal are not completely understood, nor is the relationship between dispersal patterns and modern human variation. Until recently, it was not possible to reconstruct these patterns. However, with the techniques available to modern genetics, we are able to create models of early human dispersal and of how this corresponds to modern human diversity. In Chapter 26, Alan Templeton, a Washington University population geneticist, uses patterns of trait differentiation, genetic surveys, and analysis of DNA haplotype trees to provide strong evidence that there are not now nor have there ever been distinct human "subspecies" or "races" among modern *Homo sapiens.*

Although Templeton's article is currently one of the best and most complete scientific demonstrations of this fact, the idea that biological races do not exist in human populations is not new. In fact, as can be seen in many of the articles in this section, most population geneticists and anthropologists have been making this point for years. In an article originally published in *Newsweek,* Begley (Chapter 27) outlines some of the typical problems that we face when trying to divide humans into biological groups based simply on a single trait, such as skin color. Jefferson Fish, in an article addressed to American psychologists, who for the most part still accept a color-coded division of human populations, outlines the problems created by using simple-minded racial categories and attempting to relate them to complex behaviors, such as intelligence and personality. Professor Fish has first-hand experience with the problems of racial identification. He is a white, Jewish psychologist married to a black anthropologist, whose daughter would be considered a "black" American by most, but is living in Brazil where she is considered (by some) to be white.

However, if no races exist, why is there so much racism? The belief that biological races exist among humans and racism are historical realities even if race is not a biological reality. At the time of Darwin there were two major "scientific" explanations of races in Western Europe. In the first, western "civilized," white humans were created by God, whereas other "primitive" peoples, living mainly in countries colonized by Europeans, were created before Adam (so-called pre-Adamites) and were biologically, unchangeably inferior. This made it easy to rationalize their subjugation and generally inhumane treatment. The second view was that all humans were created by God but that those living in the colonies had degenerated due to climatic factors and to isolation from civilization. This was the liberal view and led to attempts to missionize or civilize the "savages."

Around the turn of the twentieth century, Darwin's *Origins* was generally accepted, as was Mendel's genetics, and Lemark's theory of the inheritance of acquired characteristics was proven not to be a viable explanation for biological change. This led many to believe that all biological and ultimately behavioral variation among humans was determined by natural selection and by genetics. Furthermore, natural selection led to survival of the fittest individuals and groups because they had the best combination of genes (Social Darwinism). Some individuals and some racial groups were considered by Western "civilized" men to be biologically and genetically (and therefore unchangeably) inferior. Since these people or populations could not be changed by improving their environment, the majority of Western scientists thought we must limit their breeding and ensure and enhance breeding among those more fit, or the "well born." This, of course, was eugenics and was the prevalent scientific approach until its ultimate climax in Hitler's Germany.

Around 1910, Franz Boaz, one of the fathers of American anthropology, developed the major alternative theory to eugenics. He and his students and colleagues understood the dangers of eugenics and fought racism and fascism perpetuated by this movement until the end of World War II. Boaz argued that most differences in complex behavior, and in some morphological traits, are the result of the different individual and group histories that people and groups experience during their lifetimes. He and his colleagues presented ample evidence that physical and social environment greatly influenced some morphological traits (such as cranial shape) and most complex behavior. People from different parts of the world as well as people living together but brought up differently behave differently—not better or worse but differently. In 1910, this was a unique perspective. Boaz argued in his book *The Mind of Primitive Man* (1911) that all normal human thought processes and mental abilities are similar. They are just the products of different experiences. People living within the same social sphere have more shared experiences and are taught similar things. This is the basis of the anthropological concept of culture, and without understanding the powerful influence that culture has on an individual and on groups of individuals, it is difficult to understand how social environment can so strongly influence behavior. Culture is unique to humans and is what makes humans unique.

In Chapter 29, by Phillipe Rushton, a Canadian psychologist, and in Chapter 31, by Murray and Herrnstein, a psychologist and a political scientist, we see that these authors still believe that the complex behaviors are influenced by genetics and that different "races" are endowed with better and worse genetics. The problem is, as pointed out in Chapters 30 and 32, that these authors don't understand genetics, the problems with the biological concept of race, or the importance of environment and individual and group history (e.g., culture) on behavior. Thus, in order to reach their conclusions, they are forced to do bad science (e.g., complete misunderstanding of heritability) and atrocious scholarship (e.g., correlating of brain size and penis size). You might ask, "So why do you include papers like this in this book?" Because many people, too many, still believe these authors, and their thesis can be, and has been, used for political and economic policy. For example, Murray and

Herrnstein ask why should we waste taxpayers' money on social programs or support affirmative action when it is impossible to change the behavioral propensities of a certain group of people, or to improve their performance in school or their intelligence. This is much like the eighteenth century view of pre-Adamites, and the same approach that led to Nazism in Germany. Too many people are still living in the past and have not gained anything from the last 100 years of scholarship and science.

I have included the page summarizing the world to add some perspective, even though this page comes from an anonymous and unconfirmed e-mail. However, I think it gives us something to think about (if anyone can identify the author or compiler of this, I would like to acknowledge it in the next printing). The chapter entitled "Health Trends" gives us some perspective of the differential treatment and outcome that can result from a generally racist history and social policy.

In Chapter 37, Jonathan Marks, a physical anthropologist specializing in human variation, reiterates the problems one encounters in attempting to define race as a biological entity. Lind (Chapter 38) puts the reemergence of academic racism into political and economic perspective by describing who pays for the "research" and publications, and who pushes the rhetoric.

In the last chapter of this section, I attempt to illustrate how history may be repeating itself. As I mentioned above, many people still believe that race is real, that much of human behavior and behavioral differences between individuals are biologically based, and that environment has little to do with how we behave. These fixed behavioral patterns are the end product of natural selection on earlier human populations, and variation in the expression of these traits is thought to be the result of differential fitness on living human populations. This sounds very much like Social Darwinism and the eugenics of the past. As we will see in the next section of the book, the new fields of evolutionary psychology, evolutionary anthropology, behavioral ecology, as well as a number of others bring this dubious marriage of genetics and the biological basis of human behavior into the late 1990s and beyond.

# Chapter 26

# *Human Races: A Genetic and Evolutionary Perspective*

## Alan R. Templeton

The word "race" is rarely used in the modern, nonhuman evolutionary literature because its meaning is so ambiguous. When it is used, it is generally used as a synonym for "subspecies" (Futuyma 1986:107–109), but this concept also has no precise definition. The traditional meaning of a subspecies is that of a geographically circumscribed, genetically differentiated population (Smith et al. 1997). The problem with this definition from an evolutionary genetic perspective is that many traits and their underlying polymorphic genes show independent patterns of geographical variation (Futuyma 1986:108–109). As a result, some combination of characters will distinguish virtually every population from all others. There is no clear limit to the number of races that can be recognized under this concept, and indeed this notion of subspecies quickly becomes indistinguishable from that of a local population. One way around this difficulty is to place minimal quantitative thresholds on the amount of genetic differentiation that is required to recognize subspecies (Smith et al. 1997). A second solution is to allow races or subspecies to be defined only by the geographical patterns found for particular "racial" traits or characters.

A similar problem is faced in defining species. For example, the biological species concept focuses attention on characters related to reproductive incompatibility as those important in defining a species. These reproductive traits have priority in defining a species when in conflict with other traits, such as morphology (Mayr 1970). Unfortunately, there is no such guidance at the subspecies level, although in practice easily observed morphological traits (the very ones deemed not important

Reproduced by permission of the American Anthropological Association from *American Anthropologist* 100:3, September 1998. Not for further reproduction. (Modified from original version.)

under the biological species concept) are used. There is no evolutionary justification for this dominance of easily observed morphological traits; indeed, it merely arises from the sensory constraints of our own species. Therefore, most evolutionary biologists reject the notion that there are special "racial" traits.

Because of these difficulties, the modern evolutionary perspective of a "subspecies" is that of a distinct evolutionary lineage within a species (Shaffer and McKnight 1996) [although one should note that many current evolutionary biologists completely deny the existence of any meaningful definition of subspecies, as argued originally by Wilson and Brown (1953)—see discussions in Futuyma (1986:108–109) and Smith et al. 1997:13)]. The Endangered Species Act requires preservation of vertebrate subspecies (Pennock and Dimmick 1997), and the distinct evolutionary lineage definition has become the de facto definition of a subspecies in much of conservation biology (Amato and Gatesy 1994, Brownlow 1996, Legge et al. 1996, Miththapala et al. 1996, Pennock and Dimmick 1997, Vogler 1994). This definition requires that a subspecies be genetically differentiated due to barriers to genetic exchange that have persisted for long periods of time; that is, the subspecies must have historical continuity in addition to current genetic differentiation. It cannot be emphasized enough that *genetic differentiation alone is insufficient to define a subspecies.* The additional requirement of historical continuity is particularly important because many traits should reflect the common evolutionary history of the subspecies, and therefore in theory there is no need to prioritize the informative traits in defining subspecies. Indeed, the best traits for identifying subspecies are now simply those with the best phylogenetic resolution. In this regard, advances in molecular genetics have greatly augmented our ability to resolve genetic variation and provide the best current resolution of recent evolutionary histories (Avise 1994), thereby allowing the identification of evolutionary lineages in an objective, explicit fashion (Templeton 1994, Templeton 1998a, b, Templeton et al. 1995).

The purpose of this chapter is to examine the existence of races in humans using an evolutionary genetic perspective. The fundamental question is: Are human populations genetically differentiated from one another in such a fashion as to constitute either sharply genetically differentiated populations or distinct evolutionary sublineages of humanity? These questions will be answered with molecular genetic data and through the application of the same, explicit criteria used for the analyses of nonhuman organisms. This last point is critical if the use of the word "race" in humanity is to have any general biological validity. This chapter will not address the cultural, social, political, and economic aspect of human "races."

## ARE HUMAN "RACES" GEOGRAPHICALLY CIRCUMSCRIBED, SHARPLY DIFFERENTIATED POPULATIONS?

The validity of the traditional subspecies definition of human races can be addressed by examining the patterns and amount of genetic diversity found within and among human populations. One common method of quantifying the amount of within-to-among genetic diversity is through the $F_{st}$ statistic of Wright (1969) and some of its more modern variants that have been designed specifically for molecular data, such as $K_{st}$ (Hudson et al. 1992) or $N_{st}$ (Lynch and Crease 1990). $F_{st}$ and related statistics range from 0 (all the genetic diversity within a species is shared equally by all populations with no genetic differences among populations) to 1 (all the genetic diversity within a species is found as fixed differences among populations with no genetic diversity within populations). The $F_{st}$ value of humans (based on 16 populations from Africa, Europe, Asia, the Americas, and the Australo-Pacific region) is 0.156 (Barbujani et al. 1997), thereby indicating that most human genetic diversity exists as differences among individuals within populations, and only 15.6 percent can be used to genetically differentiate the major human "races." To put the human $F_{st}$ value into perspective, humans need to be compared to other species. $F_{st}$'s for many plants, invertebrates, and small bodied vertebrates are typically far larger than the human value, most of these organisms have poor dispersal abilities, so this is to be expected. A more valid comparison would be the $F_{st}$ values of other large-bodied mammals with excellent dispersal abilities. Figure 26–1 shows the values of $F_{st}$'s and related statistics for several

large-bodied mammals. As can be seen, the human $F_{st}$ value is one of the lowest, even though the human geographical distribution is the greatest. A standard criterion for a subspecies or race in the nonhuman literature under the traditional definition of a subspecies as a geographically circumscribed, sharply differentiated population is to have $F_{st}$ values of at least 0.25 to 0.30 (Smith et al. 1997). Hence, as judged by the criterion in the nonhuman literature, the human $F_{st}$ value is too small to have taxonomic significance under the traditional subspecies definition.

This does not mean that the low human $F_{st}$ value is without any evolutionary significance. Suppose for the moment that the $F_{st}$ values in humans truly reflect a balance between gene flow versus local drift/selection and are not due to isolated human lineages. One convenient method for quantifying this balance is Nm, the product of local effective population size (N) with m, the migration rate between demes. Under the idealized population structure known as the island model, the relationship between $F_{st}$ and Nm is (Wright 1969):

$$F_{st} = \frac{1}{4Nm + 1}$$

Most real populations do not fit an island model (which assumes that gene flow is independent of geographical distance). Nm is therefore not the actual number of individuals exchanged per generation, but rather is an effective number of migrating individuals per generation relative to this simple, idealized model of population structure. This allows comparisons in effective amounts of gene flow across different species with respect to a common standard. For the human $F_{st}$ value of 0.156, Nm = 1.35. This result is consistent with the work of Santos et al. (1997) who examined several human data sets with a variety of statistical procedures and always obtained Nm > 1. With Nm on the order of 1, massive movements of large numbers of individuals are not needed to explain the level of genetic differentiation observed in humans. Moreover, Nm = 1.35 does not mean that precisely 1.35 effective individuals migrate among the "races" every generation; rather, this is the long-term average. Assuming a generation time of twenty years, the levels of racial differentiation in humanity could be explained by interchanging 1.35 effective individuals every 20 years, or 13.5 every 200 years, or 135 every 2,000 years. Since humans often move as populations, gene flow could be very sporadic on a time scale measured in thousands to tens of thousands of years and still yield an effective number of migrants of 1.35.

An Nm value of 1.35 would insure that the population evolves as a single evolutionary lineage over long periods of time (Crow and Kimura 1970). Nevertheless, population genetic theory also indicates that fluctuations around an average Nm of order one is conducive both to the rapid spread of selectively favored genes throughout

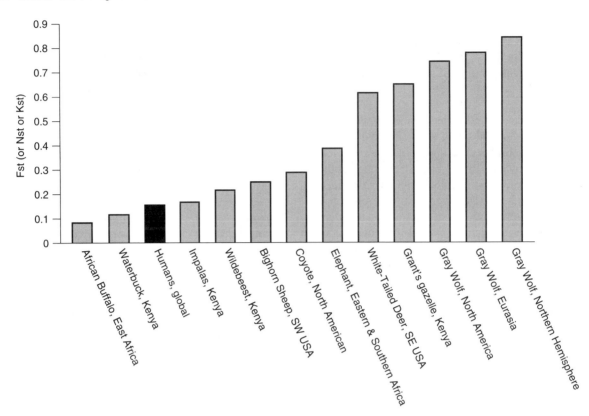

**Figure 26–1** $F_{st}$ (or $K_{st}$ or $N_{st}$) values for various species of large-bodied mammals with excellent dispersal abilities. The figure shows $F_{st}$ (or its multiallelic analogue, $G_{st}$) values for African buffalo (Templeton and Georgiadis 1996), humans (Barbujani et al. 1997), Bighorn sheep (Boyce et al. 1997), elephants (Georgiadis et al. 1994), and white-tailed deer (Ellsworth et al. 1994); $K_{st}$ values for waterbuck, impalas, wildebeest, and Grant's gazelle (Arctander et al. 1996); and $N_{st}$ values for coyotes (Lehman and Wayne 1991) and wolves (Wayne et al. 1992). The geographical scale of the study is indicated by the species name. Values are given in order of size, with the human value indicated in black and nonhuman values in gray.

the species and to local population differentiation and adaptation (Barton and Rouhani 1993). If anatomically modern traits did indeed first evolve in Africa, the human Nm value implies that such traits could rapidly spread throughout all of humanity through gene flow if selectively favored, even though local populations could still display genetic differentiation for other loci. Studies on nonhuman organisms indicate that Nm values can be larger than those in humans and yet the species can still display much local differentiation and adaptation, as predicted by this theory. For example, populations of *Drosophila mercatorum* on the slopes versus the saddle of the Kohala mountains on the island of Hawaii (a distance of 3 km) have an estimated Nm of between 4 to 8 (DeSalle et al. 1987). Nevertheless, these populations show extreme differentiation and local adaptation for the abnormal abdomen syndrome, a complex polygenic suite of phenotypes that affects morphology, developmental time, female fecundity, male sexual maturation, and longevity in adaptively significant ways (Hollocher and Templeton 1994, Hollocher et al. 1992, Templeton et al. 1993, Templeton et al. 1989). Similarly, garter snake populations in Lake Erie have an Nm value be-

tween 2.7 and 37.6 among sites with populations that differ greatly in the amount of melanism (King and Lawson 1995; 1997; Lawson and King 1996). These examples (and many more could have been given) clearly show that Nm values higher than the estimated Nm value for humans are still compatible with much local differentiation across space even though the gene flow is sufficiently high to ensure that the species as a whole evolves as a single lineage over time.

The above discussion was predicated upon the *assumption* that the human $F_{st}$ value arose from the balance of gene flow versus local drift and selection. Unfortunately, the $F_{st}$ statistic *per se* cannot discriminate among potential causes of genetic differentiation (Templeton 1998a). Although human "races" do not satisfy the standard quantitative criterion for being traditional subspecies (Smith et al. 1997), this does not necessarily mean that races do not exist in the evolutionary lineage sense. Under the lineage concept of subspecies, all that is needed is sufficient genetic differentiation to define the separate lineages. If the lineages split only recently, the overall level of divergence could be quite small. Therefore, the quantitative levels of genetic diversity among human populations do not rule out the possibility that human "races" are valid under the evolutionary lineage definition of subspecies. The remainder of this paper will focus upon this more modern definition of subspecies.

## ARE HUMAN "RACES" DISTINCT EVOLUTIONARY LINEAGES?

### Models of Human Evolution and Human Races

When a biological race is defined as a distinct evolutionary lineage within a species, the question of race can only be answered in the context of the recent evolutionary history of the species. The two dominant models of recent human evolution during the last half of this century are the candelabra (Figure 26–2) and trellis (Figure 26–3) models. Both models accept the evolutionary origin of the genus *Homo* in Africa and the spread of *Homo erectus* out of Africa a million years ago or more. Candelabra models posit that the major Old World geographical groups (Europeans, sub-Saharan Africans, and Asians) split from one another and since have had nearly independent evolutionary histories (but perhaps with some subsequent admixture). Therefore, the evolutionary relationships among Africans, Europeans, and Asians can be portrayed as an evolutionary tree—in this case with the topology of a candelabra (Figure 26–2). The major human geographical populations are portrayed as the branches on this candelabra and are therefore valid "races" under the evolutionary lineage definition. The ancient origin candelabra model regarded the split be-

tween the major "races" as occurring with the spread of *Homo erectus* (Figure 26–2A) followed by independent evolution of each "race" into its modern form. This version has been thoroughly discredited and has no serious advocates today. However, a recent origin candelabra model known as the out-of-Africa replacement hypothesis (Figure 26–2B) has become widely accepted. Under this model, anatomically modern humans evolved first in Africa. Next, a small group of these anatomically modern humans split off from the African population and colonized Eurasia about 100,000 years ago, driving the *Homo erectus* populations to complete genetic extinction everywhere (the "replacement" part of the hypothesis). The ancient (Figure 26–2A) and recent (Figure 26–B) candelabra models differ only in their temporal placement of the ancestral node but share the same tree topology that portrays Africans, Europeans, and Asians as distinct branches on an evolutionary tree. It is this branching *topology* that defines "races" under the evolutionary lineage definition, and not the *time* since the common ancestral population. Hence, human "races" are valid evolutionary lineages under either candelabra model.

The trellis model (Figure 26–3) posits that *Homo erectus* populations not only had the ability to move out of Africa, but also back in, resulting in recurrent genetic interchange among Old World human populations (Lasker and Crews 1996; Wolpoff and Caspari 1997). Under the trellis model, anatomically modern traits could evolve anywhere in the range of *Homo erectus* (which includes Africa) and subsequently spread throughout all of humanity by selection and gene flow. Hence, an African origin for anatomically modern humans is compatible with

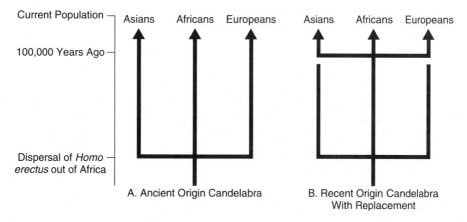

**Figure 26–2** Candelabra models of recent human evolution. (A) illustrates the ancient origin version of the candelabra model. Under this hypothesis, the major human "races" split from one another at the time of dispersal of *Homo erectus* out of Africa. After that initial split, the various "races" behaved as separate evolutionary lineages and independently evolved into their modern forms. (B) illustrates the recent origin version of the candelabra model with replacement. Under this hypothesis, an initial candelabra existed as illustrated in A. However, anatomically modern humans then arose in Africa and dispersed out of Africa around 100,000 years ago. This second dispersal event was marked by the complete genetic extinction of the earlier *Homo erectus* populations (indicated by the broken lineages in B) and by a split of these anatomically modern humans into separate evolutionary lineages that then independently acquired their modern "racial" variation.

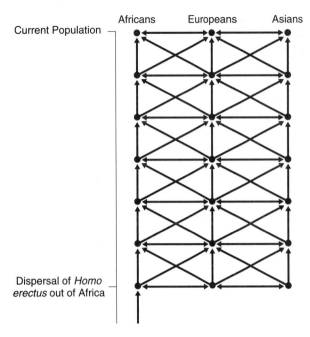

Current Population

Africans    Europeans    Asians

Dispersal of *Homo erectus* out of Africa

**Figure 26–3** The trellis model of recent human evolution. Under this hypothesis, *Homo erectus* dispersed out of Africa and established populations in Africa and southern Eurasia, as indicated by the circles. These populations were interconnected by gene flow so that there were no evolutionary sublineages of humanity nor independent evolution of the various "races." Double-headed arrows indicate gene flow among contemporaneous populations, and single-headed arrows indicate lines of genetic descent.

either model. The two models do differ in their interpretation of interpopulational genetic differences. Populational genetic differences reflect the time of divergence from a common ancestral population under the candelabra models. With the trellis model, the genetic distances reflect the amount of genetic interchange and not time of divergence from an ancestor. However, the most important distinction between the candelabra and trellis models for the discussion at hand is that under the trellis model there was no separation of humanity into evolutionary lineages and hence human "races" are not valid subspecies. In summary, human "races" as evolutionary lineages do exist under the candelabra models but do not exist under the trellis model.

Although these two models are frequently presented as mutually exclusive alternatives (Wolpoff and Caspari 1997), there is no biological reason why some human populations may be genetically differentiated because they are historical lineages, whereas other populations are differentiated because of recurrent but restricted gene flow. Moreover, the genetic differences between any two human populations may represent a mixture of both gene flow and historical events. Much genetic evidence is equally compatible with both models and hence is noninformative. The emphasis in this chapter will therefore be upon

data sets that discriminate between gene flow and historical splits as non-mutually exclusive causes of differentiation among human populations.

### Genetic Diversity Levels within and among Human Populations

Do the levels of genetic diversity found within and among human "races" discriminate between evolutionary lineage versus genetic interchange models of recent human evolution? As pointed out earlier, F statistics and related measures of within to among diversity levels do not discriminate per se. However, one conclusion reached in that section has great relevance to the debate over the validity of human races as evolutionary lineages; namely, that the estimated gene flow levels in humans are compatible with low differentiation across geographical space even though the species as a whole could evolve as a single lineage over time. Much skepticism about the trellis model stems from the belief that a delicate balance is required between gene flow (to insure all humans are a common evolutionary lineage over time) and local genetic drift/selection (to maintain humans as a polytypic species at any given moment in time) (Aiello 1997; Nei and Takezaki 1996). Indeed, even proponents of the trellis model have argued that only rarely can a species be polytypic under a trellis model. For example, Wolpoff and Caspari (1997:282) state that "the human pattern . . . of a widespread polytypic species with many different ecological niches . . . is a very rare one." However, polytypic species are not rare (Futuyma 1986; Mayr 1970). Moreover, as illustrated by the examples given earlier, polytypic species occur over a broad range of values for Nm and are a robust evolutionary outcome. There is no difficulty either in population genetic theory or observation for the conclusion that humans can be both a polytypic species and a single evolutionary lineage

Although F statistics are compatible with either model of human evolution, the claim is made in much of the recent literature that within "race" diversity levels support the recent candelabra model. Africans have higher amounts of genetic diversity than non-Africans for many nuclear loci (Armour et al. 1996, Jorde et al. 1997, Perez-Lezaun et al. 1997), mitochondrial DNA (mtDNA) (Comas et al. 1997, Francalacci et al. 1996), and some regions of Y-DNA (Hammer et al. 1997). These results are often interpreted as supporting the recent candelabra model by assuming that only a small number of individuals left Africa to colonize Eurasia with little or no subsequent gene flow. As a result, a bottleneck effect reduced the levels of genetic variation in non-Africans. This interpretation of genetic diversity also implies that at least Africans and non-Africans are distinct evolutionary lineages and hence are valid races. However, alternative explanations of diversity levels exist. Africans are expected to have higher genetic diversity simply because their population sizes were larger during much of the last million years (Harpending et al. 1996; Relethford and Harpending 1994, 1995). Indeed, the patterns of genetic diversity found in humans are more consistent with differences in population sizes and growth rates than with differences in population ages from presumed bottlenecks (Harding et al. 1997, Perez-Lezaun et al. 1997). The danger of using diversity levels as an indicator of population age from a bottleneck is illustrated by the observation that mitochondrial DNA diversity *within Africa* is higher in food producing populations than in hunter-gatherers (Watson et al. 1996). By equating diversity to age, this result would imply that agricultural peoples in Africa represent the ancestral populations, whereas the hunter-gatherers are the recent descendant populations. Such a conclusion is not credible, and the diversity levels within Africa are interpreted as reflecting effective size differences (Watson et al. 1996).

The within-"race" genetic diversity levels do not support the idea that Eurasians split off from Africans via

a small founder population, but they do not necessarily falsify the notion that a Eurasian/African split occurred without a bottleneck. Therefore, the within-population genetic diversity data is inconclusive on the status of Eurasians and Africans as separate evolutionary lineages and thereby valid races.

*Genetic Distances and Evolutionary "Trees"*

If human populations can truly be represented as branches on an evolutionary tree, then the resulting genetic distances should satisfy several constraints. Genetic distances are measures of the degree to which two populations are genetically divergent. For example, under the candelabra model, all non-African human populations "split" from the Africans at the same time, and therefore all genetic distances between African and non-African populations have the same expected value (Figure 26–4A). When genetic distances instead reflect the

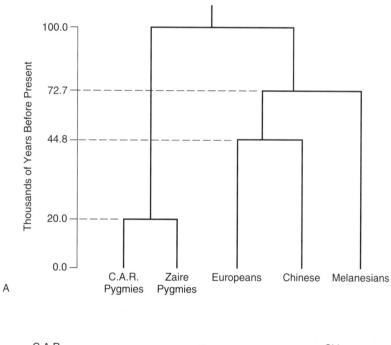

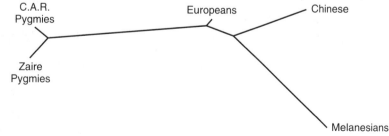

**Figure 26–4** Genetic distances and recent human evolution. (A) shows an evolutionary tree of human populations as estimated from the genetic distance data given in Bowcock et al. (1991). Human population evolution is depicted as a series of splits, and the numbers on the left indicate the estimated times of divergence in thousands of years. This figure is redrawn from Figure 2.4.4 on page 91 of Cavalli-Sforza et al. (1996). (B) shows the same genetic distance data drawn with the nearest-neighbor method but without all the constraints of a tree. This figure is redrawn from Figure 2.4.5 on page 91 of Cavalli-Sforza et al. (1996).

amount of gene flow, treeness constraints are no longer applicable. Because gene flow is commonly restricted by geographical distance (Wright 1943), gene flow models are expected to yield a strong positive relationship between geographical distance and genetic distance. Figure 26–4B shows the neighbor-joining phenogram of the same genetic distance data used to generate the tree in Figure 26–4A, but without imposing all the constraints of "treeness" (Cavalli-Sforza et al. 1996). Note that Europeans fall between Africans and Asians as predicted by their geographical location—in contrast to the candelabra model prediction of equal genetic distances of Europeans and Asians to Africans.

The failure of human genetic distances to fit treeness is ubiquitous whenever tested (Bowcock et al. 1991, Cavalli-Sforza et al. 1996, Nei and Roychoudhury 1974, 1982). Nevertheless, these same authors persist in presenting the relationships of the major human "races" as an evolutionary tree. Worse, many recent papers do not even test for treeness. The cophenetic correlations for the new data sets given in Nei and Takezaki (1996) are 0.75 for the microsatellite data of Bowcock et al. (1994), 0.69 for the microsatellite data of Deka et al. (1995), 0.79 for the restriction fragment length data of Mountain and Cavalli-Sforza (1994), and 0.45 for the *Alu* insertion polymorphism data of Batzer et al. (1994). Not one of the data sets fits treeness.

In marked contrast, the genetic distance data fit well to a restricted gene flow model. In their analyses of the older data sets, Nei and Roychoudhury (1974, 1982) not only rejected treeness, but showed that the deviations were those expected from genetic interchange among the "races." Similarly, Bowcock et al. (1991) not only rejected treeness for their data, but also showed that their data fit well to a model of "continuous admixture, in time, in space, or in both: a chain of populations somewhat similar to a stepping-stone model in which the ancestors of Europeans are geographically intermediate between the two extremes, Africans and Asians" (p. 841). The phrase "continuous admixture" is an oxymoron, as will be evident later, but in this case it is used as a synonym for recurrent gene flow (Cavalli-Sforza, personal communication). The "stepping-stone model" is a classic isolation by distance model, so Bowcock et al. (1991) show an excellent fit of their data to the recurrent gene flow model of isolation by distance. Santos et al. (1997) analyzed several human data sets with a variety of statistical procedures and found that the pattern is one of isolation by distance with high gene flow between geographically close populations. Finally, Cavalli-Sforza et al. (1996) assembled a comprehensive human data set and concluded that "the isolation-by-distance models hold for long distances as well as for short distances, and for large regions as well as for small and relatively isolated populations" (p. 124). Figure 26–5 is a redrawing of one of the figures from Cavalli-Sforza et al. (1996) that

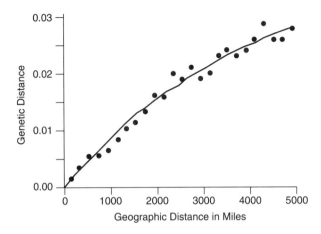

**Figure 26–5** Genetic distances and isolation by geographical distance. The global human genetic distances (the ordinate) are plotted against geographical distance in miles (the abscissa). The circles indicate the observed values and the curved line is the theoretical expectation under an isolation by distance model. This figure is redrawn from Figure 2.9.2 on page 123 of Cavalli-Sforza et al. (1996).

illustrates how well an isolation by distance model fits the human data.

Given that there is no tested human genetic distance data set consistent with treeness and that isolation by distance fits the human data well, proponents of the recent candelabra model have attempted to salvage the candelabra model by postulating a complex set of "admixtures between branches that had separated a long time before" (Cavalli-Sforza et al. 1996: 19). The key phrase in this proposal is *between branches that had separated a long time before* (Terrell and Stewart 1996). Admixture occurs when genetic interchange is reestablished between populations that had separated in the past and undergone genetic divergence (i.e., the gene flow patterns have been discontinuous). Proponents of the recent candelabra model then attempt to reconcile the genetic distance data with an admixture model that mimics some of the effects (and the good fit) of recurrent gene flow. By invoking admixture events as needed, human "races" can still be treated as separate evolutionary lineages, but now with the qualification that the "races" were purer in the past—the paradigm of the "primitive isolate" (Terrell and Stewart 1996). However, even advocates of the recent candelabra model acknowledge that these postulated admixture events are "extremely specific" and "unrealistic" (Bowcock et al. 1991: 841).

Although complex, multiple ad hoc admixture events are invoked to reconcile the recent candelabra model with the genetic distance data, they still fail to do so. In contrast, isolation by distance fits the human data well and all that it requires is that humans tend to mate primarily with others born nearby but often outside one's own natal group (Lasker and Crews 1996, Santos et al. 1997).

The hypothesis of admixture can be tested directly. When admixture occurs between branches that have differentiated under past isolation, genetic clines are set up simultaneously for all differentiated loci. This results in a strong geographical concordance in the clines for all genetic systems, both neutral and selected. In contrast, isolation by distance may result in geographical concordance for systems under similar selective regimes (Endler 1977, King and Lawson 1997), but otherwise no concordance is expected. Hence, the lack of concordance of "African traits" with molecular genetic distances is not surprising under an isolation by distance model. The lack of concordance in the geographical distribution of different elements has been thoroughly and extensively documented by others and has been one of the primary traditional arguments against the biological validity of human races (Cavalli-Sforza et al. 1996, Futuyma 1986). This lack of concordance across genetic systems falsifies the hypothesis of admixture of previously isolated branches and the idea that "races" were "pure" in the past.

The genetic distance data are therefore informative about the status of human "races" as evolutionary lineages. Genetic distance analyses strongly and uniformly indicate that human "races" cannot be represented as branches on an evolutionary tree as under the candelabra models, even by invoking ad hoc admixture events. Genetic distances, when properly analyzed, undermine the biological validity of human races as evolutionary lineages.

*Haplotype Trees*

The final type of genetic evidence to be considered is that arising from phylogenetic reconstructions of the genetic variation found in homologous regions of DNA that show little or no recombination. All the homologous copies of DNA in such a DNA region that are identical at every nucleotide (or in practice, identical at all scored nucleotide sites) constitute a single haplotype class. A mutation at any site in this DNA region will usually create a new haplotype that differs initially from its ancestral haplotype by that single mutational change. As time proceeds, some haplotypes can acquire multiple mutational changes from their ancestral type. All the different copies of a haplotype for each of the haplotypes in a species are subject to mutation, resulting in a diversity of haplotypes in the gene pool that vary in their mutational closeness to one another. If there is little or no recombination in the DNA region (as is the case for human mitochondrial DNA or for small segments of nuclear DNA), the divergence of haplotypes from one another reflects the order in which mutations occurred in evolutionary history. When mutational accumulation reflects evolutionary history, it is possible to estimate a network that shows how mutational changes transform one haplotype into

another or from some common ancestral haplotype. Such a network represents an unrooted evolutionary tree of the haplotype variation in that DNA region and is called a haplotype tree. In some circumstances, the ancestral haplotype is known or can be inferred, thereby providing a rooted haplotype tree.

Fortunately, there is much information in haplotype trees that can be used to test the hypothesis that human "races" are evolutionary sublineages whose past purity has been somewhat diminished by admixture. For example, in order to reconcile the candelabra model with the genetic distance data, it is necessary to regard Europeans as a heavily admixed population (Bowcock et al. 1991, Cavalli-Sforza et al. 1996). When admixture occurs, haplotypes should coexist in the admixed population's gene pool that differ by multiple mutational events with no existing intermediate haplotypes (Manderscheid and Rogers 1996, Templeton et al. 1995). The detection of such highly divergent haplotypes requires large sample sizes of the presumed admixed population in order to have statistical power. When large sample surveys have been performed upon the presumed admixed European populations, no highly divergent haplotypes or evidence for admixture are observed for either mtDNA (Manderscheid and Rogers 1996) or Y-DNA (Cooper et al. 1996). In contrast, isolation by distance (the trellis model) produces gene pools without strongly divergent haplotypes (i.e., most haplotypes differ by one or at most just a few mutational steps from some other haplotype found in the same population), as is observed.

The candelabra and trellis hypotheses are models of how genes spread across geographical space and through time, and hence a geographical analysis of haplotype trees provides a direct test of these two models. Statistical techniques exist that separate the influences of historical events (such as population range expansions) from recurrent events (such as gene flow with isolation by distance) when there is adequate sampling both in terms of numbers of individuals and of numbers and distribution of sampling sites (Templeton et al. 1995). This statistical approach first converts the haplotype tree into a nested statistical design. The lowest level of analysis is the haplotypes themselves, and the first level of nesting is created by starting at the tips of the haplotype network and moving one mutational step in, forming a union of any haplotypes that are reached by such a single mutational step or that converge upon a common node. The first set of "one-step clades" (Templeton et al. 1987) on the tips of the haplotype network is then pruned off and the process repeated until all haplotypes are included in one-step clades. Now one has a tree of one-step clades, and this tree can be nested into "two-step clades" using exactly the same nesting rules, but using one-step clades instead of haplotypes as the base unit. These nesting rules are used at successively higher levels until the next level of nesting would place the entire original haplotype tree into a single clade (for more details, see Templeton and Sing 1993).

The age of a higher order nesting clade has to be as old or older than the clades nested within it. Thus, even in the absence of a root for the haplotype tree, the nested design provides relative age information. By studying how a series of nested clades is distributed in space, it is therefore possible to make inferences about how haplotype lineages spread geographically through time. Moreover, the geographical range of a clade relative to that of the other clades it is nested with at the next higher level indicates how far spatially a haplotype lineage can spread during the time it takes to accumulate a single mutation. Hence, the nested design based on the haplotype tree automatically adds a temporal dimension to the spatial data gathered with the sample of current haplotypes. It is therefore possible to reconstruct the historical dynamics of the geographical spread of haplotype lineages, with the dynamical resolution being limited by the average amount of time it takes a lineage to accumulate a single mutation. Moreover, by making the analysis nested, no assumption of homogeneity is being made about how lineages spread geographically over time; that is, at one time or place, haplotype lineages may have spread through gene flow restricted by geographical distance, at another time or place, there may have been a rapid range expansion; and at yet another time or place, all genetic interchange between two geographical regions may have been severed. The nested analysis does not exclude any of these possibilities a priori, but rather regards all of them (or any mixture) as legitimate factors influencing the movement of haplotype lineages through time and space (Templeton et al. 1995). This statistical approach therefore treats historical and recurrent events as joint possibilities rather than as mutually exclusive alternatives.

However, these different factors leave different signatures in the nested analyses. If gene flow restricted by isolation by distance dominated during the place and time when a certain subset of mutations occurred, then the older clades defined by these mutations should be more widespread and the younger but evolutionarily close clades should be in the same general area as the older clades. This expectation follows from the simple fact that under isolation by distance, genes spread only a little every generation, and the longer a gene lineage exists, the more generations it has to spread geographically and to accumulate additional mutations. If two geographical regions split from one another (i.e., severed genetic interchange), then the clades that mark those geographical regions and that time of isolation would accumulate many mutational differences but without movement into each other's space. Finally, if a subset of the original population (containing only a subset of the haplotype variation that existed at that time) suddenly expanded into and colonized a new geographical region, then the subset of haplotypes they carried and the lin-

eages derived from them would have widespread geographical distributions for their frequency relative to the population as a whole. Thus, gene flow and different historical events leave distinct genetic-spatial signatures in a nested analysis and are thereby distinguishable. Moreover, the areas affected by these forces and events can be inferred, as well as their time relative to the nested design of the haplotype tree.

The ability to discriminate the genetic signatures of range expansions from recurrent but restricted gene flow is critical to discriminating the candelabra from the trellis models and thereby inferring the evolutionary validity of race. The criteria used to identify range expansions in this nested approach have been empirically validated by analyzing data sets with strong prior evidence of range expansion and were found to be accurate and not prone to false positives (Templeton 1998a). Application of this statistical approach to human mtDNA haplotype trees yields the significant results summarized in Figure 26–6 (Templeton 1993, 1997, 1998a).

As shown in Figure 26–6, human mtDNA yields a pattern of isolation by distance between Africans and Eurasians throughout the *entire* time period marked by mtDNA coalescence (Templeton 1993, 1997), thereby significantly rejecting both the candelabra hypothesis of no gene flow between Africans and non-Africans and the admixture models used to reconcile the candelabra models with the genetic distance data. Recurrent gene flow in this analysis is relative to the time scale defined by the coalescence and mutation rates of mtDNA, so gene flow among Old World human populations could have been sporadic on a time scale of several tens of thousands of years.

Figure 26–6 also reveals that range expansions played a significant role in recent human evolution. Among the statistically significant range expansions is a relatively recent range expansion across Europe (Templeton 1993, 1997); an inference supported by other mtDNA data sets (Calafell et al. 1996, Comas et al. 1997, Francalacci et al. 1996). A recent study on mtDNA isolated from a Neanderthal (Krings et al. 1997) is suggestive (but not conclusive as the sample size is one) that Neanderthals were replaced in Europe. This inference is compatible with the statistically significant European expansion shown in Figure 26–6, but further data is obviously needed to determine if this recent European expansion event was also a replacement event. The other recent expansions (into northern Asia, the Pacific, and the Americas) appear to be range expansions into previously unoccupied areas.

Genetic interchange between Africans and Eurasians over long periods of human evolutionary history is also strongly suggested by a hemoglobin beta locus tree (Harding et al. 1997). The coalescence of an autosomal gene is expected to be about four times as old as that of mtDNA or Y-DNA, and this seems to be the case for the

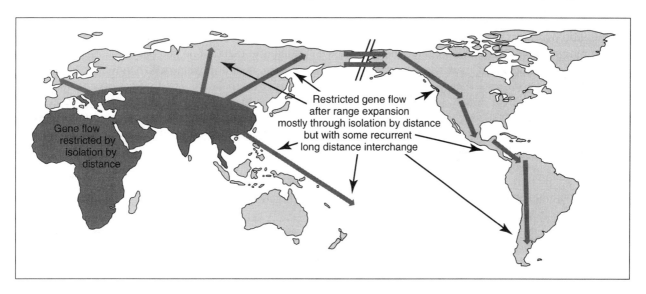

**Figure 26–6** Statistically significant inferences from geographical analyses of human mtDNA haplotype trees. As far back as is observable with mtDNA, there was gene flow restricted by isolation by distance in human populations living in Africa and southern Eurasia. More recent statistically significant range expansion events are indicated by arrows. There were expansions into Europe, northern Asia, the Pacific, and the Americas. Two arrows are indicating going into North America because this expansion either involved a colonization event with a large number of people, an extended colonization, or at least two separate colonization events. The lines drawn through these arrows indicate that after the colonization there was a significant reduction, perhaps cessation, of gene flow between Asia and North America. After the colonization of North America, there were further significant expansions into the remainder of the Americas. After these expansion events, there is statistically significant gene flow once again. Most of this post-expansion gene flow fits the expectations of isolation by distance, but some post-expansion gene flow occurred through long distance interchanges.

beta locus (Harding et al. 1997). Consequently, the patterns of widespread gene flow across Africa and Asia observed with the hemoglobin locus predate the hypothesized "replacement" event of the recent candelabra model (Harding et al. 1997). Obviously, if such a replacement had occurred, these earlier genetic signatures of gene flow should have been obliterated.

Finally, genetic interchange between Africans and Eurasians is additionally suggested by a nested clade analysis of a Y-DNA haplotype tree (Hammer et al. 1998). Interestingly, a range expansion out of Africa and into Eurasia is detected in this nested analysis. However, in light of the mtDNA and hemoglobin results, this expansion was not a replacement event, at least for the maternal demographic component. Following this out of Africa expansion, the nested analysis reveals a pattern of significant recurrent gene flow restricted by isolation by distance, including interchange between African and Eurasian populations. Moreover, there was a subsequent range expansion out of Asia and into Africa, as was also detected in the hemoglobin analysis. The Y-chromosome therefore shows more evidence of long-range population movements than the mtDNA. One possible explanation for this pattern is that males dispersed more than females during long-range population movements. However, both mtDNA and Y-DNA show recurrent gene flow with isolation by distance interconnecting African and

Eurasian populations, indicating that both males and females have dispersed during short-range migrations. Regardless, there is clearly genetic interchange between Africans and Eurasians due to a mixture of gene flow mediated by isolation by distance and population movements. No genetic split between Africans and Eurasians is found in the Y-DNA, as was also true for the mtDNA and hemoglobin beta region.

Combined, the mtDNA, Y-DNA, and hemoglobin data sets reveal that human evolution from about a million years ago to the last tens of thousands of years has been dominated by two evolutionary forces: (1) population movements and associated range expansions (perhaps with some local replacements, but definitely with no global replacement within the last 100,000 years), and (2) gene flow restricted by isolation by distance. The only evidence for any split or fragmentation event in human evolutionary history within this time frame is the one detected with mtDNA (Figure 26–6) involving the colonization of the Americas (Templeton 1998a). However, this colonization was due to either multiple colonization events, or involved movements by large numbers of peoples (Templeton 1998a), resulting in extensive sharing of genetic polymorphisms of New World with Old World human populations. Moreover, the genetic isolation between the Old and New Worlds was brief and no longer exists. Other than this temporary fragmentation event, the major human populations have been interconnected by gene flow (recurrent at least on a time scale of the order of tens of thousands of years) during the last one to two hundred thousand years. Gene flow may have been more sporadic earlier, but multiple genetic interchanges certainly occurred among Old World populations $\geq$ 200,000 years ago. Hence, the haplotype analyses of geographical associations strongly reject the existence of evolutionary sublineages of humans, reject the separation of Eurasians from Africans 100,000 years ago, and reject the idea of "pure races" in the past. Thus, human "races" have no biological validity under the evolutionary lineage definition of subspecies.

## Conclusions

The genetic data are consistently and strongly informative about human races. Humans show only modest levels of among population differentiation when compared to other large-bodied mammals, and this level of differentiation is well below the usual threshold used to identify subspecies (races) in nonhuman species. Hence, human races do not exist under the traditional concept of a subspecies as being a geographically circumscribed population showing sharp genetic differentiation. A more modern definition of race is that of a distinct evolutionary lineage within a species. The genetic evidence strongly rejects the existence of distinct evolutionary lineages within humans. The widespread representation of human "races" as branches on an intraspecific population tree is genetically indefensible and biologically misleading, even when the ancestral node is presented as being at 100,000 years ago. Attempts to salvage the idea of human "races" as evolutionary lineages by invoking greater racial purity in the past followed by admixture events are unsuccessful and falsified by multi-locus comparisons of geographical concordance and by haplotype analyses. Instead, all of the genetic evidence shows that there never was a split or separation of the "races" or between Africans and Eurasians. Recent human evolution has been characterized by both population range expansion (with perhaps some local replacements but no global replacement within the last 100,000 years) and recurrent genetic interchange. The 100,000 years ago "divergence time" between Eurasians and Africans that is commonly found in the recent literature is really only an "effective divergence time" *in sensu* Nei and Roychoudhury (1974, 1982). Since no split occurred between Africans and Eurasians, it is meaningless to assign a date to an "event" that never happened. Instead, the effective divergence time represents the average time to between population coalescence under restricted gene flow (Slatkin 1991).

Because of the extensive evidence for genetic interchange through population movements and recurrent gene flow going back at least hundreds of thousands of years ago, there is only one evolutionary lineage of humanity and there are no subspecies or races under either the traditional or phylogenetic definitions. Human evolution and population structure has been and is characterized by many locally differentiated populations coexisting at any given time, but with sufficient genetic contact to make all of humanity a single lineage sharing a common, long-term evolutionary fate.

## Acknowledgements

I would like to thank Dr. Robert Sussman and three anonymous reviewers for their excellent suggestions for improving an earlier draft of this paper.

## References

Aiello, L. C. (1997) "Review of *Race and Human Evolution: A Fatal Attraction* by M. Wolpoff and R. Caspari." *Nature,* 386:350.

Amato, G.; Gatesy, J. (1994) "PCR assays of variable nucleotide sites for identification of conservation units." In *Molecular Ecology and Evolution: Approaches and Applications* (pp. 215–226). B. Schierwater, B. Streit, G. P. Wagner, and R. DeSalle, eds. Basel: Birkhäuser Verlag.

Arctander, P.; Kat, P. W.; Simonsen, B. T.; Siegismund, H. R. (1996) "Population genetics of Kenyan impalas—consequences for conservation." In *Molecular Genetic Approaches in Conservation* (pp. 399–412). T. B. Smith and R. K. Wayne, eds. Oxford: Oxford University Press.

Amour, J. A. L.; Anttinen, T.; May, C. A.; Vega, E. E.; Sajantila, A.; Kidd, J. R.; Kidd, K. K.; Bertranpetit, J.; Paabo, S.; Jeffreys, A. J. (1996) "Minisatellite diversity supports a recent African origin for modern humans." *Nature Genetics,* 13(2):154–160.

Avise, J. C. (1994) *Molecular Markers, Natural History and Evolution.* New York: Chapman & Hall.

Barbujani, G.; Magagni, A.; Minch, E.; Cavalli-Sforza, L. L. (1997) "An apportionment of human DNA diversity." *Proceedings of the National Academy of Sciences, USA,* 94:4516–4519.

Barton, N. H.; Rouhani, S. (1993) "Adaptation and the 'shifting balance.'" *Genetical Research,* 61:57–74.

Batzer, M. A.; Stoneking, M.; Alegria-Hartman, M.; Bazan, H.; Kass, D. H.; Shaikh, T. H.; Novick, G. E.; Ioannou, P. A.; Scheer, W. D.; Herrera, R. J.; Deininger, P. L. (1994) "Africa origin of human-specific polymorphic *Alu* insertions." *Proceedings of the National Academy of Sciences, USA,* 91:12288–12292.

Bowcock, A. M.; Kidd, J. R.; Mountain, J. L.; Hebert, J. M.; Carotenuto, L.; Kidd, K. K.; Cavalli-Sforza, L. L. (1991) "Drift, admixture, and selection in human evolution: A study with DNA polymorphisms." *Proc. Natl. Acad. Sci., USA,* 88:839–843.

Bowcock, A. M.; Ruiz-Linares, A.; Tomfohrde, J.; Minch, E.; Kidd, J. R.; Cavalli-Sforza, L. L. (1994) "High resolution of human evolutionary trees with polymorphic microsatellites." *Nature,* 368:455–457.

Boyce, W. M.; Hedrick, P. W.; Mugglicockett, N. E.; Kalinowski, S.; Penedo, M. C. T.; Ramey, R. R. (1997) "Genetic variation of major histocompatibility complex and microsatellite loci—a comparison in bighorn sheep." *Genetics,* 145(2):421–433.

Brownlow, C. A. (1996) "Molecular taxonomy and the conservation of the red wolf and other endangered carnivores." *Conservation Biology,* 10(2):390–396.

Calafell, F.; Underhill, P.; Tolun, A.; Angelicheva, D.; Kalaydjieva, L. (1996) "From Asia to Europe: Mitochondrial DNA sequence variability in Bulgarians and Turks." *Annals of Human Genetics,* 60:35–49.

Cavalli-Sforza, L.; Menozzi, P.; Piazza, A. (1996) *The History and Geography of Human Genes.* Princeton, NJ: Princeton University Press.

Cavalli-Sforza, L. L. (1997) "Genes, peoples, and languages." *Proceedings of the National Academy of Sciences, USA,* 94:7719–7724.

Comas, D.; Calafell, F.; Mateu, E.; Perezlezaun, A.; Bosch, E.; Bertranpetit, J. (1997) "Mitochondrial DNA variation and the origin of the Europeans." *Human Genetics,* 99(4):443–449.

Cooper, G.; Amos, W.; Hoffman, D.; Rubinsztein, D. C. (1996) "Network analysis of human Y microsatellite haplotypes." *Human Molecular Genetics,* 5(11):1759–1766.

Crow, J. F.; Kimura, M. (1970) *An Introduction to Population Genetic Theory.* New York: Harper & Row.

Deka, R.; Jin, L.; Shriver, M. D.; Yu, L. M.; DeCroo, S.; Hundrieser, J.; Bunker, C. H.; Ferrell, R. E.; Chakraborty, R. (1995) "Population genetics of dinucleotide $(dC-dA)_n$-$(dG-dT)_n$ polymorphisms in world populations." *American Journal of Human Genetics,* 56:461–474.

DeSalle, R.; Templeton, A.; Mori, I.; Pletscher, S.; Johnston, J. S. (1987) "Temporal and spatial heterogeneity of mtDNA polymorphisms in natural populations of *Drosophila mercatorum.*" *Genetics,* 116:215–223.

Ellsworth, D. L.; Honeycutt, R. L.; Silvy, N. J.; Bickham, J. W.; Klimstra, W. D. (1994) "Historical biogeography and contemporary patterns of mitochondrial DNA variation in white-tailed deer from the Southeastern United States." *Evolution,* 48(1):122–136.

Endler, J. A. (1977) *Geographic Variation, Speciation, and Clines.* Princeton, NJ: Princeton University Press.

Francalacci, P.; Bertranpetit, J.; Calafell, F.; Underhill, P. A. (1996). "Sequence diversity of the control region of mitochondrial DNA in Tuscany and its implications for the peopling of Europe." *American Journal of Physical Anthropology,* 100(4):443–460.

Futuyma, D. J. (1986) *Evolutionary Biology.* Sunderland, MA: Sinauer Associates.

Georgiadis, N.; Bischof, L.; Templeton, A.; Patton, J.; Karesh, W.; Western, D. (1994) "Structure and history of African elephant populations: I. Eastern and Southern Africa." *Journal of Heredity,* 85:100–104.

Hammer, M. F.; Spurdle, A. B.; Karafet, T.; Bonner, M. R.; Wood, E. T.; Novelletto, A.; Malaspina, P.; Mitchell, R. J.; Horai, S.; Jenkins, T.; Zegura, S. L. (1997) "The geographic distribution of human Y chromosome variation." *Genetics,* 145(3):787–805.

Hammer, M. F.; Karafet, T.; Rasanayagam, A.; Wood, E. T.; Altheide, T. K.; Jenkins, T.; Griffiths, R. C.; Templeton, A. R.; Zegura, S. L. (1998) "Out of Africa and back again: Nested cladistic analysis of human Y chromosome variation." *Molecular Biology & Evolution,* in press.

Harding, R. M.; Fullerton, S. M.; Griffiths, R. C.; Bond, J.; Cox, M. J.; Schneider, J. A.; Moulin, D. S.; Clegg, J. B. (1997) "Archaic African *and* Asian lineages in the genetic ancestry of modern humans." *American Journal of Human Genetics,* 60:772–789.

Harpending, H. C.; Relethford, J. H.; Sherry, S. T. (1996) "Methods and models for understanding human diversity." In *Molecular Biology and Human Diversity* (pp. 283–299). A.J. Boyce and C.G.N. Mascie-Taylor, eds. Cambridge: Cambridge University Press.

Hollocher, H.; Templeton, A. R. (1994) "The molecular through ecological genetics of abnormal abdomen in *Drosophila mercatorum.* VI. The nonneutrality of the Y-chromosome rDNA polymorphism." *Genetics,* 136(4): 1373–1384.

Hollocher, H.; Templeton, A. R.; DeSalle, R.; Johnston, J. S. (1992) "The molecular through ecological genetics of *abnormal abdomen.* IV. Components of genetic-variation in a natural-population of *Drosophila mercatorum.*" *Genetics,* 130(2):355–366.

Hudson, R. R.; Boos, D. D.; Kaplan, N. L. (1992) "A statistical test for detecting geographical subdivision." *Mol. Biol. Evol.,* 9:138–151.

Jorde, L. B.; Rogers, A. R.; Bamshad, M.; Watkins, W. S.; Krakowiak, P.; Sung, S.; Kere, J.; Harpending, H. C. (1997) "Microsatellite diversity and the demographic history of modern humans." *Proceedings of the National Academy of Sciences, USA,* 94:3100–3103.

King, R. B.; Lawson, R. (1995) "Color-pattern variation in Lake Erie water snakes—the role of gene flow." *Evolution,* 49(5):885–896.

King, R. B.; Lawson, R. (1997) "Microevolution in island water snakes." *BioScience,* 47:279–286.

Krings, M.; Stone, A.; Schmitz, R. W.; Krainitzki, H.; Stoneking, M.; Pääbo, S. (1997) "Neandertal DNA sequences and the origin of modern humans." *Cell,* 90:19–30.

Lasker, G. W.; Crews, D. E. (1996) "Behavioral influences on the evolution of human genetic diversity." *Molecular Phylogenetics and Evolution,* 5:232–240.

Lawson, R.; King, R. B. (1996) "Gene flow and melanism in Lake Erie garter snake populations." *Biological Journal of the Linnean Society,* 59:1–19.

Legge, J. T.; Roush, R.; Desalle, R.; Vogler, A. P.; May, B. (1996) "Genetic criteria for establishing evolutionarily significant units in cryans buckmoth." *Conservation Biology,* 10(1):85–98.

Lehman, N.; Wayne, R. K. (1991) "Analysis of coyote mitochondrial-DNA genotype frequencies: Estimation of the effective number of alleles." *Genetics,* 128(2):405–416.

Lynch, M.; Crease, T. J. (1990) "The analysis of population survey data on DNA sequence variation." *Molecular Biology and Evolution,* 7:377–394.

Manderscheid, E. J.; Rogers, A. R. (1996) "Genetic admixture in the late Pleistocene." *American Journal of Physical Anthropology,* 100(1):1–5.

Mayr, E. (1970) *Populations, Species, and Evolution.* Cambridge, MA: The Belknap Press of Harvard University Press.

Miththapala, S.; Seidensticker, J.; O'Brien, S. J. (1996) "Phylo-geographic subspecies recognition in leopards (*Panthera pardus*)—molecular genetic variation." *Conservation Biology,* 10(4):1115–1132.

Mountain, J. L.; Cavalli-Sforza, L. L. (1994) "Inference of human evolution through cladistic analysis of nuclear DNA restriction polymorphisms." *Proceedings of the National Academy of Sciences, USA,* 91:6515–6519.

Nei, M.; Roychoudhury, A. K. (1974) "Genic variation within and between the three major races of man, Caucasoids, Negroids, and Mongoloids." *Amer. J. Human Genetics,* 26:421–443.

Nei, M.; Roychoudhury, A. K. (1982) "Genetic relationship and evolution of human races." *Evol. Biol.,* 14:1–59.

Nei, M.; Takezaki, N. (1996) "The root of the phylogenetic tree of human populations." *Molecular Biology and Evolution,* 13:170–177.

Pennock, D. S.; Dimmick, W. W. (1997) "Critique of the evolutionarily significant unit as a definition for distinct population segments under the U.S. Endangered Species Act." *Conservation Biology,* 11(3):611–619.

Perez-Lezaun, A.; Calafell, F.; Mateu, E.; Comas, D.; Ruiz-Pacheco, R.; Bertranpetit, J. (1997) "Microsatellite variation and the differentiation of modern humans." *Human Genetics,* 99(1):1–7.

Relethford, J. H.; Harpending, H. C. (1994) "Craniometric variation, genetic theory, and modern human origins." *American Journal of Physical Anthropology,* 95(3):249–270.

Relethford, J. H.; Harpending, H. C. (1995) "Ancient differences in population size can mimic a recent African origin of modern humans." *Current Anthropology,* 36:667–674.

Santos, E. J. M.; Epplen, J. T.; Epplen, C. (1997) "Extensive gene flow in human populations as revealed by protein and microsatellite DNA markers." *Human Heredity,* 47(3):165–172.

Shaffer, H. B.; McKnight, M. L. (1996) "The polytypic species revisited—genetic differentiation and molecular phylogenetics of the tiger salamander *Ambystoma tigrinum* (Amphibia, Caudata) complex." *Evolution,* 50(1):417–433.

Slatkin, M. (1991) "Inbreeding coefficients and coalescence times." *Genet. Res.,* 58:167–175.

Smith, H. M.; Chiszar, D.; Montanucci, R. R. (1997) "Subspecies and classification." *Herpetological Review,* 28:13–16.

Templeton, A. R. (1993) "The 'Eve' hypothesis: A genetic critique and reanalysis." *Amer. Anthropol.,* 95:51–72.

Templeton, A. R. (1994) "The role of molecular genetics in speciation studies." In *Molecular Ecology and Evolution: Approaches and Applications* (pp. 455–477). B. Schierwater, B. Streit, G.P. Wagner, and R. DeSalle, eds. Basel: Birkhäuser-Verlag.

Templeton, A. R. (1997) "Testing the out-of-Africa replacement hypothesis with mitochondrial DNA data." In *Conceptual Issues in Modern Human Origins Research* (pp. 329–360). G.A. Clark and C. M. Willermet, eds. New York: Aldine de Gruyter.

Templeton, A. R. (1998a) "Nested clade analyses of phylogeographic data: Testing hypotheses about gene flow and population history." *Molecular Ecology:* in press.

Templeton, A. R. (1998b) "Species and speciation: Geography, population structure, ecology, and gene trees." In *Endless Forms: Species and Speciation.* D.J. Howard and S.H. Berlocher, eds. Oxford: Oxford University press.

Templeton, A. R.; Boerwinkle, E.; Sing, C. F. (1987) "A cladistic analysis of phenotypic associations with haplotypes inferred from restriction endonuclease mapping. I. Basic theory and an analysis of alcohol dehydrogenase activity in *Drosophila.*" *Genetics,* 117:343–351.

Templeton, A. R.; Georgiadis, N. J. (1996) "A landscape approach to conservation genetics: Conserving evolutionary processes in the African Bovidae." In *Conservation Genetics: Case Histories from Nature* (pp. 398–430). J.C. Avise and J.L. Hamrick, eds. New York: Chapman & Hall.

Templeton, A. R.; Hollocher, H.; Johnston, J. S. (1993) "The molecular through ecological genetics of abnormal abdomen in *Drosophila mercatorum.* V. Female phenotypic expression on natural genetic backgrounds and in natural environments." *Genetics,* 134:475–485.

Templeton, A. R.; Hollocher, H.; Lawler, S.; Johnston, J. S. (1989) "Natural selection and ribosomal DNA in *Drosophila.*" *Genome,* 31:296–303.

Templeton, A. R.; Routman, E.; Phillips, C. (1995). "Separating population structure from population history: A cladistic analysis of the geographical distribution of mitochondrial DNA haplotypes in the Tiger Salamander, *Ambystoma tigrinum.*" *Genetics,* 140:767–782.

Templeton, A. R.; Sing, C. F. (1993) "A cladistic analysis of phenotypic associations with haplotypes inferred from restriction endonuclease mapping. IV. Nested analyses with cladogram uncertainty and recombination." *Genetics,* 134:659–669.

Terrell, J. E.; Stewart, P. J. (1996) "The paradox of human population genetics at the end of the twentieth century." *Reviews in Anthropology,* 25:13–33.

Vogler, A. P. (1994) "Extinction and the formation of phylogenetic lineages: Diagnosing units of conservation management in the tiger beetle *Cicindela dorsalis.*" In *PCR Assays of Variable Nucleotide Sites for Identification of Conservation Units* (pp. 261–273). B. Schierwater, B. Streit, G.P. Wagner, and R. DeSalle, eds. Basel: Birkhäuser Verlag.

Watson, E.; Bauer, K.; Aman, R.; Weiss, G.; van Haeseler, A.; Pääbo, S. (1996) "mtDNA sequence diversity in Africa." *American Journal of Human Genetics,* 59:437–444.

Wayne, R. K.; Lehman, N.; Allard, M. W.; Honeycutt, R. L. (1992) "Mitochondrial DNA variability of the gray wolf: Genetic consequences of population decline and habitat fragmentation." *Conservation Biology,* 6(4):559–569.

Wilson, E. O.; Brown, W. L. (1953) "The subspecies concept and its taxonomic applications." *Systematic Zoology,* 2:97–111.

Wolpoff, M.; Caspari, R. (1997) *Race and Human Evolution.* New York: Simon & Schuster.

Wright, S. (1931) "Evolution in Mendelian populations." *Genetics,* 16:97–159.

Wright S. (1943) "Isolation by distance." *Genetics,* 28:114–138.

Wright, S. (1969) *Evolution and the Genetics of Populations* (3 vols.). *Volume 2. The Theory of Gene Frequencies.* Chicago: University of Chicago Press.

# Chapter 27

# *Three Is Not Enough*

## Sharon Begley

*Surprising new lessons from the controversial science of race.*

To most Americans race is as plain as the color of the nose on your face. Sure, some light-skinned blacks, in some neighborhoods, are taken for Italians, and some Turks are confused with Argentines. But even in the children of biracial couples, racial ancestry is writ large—in the hue of the skin and the shape of the lips, the size of the brow, and the bridge of the nose. It is no harder to trace than it is to judge which basic colors in a box of Crayolas were combined to make tangerine or burnt umber. Even with racial mixing, the existence of primary races is as obvious as the existence of primary colors.

Or is it? C. Loring Brace has his own ideas about where race resides, and it isn't in skin color. If our eyes could perceive more than the superficial, we might find race in chromosome 11: There lies the gene for hemoglobin. If you divide humankind by which of two forms of the gene each person has, then equatorial Africans, Italians, and Greeks fall into the "sickle-cell race"; Swedes and South Africa's Xhosas (Nelson Mandela's ethnic group) are in the healthy-hemoglobin race. Or do you prefer to group people by whether they have epicanthic eye folds, which produce the "Asian" eye? Then the !Kung San (Bushmen) belong with the Japanese and Chinese. Depending on which trait you choose to demarcate races, "you won't get anything that remotely tracks conventional [race] categories," says anthropologist Alan Goodman, dean of natural science at Hampshire College.

The notion of race is under withering attack for political and cultural reasons—not to mention practical ones like what to label the child of a Ghanaian and a Norwegian. But scientists got there first. Their doubts about the conventional racial categories—black, white,

| NEWSWEEK POLL | | |
|---|---|---|
| Race relations in the U.S. are: | | |
| | **Blacks** | **Whites** |
| Excellent | 2% | 1% |
| Good | 10% | 22% |
| Fair | 45% | 44% |
| Poor | 41% | 31% |
| The *Newsweek* Poll, Feb. 1–3, 1995. | | |

Asian—have nothing to do with a sappy "we are all the same" ideology. Just the reverse. "Human variation is very, very real," says Goodman. "But race, as a way of organizing [what we know about that variation], is incredibly simplified and bastardized." Worse, it does not come close to explaining the astounding diversity of humankind—not its origins, not its extent, not its meaning. "There is no organizing principle by which you could put 5 billion people into so few categories in a way that would tell you anything important about humankind's diversity," says Michigan's Brace, who will lay out the case against race at the annual meeting of the American Association for the Advancement of Science.

About 70 percent of cultural anthropologists, and half of physical anthropologists, reject race as a biological category, according to a 1989 survey by Central Michigan University anthropologist Leonard Lieberman and colleagues. The truths of science are not decided by majority vote, of course. Empirical evidence, woven into a theoretical whole, is what matters. The threads of the argument against the standard racial categories:

193

• **Genes:** In 1972, population biologist Richard Lewontin of Harvard University laid out the genetic case against race. Analyzing 17 genetic markers in 168 populations such as Austrians, Thais, and Apaches, he found that there is more genetic difference within one race than there is between that race and another. Only 6.3 percent of the genetic differences could be explained by the individuals' belonging to different races. That is, if you pick at random any two "blacks" walking along the street, and analyze their 23 pairs of chromosomes, you will probably find that their genes have less in common than do the genes of one of them with that of a random "white" person. Last year the Human Genome Diversity Project used 1990s genetics to extend Lewontin's analysis. Its conclusion: Genetic variation from one individual to another of the same "race" swamps the average differences between racial groupings. The more we learn about humankind's genetic differences, says geneticist Luca Cavalli-Sforza of Stanford University, who chairs the committee that directs the biodiversity project, the more we see that they have almost nothing to do with what we call race.

• **Traits:** As sickle-cell "races" and epicanthic-fold "races" show, there are as many ways to group people as there are traits. That is because "racial" traits are what statisticians call nonconcordant. Lack of concordance means that sorting people according to *these* traits produces different groupings than you get sorting them by *those* (equally valid) traits. When biologist Jared Diamond of UCLA surveyed half a dozen traits for a recent issue of *Discover* magazine, he found that, depending on which traits you pick, you can form very surprising "races." Take the scooped-out shape of the back of the front teeth, a standard "Asian" trait. Native Americans and Swedes have these shovel-shaped incisors, too, and so would fall in the same race. Is biochemistry better? Norwegians, Arabians, north Indians and the Fulani of northern Nigeria, notes Diamond, fall into the "lactase race" (the lactase engine digests milk sugar). Everyone else—other Africans, Japanese, Native Americans—forms the "lactase-deprived race" (their ancestors did not drink milk from cows or goats and hence never evolved the lactase gene). How about blood types, the familiar A, B, and O groups? Then Germans and New Guineans, populations that have the same percentages of each type, are in one race; Estonians and Japanese comprise a separate one for the same reason, notes anthropologist Jonathan Marks of Yale University. Depending on which traits are chosen, "we could place Swedes in the same race as either Xhosas, Fulani, the Ainu of Japan, or Italians," writes Diamond.

• **Subjectivity:** If race is a valid biological concept, anyone in any culture should be able to look at any individual and say, Aha, you are a . . . It should not be the case, as French tennis star Yannick Noah said a few years ago, that "in Africa I am white, and in France I am black" (his mother is French and his father is from Cameroon).

"While biological traits give the impression that race is a biological unit of nature," says anthropologist George Armelagos of Emory University, "it remains a cultural construct. The boundaries between races depends on the classifier's own cultural norms."

• **Evolution:** Scholars who believe in the biological validity of race argue that the groupings reflect human prehistory. That is, populations that evolved together, and separately from others, constitute a race. This school of thought holds that blacks should all be in one race because they are descended from people who stayed on the continent where humanity began. Asians, epitomized by the Chinese, should be another race because they are the children of groups who walked north and east until they reached the Pacific. Whites of the pale, blond variety should be another because their ancestors filled Europe. Because of their appearance, these populations represent the extremes, the archetypes, of human diversity—the reds, blues, and yellows from which you can make every other hue. "But if you use these archetypes as your groups you have classified only a very tiny proportion of the world's people, which is not very useful," says Marks, whose incisive new book *Human Biodiversity* (321 pages. Walter de Gruyter. $23.95) deconstructs race. "Also, as people walked out of Africa, they were differentiating along the way. Equating 'extreme' with 'primordial' is not supported by history."

Often, shared traits are a sign of shared heritage—racial heritage. "Shared traits are not random," says Alice Brues, an anthropologist at the University of Colorado. "Within a continent, you of course have a number of variants [on basic traits], but some are characteristic of the larger area, too. So it's natural to look for these major divisions. It simplifies your thinking." A wide distribution of traits, however, makes them suspect as evidence of a shared heritage. The dark skin of Somalis and Ghanaians, for instance, indicates that they evolved under the same selective force (a sunny climate). But that's all it shows. It does *not* show that they are any more closely related, in the sense of sharing more genes, than either is to Greeks. Calling Somalis and Ghanaians "black" therefore sheds no further light on their evolutionary history and implies—wrongly—that they are more closely related to each other than either is to someone of a different "race." Similarly, the long noses of North Africans and northern Europeans reveal that they evolved in dry or cold climates (the nose moistens air before the air reaches the lungs, and longer noses moisten more air). The tall, thin bodies of Kenya's Masai evolved to dissipate heat; Eskimos evolved short, squat bodies to retain it. Calling these peoples "different races" adds nothing to that understanding.

Where did the three standard racial divisions come from? They entered the social, and scientific, consciousness during the Age of Exploration. Loring Brace doesn't think it's a coincidence that the standard races represent peoples who, as he puts it, "lived at the end of the Europeans' trade routes"—in Africa and China—in the days after Prince Henry the Navigator set sail. Before Europeans took to the seas, there was little perception of races. If villagers began to look different to an Englishman riding a horse from France to Italy and on to Greece, the change was too subtle to inspire notions of races. But if the English sailor left Lisbon Harbor and dropped anchor off the Kingdom of Niger, people looked so different he felt compelled to invent a scheme to explain the world—and, perhaps, distance himself from the Africans.

This habit of sorting the world's peoples into a small number of groups got its first scientific gloss from Swedish taxonomist Carolus Linnaeus. (Linnaeus is best known for his system of classifying living things by genus and species—*Escherichia coli, Homo sapiens,* and the rest.) In 1758 he declared that humanity falls into four races: white (Europeans), red (Native Americans), dark (Asians), and black (Africans). Linnaeus said that Native Americans (who in the 1940s got grouped with Asians) were ruled by custom. Africans were indolent and negligent, and Europeans were inventive and gentle, said Linnaeus. Leave aside the racist undertones (not to mention the oddity of ascribing gentleness to the group that perpetrated the Crusades and Inquisition): that alone should not undermine its validity. More worrisome is that the notion and the specifics of race predate genetics, evolutionary biology, and the science of human origins. With the revolutions in those fields, how is it that the eighteenth-century scheme of race retains its powerful hold? Consider these arguments:

- **If I parachute into Nairobi, I know I'm not in Oslo:** Colorado's Alice Brues uses this image to argue that denying the reality of race flies in the face of common sense. But the parachutists, if they were familiar with the great range of human diversity, could also tell that they were in Nairobi rather than Abidjan—east Africans don't look much like west Africans. They could also tell they were in Istanbul rather than Oslo, even though Turks and Norwegians are both called Caucasian.
- **DOA, male, 5'11" ... black:** When U.S. police call in a forensic anthropologist to identify the race of a skeleton, the scientist comes through 80 to 85 percent of the time. If race has no biological validity, how can the sleuths get it right so often? The forensic anthropologist could, with enough information about bone structure and genetic markers, identify the region from which the corpse came—south and west Africa, Southeast Asia and China, Northern and Western Europe. It just so happens that the police would call corpses from the first two countries black, from the middle two Asian, and the last pair white. But lumping these six distinct populations into three groups of two serves no biological purpose, only a social convention. The larger grouping may reflect how society views humankind's diversity, but does not explain it.

- **African Americans have more hypertension:** If race is not real, how can researchers say that blacks have higher rates of infant mortality, lower rates of osteoporosis, and a higher incidence of hypertension? Because a social construct can have biological effects, says epidemiologist Robert Hahn of the U.S. Centers for Disease Control and Prevention. Consider hypertension among African Americans. Roughly 34 percent have high blood pressure, compared with about 16 percent of whites. But William Dressler finds the greatest incidence of hypertension among blacks who are upwardly mobile achievers. "That's probably because in mundane interactions, from the bank to the grocery store, they are treated in ways that do not coincide with their self-image as respectable achievers," says Dressler, an anthropologist at the University of Alabama. "And the upwardly mobile are more likely to encounter discriminatory white culture." Lab studies show that stressful situations—like being followed in grocery stores as if you were a shoplifter—elevate blood pressure and lead to vascular changes that cause hypertension. "In this case, race captures social factors such as the experience of discrimination," says sociologist David Williams of the University of Michigan. Further evidence that hypertension has more to do with society than with biology: Black Africans have among the lowest rates of hypertension in the world.

If race is not a biological explanation of hypertension, can it offer a biological explanation of something as complex as intelligence? Psychologists are among the strongest proponents of retaining the three conventional racial categories. It organizes and explains their data in the most parsimonious way, as Charles Murray and Richard Herrnstein argue in "The Bell Curve." But anthropologists say that such conclusions are built on a foundation of sand. If nothing else, argues Brace, every ethnic group evolved under conditions where intelligence was a requirement for survival. If there are intelligence "genes," they must be in all ethnic groups equally: Differences in intelligence must be a cultural and social artifact.

Scientists who doubt the biological meaningfulness of race are not nihilists. They just prefer another way of capturing, and explaining, the great diversity of humankind. Even today most of the world's peoples marry within their own group. Intramarriage preserves features—fleshy lips, small ears, wide-set eyes—that arose by a chance genetic mutation long ago. Grouping people by geographic origins—better known as ethnicity—"is more correct both in a statistical sense and in understanding the history of human variation," says Hampshire's Goodman. Ethnicity also serves as a proxy for differences—from diet to a history of discrimination—that can have real biological and behavioral effects.

In a 1942 book, anthropologist Ashley Montagu called race "Man's Most Dangerous Myth." If it is, then our most ingenuous myth must be that we sort humankind into groups in order to understand the meaning and origin of humankind's diversity. That isn't the reason at all; a greater number of smaller groupings, like ethnicities, does a better job. The obsession with broad categories is so powerful as to seem a neurological imperative. Changing our thinking about race will require a revolution in thought as profound, and profoundly unsettling, as anything science has ever demanded. What these researchers are talking about is changing the way in which we see the world—and each other. But before that can happen, we must do more than understand the biologist's suspicions about race. We must ask science, also, why it is that we are so intent on sorting humanity into so few groups—us and Other—in the first place.

# Chapter 28

# *Why Psychologists Should Learn Some Anthropology*

## Jefferson M. Fish

Yee, Fairchild, Weizmann, and Wyatt (November 1993) are to be complimented for their thoughtful delineation of psychology's problems with race. Unfortunately, their article leaves unaddressed key questions that perplex psychologists and that continue to make the field of "race" one in which our discipline generates more heat than light. In essence, these questions have to do with what we can make of the variation in human physical appearance that so preoccupies our society. The authors are correct in stating, in essence, that race is not a meaningful concept; but they give us nothing with which to replace our scientifically inaccurate stereotypes.

Physiological psychologists, neuropsychologists, comparative psychologists, and others working in the biological realm take it as a matter of course to master the appropriate knowledge from related disciplines in the neurosciences, genetics, or other biomedical fields. When it comes to studying race, however, psychologists have not taken the trouble to inform themselves. (I might interject that the facts of the situation are quite fascinating, so those who are interested will find themselves stimulated by new knowledge and ideas, rather than confronted by a mountain of technicalities.) This knowledge provides an assumptive background that allows one to separate meaningful research questions from those that are meaningless or based on inaccurate assumptions.

The two related questions about which psychologists need to inform themselves are (1) how can we understand the range of human physical variation, some of which Americans view as "racial" and some of which they do not, and (2) how can we understand the kinds of names/labels/racial classifications applied to this human physical variation both within the United States and else-

where. As far as the knowledge needed by psychologists is concerned, physical anthropologists have long since answered the first question, and cultural anthropologists have long since answered the second one. Given the limitations of space, I will allude to some of the kinds of knowledge that exist as alternatives to our-own-folk-taxonomy-or-nothing and will suggest two well-written brief classics as a starting place for psychologists' self-education about race.

The human species evolved in Africa from earlier forms and migrated over time to all corners of the globe. Under the influences of genetic drift, natural selection, and mutation, populations in different areas came to differ over time in their physical appearance. Populations in the tropics of Africa and South America developed dark skins, presumably as protection against the sun; and populations in cold areas, which are dark for long periods of time and where people cover themselves for warmth, like northern Europe or northern North America, developed light skins, presumably to make maximum use of the sun. In our folk taxonomy, light versus dark skin is considered a racial difference. Some populations in very cold climates (e.g., the Inuit) also developed rounded bodies, because the smaller ratio of surface to volume conserves heat, whereas other populations in very hot areas (e.g., the Tutsi) developed lanky bodies—the high surface ratio is useful for shedding heat. The folk taxonomy in the United States views rounded or lanky people as kinds of Whites or Blacks—although one could equally well view light- or dark-skinned people as kinds of "lankys" or "roundeds." Furthermore, the physical features we view as racial (skin color, hair form, hair color, eye color, nose width, and lip thickness) do not vary together in racial "syndromes"—as anyone who rides the New York City subways can verify. There are people, for example, with tight curly blond hair, light skin, blue eyes, broad noses, and thick lips—whose existence is problematical for our racial assumptions. Other cultures, which classify people differently, actually have a word to denote them: In the northeast of Brazil, they are called *sararás*. It is the accumulation of this and other kinds of evidence that indicates that the term "race," as used by psychologists and other Americans, does not correspond to a biological entity.

Different cultures have different folk taxonomies for classifying human physical variability. Our system of *hypodescent,* using the folk category of "blood," classifies all offspring of one "Black" parent and one "White" parent—regardless of the children's physical appearance—as Black. This leads to a wide range of physical appearance among those called Black and a narrower range among those called White. If all the offspring were classified as White, then Whites would have the greater variability. Other cultures—such as those in Brazil or Haiti—have different folk taxonomies for race. Brazil's is based on physical appearance, whereas Haiti's involves elements of both physical appearance and descent. If our hypothetical couple lived in the Brazilian city of Salvador and had ten children, the children might well receive ten different "racial" classifications (or *tipos,* in Portuguese). Thus, whereas psychologists and other Americans view race as an immutable biological given, individuals can easily change their race by getting on a plane and flying from New York to Salvador or Port-au-Prince. What changes is not their physical appearance but the folk taxonomies by which they are classified. Familiarity with a variety of folk taxonomies, along with the variations in historical circumstances that led to their differential development, can help psychologists to achieve a culturally relative perspective on racial classification.

It is this kind of anthropological knowledge about race that tells us that Blacks and Whites as groups do not constitute biological entities (or "races") even though many psychologists and other Americans believe that they do. This is why psychologists cannot learn anything about the biological causation of behavior by comparing the performance of Blacks and Whites—just as a comparison of the personalities or IQs of people with large versus small ears would be similarly uninformative. Gould (1981) has documented the lamentable story of research that studies ethnocentric assumptions clothed as scientific questions.

I hope this brief comment will whet psychologists' appetites for anthropology. A good place to start is with *Patterns of Race in the Americas* by Marvin Harris (1964) and *Human Diversity* by Alexander Alland (1971).

### REFERENCES

Alland, A. (1971) *Human Diversity.* New York: Columbia University Press.

Gould, S. J. (1981) *The Mismeasure of Man.* New York: Norton.

Harris, M. (1964) *Patterns of Race in the Americas.* New York: Walker.

Yee, A. H.; Fairchild, H. H.; Weizmann, F.; Wyatt, G. E. (1993) "Addressing psychology's problems with race." *American Psychologist, 48,* 1132–1140.

# Chapter 29

# *Toward a Theory of Human Multiple Birthing: Sociobiology and r/K Reproductive Strategies*

## J. Philippe Rushton

## INTRODUCTION

The question of why different species have different numbers of offspring can be explained at both proximate and ultimate levels. Proximate levels emphasize the environmental and physiological mechanisms involved; ultimate explanations consider the evolutionary significance of phenomena in terms of reproductive fitness. Species have evolved numerous strategies of genetic replication ranging from asexual reproduction (not entailing the fusion of gametes), through semelparity (reproducing once in a lifetime), to iteroparity (reproducing repeatedly over the life-cycle). Each of these strategies can be examined from both proximate and ultimate perspectives.

In his Presidential address to the Fourth International Congress, MacGillivray (1984) touched on both proximate and ultimate types of explanation in his discussion of two historical hypotheses regarding human multiple birthing: "superfecundity" and "evolutionary atavism." In this chapter both these ideas will be organized within a sociobiological framework. Specifically, I suggest that human multiple egg production is an r, rather than a K, reproductive strategy and as such, is expected to underlie a variegated complex of characteristics concerning life histories, social behavior, and physiological functioning (Rushton 1985, Wilson 1975).

## THE r/K CONTINUUM

The symbols r and K originate in the mathematics of population biology and refer to two ends of a continuum of reproductive strategies organisms can adopt, ranging

from extreme r, involving maximum egg output and no parental care, to extreme K, emphasizing elaborate parental care in which the birthrate is reduced to a minimum (Wilson 1975). As can be seen in Figure 29–1, oysters, producing 500 million eggs a year exemplify the r-strategy, while the great apes, producing only one infant every 5 or 6 years, exemplify the K-strategy.

Evidence from both comparative studies and selective breeding experiments on species ranging from dandelions to fish, to mice, to men, indicate that reproductive strategies are correlated with other features of the organism's life history. Following Pianka (1970), Wilson (1975), and Barash (1982), these differences are summarized in Table 29–1. While each of the life cycle traits might independently contribute to fitness, the important point is that they are expected to covary along a single axis both between and within species. Despite some anomalies, many evolutionary biologists, having considered the literature, find the r/K continuum useful in organizing information on life histories (Barash 1982, Daly and Wilson 1983, Dawkins 1982, Wilson 1975).

From Table 29–1, it can be seen that, in terms of family characteristics, r and K strategists differ in terms of litter size, birth spacing, total number of offspring, rate of infant mortality, and degree of parental care. In regard to individual characteristics, r and K strategists differ in rate of physical maturation, sexual precocity, lifespan, body size, reproductive effort, energy use, and intelligence. Finally, in terms of population and social system characteristics, they differ in their treatment of the environment, tendency to geographically disperse, population size stability, competitiveness, degree of social organization, and altruism.

Individuals and species are, of course, only relatively r and K. Thus rabbits are K-strategists compared to fish but r-strategists compared to humans. Primates are

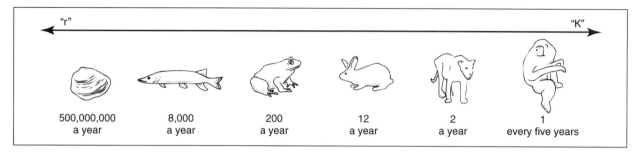

**Figure 29–1** The r/K continuum of reproductive strategies balancing egg output with parental care. (After Johanson and Edey 1981).

all relatively K-strategists, and humans are the most K of all. Indeed, as depicted in Figure 29–2, the order primates displays a natural scale going from lemur to macaque to gibbon to chimp to humans, in which there is a consistent trend toward K with progressive prolongation of gestation period and life phases (Lovejoy 1981). Note the proportionality of the four indicated phases. The postreproductive phase is restricted to humans. With each step in the natural scale, populations devote a greater proportion of their reproductive energy to subadult care, with increased investment in the survival of offspring.

## INDIVIDUAL DIFFERENCES IN K AMONG HUMANS

As a species, humans are at the K end of the continuum. What I am proposing, however, is that some people are genetically more K than others, and that K-behavior is associated with a constellation of personality attributes, all deeply embedded in evolutionary history (Rushton 1985). Several falsifiable predictions derive from this analysis. The more K the family, the greater should be the spacing between births, the fewer should be the total number of offspring, the lower should be the rate of infant mortality, and the better developed should be the

TABLE 29–1  Some Life History, Social Behavior, and Physiological Differences between r- and K-Strategists (following Pianka 1970).

| r-Strategist | K-Strategist |
|---|---|
| *Family characteristics* | |
| Large litter size | Small litter size |
| Short spacing between births | Long spacing between births |
| Many offspring | Few offspring |
| High rate of infant mortality | Low rate of infant mortality |
| Low degree of parental care | High degree of parental care |
| *Individual characteristics* | |
| Rapid rate of maturation | Slow rate of maturation |
| Early sexual reproduction | Delayed sexual reproduction |
| Short life | Long life |
| High reproductive effort | Low reproductive effort |
| Productive energy utilization | Efficient energy utilization |
| Low intelligence | High intelligence |
| *Population characteristics* | |
| Opportunistic exploiters of environment | Consistent exploiters of environment |
| Dispersing colonizers | Stable occupiers of habitat |
| Variable population size | Stable population size |
| Competition variable, often lax | Competition keen |
| *Social system characteristics* | |
| Low degree of social organization | High degree of social organization |
| Low amounts of altruism | High amounts of altruism |

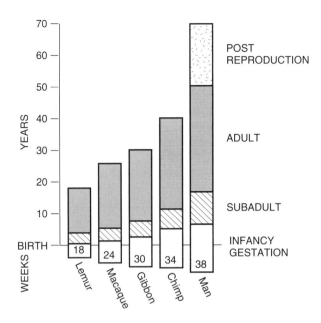

**Figure 29–2** Progressive prolongation of life phases and gestation in primates. *Science,* 211:341–350. Copyright 1981 by the American Association for the Advancement of Science. Reprinted by permission.

parental care. The more K the person, the longer should be the period of gestation, the higher the birthweight, the more delayed the onset of sexual activity, the older the age at first reproduction, the longer the life, the lower the sex drive, the higher the intelligence, the more efficient the use of energy, the lower the dispersal tendency, the more social rule following the behavior, and the greater the altruism. Significant correlations are predicted to occur among all these indices of K.

Consideration of the available evidence offers a degree of support for the K perspective (Rushton 1985). Many indices of K, for example, have been shown to be heritable, including family size and structure (Bulmer 1970), the rate of growth from 3 months to 15 years in height and intelligence (Wilson 1983), the age of onset of puberty and menopause (Bouchard 1984), the strength of the sex drive and its relation to age of first intercourse, intercourse frequency, and total number of partners (Martin et al. 1977), body mass (Stunkard et al. 1986), susceptibility to infectious diseases (Gedda et al. 1984), the onset of degenerative diseases associated with aging (Omenn 1977), longevity (Carmelli and Anderson 1981, Hrubec et al. 1984), and a wide range of relevant personality traits, including intelligence (Bouchard 1984), social rule following (Mednick et al. 1984), and altruism (Rushton et al. 1986).

### THE NATURE OF MULTIPLE BIRTHING

The more K the species, the smaller, on average, will be its litter size. Primates, including *Homo sapiens,* tend to

have single offspring. However, all types of primates occasionally have multiple births. Multiple births are here considered to be indices of "litter size" and to represent an r-reproductive strategy. This directly follows in cases where multiple births result from the production of more than one egg at a time as occurs with DZ but not MZ twins. That DZ twins, more than MZs, are the result of an r-reproductive strategy, is suggested by evidence that their production is (1) known to be genetically influenced and otherwise related to having large families (Bulmer 1970, but see Parisi et al. 1983), (2) increased by fertility drugs (Webster and Elwood 1985, Wyshak 1978), and (3) related to their mothers having higher levels of naturally occurring serum gonadotropin and estradiol (Martin et al. 1984). Moreover, the tendency to produce DZ twins is related to several other r dimensions. Compared to mothers of singletons, mothers of DZ twins typically have a lower age of menarche, a shorter menstrual cycle, and a higher number of marriages (Wyshak 1981), a higher rate of coitus (James 1984), more illegitimate children (Eriksson and Fellman 1967, Nylander 1981), a closer spacing of births (Allen 1981), a greater fecundity (Allen and Schachter 1971, Bulmer 1959, Parisi and Caperna 1981, Pollard 1969), more pregnancy wastage (Wyshak 1981), a larger family (Bulmer 1976), an earlier menopause (Wyshak 1978), an earlier mortality measured by cancer of the pancreas (but not for other sites), by diabetes, other endocrine diseases, and allergies (Wyshak 1984). They do not, however, appear to have an earlier age at first live birth (Wyshak 1981).

Twins themselves, of course, have shorter gestation periods, lower birth weights, and a greater incidence of infant mortality when compared with singletons (Bulmer 1970). In these respects, however, and possibly counter to predictions from K theory, MZ twins fare even worse than DZ twins, although this may be due to MZ twins more often being monochorial. Subsequently, DZ twins, compared with MZ twins, have a greater susceptibility to major health disorders such as schizophrenia, diabetes, hypertension, heart diseases, ulcers, and neuroses (Keudler and Robinette 1983), and generally to have an earlier mortality (Hrubec et al. 1984).

Given that the production of DZ twins represents an r-strategy relative to the production of MZ twins or singletons, it would be informative to contrast the personalities and life histories of such twins. Usually, however, this is not feasible because of the underrepresentation of DZ twins in most studies and the possibly K nature of most DZ volunteers. Volunteering for research has often been considered a measure of altruism (Rushton 1980), a trait clearly related to K (see Table 29–1), and on which individual differences are partly heritable (Rushton et al. 1986). It is known that although MZ and DZ same sex twins co-occur in nearly equal frequencies in Caucasian populations, DZ pairs volunteer about one-third less often for research than do MZ pairs (Lykken et al. 1978). Explanations for this range from difference in narcissistic motivation on the part of the twins (Lykken et al. 1978), to the method of construction of twin registers by researchers (Kendler and Holm 1985, Martin and Wilson 1982). K theory suggests an additional explanation: DZ twins, on average, are less altruistic, as well as more likely to be geographically dispersed (see Table 29–1) than MZs or singletons, and, therefore, less inclined to volunteer to help research. Moreover, this lack of altruism and tendency to disperse is postulated to be part of a syndrome of personality and life-cycle traits. Following the recommendations of Lykken et al. (1978) and others, therefore, it may be advisable to offer financial incentives to increase the representation of DZ twins. It would then be instructive to compare mean differences between MZs and DZs on life-history phenomena to test other predictions from K theory. Since males appear to be less altruistic, on average, than females (Rushton 1980, Rushton et al. 1986), this disposition may also underlie the underrepresentation of males in volunteer twin studies.

## GROUP DIFFERENCES IN MULTIPLE BIRTHING

Population differences exist in frequency of multiple birthing such that higher socioeconomic < lower socioeconomic, and Mongoloids < Caucasoids < Negroids. With respect to social class, studies have found the frequency to be greater among lower social class women in both European and African samples (Golding 1986, Nylander 1981). With respect to race, although MZ twinning is nearly constant at about three and a half per thousand in all groups, DZ twinning varies; the approximate rate per 1000 births among Mongoloids is 3; among Caucasoids, 8; and among Negroids, < 16; with some African populations having twinning rates as high as 57 per 1,000 (Bulmer 1970, Nylander 1975). The incidence of non-MZ triplets and quadruplets shows comparable rank orders. For triplets, the rate per million among Mongoloids is 10; among Caucasoids, 100; and among Negroids 1700; and for quadruplets, per million, among Mongoloids, 0.000; among Caucasoids, 1.0; and among Negroids, 60 (Bulmer 1970, Nylander 1975). Moreover, data from racially mixed matings suggests that the DZ twinning rate is largely determined by the race of the mother independently of the race of the father, as shown for Mongoloid-Caucasoid crossings in Hawaii, and Caucasoid-Negroid crosses in Brazil (Bulmer 1970).

If the analysis of multiple birthing presented here is correct, then the differences observed between populations in other K related characteristics such as activity level, intelligence, longevity, rate of maturation, sexual behavior, and social rule following (Rushton 1984, 1985a, 1985b, Rushton and Bogaert in press), may take on deeper evolutionary significance. On many of these measures the rank order of whites is between that of blacks and Orientals, as it is in rate of multiple birthing, and gonadotropin levels (Nylander 1981, Soma et al. 1975). The need for further research on these inter- and intrapopulation patterns is clearly warranted. A perspective from evolutionary biology may prove fruitful.

## ACKNOWLEDGMENT

Supported in part by a grant from The Pioneer Fund, Inc.

## REFERENCES

Allen, G. (1981) "The twinning and fertility paradox." In *Twin Research 3: Part A, Twin Biology and Multiple Pregnancy.* L. Gedda, P. Parisi, W. L. Nance, eds. New York: Alan R Liss.

Allen, G., Schachter, J. (1971) "Ease of conception in mothers of twins." *Soc. Biol.,* 18:18–27.

Barash, D. P. (1982) *Sociobiology and Behavior,* 2nd edition. New York: Elsevier.

Bouchard, T. J., Jr. (1984) "Twins reared together and apart: What they tell us about human diversity." In *Individuality and Determinism.* S. W. Fox, ed. New York: Plenum.

Bulmer, M. G. (1959) "The effect of parental age, parity and duration of marriage on the twinning rate." *Ann. Hum. Genet.,* 23:454–458.

Bulmer, M. G. (1970) *The Biology of Twinning in Man.* Oxford: Clarendon Press.

Carmelli, D.; Andersen, S. (1981) "A longevity study of twins in the Mormon genealogy." In *Twin Research 3: Part A, Twin Biology and Multiple Pregnancy.* L. Gedda, P. Parisi, W. E. Nance, eds. New York: Alan R Liss.

Daly, M.; Wilson, M. (1983) *Sex, Evolution and Behavior,* 2nd edition. Boston: Willard Grant Press.

Dawkins, R. (1982) *The Extended Phenotype.* San Francisco: Freeman.

Eriksson, A. W.; Fellman, J. (1967) "Twinning and legitimacy." *Hereditas,* 47:395–402.

Gedda, L.; Rajani, G.; Brenci, G.; Lun, M. T.; Talone, C.; Oddi, G. (1984) "Heredity and infectious diseases: A twin study." *Acta Genet. Med. Gemellol.,* 33:497–500.

Golding, J. (1986) "Social class and twinning (Abstract)." *Acta Genet. Med. Gemellol.,* 35:207.

Hrubec, Z.; Floderus-Myrhed, B.; de Faire, U.; Sarna, S. (1984) "Familial factors in mortality with control of epidemiological covariables. Swedish twins born 1886–1925." *Acta Genet. Med. Gemell.,* 33:403–412.

James, W. H. (1984) "Coitus-induced ovulation and its implications for estimates of some reproductive parameters." *Acta Genet. Med. Gemellol.,* 33:547–555.

Johanson, D. C.; Edey, M. A. (1981) *Lucy: The Beginnings of Human Kind.* New York: Simon & Schuster.

Kendler, K. S.; Holm, N. V. (1985) "Differential enrollment in twin registries: Its effects on prevalence and concordance rates and estimates of genetic parameters." *Acta Genet. Med. Gemellol.,* 34:125–140.

Kendler, K. S.; Robinette, C. D. (1983) "Schizophrenia in the National Academy of Sciences—National Research Council Twin Registry: A 16-year update." *Am. J. Psychiatry,* 140:1551–1563.

Lovejoy, C. O. (1981) "The origin of man." *Science,* 211:341–350.

Lykken, D. T.; Tellegan, A.; DuRubeis, R. (1978) "Volunteer bias in twin research: The rule of two-thirds." *Soc. Biol.,* 25:1–9.

MacGillivray, I. (1984) "Presidential address: The Aberdeen contribution to twinning." *Acta Genet. Med. Gemellol.,* 33:5–11.

Martin, N. G.; Beaini, J. L. E.; Olsen, M. E.; Bhatnagar, A. S.; Macourt, D. (1984) "Gonadotropin levels in mothers who have had two sets of DZ twins." *Acta Genet. Med. Gemellol.,* 33:131–139.

Martin, N. G.; Eaves, L. J.; Eysenck, H. J. (1977) "Genetical, environmental and personality factors influencing the age of first sexual intercourse in twins." *J. Biosoc. Sci.,* 9:91–97.

Martin, N. G.; Wilson, S. R. (1982). "Bias in the estimation of heritability from truncated samples of twins." *Behav. Genet.,* 12:467–472.

Mednick, S. A.; Gabrielli, W. F.; Hutchings, B. (1984) "Genetic influences in criminal convictions: Evidence from an adoptive cohort." *Science,* 224:891–894.

Nylander, P. P. S. (1975) "Frequency of multiple births." In *Human Multiple Reproduction.* I. MacGillivray, P. P. S. Nylander, G. Corney, eds. Philadelphia: WB Saunders.

Nylander, P. P. S. (1981) "The factors that influence twinning rates." *Acta Genet. Med. Gemellol.,* 30:189–202.

Omenn, G. S. (1977) "Behavior genetics." In *Handbook of the Psychology of Aging.* J. E. Birren, K. W. Schaie, eds. New York: Van Nostrand and Reinhold.

Parisi, P.; Caperna, G. (1981) "The changing incidence of twinning: One century of Italian statistics." In *Twin Research 3: Part A. Twin Biology and Multiple Pregnancy* (pp. 35–48). L. Gedda, P. Parisi, W. E. Nance, eds. New York: AR Liss.

Parisi, P.; Gatti, M.; Prinzi, G.; Caperna, G. (1983) "Familial incidence of twinning." *Nature,* 304:626–628.

Pianka, E. R. (1970) "On r- and K-selection." *Am. Naturalist,* 104:592–597.

Pollard, G. N. (1969) "Multiple births in Australia, 1944–63." *J. Biosoc. Sci.,* 1:389–404.

Rushton, J. P. (1980) *Altruism, Socialization, and Society.* Englewood Cliffs, NJ: Prentice-Hall.

Rushton, J. P. (1984) "Sociobiology: Toward a theory of individual and group differences in personality and social behavior." In *Annals of Theoretical Psychology,* Vol 2. (pp. 1–81). J. R. Royce, L. P. Mos, eds. New York: Plenum.

Rushton, J. P. (1985a) "Differential K theory: The sociobiology of individual differences." *Person. Individ. Diff.,* 6:441–452.

Rushton, J. P. (1985b): "Differential K theory and race differences in E and N." *Person. Individ. Diff.,* 6:769–770.

Rushton, J. P.; Bogaert, A. F. (in press) "Race differences in sexual behavior: Testing an evolutionary hypothesis." *J. Res. Person.*

Rushton, J. P.; Fulker, D. W.; Neale, M. C.; Nias, D. K. B.; Eysenck, H. J. (1986) "Altruism and aggression: The heritability of individual differences." *J. Pers. Soc. Psychol.,* 50:1192–1198.

Stunkard, A. J.; Sorensen, T. I. A.; Hanis, C.; Teasdale, T. W.; Chakraborty, R.; Schull, W. J.; Schulsinger, F. (1986) "An adoption study of human obesity." *New Engl. J. Med.,* 314:193–198.

Webster, F.; Elwood, J. M. (1985): "A study of the influence of ovulation stimulants and oral contraception on twin births in England." *Acta Genet. Med. Gemellol.,* 34:105–108.

Wilson, E. O. (1975) *Sociobiology: The New Synthesis.* Cambridge, MA: Harvard University Press.

Wilson, R. S. (1983) "The Louisville Twin Study: Developmental synchronies in behavior." *Child. Dev.,* 54:298–316.

Wyshak, G. (1978) "Menopause in mothers of multiple births and mothers of singletons only." *Soc. Biol.,* 25:52–61.

Wyshak, G. (1978) "Statistical findings on the effects of fertility drugs on plural births." In *Twin Research 2: Part B, Biology and Epidermiology.* W. E. Nance, ed. New York: Alan R Liss.

Wyshak, G. (1981) "Reproductive and menstrual characteristics of mothers of multiple births and mothers of singletons only: A discriminant analysis." In *Twin Research 3: Part A, Twin Biology and Multiple Pregnancy.* L. Gedda, P. Parisi, W. E. Nance, eds. New York: Alan R Liss.

Wyshak, G. (1984) "Health characteristics of mothers of twins." *Acta Genet. Med. Gemellol.,* 33:141–145.

# Chapter 30

# *Differential K Theory and Racial Hierarchies*

Frederic Weizmann, Neil I. Wiener,
David L. Wiesenthal, and Michael Ziegler

Many critics have charged that human sociobiology embodies a form of biological determinism that serves to justify existing social inequalities on the grounds that they reflect underlying biological differences. Sociobiologists themselves, however, have tended to focus largely on those features of human individual and social existence that are universal (with the major exception of gender). Indeed, several eminent sociobiologists (Barash 1979, Trivers 1981) have defended the discipline from charges of racism or conservative political bias precisely on the grounds that sociobiology has not concerned itself with group differences.

Rushton's Differential K theory (e.g., Ellis 1987, Rushton 1985, 1988a, 1988b, 1989a, Rushton and Bogaert 1987, 1988) represents a significant departure from this precedent. This theory is based on the assumption that racial and social class differences are deeply rooted in evolutionary history. It borrows its specific evolutionary ideas from life-history theory, that area of evolutionary ecology concerned with the evolution of major individual characteristics across the life span (e.g., fecundity, developmental rate, age at sexual maturity, longevity, and mode of parental investment).

Specifically, Rushton (1985) has proposed that blacks invest more heavily in traits and activities directly relevant to sex and reproduction than do whites, who in turn invest more than Orientals. According to Rushton, however, this leaves blacks with far fewer resources available for non-procreative purposes than the other two racial groups. These differences in the allocation of resources leads to differences in a number of other traits, psychological, social, and physical. Thus Rushton argues that blacks are the least intelligent, least sexually restrained, most criminal, and least altruistic of the races.

From *Canadian Psychology,* Vol. 31, No. 1, 1990

Orientals are on the opposite extreme for all these traits, and whites fall in the middle. A similar ordering exists for social class; lower social class individuals resemble blacks behaviorally, and "upper income" [sic] individuals resemble whites and Orientals.

Rushton's Differential K theory incorporates a number of familiar vulgar stereotypes, integrated by the hypothesis that these differences define a hierarchy of evolutionary progress (Rushton 1989a), in which Orientals are the most advanced, blacks the most primitive, and whites intermediate between the two. Although Rushton and Bogaert (1988) claim that the differences between racial groups in sexual behavior are stronger than the differences between social classes, they propose that social class differences also reflect evolutionary differences. While the idea of such an evolutionary hierarchy among human races (e.g., Haller 1965) is not new, Rushton's placing of Orientals rather than whites at the top of the hierarchy is, perhaps, something of an innovation: The genetic ordering of social classes, however, is entirely consistent with older eugenic traditions (Cravens 1978).

Rushton uses the very existence of racial and social differences as evidence for the applicability of this evolutionary model, and the model, in turn, is then used to explain these same differences. Thus only the scientific soundness and relevance of the underlying biological evolutionary model can save Differential K theory from circularity. The claims for Differential K theory are hardly modest: Rushton (1985) has suggested that the K-dimension may underlie "much of the field of personality" (p. 445). The extravagance of its claims and the attention it has received justify a careful examination of Differential K theory, especially since it does exactly what critics of human sociobiology have charged; namely, it provides a biological rationale for existing patterns of social inequality.

## r- AND K-SELECTION

As an evolutionary scheme, Differential K theory represents an extension of the concepts of r- and K-selection to humans. Although building on earlier research and theory, these terms were first introduced by MacArthur and Wilson (1967) in their influential work on island ecology. In this work, they examined the nature and consequences of selection pressures on organisms colonizing uncrowded islands and compared them with the pressures that obtain as the habitat becomes more crowded and population densities increase.

In the first instance, they theorized that selection would favor traits supporting rapid and prolific population growth. In the second, selection would favor traits supporting the efficient exploitation of environmental resources, rather than sheer prolificacy. These ideas quickly became generalized beyond island settings; *r-selection* was hypothesized to operate in any unstable, fluctuating, or ephemeral habitat, and *K-selection* was hypothesized to typify the selection pressures operating in more stable and persisting environments, such as the tropics (Murray 1979). (Readers should note that this implies that human populations who have persisted longest in the tropical ancestral habitat, i.e., blacks, should be more K-selected than other human groups.) Species began to be described as being r-strategists or K-strategists. Each of these evolutionary strategies came to be strongly identified with a particular complex of specific life-history traits, as articulated by Pianka in an influential article in 1970 (Boyce 1984, Stearns 1977).

Population regulation for r-selected species was assumed to be independent of population density, and such species were characterized as discovering new or empty habitats, reproducing rapidly and prolifically, and using up resources before competitors appeared or before the habitat itself disappeared (Murray 1979). In order to maximize reproduction, parents would invest as little as possible in individual offspring. Achieving maximal reproduction also meant that traits leading to increased reproduction would be selected even at the cost of traits supporting individual maintenance and survival (e.g., Pianka 1970, Stearns, 1976, 1977). K-selected species were presumed to evolve under conditions where population density would regulate population growth. Under these conditions there would be greater competition for scarce resources, and so selection would favor the production of fewer offspring who were better equipped to meet the challenges of intraspecific competition (e.g., Pianka 1970, Stearns 1976, 1977).

In the late 1970s, criticisms of the r/K model, especially in the more generalized form popularized by Pianka (1970) and others, began to appear. In one influential critique, Stearns (1977) pointed out that life-history theorists tended to ignore the importance of developmental plasticity and the role of developmental influ-

ences in shaping the phenotype (Schlichting 1986, Stearns 1977). However, there is often considerable plasticity in those life-history characteristics frequently assumed to be the consequences of r-or K-selection. Marmosets, for example, are small colonizing primates who can produce two sets of twins a year when food is plentiful (Hrdy 1981, p. 40). When food is scarce, however, the spacing between births is increased, as is the likelihood that one member of the twin pair may die. Hrdy has written " . . . marmosets, like many small animals, must be ecological double agents, shuttling back and forth along a continuum ranging from r- to K-selected strategies—from reliance on proliferation to reliance on competition" (p. 41).

Plasticity may be especially adaptive when environmental conditions are changing rapidly and unpredictably (Roughgarten 1979), precisely the conditions under which r-selection may be most evident. Insofar as plasticity itself is an adaptive response to evolutionary selection, however, it undercuts the idea that there is a general relationship between selection and any specific set of traits. On the contrary, plasticity in r/K behavior, conjoined with the many examples of organisms that possess both r-selected and K-selected traits (marine turtles, for example, both lay numerous eggs and have long life spans), suggest that there is little evidence for the existence of complexes of r or K traits at the level of the genes.

Stearns also criticized the empirical robustness of the r/K model in his 1977 review. He noted that only 18 of the 35 studies reviewed provided positive evidence for the model, and most of these had significant methodological limitations. As Begon and Mortimer (1981) have noted, it has been the better designed studies that have failed to support the r/K model.

In fairness, it should be pointed out that these negative empirical findings, as well as the general criticisms noted above, apply more to the ambitious claims of the extended versions of the model than they do to the more modest idea of r/K selection itself (Boyce 1984). The original model of r/K selection did not imply that r- or K-selection was to be identified with a specified group of life-history traits (Boyce 1984). However, it is precisely this extended and oversimplified version of the r/K model, with its rigid specification of traits, that has been embodied in Differential K theory.

## DIFFERENTIAL K THEORY

Based on his analysis of the r/K literature, Rushton (1985) concludes that there is an evolutionary trend towards K within the mammalian order. Not only are primates highly K-selected, but humans are the most K-selected of the primates. Rushton (1985, Rushton and Bogaert 1987, 1988) and his associates (Ellis 1987) argue that while humans as a species are K-selected, there are nonetheless relative differences among groups in this regard. That is, they assume that if r/K selection can account for evolutionary differences between species, then differences in evolutionary reproductive strategies may also account for a number of differences among human groups. Translating our earlier description of Rushton's hypotheses into r/K terminology, Rushton (1985) has hypothesized that because of imputed differences in evolutionary history, Negroes (blacks) are less K-selected than Caucasians (whites), who in turn are less K-selected than Orientals.

One major problem with Differential K theory is that neither the biological theory nor the data on which it rests provide a solid foundation for its extension to humans. While there is no a priori reason why r/K selection cannot operate within species, Rushton provides no evidence regarding those environmental factors that might have differentially selected for r- or K-traits among human groups. In fact, Stearns (1983) found little evidence that life-history selection occurs at the level of either the subspecies (i.e., varieties or races) or the species. He reported that the selection of life-history traits that form the basic ground-plan of the organism are more evident at biological levels more inclusive (e.g., class, family, and order) and evolutionarily older than the species level.

Rushton has argued that there are biological differences among the races, so that less strongly K-selected (i.e., more r-selected) groups are hypothesized to have larger genitalia, lower age at menarche, higher levels of multiple births, and a higher rate of infant mortality, all of which can be interpreted fairly directly as manifestations of a more r-like, less K-like strategy. He and his colleagues have also argued, however, that evolutionary r/K differences would also lead to differences in a variety of traits whose relationship to r/K selection is neither immediately obvious nor compelling to us. These include differences in measured intelligence, altruism (undefined), attitudes toward the environment, degree of social organization, extraversion and introversion (Rushton 1985, Rushton and Bogaert 1987, 1988), law-abidingness, and economic behavior and business practices (Ellis 1987).

In his earlier writings Rushton (1985) did not offer any theoretical rationale for including such traits as altruism (undefined), degree of social organization, and abstract intelligence in his list of r/K selected traits. The way the list is presented makes it appear that these traits are simply taken from Pianka's (1970) list of traits, on which Rushton's is based. In fact, these traits do not occur in Pianka. More recently, Rushton (Rushton and Bogaert 1988) has attempted to justify their inclusion by suggesting that these traits are K-selected because they contribute to social organization, which helps insure the viability of offspring.

The ascription of r- or K-selected status to these traits seems arbitrary, however. For example, there is no reason to assume that K-selection, which involves interindividual competition, will lead to the evolution of altruism, however defined. In the absence of any knowledge about the environmental context in which selection took place, one could as easily (and more directly) argue that K-selection would place a premium on selfishness. To take another example, Rushton and his colleagues (Ellis 1987) have suggested that the higher crime rate found among American blacks indicates that they are less K-selected and more r-selected. As is well known among criminologists, however, black crime is largely directed at black victims (Bureau of the Census 1988); hence, it could be argued easily that such behavior is more strongly K- than r-selected (i.e., that it represents competition for limited resources).

In the end, then, there is neither any justification from the biological literature nor any strong theoretical justification for Rushton's ascription of r-selected or K-selected status to traits like altruism, criminality, and so on. What Rushton has done is to employ the terminology of r/K theory to justify a number of stereotypic beliefs, all the while ignoring not only the limitation of the r/K model, but frequently the very model itself.

## HERITABILITY

Rushton (1985) has claimed that traits and the group differences among them are largely heritable and that such heritability provides a basis for arguing that group differences represent the outcome of different evolutionary strategies. Leaving aside the problems of inferring conclusions about genetic variability from correlations reflecting phenotypic familial resemblance, problems that have been discussed at length in the literature (e.g., Hirsch 1970, Roughgarten, 1979, Wachs 1983, Wahlsten 1979), there are some serious limitations of the concept of heritability itself that Rushton has ignored. (For additional discussions of heritability, see Angoff 1988, Feldman and Lewontin 1975, McGuire and Hirsch 1977, Plomin 1983, Scarr 1981a, 1981b).

A *heritability coefficient* is simply a numerical estimate of the amount of additive genetic variation underlying the phenotypic variation in a given trait for a particular population. Since heritability only involves variation within a population, it says nothing about the operation of genes within individuals; thus, heritability cannot be identified with heredity, a confusion that is quite common, even among geneticists (Paul 1985). Changes in either genotypes or environments can lead to different heritability estimates (Falconer 1960, p. 166). In fact, Angoff (1988) has recently suggested that obtaining a reliable heritability estimate for intelligence may be impossible, since estimates of the heritability of intelligence vary so widely. Given the difficulty of ascertaining the heritability of human traits, such a conclusion is not surprising.

The descriptive nature of heritability also means that one cannot generalize heritabilities from one population to another. For example, all of the variation in a genetically homogeneous population is necessarily environmental, which results in a heritability estimate of .00; however, one cannot generalize this figure to more genetically heterogeneous populations.

Similarly, it is important to emphasize that within-group heritability scores, whether high or low, are absolutely silent regarding the cause of between-group differences. Heritability is a descriptive measure that cannot be generalized beyond the range of genotypes or environments on which the estimates were originally made, a point disputed to our knowledge only by Rushton (1989b). Since groups may differ genetically and/or environmentally, average differences can be caused by either and/or both factors, and they cannot be disentangled without employing a highly specialized and demanding methodology (Zuckerman and Brody, 1988). Zuckerman and Brody point out that Rushton never uses or cites studies that employ methods that can separate genetic and environmental factors as causes of group differences. Of the several such studies Zuckerman and Brody found in the area of intellectual differences, none report any evidence that group differences in intelligence are genetic.

Even differences between groups that are totally due to genetic influences may not generalize to other environments. Changing the environment of rearing may change the magnitude or even the direction of group differences. Whether group differences are genetic has only to do with the causes of variation between groups within a given environment and does not necessarily predict what the pattern of group differences will be in other environments. For this reason, evolutionary hypotheses about the development of population traits need to be tested in the environments in which they were presumed to have evolved, a condition that most data on racial differences do not meet.

The usefulness of heritability measures is that they provide an index of the amount of genetic variation available for selection. Without such variation, selection has no raw material on which to work. While heritability is necessary for selection to occur, however, the very process of selecting for a trait, if successful, reduces genetic variation, and thus works towards lowering heritability, at least within the range of environments within which the selective pressures operate.

For that reason, traits on which selection may be presumed to have operated quite strongly often tend to have relatively low heritabilities (e.g., Falconer 1960, Mousseau and Roff 1987). More generally, any traits that are universal have low heritabilities, since the requisite genes for producing the traits are also universal. While such traits may help exemplify the effects of natural selection, however, they hold little promise for those seeking to find an evolutionary sanction to rationalize beliefs about racial inequality. Hence Rushton's (1984, Rushton et al. 1986) assumption that data indicating that high heritability constitutes evidence that a trait has been the subject of selective pressures is simply wrong.

Rushton (1985) further compounds this misunderstanding of the relationship between heritability and natural selection by misconstruing the relationship between heritability and plasticity. Thus in accord with recent versions of sociobiological theory (Lumsden and Wilson 1981) that provide an explicit, if highly limited, role for learning and cultural influences, Rushton acknowledges (Rushton and Bogaert 1987) that there is some room for individual change in r/K selected traits. However, Rushton explains this plasticity on the grounds that the correlations indicating the heritability are of only moderate size (Rushton and Bogaert 1987), implying that heritability limits plasticity.

High heritability, however, does not limit changeability or imply lack of educability, nor does low heritability necessarily imply plasticity (e.g., Angoff 1988, Hirsch 1970, Hunt 1961, Oyama 1985, Scarr-Salapatek 1971, Weizmann 1971). The fact that heritabilities for various traits can change during development indicates that heritability estimates respond to change, they do not constrain it. As research dating back to T. H. Morgan (Morgan et al. 1915) indicates, however, even minor environmental variations can produce markedly different phenotypes.

## RACE

Rushton nowhere discusses the basis for his racial classification beyond stating that his three major racial categories follow "common usage" (Rushton 1988a, p. 1009). Given the weight that Rushton places on racial classification, however, his response is unacceptable. Common usage is not a justification for a scientific category. The tripartite racial classification of common usage has been widely discredited as a biological concept (Molnar 1975, p. 97), even if it has not disappeared as an explanatory variable in some circles. In particular, the biological concept of race has been found wanting on a number of grounds. There is no evidence supporting a typological conception of race, that is, the view that there is a prototypical individual who is representative of a race (Benton and Harwood 1975, Molnar 1975, Williams 1973). The population variance among population groups inhabiting particular regions contradicts any concept of racial homogeneity (King 1981, Molnar 1975, Stringer and Andrews 1988). In fact, no morphological characteristic or combination of characteristics (such as skin color, skull shape, or stature) reliably defines a subgroup of *Homo sapiens* (Molnar 1975, Williams 1973).

Clines, which are geographical gradients of gene frequencies between distant populations, indicate that group characteristics vary continuously, and there are no clearcut divisions between groups (Benton and Harwood 1975, King 1981, Molnar 1975).

## Plasticity, Change, and Group Differences

Change presents particular difficulties for sociobiological genetic explanations because the rapidity and the extent of many population changes cannot be accounted for by any known model of genetic change. If substantial changes within a population are due to environmental changes, then similar explanations may also apply to differences between groups. Many of the traits and behaviors that Rushton and his colleagues describe have undergone rapid and substantial change. For example, not only have IQ gains (Angoff 1988, Flynn 1987) been reported for many groups and nationalities that rival or exceed the average 15-point black-white difference that Rushton (1988a) reports, but the gap between whites and blacks on standardized tests of intellectual achievement lessened considerably in the 1960s and 1970s (see Angoff 1988).

## Human Fertility

It is worth examining some aspects of human fertility and population growth, since they are central to Differential K theory. Recent research on the sensitivity of human fertility to changing environmental and social conditions (Coale and Watkins, 1986) has led researchers to conclude that the declining birthrate in Europe over the last century constituted a "social revolution" (Watkins 1986, p. 420). The speed with which the initiation of family limitation spread throughout the provinces of Europe (Coale and Watkins 1986) was most dramatic. National fertility levels (i.e., birth rates) declined from 90 percent to 60 percent of their previous levels in only 18 to 30 years (Coale and Watkins 1986). Similar trends occurred in North America. During the sixteenth century, Quebec had one of the highest birth rates in the world. Since the Great Depression of the 1930s, however, the birth rate has fallen from a total fertility rate of 4.3 in 1926, just prior to the Depression, to the current rate of 1.4 (Lachapelle 1988), a figure much below the replacement rate. Similarly, while the birth rate in the United States is now comparable to the low rates found in other industrialized countries, in colonial days women had, on average, eight children (Kiser et al. 1968).

Past research tended to ignore the effects of age, SES-related factors, or rural/urban residence patterns on ethnic and racial differences in fertility. In more recent research in which these factors have been better controlled, many previously observed racial and ethnic differences weakened or disappeared (Bean and Swicegood 1985). This change in emphasis has been particularly apparent in studies of black fertility. Bean and Swicegood, citing the work of Lee and Lee, indicate that the only case in which American nonwhite fertility exceeded that of whites was among less educated farm residents, while fertility among more highly educated blacks was actually lower than that found among similarly educated whites (1985, p. 10).

Bean and Swicegood (1985) conclude that one can predict the birthrates of female minority group members from the educational attainments of their respective mothers (p. 21). Among women with eight or fewer years of education, black fertility exceeds that of whites by 1.42 children. For women with four or more years of university, blacks averaged only 0.08 more children than whites (Johnson 1979, cited by Bean and Swicegood). Similarly, Kiser et al. (1968) reported that, for the period 1950 to 1960, the fertility rates of nonwhite American women reporting one or more years of college tended to be lower than those of white women. At other educational levels, the extent to which the fertility of nonwhite women exceeded that of white women tended to be inversely related to educational level. Among wives of professional men, the average number of children was frequently lower for non-white than for white women (p. 291).

The high degree of plasticity evident from the human fertility data certainly seems to indicate that humans can change fertility rates quite drastically in response to environmental change. The data regarding the relationship of environmental factors to lowered fertility rates in black and Hispanic populations are particularly opposite in view of Rushton's (1989a) recently expressed fears that when selection pressures are relaxed, natural selection will favour "r-genotypes" [sic] because of their more rapid rate of reproduction.

Perhaps the most dramatic illustration of the absurdity of Rushton's linking of race or population differences in fertility with what he assumes are gene-based differences in r- or K-selected traits is the fact that one of the highest fertility rates found anywhere in the world is that of the Hutterites of the Western United States and Canada (Potts and Selman 1979). The fertility rate of this group of Swiss-German descent is so high that demographers consider it to be close to the theoretical possible maximum and employ it as the standard against which other groups are compared (Potts and Selman 1979). This high fertility rate, however, has not evidently diminished the parental investment of the Hutterites in their young. Observers report that all members of the Hutterite community express concern for all of the children in the colony (Hostetler and Huntington 1967). It should be noted that the Hutterite's "racial" compatriots in Switzerland and Germany presently have very low birthrates.

## TWINNING

A second important area for testing Differential K theory is group differences in the rate of dizygotic (DZ) twinning. DZ twinning rate is considered to be an indicator of the tendency to have multiple births ("litter size" in Rushton's phrase). "Racial differences in the r/K sexual strategies were predicted because human populations are known to differ in egg production: namely, lower socioeconomic > higher socioeconomic, and Negroid > Caucasoids > Mongoloids" (Rushton and Bogaert 1988, p. 261).

Rushton's emphasis on genetic explanations for such group differences, however, ignores more obvious and plausible explanations that are clearly specifiable and testable; that is, that DZ twinning results from dietary or other environmental factors that increase follicle stimulating hormone or follicle stimulating releasing hormone (FHS or FSRH). Nylander (1981) suggests that the high rate of DZ twinning in Western Nigeria occurs because "some environmental factor (e.g., a substance in the diet) may be acting like a fertility pill . . . causing high serum FSH and increased tendency to multiple births" (p. 201). James (1985) suggests that specific dietary substances such as milk products may be one such factor, since the consumption of milk products correlates 0.78 with DZ twinning rates in Europe.

James (1985) has recently reported that geographic latitude correlates substantially with DZ twinning rates in both Europe and America. It is interesting to note that given Rushton's assumptions about the meaning of twinning, this finding would lead to the conclusion that the higher twinning rates that characterize inhabitants of those regions employ a more r-selected reproductive strategy. This would also suggest that whites and Orientals are more r-selected (or less K-selected) than blacks.

In addition to ignoring environmental factors in twinning, Rushton also ignores the remarkable shifts in DZ twinning rates that have occurred in a large number of geographical regions in very short periods of time (James 1986); such rates declined in all European countries for which data is available during the 1960s, and most continued to decline through the 1970s. The DZ twinning rate in England, Wales, Finland, Eire, Holland, Greece, and Spain declined nearly 40 percent during this time (James 1986). New Zealand's DZ twinning rate declined more than 40 percent from the late 1950s to 1973 (James 1982). Similarly, Trinidad and Tobago's rate declined 40 percent during the period 1961 to 1975 (James 1982). These widespread and substantial changes are based on reliable data and are independent of maternal age.

The largest change in DZ twinning rate has occurred, however, in Western Nigeria, a region known to have one of the highest rates of twinning in the world. While Nylander (1969) reported a twinning rate of 45 to 53 per 1,000 births for the mainly Yoruba area of West-

ern Nigeria in 1969, more recent investigators (Marinho et al. 1986) found that the rate had declined to 23.8 per 1000 for the same area by 1982–1983. That is, the DZ twinning rate had declined 50 percent in just fourteen years. Not only is the rapidity of such a large change quite remarkable, but it acquires additional significance from the fact that it is the high DZ twinning rates in Nigeria that have constituted one of the important bases for the generalization that blacks have a higher twinning rate than whites and Orientals.

As in the case of the changes in human fertility, it seems overwhelmingly clear that something other than genetic shifts is affecting DZ twinning rates. Thus the evidence provides no support for Rushton's views regarding the genetic basis for racial differences in this area.

Rushton's parallel claim (Rushton and Bogaert 1987) that there is a genetic basis for socioeconomic differences in DZ twinning rates is even weaker because, contrary to Rushton's assertion, the evidence that there are any consistent class related differences in DZ twinning rates is itself highly questionable. Rushton and Bogaert (1987) make it appear that Nylander's data support the claim of class differences in twinning rates in both Europe and Nigeria. Nylander (1979, 1981) however, reports no evidence for class differences in Nigeria. Because there is no familial tendency towards twinning in Nigeria, however, this suggests that these class differences are not genetically based.

## GENITAL SIZE

In accord with their formulation that blacks are more r-selected than whites or Orientals, Rushton and Bogaert (1987) assert that blacks have larger genitalia than whites, who in turn have larger genitalia than Orientals. One of the major sources for their conclusions is an alleged report of an anonymous French Army Surgeon (1896), a curious source for reliable data. While Rushton and Bogaert (1987, Rushton 1988a) describe the work as an example of the "ethnographic record," it might more accurately be described as an example of nineteenth century "anthroporn." [The anonymous author regales the reader with descriptions of sexual perversions of all sorts, as well as pseudoscientific descriptions of human physical traits, including genitalia of varying size, shape, texture, and color, and the strange sexual customs of a large number of "semi-civilized" peoples. It even contains a recipe for do-it-yourself penis enlargement employing an eggplant and hot peppers!]

This work is filled with internal contradictions. For example, an average African American penis is said to be 7 ¾ to 8 inches long on p. 56, while on p. 242 it is stated that it "generally exceeds" 9 inches. Similarly, while the French Army surgeon announces on p. 56 that he once discovered a 12-inch penis, an organ of that size becomes "far from rare" on p. 243. As one might presume from such a work, there is no indication of the statistical procedures used to compute averages, what terms such as "often" mean, how subjects were selected, how measurements were made, what the sample sizes were, and so on.

Of course a 100-year-old volume of tall tales about the semi-civilized peoples should not be criticized for methodological flaws and internal inconsistencies. The use of such material in a scholarly article raises questions, however, regarding the methodological standards of those who mine such a source for evidence of biologically based race differences. It should be noted that the French Army surgeon (1896) is not an unimportant source. It is Rushton's (Rushton 1988a, Rushton and Bogaert 1987) only source for the "data" on racial differences in clitoral size and on the placement of female genitalia. It is also the only source that contains comparative "data" on male genitalia from all three racial groups, and the only source (e.g., Rushton, 1988a) at all for data on erectile "angle and texture" ("Orientals parallel to the body and stiff, blacks at right angles and flexible," p. 1015).

Much of Rushton's other data (Rushton 1988a, Rushton and Bogaert 1987) on penis size relies heavily on studies based on Kinsey's data, which, as Zuckerman and Brody (1988) point out, can hardly be considered representative. Two more recent publications, however, allow some comparisons to be made between white (Czech) and black (Nigerian) flaccid penises. Farkas (1971) found the average penis length of 177 Czech Army recruits to be 72.18 mm with a circumference of 95.65 mm. Using the same methods of measurement, Ajami, Jain, and Saxena (1985) found the average penis length of Nigerian medical students to be 81.6 mm with a circumference of 88.3 mm.

These sources provided enough numerical detail to test the significance of the size differences. When these tests were carried out, black penises were indeed found to be significantly longer than white ($t = 7.98$ $p < .001$), but white penises had significantly larger circumferences than black ($t = 8.96$ $p < .001$). Thus, while the length of the penis, which perhaps receives more attention because of its visible salience, "favored" blacks in this comparison, circumference did not. Farkas (1971) measured and reported differences in penis size between Bulgarian and Czech males and concluded that penis size differences were attributable to "ethnic, social, alimentary, geographical and other factors" (p. 328). Clearly then, one cannot simply generalize findings obtained from one white (or black) group to whites (or blacks) in general, let alone use them as bases for general black/white comparisons.

However, whether there are some average racial differences in genital size does not seem important, and, like Zuckerman and Brody (1988), we do not find the topic terribly relevant. As Zuckerman and Brody note,

Rushton manifests a "strange naivete" in his attitude toward sex. He ignores the fact that humans dissociate sex and procreation in ways influenced by religion and socio-cultural factors (Zuckerman and Brody 1988).

Rushton's understanding of human sexuality seems to pre-date that of Masters and Johnson (1966) and other modern sexologists. Indeed, following Weinrich (1977), Rushton (1985) assumes that larger genitalia indicates more frequent copulation, while oral-genital contact indicates less. While he assumes that copulation is always aimed at procreation, birth control notwithstanding, oral-genital sex and noncoital sexuality are not taken as indicative of a lack of sexual restraint, as one might think, but as instances of less reproductively oriented (i.e., more K-selected behavior [Rushton, 1985]). Perhaps Rushton and Weinrich make such an interpretation simply because Kinsey data indicate that blacks indulge in less oral-genital and noncoital sex than do whites.

While Kinsey data on sexual behavior are outdated and based on nonrepresentative, nonrandom samples, Rushton and Bogaert (1987, 1988) make a number of racial comparisons relevant to Differential K theory using these data, as presented and described in Gebhard and Johnson (1979). Based on these comparisons, Rushton and Bogaert (1987) conclude that blacks are more precocious and less sexually restrained than whites. The authors seem to have omitted a number of comparisons that run counter to their conclusions, however. For example, although Rushton and Bogaert are quite emphatic about the sexual nature (" . . . mock copulation" p. 546) of African dance, they do not cite Kinsey's data indicating that blacks in his sample dance less than white college students. Rushton and Bogaert also do not mention that the Kinsey survey revealed that blacks are more prudish regarding nudity, are less likely to have a prostitute as their first coital partner, and are less eager, relative to whites, to have large families. (These data are contained in Gebhard and Johnson 1979, Tables 42, 220, 258, 259, 299, 302, and 303.) All of these comparisons appear relevant to Differential K theory, but all of them contradict its predictions. In addition, by carefully selecting the comparisons from the vast number that could be made, Rushton and Bogaert render the reported levels of statistical significance moot.

## BRAIN SIZE AND INTELLIGENCE

Rushton (e.g., Rushton, 1988a) has argued that human races differ in average cranial capacity as well as in brain weight and that there is a correlation between brain size and intelligence. Craniometry, of course, has been long discredited for reasons clearly articulated in Gould's (1981) excellent historical review of the topic. As a scientific tool, craniometry has shown itself to be not merely useless, but positively harmful.

In a review of the topic, Tobias (1970) listed a number of the difficulties involved in measuring and making meaningful comparisons of brain weight. These include equating subjects on age, sex, body size, cause of death, time since death, method of preservation, temperature, and the methods employed in removing and preparing the brain. In addition, brain development is plastic, and brain size may be affected by early environmental factors. Because of all these difficulties, Tobias (1970) concluded that no adequate racial comparative studies had actually been conducted.

Nonetheless, Rushton (1988a) presents comparative cranial data from several sources indicating the expected order of cranial capacity, that is, Orientals > whites > blacks. Although he cites Tobias's (1970) paper, Rushton does not discuss the comparability of the samples nor any of the methodological problems raised by Tobias.

In response to Rushton's (1988a) claims, Zuckerman and Brody (1988) cited a well-known study by Herskovits (1930) that reported only a negligible difference in brain size between American Blacks and British university students. In a rejoinder, Rushton (1988b) cited some additional data provided by Tobias (1970, p. 9), in which Tobias had reported brain sizes for eight different racial subgroups and nationalities corrected for brain/body ratios. For illustrative purposes, Tobias used a formula that translated brain weight into an estimate of the number of neurons available for general adaptive purposes over and above that necessary for maintaining bodily functioning. In his article, Tobias also pointed out that, because there are other cells in the brain besides neurons and because the density and complexity of neurons varies from one part of the brain to another, one had to make a number of implausible assumptions in applying the formula (see Tobias 1970).

Ignoring Tobias's (1970) cautions as well as his conclusions that the racial differences he reports are negligible, Rushton (1988b) used Tobias's illustrative data to compute average racial differences in neuronal number. Rushton (1989a) then reported that Orientals averaged 250 million more neurons than whites who, in turn averaged 100 million more neurons than blacks and concluded that these differences were "sufficient to underlie the cultural differences observed" (p. 1036).

Actually, a most impressive characteristic of Tobias's (1970) data was the variability of the subgroups making up each interracial sample. Zuckerman and Brody (1988) were also impressed by the variability in the craniometric data they examined. In fact, while the Swedish brains were the largest ones among all the racial and ethnic groups described in Tobias's report, they were the smallest ones obtained from any of the Caucasian groups in the Herskovits (1930) study. Interestingly

enough, the brain size of American blacks reported in Tobias's summary were larger than any of the white groups, which included American, French, and English whites) except those from the Swedish subsample, and were estimated to contain some 200 million more neurons than American whites.

Rushton ignores the intraracial variability in cranial size, as well as in other traits, on the grounds that by aggregating scores across each race, unique or idiosyncratic variance (i.e., error) will average out (Rushton and Bogaert 1987). This applies only to random error, however; constant or systematic error cumulates (Gulliksen 1950). As Molnar (1975) has pointed out, ignoring variability that occurs within broad racial groups obscures important differences (p. 97). While the existence of racial differences would not necessarily imply genetic causation in any case, even aggregating data on cranial size across race does not support the idea that there are such differences. Vanderwolf (1989) recently reviewed the literature on racial differences in brain size in the light of Rushton's claims and concluded that Rushton's own survey of the literature was "less than careful" and that, in fact, there was no good evidence supporting these claims.

Rushton also cites several studies to support his hypothesis of a positive relationship between brain size and intelligence. Although Rushton (1988a) correctly reports that Van Valen (1974), the author of one well-known study in the area, computed a correlation coefficient of .30 between brain size and intelligence, that statement by itself is misleading. The average correlation of the studies reported by Van Valen is actually about .10, little different from chance. In order to obtain the .30 correlation, Van Valen argued that the low correlation was actually due to the poor measures of intelligence employed. He then applied a statistical correction to the original correlation based on his "guess" about the amount of information lost due to poor measures, thus obtaining the final "correlation" of .30. This seems to be a somewhat dubious procedure, and Van Valen admitted that his study does not prove that a relationship between brain size and intelligence exists. Indeed, he stated that he knows of no study that directly correlates brain size (or cranial capacity) and intelligence.

Rushton (1989a) also cites several studies by Passingham (1982) in support of his hypothesis. As Rushton himself notes, however, although Passingham concurred with Van Valen's (1974) estimates of a .30 correlation between brain size and intelligence, when Passingham controlled for stature, the correlation vanished. Rushton also cites the results of a second study by Passingham (1982) in which a positive relationship between cranial size and intelligence was reported. As Passingham admits, however, the study was methodologically flawed (IQ was not actually measured, but was estimated from occupational status), and the effect was so small and the groups overlapped to such an extent that Passingham was reluctant to draw any positive conclusions from his findings. In short, there is not reliable evidence indicating that brain size is correlated with intelligence.

## CONCLUSIONS AND DISCUSSION

We have demonstrated that Rushton's Differential K theory has no foundation whatsoever in evolutionary biology, rather, the theory reflects a number of basic misunderstandings about the nature of evolution and genetics. We have also demonstrated that many of Rushton's claims about racial and group differences, including some which are central to his theorizing, are either false, highly overstated, or are much more likely to reflect social and environmental causes than genetic ones.

At a more general level, Rushton's work represents the juxtaposition of two ideas, the first, a belief in an evolutionary hierarchy, a scala naturae, an idea that in its preevolutionary form can be traced to the Greeks. It constitutes, as the historian Arthur Lovejoy (1936) wrote, one of the five or six most basic themes in Western thought.

The idea of the scala naturae quickly became integrated into evolutionary theory, and as Hodos and Campbell (1969) note, the phylogenetic tree, a genealogy, quickly became transformed into a ladder of evolutionary progress with humans at the apex. While the idea that the human races are hierarchically ordered also antedated evolutionary theory, it quickly took its place within the new evolutionary version of the ladder of progress: It was not simply humans who represented the surge of evolutionary progress but, more specifically, white Northern European males.

Blacks, whites, and Orientals were regarded by some as having evolved separately. Coon (1962), for example, hypothesized that the various races evolved independently from different *Homo erectus* ancestors. More commonly, various races were regarded as representing different states of human evolution (Haller 1965). Blacks were hypothesized to represent the later, somewhat degenerate stage, or (as in Rushton) an earlier less advanced one. Thinkers like Herbert Spencer and Lewis Henry Morgan also posited stages of cultural evolution paralleling the putative physical evolution of the groups (Haller 1965).

Hodos and Campbell (1969) point out that while the idea of a scala naturae is scientifically unjustified, it nonetheless continues to exercise a great deal of influence on scientific thought. Certainly those who, like Rushton, argue for the fundamental reality and importance of racial differences often seem to assume that there is such a ladder of evolutionary progress (e.g., Jensen 1980, p. 176).

Rushton's second guiding idea is that there is an inverse relationship between deployment of energy for sex and reproductive purposes on the one hand, and "higher" moral and intellectual purposes on the other. The idea that the poor, and later the feeble-minded, the racially, ethnically, and socially undesirable, were promiscuous and would outbreed the more desirable or advanced segments of the population is an old and powerful one that has often been "biologized" and merged with the belief in a racial evolutionary hierarchy. In this form, these ideas helped fuel the eugenics movements in both Europe and North America (e.g., Kevles 1985, Weizmann 1988) and constituted a major influence on the formulation of Nazi racial doctrine as well (e.g., Chase 1977, Mosse 1978, Muller-Hill 1988).

It is, of course, logically impossible to prove that there are no fundamental genetically based differences in behavior among human groups and races; that would amount to proving the null hypothesis. Propositions of human equality, therefore, always remain fragile and vulnerable to any who care to challenge them. At the same time, however, there are so many enormous methodological, ethical, and practical difficulties involved in establishing important gene or evolutionary-based race and group differences in behavior that one can question whether the study of such differences should command any of our limited scientific resources.

Leaving aside the thorny issue of defining race in order to establish that race differences in behavior have genetic bases, one would have to systematically compare the same race in different environments, and hybrids in all environments. Ideally, one should also be able to employ the experimental techniques that behavior geneticists use to study the interaction of genes and environments in animals, techniques such as cross-fostering and interuterine transplantation. Obviously, such a program would be neither feasible nor desirable. In its absence, however, the collecting and cataloguing of the ad hoc racial differences in behavior says nothing about the evolutionary, genetic, or environmental origins and causes of such differences. It also betrays a rather naive and outdated inductivist view of science.

## REFERENCES

A French Army Surgeon. (1896) *Untrodden Fields of Anthropology: Observations on the Esoteric Manners and Customs of Semi-Civilized Peoples; Being a Record of Thirty Years' Experience in Asia, Africa and America*. Paris: Librairie De Bibliophiles.

Ajami, M. L.; Jain, S. P.; Saxena, S. K. (1985) "Antropometric study of male external genitalia of 320 healthy Nigerian adults." *Antropoligisher Anzeiger*, 43, 179–186.

Angoff, W. H. (1988) "The nature-nurture debate, aptitudes, and group differences." *American Psychologist, 43,* 713–721.

Barash, D. (1979) *The Whisperings Within.* London: Penguin.

Bean, F. D.; Swicegood, G. (1985) *Mexican American Fertility Patterns.* Austin: University of Texas Press.

Begon, M.; Mortimer, M. (1981) *Population Ecology: A United Study of Animals and Plants.* Oxford: Blackwell Scientific Publications.

Benton, M.; Harwood, J. (1975) *The Race Concept.* Newton Abbot, UK: David and Charles.

Boyce, M. S. (1984) "Restitution of r- and K-selection as a model of density dependent selection." *Annual Review of Ecology and Systematics, 15,* 427–444.

Bureau of the Census. (1988) *Statistical abstract of the United States 1988,* 108th ed. Washington, DC: U.S. Department of Commerce.

Chase, A. (1977) *The Legacy of Malthus: The Social Costs of the New Scientific Racism.* New York: Knopf.

Coale, A. J.; Watkins, S. C. (Eds.) (1986) *The Decline of Fertility in Europe: The Revised Proceedings of a Conference on the Princeton European Fertility Project.* Princeton, NJ: Princeton University Press.

Coon, C. S. (1962) *The Origin of Races.* New York: Knopf.

Cravens, H. (1978) *The Triumph of Evolution: American Scientists and the Heredity-Environment Controversy, 1900–1941.* Philadelphia: University of Pennsylvania Press.

Ellis, L. (1987) "Criminal behavior and r/K selection: An extension of gene-based evolutionary theory." *Deviant Behavior, 8,* 149–176.

Falconer, D. S. (1960) *Introduction to Quantitative Genetics.* New York: Ronald.

Farkas, L. G. (1971) "Basic morphological data of external genitals in 177 healthy central European men." *American Journal of Physical Anthropology, 34,* 325–328.

Feldman, M. W.; Lewontin, R. C. (1975) "The heritability hang-up." *Science, 190,* 1163–1168.

Flynn, J. R. (1987) "Massive IQ gains in 14 nations: What IQ tests really measure." *Psychological Bulletin, 101,* 171–191.

Gebhard, P.; Johnson, A. (1979) *The Kinsey Data: Marginal Tabulations of the 1938–1963 Interviews Conducted by the Institute for Sex Research.* Toronto, Ontario: W.B. Saunders.

Gould, S. J. (1981) *The Mismeasure of Man.* New York: Norton.

Gulliksen, H. (1950) *Theory of Mental Tests.* New York: Wiley.

Haller, J. S., Jr. (1965) *Outcasts from Evolution.* New York: McGraw-Hill.

Herskovits, M. J. (1930) *The Anthropometry of the American Negro.* New York: Columbia University Press.

Hirsch, J. (1970) "Behavior genetic analysis and its biosocial consequences." *Seminars in Psychiatry, 2,* 89–105.

Hodos, W.; Campbell, C. B. G. (1969) "*Scalae naturae:* Why there is no theory in comparative psychology." *Psychological Review, 76,* 337–519.

Hostetler, J.; Huntington, G. (1967) *The Hutterites in North America.* New York: Holt, Rinehart, and Winston.

Hrdy, S. B. (1981) *The Woman That Never Evolved.* Cambridge, MA: Harvard University Press.

Hunt, J. McV. (1961) *Intelligence and Experience.* New York: Ronald Press.

James, W. H. (1982) "Second survey of secular trends in twinning rates." *Journal of Biosocial Science, 14,* 481–497.

James, W. H. (1985) "Dizygotic twinning, birth weight and latitude." *Annuals of Human Biology, 12,* 441–447.

James. W. H. (1986) "Recent secular trends in dizygotic twinning rates in Europe." *Journal of Biosocial Science, 18,* 497–504.

Jensen, A. R. (1980) *Bias in Mental Testing.* London: Methoen.

Kevles, D. J. (1985) *In the Name of Eugenics.* Los Angeles: University of California Press.

King, J. C. (1981) *The biology of race* (rev. ed.), Berkeley: University of California Press.

Kiser, C. V.; Grabill, W. H.; Campbell, A. A. (1968) *Trends and Variations in Fertility in the United States.* Cambridge, MA: Harvard University Press.

Lachapelle, R. (1988, Autumn) "Changes in fertility among Canada's linguistic groups." *Canadian Social Trends,* 1–8.

Lovejoy, A. O. (1936) *The Great Chain of Being.* Cambridge, MA: Harvard University Press.

Lumsden, C. J.; Wilson, E. O. (1981) *Genes, Mind and Culture. The Evolutionary Process.* Cambridge, MA: Harvard University Press.

MacArthur, R. H.; Wilson, E. O. (1967) *The Theory of Island Biogeography.* Princeton, NJ: Princeton University Press.

Marinho, A. O.; Ilesanmi, A. O.; Ladel, O. A.; Asuni, O. H.; Omigbodun, A.; Oyejide, C. O. (1986) "A fall in the rate of multiple births in Ibadan and Igbo Ora, Nigeria." *Acta Geneticae et Medicae Gemellologiae, 35,* 201–204.

Masters, W. H.; Johnson, V. E. (1966) *Human Sexual Response.* Boston: Little Brown.

McGuire, T. R.; Hirsch, J. (1977) "General intelligence (g) and heritability ($H^2$,$h_2$)." In *The Structuring of Experience* (pp. 25–72). I. C. Uzgiris and F. Weizmann, eds. New York: Plenum Press.

Molnar, S. (1975). *Races, Types, and Ethnic Groups: The Problem of Human Variation.* Englewood Cliffs, NJ: Prentice Hall.

Morgan, T. H.; Sturtevant, A. H.; Muller, H. J.; Bridges, C. B. (1915) *The Mechanism of Mendelian Heredity.* New York: Holt.

Mosse, G. L. (1978) *Toward the Final Solution: A History of European Racism.* New York: Fertig.

Mousseau, T. A.; Roff, D. A. (1987) "Natural selection and the heritability of fitness components." *Heredity, 59,* 181–197.

Muller-Hill, B. (1988) *Murderous Science: Elimination by Scientific Selection of Jews, Gypsies and Others, Germany 1933–1945.* New York: Oxford University Press.

Murray, B. G., Jr. (1979) *Population Dynamics: Alternative Models.* New York: Academic Press.

Nylander, P. P. S. (1969) "The frequency of twinning in a rural community in Western Nigeria." *Annals of Human Genetics, 33,* 41–44.

Nylander, P. P. S. (1979) "The twinning incidence in Nigeria." *Acta Geneticae et Medicae Gemellologiae, 28,* 261–263.

Nylander, P. P. S. (1981) "The factors that influence twinning rates." *Acta Geneticae et Medicae Gemellologiae, 30,* 189–202.

Oyama, S. (1985) *The Ontogeny of Information: Developmental Systems and Evolution.* Cambridge, UK: Cambridge University Press.

Passingham, R. E. (1982) *The Human Primate.* San Francisco: Freeman.

Paul, D. B. (1985) "Textbook treatments of the genetics of intelligence." *Quarterly Review of Biology,* 60, 317–327.

Pianka, E. R. (1970) "On "r" and "K" selection." *American Naturalist,* 104, 592–597.

Plomin, R. (1983) "Developmental behavior genetics." *Child Development,* 54, 253–259.

Potts, M.; Selman, P. (1979) *Society and Fertility.* Plymouth, UK: Macdonald and Evans.

Roughgarten, J. (1979) *Theory of Population Genetics and Evolutionary Ecology: An Introduction.* New York: Macmillan.

Rushton, J. P. (1984) "Sociobiology: Toward a theory of individual and group differences in personality and social behavior." In *Annals of Theoretical Psychology.* J. R. Royce and L. P. Mos, eds. New York: Plenum Press.

Rushton, J. P. (1985) "Differential K Theory: The sociobiology of individual and group differences." *Personality and Individual Differences,* 6, 441–452.

Rushton, J. P. (1988a) "Race differences in behaviour: A review and evolutionary analysis." *Journal of Personality and Individual Differences,* 9, 1009–1024.

Rushton, J. P. (1988b) "The reality of racial differences: A rejoinder with new evidence." *Journal of Personality and Individual Differences,* 9, 1035–1040.

Rushton, J. P. (1989a) *Evolutionary Biology and Heritable Traits.* Presented at the annual meeting of the American Association for the Advancement of Science, San Francisco, CA.

Rushton, J. P. (1989b) "The generalizability of genetic estimates." *Journal of Personality and Individual Differences,* 10, 985–989.

Rushton, J. P.; Bogaert, A. F. (1987) "Race differences in sexual behavior: Testing an evolutionary hypothesis." *Journal of Personality and Individual Differences,* 20, 529–551.

Rushton, J. P.; Bogaert, A. F. (1988) "Race versus social class differences in sexual behavior: A follow-up test of the r/K dimension." *Journal of Research in Personality and Individual Differences,* 22, 259–272.

Rushton, J. P.; Fulker, D. W.; Neale, M. C.; Nias, D. K. B.; Eysenck, H. J. (1986) "Altruism and aggression: The heritability of individual differences." *Journal of Personality and Social Psychology,* 50, 1192–1198.

Scarr, S. (1981a) "Genetics and the development of intelligence." In *Race, Social Class and Individual Differences* (pp. 3–59). S. Scarr, ed. Hillsdale, NJ: Erlbaum.

Scarr, S. (1981b) "Unknowns in the IQ equation." In *Race, Social Class and Individual Differences* (pp. 61–64). S. Scarr, ed. Hillsdale, NJ: Erlbaum.

Scarr-Salapatek, S. (1971) "Unknowns in the IQ equation [Review of *Environment, Heredity and Intelligence: The IQ Argument and IQ*]." *Science,* 174, 1223–1228.

Schlichting, C. D. (1986) "The evolution of phenotypic plasticity in plants." *Annual Review of Ecology and Systematics,* 17, 667–695.

Stearns, S. C. (1976) "Life history tactics. A review of the ideas." *Quarterly Review of Biology,* 51, 3–47.

Stearns, S. C. (1977) "The evolution of life-history traits: A critique of the theory and a review of the data." *Annual Review of Ecology and Systematics,* 8, 145–171.

Stearns, S. C. (1983) "The influence of size and phylogeny on patterns of covariation among life-history traits in the mammals." *Oikos,* 41, 173–187.

Stringer, C. B.; Andrews, P. (1988) "Genetic and fossil evidence for the origin of modern humans." *Science,* 239, 1263–1268.

Tobias, P. V. (1970) "Brain-size, grey matter and race—fact or fiction." *American Journal of Physical Anthropology,* 32, 3–26.

Trivers, R. L. (1981) "Sociobiology and politics." In *Sociobiology and Human Politics* (pp. 1–45). E. White, ed. Lexington: Lexington Books (D.C. Heath and Co.).

Vanderwolf, C. H. (1989) "Dialogue: Published data on brain weight, volume examined." *Western News,* 25(10), 9.

Van Valen, L. (1974) "Brain size and intelligence in man." *American Journal of Physical Anthropology,* 40, 417–424.

Wachs, T. D. (1983) "The use and abuse of environments in behavior genetic research." *Child Development,* 54, 396–408.

Wahlsten, D. (1979) "A critique of the concepts of heritability and heredity." In *Theoretical Advances in Behavior Genetics* (pp. 425–481). J. R. Royce and L. P. Mos, eds. Germantown: Sijthoff and Noordhoff.

Watkins, S. C. (1986) *The Decline of Fertility in Europe: The Revised Proceedings of a Conference on the Princeton European Fertility Project.* Princeton, NJ: Princeton University Press.

Weinrich, J. D. (1977) "Human sociobiology: Pair-bonding and resource predictability (effects of social class and race)." *Behavioral Ecology and Sociobiology,* 2, 91–118.

Weizmann, F. (1971) "Correlational statistics and the nature-nurture problem." *Science,* 171, 589.

Weizmann, F. (1988) *Eugenics and Child Development: The Role of Eugenics in the Work of Arnold Gesell.* Paper presented at the annual Cheiron Society meeting on the history of the behavioral sciences, Princeton.

Western, D. (1979) "Size, life history and ecology in mammals." *African Journal of Ecology,* 17, 185–204.

Williams, B. J. (1973) *Evolution and Human Origins.* New York: Harper and Row.

Zuckerman, M.; Brody, N. (1988) "Oysters, rabbits and people [A critique of "Race differences in behaviour" by J. P. Rushton]." *Journal of Personality and Individual Differences,* 9, 1025–1033.

# Chapter 31

# *Race, Genes, and IQ—An Apologia*

## Charles Murray and Richard J. Herrnstein

### I.

The private dialogue about race in America is far different from the public one, and we are not referring just to discussions among white rednecks. Our impression is that the private attitudes of white elites toward blacks is strained far beyond any public acknowledgment, that hostility is not uncommon, and that a key part of the strain is a growing suspicion that fundamental racial differences are implicated in the social and economic gap that continues to separate blacks and whites, especially alleged genetic differences in intelligence.

We say "our impression" because we have been in a unique position to gather impressions. Since the beginning of 1990, we have been writing a book about differences in intellectual capacity among people and groups and what those differences mean for America's future. As authors do, we have gotten into numberless conversations that begin, "What are you working on now?" Our interlocutors have included scholars at the top-ranked universities and think tanks, journalists, high public officials, lawyers, financiers, and corporate executives. In the aggregate, they have split about evenly between left and right of the political center.

With rare exceptions, these people have shared one thing besides their success. As soon as the subject turned to the question of IQ, they focused on whether there was any genetic race differences in intelligence. And they tended to be scared stiff about the answer. This experience has led us to be scared as well, about the consequences of ignorance. We have been asked whether the question of racial genetic differences in intelligence should even be raised in polite society. We believe there's no alternative. A taboo issue, filled with potential for hurt and anger, lurks just beneath the surface of American life. It is essential that people begin to talk about this in the open. Because raising this

From *The New Republic,* October 31, 1994. Reprinted by permission from Charles Murray.

question at all provokes a host of fears, it is worth stating at the outset a clear conclusion of our research: The fascination with race, IQ, and genes is misbegotten. There are all sorts of things to be worried about regarding intelligence and American life, and even regarding intelligence and ethnicity. But genetics isn't one of them.

### II.

First, the evidence, beginning with this furiously denied fact: Intelligence is a useful construct. Among the experts, it is by now beyond much technical dispute that there is such a thing as a general factor of cognitive ability on which human beings differ and that this general factor is measured reasonably well by a variety of standardized tests, best of all by IQ tests designed for that purpose. These points are no longer the topic of much new work in the technical journals because most of the questions about them have been answered.

Intelligence as measured by IQ tests is predictive of many educational, economic, and social outcomes. In America today, you are much better off knowing a child's IQ score than her parents' income or education if you want to predict whether she will drop out of high school, for example. If you are an employer trying to predict an applicant's job productivity and are given a choice of just one item of information, you are usually better off asking for an IQ score than a résumé, college transcript, letter of recommendation, or even a job interview. These statements hold true for whites, blacks, Asians, and Latinos alike.

This is not to say that IQ is destiny—in each of these instances, IQ is merely a better predictor than the alternatives, not even close to a perfect one. But it should be stated that the pariah status of intelligence as a construct and IQ as its measure for the past three decades has been a function of political fashion, not science.

Ethnic differences in measured cognitive ability have been found since intelligence tests were invented. The battle over the meaning of these differences is largely responsible for today's controversy over intelligence testing itself. The first thing to remember is that the differences among individuals are far greater than the differences among groups. If all the ethnic differences in intelligence evaporated overnight, most of the intellectual variation in America would endure. The remaining inequality would still strain the political process, because differences in cognitive ability are problematic even in ethnically homogeneous societies.

Even using the word "race" is problematic, which is why we use the word ethnicity as well as race in this article. What does it mean to be "black" in America, in racial terms, when the word black (or African American) can be used for people whose ancestry is more European than African? How are we to classify a person whose parents hail from Panama but whose ancestry is predominantly African? Is he Latino? Black? The rule we follow here is a simple one: to classify people according to the way they classify themselves.

## III.

We might start with a common question in America these days: Do Asians have higher IQs than whites? The answer is probably yes, if Asian refers to the Japanese and Chinese (and perhaps also Koreans), whom we will refer to here as East Asians. How much higher is still unclear. The best tests of this have involved identical IQ tests given to populations that are comparable except for race. In one test, samples of American, British, and Japanese students aged 13 to 15 were given a test of abstract reasoning and spatial relations. The U.S. and U.K. samples had scores within a point of the standardized mean of 100 on both the abstract and spatial relations parts of the test; the Japanese scored 104.5 on the test for abstract reasoning and 114 on the test for spatial relations—a large difference, amounting to a gap similar to the one found by another leading researcher for Asians in America. In a second set of studies, 9-year-olds in Japan, Hong Kong, and Britain, drawn from comparable socioeconomic populations, were administered the Ravens Standard Progressive Matrices. The children from Hong Kong averaged 113; from Japan, 110; and from Britain, 100.

Not everyone accepts that the East Asian–white difference exists. Another set of studies gave a battery of mental tests to elementary school children in Japan, Taiwan, and Minneapolis, Minnesota. The key difference between this study and the other two was that the children were matched carefully on many socioeconomic and demographic variables. No significant difference in overall IQ was found, and the authors concluded that "this study offers no support for the argument that there are differences in the general cognitive functioning of Chinese, Japanese, and American children."

Where does this leave us? The parties in the debate are often confident, and present in their articles are many flat statements that an overall East Asian–white I.Q. difference does, or does not, exist. In our judgment, the balance of the evidence supports the notion that the overall East Asian mean is higher than the white mean. Three IQ points most resembles a consensus, tentative though it still is. East Asians have a greater advantage in a particular kind of nonverbal intelligence.

The issues become far more fraught, however, in determining the answer to the question: Do African Americans score differently from whites on standardized tests of cognitive ability? If the samples are chosen to be representative of the American population, the answer has been yes for every known test of cognitive ability that meets basic psychometric standards. The answer is also yes for almost all studies in which the black and white samples are matched on some special characteristics—juvenile delinquents, for example, or graduate students—but there are exceptions.

How large is the black–white difference? The usual answer is what statisticians call one standard deviation. In discussing I.Q. tests, for example, the black mean is commonly given as 85, the white mean as 100 and the standard deviation as fifteen points. But the differences observed in any given study seldom conform exactly to one standard deviation. In 156 American studies conducted during this century that have reported the IQ means of a black sample and a white sample, and that meet basic requirements of interpretability, the mean black–white difference is 1.1 standard deviations, or about sixteen I.Q. points.

More rigorous selection criteria do not diminish the size of the gap. For example, with tests given outside the South only after 1960, when people were increasingly sensitized to racial issues, the number of studies is reduced to twenty-four, but the mean difference is still 1.1 standard deviations. The National Longitudinal Survey of Youth (NLSY) administered an IQ test in 1980 to by far the largest and most carefully selected national sample (6502 whites, 3022 blacks) and found a difference of 1.2 standard deviations.

Evidence from the SAT, the ACT, and the National Assessment of Educational Progress gives reason to think that the black–white IQ difference has shrunk by perhaps three IQ points in the last twenty years. Almost all the improvement came in the low end, however, progress has stalled for several years and the most direct evidence, from IQ tests of the next generation in the NLSY, points to a widening black–white gap rather than a shrinking one.

It is important to understand that even a difference of 1.2 standard deviations means considerable overlap in the cognitive ability distribution for blacks and whites, as shown for the NLSY population in Figure 31–1. For any

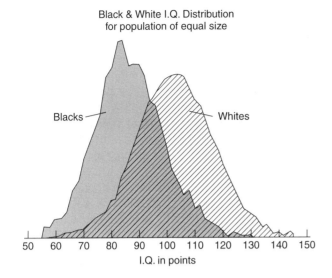

Black & White I.Q. Distribution
for population of equal size

**Figure 31–1** Adapted from an illustration by Jim Holloway for the *New Republic*

equal number of blacks and whites, a large proportion have IQs that can be matched up. For that matter, millions of blacks have higher IQs than the average white. Tens of thousands have IQs that put them in the top few percentiles of the white distribution. It should be no surprise to see (as everyone does every day) African Americans functioning at high levels in every intellectually challenging field. This is the distribution to keep in mind whenever thinking about individuals.

But an additional complication must be taken into account: In the United States, there are about six whites for every black. This means that the IQ overlap of the two populations as they actually exist in the United States looks very different from the overlap in Figure 31–1. Figure 31–2 presents the same data from the NLSY when the distributions are shown in proportion to the actual population of young people in the NLSY. This figure shows why a black–white difference can be problematic to society as a whole. At the lower end of the IQ range, there are about equal numbers of blacks and whites. But throughout the upper half of the range, the disproportions between the number of whites and blacks at any given IQ level are huge. To the extent that the difference represents an authentic difference in cognitive functioning, the social consequences are huge as well. But is the difference authentic? Is it, for example, attributable to cultural bias or other artifacts of the test? There are several ways of assessing this. We'll go through them one by one.

*External Evidence of Bias*

Tests are used to predict things—most commonly, to predict performance in school or on the job. The ability of a test to predict is known as its validity. A test with

high validity predicts accurately; a test with poor validity makes many mistakes. Now suppose that a test's validity differs for the members of two groups. To use a concrete example: The SAT is used as a tool in college admissions because it has a certain validity in predicting college performance. If the SAT is biased against blacks, it will underpredict their college performance. If tests were biased in this way, blacks as a group would do better in college than the admissions office expected based just on their SATs. It would be as if the test underestimated the "true" SAT score of the blacks, so the natural remedy for this would be to compensate the black applicants by, for example, adding the appropriate number of points to their scores.

Predictive bias can work in another way, as when the test is simply less reliable—that is, less accurate—for blacks than for whites. Suppose a test used to select police sergeants is more accurate in predicting the performance of white candidates who become sergeants than in predicting the performance of black sergeants. It doesn't underpredict for blacks, but rather fails to predict at all (or predicts less accurately). In these cases, the natural remedy would be to give less weight to the test scores of blacks than to those of whites.

The key concept for both types of bias is the same: A test biased against blacks does not predict black performance in the real world in the same way that it predicts white performance in the real world. The evidence of bias is external in the sense that it shows up in differing validities for blacks and whites. External evidence of bias has been sought in hundreds of studies. It has been evaluated relative to performance in elementary school, in the university, in the military, in unskilled and skilled jobs, in the professions. Overwhelmingly, the evidence is that the standardized tests used to help make school and

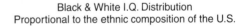

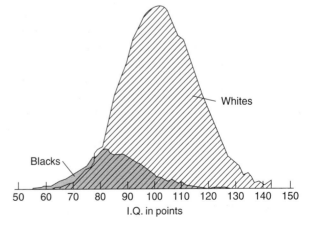

**Figure 31–2** Adapted from an illustration by Jim Holloway for the *New Republic*

job decisions do not underpredict black performance. Nor does the expert community find any other systematic difference in the predictive accuracy of tests for blacks and whites.

### Internal Evidence of Bias

The most common charges of cultural bias involve the putative cultural loading of items in a test. Here is an SAT analogy item that has become famous as an example of cultural bias:

> RUNNER: MARATHON (A) envoy: embassy (B) martyr: massacre (C) oarsman: regatta (D) referee: tournament (E) horse: stable

The answer is "oarsman: regatta"—fairly easy if you know what both a marathon and a regatta are, a matter of guesswork otherwise. How would a black youngster from the inner city ever have heard of a regatta? Many view such items as proof that the tests must be biased against people from disadvantaged backgrounds. "Clearly," writes a critic of testing, citing this example, "this item does not measure students' 'aptitude' or logical reasoning ability, but knowledge of upper-middle class recreational activity." In the language of psychometrics, this is called internal evidence of bias.

The hypothesis of bias again lends itself to direct examination. In effect, the SAT critic is saying that culturally loaded items are producing at least some of the black-white difference. Get rid of such items, and the gap will narrow. Is he correct? When we look at the results for items that have answers such as "oarsman: regatta" and the results for items that seem to be empty of any cultural information (repeating a sequence of numbers, for example), are there any differences?

The technical literature is again clear. In study after study of the leading tests, the idea that the black–white difference is caused by questions with cultural content has been contradicted by the facts. Items that the average white test-taker finds easy relative to other items, the average black test-taker does, too; the same is true for items that the average white and black find difficult. Inasmuch as whites and blacks have different overall scores on the average, it follows that a smaller proportion of blacks get right answers for either easy or hard items, but the order of difficulty is virtually the same in each racial group. How can this be? The explanation is complicated and goes deep into the reasons why a test item is "good" or "bad" in measuring intelligence. Here, we restrict ourselves to the conclusion: *The black–white difference is generally wider on items that appear to be culturally neutral than on items that appear to be culturally loaded.* We italicize this point because it is so well established empirically yet comes as such a surprise to most people who are new to this topic.

### Motivation to Try

Suppose the nature of cultural bias does not lie in predictive validity or in the content of the items but in what might be called "test willingness." A typical black youngster, it is hypothesized, comes to such tests with a mindset different from the white subject's. He is less attuned to testing situations (from one point of view), or less inclined to put up with such nonsense (from another). Perhaps he just doesn't give a damn, since he has no hopes of going to college or otherwise benefiting from a good test score. Perhaps he figures that the test is biased against him anyway, so what's the point. Perhaps he consciously refuses to put forth his best effort because of the peer pressure against "acting white" in some inner-city schools.

The studies that have attempted to measure motivation in such situations generally have found that blacks are at least as motivated as whites. But these are not wholly convincing, for why shouldn't the measures of motivation be just as inaccurate as the measures of cognitive ability are alleged to be? Analysis of internal characteristics of the tests once again offers the best leverage in examining this broad hypothesis. Here, we will offer just one example involving the "digit span" subtest, part of the widely used Wechsler intelligence tests. It has two forms: forward digit span, in which the subject tries to repeat a sequence of numbers in the order read to him, and backward digit span, in which the subject tries to repeat the sequence of numbers backward. The test is simple, uses numbers familiar to everyone and calls on no cultural information besides numbers. The digit span is informative regarding test motivation not just because of the low cultural loading of the items but because the backward form is a far better measure of "*g*," the psychometrician's shorthand for the general intelligence factor that I.Q. tests try to measure. The reason that the backward form is a better measure of *g* is that reversing the numbers is mentally more demanding than repeating them in the heard order, as you can determine for yourself by a little self-testing.

The two parts of the subtest have identical content. They occur at the same time during the test. Each subject does both. But in most studies the black–white difference is about twice as great on backward digits as on forward digits. The question then arises: How can lack of motivation (or test willingness) explain the difference in performance on the two parts of the same subtest?

This still leaves another obvious question: Are the differences in overall black and white test scores attributable to differences in socioeconomic status? This question has two different answers depending on how the question is understood, and confusion is rampant. There are two essential answers and two associated rationales.

First version: If you extract the effects of socioeconomic class, what happens to the magnitude of the black–white difference? Blacks are disproportionately in the lower socioeconomic classes, and class is known to be associated with IQ. Therefore, many people suggest, part of what appears to be an ethnic difference in IQ scores is actually a socioeconomic difference. The answer to this version of the question is that the size of the gap shrinks when socioeconomic status is statistically extracted. The NLSY gives a result typical of such analyses. The black–white difference in the NLSY is 1.2. In a regression equation in which both race and socioeconomic background are entered, the difference between whites and blacks shrinks to less than .8 standard deviation. Socioeconomic status explains 37 percent of the original black–white difference. This relationship is in line with the results from many other studies.

The difficulty comes in interpreting what it means to "control" for socioeconomic status. Matching the status of the groups is usually justified on the grounds that the scores people earn are caused to some extent by their socioeconomic status, so if we want to see the "real" or "authentic" difference between them, the contribution of status must be excluded. The trouble is that socioeconomic status is also a result of intelligence, as people of high and low cognitive ability move to high and low places in the class structure. The reason parents have high or low socioeconomic status is in part a function of their intelligence, and their intelligence also affects the IQ of the children via both genes and environment.

Because of these relationships, "controlling" for socioeconomic status in racial comparisons is guaranteed to reduce IQ differences in the same way that choosing black and white samples from a school for the intellectually gifted is guaranteed to reduce IQ differences (assuming raceblind admissions standards). These complications aside, a reasonable guideline is that controlling for socioeconomic status reduces the overall black–white difference by about one-third.

Second version: As blacks move up the socioeconomic ladder, do the differences with whites of similar socioeconomic status diminish? The first version of the SES/IQ question referred to the overall score of a population of blacks and whites. The second version concentrates on the black–white difference within socioeconomic classes. The rationale goes like this: Blacks score lower on average because they are socioeconomically at a disadvantage. This disadvantage should most seriously handicap children in the lower socioeconomic classes, who suffer from greater barriers to education and job advancement than do children in the middle and upper classes. As blacks advance up the socioeconomic ladder, their children, less exposed to these barriers, will do better and, by extension, close the gap with white children of their class.

This expectation is not borne out by the data. A good way to illustrate this is to use an index of parental SES based on their education, income, and occupation

and to match it against the mean IQ score, as shown in Figure 31–3. IQ scores increase with economic status for both races. But as the figure shows, the magnitude of the black–white difference in standard deviations does not decrease. Indeed, it gets larger as people move up from the very bottom of the socioeconomic ladder. The pattern shown in the figure is consistent with many other major studies, except that the gap flattens out. In other studies, the gap has continued to increase throughout the range of socioeconomic status.

## IV.

This brings us to the flashpoint of intelligence as a public topic: the question of genetic differences between the races. Expert opinion, when it is expressed at all, diverges widely. In the 1980s Mark Snyderman, a psychologist, and Stanley Rothman, a political scientist, sent a questionnaire to a broad sample of 1020 scholars, mostly academicians, whose specialties give them reason to be knowledgeable about IQ. Among other questions, they asked "Which of the following best characterizes your opinion of the heritability of the black–white difference in IQ?" The answers were divided as follows: The difference is entirely due to environmental variation: 15 percent. The difference is entirely due to genetic variation: 1 percent. The difference is a product of both genetic and environmental variation: 45 percent. The data are insufficient to support any reasonable opinion: 24 percent. No response: 14 percent.

This pretty well sums up the professional judgment on the matter. But it doesn't explain anything about the environment/genetic debate as it has played out in the profession and in the general public. And the question, of course, is fascinating. So what could help us

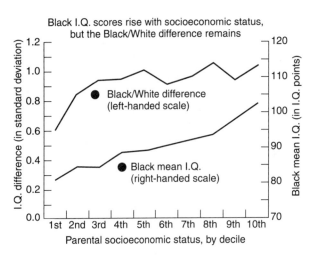

**Figure 31–3** Adapted from an illustration by Jim Holloway for the *New Republic*

understand the connection between heritability and group differences? A good place to start is by correcting a common confusion about the role of genes in individuals and in groups.

Most scholars accept that IQ in the human species as a whole is substantially heritable, somewhere between 40 percent and 80 percent, meaning that much of the observed variation in IQ is genetic. And yet this information tells us nothing for sure about the origin of the differences between groups of humans in measured intelligence. This point is so basic, and so misunderstood, that it deserves emphasis: that a trait is genetically transmitted in a population does not mean that group differences in that trait are also genetic in origin. Anyone who doubts this assertion may take two handfuls of genetically identical seed corn and plant one handful in Iowa, the other in the Mojave Desert, and let nature (i.e., the environment) take its course. The seeds will grow in Iowa, not in the Mojave, and the result will have nothing to do with genetic differences.

The environment for American blacks has been closer to the Mojave and the environment for American whites has been closer to Iowa. We may apply this general observation to the available data and see where the results lead. Suppose that all the observed ethnic differences in tested intelligence originate in some mysterious environmental differences—mysterious, because we know from material already presented that socioeconomic factors cannot be much of the explanation. We further stipulate that one standard deviation (fifteen IQ points) separates American blacks and whites and that one-fifth of a standard deviation (three IQ points) separates East Asians and whites. Finally, we assume that IQ is 60 percent heritable (a middle-ground estimate). Given these parameters, how different would the environments for the three groups have to be in order to explain the observed difference in these scores?

The observed ethnic differences in IQ could be explained solely by the environment if the mean environment of whites is 1.58 standard deviations better than the mean environment of blacks and .32 standard deviation worse than the mean environment for East Asians, when environments are measured along the continuum of their capacity to nurture intelligence. Let's state these conclusions in percentile terms: The average environment of blacks would have to be at the sixth percentile of the distribution of environments among whites and the average environment of East Asians would have to be at the sixty-third percentile of environments among whites for the racial differences to be entirely environmental.

Environmental differences of this magnitude and pattern are wildly out of line with all objective measures of the differences in black, Asian, and white environments. Recall further that the black–white difference is smallest at the lowest socioeconomic levels. Why, if the black–white difference is entirely environmental, should the advantage of the "white" environment compared to the "black" be greater among the better-off and better-educated blacks and whites? We have not been able to think of a plausible reason. Can you? An appeal to the effects of racism to explain ethnic differences also requires explaining why environments poisoned by discrimination and racism for some other groups—against the Chinese or the Jews in some regions of America for example—have left them with higher scores than the national average.

However discomfiting it may be to consider it, there are reasons to suspect genetic considerations are involved. The evidence is circumstantial, but provocative. For example, ethnicities differ not just in average scores but in the profile of intellectual capacities. A full-scale IQ score is the aggregate of many subtests. There are thirteen of them in the Wechsler Intelligence Scale for Children, for example. The most basic division of the subtests is into a verbal IQ and a performance IQ. In white samples the verbal and performance IQ subscores tend to have about the same mean, because IQ tests have been standardized on predominantly white populations. But individuals can have imbalances between these two IQs. People with high verbal abilities are likely to do well with words and logic. In school they excel in history and literature; in choosing a career to draw on those talents, they tend to choose law or journalism or advertising or politics. In contrast, people with high performance IQs—or, using a more descriptive phrase, "visuospatial abilities"—are likely to do well in the physical and biological sciences, mathematics, engineering, or other subjects that demand mental manipulation in the three physical dimensions or the more numerous dimensions of mathematics.

East Asians living overseas score about the same or slightly lower than whites on verbal IQ and substantially higher on visuospatial IQ. Even in the rare studies that have found overall Japanese or Chinese IQs no higher than white IQs, the discrepancy between verbal and visuospatial IQ persists. For Japanese living in Asia, a 1987 review of the literature demonstrated without much question that the verbal-visuospatial difference persists even in examinations that have been thoroughly adapted to the Japanese language and, indeed, in tests developed by the Japanese themselves. A study of a small sample of Korean infants adopted into white families in Belgium found the familiar elevated visuospatial scores.

This finding has an echo in the United States, where Asian American students abound in science subjects, in engineering and in medical schools, but are scarce in law schools and graduate programs in the humanities and social sciences. Is this just a matter of parental pressures or of Asian immigrants uncomfortable with English? The same pattern of subtest scores is found in Inuits and American Indians (both of Asian origin) and in fully assimilated second- and third-generation Asian Americans. Any simple socioeconomic, cultural, or linguistic explanation is out of the question, given the diversity of living conditions, native languages, educational systems and cultural practices experienced by these groups and by East Asians living in Asia. Their common genetic history cannot plausibly be dismissed as irrelevant.

Turning now to blacks and whites (using these terms to refer exclusively to Americans), ability profiles also have been important in understanding the nature, and possible genetic component, of group differences. The argument has been developing around what is known as Spearman's hypothesis. This hypothesis says that if the black–white difference on test scores reflects a real underlying difference in general mental ability (*g*), then the size of the black–white difference will be related to the degree to which the test is saturated with *g*. In other words, the better a test measures *g*, the larger the black–white difference will be.

By now, Spearman's hypothesis has been borne out in fourteen major studies, and no appropriate data set has yet been found that contradicts Spearman's hypothesis. It should be noted that not all group differences behave similarly. For example, deaf children often get lower test scores than hearing children, but the size of the difference is not correlated positively with the test's loading on *g*. The phenomenon seems peculiarly concentrated in comparisons of ethnic groups. How does this bear on the genetic explanation of ethnic differences? In plain though somewhat imprecise language: The broadest conception of intelligence is embodied in *g*. At the same time, *g* typically has the highest heritability (higher than the other factors measured by IQ tests). As mental measurement focuses most specifically and reliably on *g*, the observed black–white mean difference in cognitive ability gets larger. This does not in itself demand a genetic explanation of the ethnic difference but, by asserting that "the better the test, the greater the ethnic difference," Spearman's hypothesis undercuts many of the environmental explanations of the difference that rely on the proposition (again, simplifying) that the apparent black–white difference is the result of bad tests, not good ones.

There are, of course, many arguments against such a genetic explanation. Many studies have shown that the disadvantaged environment of some blacks has depressed their test scores. In one study, in black families in rural Georgia, the elder sibling typically had a lower IQ than the younger. The larger the age difference is between the siblings, the larger is the difference in IQ. The implication is that something in the rural Georgia environment was depressing the scores of black children as they grew older. In neither the white families of Georgia, nor white or black families in Berkeley, California, were there comparable signs of a depressive effect of the environment.

Another approach is to say that tests are artifacts of a culture, and a culture may not diffuse equally into every household and community. In a heterogeneous society, subcultures vary in ways that inevitably affect scores on IQ tests. Fewer books in the home mean less exposure to the material that a vocabulary subtest measures; the varying ways of socializing children may influence whether a child acquires the skills, or a desire for the skills, that tests test; the "common knowledge" that tests supposedly draw on may not be common in certain households and neighborhoods.

So far, this sounds like a standard argument about cultural bias, and yet it accepts the generalizations that we discussed earlier about internal evidence of bias. The supporters of this argument are not claiming that less exposure to books means that blacks score lower on vocabulary questions but do as well as whites on culture free items. Rather, the effects of culture are more diffuse.

Furthermore, strong correlations between home or community life and IQ scores are readily found. In a study of 180 Latino and 180 non-Latino white elementary school children in Riverside, California, the researcher examined eight sociocultural variables: (1) mother's participation in formal organizations, (2) living in a segregated neighborhood, (3) home language level, (4) socioeconomic status based on occupation and education of head of household, (5) urbanization, (6) mother's achievement values, (7) home ownership, and (8) intact biological family. She then showed that once these sociocultural variables were taken into account, the remaining group and IQ differences among the children fell to near zero.

The problem with this procedure lies in determining what, in fact, these eight variables control for: cultural diffusion, or genetic sources of variation in intelligence as ordinarily understood? By so drastically extending the usual match for socioeconomic status, the possibility is that such studies demonstrate only that parents matched on IQ will produce children with similar IQs—not a startling finding. Also, the data used for such studies continue to show the distinctive racial patterns in the subtests. Why should cultural diffusion manifest itself by differences in backward and forward digit span or in completely nonverbal items? If the role of European white cultural diffusion is so important in affecting black IQ scores, why is it so unimportant in affecting Asian IQ scores?

There are other arguments related to cultural bias. In the American context, Wade Boykin is one of the most prominent academic advocates of a distinctive black culture, arguing that nine interrelated dimensions put blacks at odds with the prevailing Eurocentric model. Among them are spirituality (blacks approach life as "essentially vitalistic rather than mechanistic, with the conviction that non-material forces influence people's everyday lives"); a belief in the harmony between humankind and nature; an emphasis on the importance of movement, rhythm, music and dance, "which are taken as central to psychological health"; personal styles that he characterizes as "verve" (high levels of stimulation and energy) and "affect" (emphasis on emotions and expressiveness); and "social time perspective," which he defines as "an orientation in which time is treated as passing through a social space rather than a material one." Such analyses purport to explain how large black–white differences in test scores could coexist with equal predictive validity of the test for such things as academic and job performance and yet still not be based on differences in "intelligence," broadly defined, let alone genetic differences.

John Ogbu, a Berkeley anthropologist, has proposed a more specific version of this argument. He suggests that we look at the history of various minority groups to understand the sources of differing levels of intellectual attainment in America. He distinguishes three types of minorities: "autonomous minorities" such as the Amish, Jews, and Mormons, who, while they may be victims of discrimination, are still within the cultural mainstream; "immigrant minorities," such as the Chinese, Filipinos, Japanese, and Koreans within the United States, who moved voluntarily to their new societies and, while they may begin in menial jobs, compare themselves favorably with their peers back in the home country; and, finally, "castelike minorities," such as black Americans, who were involuntary immigrants or otherwise are consigned from birth to a distinctively lower place on the social ladder. Ogbu argues that the differences in test scores are an outcome of this historical distinction, pointing to a number of castes around the world—the untouchables in India, the Buraku in Japan, and Oriental Jews in Israel—that have exhibited comparable problems in educational achievement despite being of the same racial group as the majority.

Indirect support for the proposition that the observed black–white difference could be the result of environmental factors is provided by the worldwide phenomenon of rising test scores. We call it "the Flynn effect" because of psychologist James Flynn's pivotal role in focusing attention on it, but the phenomenon itself was identified in the 1930s when testers began to notice that IQ scores often rose with every successive year after a test was first standardized. For example, when the Stanford-Binet I.Q. was restandardized in the mid-1930s, it was observed that individuals earned lower IQs on the new tests than they got on the Stanford-Binet that had been standardized in the mid-1910s; in other words, getting a score of 100 (the population average) was harder to do on the later test. This meant that the average person could answer more items on the old test than on the new test. Most of the change has been concentrated in the nonverbal portions of the tests.

The tendency for IQ scores to drift upward as a function of years since standardization has now been substantiated in many countries and on many IQ tests besides the Stanford-Binet. In some countries, the upward drift since World War II has been as much as a point per year for some spans of years. The national averages have in fact changed by amounts that are comparable to the fifteen or so IQ points separating whites and blacks in America. To put it another way, on the average, whites today may differ in IQ from whites, say, two generations ago as much as whites today differ from blacks today. Given their size and speed, the shifts in time necessarily have been due more to changes in the environment than to changes in the genes. The question then arises: Couldn't the mean of blacks move fifteen points as well through environmental changes? There seems no reason why not—but also no reason to believe that white and Asian means can be made to stand still while the Flynn effect works its magic.

### V.

As of 1994, then, we can say nothing for certain about the relative roles that genetics and environment play in the formation of the black–white difference in IQ. All the evidence remains indirect. The heritability of individual differences in IQ does not necessarily mean that ethnic differences are also heritable. But those who think that ethnic differences are readily explained by environmental differences haven't been tough-minded enough about their own argument. At this complex intersection of complex factors, the easy answers are unsatisfactory ones.

Given the weight of the many circumstantial patterns, it seems improbable to us—though possible—that genes have no role whatsoever. What might the mix of genetic and environmental influences be? We are resolutely agnostic on that.

Here is what we hope will be our contribution to the discussion. We put it in italics; if we could, we would put it in neon lights: *The answer doesn't much matter.* Whether the black–white difference in test scores is produced by genes or the environment has no bearing on any of the reasons why the black–white difference is worth worrying about. If tomorrow we knew beyond a shadow of a doubt what role, if any, were played by genes, the news would be neither good if ethnic differences were predominantly environmental, nor awful if they were predominantly genetic.

The first reason for this assertion is that what matters is not whether differences are environmental or genetic, but how hard they are to change. Many people have a fuzzy impression that if cognitive ability has been depressed by a disadvantaged environment, it is easily remedied. Give the small child a more stimulating environment, give the older child a better education, it is thought, and the environmental deficit can be made up.

This impression is wrong. The environment unquestionably has an impact on cognitive ability, but a record of interventions going back more than fifty years has demonstrated how difficult it is to manipulate the environment so that cognitive functioning is improved. The billions of dollars spent annually on compensatory education under Title I of the Elementary and Secondary Education Act have had such a dismal evaluation record that improving general cognitive functioning is no longer even a goal. Preschool education fares little better. Despite extravagant claims that periodically get their fifteen minutes of fame, preschool education, including not just ordinary Head Start but much more intensive programs such as Perry Preschool, raises IQ scores by a few points on the exit test, and even those small gains quickly fade. Preschool programs may be good for children in other ways, but they do not have important effects on intelligence. If larger effects are possible, it is only through truly heroic efforts, putting children into full-time, year-round, highly enriched day care from within a few months of birth and keeping them there for the first five years of life—and even those effects, claimed by the Milwaukee Program and the Abecedarian Project, are subject to widespread skepticism among scholars.

In short: If it were proved tomorrow that ethnic differences in test scores were entirely environmental, there would be no reason to celebrate. That knowledge would not suggest a single educational, preschool, daycare, or prenatal program that is not already being tried, and would give no reason to believe that tomorrow's effects from such programs will be any more encouraging than those observed to date. Radically improved knowledge about child development and intelligence is required, not better implementation of what is already known. No breakthroughs are in sight.

The second reason that the concern about genes is overblown is the mistaken idea that genes mean there is nothing to be done. On the contrary, the distributions of genetic traits in a population can change over time, because people who die are not replaced one-for-one by babies with matched DNA. Just because there might be a genetic difference among groups in this generation does not mean that it cannot shrink. Nor, for that matter, does genetic equality in this generation mean that genetic differences might not arise within a matter of decades. It depends on which women in which group have how many babies at what ages. More broadly, genetic causes do not leave us helpless. Myops see fine with glasses and many bald men look as if they have hair, however closely myopia and baldness are tied to genes. Check out visual aids and gimmicks on any Macintosh computer to see how technology can compensate for innumeracy and illiteracy.

Now comes the third reason that the concern about genes needs rethinking. It is to us the most compelling: There is no *rational* reason why any encounter between individuals should be affected in any way by the knowledge that a group difference is genetic instead of environmental. Suppose that the news tomorrow morning is that the black–white difference in cognitive test scores is rooted in genetic differences. Suppose further that tomorrow afternoon, you—let us say you are white—encounter a random African American. Try to think of any way in which anything has changed that should affect your evaluation of or response to that individual and you will soon arrive at a truth that ought to be assimilated by everyone: Nothing has changed. That an individual is a member of a group with a certain genetically based mean and distribution in any characteristic, whether it be height, intelligence, predisposition to schizophrenia, or eye color has no effect on that reality of that individual. A five-foot man with six-foot parents is still five feet tall, no matter how much height is determined by genes. An African American with an IQ of 130 still has an IQ of 130, no matter what the black mean may be or to what extent IQ is determined by genes. Maybe for some whites, behavior toward black individuals would change if it were known that certain ethnic differences were genetic—but not for any good reason.

We have been too idealistic, one may respond. In the real world, people treat individuals according to their membership in a group. Consider the young black male trying to catch a taxi. It makes no difference how honest he is; many taxi drivers will refuse to pick him up because young black males disproportionately account for taxi robberies. Similarly, some people fear that talking about group differences in IQ will encourage employers to use ethnicity as an inexpensive screen if they can get away with it, not bothering to consider black candidates.

These are authentic problems that need to be dealt with. But it puzzles us to hear them raised as a response to the question, "What difference does it make if genes are involved?" Two separate issues are being conflated: the reality of a difference versus its source. An employer has no more incentive to discriminate by ethnicity if he knows that a difference in ability is genetic than if he knows it is "only" environmental. To return to an earlier point, the key issue is how intractable the difference is. By the time someone is applying for a job, his cognitive functioning can be tweaked only at the margins, if at all, regardless of the original comparative roles of genes and environment in producing that level of cognitive functioning. The existence of a group difference may make a difference in the behavior of individuals toward other individuals, with implications that may well spill over into policy, but the source of the difference is irrelevant to the behavior.

## VI.

In *The Bell Curve*, we make all of the above points, document them fully and are prepared to defend them against all comers. We argue that the best and indeed only answer to the problem of group differences is an energetic and uncompromising recommitment to individualism.

To judge someone except on his or her own merits was historically thought to be un-American, and we urge that it become so again.

But as we worked on the discussion in the book, we also became aware that ratiocination is not a sufficient response. Many people instinctively believe that genetically caused group differences in intelligence must be psychologically destructive in a way that environmentally caused differences are not. In a way, our informal survey of elites during the writing of the book confirmed this. No matter what we said, we found that people walked away muttering that it *does* make a difference if genes are involved. But we nonetheless are not persuaded. It seems to us that, on the contrary, human beings have it in them to live comfortably with all kinds of differences, group and individual alike.

We did not put those thoughts into the book. Early on, we decided that the passages on ethnic differences in intelligence had to be inflexibly pinned to data. Speculations were out, and even provocative turns of phrase had to be guarded against. The thoughts we are about to express are decidedly speculative, and hence did not become part of our book. But if you will treat them accordingly, we think they form the basis of a conversation worth beginning, and we will open it here.

As one looks around the world at the huge variety of ethnic groups that have high opinions of themselves, for example, one is struck by how easy it is for each of these clans, as we will call them, to conclude that it has the best combination of genes and culture in the world. In each clan's eyes, its members are blessed to have been born who they are—Arab, Chinese, Jew, Welsh, Russian, Spanish, Zulu, Scots, Hungarian. The list could go on indefinitely, breaking into ever smaller groups (highland Scots, Glaswegians, Scotch-Irish). The members of each clan do not necessarily think their people have gotten the best break regarding their political or economic place in the world, but they do not doubt the intrinsic, unique merits of their particular clan.

How does this clannish self-esteem come about? Any one dimension, including intelligence, clearly plays only a small part. The self-esteem is based on a mix of qualities. These packages of qualities are incomparable across clans. The mixes are too complex, the metrics are too different, the qualities are too numerous to lend themselves to a weighting scheme that everyone could agree upon. The Irish have a way with words; the Irish also give high marks to having a way with words in the pantheon of human abilities. The Russians see themselves as soulful; they give high marks to soulfulness. The Scotch-Irish who moved to America tended to be cantankerous, restless, and violent. Well, say the American Scotch-Irish proudly, these qualities made for terrific pioneers.

We offer this hypothesis: Clans tend to order the world, putting themselves on top, not because each clan has an inflated idea of its own virtues, but because each is using a weighting algorithm that genuinely works out that way. One of us had a conversation with a Thai many years ago about the Thai attitude toward Americans. Americans have technology and capabilities that the Thais do not have, he said, just as the elephant is stronger than a human. But," he said with a shrug, "who wants to be an elephant?" We do not consider his view quaint. There is an internally consistent logic that legitimately might lead a Thai to conclude that being born Thai gives one a better chance of becoming a complete human being than being born American. He may not be right, but he is not necessarily wrong.

If these observations have merit, why is it that one human clan occasionally develops a deep-seated sense of ethnic inferiority vis-à-vis another clan? History suggests that the reasons tend to be independent of any particular qualities of the two groups, but instead are commonly rooted in historical confrontations. When one clan has been physically subjugated by another, the psychological reactions are complex and long-lasting. The academic literature on political development is filled with studies of the reactions of colonized peoples that prove this case. These self-denigrating reactions are not limited to the common people; if anything, they are most profound among the local elites. Consider, for example, the deeply ambivalent attitudes of Indian elites toward the British. The Indian cultural heritage is glittering, but that heritage was not enough to protect Indian elites from the psychological ravages of being subjugated.

Applying these observations to the American case and to relations between blacks and whites suggests a new way of conceptualizing the familiar "legacy of slavery" arguments. It is not just that slavery surely had lasting effects on black culture, nor even that slavery had broad negative effect on black self-confidence and self-esteem, but more specifically that the experience of slavery perverted and stunted the evolution of the ethnocentric algorithm that American blacks would have developed in the normal course of events. Whites did everything in their power to explain away or belittle every sign of talent, virtue, or superiority among blacks. They had to—if the slaves were superior in qualities that whites themselves valued, where was the moral justification for keeping them enslaved? And so everything that African Americans did well had to be cast in terms that belittled the quality in question. Even to try to document this point leaves one open to charges of condescension, so successfully did whites manage to coopt the value judgments. Most obviously, it is impossible to speak straightforwardly about the dominance of many black athletes without being subject to accusations that one is being backhandedly antiblack.

The nervous concern about racial inferiority in the United States is best seen as a variation on the colonial experience. It is in the process of diminishing as African

Americans define for themselves that mix of qualities that makes the American black clan unique and (appropriately in the eyes of the clan) superior. It emerges in fiction by black authors and in a growing body of work by black scholars. It is also happening in the streets. The process is not only normal and healthy; it is essential.

In making these points, there are several things we are not saying that need to be spelled out. We are not giving up on the melting pot. Italians all over America who live in neighborhoods without a single other Italian, and who may technically have more non-Italian than Italian blood, continue to take pride in their Italian heritage in the ways we have described. The same may be said of other ethnic clans. For that matter, we could as easily have used the examples of Texans and Minnesotans as of Thais and Scotch-Irish in describing the ways in which people naturally take pride in their group. Americans often see themselves as members of several clans at the same time—and think of themselves as 100 percent American as well. It is one of America's most glorious qualities.

We are also not trying to tell African Americans or anyone else what qualities should be weighted in their algorithm. Our point is precisely the opposite: No one needs to tell any clan how to come up with a way of seeing itself that is satisfactory; it is one of those things that human communities know how to do quite well when left alone to do it. Still less are we saying that the children from any clan should not, say, study calculus because studying calculus is not part of the clan's heritages. Individuals strike out on their own, making their way in the Great World according to what they bring to their endeavors as individuals—and can still take comfort and pride in their group affiliations. Of course there are complications and tensions in this process. The tighter the clan, the more likely it is to look suspiciously on their children who depart for the Great World—and yet also, the more proudly it is likely to boast of their successes once they have made it, and the more likely that the children will one day restore some of their ties with the clan they left behind. This is one of the classic American dramas.

We are not preaching multiculturalism. Our point is not that everything is relative and the accomplishments of each culture and ethnic group are just as good as those of every other culture and ethnic group. Instead, we are saying a good word for a certain kind of ethnocentrism. Given a chance, each clan will add up its accomplishments using its own weighting system, will encounter the world with confidence in its own worth and, most importantly, will be unconcerned about comparing its accomplishments line-by-line with those of any other clan. This is wise echnocentrism.

In the context of intelligence and IQ scores, we are urging that it is foolish ethnocentrism on the part of Eu-

ropean Americans to assume that mean differences in IQ among ethnic groups must mean that those who rank lower on that particular dimension are required to be miserable about it—all the more foolish because the group IQ of the prototypical American clan, white Protestants, is some rungs from the top.

It is a difficult point to make persuasively, because the undoubted reality of our era is that group differences in intelligence are intensely threatening and feared. One may reasonably ask what point there is in speculating about some better arrangement in which it wouldn't matter. And yet there remain stubborn counterfactuals that give reason for thinking that inequalities in intelligence need not be feared—not just theoretically, but practically.

We put it as a hypothesis that lends itself to empirical test: hardly anyone feels inferior to people who have higher IQs. If you doubt this, put it to yourself. You surely have known many people who are conspicuously smarter than you are, in terms of sheer intellectual horsepower. Certainly we have. There have been occasions when we thought it would be nice to be as smart as these other people. But, like the Thai who asked, "Who wants to be an elephant?" we have not felt inferior to our brilliant friends, nor have we wanted to trade places with them. We have felt a little sorry for some of them, thinking that despite their high intelligence they lacked other qualities that we possessed and that we valued more highly than their extra IQ points.

When we have remarked upon this to friends, their reaction has often been, "That's fine for you to say, because you're smart enough already." But we are making a more ambitious argument: It is not just people with high IQs who don't feel inferior to people with even higher IQs. The rule holds true all along the IQ continuum.

It is hard to get intellectuals to accept this, because of another phenomenon that we present as a hypothesis, but are fairly confident can be verified: People with high IQs tend to condescend to people with lower IQs. Once again, put yourself to the test. Suppose we point to a person with an IQ thirty points lower than yours. Would you be willing to trade places with him? Do you instinctively feel a little sorry for him? Here, we have found the answers from friends to be more reluctant, and usually a little embarrassed, but generally they have been "no" and "yes," respectively. Isn't it remarkable: just about everyone seems to think that his level of intelligence is enough, that any less than his isn't as good, but that any more than his isn't such a big deal.

In other words, we propose that the same thing goes on within individuals as within clans. In practice, not just idealistically, people do not judge themselves as human beings by the size of their IQs. Instead, they bring to bear a multidimensional judgment of themselves that lets them take satisfaction in who they are. Surely a person with an

IQ of 90 sometimes wishes he had an IQ of 120, just as a person with an IQ of 120 sometimes wishes he had an IQ of 150. But it is presumptuous, though a curiously common presumption among intellectuals, to think that someone with an IQ of 90 must feel inferior to those who are smarter, just as it is presumptuous to think a white person must feel threatened by a group difference that probably exists between whites and Japanese, a gentile must feel threatened by a group difference that certainly exists between gentiles and Jews or a black person must feel threatened by a group difference between blacks and whites. It is possible to look ahead to a world in which the glorious hodgepodge of inequalities of ethnic groups—genetic and environmental, permanent and temporary—can be not only accepted but celebrated.

This difficult topic calls up an unending sequence of questions. How can intelligence be treated as just one of many qualities when the marketplace puts such a large monetary premium on it? How can one hope that people who are on the lower end of the IQ range find places of dignity in the world when the niches they used to hold in society are being devalued? Since the world tends to be run by people who are winners in the IQ lottery, how can one hope that societies will be structured so that the lucky ones do not continually run society for their own benefit?

These are all large questions, exceedingly complex questions—but they are no longer about ethnic variations in intelligence. They are about *human* variation in intelligence. They, not ethnic differences, are worth writing a book about—and that's what we did. Ethnic differences must be dreaded only to the extent that people insist on dreading them. People certainly are doing so—that much is not in dispute. What we have tried to do here, in a preliminary and no doubt clumsy way, is to begin to talk about the reasons why they need not.

# Chapter 32

# *The Poor Person's Guide to* The Bell Curve

## Jeremy Bernstein

I have, of course, never read *The Bell Curve*. I doubt that anyone has actually read it except possibly its authors, Richard J. Herrnstein and Charles Murray, and I am not entirely sure about them either. No matter. The important thing is that I have read *about The Bell Curve*. To have read it would have made the writing of this guide quite impossible. It would have confused matters irreparably. But now to the task at hand.

I begin with a simple, almost self-evident principle that for the sake of clarity I call Bernstein's First Law.

*Bernstein's First Law: All tests measure something.*

A case in point: I was once tested on my ability to crawl under a limbo stick after having drunk a jigger of Jamaican rum. I found that I could do it if the stick was set at my actual height.

Conclusion: IQ tests measure *something*. The problem is what to call it.

There has been a terrible fuss because the thing the tests measure has been called Intelligence Quota. Therefore, having a small one qualifies a person as a moron—something that is regarded as undesirable in some parts of our society. I propose to solve this problem by renaming it Quot. No stigma is attached to having a large or small Quot, any more than one is stigmatized by having a large or small telephone number.

The real question is how to pronounce Quot. Here I can be helpful. The word comes from James Joyce's *Finnegan's Wake*. Recall the sentence, "Three quots from Mister Motz." Herman Motz was the owner of a liquor store in Zurich where Joyce shopped. Joyce had trouble

JEREMY BERNSTEIN wears many hats, one of which is professor of physics at the Stevens Institute of Technology in Hoboken, N.J. The inspiration for this essay came while he was munching on a hoagie.

with his rrr's—hence his pronunciation of "quart." This problem much amused Motz, whose little joke seeped into *Finnegan's Wake*. In short, "Quots" rhymes with "Motz."

Does Quot size correlate to any other recognizable genetic feature? This is an important matter. It is so important that I give the evidence for a correlation between Quots and hats in my first graph, graph #1. I believe this diagram, which I have painstakingly sketched by hand, is about as accurate as the ones in *The Bell Curve*.

Note that beret wearers have almost perfect bell-curved Quots. That is because most of them are French.

I next turn to the delicate question, "Should you be told the size of your Quot?" The simple answer is no. If you have a large Quot and are so informed, it will give you a swelled head. And nobody wants to be confronted with the

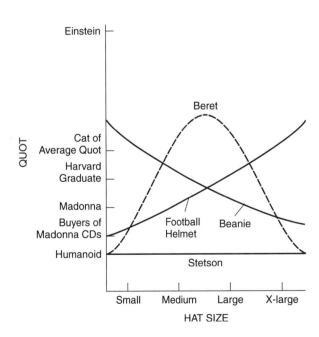

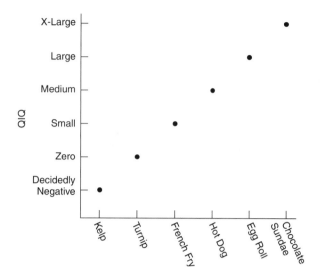

heartbreak of a small Quot. When I was about 11 years old, I was told that my Quot was substantially smaller than my sister's. This information did me no good. I blamed my parents. I asked them what *their* Quots were, and they told me it was none of my business.

If you find that you or your loved ones have small Quots, is there anything you can do about it? Yes! That is the really good news I bring you. Enlarging your Quot is all a matter of proper nutrition. This is spelled out in the second graph, graph #2. The term "QIQ" stands for Quot Improvement Quota. For the sake of economy, I have measured QIQs in the same units I used to measure hat size.

This graph is a treasure trove of information. For example, it explains why patrons of health food stores often seem a little slow. A good hot pastrami sandwich would do wonders.

Finally, I would like to present a third graph, graph #3, showing the result of a recent scientific experiment in which I was myself the subject. It takes advantage of the latest high-tech Quot meters. These devices, which can be inconspicuously disguised as Walkmans, earmuffs, or cellular telephones, constantly monitor your Quot. The results speak for themselves.

It is clear from the graph that the period between 10:30 A.M. is a very dicey one. Forewarned is forearmed.

Readers of this guide have no need to buy *The Bell Curve.* I have saved you $30! My advice is to redirect this money toward a good Quot-enhancing dinner. Don't forget the three basic food groups: vanilla, chocolate, and butter pecan.

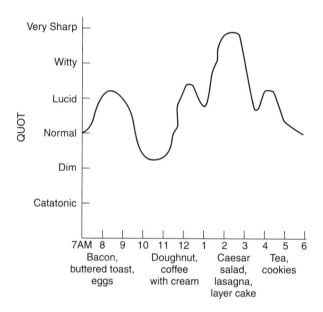

# Chapter 33

# *Critique of* The Bell Curve

## Stephen Jay Gould

### THE BELL CURVE

*The Bell Curve* by Richard J. Herrnstein and Charles Murray provides a superb and unusual opportunity for insight into the meaning of experiment as a method in science. Reduction of confusing variables is the primary desideratum in all experiments. We bring all the buzzing and blooming confusion of the external world into our laboratories and, holding all else constant in our artificial simplicity, try to vary just one potential factor at a time. Often, however, we cannot use such an experimental method, particularly for most social phenomena when importation into the laboratory destroys the subject of our investigation—and then we can only yearn for simplifying guides in nature. If the external world therefore obliges and holds some crucial factors constant for us, then we can only offer thanks for such a natural boost to understanding.

When a book garners as much attention as *The Bell Curve* has received, we wish to know the causes. One might suspect content itself—a startling new idea, or an old suspicion now verified by persuasive data—but the reason might well be social acceptability, or just plain hype. *The Bell Curve* contains no new arguments and presents no compelling data to support its anachronistic Social Darwinism. I must therefore conclude that its initial success in winning such attention must reflect the depressing temper of our time—a historical moment of unprecedented ungenerosity, when a mood for slashing social programs can be so abetted by an argument that beneficiaries cannot be aided due to inborn cognitive limits expressed as low IQ scores.

*The Bell Curve* rests upon two distinctly different but sequential arguments, which together encompass the classical corpus of biological determinism as a social philosophy. The first claim (Chapters 1–12) rehashes the

From *Mismeasure of Man*, W. W. Norton and Company, 1996.

tenets of Social Darwinism as originally constituted. ("Social Darwinism" has often been used as a general term for any evolutionary argument about the biological basis of human differences, but the initial meaning referred to a specific theory of class stratification within industrial societies, particularly to the idea that a permanently poor underclass consisting of genetically inferior people had precipitated down into their inevitable fate.)

This Social Darwinian half of *The Bell Curve* arises from a paradox of egalitarianism. So long as people remain on top of the social heap by accident of a noble name or parental wealth, and so long as members of despised castes cannot rise whatever their talents, social stratification will not reflect intellectual merit, and brilliance will be distributed across all classes. But if true equality of opportunity can be attained, then smart people rise and the lower classes rigidify by retaining only the intellectually incompetent.

This nineteenth-century argument has attracted a variety of twentieth-century champions, including Stanford psychologist Lewis M. Terman, who imported Binet's original test from France, developed the Stanford-Binet IQ test, and gave a hereditarian interpretation to the results (one that Binet had vigorously rejected in developing this style of test); Prime Minister Lee Kuan Yew of Singapore, who tried to institute a eugenics program of rewarding well-educated women for higher birthrates; and Richard Herrnstein, co-author of *The Bell Curve* and author of a 1971 *Atlantic Monthly* article that presented the same argument without documentation. The general claim is neither uninteresting nor illogical, but does require the validity of four shaky premises, all asserted (but hardly discussed or defended) by Herrnstein and Murray. Intelligence, in their formulation, must be depictable as a single number, capable of ranking people in linear order, genetically based, and effectively immutable. If any of these premises are false, the entire argument collapses. For example, if all are true except immutability, then programs for early intervention in education might work to boost IQ permanently, just as a pair of eyeglasses may correct a genetic defect in vision. The central argument of *The Bell Curve* fails because most of the premises are false.

The second claim (Chapters 13–22), the lightning rod for most commentary, extends the argument for innate cognitive stratification by social class to claim for inherited racial differences in IQ—small for Asian superiority over Caucasian, but large for Caucasians over people of African descent. This argument is as old as the study of race. The last generation's discussion centered upon the sophisticated work of Arthur Jensen (far more elaborate and varied than anything presented in *The Bell Curve*, and therefore still a better source for grasping the argument and its fallacies) and the cranky advocacy of William Shockley.

The central fallacy in using the substantial heritability of within-group IQ (among whites, for example) as an explanation for average differences between groups (whites vs. blacks, for example) is now well known and acknowledged by all, including Herrnstein and Murray, but deserves a restatement by example. Take a trait far more heritable than anyone has ever claimed for IQ, but politically uncontroversial—body height. Suppose that I measure adult male height in a poor Indian village beset with pervasive nutritional deprivation. Suppose the average height of adult males is 5 feet 6 inches, well below the current American mean of about 5 feet 9 inches. Heritability within the village will be high—meaning that tall fathers (they may average 5 feet 8 inches) tend to have tall sons, while short fathers (5 feet 4 inches on average) tend to have short sons. But high heritability within the village does not mean that better nutrition might not raise average height to 5 feet 10 inches (above the American mean) in a few generations. Similarly the well-documented fifteen-point average difference in IQ between blacks and whites in America, with substantial heritability of IQ in family lines within each group, permits no conclusion that truly equal opportunity might not raise the black average to equal or surpass the white mean.

Since Herrnstein and Murray know and acknowledge this critique, they must construct an admittedly circumstantial case for attributing most of the black–white mean difference to irrevocable genetics—while properly stressing that the average difference doesn't help at all in judging any particular person because so many individual blacks score above the white mean in IQ. Quite apart from the rhetorical dubiety of this old ploy in a shop-worn genre—"some-of-my-best-friends-are-group-x"—Herrnstein and Murray violate fairness by converting a complex case that can only yield agnosticism into a biased brief for permanent and heritable difference. They impose this spin by turning every straw on their side into an oak, while mentioning but downplaying the strong circumstantial case for substantial malleability and little

average genetic difference (impressive IQ gains for poor black children adopted into affluent and intellectual homes; average IQ increases in some nations since World War II equal to the entire fifteen-point difference now separating blacks and whites in America; failure to find any cognitive differences between two cohorts of children born out of wedlock to German women, and raised in Germany as Germans, but fathered by black and white American soldiers).

Disturbing as I find the anachronism *The Bell Curve*, I am even more distressed by its pervasive disingenuousness. The authors omit facts, misuse statistical methods, and seem unwilling to admit the consequences of their own words.

## DISINGENUOUSNESS OF CONTENT

The ocean of publicity that has engulfed *The Bell Curve* has a basis in what Murray and Herrnstein (*New Republic*, October 31, 1994) call "the flashpoint of intelligence as a public topic: the question of genetic differences between the races." And yet, since the day of publication, Murray has been temporizing and denying that race is an important subject in the book at all; instead, he blames the press for unfairly fanning these particular flames. He writes with Herrnstein (who died just a month before publication) in the *New Republic*: "Here is what we hope will be our contribution to the discussion. We put it in italics; if we could we would put it in neon lights: *The answer doesn't much matter.*"

Fair enough in the narrow sense that any individual may be a rarely brilliant member of an averagely dumb group (and therefore not subject to judgment by the group mean), but Murray cannot deny that *The Bell Curve* treats race as one of two major topics, with each given about equal space; nor can he pretend that strongly stated claims about group differences have no political impact in a society obsessed with the meanings and consequences of ethnicity. The very first sentence of *The Bell Curve*'s preface acknowledges equality of treatment for the two subjects of individual and group differences: "This book is about differences in intellectual capacity among people and groups and what these differences mean for America's future." And Murray and Herrnstein's *New Republic* article begins by identifying racial difference as the key subject of interest: "The private dialogue about race in America is far different from the public one."

## DISINGENUOUSNESS OF ARGUMENT

*The Bell Curve* is a rhetorical masterpiece of scientism, and the particular kind of anxiety and obfuscation that numbers impose upon nonprofessional commentators.

The book runs to 845 pages, including more than 100 pages of appendices filled with figures. So the text looks complicated, and reviewers shy away with a knee-jerk claim that, while they suspect fallacies of argument, they really cannot judge. So Mickey Kaus writes in the *New Republic* (October 31, 1994): "As a lay reader of *The Bell Curve*, I'm unable to judge fairly," as does Leon Wieseltier in the same issue: "Murray, too, is hiding the hardness of his politics behind the hardness of his science. And his science for all I know is soft.... Or so I imagine. I am not a scientist. I know nothing about psychometrics." Or Peter Passell in the *New York Times* (October 27, 1994): "But this reviewer is not a biologist, and will leave the argument to experts."

In fact, *The Bell Curve* is extraordinarily one-dimensional. The book makes no attempt to survey the range of available data, and pays astonishingly little attention to the rich and informative history of this contentious subject. (One can only recall Santayana's dictum, now a cliché of intellectual life: "Those who cannot remember the past are condemned to repeat it."). Virtually all the analysis rests upon a single technique applied to a single set of data—all probably done in one computer run. (I do agree that the authors have used the most appropriate technique—multiple regression—and the best source of information—the National Longitudinal Survey of Youth—though I shall expose a core fallacy in their procedure below. Still, claims as broad as those advanced in *The Bell Curve* simply cannot be adequately defended—that is, either properly supported or denied—by such a restricted approach.)

The blatant errors and inadequacies of *The Bell Curve* could be picked up by lay reviewers if only they would not let themselves be frightened by numbers—for Herrnstein and Murray do write clearly and their mistakes are both patent and accessible. I would rank the fallacies in two categories: omissions and confusions and content.

1. *Omissions and confusions*: While disclaiming on his own ability to judge, Mickey Kaus (in the *New Republic*) does correctly identify "the first two claims" that are absolutely essential "to make the pessimistic 'ethnic difference' argument work": "(1) that there is a single, general measure of mental ability; (2) that the IQ tests that purport to measure this ability . . . aren't culturally biased."

Nothing in *The Bell Curve* angered me more than the authors' failure to supply any justification for their central claim, the *sine qua non*, of their entire argument: the reality of IQ as a number that measures a real property in the head, the celebrated "general factor" of intelligence (known as *g*) first identified by Charles Spearman in 1904. Murray and Herrnstein simply proclaim that the issue has been decided, as in this passage from their *New Republic* article: "Among the experts, it is by now beyond

much technical dispute that there is such a thing as a general factor of cognitive ability on which human beings differ and that this general factor is measured reasonably well by a variety of standardized tests, best of all by IQ tests designed for that purpose."

Such a statement represents extraordinary obfuscation, achieved by defining "expert" as "that group of psychometricians working in the tradition of *g* and its avatar IQ." The authors even admit (pp. 14–19) that three major schools of psychometric interpretation now contend, and that only one supports their view of *g* and IQ—the classicists as championed in *The Bell Curve* ("intelligence as a structure"), the revisionists ("intelligence as information processing"), and the radicals ("the theory of multiple intelligences").

This vital issue cannot be decided, or even understood without discussing the key and only rationale that *g* has maintained since Spearman invented the concept in 1904—factor analysis. The fact that Herrnstein and Murray barely mention the factor analytic argument (the subject receives fleeting attention in two paragraphs) provides a central indictment and illustration of the vacuousness in *The Bell Curve*. How can authors base an eight-hundred-page book on a claim for the reality of IQ as measuring a genuine, and largely genetic, general cognitive ability—and then hardly mention, either pro or con, the theoretical basis for their certainty? Various clichés like "*Hamlet* without the Prince of Denmark" come immediately to mind.

Admittedly, factor analysis is a difficult and mathematical subject, but it can be explained to lay readers with a geometrical formulation developed by L. L. Thurstone in the 1930s and used by me in Chapter 7 of *The Mismeasure of Man*. A few paragraphs cannot suffice for adequate explanation, so, although I offer some sketchy hints below, readers should not question their own IQs if the topic still seems arcane.

In brief, a person's performances on various mental tests tend to be positively correlated—that is, if you do well on one kind of test, you tend to do well on the others. This result is scarcely surprising and is subject to either purely genetic (the innate thing in the head that boosts all scores) or purely environmental interpretation (good books and good childhood nutrition to enhance all performances). Therefore, the positive correlations say nothing in themselves about causes.

Charles Spearman used factor analysis to identify a single axis—which he called *g*—that best identifies the common factor behind positive correlations among the tests. But Thurstone later showed that *g* could be made to disappear by simply rotating the factor axes to different positions. In one rotation, Thurstone placed the axes near the most widely separated of attributes among the tests—thus giving rise to the theory of multiple intelligences (verbal, mathematical, spatial, etc., with no overarching *g*). This theory (the "radical" view in Herrnstein and Murray's classification) has been supported by many prominent psychometricians, including J. P. Guilford in the 1950s, and most prominently today by Howard Gardner. In this perspective, $g$ cannot have inherent reality, for $g$ emerges in one form of mathematical representation for correlations among tests, and disappears (or at least greatly attenuates) in other forms that are entirely equivalent in amounts of information explained. In any case, one can't grasp the issue at all without a clear exposition of factor analysis—and *The Bell Curve* cops out completely on this central concept.

On Kaus's second theme of "cultural bias," *The Bell Curve*'s presentation matches Arthur Jensen's, and that of other hereditarians, in confusing a technical (and proper) meaning of bias (I call it "S-bias" for "statistical") with the entirely different vernacular concept (I call it "V-bias") that agitates popular debate. All these authors swear up and down (and I agree with them completely) that the tests are not biased—in the statistician's definition. Lack of S-bias means that the same score, when achieved by members of different groups, predicts the same consequence—that is, a black person and a white person with an identical IQ score of 100 will have the same probabilities for doing anything that IQ is supposed to predict. (I should hope that mental tests aren't S-biased, for the testing profession isn't worth very much if practitioners can't eliminate such an obvious source of unfairness by careful choice and framing of questions.)

But V-bias, the source of public concerns, embodies an entirely different issue that, unfortunately, uses the same word. The public wants to know whether blacks average 85 and whites 100 because society treats blacks unfairly—that is, whether lower black scores record biases in this social sense. And this crucial question (to which we do not know the answer) cannot be addressed by a demonstration that S-bias doesn't exist (the only issue treated, however correctly, by *The Bell Curve*).

2. *Content:* As stated above, virtually all the data in *The Bell Curve* derive from one analysis—a plotting, by a technique called multiple regression, of the social behaviors that agitate us, such as crime, unemployment, and births out of wedlock (treated as dependent variables), against both IQ and parental socioeconomic status (treated as independent variables). The authors first hold IQ constant and consider the relationship of social behaviors to parental socioeconomic status. They then hold socioeconomic status constant and consider the relationship of the same social behaviors to IQ. In general, they find a higher correlation with IQ than with socioeconomic status; for example, people with low IQ are more likely to drop out of high school than people whose parents have low socioeconomic status.

But such analyses must engage two issues—form *and* strength of the relationship—and Herrnstein and Murray only discuss the issue that seems to support their viewpoint, while virtually ignoring (and in one key passage almost willfully and purposely hiding) the other factor that counts so profoundly against them. Their numerous graphs only present the *form* of the relationships—that is, they draw the regression curves of their variables against IQ and parental socioeconomic status. But, in violation of all statistical norms that I've ever learned, they plot *only* the regression curve and do not show the scatter of variation around the curve, so their graphs show nothing about the *strength* of the relationship—that is, the amount of variation in social factors explained by IQ and socioeconomic status.

Now why would Herrnstein and Murray focus on the form and ignore the strength? Almost all of their relationships are very weak—that is, very little of the variation in social factors can be explained by either IQ or socioeconomic status (even though the form of this small amount tends to lie in their favored direction). In short, IQ is not a major factor in determining variation in nearly all the social factors they study—and their vaunted conclusions thereby collapse, or become so strongly attenuated that their pessimism and conservative social agenda gain no significant support.

Herrnstein and Murray actually admit as much in one crucial passage on page 117, but then they hide the pattern. They write: "It almost always explains less than 20 percent of the variance, to use the statistician's term, usually less than 10 percent and often less than 5 percent. What this means in English is that you cannot predict that a given person will do from his IQ score. . . . On the other hand, despite the low association at the individual level, large differences in social behavior separate groups of people when the groups differ intellectually on the average." Despite this disclaimer, their remarkable next sentence makes a strong causal claim: "We will argue that intelligence itself, not just its correlation with socioeconomic status, is responsible for these group differences." But a few percent of statistical determination is not equivalent to causal explanation (and correlation does not imply cause in any case, even when correlations are strong—as in the powerful, perfect, positive correlation between my advancing age and the rise of the national debt). Moreover, their case is even worse for their key genetic claims—for they cite heritabilities of about 60 percent for IQ, so you must nearly halve the few percent explained if you want to isolate the strength of genetic determination by their own criteria!

My charge of disingenuousness receives its strongest affirmation in a sentence tucked away on the first page of Appendix 4, page 593, where the authors state: "In the text, we do not refer to the usual measure of goodness of fit for multiple regressions, $R^2$, but they are presented here for the cross-sectional analysis." Now why would they exclude from the text, and relegate to an appendix that very few people will read or even consult, a number that, by their own admission, is "the usual measure of goodness of fit"? I can only conclude that they did not choose to admit in the main text the extreme weakness of their vaunted relationships.

Herrnstein and Murray's correlation coefficients are generally low enough by themselves to inspire lack of confidence. (Correlation coefficients measure the strength of linear relationships between variables; positive values run from 0.0 for no relationship to 1.0 for perfect linear relationship.) Although low figures are not atypical in the social sciences for large surveys involving many variables, most of Herrnstein and Murray's correlations are very weak—often in the 0.2 to 0.4 range. Now, 0.4 may sound respectably strong, but—and now we come to the key point—$R^2$ is the square of the correlation coefficient, and the square of a number between 0 and 1 is less than the number itself, so a 0.4 correlation yields an r-squared of only 0.16. In Appendix 4, then, we discover that the vast majority of measures for $R^2$, excluded from the main body of the text, have values less than 0.1. These very low values of $R^2$ expose the true weakness, in any meaningful vernacular sense, of nearly all the relationships that form the heart of *The Bell Curve*.

## DISINGENUOUSNESS OF PROGRAM

Like so many conservative ideologues who rail against a largely bogus ogre of suffocating political correctness, Herrnstein and Murray claim that they only seek a hearing for unpopular views so that that truth will out. And here, for once, I agree entirely. As a card-carrying First Amendment (near) absolutist, applaud the publication of unpopular views that some people consider dangerous. I am delighted that *The Bell Curve* was written—so that its errors could be exposed, for Herrnstein and Murray are right in pointing out the difference between public and private agendas on race, and we must struggle to make an impact upon the private agendas as well.

But *The Bell Curve* can scarcely be called an academic treatise in social theory and population genetics. The book is a manifesto of conservative ideology, and its sorry and biased treatment of data records the primary purpose—advocacy above all. The text evokes the dreary and scary drumbeat of claims associated with conservative think tanks—reduction or elimination of welfare, ending of affirmative action in schools and workplaces, cessation of Head Start and other forms of preschool education, cutting of programs for slowest learners and application of funds to the gifted (Lord knows I would love to see more attention paid to talented students, but not at this cruel and cynical price).

The penultimate chapter presents an apocalyptic vision of a society with a growing underclass permanently mired in the inevitable sloth of their low IQs. They will take over our city centers, keep having illegitimate babies (for many are too stupid to practice birth control), commit more crimes, and ultimately require a kind of custodial state, more to keep them in check (and out of our high IQ neighborhoods) than with any hope for an amelioration that low IQ makes impossible in any

case. Herrnstein and Murray actually write (p. 526): "In short, by custodial state, we have in mind a high-tech and more lavish version of the Indian reservation for some substantial minority of the nation's population, while the rest of America tries to go about its business."

The final chapter then tries to suggest an alternative, but I have never read anything so feeble, so unlikely, so almost grotesquely inadequate. They yearn romantically for the "good old days" of towns and neighborhoods where all people could be given tasks of value and self-esteem could be found for all steps in the IQ hierarchy (so Forrest Gump might collect the clothing for the church raffle, while Mr. Murray and the other bright folks do the planning and keep the accounts. Have they forgotten about the town Jew and the dwellers on the other side of the tracks in many of these idyllic villages?). I do believe in this concept of neighborhood, and I will fight for its return. I grew up in such a place within that mosaic known as Queens, New York City, but can anyone seriously find solutions (rather than important palliatives) to our social ills therein?

However, if Herrnstein and Murray are wrong about IQ as an immutable thing in the head, with humans graded in a single scale of general capacity, leaving large numbers of custodial incompetents at the bottom, then the model that generates their gloomy vision collapses, and the wonderful variousness of human abilities, properly nurtured, reemerges. We must fight the doctrine of *The Bell Curve* both because it is wrong and because it will, if activated, cut off all possibility of proper nurturance for everyone's intelligence. Of course we cannot all be rocket scientists or brain surgeons (to use the two current slang synecdoches for smartest of the smart), but those who can't might be rock musicians or professional athletes (and gain far more social prestige and salary thereby)—while others will indeed serve by standing and waiting.

I closed Chapter 7 in *The Mismeasure of Man* on the unreality of *g* and the fallacy of regarding intelligence as a single innate thing-in-the-head (rather than a rough vernacular term for a wondrous panoply of largely independent abilities) with a marvelous quote from John Stuart Mill, well worth repeating to debunk this generation's recycling of biological determinism for the genetics of intelligence.

> The tendency has always been strong to believe that whatever received a name must be an entity or being, having an independent existence of its own. And if no real entity answering to the name could be found, men did not for that reason suppose that none existed, but imagined that it was something particularly abstruse and mysterious.

How strange that we would let a single false number divide us, when evolution has united all people in the recency of our common ancestry—thus undergirding with a shared humanity that infinite variety that custom can never stale. *E pluribus unum.*

# Chapter 34

# *What Color Is Black?*

## Tom Morganthau

*And what color is white? The markers of racial identity are every conceivable hue—and suddenly matters of ideology and attitude as much as pigmentation.*

Nearly 400 years after the first African came ashore at Jamestown—and 40 years after Rosa Parks launched the Montgomery bus boycott—Americans are still preoccupied with race. Race divides us, defines us and in a curious way, unites us—if only because we still think it matters. Race-based thinking permeates our law and policy, and the sense of racial grievance, voiced by blacks and whites alike, infects our politics. Blacks cleave to their roles as history's victims; whites grumble about reverse discrimination. The national mood on race, as measured by *Newsweek's* latest poll, is bleak: 75 percent of whites—and 86 percent of blacks—say race relations are "only fair" or "poor."

But the world is changing anyway. By two other measures in the same *Newsweek* poll—acceptance of interracial marriage and the willingness to reside in mixed-race neighborhoods—tolerance has never been higher. The nation's racial dialogue, meanwhile, is changing so rapidly that the familiar din of black–white antagonism seems increasingly out of date. Partly because of immigration—and partly because diversity is suddenly hip—America is beginning to revise its two-way definition of race. Though this process will surely take years, it is already blurring our sense that racial identity is fixed, immutable, and primarily a matter of skin color. What color is black? It is every conceivable shade and hue from tan to ebony—and suddenly a matter of ideology and identity as much as pigmentation.

The politics of racial identity are public and deeply personal. Twenty-eight years after the last state antimiscegenation law was struck down, an interracial genera-

From *Newsweek*, February 13, 1995.

tion is demanding its place at the American table. They are not the first biracial Americans; that honor belongs to youngsters who grew up in Colonial Jamestown. But they are the first to stake a claim to mainstream status, discomfiting in the process blacks and whites who are reluctant to reconsider familiar racial categories. They are aided by older cousins who, if nothing else, are changing the talk of the nation, producing powerful memoirs about life on the color line.

It is important to note, meanwhile, that the idea of race itself is now coming under attack by science. To scientists who have looked into the question, race is a notoriously slippery concept that eludes any serious attempt at definition: It refers mostly to observable differences in skin color, hair texture, and the shape of one's eyes or nose. Considering the whole range of biological variation

---

**Newsweek Poll**

Are the numbers of immigrants entering the U.S. from each of the following areas too many, too few or about right?

(percent saying too many)

| Area | Blacks | Whites |
| --- | --- | --- |
| Europe | 36% | 30% |
| Latin America | 40% | 59% |
| Africa | 24% | 35% |
| Asia | 39% | 45% |

The *Newsweek* Poll, Feb. 1–3, 1995

within the human species, these differences are at best superficial—and try as they will, scientists have been broadly unable to come up with any significant set of differences that distinguishes one racial group from another. (*The Bell Curve,* a best-selling book by Richard Herrnstein and Charles Murray, revives the old controversy about black–white differences in intelligence, but surely does not settle it.) The bottom line, to most scientists working in these fields, is that race is a mere "social construct"—a gamy mixture of prejudice, superstition, and myth.

This assault on racialist thinking is compounded by the visible results of thirty years of accelerating immigration from Latin America, the Caribbean, and Asia. That trend, still continuing, has added approximately 18 million people to the American melting pot, most of whom are eligible to be labeled "persons of color." One obvious consequence is the prediction that Hispanics, now 25 million strong and nearly 10 percent of the population (blacks are almost 13 percent, and non-Hispanic whites are 74 percent), will be the nation's largest minority by the year 2010. But Latinos are neither a "race" nor an "ethnic group." They are a disparate collection of nationalities variously descended from Europeans, African slaves, and American Indians. The new immigrants also include some 3.5 million Chinese, Japanese, Koreans, Filipinos, Vietnamese, and Laotian Hmong. And hundreds of thousands of dark-skinned East Indians, Pakistanis, and Bangladeshis—who, despite their color, are Caucasians.

All of this portends an era of increasing multiethnic and multiracial confusion: Diversity "R" Us. The question now is whether America's traditional concept of race is relevant to the nation's changing demographics—and the answer, almost certainly, is "no." Americans have long tended to take a "binary" approach toward race—to assume, based on our own historical experience, that only two races count and that skin color is the dividing line between them. This belief is rooted in what historians call the "one-drop rule," which is a relic of slavery and segregation. But as Harvard sociologist Orlando Patterson says, "The U.S. approach to racial identity has been most unusual. In much of the rest of the world, people make [social and class] distinctions based on gradations of color." Now, Patterson says, the arrival of millions of new immigrants from racially mixed societies is undermining the de facto consensus on the meaning of race in the American context. "We've had this large group of people coming from parts of Latin America . . . [who] don't consider themselves white or black," he says. "They don't want to play the binary game."

The demand for a more flexible view of race and ethnicity is not limited to immigrants—for many native-born Americans are refusing to play the binary game as well. Ramona Douglass of Chicago is the child of a multi-racial couple: Her mother was Sicilian-American and her father was half African American and half Ogalala Sioux. Douglass says she is frustrated that native-born multiethnics are "invisible" to the rest of society. She is president of a group, the Association of MultiEthnic Americans, that is lobbying Washington to add a multiracial category to the questionnaire for the next census. Currently, respondents are asked to choose between White, Black, Asian or Pacific Islander, American Indian, Eskimo or Aleut; and the catchall designator "Other." (The questionnaire provides a separate Hispanic/Spanish-origin box in addition to these racial categories.) Simply changing the census form, Douglass argues, would help to acknowledge the nation's increasing diversity "in a positive way."

This seemingly innocuous revision is fast becoming a hideously complicated issue. Federal officials are well aware that the census form forces millions of Americans to identify themselves as "Other," which sounds faintly diminishing. They are also aware that the current racial categories do not depict the nation's increasingly fluid demographics. "The problem is that the country is changing at a very rapid rate now, and the categories have not changed for the last twenty years," says Ohio Rep. Thomas C. Sawyer. "The [census] numbers may be precise, but they are precisely wrong. They do not reflect the reality of who people think they are." In 1990, census officials say, Americans used a write-in blank on the census forms to identify nearly 300 "races," 600 Indian tribes, 70 Hispanic groups and 75 combinations of multiracial ancestry—including one person self-identified as "black/Hmong."

Viewed as a matter of individual choice, the census-form issue looks like healthy self-assertion for those who feel themselves confined by America's traditional beliefs about race identity. It is that—but it is also a potentially major political issue. If significant numbers of

---

### Newsweek Poll

Should the U.S. Census add a multiracial category so people aren't forced to deny part of a family member's heritage by choosing a single racial category?

|  | **Blacks** | **Whites** |
| --- | --- | --- |
| Add category | 49% | 36% |
| Don't add | 42% | 51% |

Should the U.S. Census stop collecting information on race and ethnicity?

|  | **Blacks** | **Whites** |
| --- | --- | --- |
| Should stop | 48% | 47% |
| Should not stop | 44% | 41% |

The *Newsweek* Poll, Feb. 1–3, 1995.

blacks and Hispanics begin to check the proposed multiracial box, the shift could trigger changes in census-based formulas used to distribute federal aid to minorities. It could also undermine part of the Voting Rights Act that requires so-called minority districting for blacks and Hispanics in congressional elections. And some speculate that it could lead to an expansion of affirmative action for previously ineligible minority groups.

All this remains so much speculation until (and unless) the census form is changed. But the demand for recognition by emerging multiethnic and multiracial groups is a clear rejection of the binary view of race and

---

**Newsweek Poll**

How important is it that voting districts be drawn so that blacks can obtain representation in elective office comparable to their numbers in the population?

|  | Blacks | Whites |
| --- | --- | --- |
| Somewhat or very important | 92% | 59% |

The *Newsweek* Poll, Feb. 1–3, 1995.

---

the one-drop rule as well. As such, it implicitly threatens the tradition of black solidarity on the long march toward social equality. Black intellectuals and political activists already recognize that possibility, and some are worried by the prospect of change. Since a great many black Americans can clearly claim to be biracial, the worst-case scenario is that black solidarity will slowly erode because of "defections" to multiethnic status. But not everyone agrees. "I don't think there are *any* political implications," says Bill Lynch, a former deputy mayor of New York. "It's no different from checking the 'Other' box."

And what if multiethnicity is the way out of our binary stalemate? Orlando Patterson, for one, takes exactly that view. "If your object is the eventual integration of the races, a mixed-race or middle group is something you'd want to see developing," he says. "The middle group grows larger and larger, and the races eventually blend." Patterson knows that whites are wary and that blacks warier still. But he thinks the amount of social interaction between the races is already "surprising," and he insists there is "nothing fundamental" about American society to block the ultimate blending of black and white. All it requires is patience, faith—and a measure of good will.

# Chapter 35

# *A Summary of the World*

If we could shrink the Earth's population to a village of precisely 100 people, with all existing human ratios remaining the same, it would look like this:

- There would be 57 Asians, 21 Europeans, 14 from the Western Hemisphere (North and South America), and 8 Africans.
- 51 would be female; 49 would be male.
- 70 would be nonwhite; 30 white.
- 70 would be non-Christian; 30 Christian.
- 50% of the entire world's wealth would be in the hands of only 6 people, and all 6 would be citizens of the United States.

- 80 would live in substandard housing.
- 70 would be unable to read.
- 50 would suffer from malnutrition.
- 1 would be near death; 1 would be near birth.
- Only 1 would have a college education.
- 0 would own a computer.

When one considers our world from such an incredibly compressed perspective, the need for both tolerance and understanding becomes glaringly apparent. . . .

    . . . Have a small day.

# Chapter 36

# *New Vital Statistics Confirm Worsening of Black Health*

## International Society on Hypertension in Blacks

As anticipated, the most recent vital statistics confirm the deepening health crisis for black Americans.[1] The final mortality data for 1989 demonstrate a continued reduction in life expectancy for black men, and no change for both sexes combined (Table 36–1). These trends are in striking contrast to the extension of life by 0.4 years for whites of both sexes.

The situation is equally bad, if more complicated, for children under 1 year of age. In 1989, the National Center for Health Statistics introduced a new reporting system for infant mortality. In the old system, a child born to "mixed parentage where only one parent was white . . . was assigned to the other parent's race.[1] It had also been recognized for several years that inconsistencies exist in the reporting of race on birth and death certificates. Thus, a child designated as black or Hispanic at birth might be coded as white at death. Moving fatal events from one racial category to another would obviously provide a falsely low estimate of mortality rates. Use of the old system, based on the child's race on the death certificate, demonstrates a slight increase in infant mortality among blacks from 1988 to 1989, accompanied by a decrease among whites (Table 36–2). Use of mother's race to classify the infant provides new estimates that are sizably worse than previously thought (Table 36–2).

As noted above, despite some confusion caused by the preliminary estimates,[2] the trends are not unexpected. The economic status of the black population in the United States has worsened markedly over the last decade and a half. Based on constant dollars, 30 percent more blacks had an annual income of less than $5000 in 1987 than in 1970.[3] As recently reported, fully 60 percent of the expansion in income from 1977 through 1989 was concentrated within the wealthiest 1 percent of all U.S. families.[4] It seems likely, therefore, that the enormous growth in social inequality, as evidenced in the widening gap in income, has contributed heavily to the worsening of the social conditions determining health in the black community. These findings have created an urgent need to focus greater public attention on the adverse trends identified by the data presented here.

TABLE 36–1　Life Expectancy (in Years) Among Blacks and Whites in the United States

| Year | White | | Black | |
|------|-------|-------|-------|-------|
| | Men | Women | Men | Women |
| 1989 | 72.7 | 79.2 | 64.8 | 73.5 |
| 1988 | 72.3 | 78.9 | 64.9 | 73.4 |
| 1987 | 72.2 | 78.9 | 65.2 | 73.6 |
| 1986 | 72.0 | 78.8 | 65.2 | 73.5 |
| 1985 | 71.9 | 78.7 | 65.3 | 73.5 |
| 1984 | 71.8 | 78.7 | 65.6 | 73.7 |
| 1980 | 70.7 | 78.1 | 63.8 | 72.5 |

From *Ethnicity and Disease*, Vol. 2, 1992.

TABLE 36–2　Infant Mortality among Blacks and Whites in the United States*

| Year | White | Black |
|------|-------|-------|
| 1989 | | |
| 　Race of Mother† | 8.1 | 18.6 |
| 　Race of Child‡ | 8.2 | 17.7 |
| 1988 | 8.5 | 17.6 |
| 1987 | 8.6 | 17.9 |
| 1986 | 8.9 | 18.0 |
| 1985 | 9.3 | 18.2 |
| 1984 | 9.4 | 18.4 |
| 1980 | 11.0 | 21.4 |

*Rates per 1000 live births.

†Deaths based on race of decedent; live births based on race of mother.

‡Deaths based on race of decedent; live births based on race of child.

## REFERENCES

1. National Center for Health Statistics. Advance report of final mortality statistics, 1989. Monthly vital statistics report; vol. 40, no. 8, suppl. 2. Hyattsville, Md: Public Health Service; 1992

2. Gap in black-white life expectancy narrows in 1989–1990. *Ethnicity Dis.* 1991; 1:402–403. Health Trends.

3. Horton, E. P., Smith, J. C., eds., *Statistical record of black America.* Detroit, Mich: Gale Research Inc.; 1990.

4. 1980s: a very good time for the very rich. *New York Times.* March 5, 1992:1.

# Chapter 37

# ☐ Black   ☐ White   ☑ Other

## Jonathan Marks

*Racial categories are cultural constructs masquerading as biology.*

While reading the Sunday edition of the *New York Times* one morning last February, my attention was drawn by an editorial inconsistency. The article I was reading was written by attorney Lani Guinier. (Guinier, you may remember, had been President Clinton's nominee to head the civil rights division at the Department of Justice in 1993. Her name was hastily withdrawn amid a blast of criticism over her views on political representation of minorities.) What had distracted me from the main point of the story was a photo caption that described Guinier as being "half-black." In the text of the article, Guinier had described herself simply as "black."

How can a person be black and half black at the same time? In algebraic terms, this would seem to describe a situation where $x = \frac{1}{2} x$, to which the only solution is $x = 0$.

The inconsistency in the *Times* was trivial, but revealing. It encapsulated a longstanding problem in our use of racial categories—namely, a confusion between biological and cultural heredity. When Guinier is described as "half-black," that is a statement of biological ancestry, for one of her two parents is black. And when Guinier describes herself as black, she is using a cultural category, according to which one can either be black or white, but not both.

Race—as the term is commonly used—is inherited, although not in a strictly biological fashion. It is passed down according to a system of folk heredity, an all-or-nothing system that is different from the quantifiable heredity of biology. But the incompatibility of the two notions of race is sometimes starkly evident—as when the state decides that racial differences are so important that interracial marriages must be regulated or

outlawed entirely. Miscegenation laws in this country (which stayed on the books in many states through the 1960s) obliged the legal system to define who belonged in what category. The resulting formula stated that anyone with one-eighth or more black ancestry was a "negro." (A similar formula, defining Jews, was promulgated by the Germans in the Nuremberg Laws of the 1930s.)

Applying such formulas led to the biological absurdity that having one black great-grandparent was sufficient to define a person as black, but having seven white great-grandparents was insufficient to define a person as white. Here, race and biology are demonstrably at odds. And the problem is not semantic but conceptual, for race is presented as a category of nature.

Human beings come in a wide variety of sizes, shapes, colors, and forms—or, because we are visually oriented primates, it certainly seems that way. We also come in larger packages called populations; and we are said to belong to even larger and more confusing units, which have long been known as races. The history of the study of human variation is to a large extent the pursuit of those human races—the attempt to identify the small number of fundamentally distinct kinds of people on earth.

This scientific goal stretches back two centuries, to Linnaeus, the father of biological systematics, who radically established *Homo sapiens* as one species within a group of animals he called Primates. Linnaeus's system of naming groups within groups logically implied further breakdown. He consequently sought to establish a number of subspecies within *Homo sapiens*. He identified five: four geographical species (from Europe, Asia, Africa, and America) and one grab-bag subspecies called *monstrosus*. This category was dropped by subsequent researchers (as

From *Natural History* December, 1994.

was Linnaeus's use of criteria such as personality and dress to define his subspecies.)

While Linneaus was not the first to divide humans on the basis of the continents on which they lived, he had given the division a scientific stamp. But in attempting to determine the proper number of subspecies, the heirs of Linnaeus always seemed to find different answers, depending upon the criteria they applied. By the mid-twentieth century, scores of anthropologists—led by Harvard's Earnest Hooton—had expended enormous energy on the problem. But these scholars could not convince one another about the precise nature of the fundamental divisions of our species.

Part of the problem—as with the *Times's* identification of Lani Guinier—was that we humans have two constantly intersecting ways of thinking about the divisions among us. On the one hand, we like to think of "race"—as Linneaus did—as an objective, biological category. In this sense, being a member of a race is supposed to be equivalent of being a member of a species or phylum—except that race, on the analogy of subspecies, is an even narrower (and presumably more exclusive and precise) biological category.

The other kind of category into which we humans allocate ourselves—when we say "Serb" or "Hutu" or "Jew" or "Chicano" or "Republican" or "Red Sox fan"—is cultural. The label refers to little or nothing in the natural attributes of its members. These members may not live in the same region and may not even know many others like themselves. What they share is neither strictly nature nor strictly community. The groupings are constructions of human social history.

Membership in these *un*biological groupings may mean the difference between life and death, for they are the categories that allow us to be identified (and accepted and vilified) socially. While membership in (or allegiance to) these categories may be assigned or adopted from birth, the differentia that marks members from nonmembers are symbolic and abstract; they serve to distinguish people who cannot be readily distinguished by nature. So important are these symbolic distinctions that some of the strongest animosities are often expressed between very similar-looking peoples. Obvious examples are Bosnian Serbs and Muslims, Irish and English, Huron and Iroquois.

Obvious natural variation is rarely so important as cultural difference. One simply does not hear of a slaughter of the short people at the hands of the tall, the glabrous at the hands of the hairy, the red-haired at the hands of the brown-haired. When we do encounter genocidal violence between different-looking peoples, the two groups are invariably socially or culturally distinct as well. Indeed, the tragic frequency of hatred and genocidal violence between biologically indistinguishable peoples implies that biological differences such as skin color are not motivations, but rather excuses. They allow

nature to be invoked to reinforce group identities and antagonisms that would exist without these physical distinctions. But are there any truly "racial" biological distinctions to be found in our species?

Obviously, if you compare two people from different parts of the world (or whose ancestors came from different parts of the world), they will differ physically, but one cannot therefore define three or four or five basically different kinds of people, as a biological notion of race would imply. The anatomical properties that distinguish people—such as pigmentation, eye form, body build—are not clumped in discrete groups, but distributed along geographical gradients, as are nearly all the genetically determined variants detectable in the human gene pool.

These gradients are produced by three forces. Natural selection adapts populations to local circumstances (like climate) and thereby differentiates them from other populations. Genetic drift (random fluctuations in a gene pool) also differentiates populations from one another, but in nonadaptive ways. And gene flow (via intermarriage and other child-producing unions) acts to homogenize neighboring populations.

In practice, the operations of these forces are difficult to discern. A few features, such as body build and the graduated distribution of the sickle cell anemia gene in populations from western Africa, southern Asia, and the Mediterranean can be plausibly related to the effects of selection. Others, such as the graduated distribution of a small deletion in the mitochondrial DNA of some East Asian, Oceanic, and Native American peoples, or the degree of flatness of the face, seem unlikely to be the result of selection and are probably the results of random biohistorical factors. The cause of the distribution of most features, from nose breadth to blood group, is simply unclear.

The overall result of these forces is evident, however. As Johann Friedrich Blumenbach noted in 1775, "you see that all do so run into one another, and that one variety of mankind does so sensibly pass into the other, that you cannot mark out the limits between them." (Posturing as an heir to Linnaeus, he nonetheless attempted to do so.) But from humanity's gradations in appearance, no defined groupings resembling races readily emerge. The racial categories with which we have become so familiar are the result of our imposing arbitrary cultural boundaries in order to partition gradual biological variation.

Unlike graduated biological distinctions, culturally constructed categories are ultrasharp. One can be French or German, but not both; Tutsi or Hutu, but not both; Jew or Catholic, but not both; Bosnian Muslim or Serb, but not both; black or white, but not both. Traditionally, people of "mixed race" have been obliged to choose one and thereby identify themselves ambiguously to census takers and administrative bookkeepers—a practice that is now being widely called into question.

A scientific definition of race would require considerable homogeneity within each group, and reasonably discrete differences between groups, but three kinds of data militate against this view: First, the groups traditionally described as races are not all homogeneous. Africans and Europeans for instance, are each a collection of biologically diverse populations. Anthropologists of the 1920s widely recognized *three* European races: Nordic, Alpine, and Mediterranean. This implied that races could exist within races. American anthropologist Carleton Coon identified *ten* European races in 1939. With such protean use, the term race came to have little value in describing actual biological entities within *Homo sapiens*. The scholars were not only grappling with a broad north-south gradient in human appearance across Europe, they were trying to bring the data into line with their belief in profound and fundamental constitutional differences between groups of people.

But there simply isn't one European race to contrast with an African race, nor three, nor ten: the question (as scientists long posed it) fails to recognize the actual patterning of diversity in the human species. Fieldwork revealed, and genetics later quantified, the existence of far more biological diversity within any group than between groups. Fatter and thinner people exist everywhere, as do people with type O and type A blood. What generally varies from one population to the next is the *proportion* of people in these groups expressing the trait or gene. Hair color varies strikingly among Europeans and native Australians, but little among other peoples. To focus on discovering differences between presumptive races, when the vast majority of detectable variants do not help differentiate them, was thus to define a very narrow—if not largely illusory—problem in human biology. (The fact that Africans are biologically more diverse than Europeans, but have rarely been split into races, attests to the cultural basis of these categorizations.)

Second, differences between human groups are only evident when contrasting geographical extremes. Noting these extremes, biologists of an earlier era sought to identify representatives of "pure," primordial races—presumably located in Norway, Senegal, and Thailand. At no time, however, was our species composed of a few populations within which everyone looked pretty much the same. Ever since some of our ancestors left Africa to spread out through the Old World, we humans have always lived in the "in-between" places. And human populations have also always been in genetic contact with one another. Indeed, for tens of thousands of years, humans have had trade networks; and where goods flow, so do genes. Consequently, we have no basis for considering *extreme* human forms the most pure or most representative, of some ancient primordial populations. Instead, they represent populations adapted to the most disparate environments.

And third, between each presumptive "major" race are unclassifiable populations and people. Some populations of India, for example, are darkly pigmented (or "black"), have European-like ("Caucasoid") facial features, but inhabit the continent of Asia (which should make them "Asian"). Americans might tend to ignore these "exceptions" to the racial categories, since immigrants to the United States from West Africa, Southeast Asia, and northwest Europe far outnumber those from India. The very existence of these unclassifiable peoples undermines the idea that there are just three human biological groups in the Old World. Yet acknowledging the biological distinctiveness of such groups leads to a rapid proliferation of categories. What about Australians? Polynesians? The Ainu of Japan?

Categorizing people is important to any society. It is, at some basic psychological level, probably necessary to have a group identity about who and what you are, in contrast to who and what you are not. The concept of race, however, specifically involves the recruitment of biology to validate those categories of self-identity.

Mice don't have to worry about that the way humans do. Consequently, classifying them into subspecies entails less of a responsibility for a scientist than classifying humans into subspecies does. And by the 1960s, most anthropologists realized they could not defend any classification of *Homo sapiens* into biological subspecies or races that could be considered reasonably objective. They therefore stopped doing it, and stopped identifying the endeavor as a central goal of the field. It was a biologically intractable problem—the old square-peg-in-a-round-hole enterprise; and people's lives, or welfares, could well depend on the ostensibly scientific pronouncement. Reflecting on the social history of the twentieth century, that was a burden anthropologists would no longer bear.

This conceptual divorce in anthropology—of cultural from biological phenomena—was one of the most fundamental scientific revolutions of our time. And since it affected assumptions so rooted in our everyday experience, and resulted in conclusions so counterintuitive—like the idea that the earth goes around the sun, and not vice versa—it has been widely underappreciated.

Kurt Vonnegut, in *Slaughterhouse Five*, describes what he remembered being taught about human variation: "At that time, they were teaching that there was absolutely no difference between anybody. They may be teaching that still." Of course there are biological differences between people, and between populations. The question is: How are those differences patterned? And the answer seems to be: Not racially. Populations are the only readily identifiable units of humans, and even they are fairly fluid, biologically similar to populations nearby, and biologically different from populations far away.

In other words, the message of contemporary anthropology is: You may group humans into a small number of races if you want to, but you are denied biology as a support for it.

# Chapter 38

# *Brave New Right*

## Michael Lind

Suddenly, hereditarianism is back on the American right. "Race, Pathology, and IQ," read the headline of one of two excerpts from *The Bell Curve* in *The Wall Street Journal* on October 10, 1994. "Race, Intelligence, and Science," was the rubric that glowed on the sleeve of the September 12, 1994 issue of *National Review.* The latter contained a rave review of a different book, by Canadian psychologist J. Phillipe Rushton, titled *Race, Intelligence and Behavior.* Rushton's book offered far-out views about differences in intelligence, work habits, and genital size among whites, black, and Asians.

The rehabilitation of would-be scientific race theory on the right—cautious in the work of Murray and Herrnstein, blatant in the writings of Rushton—raises an interesting question: Why now? After all, there is nothing new about the claim that IQ scores prove that blacks are inherently inferior to whites in intelligence. Arthur J. Jensen and William Shockley stirred controversy by promoting it in the 1960s and 1970s, as did Roger Pearson and Rushton in the 1980s and early 1990s. Much of this debate, moreover, has taken place in public. Rushton's views on race have made him a figure of controversy in Canada for years. And he is not unknown in this country (he has appeared on "Geraldo"). Herrnstein himself set off a firestorm with his article "IQ" in *The Atlantic Monthly* in December 1971. Why have these theories about race become respectable on the right for the first time since the civil rights revolution?

The change in the conservative line on race, IQ and inequality does not mirror any change in mainstream scientific thinking on these subjects. To be sure, speculation about the influence of biology on human nature has become more respectable since the 1970s, when radical leftists at a public speech threw blood on one of America's leading sociobiologists, Edmund O. Wilson. Both radical environmentalism and the crude kind of sociobi-

ology that tried to directly connect specific behavioral traits with genes appear to be giving way in the scholarly community to a nuanced consensus view that human potential is flexible but constrained at the margins by heredity. There has even been interesting research done into the connection between language families and genetic groups by Luigi Cavalli-Sforza and other scholars.

These recent developments in mainstream genetics and anthropology have been utterly ignored by the conservative press, and have apparently played no part in the revival of hereditarian theory on the right. As a group, the neo-hereditarian thinkers look less like a school of dissident experts than an eccentric and impassioned sect. None of the well-known hereditarian theorists has been formally trained in mathematical genetics, population biology, or ecology. They tend to be amateurs who turn to armchair speculation about race and eugenics after careers in other fields (Shockley was a physicist; Herrnstein and Rushton were trained in psychology; Murray has a degree from MIT in political science). They rely extensively and sometimes uncritically on one another's work. Rather in the manner of creationists, they are inclined to portray themselves as victimized martyrs of a "liberal" or "Marxist" scientific establishment. And—by far the most important point—almost all of the leading hereditarians have been supported financially by the same institutional benefactor.

Since the late 1960s, a little-known institution called the Pioneer Fund has been the major financial sponsor of the research of the major neo-hereditarian theorists. Among the recipients of Pioneer Fund grants (often hundreds of thousands of dollars) have been Jensen, who has argued that IQ tests prove the genetic inferiority of blacks; Shockley, promoter of a "sterilization bonus plan" deterring low-IQ people, disproportionately black, from reproducing; Robert Gordon, who argues that black–white differences in crime are closely correlated to black–white IQ differences; Ralph Scott, an

From *The New Republic* October 31, 1994.

educational psychology professor at the University of Northern Iowa who opposed busing on the basis of "genetic aspects of educability"; and Pearson, who, since the mid-1980s, has received more than $200,000 from the Pioneer Fund. Between 1986 and 1990, Rushton received more than $250,000.

In addition to supporting the research of scholars who argue for the innate intellectual inferiority of blacks, the Pioneer Fund has also subsidized the Federation for American Immigration Reform (FAIR), which supports immigration restriction, and an English-only advocacy group called U.S. English. (Former U.S. Civil Rights Commission member Linda Chavez resigned as president of U.S. English after the anti-Catholic and anti-Hispanic views of its founder became known.) During the past decade the Pioneer Fund has given more than half a million dollars to support "twin studies" at the University of Minnesota. The researchers at the Minnesota Center for Twin and Adoption Research are investigating, among other things, possible genetic origins for professional aptitude, religious tolerance, and even political radicalism. One of the directors of the Minnesota Center, psychologist Thomas J. Bouchard, co-authored a paper with Rushton in 1989 in which the two beneficiaries of Pioneer Fund grants argued that blacks are inherently more likely to get AIDS. The reason, Bouchard and Rushton claimed, is an inherited "reproductive strategy" that gives blacks a propensity to engage in promiscuous sex. All these authors are cited in the bibliography of Murray and Herrnstein's *The Bell Curve.*

What exactly is the Pioneer Fund? It was founded in 1937 with the money from a textile tycoon, Wickliffe Draper, whose other projects included paying for the translation of eugenics texts from German into English (after World War II, Draper supported Senator Joseph McCarthy, opposed federal civil rights laws and favored the "repatriation" of black Americans to Africa). The Fund's stated purpose was to promote "race betterment" through the reproduction of descendants of "white persons who settled in the original thirteen colonies prior to the adoption of the Constitution and/or from related stocks." An early project was cash grants to pilots in the all-white U.S. Army Air Corps to encourage them to have more children. One of the Pioneer Fund's founders, Frederick Osborn, at one time president of the American Eugenics Society, described Nazi eugenic policy in 1936 as the "most important experiment which has ever been tried."

The central role of the Pioneer Fund in the neo-hereditarian movement makes the new support for these researchers on the part of the mainstream right all the more perplexing. Why are mainstream conservatives suddenly welcoming thinkers in this tainted tradition? The answer, I suggest, has less to do with changes in the American intellectual community or American society as a whole than with the ongoing transformation of American conservatism. In a remarkably short period of time, the broadly based, optimistic conservatism of the Reagan years, with its focus on the economy and foreign policy, has given way to a new "culture war" conservatism, obsessed with immigration, race, and sex. This emergent post-cold war right has less to do with the Goldwater-Reagan right than the older American right of Father Coughlin and Gerald L.K. Smith's Christian Nationalist Crusade. In its apocalyptic style as well as its apocalyptic obsessions, this new conservatism owes more to Pat Robertson and Patrick Buchanan than to William F. Buckley Jr. and Irving Kristol. The growing importance, within the Republican Party, of the Deep South no doubt also plays a role; Goldwater's and Reagan's Sun Belt conservatism is being rewritten in Southern Gothic style. Race, sex, breeding, class—these are the classic themes of Tidewater reaction.

It is not surprising, then, that long-suppressed ideas about hereditary racial inequality are now reemerging. Their entry, or rather their return, is made easier by the crumbling of taboos that has accompanied the popular backlash against the excesses of political correctness. The nastiest elements on the right now answer any criticism with the charge that they are victims of "P.C."

In addition to these general trends, the most important particular factor behind the rehabilitation of hereditarianism on the right may be the recent evolution of the debate among conservatives about race and poverty. For several years a right-wing backlash has been growing against the integrationism and environmentalism not of liberals, but of certain prominent conservatives. A few years ago, in a perceptive article for *The American Spectator,* David Frum identified two schools of thought among conservatives about poverty in general, and black urban poverty in particular. One school, whose major spokesman was Jack Kemp, believed that poor black Americans would respond to the proper economic incentives with entrepreneurial ardor. These conservatives stressed free market reforms such as "enterprise zones" and the subsidized sale of public housing to tenants, reforms that, it was claimed, might break the underclass dependency on a paternalistic state. The "culturalist" school, identified with thinkers like William Bennett and James Q. Wilson, were more impressed by signs of familial breakdown in the inner city and the perpetuation of a "culture of poverty." The ghetto poor could not be expected to take advantage of new economic opportunities unless their values changed first. When Frum wrote, a third school of pessimistic neo-hereditarians was not engaged in the debate; Kemp, Bennett, and Wilson were environmentalists, finding the sources of black poverty elsewhere than in the inherited traits of poor blacks.

For all their differences, the free-marketeers and "culturalists" agreed that the problems of the black urban underclass could not be addressed without government activism. In effect, Kemp and Wilson (who has come to represent the "culturalist" school more than Bennett) had reasoned their way back to the conclusions of Daniel Patrick Moynihan in 1965 about the need to address the black family breakdown through substantial social programs. The conservatives who had thought the most about race and poverty were arguing, in effect, for a conservative version of Lyndon Johnson's War on Poverty. Whether it took the form of massive subsidies to public housing tenants or a national network of high quality orphanages for the children of broken ghetto families, there would have to be government-backed social engineering on a grand scale. It soon became clear that a conservative war on poverty would be enormously expensive. In the Bush administration, conservative hate object Richard Darman actually led the struggle to defeat Kemp's proposals for higher spending on the urban poor. A national system of quality orphanages and boarding schools, of the kind that Wilson favors, would cost billions.

A call for activist government paid for by higher taxes to help the ghetto poor was not what most conservatives wanted to hear from their experts on urban poverty. Wilson's proposals probably never had a chance in the era of Bob Dole, Newt Gingrich, and a bitter Republican obstructionism. As for Kemp, the reaction against his "bleeding-heart, big-government" conservatism on the right was setting in even while he was still George Bush's secretary of housing and urban development. Conservatives who revered the hero of the Kemp-Roth tax cuts himself began to mutter about the new Kemp, the Kemp who was too eager to embrace big government—and too soft on blacks.

The gradual isolation of Kemp within the conservative movement has probably ruined his presidential hopes. Empower America, founded as a springboard for his 1996 GOP presidential nomination, is slowly falling apart, with Vin Weber distancing himself. The marginalization of Kemp has been most clearly visible in *National Review,* which has criticized Kemp's views on immigration as too soft and cast him as the defender of the black poor in a strange debate over whether there is a crime problem in America or just a "black crime" problem.

The crypto-nativist rationale for restricting high levels of immigration (there are other, non-nativist arguments) can only be strengthened by the fact that scholars as esteemed as Murray and Herrnstein fret over the danger posed by "an immigrant population with low cognitive ability." Not only must low-IQ immigrants be kept out, according to Herrnstein and Murray, but low-IQ native-born Americans must be discouraged from reproducing. Though the authors of *The Bell Curve* refuse to endorse eugenic measures other than an end to welfare and easy access to contraceptives, the logic of their arguments points in the direction of the sterilization of the "feeble-minded," a policy common in the United States throughout most of this century.

It remains to be seen how far the eugenic enthusiasms of the neo-hereditarian right can go before they collide with conservative religious convictions. In the early twentieth century, advocates of eugenic sterilization (not only political conservatives, but liberals and socialists) found their most committed adversary in the Catholic Church. The employment of a distorted version of Darwinism in the defense of the economic and racial status quo is also problematic in light of the resolute anti-Darwinism of Protestant evangelicals. In the nineteenth century the most radical American racists tended to be secular intellectuals; the biblical account of the common origin and salvation of mankind prevented devout Protestant conservatives, no matter how bigoted, from treating the different races as separate species of subspecies. In what is surely one of the great ironies of our time, at the end of the twentieth century, as at the end of the nineteenth, the excesses encouraged by eugenic theory in the United States may only be checked within the conservative movement by the dogmas of resurgent fundamentalism.

# Chapter 39

# *The Nature of Human Universals*

## Robert W. Sussman

The two books I review in this paper focus on the biological basis of human nature and on universal aspects of humanness. Carl N. Degler is a historian who has written a number of books on the history of racism and sexism in the United States. His book *In Search of Human Nature: The Decline and Revival of Darwinism in American Social Thought* traces the history and changes in these topics from Darwin's time to the present. In *Human Universals,* Donald E. Brown attempts to convince us that human universals do indeed exist and then he lists them for us.

As his title implies, Degler has two main themes. The first, the decline of Darwinism, is a history of racism and sexism in United States thought since Darwin. The second theme, the revival of Darwinism, is a review of the recent resurgence, popularity, and scientific interest in the study of the biological underpinnings of human behavior. Degler's basic thesis is that, over the past century, racism and sexism have often been justified by emphasizing biologically based differences between racial and ethnic groups, and between the sexes. In arguing against this view, he reviews studies that have consistently shown greater differences within than between different races and genders in major and important measures of behavior.

In the final section of the book, however, Degler praises new efforts to search for general aspects of human nature that transect human groups. It is assumed that humans have adapted to their environment over evolutionary history and, in doing so, share certain aspects of their nature in common. I found Degler's review of the "decline" of Darwinism excellent. His discussion of its "revival" was less inspiring.

In his book, Donald Brown is worried that anthropologists have been too skeptical about the universals and have too much faith in cultural relativism. So he attempts to define human universals for us, present a history of their study, and explain them; and then he provides us with a list of (as the jacket cover touts) some four hundred human universals.

Beginning at the end of the nineteenth century, many biological and social scientists applied the principle of the survival of the fittest to explain "biologically based" differences in the behavior of racial groups, though many confused the inheritance of acquired characteristics with that of genetically based ones. With the acceptance of Mendelian or the "new" genetics in the early 1990s, the belief that racial differences were biologically based and could not be changed by the environment was generally espoused. That these differences were permanently fixed in the genes was the major rationale for the eugenics movement. In a similar manner, writes Degler, scientists used Darwinism to explain and justify differences in the treatment of women in the late nineteenth and twentieth centuries. Sexual selection and genetics became the rationale for the Victorian family and for many discriminatory educational policies.

In 1883, fearing the effects of bad genetics on human behavior, Darwin's cousin, Francis Galton (a geneticist and statistician) coined the term eugenics from the Greek, "well born." Galton recommended that we breed better people. Once Lamarckian inheritance was overturned in favor of Mendelian genetics, the eugenics movement became extremely popular among scientists and politicians; after all, hereditary change and not environmental manipulation was seen as the only way to better the human race. The systematic practice of involuntary sterilization, begun to control crime, became the technology of eugenics; and by 1930 thirty states had enacted sterilization laws.

IQ tests were often used to prove mental deficiency and were increasingly drawn upon to compare the "intelligence" of ethnic and racial groups. Two well-known psychologists, Robert Yerkes and Carl Brigham, were

From *Reviews in Anthropology*, Volume 24, 1995. Reprinted by permission from Gordon and Breach Publishers.

among the most diligent in using these tests and were extremely active in the eugenics movement. In fact, in his well received book, *A Study of American Intelligence,* Brigham (1923) drew from the results of army testing and wrote, "American intelligence is declining and will proceed with an accelerating rate as the racial admixture becomes more and more extensive" (quoted in Degler, pp. 51–52). He then urged the government to severely limit immigration of the undesirable groups. Congress passed the Immigration Act in 1924.

Franz Boas was a Jewish immigrant who had left Germany because of the rising racial prejudice in that country at the end of the nineteenth century. Degler points out the importance of Boas and a handful of other scientists in offering an alternative to the idea that behavioral traits were fixed in the genes. As early as 1911, Boas challenged the view that differences in race, ethnic group, and social class were derived from innate capacities. Boas' radical view at that time was that these "differences were the product of different histories, not different biological experiences" (Degler, p. 62). He introduced a then innovative use of the term "culture" (1911), applying it not as another word for civilization but in a plural form to express that different societies exhibit distinctive cultures, and that this underlies differences among people. With the introduction of this concept, environment could again be seen as a major cause of behavioral variability among peoples. Boas, along with his students and colleagues, continued to develop this idea of culture, and it became the paradigm of anthropology—to my mind perhaps the most important contribution of anthropology to modern science and to social policy.

Degler reviews many of the important studies that provided evidence of the importance of culture in ethnic and racial differences in morphology and behavior. One example is Boas' study of head shape, whose measurement was thought to be the most reliable indicator of human types or races. Boas (1912) showed that the head shapes of children born to immigrants in the United States changed after mothers had been in the United States for as little as ten years.

In another extremely important series of studies, Otto Klineberg, a colleague of Boas at Columbia University, argued against the use of IQ tests to support the hypothesis of biological inferiority of certain races or ethnic groups. Klineberg (1935) first focused on the theory that Nordics were mentally superior to Mediterranean and Alpine people. He found that European urban boys scored higher on achievement tests than did rural boys regardless of ethnic group and, further, that the differences among these groups were small and unreliable.

Klineberg (1928, 1935) also studied the tests being administered to American army personnel, which often were used to justify racial slanders. Among other things, Klineberg found that northern blacks scored higher on IQ tests than southern blacks; northern whites scored

higher than southern whites; and northern blacks scored higher than southern whites. Yerkes (1923) had explained these differences as the result of "selective migration ... the more energetic, progressive, mentally alert members of the race have moved northward" (quoted in Degler, p. 181). But in testing southern-born black children in New York City, Klineberg found that the longer they lived in the north the higher their scores. The conclusion was that environment alone and not heredity or selective migration accounted for the test score differences.

The writings of Boas, Klineberg, and other scientists fighting racially and sexually based prejudices of the early 1900s should be reread by scientists of all fields today because many of these early arguments are still valid against the racism, sexism, and much of the biological determinism that we see in the current literature. By 1930, many scientists believed that the inability to define intelligence or to control for such factors as education, social status, and language prevented any proof of racial inferiority or superiority that would meet the traditional standards for scientific acceptance. In 1916 Boas asserted that "unless the contrary can be proved, we must assume that all complex activities are socially determined, not hereditary" (quoted in Degler, p. 148).

Kroeber, a student of Boas, developed the idea of culture even further and warned that until biological bases for behavioral differences "are established and exactly defined," the historian must assume their nonexistence. "If he does not his work becomes a vitiated mixture of history and biology" (quoted in Degler, p. 92). It is my belief that these warnings still hold true for much of what is advanced today in the name of biological determinism and human universals. In fact, many of the arguments raised by Degler in the first half of his book can be used against theories he praises in the last half, as well as those discussed by Donald Brown.

In his final five chapters, Degler attempts to show that, even though Darwinism was a bad explanation for racial and sexual differences among humans, it might in fact be a good way to explain general aspects of human nature. He believes that, in the recent resurgence of biology to explain human behavior, there is no attempt to divide human groups into those more or less genetically well endowed. Instead, this new Darwinism simply attempts to put human behavior into an evolutionary perspective. Donald Brown also believes that ". . . evolutionary theory offers the only explanatory framework for universals that is potentially all-inclusive" (p. 99).

We might all agree that, since we are subject to the laws of natural selection, our biology and behavior should reflect this. Human nature does exist and indeed it is dependent upon human heredity. After all, humans are more like one another than they are like gorillas, and gorilla nature differs from that of chimpanzees. We must then ask 'What is human nature (as, for example, opposed to gorilla nature)?" and "Once we know what it is, how does this help us understand, explain, predict, (control?) human behavior, evolution, or whatever?" Do Degler or Brown have the answers to these questions, or do they at least get us any closer to these answers than all of those who have pondered the problem of human nature and nurture in the past? I think not.

Degler, in speaking of the revival of Darwinism in America believes that the new biological approach is better than the old one. After all, it is based on the assumption, expressed above, that all humans share a common heredity. The basis of this new approach is as follows: "The new biology, the biology of Darwinism, evolutionary theory, and genetics, dealt with the whole species, not with the races or subgroups within the species" (Degler, p. 219). Degler believes that the root of this new direction was (in my opinion, often sensationalized) ethological research that sought to find some relationships between animal and human behavior. "Undoubtedly the most frequently expressed philosophical outlook moving social scientists beyond an environmental or cultural explanation for human behavior was an appreciation of the Darwinian emphasis upon the continuity between animals and human beings" (p. 237).

Degler points out, as does Donald Brown, that this new approach gained notoriety with the publication of E. O. Wilson's *Sociobiology: The New Synthesis* (1975) in which he attempted to show the relevance of animal ethology to the study of human behavior. Degler believes that, unlike the (perhaps unconscious) motivation for earlier attempts to explain the biological basis of human behavior, sociobiological explanations are not driven by conservative politics. (Though I would argue that most proponents of these new theories are middle class, white, western European males and that the media coverage of this field has been quite politically conservative.) However, Degler does suggest, although not in so many words, that the motivation for this new biological determinism is the desire of biologists, mainly animal ethologists, to assume that they have some expertise in explaining human behavior (usually a false assumption, I would argue) and the fact that many social scientists believe that by becoming sociobiologists they are being more scientific, like their colleagues in biology: ". . . in seeking to uncover the reasons why many social scientists were attracted to biological ideas, the power and success of the biological sciences cannot be ignored" (Degler, p. 241).

Degler is impressed by the 2500 items in the bibliography of Wilson's book in that it "amply testified to the wealth of research that had been published in the preceding twenty to thirty years" (p. 243). The last chapter, "Man: From Sociobiology to Sociology," Degler notes, was on the relevance of animal ethology to the study of human behavior. What Degler fails to note is that, although there are more than 500 papers on insect research referenced in Wilson's book (the subject of his

own expertise), only twenty papers dealing with original research on human behavior and ethnology are cited.

The remainder of Degler's book and the subject of Donald Brown's is to outline "human universals" and to attempt to determine the biological basis of human nature. Both authors believe that biologically based human universals are inherited and the product of natural selection through such processes as kin selection, reciprocal altruism, sexual selection, and the desire for all organisms to attain dominance—all of which are assumed to lead to greater reproductive success. Although these mechanisms undoubtedly work in certain contexts, and they have been accepted as the major forces of behavioral evolution by many contemporary scientists (including Degler and Brown), empirical research on these hypotheses has been inconclusive at best. However, neither Degler nor Brown dwell on these evolutionary processes, nor will I, except to offer a short list of critical reviews on these subjects. See, for example, Bekoff (1981) and Gouzoules (1984) on kin selection, Casti (1989) on reciprocal altruism, Bartlett et al. (1994) on sexual selection in explaining infanticide, and Dewsbury (1982) and Bercovitch (1991) on the relationship between dominance and reproductive success.

After accepting the fact that human universals do exist, that the important ones are biologically based (e.g., the results of inheritance), and that their existence has been brought about by selection, both authors enumerate some of these. For example, a partial list of Brown's "human universals" includes: language, incest taboos, units of time, classifications for parts of the body, binary discrimination, ability to order continua, gestures, ability to distinguish normal from abnormal mental states, emotional reaction (generally with fear) to snakes, Oedipus complex as a part of the male psychology, propensity for right-handedness, knowledge of how to use fire, propensity to take substances to alter mood, territoriality, children not being left to grow up on their own, ability to learn by trial and error, practice of magic, attempt to control the weather, practice of divination, dancing and music, children's music, dominance hierarchies, male dominance over females. "Universals," Brown explains, "comprise a heterogenous set—cultural, social, linguistic, individual, unrestricted, implicational, etc.—a set that may defy any single overarching explanation. If, however, a single source for universals had to be sought, human nature would be the place to look" (p. 142).

The traits listed above are among Brown's "absolute universals," which he distinguishes from "near-universals," "statistical universals," "implicational universals," and a number of others. The *Webster New World Dictionary* definition of "universal" is "of, for, or including all or the whole; unlimited; or of the universe; present everywhere." Something is, thus, universal or it is not. A near-universal is like something that is "almost unique." Unfortunately, the result of vague definitions of this sort is a loose laundry list of presumably genetically based "universal" behaviors.

In fact, I see three major, interrelated problems with this approach. First, these *presumed* "universals" are assumed to be hereditary, genetically based behaviors derived from natural selection over the history of humans, and yet the relationship between genetics and behavior among them is extremely vague at best. What, for example, are the genes that control our fear of snakes, our ability to practice magic, or our attempt to control the weather? Are these single gene traits, polygenic, or pleiotropic traits? Although inheritance of these traits is crucial for the operation of natural selection, very little is known about the inheritance of social behavior in human or non-human primates (Bartlett et al. 1994, Lande and Arnold 1983, Richard and Schulman 1982).

Second, many of the traits included as universals by both Degler and Brown are either not universal at all or, as warned by Kroeber, are "a vitiated mixture of history and biology." For example, it is by no means accepted that the Oedipus complex is universal, or that it exists at all (Fisher and Greenberg 1977, Grünbaum 1984). In relation to the universal ability to recognize abnormal mental states, psychiatrists using the Diagnostic and Statistical Manual (DSM) of the American Psychiatric Association have constantly changed the criteria used to define and describe psychiatric disorders. This manual has been revised approximately every ten years since first written in the early 1950s. Furthermore, it has been shown that ethnic groups interpret physical and emotional symptoms differently and use varied criteria to identify what is and what is not an "abnormal" mental state (Sussman et al. 1987, Trimble et al. 1984).

Both authors include a chapter on incest taboo/ avoidance as a human universal; for example Degler claims that "The so-called incest taboo . . . is one of the few undisputed 'universals' of human behavior" (p. 245). However, after detailed discussion Degler and Brown are unable to distinguish nature from nurture in human incest avoidance. Degler first criticizes Lévi-Strauss' ambivalence in stating that "the taboo is the link between culture and nature . . . (the prohibition of incest is where nature transcends itself" (quoted in Degler, p. 254) Then at the end of his chapter he seems to come to a similar conclusion: "Just because incest is prohibited by nature, its practice is a sign and a measure of human transcendence over nature or the animal" (p. 268). Brown, on the other hand, just sounds confused:

What lessons, in conclusion, may be derived from the recent efforts to understand the incest taboo/avoidance? One is the sobering reflection that an alleged universal that has exercised the anthropological imagination for over 100 years is still not explained to everyone's satisfaction. It is not even certain that the phenomenon is a universal. The incest taboo clearly is not universal, though it surely is a statistical universal and might be a near universal. On the other hand, incest avoidance may be universal. (p. 128)

My third problem with this grab-bag of universals is that they include traits that are of very different levels of abstraction, and there is no attempt to integrate or organize them in any meaningful way. For example, human behavior is constrained to some extent by the structure of the human mind and of the morphophysiology of the sense organs. Certainly, many of the cross-cultural similarities in language and language acquisition are due to these organic structures. Secondly, there are so-called "universals" that are the result of limited possibilities—that is, there would be no other conceivable way in which these behaviors could be carried out. For example, both Degler and Brown mention the way in which humans classify the world into "binary discriminations" and also "continua" (Brown, p. 134). But as George Gaylord Simpson (1961) stated in *Principles of Animal Taxonomy:*

> The necessity of aggregating things into classes is a completely general characteristic of living things . . . (a) minimal requirement of being and staying alive. The relationships among things that must in some way be taken into account are of many different kinds and are themselves intricately related. . . . Among these things are two . . . that seem to be particularly fundamental . . . "association by contiguity" and "association by similarity." (p. 3)

Finally, there are those limitations placed on us by our genetically based morphophysiology that restrict our cultural and social behavior. This includes such things as bipedalism, right-handedness, sexually based hormonal distinctions, and differences related to childbirth and nursing, death, etc. In the early 1900s, Hertz recognized difficulty in separating culture and biology in dealing with the way in which different peoples handle these sorts of impositions. Concerning death, Hertz (1960) stated: "To the organic event is added a complex mass of beliefs, emotions and activities which give it its distinctive character" (p. 27). And about the right hand: "An almost insignificant bodily asymmetry is enough to turn in one direction and the other contrary representations which are already completely formed" (p. 111).

Making an unorganized laundry list of universals is a fruitless exercise. Leach (1961) attempted to describe the difficulty in trying to describe very complex phenomena without any attempt to understand underlying principles.

> I would maintain that quite simple mechanical models can have relevance for social anthropology despite the acknowledged fact that the detailed empirical facts of social life display the utmost complexity. . . . If I have a piece of rubber sheet and draw a series of lines on it to symbolize the functional interconnections of some set of social phenomena and I then start stretching the rubber

about, I can change the manifest shape of my original geometric figure out of all recognition and yet clearly there is a sense in which it is the *same* figure all the time. (p. 7)

In a similar vein, one might say that attempting to list all of the behaviors that are in some way shared by all, most, or many of the cultures of the world is like attempting to describe all of the possible permutations of a game of chess. This, of course, would lead to an enormous number of possibilities and would be extremely confusing if one did not first know the rules of the game. Once we know some of these rules, it may be possible to determine what might be important to know about biological influences on human behavior. So far, we are still just talking about statistical permutations.

If I am correct and these behaviors are not biologically based human universals but loosely defined cultural manifestations of, often at best, loosely defined biological limitations, we might ask, what criteria did Brown use to compile his list of human "universals," or to choose which human behaviors are biologically based? Brown explains that his list of absolute universals "draws heavily from Murdock (1945), Tiger and Fox (1971), and Hockett (1973). . . . In some cases I have added items to the list because of my own experience or that of a colleague or student has convinced me that the items ought to be there even though appropriate references could not be found. In a few cases I have counted something as a universal even though that required setting aside ethnographic testimony" (p. 140)(!!!). This seems like a very loose scientific methodology indeed.

Is Degler's method for determining the biological basis for human nature any better than that of Brown? For Degler, biologically based human behaviors can be found by seeking out "possible universals among human beings that might have some analogues with those identified by animal ethologists" (p. 237). These criteria are very similar to those used by Wilson who considered behaviors to be biologically determined if they were relatively constant throughout the order Primates, and were the ones most likely to have persisted in relatively unaltered form into the evolution of *Homo* (1975:551). Brown also assumes that: "As species-typical phenomena, human universals are specially privileged considerations in developing a cross-culturally valid conception of human nature" (p. 86).

Using these criteria of conservative behaviors, Wilson comes up with a list of general human traits that are still assumed by many sociobiologists to be human universals. These traits include: territoriality, aggressive dominance hierarchies, permanent male-female bonds, male dominance over females, and extended maternal care leading to matrilineality. In fact, each of the above traits is included by either Degler or Brown (or both) in their list of human universals. These traits therefore are considered

elements of human nature because they are assumed to be relatively constant throughout the order Primates and/or species-typical human behaviors (human universals). As a final exercise, let me briefly examine each of the above traits to see just how common they are among humans and other primates.

*Territoriality:* The concept of "territory" was first developed in studies on birds. The essence of the concept is that an animal or group of animals "defends" all or part of its range. Thus there are two major components: space and active defense of that space. However, many animals maintain exclusive areas simply by vocalizing, displaying, or in some way signaling to possible intruders, and very rarely, if ever, actually fighting at borders (see Waser and Wiley 1980). The concept, thus, is not in any way simple, and there are real difficulties in relating various spacing methods used by different animals to the strict concept of territoriality. In any case, group spacing mechanisms are extremely variable. Groups of gibbons and the South American monkey *Callicebus* could be considered territorial in that they actually have ritualized battles at borders of their almost exclusive ranges. A number of other primates have specialized loud calls that presumably help them maintain exclusive areas (e.g., *Colobus, Indri,* and howler monkeys, and orangutan males). However, most species of primates have overlapping group ranges and often share resources. This is especially true of many savannah forms such as baboons and chimpanzees. In ring-tailed lemurs and gorillas, several groups may have almost coincidental home ranges. Thus in primates, territoriality in the strict sense of the word is very rare (see Fedigan 1992).

In humans, the concept of territory, as used to define bird defense of area, is not at all useful. Most hunters and gatherers do not have exclusive, defended ranges. Agricultural peoples have a multitude of ways of dealing with land use. Lumping these into a simple concept of territory is nonsensical. Finally, modern warfare usually has little to do with directly defending borders. How is a political decision to send troops to Somalia similar to a bird or a gibbon displaying at the border of its range?

*Aggressive Dominance Hierarchies:* Again we are dealing with a very complex concept. Dominance hierarchies in animals are defined by a number of criteria, including priority of access to food, space, or mates; grooming direction; leader of group progression; or winner in aggressive encounters. These often are not positively correlated (Bernstein 1981)—that is, the animal who wins fights does not always lead the group. In fact, defining the group hierarchy by any one of these criteria usually does not in any way help us to understand the complexities of group structure.

Furthermore, there are many primate species in which dominance hierarchies are unclear, ambiguous, or absent altogether (Walters and Seyfarth 1987). For example, they have not been demonstrated in most prosimians, in many New and Old World arboreal monkeys, in patas monkeys, or in gibbons. They do seem to be present in baboons, macaques, and chimpanzees. However, even among these primates, hierarchies are often unstable, and the genetic influence and consequences of hierarchies are unknown. For example, in baboons, rank changes may occur on average every two weeks among males and every two months among females (Hausfater 1975); and in many studies of baboons and macaques in which paternity is known, little correlation between rank and reproductive success has been found. Generally, the relationship between rank and reproductive success remains obscure (Bercovitch 1991).

When we consider humans, the presence of dominance hierarchies based on aggression becomes even more problematic. Remember, in ethology, an aggressive dominance hierarchy is determined by winners and losers of head-to-head aggressive encounters and is normally defined within a closed social group. You might ask yourself the following questions: Is your status in society based on your fighting ability or aggressiveness? As you walk down the street or the halls of your work place, do you display aggressively or are you forced to give way to people as they pass? How many face-to-face fights have you had in your lifetime? What is your status (based on aggressive encounters) in your social group? And, by the way, what is your social group? Are these questions meaningful in human societies? I think not.

*Male Dominance over Females:* Male dominance over females is not by any means a conservative trait in primates. Smuts (1987) has identified five major types of dyadic dominance relationships between adult male and female nonhuman primates. In three of the five, males are not dominant to females. These include (1) species in which sexual dimorphism in body size is slight and in which females are clearly dominant to males (e.g., many lemuriforms); (2) species in which sexual dimorphism is slight and the sexes are codominant (many prosimians, callitrichids, many New World monkeys, and gibbons); (3) species in which males are larger than females but females sometimes dominate, often through female-female coalitions (squirrel monkeys, talapoins, vervets, many macaques, and possibly patas and Syke's monkeys). In fact, the only species in which females rarely, if ever, dominate males are those in which males are much larger than females. These species include baboons and great apes (the only primate species that most sociobiologists know anything about). Of course, sexual dimorphism in humans is slight, and female coalitions are quite common. Brown believes that male dominance over females is universal and states: "women prove everywhere to be second-class citizens in the public-political domain" (p. 91). I say, "Tell it to the queen!" (Well, I guess it must be just a partial, statistical, implicational, or near-universal.)

*Permanent Male-Female Bonds or the Nuclear Family:* These are extremely rare among primates, most primates having promiscuous mating systems. Among humans, of 862 cultures listed in Murdock's (1967) ethnographic atlas, 16 percent have pair bonds, whereas 83 percent are polygynous (Pasternak 1976).

*Matrilineality:* Sixteen of the 179 hunting and gathering societies listed in Murdock's atlas are matrilineal.

Thus, these evolutionary and "genetically conservative universal" traits are neither conservative nor universal. The problem with these authors' approach to the old nature-nurture question is that they do not have any better criteria by which to formulate human nature than did earlier Social Darwinists. In fact, one of the best criticisms of this approach is one that Wilson himself uses to criticize earlier Social Darwinists "... their particular handling of the problem tended to be inefficient and misleading. They selected one plausible hypothesis or another based on a review of a small sample of animal species [or human groups, I might add] then advocated the explanation to the limit" (Wilson 1975:551). I am not saying there is no biological basis to human behavior but, as stated by Boas over 70 years ago, "unless the contrary can be proved, we must assume that all complex activities are socially determined, not hereditary" (in Degler, p. 148).

## References

Bartlett, T. Q.; Sussman, R. W.; Cheverud, J. M. (1994) "Infant killing in primates: A review of observed cases with specific reference to the sexual selection hypothesis." *American Anthropologist*, 95:958–990.

Bekoff, M. (1981) "Mammalian sibling interactions." In *Parental Care in Mammals.* (pp. 307–347). D. J. Gubernick and P. H. Klopfer, eds. New York: Plenum Press.

Bercovitch, F. B. (1991) "Social stratification, social strategies, and reproductive success in primates." *Ethology and Sociobiology*, 12:315–333.

Bernstein, I. S. (1981) "Dominance: The baby and the bathwater." *Behavior and Brain Sciences*, 4:419–457.

Brigham, C. C. (1923) *A Study of American Intelligence.* Princeton, NJ: Princeton University Press.

Brown, D. E. (1991) *Human Universals.* Philadelphia: Temple University Press.

Boas, F. (1911) (1963) *The Mind of Primitive Man.* New York: Collier Books.

Boas, F. (1912) *Changes in Bodily Form of Descendants of Immigrants.* New York: Columbia University Press.

Casti, J. L. (1989) *Paradigms Lost.* New York: William Morrow.

Degler, C. N. (1991) *In Search of Human Nature.* New York: Oxford University Press.

Dewsbury, D. A. (1982) "Dominance rank, copulatory behavior, and differential reproduction." *Quarterly Review of Biology*, 57:135–159.

Fedigan, L. M. (1992) *Primate Paradigms.* Chicago: University of Chicago Press.

Fisher, S.; Greenberg, R. P. (1977) *The Scientific Credibility of Freud's Theories and Therapy.* New York: Basic Books.

Gouzoules, S. (1984) "Primate mating systems, kin associations, and cooperative behavior: Evidence for kin recognition?" *Yearbook of Physical Anthropology,* 27:99–134.

Grünbaum, A. (1984) *The Foundation of Psychoanalysis: A Philosophical Critique.* Berkeley: University of California Press.

Hausfater, G. (1975) *Dominance and Reproduction in Baboons (Papio cynocephalus).* Basel: S. Karger.

Hertz, R. (1960) *Death and the Right Hand.* Glencoe, IL: Free Press.

Hockett, C. F. (1973) *Man's Place in Nature.* New York: McGraw-Hill.

Klineberg, O. (1928). "An experimental study of speed and other factors in 'racial' differences." *Archives of Psychology,* 15:49–50.

Klineberg, O. (1935) *Racial Differences.* New York: Harper and Brothers.

Lande, R.; Arnold, S. (1983) "The measurement of selection on correlated characters." *Evolution,* 37:1210–1226.

Leach, E. R. (1961) *Rethinking Anthropology.* London: Athlone Press.

Murdock, G. P. (1945) "The common denominator of cultures." In *The Science of Man in the World Crisis.* (pp. 123–142). R. Linton, ed. New York: Columbia University Press.

Murdock, G. P. (1967) *Ethnographic Atlas.* Pittsburgh: University of Pittsburgh Press.

Pasternak, B. (1976) *Introduction to Kinship and Social Organization.* Englewood Cliffs, NJ: Prentice-Hall.

Richard, A. F.; Schulman, S. R. (1982) "Sociobiology: Primate field studies." *Annual Review of Anthropology,* 11:231–255.

Simpson, G. G. (1961) *Principles of Animal Taxonomy.* New York: Columbia University Press.

Smuts, B. B. (1987) "Gender, aggression, and influence." In *Primate Societies.* (pp. 400–412). B. B. Smuts, D. L. Cheney, R. M. Seyfarth, R. W. Wrangham, and T. T. Struhsaker, eds. Chicago: University of Chicago Press.

Sussman, L. K.; Robins, L. N.; Earls, F. (1987) "Treatment-seeking for depression by black and white Americans." *Social Science and Medicine,* 24:187–196.

Tiger, L; Fox, R. (1971) *The Imperial Animal.* New York: Holt, Rinehart and Winston.

Trimble, J. E.; Manson, S. M.; Dinges, N. C.; Medicine, B. (1984) "American Indian concepts of mental health: Reflections and directions." In *Cultural Concepts of Mental Health and Therapy* (pp. 199–220). P. Pedersen and A. Marsella, eds. Beverly Hills: Sage Publications.

Walters, J. R.; Seyfarth, R. M. (1987) "Conflict and cooperation." In *Primate Societies* (pp. 306–317). B. B. Smuts, D. L. Cheney, R. M. Seyfarth, R. W. Wrangham, and T. T. Struhsaker, eds. Chicago: University of Chicago Press.

Waser, P.; Wiley, R. H. (1980) "Mechanisms and evolution of spacing in animals." In *Handbook of Behavioral Neurobiology,* Vol. 3. (pp. 159–233). P. Marler and J. G. Vandenbergh, eds. New York: Plenum Press.

Wilson, E. O. (1975) *Sociobiology: The New Synthesis.* Cambridge, MA: Harvard University Press.

Yerkes, R. M. (1923) "Testing the human mind." *Atlantic Monthly,* 131:363–364.

# Part IV

# THE NEW BIOLOGICAL DETERMINISM

It is commonly believed that sociobiology (see Chapters 13–15) is no longer a major component of behavioral biology. However, many of the preconceptions now pervasive in the field are derived from sociobiological premises. Although the current proponents of this approach rarely refer to themselves as sociobiologists, the theoretical underpinnings are the same (e.g., Daly and Wilson 1988, Dunbar 1988, Emlen 1995, Scarr 1993, Tooby and Cosmides 1992). Furthermore, the perceptions of human nature are much the same as they were in the 1950s (e.g., Brown 1991, Degler 1991, Russell 1993, Wrangham and Peterson 1996, Wright 1994).

This approach has reached a wide popular audience, especially through the writings of Robert Wright, a senior editor of *The New Republic,* who has recent articles in *Time, Newsweek, The New Yorker,* and *Atlantic Monthly* on the new sociobiology. In his book, *The Moral Animal, Why We Are the Way We Are: The New Science of Evolutionary Psychology,* Wright (1994:6–7) writes:

> . . . Wilson's book drew so much fire, provoked so many charges of malign political intent, so much caricature of sociobiology's substance, that the word became tainted. Most practitioners of the field he defined now prefer to avoid his label. Though bound by allegiance to a compact and coherent set of doctrines, they go by different names: behavioral ecologists, Darwinian anthropologists, evolutionary psychologists, evolutionary psychiatrists. People sometimes ask: Whatever happened to sociobiology? The answer is that it went underground, where it has been eating away at the foundations of academic orthodoxy.

Although the basic premises of sociobiology were criticized extensively in the 1970s and 1980s, the new "underground" biological determinism of the 1990s has yet to face major challenges. In this section of the book, three widely accepted concepts within this new sociobiology are presented, with rebuttals to each: (1) behavioral differences between the sexes and the genetic basis of infidelity among humans, (2) the biology of violence, and (3) infanticide as an evolutionary strategy. I believe each of these concepts is based more upon preconceptions about nonhuman and human behavior than upon existing data.

*Is there a gene for infidelity?* A recent cover of *Newsweek* (August 15, 1994) reads: "Infidelity: It may be in our genes." This view of "natural" human behavior rests on two simple predictions of modern evolutionary psychology (see Chapter 40). First, to spread their genes, the most fit men attempt to sire the maximum number of children and, second, that women should attempt to mate with males who will make the maximum investment in children. We could call these two types of males cavorting males and nurturing males. This view of human society is based on a widely accepted sociobiological tenet. A female mammal, once fertilized, gains little by repeated matings, whereas males are less constrained by their reproductive biology and can increase their reproductive output by continuing to mate with as many females as possible (Dunbar 1988). Furthermore, it is believed that most primates show male-biased dispersal and males provide little direct paternal care (Bradbury and Vehrencamp 1977; Pusey and Packer 1987; Trivers 1972; Wrangham 1980).

There are problems with the data used to support this theory and with the theory itself. In a recent article, "Myth of the Typical Primate," Strier (1994:233) points out that "data on species that were once considered peripheral to questions about human behavioral evolution are now challenging many long-standing perceptions of comparative behavioral ecology." Among these perceptions is that male-biased dispersal and female philopatry are "typical" in nonhuman primates. In fact, Strier points out that, even when just comparing polygynous and polygamous species, over 50 percent exhibit dispersal by females or by both sexes.

The assumption that the costs of reproduction are extremely high for females and cheap for males has been challenged by Hrdy (1988) and Tang-Martinez (Chapter 42). The data reveal that the costs for males has been greatly underestimated. " . . . such data have also forced us to reinterpret the behavior of males.... by shifting our focus from the production of infants to the survival of infants, we are forced to take into account a whole range of male and female activities that have drastic repercussions on the survival of offspring" (Hrdy 1988:167).

Theoretically, the hypothesis is contradictory and leads to circular reasoning. If the most fit male (the cavorter) spends his time searching for females with which to mate and increases his fitness even further by killing the infants of his rivals, then he has little time to help any one female nurture her offspring, or protect it from infanticidal males. However, the nurturing male is not fit because he doesn't have time to cavort! And, if he decides to cavort, an infanticidal male may kill his offspring. What type of male is a female to choose (if she has any choice)?

The evolutionary psychologists have an answer (see Chapter 41). Fit males are infidels, and females choose males that can either fool them (fit cavorting males that at least show a semblance of supporting their offspring), or unfit, nurturing males (who don't cavort). In the latter case, the female's best strategy is to fool the unfit male by cavorting with more fit, cavorting males and cuckholding her nurturing partner. "The theoretical upshot of all this is another evolutionary arms race. As men grow more attuned to the threat of cuckoldry, women should get better at convincing a man that their adoration borders on awe, their fidelity on the saintly." (Wright 1994:72). Thus, according to the evolutionary psychologist, yes, we are by nature infidels, and evolving to get better at it all the time!

*The biological basis of violence.* In Chapter 43, Wright asks if it is "right to compare violent inner-city males—or any other violent human males—to nonhuman primates," or to "think that rape in some sense can be a 'natural' response to certain circumstances"? To Wright, thinking about genes for violence from an evolutionary point of view can explain why "inner-city thugs may be functioning as 'designed'" by long-term evolutionary adaptations that predetermine their responses to their poverty-stricken (low-status) environment. In this light, Wright quotes Daly and Wilson: "competition can sometimes be fiercest near the bottom of the scale, where the man on track for total (reproductive) failure has nothing to lose by the most dangerous competitive tactics, and therefore may throw caution to the winds."

I presume that these authors are equating inner-city males to subordinate nonhuman primate males and making the false assumption that in nonhuman primates dominance status is always associated with reproductive fitness. They also are making the false assumption that poverty and violence in the inner city is in some way related to reproductive success or lack thereof. Finally, these authors seem to be assuming that it is "natural" for inner city males to be violent. This approach cannot explain why the majority of inner-city males are not violent—a fact perhaps missed by the new sociobiologists.

Wright goes on to explain that evolutionary psychology depicts some things "often thought to be 'pathological' as 'natural'." He includes as natural unyielding hatred, mild depression, and the tendency for men to treat women as their personal property. "Of course, to call these things 'natural' isn't to call them good." Wright continues, "If anything, evolutionary psychology might be invoked on behalf of the doctrine of Original Sin: We are in some respects born bad, and redemption entails struggle against our nature."

Original sin seems to be a recurring theme. As I pointed out in Chapter 20, these theories appear to be "good to think" because they fit our traditional Euro-Christian beliefs and the data often are being interpreted in ways that reinforce these beliefs. The morality and ethics of Western "civilized" humans are often reiterated in our scientific stories, myths, and ideologies.

In Chapter 44, Allen further examines the evidence (or lack thereof) for the genetics or inheritance of human violence. He shows parallels between eugenics of the early 1900s and the current focus on biological determinism, and between some aspects of the political and economic climate then and now. Allen warns that: "In most of the formulations in which it has appeared in the past and at the present, the phrase 'Biology is destiny!' leads to disastrous human consequences." Kevles and Kevles (Chapter 45) reiterate the need to look at the environmental and social causes for violence and not so quickly to jump on the biology bandwagon.

*Infanticide—throw out the baby.* As seen in Chapters 46 to 48 of this reader, Hrdy developed an elegant theory of sexual selection to explain a handful of cases of infanticide among langurs. She suggested that an infanticidal male gains reproductive advantage by selectively killing the unweaned offspring of his male rivals. In addition to the relative gain in genetic representation, the infanticidal act shortens the interbirth interval. This ensures the earliest possible opportunity for the infanticidal male to mate with the infant-deprived female, the advantage being that the female can conceive again sooner—the presumed functional cause for infanticide (Hrdy 1979, Hrdy and Hausfater 1984, van Schaik and Dunbar 1990).

The sexual selection hypothesis has become entrenched as an explanatory hypothesis for infant killing in nonhuman primates, and to explain the patterns of child abuse in human society as seen in the newspaper article reprinted as Chapter 46 (see, also, Daly and Wilson 1988, Emlen 1995; Russell 1993). Furthermore, increasingly, the threat of infanticide has begun to be viewed as a central factor in theories of primate social evolution. It also has been identified as a major reason for group-living among primates (Dunbar 1984, Newton 1988, Pereira and Weiss 1991, van Schaik and Dunbar 1990, van Schaik and Kappeler 1993).

This has been extended to explain the human family. "Long-term pairbonding is found in many human societies, and we ask whether in humans, too, females prefer bonding to a particular male in order to reduce the risk of infanticide on their children" (van Schaik and Dunbar 1990:55).

A serious problem with the data for infanticide is the fact that the context rarely fits the pattern predicted for sexual selection. Furthermore, the fundamental assumption of the sexual selection hypothesis concerns the genetic basis of infant killing. Although the inheritance of the "infanticidal trait" (Hrdy 1979, 1984, Newton 1988) is crucial for the operation of the model, there is no evidence supporting its genetic inheritance (Sussman et al., Chapter 47).

In rebutting these arguments, Hrdy et el. (Chapter 48) imply that the critics of sexual selection theory are too interested in the data and the "sacredness of the context." Those supporting it seek general patterns and use theory to explain them; they "derive their greatest pleasure from noting that so many findings could have been correctly predicted on the basis of pitifully incomplete data sets merely by relying on logic, comparisons, and extrapolations guided by evolutionary theory." However, as emphasized by Fischer (1970) in pointing out fallacies in methodology, a statement is not true by simply establishing the possibility of its truth. To date, the data for infanticide do not support the theory. For the sexual selection theory to be demonstrated, it must be shown that infanticidal males are more successful in leaving offspring than males that do not kill infants, and that this trait is inherited by their offspring. The investigator, "must not merely provide good relevant evidence but the best relevant evidence" and "the burden of proof . . . always rests upon its author. Not his critics, not his readers, not his graduate students, not the next generation" (Fischer 1970:62–63). The sexual selection hypothesis may not be incorrect, but it must be formulated so that it is testable and it remains to be tested, not unilaterally accepted as fact.

Allen (Chapter 44) lists number of problems with assuming a significant genetic basis for various social behaviors. These include: (1) Poorly defined phenotypes—many of the terms being used, such as dispersal and nurturing, include very different sets of behaviors in different species. Other value-laden terms (e.g., infidelity, cuckoldry, infanticide) are defined by the mores of a given society at given point in history. (2) Reduction of complex processes to a single entity—while mating is a single event, mating behavior is not. It is made up of a complex of intellectual, emotional, and behavioral components that cannot be reduced to a single trait as would be expected in standard genetic analysis. (3) Uncritical and selective use of information—what might be called "stacking the deck." (4) The tendency in all such research to resort to extreme forms of genetic reductionism, including references to *"the gene* for infidelity", *"the gene* for infanticide", *"the gene* for (fill in behavior of your choice)."* This level of simplification rarely applies to relatively simple morphological traits, much less to complex, plastic traits such as social behavior. For example, Greenspan (Chapter 4, this volume), studying the genetic components of male courtship in fruit flies, notes: ". . . behavior is regulated by a myriad of interacting genes, each of which handles diverse responsibilities in the body. . . . the genetic influences on behavior will be at least as complicated in people as they are in fruit flies. Hence, the notion of many, multipurpose genes making small contributions is likely to apply." Few if any of those investigators propounding theories of a genetic basis for nonhuman and human social behaviors are actually trained geneticists. As Allen concludes: "Their naiveté about making genetical analyses and corresponding claims of genetic causality is thus all the more blatant because it would not stand up to any standard genetic scrutiny."

It appears that many of our current preconceptions are clearly defined, enthusiastically welcomed, and easily reproduced, such that we have a "disturbing predisposition towards belief before investigation" (Reader 1988:78). Again, as stated by Boas over 70 years ago, "unless the contrary can be proved, we must assume that all complex activities are socially determined, not hereditary" (see Chapter 39).

## REFERENCES

Bradbury, J. W.; Vehrencamp S. L. (1977) "Social organization and foraging in emballonurid bats." *Beh. Ecol Sociobiol.*, 2:1–17.

Brown, D. E. (1991) *Human Universals.* Philadelphia: Temple University Press.

Daly, M.; M. Wilson. (1988) *Homicide.* New York: Aldine de Gruyter.

Degler, C. N. (1991) *In Search of Human Nature.* New York: Oxford University Press..

Dunbar, R. I. (1984) *Reproductive Decisions: An Economic Analysis of Gelada Baboon Social Strategies.* Princeton, NJ: Princeton University Press.

Dunbar, R. I. (1988) *Primate Social Systems.* New York: Cornell University Press.

Emlen, S. T. (1995) "An evolutionary theory of the family." *Proc. Nat. Acad. Sci.*, 92:8092–8099.

Fischer, D. H. (1970) *Historian's Fallacies: Towards a Logic of Historical Thought.* New York: Harper and Row.

Hrdy, S. B. (1979) "Infanticide among animals: A review, classification, and examination of the implications for reproductive strategies for females." *Ethol. Sociobiol.*, 1:13–40.

Hrdy, S. B. (1984) "Assumptions and evidence regarding the sexual selection hypothesis: A reply to Boggess." In *Infanticide: Comparative and Evolutionary Perspectives* (pp. 315–319). G. Hausfater, and S. B. Hrdy, eds. New York: Aldine.

Hrdy, S. B. (1988) "Raising Darwin's consciousness: Females and evolutionary theory." In *The Evolution of Sex.* R. Bellig and G. Stevens, eds. San Fransisco: Harper and Row.

Hrdy, S. B.; Hausfater, G. (1984) "Comparative and evolutionary perspective on infanticide: Introduction and overview." In *Infanticide: Comparative and Evolutionary Perspectives* (pp xiii – xxxv). G. Hausfater and S. B. Hrdy, eds. New York: Aldine.

Newton, P. N. (1988) "The variable social organization of Hanuman langurs *(Presbytis entellus),* infanticide and the monopolization of females." *Intl. J. Primatol.,* 9:59–77.

Pereira M. E.; M. L. Weiss (1991) "Female mate choice, male migration, and the threat of infanticide in ringtailed lemurs." *Beh. Bio. Sociobiol,* 18:141–152.

Pusey, A. E.; Packer, C. (1987) "Dispersal and philopatry." In *Primate Societies* (pp. 250–266). B. B. Smuts, D. L. Cheney, R. M. Seyfarth, and Wrangham, and T. T. Struhsaker, eds. Chicago: University of Chicago Press.

Reader, J. (1988) *Missing Links.* London: Penguin.

Russell, R. J. (1993) *The Lemur's Legacy: The Evolution of Power, Sex, and Love.* New York, G. P. Putnam's Sons.

Scarr, S. (1993) "Biological and cultural diversity: The legacy of Darwin for development." *Child Development,* 64:1333–1353.

Strier, K. B. (1994) "Myth of the typical primate." *Ybk. Phys. Anthropol.,* 37:233–271.

Tooby, J.; Cosmides, L. (1992) "The psychological foundations of culture." In J. H. Barkow, L. Cosmides, and J. Tooby, *The Adapted Mind: Evolutionary Psychology and the Generation of Culture.* New York: Oxford University Press.

Trivers, R. L. (1972) "Parental investment and sexual selection." In *Sexual Selection and the Descent of Man, 1871–1971* (pp. 136–179). B. Campbell, ed. Chicago: Aldine.

van Schaik, C. P.; Dunbar, R. I. M. (1990) "The evolution of monogamy in large primates: A new hypothesis and some crucial tests." *Behaviour,* 115:30–62.

van Schaik, C. P.; Kappeler, P. M. (1993) "Life history, activity period and lemur social systems." In *Lemur Social Systems and Their Ecological Basis* (pp. 241–260) P. M. Kappeler and J. U. Ganzhorn, eds. New York: Plenum.

Watts, D. P. (1990) "Ecology of gorillas and its relation to female transfer in mountain gorillas." *Intl. J. Primatol.,* 11:21–45.

Wrangham, R. W. (1980) An ecological model of female bonded primate groups. *Behaviour,* 75:262–300.

Wrangham, R. W.; Peterson, D. (1996) *Demonic Males.* Boston: Houghton Mufflin.

Wright, R. (1994) *The Moral Animal: Evolutionary Psychology and Everyday Life.* New York: Vintage.

# Chapter 40

# *Male and Female*

## Robert Wright

---

*In the most distinct classes of the animal kingdom, with mammals, birds, reptiles, fishes, insects, and even crustaceans, the differences between the sexes follow almost exactly the same rules; the males are almost always the wooers. . . .*

The Descent of Man *(1981)*

Darwin was wrong about sex.

He wasn't wrong about the males being the wooers. His reading of the basic characters of the two sexes holds up well today. "The female, . . . with the rarest exception, is less eager than the male. . . . [S]he is coy, and may often be seen endeavouring for a long time to escape from the male. Every one who has attended to the habits of animals will be able to call to mind instances of this kind. . . . The exertion of some choice on the part of the female seems almost as general a law as the eagerness of the male."

Nor was Darwin wrong about the *consequences* of this asymmetrical interest. He saw that female reticence left males competing with one another for scarce reproductive opportunities, and thus explained why males so often have built-in weapons—the horns of stags, the hornlike mandibles of stag beetles, the fierce canines of chimpanzees. Males not hereditarily equipped for combat with other males have been excluded from sex, and their traits have thus been discarded by natural selection.

Darwin also saw that the choosiness of females gives great moment to their choices. If they prefer to mate with particular kinds of males, those kinds will proliferate. Hence the ornamentation of so many male animals—a lizard's inflatable throat sack, brightly colored during the mating season; the immense, cumbersome tail of the peacock; and, again, the stag's horns, which seem more elaborate than the needs of combat alone would dictate. These decorations have evolved not be-

cause they aid in daily survival—if anything, they complicate it—but because they can so charm a female as to outweigh the everyday burdens they bring. (How it came to be in the genetic interest of females to be charmed by such things is another story, and a point of subtle disagreement among biologists.)

Both of these variants of natural selection—combat among males and discernment by females—Darwin called "sexual selection." He took great pride in the idea, and justifiably so. Sexual selection is a nonobvious extension of his general theory that accounts for seeming exceptions to it (like garish colors that virtually say "kill me" to predators), and that has not just endured over time but grown in scope.

What Darwin was wrong about was the evolutionary *cause* of female coyness and male eagerness. He saw that this imbalance of interest creates competition among males for precious reproductive slots, and he saw the consequences of this competition; but he didn't see what had created the imbalance. His attempt late in life to explain the phenomenon was unsuccessful. And, in fairness to him, whole generations of biologists would do no better.

Now that there is a consensus on the solution, the long failure to find it seems puzzling. It's a very simple solution. In this sense, sex is typical of many behaviors illuminated by natural selection; though the illumination has gotten truly powerful only within the last three decades, it could in principle have done so a century earlier, so plainly does it follow from Darwin's view of life. There is some subtle logic involved, so Darwin can be

From *The Moral Animal: Evolutionary Psychology and Everyday Life.* Vintage, New York, 1994.

257

forgiven for not having seen the full scope of his theory. Still, if he were around today to hear evolutionary biologists talk about sex, he might well sink into one of his self-effacing funks, exclaiming at his obtuseness in not getting the picture sooner.

## PLAYING GOD

The first step toward understanding the basic imbalance of the sexes is to assume hypothetically the role natural selection plays in designing a species. Take the human species, for example. Suppose you're in charge of installing, in the minds of human (or prehuman beings), rules of behavior that will guide them through life, the objective of the game being to maximize each person's genetic legacy. To oversimplify a bit: You're supposed to make each person behave in such a way that he or she is likely to have lots of offspring—offspring, moreover, who themselves have lots of offspring.

Obviously, this isn't the way natural selection actually works. It doesn't consciously design organisms. It doesn't consciously do anything. It blindly preserves hereditary traits that happen to enhance survival and reproduction. Still, natural selection works *as if* it were consciously designing organisms, so pretending you're in charge of organism design is a legitimate way to figure out which tendencies evolution is likely to have ingrained in people and other animals. In fact, this is what evolutionary biologists spend a good deal of time doing: looking at a trait—mental or otherwise—and figuring out what, if any, engineering challenge it is a solution to.

When playing the Administrator of Evolution and trying to maximize genetic legacy, you quickly discover that this goal implies different tendencies for men and women. Men can reproduce hundreds of times a year, assuming they can persuade enough women to cooperate, and assuming there aren't any laws against polygamy—which there assuredly weren't in the environment where much of our evolution took place. Women, on the other hand, can't reproduce more often than once a year. The asymmetry lies partly in the high price of eggs; in all species they're bigger and rarer than minuscule, mass-produced sperm. (That, in fact, is biology's official definition of a female: the one with the larger sex cells.) But the asymmetry is exaggerated by the details of mammalian reproduction; the egg's lengthy conversion into an organism happens inside the female, and she can't handle many projects at once.

So, while there are various reasons why it could make Darwinian sense for a woman to mate with more than one man (maybe the first man was infertile, for example), there comes a time when having more sex just isn't worth the trouble. Better to get some rest or grab a bite to eat. For a man, unless he's really on the brink of collapse or starvation, the time never comes. Each new partner offers a very real chance to get more genes into the next generation—a much more valuable prospect, in the Darwinian calculus, than a nap or a meal. As the evolutionary psychologists Martin Daly and Margo Wilson have succinctly put it: For males "there is always the possibility of doing better."

There's a sense in which a female can do better, too, but it has to do with quality, not quantity. Giving birth to a child involves a huge commitment of time, not to mention energy, and nature has put a low ceiling on how many such enterprises she can undertake. So each child, from her (genetic) point of view, is an extremely precious gene machine. Its ability to survive and then, in turn, produce its own young gene machines is of mammoth importance. It makes Darwinian sense, then, for a woman to be selective about the man who is going to help her build each gene machine. She should size up an aspiring partner before letting him in on the investment, asking herself what he'll bring to the project. This question then entails a number of subquestions that, in the human species especially, are more numerous and subtle than you might guess.

Before we go into these questions, a couple of points must be made. One is that the woman needn't literally ask them, or even be aware of them. Much of the relevant history of our species took place before our ancestors were smart enough to ask much of anything. And even in the more recent past, after the arrival of language and self-awareness, there has been no reason for every evolved behavioral tendency to fall under conscious control. In fact, sometimes it is emphatically *not* in our genetic interest to be aware of exactly what we are doing or why. (Hence Freud, who was definitely onto something, though some evolutionary psychologist would say he didn't know exactly what.) In the case of sexual attraction, at any rate, everyday experience suggests that natural selection has wielded its influence largely via the emotional spigots that turn on and off such feelings as tentative attraction, fierce passion, and swoon-inducing infatuation. A woman doesn't typically size up a man and think: "He seems like a worthy contributor to my genetic legacy." She just sizes him up and feels attracted to him—or doesn't. All the "thinking" has been done—unconsciously, metaphorically—by natural selection. Genes leading to attractions that would end up being good for her ancestors' genetic legacies have flourished, and those leading to less productive attractions have not.

Understanding the often unconscious nature of genetic control is the first step toward understanding that—in many realms, not just sex—we're all puppets, and our best hope for even partial liberation is to try to decipher the logic of the puppeteer. The full scope of the logic will take some time to explain, but I don't think I'm spoiling the end of the movie by noting here that the puppeteer seems to have exactly zero regard for the happiness of the puppets.

The second point to grasp before pondering how natural selection has "decided" to shape the sexual preferences of women (and of men) is that it isn't foresightful. Evolution is guided by the environment in which it takes place, and environments change. Natural selection had no way of anticipating, for example, that someday people would use contraception, and that their passions would thus lead them into time-consuming and energy-sapping sex that was sure to be fruitless; or that X-rated videotapes would come along and lead indiscriminately lustful men to spend leisure time watching them rather than pursuing real, live women who might get their genes to the next generation.

This isn't to say that there's anything wrong with "unproductive" sexual recreation. Just because natural selection created us doesn't mean we have to slavishly follow its peculiar agenda. (If anything, we might be tempted to spite it for all the ridiculous baggage it's saddled us with.) The point is just that it isn't correct to say that people's minds are designed to maximize their fitness, their genetic legacy. What the theory of natural selection says, rather, is that people's minds were designed to maximize fitness *in the environment in which those minds evolved.* This environment is known as the EEA—the environment of evolutionary adaptation. Or, more memorably: the "ancestral environment." At times, in pondering whether some mental trait is an evolutionary adaptation, I will ask whether it seems to be in the "genetic interest" of its bearer. For example: Would indiscriminate lust be in the genetic interest of men? But this is just a kind of shorthand. The question, properly put, is always whether a trait would be in the "genetic interest" of someone in the EEA, not in modern America or Victorian England or anywhere else. Only traits that would have propelled the genes responsible for them through the generations in our ancestral social environment should, in theory, be part of human nature today.

What was the ancestral environment like? The closest things to a twentieth-century example is a hunter-gatherer society, such as the !Kung San of the Kalahari Desert in Africa, the Inuit (Eskimos) of the Arctic region, or the Ache of Paraguay. Inconveniently, hunter-gatherer societies are quite different from one another, rendering simple generalization about the crucible of human evolution difficult. This diversity is a reminder that the idea of a single EEA is actually a fiction, a composite drawing; our ancestral social environment no doubt changed much in the course of human evolution. Still, there are recurring themes among contemporary hunter-gatherer societies, and they suggest that some features probably stayed fairly constant during much of the evolution of the human mind. For example: People grew up near close kin in small villages where everyone knew everyone else and strangers didn't show up very often. People got married—monogamously or polygamously—and the female typically was married by the time she was old enough to be fertile.

This much, at any rate, is a safe bet: Whatever the ancestral environment was like, it wasn't much like the environment we're in now. We aren't designed to stand on crowded subway platforms, or to live in suburbs next door to people we never talk to, or to get hired or fired, or to watch the evening news. This disjunction between the contexts of our design and of our lives is probably responsible for much psychopathology, as well as much suffering of a less dramatic sort. (And, like the importance of unconscious motivation, it is an observation for which Freud gets some credit; it is central to his *Civilization and Its Discontents.)*

To figure out what women are inclined to seek in a man, and vice versa, we'll need to think more carefully about our ancestral social environment(s). And, as we'll see, thinking about the ancestral environment also helps explain why females in our species are less sexually reserved than females in many other species. But for purposes of making the single, largest point of this chapter—that, whatever the typical level of reserve for females in our species, it is higher than the level for males—the particular environment doesn't much matter. For this point depends only on the premise that an individual female can, over a lifetime, have many fewer offspring than an individual male. And that has been the case, basically, forever: since before our ancestors were human, before they were primates, before they were mammals—way, way back through the evolution of our brain, down to its reptilian core. Female snakes may not be very smart, but they're smart enough to know, unconsciously, at least, that there are some males it's not a good idea to mate with.

Darwin's failure, then, was a failure to see what a deeply precious commodity females are. He saw that their coyness had made them precious, but he didn't see that they were *inherently* precious—precious by virtue of their biological role in reproduction and the resulting slow rate of female reproduction. Natural selection had seen this—or, at least, had "seen" it—and female coyness is the result of this implicit comprehension.

## ENLIGHTENMENT DAWNS

The first large and clear step toward human comprehension of this logic was made in 1948 by the British geneticist A. J. Bateman. Bateman took fruit flies and ran them through a dating game. He would place five males and five females in a chamber, let them follow their hearts, and then, by examining the traits of the next generation, figure out which offspring belonged to which parents. He found a clear pattern. Whereas almost all females had about the same number of offspring, regardless of whether they mated with one, two, or three males, male legacies differed according to a simple rule: the more females you mate with, the more offspring you have. Bateman saw the import: natural selection encourages "an undiscriminating eagerness in the males and a discriminating passivity in the females."

Bateman's insight long lay essentially unappreciated. It took nearly three decades, and several evolutionary biologists, to give it the things it lacked: full and rigorous elaboration on the one hand, and publicity on the other.

The first part—the rigor—came from two biologists who are good examples of how erroneous some stereotypes about Darwinism are. In the 1970s, opposition to sociobiology often took the form of charges that its practitioners were closet reactionaries, racists, fascists, and so on. It is hard to imagine two people less vulnerable to such charges than George Williams and Robert Trivers, and it is hard to name anyone who did more than they to lay the foundations of the new paradigm.

Williams, a professor emeritus at the State University of New York, has worked hard to dispel vestiges of Social Darwinism, with its underlying assumption that natural selection is a process somehow worthy of obedience or emulation. Many biologists share his view, and stress that we can't derive our moral values from its "values." But Williams goes further. Natural selection, he says, is an "evil" process, so great is the pain and death it thrives on, so deep is the selfishness it engenders.

Trivers, who was an untenured professor at Harvard when the new paradigm was taking shape and is now at Rutgers University, is much less inclined than Williams toward moral philosophy. But he evinces an emphatic failure to buy the right-wing values associated with Social Darwinism. He speaks proudly of his friendship with the late Black Panther leader Huey Newton (with whom he once co-authored an article on human psychology). He rails against the bias of the judicial system. He sees conservative conspiracies where some people don't.

In 1966 Williams published his landmark work, *Adaptation and Natural Selection: A Critique of Some Current Evolutionary Thought.* Slowly this book has acquired a nearly holy stature in its field. It is a basic text for biologists who think about social behavior, including human social behavior, in light of the new Darwinism. Williams' book dispelled confusions that had long plagued the study of social behavior, and it laid down foundational insights that would support whole edifices of work on the subjects of friendship and sex. In both cases Trivers would be instrumental in building edifices.

Williams amplified and extended the logic behind Bateman's 1948 paper. He cast the issue of male versus female genetic interests in terms of the "sacrifice" required for reproduction. For a male mammal, the necessary sacrifice is close to zero. His "essential role may end with copulation, which involves a negligible expenditure of energy and materials on his part, and only a momentary lapse of attention from matters of direct concern to

his safety and well-being." With little to lose and much to gain, males can profit, in the currency of natural selection, by harboring "an aggressive and immediate willingness to mate with as many females as may be available." For the female, on the other hand, "copulation may mean a commitment to a prolonged burden, in both the mechanical and physiological sense, and its many attendant stresses and dangers." Thus, it is in her genetic interest to "assume the burdens of reproduction" only when circumstances seem propitious. And "one of the most important circumstances is the inseminating male"; since "unusually fit fathers tend to have unusually fit offspring," it is "to the female's advantage to be able to pick the most fit male available. . . . "

Hence, courtship: "the advertisement, by a male, of how fit he is." And just as "it is to his advantage to pretend to be highly fit whether he is or not," it is to the female's advantage to spot false advertising. So natural selection creates "a skilled salesmanship among the males and an equally well-developed sales resistance and discrimination among females." In other words: males should, in theory, tend to be show-offs.

A few years later, Trivers used the ideas of Bateman and Williams to create a full-blown theory that ever since has been shedding light on the psychology of men and women. Trivers began by replacing William's concept of "sacrifice" with "investment." The difference may seem slight, but nuances can start intellectual avalanches, and this one did. The term *investment,* linked to economics, comes with a ready-made analytical framework.

In a now-famous paper published in 1972, Trivers formally defined "parental investment" as "any investment by the parent in an individual offspring that increases the offspring's chance of surviving (and hence [the offspring's] reproductive success) at the cost of the parent's ability to invest in other offspring." Parental investment includes the time and energy consumed in producing an egg or a sperm, achieving fertilization, gestating or incubating the egg, and rearing the offspring. Plainly, females will generally make the higher investment up until birth, and less plainly but in fact typically, this disparity continues after birth.

By quantifying the imbalance of investment between mother and father in a given species, Trivers suggested, we could better understand many things—for example, the extent of male eagerness and female coyness, the intensity of sexual selection, and many subtle aspects of courtship and parenthood, fidelity and infidelity. Trivers saw that in our species the imbalance of investment is not as stark as in many others. And he correctly suspected that the result is much psychological complexity.

At last, with Trivers's paper "Parental Investment and Sexual Selection," the flower had bloomed; a simple extension of Darwin's theory—so simple that Darwin would have grasped it in a minute—had been glimpsed in 1948, clearly articulated in 1966, and was now, in

1972, given full form. Still, the concept of parental investment lacked one thing: publicity. It was E. O. Wilson's book *Sociobiology* (1975) and Richard Dawkins's *The Selfish Gene* (1976) that gave Trivers's work a large and diverse audience, getting scores of psychologists and anthropologists to think about human sexuality in modern Darwinian terms. The resulting insights are likely to keep accumulating for a long time.

## TESTING THE THEORY

Theories are a dime a dozen. Even strikingly elegant theories, which, like the theory of parental investment, seem able to explain much with little, often turn out to be worthless. There is justice in the complaint (from creationists, among others) that some theories about the evolution of animal traits are "just so stories"—plausible, but nothing more. Still, it is possible to separate the merely plausible from the compelling. In some sciences, testing theories is so straightforward that it is only a slight exaggeration (though it is always, in a certain strict sense, an exaggeration) to talk of theories being "proved." In others, corroboration is roundabout—an ongoing, gradual process by which confidence approaches the threshold of consensus, or fails to. Studying the evolutionary roots of human nature, or of anything else, is a science of the second sort. About each theory we ask a series of questions, and the answers nourish belief or doubt or ambivalence.

One question about the theory of parental investment is whether human behavior in fact complies with it in even the most basic ways. Are women more choosy about sex partners than men? (This is not to be confused with the very different question, to which we'll return, of which sex, if either, is choosier about *marriage* partners.) Certainly there is plenty of folk wisdom suggesting as much. More concretely, there's the fact that prostitution—sex with someone you don't know and don't care to know—is a service sought overwhelmingly by males, now as in Victorian England. Similarly, virtually all pornography that relies sheerly on visual stimulation—pictures or films of anonymous people, spiritless flesh—is consumed by males. And various studies have shown men to be, on average, much more open to casual, anonymous sex than women. In one experiment, three-fourths of the men approached by an unknown woman on a college campus agreed to have sex with her, whereas none of the women approached by an unknown man were willing.

It used to be common for doubters to complain that this sort of evidence, drawn from Western society, reflects only its warped values. This tack has been problematic since 1979, when Donald Symons published *The Evolution of Human Sexuality*, the first comprehensive anthropological survey of human sexual behavior from

the new Darwinian perspective. Drawing on cultures East and West, industrial and preliterate, Symons demonstrated the great breadth of the patterns implied by the theory of parental investment: Women tend to be relatively selective about sex partners; men tend to be less so, and tend to find sex with a wide variety of partners an extraordinarily appealing concept.

One culture Symons discussed is about as far from Western influence as possible: the indigenous culture of the Trobriand Islands in Melanesia. The prehistoric migration that populated these islands broke off from the migrations that peopled Europe at least tens of thousands of years ago, and possibly more than 100,000 years ago. The Trobrianders' ancestral culture was separated from Europe's ancestral culture even earlier than was that of Native Americans. And indeed, when visited by the great anthropologist Bronislaw Malinowski in 1915, the islands proved startlingly remote from the currents of Western thought. The natives, it seemed, hadn't even gotten the connection between sex and reproduction. When one seafaring Trobriander returned from a voyage of several years to find his wife had two children, Malinowski was tactful enough not to suggest that she had been unfaithful. And "when I discussed the matter with others, suggesting that at least one of these children could not be his, my interlocutors did not understand what I meant."

Some anthropologists have doubted that the Trobrianders could have been so ignorant. And although Malinowski's account of this issue seems to have a ring of authority, there is no way of knowing whether he got the story straight. But it is important to understand that he could, in principle, be right. The evolution of human sexual psychology seems to have preceded the discovery by humans of what sex is for. Lust and other such feelings are natural selection's way of getting us to act as if we wanted lots of offspring and knew how to get them, whether or not we actually do. Had natural selection *not* worked this way—had it instead harnessed human intelligence so that our pursuit of fitness was entirely conscious and calculated—then life would be very different. Husbands and wives would, for example, spend no time having extramarital affairs with contraception; they would either scrap the contraception or scrap the sex.

Another un-Western thing about Trobriand culture was the lack of Victorian anxiety about premarital sex. By early adolescence, both girls and boys were encouraged to mate with a series of partners to their liking. (This freedom is found in some other preindustrial societies, though the experimentation typically ends, and marriage begins, before a girl reaches fertility.) But Malinowski left no doubt about which sex was choosier. "[T]here is nothing roundabout in a Trobriand wooing. . . . Simply and directly a meeting is asked for with the avowed intention of sexual gratification. If the invitation is accepted, the satisfaction of the boy's desire eliminates the romantic frame of mind, the craving for the unattainable and mysterious. If he is rejected, there is not much room for personal tragedy, for he is accustomed from childhood to having his sexual impulses thwarted by some girl, and he knows that another intrigue cures this type of ill surely and swiftly. . . ." And: "In the course of every love affair the man has constantly to give small presents to the woman. To the natives the need of one-sided payment is self-evident. This custom implies that sexual intercourse, even where there is mutual attachment, is a service rendered by the female to the male."

There were certainly cultural forces reinforcing coyness among Trobriand women. Though a young woman was encouraged to have an active sex life, her advances would be frowned on if too overt and common because of the "small sense of personal worth that such urgent solicitation implies." But is there any reason to believe this norm was anything other than a culturally mediated reflection of deeper genetic logic? Can anyone find a single culture in which women with unrestrained sexual appetites *aren't* viewed as more aberrant than comparably libidinous men? If not, isn't it an astonishing coincidence that all peoples have independently arrived at roughly the same cultural destination, with no genetic encouragement? Or is it the case that this universal cultural element was present half a million or more years ago, before the species began splitting up? That seems a long time for an essentially arbitrary value to endure, without being extinguished in a single culture.

This exercise holds a couple of important lessons. First: One good reason to suspect an evolutionary explanation for something—some mental trait or mechanism of mental development—is that it's universal, found everywhere, even in cultures that are as far apart as two cultures can be. Second: The general difficulty of explaining such universality in utterly cultural terms is an example of how the Darwinian view, though not *proved* right in the sense that mathematical theorems are proved right, can still be the view that, by the rules of science, wins; its chain of explanation is shorter than the alternative chain and has fewer dubious links; it is a simpler and more potent theory. If we accept even the three meager assertions made so far—(1) that the theory of natural selection straightforwardly implies the "fitness" of women who are choosy about sexual partners and of men who often aren't; (2) that this choosiness and unchoosiness, respectively, is observed worldwide; and (3) that this universality can't be explained with equal simplicity by a competing, purely cultural, theory—if we accept these things, and if we're playing by the rules of science, we have to endorse the Darwinian explanation: Male license and (relative) female reserve are to some extent innate.

Still, it is always good to have more evidence. Though absolute "proof" may not be possible in science, varying degrees of confidence are. And while evolutionary explanations rarely attain the 99.99 percent confi-

dence sometimes found in physics or chemistry, it's always nice to raise the level from, say 70 to 97 percent.

One way to strengthen an evolutionary explanation is to show that its logic is obeyed generally. If women are choosy about sex because they can have fewer kids than men (by virtue of investing more in them), and if females in the animal kingdom generally can have fewer offspring than males, then female animals in general should be choosier than males. Evolutionary theories can generate falsifiable predictions, as good scientific theories are expected to do, even though evolutionary biologists don't have the luxury of rerunning evolution in their labs, with some of its variables controlled, and predicting the outcome.

This particular prediction has been abundantly confirmed. In species after species, females are coy and males are not. Indeed, males are so dim in their sexual discernment that they may pursue things other than females. Among some kinds of frogs, mistaken homosexual courtship is so common that a "release call" is used by males who find themselves in the clutches of another male to notify him that they're both wasting their time. Male snakes, for their part, have been known to spend a while with dead females before moving on to a live prospect. And male turkeys will avidly court a stuffed replica of a female turkey. In fact, a replica of a female turkey's head suspended fifteen inches from the ground will generally do the trick. The male circles the head, does its ritual displays, and then (confident, presumably, that its performance has been impressive) rises into the air and comes down in the proximity of the female's backside, which turns out not to exist. The more virile males will show such interest even when a wooden head is used, and a few can summon lust for a wooden head with no eyes or beak.

Of course, such experiments only confirm in vivid form what Darwin had much earlier said was obvious: Males are very eager. This raises a much-cited problem with testing evolutionary explanations: the odd sense in which a theory's "predictions" are confirmed. Darwin didn't sit in his study and say, "My theory implies coy, picky females and mindlessly lustful males," and then take a walk to see if he could find examples. On the contrary, the many examples are what prompted him to wonder which implication of natural selection had created them—a question not correctly answered until midway through the following century, after even more examples had piled up. This tendency for Darwinian "predictions" to come after their evident fulfillment has been a chronic gripe of Darwin's critics. People who doubt the theory of natural selection, or just resist its application to human behavior, complain about the retrofitting of fresh predications to preexisting results. This is often what they have in mind when they say evolutionary biologists spend their time dreaming up "just so stories" to explain everything they see.

In a sense, dreaming up plausible stories *is* what evolutionary biologists do. But that's not by itself a damning indictment. The power of a theory, such as the theory of parental investment, is gauged by how much data it explains and how simply, regardless of when the data surfaced. After Copernicus showed that assuming the Earth to revolve around the Sun accounted elegantly for the otherwise perplexing patterns that stars trace in the sky, it would have been beside the point to say, "But you cheated. You knew about the patterns all along." Some "just so stories" are plainly better than others, and they win. Besides, how much choice do evolutionary biologists have? There's not much they can do about the fact that the database on animal life began accumulating millennia before Darwin's theory.

But there is one thing they can do. Often a Darwinian theory generates, in addition to the pseudopredictions that the theory was in fact designed to explain, additional predictions—real predictions, untested predictions that can be used to further evaluate the theory. (Darwin elliptically outlined this method in 1838, at age twenty-nine—more than twenty years before *The Origin of Species* was published. He wrote in his notebook: "The line of argument pursued throughout my theory is to establish a point as a probability by induction, & to apply it as hypothesis to other points. & see whether it will solve them.") The theory of parental investment is a good example. For there are a few oddball species, as Williams noted in 1966, in which the male's investment in the offspring roughly matches, or even exceeds, the female's. If the theory of parental investment is right, these species should defy sex stereotypes.

Consider the spindly creatures known as pipefish. Here the male plays a role like a female kangaroo's: He takes the eggs into a pouch and plugs them into his bloodstream for nutrition. The female can thus start on another round of reproduction while the male is playing nurse. This may not mean that she can have many more offspring than he in the long run—after all, it took her a while to produce the eggs in the first place. Still, the parental investment isn't grossly imbalanced in the usual direction. And, predictably, female pipefish tend to take an active role in courtship, seeking out the males and initiating the mating ritual.

Some birds, such as the phalarope (including the two species known as sea snipes), exhibit a similarly abnormal distribution of parental investment. The males sit on the eggs, leaving the females free to go get some wild oats sown. Again, we see the expected departure from stereotype. It is the phalarope *females* who are larger and more colorful—a sign that sexual selection is working in reverse, as females compete for males. One biologist observed that the females, in classically male fashion, "quarrel and display among themselves" while the males patiently incubate the eggs.

If the truth be told, Williams knew that these species defy stereotype when he wrote in 1966. But subsequent investigation has confirmed his "prediction" more broadly. Extensive parental investment by males has been shown to have the expected consequences in other birds, in the Panamanian poison-arrow frog, in a water bug whose males cart fertilized eggs around on their backs, and in the (ironically named, it turns out) Mormon cricket. So far Williams's prediction has encountered no serious trouble.

## APES AND US

There is another major form of evolutionary evidence bearing on differences between men and women: our nearest relatives. The great apes—chimpanzees, pygmy chimps (also called bonobos), gorillas, and orangutans—are not, of course, our ancestors; all have evolved since their path diverged from ours. Still, those forks in the road have come between eight million years ago (for chimps and bonobos) and sixteen million years ago (for orangutans). That's not long, as these things go. (A reference point: The australopithecine, our presumed ancestor, whose skull was ape-sized but who walked upright, appeared between six and four million years ago, shortly after the chimpanzee off-ramp. *Homo erectus*—the species that had brains midway in size between ours and apes' and used them to discover fire—took shape around 1.5 million years ago.)

The great apes' nearness to us on the evolutionary tree legitimizes a kind of detective game. It's possible—though hardly certain—that when a trait is shared by all of them and by us, the reason is common descent. In other words: the trait existed in our common, sixteen-million-year-old proto-ape ancestor, and has been in all our lineages ever since. The logic is roughly the same as tracking down four distant cousins, finding that they all have brown eyes, and inferring that at least one of their two common great-great-grandparents had brown eyes. It's far from being an airtight conclusion, but it has more credence than it had when you had seen only one of the cousins.

Lots of traits are shared by us and the great apes. For many of the traits—five-fingered hands, say—pointing this out isn't worth the trouble; no one doubts the genetic basis of human hands anyway. But in the case of human mental traits whose genetic substratum is still debated—such as the differing sexual appetites of men and women—this inter-ape comparison can be useful. Besides, it's worth taking a minute to get acquainted with our nearest relatives. Who knows how much of our psyche we share by common descent with some or all of them.

Orangutan males are drifters. They wander in solitude, looking for females, who tend to be stationary, each in her own home range. A male may settle down long enough to monopolize one, two, or even more of these ranges, though vast monopolies are discouraged by the attendant need to fend off vast numbers of rivals. Once the mission is accomplished, and the resident female gives birth, the male is likely to disappear. He may return years later, when pregnancy is again possible. In the meantime, he doesn't bother to write.

For a gorilla male, the goal is to become leader of a pack comprising several adult females, their young offspring, and maybe a few young adult males. As dominant male, he will get sole sexual access to the females; the young males generally mind their manners (though a leader may, as he ages and his strength ebbs, share females with them). On the downside, the leader does have to confront any male interlopers, each of which aims to make off with one or more of his females and thus is in an assertive mood.

The life of the male chimpanzee is also combative. He strives to climb a male hierarchy that is long and fluid compared to a gorilla hierarchy. And, again, the dominant male—working tirelessly to protect his rank through assault, intimidation, and cunning—gets first dibs on any females, a prerogative he enforces with special vigor when they're ovulating.

Pygmy chimps, or bonobos (they're actually a distinct species from chimpanzees), may be the most erotic of all primates. Their sex comes in many forms and often serves purposes other than reproduction. Periodic homosexual behavior, such as genital rubbings between females, seems to be a way of saying, "Let's be friends." Still, broadly speaking, the bonobos' sociosexual outline mirrors that of the common chimpanzees: a pronounced male hierarchy that helps determine access to females.

Amid the great variety of social structures in these species, the basic theme of this chapter stands out, at least in minimal form: Males seem very eager for sex and work hard to find it; females work less hard. This isn't to say the females don't like sex. They love it and may initiate it. And, intriguingly, the females of the species most closely related to humans—chimpanzees and bonobos—seem particularly amenable to a wild sex life, including a variety of partners. Still, female apes don't do what male apes do: search high and low, risking life and limb, to find sex, and to find as much of it, with as many different partners, as possible; it has a way of finding them.

## FEMALE CHOICE

That female apes are, on balance, more reticent than male apes doesn't necessarily mean that they actively screen their prospective partners. To be sure, the partners get screened; those who dominate other males mate, while those who get dominated may not. This competition is exactly what Darwin had in mind in defining one of the two kinds of sexual selection, and these species (like our own) illustrate how it favors the evolution of big, mean males. But what about the other kind of sexual selection? Does the female participate in the screening, choosing the male that seems the most auspicious contributor to her project?

Female choice is notoriously hard to spot, and signs of its long-term effect are often ambiguous. Are males larger and stronger than females just because tougher males have bested their rivals and gotten to mate? Or, in addition, have females come to prefer tough males, since females with this genetically ingrained preference have had tougher and therefore more prolific sons, whose many daughters then inherited their grandmother's taste?

Notwithstanding such difficulties, it's fairly safe to say that in one sense or another, females are choosy in all the great ape species. A female gorilla, for example, though generally confined to sex with a single, dominant male, normally emigrates in the course of her lifetime. When an alien male approaches her pack, engaging its leader in mutual threats and maybe even a fight, she will, if sufficiently impressed, decide to follow him.

In the case of chimps, the matter is more subtle. The dominant, or alpha, male can have any female he wants, but that's not necessarily because she prefers him; he shuts off alternatives by frightening other males. He can frighten her, too, so that any spurning of low-ranking males may reflect only her fear. (Indeed, the spurning has been known to disappear when the alpha isn't looking.) But there is a wholly different kind of chimp mating—a sustained, private consortship that may be a prototype for human courtship. A male and female chimp will leave the community for days or even weeks. And although the female may be forcibly abducted if she resists an invitation, there are times when she successfully resists, and times when she chooses to go peacefully, even though nearby males would gladly aid her in any resistance.

Actually, even going unpeacefully can involve a kind of choice. Female orangutans are a good example. They do often seem to exercise positive choice, favoring some males over others. But sometimes they resist a mating and are forcibly subdued and—insofar as this word can be applied to nonhumans—raped. There is evidence that the rapists, often adolescents, usually fail to impregnate. But suppose that they succeed with some regularity. Then a female, in sheerly Darwinian terms, is better off mating with a good rapist, a big, strong, sexually aggressive male; her male offspring will then be more likely to be big, strong, and sexually aggressive (assuming sexual aggressiveness varies at least in part because of genetic differences)—and therefore prolific. So female resistance should be favored by natural selection as a way to avoid having a son who is an inept rapist (assuming it doesn't bring injury to the female).

This isn't to say that a female primate, her protests notwithstanding, "really wants it," as human males have been known to assume. On the contrary, the more an orangutan "really wants it," the less she'll resist, and the less powerful a screening device her reticence will be. What natural selection "wants" and what any individual wants needn't be the same, and in this case they're somewhat at odds. The point is simply that, even when females demonstrate no clear preference for certain kinds of males, they may be, in practical terms, preferring a certain kind of male. And this de facto discretion may be de jure. It may be an adaptation, favored by natural selection precisely *because* it has this filtering effect.

In the broadest sense, the same logic could apply in any primate species. Once females in general begin putting up the slightest resistance, then a female that puts up a little extra resistance is exhibiting a valuable trait. For whatever it takes to penetrate resistance, the sons of strong resisters are more likely to have it than the sons of weak resisters. (This assumes, again, that the relative possession by different males of "whatever it takes" reflects underlying genetic differences.) Thus, in sheerly Darwinian terms, coyness becomes its own reward. And this is true regardless of whether the male's means of approach is physical or verbal.

## ANIMALS AND THE UNCONSCIOUS

A common reaction to the new Darwinian view of sex is that it makes perfect sense as an explanation for animal behavior—which is to say, for the behavior of *nonhuman* animals. People may chuckle appreciatively at a male turkey that tries to mate with a poor rendition of a female's head, but if you then point out that many a human male regularly gets aroused after looking at two-dimensional representations of a nude woman, they don't see the connection. After all, the man surely knows that it's only a photo he's looking at; his behavior may be pathetic, but it isn't comic.

And maybe it isn't. But if he "knows" it's a photo, why is he getting so excited? And why are women so seldom whipped up into an onanistic frenzy by pictures of men?

Resistance to lumping humans and turkeys under one set of Darwinian rules has its points. Yes, our behavior is under more subtle, presumably more "conscious," control than is turkey behavior. Men can decide not to get aroused by something—or, at least, can decide not to look at something they know will arouse them. Sometimes they even stick with those decisions. And although turkeys can make what look like comparable "choices" (a

turkey hounded by a shotgun-wielding man may decide that now isn't the time for romance), it is plainly true that the complexity and subtlety of options available to a human are unrivaled in the animal kingdom. So too is the human's considered pursuit of very long-run goals.

It all feels very rational, and in some ways it is. But that doesn't mean it isn't in the service of Darwinian ends. To a layperson, it may seem natural that the evolution of reflective, self-conscious brains would liberate us from the base dictates of our evolutionary past. To an evolutionary biologist, what seems natural is roughly the opposite: that human brains evolved not to insulate us from the mandate to survive and reproduce, but to follow it more effectively, if more pliably; that as we evolve from a species whose males forcibly abduct females into a species whose males whisper sweet nothings, the whispering will be governed by the same logic as the abduction that is a means of manipulating females to male ends, and its form serves this function. The basic emanations of natural selection are refracted from the older, inner parts of our brain all the way out to its freshest tissue. Indeed, the freshest tissue would never have appeared if it didn't toe natural selection's bottom line.

Of course, a lot *has* happened since our ancestors parted ways with the great apes' ancestors, and one can imagine a change in evolutionary context that would have removed our lineage from the logic that so imbalances the romantic interest of male and female in most species. Don't forget about the seahorses, sea snipes, Panamanian poison-arrow frogs, and Mormon crickets, with their reversed sex roles. And, less dramatically, but a bit closer to home, there are the gibbons, another of our primate cousins, whose ancestors waved good-bye to ours about twenty million years ago. At some point in gibbon evolution, circumstances began to encourage much male parental investment. The males regularly stick around and help provide for the kids. In one gibbon species the males actually carry the infants, something male apes aren't exactly known for. And talk about marital harmony: Gibbon couples sing a loud duet in the morning, pointedly advertising their familial stability for the information of would-be home-wreckers.

Well, human males too have been known to carry around infants and to stay with their families. It is possible that at some time over the last few million years something happened to us rather like what happened to the gibbons. Have male and female sexual appetites converged at least enough to make monogamous marriage a reasonable goal?

# Chapter 41

# *Our Cheating Hearts*

## Robert Wright

*Devotion and betrayal, marriage and divorce: how evolution shaped human love.*

The language of zoology used to be so reassuring. Human beings were called a "pair-bonding" species. Lasting monogamy, it seemed, was natural for us, just as it was for geese, swans, and the other winged creatures that have filled our lexicon with such labels as "lovebirds" and "lovey-dovey." Family values, some experts said, were in our genes. In the 1967 best seller *The Naked Ape,* zoologist Desmond Morris wrote with comforting authority that the evolutionary purpose of human sexuality is "to strengthen the pair-bond and maintain the family unit."

This picture has lately acquired some blemishes. To begin with, birds are no longer such uplifting role models. Using DNA fingerprinting, ornithologists can now check to see if a mother bird's mate really is the father of her offspring. It turns out that some female chickadees (as in "my little chickadee") indulge in extramarital trysts with males that outrank their mates in the social hierarchy. For female barn swallows, it's a male with a long tail that makes extracurriculars irresistible. The innocent-looking indigo bunting has a cuckoldry rate of 40 percent. And so on. The idea that most bird species are truly monogamous has gone from conventional wisdom to punctured myth in a few short years. As a result, the fidelity of other pair-bonding species has fallen under suspicion.

Which brings us to the other problem with the idea that humans are by nature enduringly monogamous: humans. Of course, you don't need a Ph.D. to see that till-death-do-we-part fidelity doesn't come as naturally to people as, say, eating. But an emerging field known as evolutionary psychology can now put a finer point on the matter. By studying how the process of natural selection shaped the mind, evolutionary psychologists are painting a new portrait of human nature, with fresh detail about the feelings and thoughts that draw us into marriage—or push us out.

The good news is that human beings are designed to fall in love. The bad news is that they aren't designed to stay there. According to evolutionary psychology, it is "natural" for both men and women—at some times, under some circumstances—to commit adultery or to sour on a mate, to suddenly find a spouse unattractive, irritating, wholly unreasonable. (It may even be natural to *become* irritating and wholly unreasonable, and thus hasten the departure of a mate you've soured on.) It is similarly natural to find some attractive colleague superior on all counts to the sorry wreck of a spouse you're saddled with. When we see a couple celebrate a golden anniversary, one apt reaction is the famous remark about a dog walking on two legs: The point is not that the feat was done well but that it was done at all.

All of this may sound like cause for grim resignation to the further decline of the American family. But what's "natural" isn't necessarily unchangeable. Evolutionary psychology, unlike past gene-centered views of human nature, illuminates the tremendous flexibility of the human mind and the powerful role of environment in shaping behavior. In particular, evolutionary psychology shows how inhospitable the current social environment is to monogamy. And while the science offers no easy cures, it does suggest avenues for change.

The premise of evolutionary psychology is simple. The human mind, like any other organ, was designed for the purpose of transmitting genes to the next generation;

From *Time,* August 15, 1994.

the feelings and thoughts it creates are best understood in these terms. Thus the feeling of hunger, no less than the stomach, is here because it helped keep our ancestors alive long enough to reproduce and rear their young. Feelings of lust, no less than the sex organs, are here because they aided reproduction directly. Any ancestors who lacked stomachs or hunger or sex organs or lust—well, they wouldn't have become ancestors, would they? Their traits would have been discarded by natural selection.

This logic goes beyond such obviously Darwinian feelings as hunger and lust. According to evolutionary psychologists, our everyday, ever-shifting attitudes toward a mate or prospective mate—trust, suspicion, rhapsody, revulsion, warmth, iciness—are the handiwork of natural selection that remain with us today because in the past they led to behaviors that helped spread genes.

How can evolutionary psychologists be so sure? In part, their faith rests on the whole data base of evolutionary biology. In all sorts of species, and in organs ranging from brains to bladders, nature's attention to the subtlest aspects of genetic transmission is evident. Consider the crafting of primate testicles—specifically, their custom tailoring to the monogamy, or lack thereof, of females. If you take a series of male apes and weigh their testicles (not recommended, actually), you will find a pattern. Chimpanzees and other species with high "relative testes weight" (testes weight in comparison to body weight) feature quite promiscuous females. Species with low relative testes weight are either fairly monogamous (gibbons, for example) or systematically polygynous (gorillas), with one male monopolizing a harem of females. The explanation is simple. When females breed with many males, male genes can profit by producing lots of semen for their own transportation. Which male succeeds in getting his genes into a given egg may be a question of sheer volume, as competing hordes of sperm do battle.

## THE TROUBLE WITH WOMEN

Patterns like these, in addition to showcasing nature's ingenuity, allow a kind of detective work. If testicles evolved to match female behavior, then they are clues to the natural behavior of females. Via men's testicles, we can peer through the mists of prehistory and see how women behaved in the social environment of our evolution, free from the influence of modern culture; we can glimpse part of a pristine female mind.

The relative testes weight of humans falls between that of the chimpanzee and the gorilla. This suggests that women, while not nearly so wild as chimpanzee females (who can be veritable sex machines), are by nature somewhat adventurous. If they were not, why would natural selection divert precious resources to the construction and maintenance of weighty testicles?

There is finer evidence, as well, of natural female infidelity. You might think that the number of sperm cells in a husband's ejaculate would depend only on how long it has been since he last had sex. Wrong. What matters more, according to a recent study, is how long his mate has been out of sight. A man who hasn't had sex for, say, a week will have a higher sperm count if his wife was away on a business trip than if she's been home with the flu. In short, what really counts is whether the woman has had the opportunity to stray. The more chances she has had to collect sperm from other males, the more profusely her mate sends in his own troops. Again: That natural selection designed such an elaborate weapon is evidence of something for the weapon to combat—female faithlessness.

So here is problem No. 1 with the pair-bond thesis: Women are not by nature paragons of fidelity. Wanderlust is an innate part of their minds, ready to surface under propitious circumstances. Here's problem No. 2: if you think women are bad, you should see men.

## THE TROUBLE WITH MEN

With men, too, clues from physiology help uncover the mind. Consider "sexual dimorphism"—the difference between average male and female body size. Extreme sexual dimorphism is typical of a polygynous species, in which one male may impregnate several females, leaving other males without offspring. Since the winning males usually secure their trophies by fighting or intimidating other males, the genes of brawny, aggressive males get passed on while the genes of less formidable males are deposited in the dustbin of history. Thus male gorillas, who get a whole haremful of mates if they win lots of fights and no mates if they win none, are twice as big as females. With humans, males are about 15 percent bigger—sufficient to suggest that male departures from monogamy, like female departures, are not just a recent cultural invention.

Anthropology offers further evidence. Nearly 1000 of the 1154 past or present human societies ever studied—and these include most of the world's "hunter-gatherer" societies—have permitted a man to have more than one wife. These are the closest things we have to living examples of the "ancestral environment"—the social context of human evolution, the setting for which the mind was designed. The presumption is that people reared in such societies—the !Kung San of southern Africa, the Ache of Paraguay, the nineteenth century Eskimo—behave fairly "naturally." More so, at least, than people reared amid influences that weren't part of the ancestral environment: TVs, cars, jail time for bigamy.

There are vanishingly few anthropological examples of systematic female polygamy, or polyandry—women monopolizing sexual access to more than one man at once. So, while both sexes are prone under the right circumstances to infidelity, men seem much more deeply inclined to actually acquire a second or third mate—to keep a harem.

They are also more inclined toward the casual fling. Men are less finicky about sex partners. Prostitution—sex with someone you don't know and don't care to know—is a service sought overwhelmingly by males the world round. And almost all pornography that relies sheerly on visual stimulation—images of anonymous people, spiritless flesh—is consumed by males.

Many studies confirm the more discriminating nature of women. One evolutionary psychologist surveyed men and women about the minimal level of intelligence they would accept in a person they were "dating." The average response for both male and female: average intelligence. And how smart would the potential date have to be before they would consent to sex? Said the women: Oh, in that case, markedly above average. Said the men: Oh, in that case, markedly below average.

There is no dispute among evolutionary psychologists over the basic source of this male open-mindedness. A woman, regardless of how many sex partners she has, can generally have only one offspring a year. For a man, each new mate offers a real chance for pumping genes into the future. According to the *Guinness Book of Records,* the most prolific human parent in world history was Moulay ("The Bloodthirsty") Ismail, the last Sharifian Emperor of Morocco, who died in 1727. He fathered more than 1000 children.

This logic behind undiscerning male lust seems obvious now, but it wasn't always. Darwin had noted that in species after species the female is "less eager than the male," but he never figured out why. Only in the late 1960s and early 1970s did biologists George Williams and Robert Trivers attribute the raging libido of males to their nearly infinite potential rate of reproduction.

## WHY DO WOMEN CHEAT?

Even then the female capacity for promiscuity remained puzzling. For women, more sex doesn't mean more offspring. Shouldn't they focus on quality rather than quantity—look for a robust, clever mate whose genes may bode well for the offspring's robustness and cleverness? There's ample evidence that women are drawn to such traits but in our species genes are not all a male has to offer. Unlike our nearest ape relatives, we are a species of "high male-parental investment." In every known hunter-gatherer culture, marriage is the norm—not necessarily monogamous marriage, and not always lasting marriage, but marriage of some sort; and via this institution, fathers help provide for their children.

In our species, then, a female's genetic legacy is best amplified by a mate with two things: good genes and much to invest. But what if she can't find one man who

has both? One solution would be to trick a devoted, generous, and perhaps wealthy but not especially brawny or brainy mate into raising the offspring of another male. The woman need not be aware of this strategy, but at some level, conscious or unconscious, deft timing is in order. One study found that women who cheat on mates tend to do so around ovulation, when they are most likely to get pregnant.

For that matter, cheating during the infertile part of the monthly cycle might have its own logic, as a way (unconsciously) to turn the paramour into a dupe; the woman extracts goods or services from him in exchange for his fruitless conquest. Of course, the flowers he buys may not help her genes, but in the ancestral environment, less frivolous gifts—notably food—would have. Nisa, a woman in a !Kung San hunter-gatherer village, told an anthropologist that "when you have lovers, one brings you something and another brings you something else. One comes at night with meat, another with money, another with beads. Your husband also does things and gives them to you."

Multiple lovers have other uses, too. The anthropologist Sarah Blaffer Hrdy has theorized that women copulate with more than one man to leave several men under the impression that they might be the father of particular offspring. Then, presumably, they will treat the offspring kindly. Her theory was inspired by langur monkeys. Male langurs sometimes kill infants sired by others as a kind of sexual icebreaker, a prelude to pairing up with the (former) mother. What better way to return her to ovulation—by putting an emphatic end to her breast-feeding—and to focus her energies on the offspring to come?

Anyone tempted to launch into a sweeping indictment of langur morality should first note that infanticide on grounds of infidelity has been acceptable in a number of human societies. Among the Yanomamö of South America and the Tikopia of the Solomon Islands, men have been known to demand, upon marrying women with a past, that their babies will be killed. And Ache men sometimes collectively decide to kill a newly fatherless child. For a woman in the ancestral environment, then, the benefits of multiple sex partners could have ranged from their sparing her child's life to their defending or otherwise investing in her youngster.

Again, this logic does not depend on a conscious understanding of it. Male langurs presumably do not grasp the concept of paternity. Still, genes that make males sensitive to cues that certain infants may or may not carry their genes have survived. A gene that says, "Be nice to children if you've had lots of sex with their mothers," will prosper over the long haul.

## THE INVENTION AND CORRUPTION OF LOVE

Genes don't talk, of course. They affect behavior by creating feelings and thoughts—by building and maintaining the brain. Whenever evolutionary psychologists talk about some evolved behavioral tendency—a polygamous or monogamous bent, say, or male parental investment—they are also talking about an underlying mental infrastructure.

The advent of male parental investment, for example, required the invention of a compelling emotion: paternal love. At some point in our past, genes that inclined a man to love his offspring began to flourish at the expense of genes that promoted remoteness. The reason, presumably, is that changes in circumstances—an upsurge in predators, say—made it more likely that the offspring of undevoted, unprotective fathers would perish.

Crossing this threshold meant love not only for the child; the first step toward becoming devoted parents consists of the man and woman developing a mutual attraction. The genetic payoff of having two parents committed to a child's welfare seems to be the central reason men and women can fall into swoons over one another.

Until recently, this claim was heresy. "Romantic love" was thought to be the unnatural invention of Western culture. The Mangaians of Polynesia, for instance, were said to be "puzzled" by references to marital affection. But lately anthropologists have taken a second look at purportedly loveless cultures, including the Mangaians, and have discovered what nonanthropologists already knew: Love between man and woman is a human universal.

In this sense the pair-bonding label is apt. Still, that term—and for that matter the term love—conveys a sense of permanence and symmetry that is wildly misleading. Evolution not only invented romantic love but from the beginning also corrupted it. The corruption lies in conflicts of interest inherent in male parental investment. It is the goal of maximizing male investment, remember, that sometimes leads a woman to infidelity. Yet it is the preciousness of this investment that makes her infidelity lethal to her mate's interests. Not long for this world are the genes of a man who showers time and energy on children who are not his.

Meanwhile, male parental investment also makes the man's naturally polygynous bent inimical to his wife's reproductive interests. His quest for a new wife could lead him to withdraw, or at least dilute, investment in his first wife's children. This reallocation of resources may on balance help his genes but certainly not hers.

The living legacy of these long-running genetic conflicts is human jealousy—or, rather, human jealousies. In theory, there should be two kinds of jealousy—one male and one female. A man's jealousy should focus on sexual infidelity, since cuckoldry is the greatest genetic threat he faces. A woman, though she'll hardly applaud a partner's strictly sexual infidelity (it does consume time and divert some resources), should be more concerned with emotional infidelity—the sort of magnetic commitment to another woman that could lead to a much larger shift in resources.

David Buss, an evolutionary psychologist at the University of Michigan, has confirmed this prediction vividly. He placed electrodes on men and women and had them envision their mates doing various disturbing things. When men imagined sexual infidelity, their heart rates took leaps of a magnitude typically induced by three cups of coffee. They sweated. Their brows wrinkled. When they imagined a budding emotional attachment, they calmed down, though not quite to their normal level. For women, things were reversed: envisioning emotional infidelity—redirected love, not supplementary sex—brought the deeper distress.

That jealousy is so finely tuned to these forms of treachery is yet more evidence that they have a long evolutionary history. Still, the modern environment has carried them to new heights, making marriage dicier than ever. Men and women have always, in a sense, been designed to make each other miserable, but these days they are especially good at it.

## MODERN OBSTACLES TO MONOGAMY

To begin with, infidelity is easier in an anonymous city than in a small hunter-gatherer village. Whereas paternity studies show that 2 percent of the children in a !Kung San village result from cuckoldry, the rate runs higher than 20 percent in some modern neighborhoods.

Contraceptive technology may also complicate marriage. During human evolution, there were no condoms or birth-control pills. If an adult couple slept together for a year or two and produced no baby, the chances were good that one of them was not fertile. No way of telling which one, but from their genes' point of view, there was little to lose and much to gain by ending the partnership and finding a new mate. Perhaps, some have speculated, natural selection favored genes inclining men and women to sour on a mate after long periods of sex without issue. And it is true that barren marriages are especially likely to break up.

Another possible challenge to monogamy in the modern world lies in movies, billboards, and magazines. There was no photography in the long-ago world that shaped the human male mind. So at some deep level, that mind may respond to glossy images of pin-ups and fashion models as if they were viable mates—alluring alternatives to dull, monogamous devotion. Evolutionary psychologist Douglas Kenrick has suggested as much. According to his research, men who are shown pictures of *Playboy* models later describe themselves as less in love with their wives than do men shown other images. Women shown pictures from *Playgirl* felt no such attitude adjustment toward spouses.

Perhaps the largest modern obstacle to lasting monogamy is economic inequity. To see why, it helps to grasp a subtle point made by Donald Symons, author of the 1979 classic *The Evolution of Human Sexuality*. Though men who leave their wives may be driven by "natural" impulses, that does not mean men have a natural impulse designed expressly to make them leave their wives. After all, in the ancestral environment, gaining a second wife didn't mean leaving the first. So why leave her? Why not stay near existing offspring and keep giving some support? Symons believes men are designed less for opportune desertion than for opportune polygyny. It's just that when polygyny is illegal, a polygynous impulse will find other outlets, such as divorce.

If Symons is right, the question of what makes a man feel the restlessness that leads to divorce can be rephrased: What circumstances, in the ancestral environment, would have permitted the acquisition of a second wife? Answer: possessing markedly more resources, power, or social status than the average Joe.

Even in some "egalitarian" hunter-gatherer societies, men with slightly more status or power than average are slightly more likely to have multiple wives. In less egalitarian preindustrial societies, the anthropologist Laura Betzig has shown, the pattern is dramatic. In Incan society, the four political offices from petty chief to chief were allotted ceilings of seven, eight, fifteen and thirty women. Polygyny reaches its zenith under the most despotic regimes. Among the Zulu, where coughing or sneezing at the king's dinner table was punishable by death, his highness might monopolize more than 100 women.

To an evolutionary psychologist, such numbers are just extreme examples of a simple fact: The ultimate purpose of the wealth and power that men seek so ardently is genetic proliferation. It is only natural that the exquisitely flexible human mind should be designed to capitalize on this power once it is obtained.

Thus it is natural that a rising corporate star, upon getting a big promotion, should feel a strong attraction to women other than his wife. Testosterone—which expands a male's sexual appetite—has been shown to rise in nonhuman primates following social triumphs, and there are hints that it does so in human males, too. Certainly the world is full of triumphant men—Johnny Carson, Donald Trump—who trade in aging wives for younger, more fertile models. (The multi-wived J. Paul Getty said, "A lasting relationship with a woman is only possible if you are a business failure.")

A man's exalted social status can give his offspring a leg up in life, so it's natural that women should lust after the high-status men who lust after them. Among the Ache, the best hunters also have more extramarital affairs and more illegitimate children than lesser hunters. In modern societies, contraception keeps much of this sex appeal from translating into offspring. But last year a study by Canadian anthropologist Daniel Pérusse found that single men of high socioeconomic status have sex with more partners than lower-status men.

One might think that the appeal of rich or powerful men is losing its strength. After all, as more women enter the work force, they can better afford to premise their marital decisions on something other than a man's income. But we're dealing here with deep romantic attractions, not just conscious calculation, and these feelings were forged in a different environment. Evolutionary psychologists have shown that the tendency of women to place greater emphasis than men on a mate's financial prospects remains strong regardless of the income or expected income of the women in question.

The upshot of all this is that economic inequality is monogamy's worst enemy. Affluent men are inclined to leave their aging wives, and young women—including some wives of less affluent men—are inclined to offer themselves as replacements.

Objections to this sort of analysis are predictable: "But people leave marriages for emotional reasons. They don't add up their offspring and pull out their calculators." True. But emotions are just evolution's executioners. Beneath the thoughts and feelings and temperamental differences marriage counselors spend their time sensitively assessing are the stratagems of the genes— cold, hard equations composed of simple variables: social status, age of spouse, number of children, their ages, outside romantic opportunities, and so on. Is the wife really duller and more nagging than she was twenty years ago? Maybe, but maybe the husband's tolerance for nagging has dropped now that she is 45 and has no reproductive future. And the promotion he just got, which has already drawn some admiring glances from a young woman at work, has not helped.

Similarly, we might ask the young, childless wife who finds her husband intolerably insensitive why the insensitivity wasn't so oppressive a year ago, before he lost his job and she met the kindly, affluent bachelor who seems to be flirting with her. Of course, maybe her husband's abuses are quite real, in which case they signal his disaffection and perhaps his impending departure—and merit just the sort of preemptive strike the wife is now mustering.

## THE FALLOUT FROM MONOGAMY'S DEMISE

Not only does male social inequality favor divorce. Divorce can also reinforce male social inequality; it is a tool of class exploitation. Consider Johnny Carson. Like many wealthy, high-status males, he spent his career dominating the reproductive years of a series of women. Somewhere out there is a man who wanted a family and a pretty wife and, if it hadn't been for Johnny Carson, would have married one of these women. And if this man has managed to find another woman, she was similarly snatched from the clutches of some other man. And so on—a domino effect: A scarcity of fertile females trickles down the social scale.

As theoretical as this sounds, it cannot help happening. There are only about 25 years of fertility per woman. When some men dominate more than 25 years' worth, some man somewhere must do with less. And when, in addition to all the serial husbands, you count the men who live with a woman for five years before deciding not to marry her, and then do it again (perhaps finally at 35 marrying a 28-year-old, the net effect is not trivial. As some Darwinians have put it, serial monogamy is tantamount to polygyny. Like polygyny, it lets powerful men grab extra sexual resources (a.k.a. women), leaving less fortunate men without mates—or at least without mates young enough to bear children. Thus rampant divorce not only ends the marriages of some men but also prevents the marriage of others. In 1960, when the divorce rate was around 25 percent, the portion of the never married population age 40 or older was about the same for men and women. By 1990, with the divorce rate running at 50 percent, the portion for men was larger by 20 percent than for women.

Viewing serial monogamy as polygyny by another name throws a kink into the family-values debate. So far, conservatives have got the most political mileage out of decrying divorce. Yet lifelong monogamy—one woman per man for rich and poor alike—would seem to be a natural rallying cry for liberals.

One other kind of fallout from serial monogamy comes plainly into focus through the lens of evolutionary psychology: the toll taken on children. Martin Daly and Margo Wilson of McMaster University in Ontario, two of the field's seminal thinkers, have written that one of the "most obvious" Darwinian predictions is that stepparents will "tend to care less profoundly for children than natural parents." After all, parental investment is a precious resource. So natural selection should "favor those parental psyches that do not squander it on nonrelatives"—who after all do not carry the parent's genes.

Indeed, in combing through 1976 crime data, Daly and Wilson found that an American child living with one or more substitute parents was about 100 times as likely to be fatally abused as a child living with biological parents. In a Canadian city in the 1980s, a child age two or younger was 70 times as likely to be killed by a parent if living with a stepparent and a natural parent than if living with two natural parents.

Of course, murdered children are a tiny fraction of all children living with stepparents; divorce and remarriage hardly amount to a child's death warrant. But consider the more common problem of nonfatal abuse. Children under 10 were, depending on their age and the study in question, three to forty times as likely to suffer parental abuse if living with a stepparent and a biological parent instead of two biological parents.

There are ways to fool Mother Nature, to induce parents to love children who are not theirs. (Hence cuckoldry.) After all, people cannot telepathically sense that a child is carrying their genes. Instead they rely on cues that in the ancestral environment would have signaled as

much. If a woman feeds and cuddles an infant day after day, she may grow to love the child, and so may the woman's mate. This sort of bonding is what makes adopted children lovable (and is one reason relationships between stepparent and child are often harmonious). But the older a child is when first seen, the less profound the attachment will probably be. Most children who acquire stepfathers are past infancy.

Polygynous cultures, such as the nineteenth century Mormons, are routinely dismissed as cruelly sexist. But they do have at least one virtue: They do not submit children to the indifference or hostility of a surrogate father. What we have now—serial monogamy, quasi-polygyny—is in this sense worse than true polygyny. It massively wastes the most precious evolutionary resource: love.

## IS THERE HOPE?

Given the toll of divorce—on children, on low-income men, and for that matter on mothers and fathers—it would be nice to come up with a magic monogamy-restoration plan. Alas, the importance of this task seems rivaled only by its difficulty. Lifelong monogamous devotion just isn't natural, and the modern environment makes it harder than ever. What to do?

As Laura Betzig has noted, some income redistribution might help. One standard conservative argument against antipoverty policies is their cost: Taxes burden the affluent and thus, by lowering work incentive, reduce economic output. But if one goal of the policy is to bolster monogamy, then making the affluent less so would help. Monogamy is threatened not just by poverty in an absolute sense but also by the relative wealth of the rich. This is what lures a young woman to a wealthy married or formerly married man. It is also what makes the man who attracts her feel too good for just one wife.

As for the economic consequences, the costs of soaking the rich might well be outweighed by the benefits, financial and otherwise, of more stable marriages, fewer divorces, fewer abused children, and less loneliness and depression.

There are other levers for bolstering monogamy, such as divorce law. In the short run, divorce brings the average man a marked rise in standard of living, while his wife, along with her children, suffers the opposite. Maybe we should not lock people into unhappy marriages with financial disincentives to divorce, but surely we should not reward men for leaving their wives, either.

## A MORAL ANIMAL

The problem of divorce is by no means one of public policy alone. Progress will also depend on people using the explosive insight of evolutionary psychology in a morally responsible way. Ideally, this insight would lead people to subject their own feelings to more acute scrutiny. Maybe for starters, men and women will realize that their constantly fluctuating perceptions of a mate are essentially illusions, created for the (rather absurd, really) purpose of genetic proliferation, and that these illusions can do harm. Thus men might beware the restlessness designed by natural selection to encourage polygyny. Now that it brings divorce, it can inflict great emotional and even physical damage on their children.

And men and women alike might bear in mind that impulses of wanderlust, or marital discontent, are not always a sign that you married the "wrong person." They may just signify that you are a member of our species who married another member of our species. Nor, as evolutionary psychiatrist Randolph L. Nesse has noted, should we believe such impulses are a sign of psychopathology. Rather, he writes, they are "expected impulses that must, for the most part, be inhibited for the sake of marriage."

The danger is that people will take the opposite tack: react to the new knowledge by surrendering to "natural" impulses, as if what's "in our genes" were beyond reach of self-control. They may even conveniently assume that what is "natural" is good.

This notion was common earlier in this century. Natural selection was thought of almost as a benign deity, constantly "improving" our species for the greater good. But evolutionary psychology rests on a quite different world view: recognition that natural selection does not work toward overall social welfare, that much of human nature boils down to ruthless genetic self-interest, that people are naturally oblivious to their ruthlessness.

George Williams, whose 1966 book *Adaptation and Natural Selection* helped dispel the once popular idea that evolution often works for "the good of the group," has even taken to calling natural selection "evil" and "the enemy." The moral life, in his view, consists largely of battling human nature.

Darwin himself believed the human species to be a moral one—in fact, the only moral animal species. "A moral being is one who is capable of comparing his past and future actions or motives, and of approving or disapproving of them," he wrote.

In a sense, yes, we are moral. We have at least the technical capacity to lead an examined life: self-awareness, memory, foresight, and judgment. Still, chronically subjecting ourselves to moral scrutiny and adjusting our behavior accordingly is hardly a reflex. We are potentially moral animals—which is more than any other animal can say—but we are not naturally moral animals. The first step to being moral is to realize how thoroughly we aren't.

# Chapter 42

# *The Curious Courtship of Sociobiology and Feminism: A Case of Irreconcilable Differences*

## Zuleyma Tang-Martinez

Sociobiology has influenced many different fields of inquiry, feminism (defined as a movement to end the oppression of women) among them. However, the relationship between feminism and sociobiology has been complex and multidimensional. On the one hand, some feminists (here referred to as sociobiological feminists or "Darwinian feminists," see Gowaty, 1992) have embraced sociobiology as a boon to our understanding of women's oppression. On the other hand, most other feminists have charged that human sociobiology is inherently misogynistic and provides a justification for the oppression of women.

The relationship between feminism and sociobiology can best be understood by examining three different approaches that feminists have taken in their encounter with sociobiology. These approaches differ significantly in their methodology, in their assumptions and, most importantly, in their conclusions. The first approach represents the more traditional feminist view of sociobiology, while the last two approaches are representative of sociobiological feminism.

1. Traditionally, most feminists (myself included) have rejected sociobiology as neither relevant nor necessary to understanding or ending the oppression of women. The objections raised by traditional feminists are both methodological and ideological. These feminists hold that the methods used by human sociobiologists are flawed and unscientific and that there is little credible evidence to support sociobiological claims about male–female differences. At the same time, traditional feminists contend that human sociobiology is biologically deterministic and that it serves only to justify and promote the

In: *Feminism and Evolutionary Biology: Boundaries, Intersections, and Frontiers.* Routledge, Chapman and Hall.

oppression of women by perpetuating the notion that male dominance and female oppression are natural outcomes of human evolutionary history. Furthermore, they argue that reliance on questionable evolutionary scenarios can be used to rationalize and exonerate obnoxious male behavior. For example, the middle-aged man who leaves his middle-aged wife for a younger woman can be excused because he is acting in accordance with sociobiological theory by behaving so as to maximize his genetic contribution to future generations by leaving an older spouse who has "low reproductive value" in favor of a younger female with higher reproductive value (see discussion of evolutionary psychology, below). Most traditional feminists would consider this excuse as a "cop-out" that condones the oppression of women. Rather than relying on genetic/evolutionary explanations, traditional feminists are more likely to look at economic, sociological, and cultural analyses as more meaningful explanations of male–female differences and male domination of women.

2. Some feminists have used a sociobiological approach, informed by a feminist perspective, to reinterpret data so as to gain insights into aspects of female power and the control of female sexuality. Hrdy (1986), in her essay entitled "Empathy, Polyandry, and the Myth of the Coy Female," provides an excellent example of this approach. By re-examining existing data, Hrdy concludes that female mammals have many different strategies for controlling their reproduction and that the presumed "coyness" of females (a concept that serves as an underpinning for much of modern sexual selection theory, e.g., Orians 1969, Trivers 1972), is an erroneous interpretation of strategies used by females to further their own reproductive interests.

Similarly, using a sociobiological approach, Smuts (1992, in press) re-interprets data on female behaviors in male dominated primate societies. She concludes that many of the behaviors shown by the females can be best understood as strategies by which females effectively resist attempted sexual coercion by males.

**3.** A third approach is to use sociobiological methodology and analyses in an attempt to understand the origins of male domination and female oppression. Feminists using this approach believe that by understanding the evolutionary origins of male dominance we will be able to formulate more effective responses to counteract female oppression. They implicitly assume that human social systems, including male-female relationships and societal practices and mores, have a biological basis and are the end result of organic revolution. Those who accept such an evolutionary or Darwinian "world view" believe that an evolutionary approach can lead to novel insights that may lead to more efficient strategies aimed at ending the oppression of women.

These three approaches are not necessarily mutually exclusive. The Darwinian feminist approaches frequently overlap (e.g., Hrdy 1981, Smuts 1992, in press). Furthermore, sociobiological feminists generally reject the allegation that their arguments represent, or lend themselves to, biological determinism [in this they resemble the approach taken by Alexander (1979) who champions a sociobiological approach while simultaneously rejecting biological determinism (see Kitcher, 1985, Chap. 9)]. Furthermore, despite the fact that sociobiological feminists at times use terminology such as "natural selection," "evolved characters," "Darwinian evolution," and "kin selection," some of them do not believe that their analyses rely on genetic effects. Most sociobiological feminists overtly reject the notion that biology equals destiny, or that human evolutionary history should be used as a justification for misogyny in modern human societies. They do believe, however, that "such knowledge (evolutionary biology) will yield more realistic expectation concerning present human conduct . . . " (Hrdy 1988, p. 126).

As an evolutionary biologist who is also a feminist, I share a common goal with sociobiological feminists: the eradication of male dominance and female oppression. However, I believe that the two sociobiological feminist approaches, and especially the second of these, are fundamentally flawed, misguided, and unscientific. I do not believe that the "scientific" methodology of human sociobiology is either rigorous or valid, or that most hypotheses advanced by human sociobiology can be satisfactorily tested and falsified, as required by the scientific method (Platt 1964, Popper 1959). Given the potential dangers (particularly in terms of sexism and racism) inherent in some of the conclusions advanced by human sociobiology, we should insist that sociobiological hypotheses on human behavior be held to the same high standards of scientific evidence and testability that we demand from other scientific endeavors.

## ASSUMPTIONS OF THE SOCIOBIOLOGICAL APPROACH

Sociobiological analyses rest on two basic assumptions. The first is that most traits are genetic adaptations. The second is that similarity between traits implies shared genetic origins and function. The problem with these assumptions is that they are treated as the starting and ending points for sociobiological analyses. Thus, no actual evidence is required to demonstrate that the trait is, in fact, genetically based or that it is heritable. Likewise, the adaptive nature of traits is often assumed and asserted without the empirical evidence to support these claims.

### Traits as Genetic Adaptations

A defining characteristic of sociobiology is that it embraces the adaptationist program. The adaptationist program assumes that most (if not all) traits, whether morphological, physiological, or behavioral, are (or are derived from traits that are) adaptive and optimal in terms of increasing the reproductive success of the carrier of the trait (Futuyma 1986, Gould and Lewontin 1979). In other words, traits are assumed to have evolved in such a way that they maximize or optimize the fitness (reproductive success) of the possessor of the trait. The mechanisms by which such optimal traits are selected are almost invariably assumed to be individual selection or kin selection. (See Futuyma 1986 for a more in-depth discussion of "adaptationism").

The sociobiological approach also assumes implicitly that all adaptive traits are genetically based and are the result of organic evolution. Learned or culturally evolved traits (some of which also increase the reproductive success of the animal showing the trait) are generally of little interest or concern to sociobiologists. This approach ignores the role of culture and the complex interactions among culture, phenotype (the traits shown by the individual), and environment. For example, Kitcher (1985) emphasizes that culture affects phenotype and the phenotypes of individuals in any one generation can, in turn, affect the culture encountered by the subsequent generation. Thus, an individual's phenotype is the result of dynamic interactions among an individual's genotype (genetic makeup) and the biotic, abiotic, social, and historical environment in which the individual develops and lives.

Lumsden and Wilson (1981), in their book *Genes, Mind, and Culture,* attempt to incorporate culture into sociobiological theory. Unfortunately, the book deteriorates into the same types of biologically determinist arguments advanced in Wilson's earlier books. The role of culture is envisioned as allowing only very limited flexibility in human behavior (the "short leash" metaphor), behaviors are still assumed to be adaptive, and genes continue to be the primary determinants of human destiny and human nature. Thus, Lumsden and Wilson (1981, pp. 357–360) state, "Only with difficulty can individual development be deflected from the narrow channels along which the great majority of human beings travel." They proceed to argue that human societies "cannot escape the inborn rules of epigenesis" without running the "risk of losing the very essence of humanness." So much for culture! Clearly, from Lumsden and Wilson's perspective, what really matters are the genes and woe be to the society that does not follow its genetic imperative.

Sociobiologists and their supporters acknowledge that the assumptions of adaptation and genetic bases for behaviors are central to their methodology. For example, Alcock (1989, pp. 512–513) states: "In order to employ an evolutionary approach to the behavior of any species, one has to *assume* that the behavior of interest has evolved. In order for behavior to evolve, it must have a *genetic foundation* and in the past, individuals with different alleles must have exhibited different behaviors that affected their inclusive fitness" (emphases mine). In other words, Alcock makes it clear that the starting point for any sociobiological exploration is the assumption of adaptation and genetic basis. Empirical evidence for either of these assumptions plays no significant role in the methodology. Furthermore, the emphasis on inclusive fitness demonstrates the reliance on individual and kin selection as the important forces selecting for behaviors.

### Similar Traits Imply Similar Genetic Origins

A second assumption of human sociobiology is that human behaviors are directly comparable to nonhuman animal (hereafter "animal") behaviors that are similar in "form" or appearance. Human sociobiologists often assume that human behaviors have the same evolutionary origin and genetic basis as animal behaviors that resemble them. For example, a sociobiologist may assume that the behavior of a man who beats his wife has the same evolutionary and genetic origins as the behavior of a male baboon who bites a female that has strayed too far from him. He or she may then further assume that if one can explain the adaptive function of male aggression against females in baboons, one will also have explained the "adaptive function" of wife-beating in humans. Alternatively, he or she may argue that while some traits may not be evolutionarily identical by descent, they nonetheless represent convergent evolution and are, therefore, evolutionary (genetic) solutions to similar problems.

One example of this equation of animal and human behaviors is provided by the sociobiological literature on rape. Thornhill and Thornhill (1983, p. 140), in their discussion of the "evolutionary and background considerations" for the evolutionary analysis of human rape, mention "forced copulations" in ducks, orangutans, and scorpionflies. Alcock (1989, p. 526) is even more explicit: "According to this view, (Thornhill and Thornhill's) rape in humans is analogous to forced copulation in *Panorpa* scorpionflies . . . Male *Panorpa* that are able to offer material benefits to females do so in return for copulations; males that cannot offer nuptial gifts attempt to force females to copulate with them. Human males unable to attract willing sexual partners might also rape as a reproductive option of last resort." Similarly, Shields and Shields (1983) introduce their analysis of human rape by citing studies of "forced copulations," "stolen fertilizations," and "rape" in species as diverse as acanthocephalan worms, insects, fishes, amphibians, birds, and mammals.

Sociobiological feminists often use the behaviors of animals to buttress their arguments on the evolutionary origins of human behaviors and tendencies. Thus, Hrdy (1981) uses the behavior of nonhuman female primates as the foundation for her treatise on the evolution of women; Smuts (1992) and Smuts and Smuts (1993) rely on studies of male aggression and sexual coercion of females in nonhuman primates and other mammals in their attempts to understand the origins of patriarchy and male aggression against women in humans. Likewise, Mesnick uses information on sexual coercion in a broad range of animals as the basis for her "sex-for-protection" hypothesis.

Whether explicitly stated or not, these approaches inherently assume that animal and human behaviors are sufficiently similar in evolutionary origin, that an understanding of animal behaviors can lead us to a valid understanding of the origins and evolution of human behaviors. However, without empirical evidence that this is the case, similarity in form and appearance of behaviors is not sufficient to conclude that the behaviors in question have a similar genetic origin or share a common or convergent evolutionary history.

## METHODOLOGIES OF HUMAN SOCIOBIOLOGY

Human sociobiologists (including sociobiological feminists) use three different methodologies in analyzing human social behavior. These methodologies are: (1) cross-species comparisons, that is, comparisons of human behaviors to nonhuman animal behaviors; (2) cross cultural studies, usually aimed at demonstrating the existence of "universal traits"; and (3) adaptive storytelling. Each of these methodologies, and how the preceding assumptions impact them, will be explained and critiqued in turn.

*Cross-Species Comparisons*

The problems with making cross-species comparisons are many, and the assumptions on which this approach is based have been discussed in some detail in the preceding section. These problems include: (1) choice of species and selective use of data; (2) assumptions about genetic similarities between similar human and animal behaviors; (3) the use of anthropomorphic terminology; and (4) the uncritical acceptance of axiomatic formulations in evolutionary biology. Because arguments based on comparisons between animals and humans are often the most convincing to nonbiologists, I will discuss each of these problems in depth.

*Choice of Species.* A major problem in cross-species comparisons is the potential for bias in the choice of the species that will be compared to humans. Most frequently, human behaviors are compared to the behaviors of other, nonhuman primates, but species as diverse as scorpionflies, ducks, and rats have also been used as models for human behaviors.

For example, as documented in the preceding discussion, sociobiological analyses of human rape have relied on studies of "rape" (ostensibly forced copulations) in other species. Conclusions on the biological bases of rape in these species are then applied to humans and it is argued that human rape is an evolved adaptive strategy.

Similarly, studies on rodents have been used by sociobiologists as well as some non-sociobiologists, to explain sexual differences in human behaviors. Research on rodents has shown that neonatal hormones can affect the development of certain areas of the brain and that sexual differences in these brain areas are reflected in differences in the sexual behaviors of adult male and female rodents (e.g., Barraclough and Gorski 1962, Gorski et al. 1978, Phoenix et al. 1959). These findings have led some researchers to suggest that similar neuroendocrine effects may be responsible for gender role differences between men and women (e.g., Money and Ehrhardt 1972; Swaab and Fliers 1985). Likewise, based on the results of the same rodent studies and on the assumption that homosexual men are more "feminine," some have argued that the brains of gay men have developed in a female direction and that this is the biological basis for their sexual preference (Le Vay 1991, Swaab and Hoffman 1990).

Typically, the leaps from the rodent studies to human neuroanatomy and behavior are made without any acknowledgment that such comparisons can be problematic and equivocal. Yet more than twenty years ago, Beach (1971) cautioned that the results of hormonal treatments on the neonatal brain could not be generalized easily even from one rodent species to another (see also Beach 1978 for a critique of facile comparisons between human sexual behavior and the sexual behaviors of nonhuman animals, specially in reference to homosexuality).

Even when human behaviors are compared to those of nonhuman primates, the reasons why a particular primate species is chosen are not always apparent. Primate species exhibit remarkable diversity in their social organization, mating systems, male-female relationships, and in their sexual and aggressive behaviors.

Despite this bewildering diversity among primate species, sociobiologists (e.g., Washburn and DeVore 1961; Washburn and Lancaster 1968) and pop-ethologists (e.g., Ardrey 1961, Pfeiffer 1969, Tiger and Fox 1971) regularly use baboon ecology, social behavior, and male-female relationships as the prototype for human evolution and social systems. This is true despite the fact that baboons are not particularly closely related to humans.

So, why have baboons been the species of choice for sociobiologists and pop-ethologists?

It seems inescapable that the main reason that baboons are the species of choice is that they allow sociobiologists and pop-ethologists to argue that behavioral traits found in both baboons and some human societies (male dominance and aggression against females) are natural consequences of our ostensibly common evolutionary histories. In saying this, I am not suggesting that there has been a conscious "conspiracy" among sociobiologists and pop-ethologists with regard to the baboon model. Fedigan (1992, p. 309) concludes an insightful and elegant critique of the "baboonization" of human evolution with the statement, "When one primate species out of at least 200 species is chosen as a model for early humans, the explanation for the choice probably lies as much in the nature of the argument being developed, as in the behavior of the animal upon which the argument is to be based."

In a recent pop-sociobiology book, Russel (1993) models human "evolution, power, sex, and love" on lemurs. He maintains that the roots of human behavior can be traced back to the mouse, ringtailed, and brown lemurs. He claims that from our lemur roots, humans derived male-female bonding, male aggression, aggressively determined dominance hierarchies, adventurous and active males, passive and timid females, sexual coercion of females, and female preferences for non-aggressive males.

In a scathing review, Sussman (1994) points out that Russel's "facts" are just plain wrong and that he misrepresents the behavior of the species he describes. For example, with regards to the ringtailed lemur, Sussman states, ". . . I have studied this species for close to 25 years and find it difficult to recognize the animal he describes . . ." Specifically, Sussman emphasizes that there are no restricted male-female bonds, that mating is always dependent on females and that there is no forced mating. Additionally, there is no relationship between female choice and levels of male aggression and all receptive females mate with a number of different males of all ranks (Sussman 1994, p. 366). Similar critiques follow each of the species cited by Russel.

Interestingly, sociobiological feminists have also used baboons (as well as male-dominant macaque societies) as the starting point for their analyses of male dominance and sexual coercion in humans (e.g., Smuts 1992, in press). The assumption in these analyses appears to be that high levels of aggression, male dominance, and sexual coercion of females by males are ancestral conditions in primates. Thus, primate societies that do not show these characteristics are considered as outside the norm and, therefore, in need of explanation. Given the great diversity of male-female relationships among primates and the fact that, as Smuts (in press) acknowledges, "Humans are an exception to the *typical primate pattern of sexual egalitarianism*" (emphasis mine), it is surprising that species in which male dominance and sexual aggression are common are chosen as the point of departure for discussions on the evolution of male dominance in human societies.

*Assumptions of Genetic Similarity.*   A major problem in sociobiological comparisons of animal and human behaviors is that the form (what the behavior looks like), the function, and the causation of behaviors have been conflated (see Purton 1978 for a detailed discussion of the dangers in such conflation). Similarity of form is assumed to indicate similarity of function either as a result of evolutionary homology (i.e., same genetic origin), or as a result of convergent evolution. However, function, causation, and genetic origin should never be inferred solely from form. Behaviors that have the same form may have very different functions in different species, and sometimes even in the same species in different contexts.

Several examples illustrate these points. Head-nodding, a behavior during which the animal presents the top of its head to its opponent, functions as a threat display in the sandwich tern (van Iersel and Bol 1958), but as an appeasement display used during greeting ceremonies in the night heron (Lorenz 1938; also discussed in Zawistowski and Hirsch 1983). Male tyrannid flycatchers have a "kitter" vocalization. In one context this vocalization functions to attract females, in another context it functions as a threat display to other males, and in a third context it functions as an appeasement display to the female during mating (Smith 1963). Behaviors with similar form but different functions are also found when comparing humans and nonhuman primates. For example, the "grin" of cercopithecine monkeys is an expression of fear (Rowell 1972, p. 97), while the grin of humans is most commonly a proximity-promoting signal. Baboon "yawns" are often threat behaviors (e.g., Jolly

1972, p. 170) while human yawns are associated with boredom or sleepiness.

To complicate this situation even further, two traits may have a similar function but different evolutionary histories and genetic origins. In biology such traits are referred to as "analogous" to one another. For example, the wings of a bat and the wings of a butterfly have the same function (flying) and superficially are even somewhat similar in appearance. However, one cannot understand the genetic and phylogenetic origins of the butterfly's wings by studying the genetic and phylogenetic origins of the bat's wings. This is because the two species are not derived from a common ancestor and do not share the same evolutionary history.

In summary, when human sociobiologists compare human and animal behaviors and assume that behaviors that are similar in appearance have similar functions and evolutionary histories, they are violating a basic principle of biology: Form alone does not provide information about function nor about shared genetic or evolutionary histories.

*Anthropomorphic Terminology.*   Another way in which human sociobiologists attempt to equate human behaviors with animal behaviors is by the use of anthropomorhpic terminology. Characteristically, a behavior that somewhat resembles a human behavior is observed in an animal and labelled with a human term. The possible evolutionary origins and adaptive significance of the animal behavior is then studied and the conclusions are advanced as explanations for the behavior in humans. The assumption is that since we are dealing with the "same" behavior, based on the fact that the researcher has labelled the animal behavior with the human term and that the animal behavior has a resemblance to human behavior (see previous section), then an explanation of the behavior in animals must also be applicable to the human behavior.

A common pattern is for human sociobiologists to assume that the animal behavior (assigned the heavily loaded anthropomorphic label) and the human behavior are the same because they look similar (i.e., superficial similarity of form). Then an evolutionary analysis of the behavior in the animal is extended to claim that the behavior in humans has a similar evolutionary origin. Thus, the explanation in one species is assumed to be directly applicable, perhaps with minor modifications, to the other.

*Acceptance of Dogmatic Assumptions.*   Most modern biological discussions of mating systems, sexual selection, or male-female interactions start with the premise that females have been selected to be sexually discriminating ("coy"), while males have been selected to be sexually indiscriminate (e.g., Orians 1969, Trivers 1972, Daly and Wilson 1983, and countless others). This assumption is based on the "principle of anisogamy," which holds that eggs are very costly to produce (they are large in size and contain large amounts of expensive nutrients, such as yolk), while sperm are cheap (they are tiny, compared to eggs, and generally are nothing more that a packet of chromosomes without nutrients). As a result of this asymmetry, females have to be very discriminating in selecting mates because they cannot afford to lose their large investment in eggs. Males, on the contrary, have little to lose in mating with any and all females that happen to come along because their investment in sperm is minimal, sperm are cheap, and the male can always produce millions more sperm. Consequently, males compete for as many matings as possible while females set the limits by mating only with superior males. This premise has achieved dogmatic proportions in modern biology and almost every aspect of male-female relationships, as well as male-female differences in parental care of young, has, at one time or another, been explained or justified by referring to this paradigm.

Until recently no one questioned whether the one egg to one sperm comparison is a valid one. Yet, one ejaculation produces millions of sperm and, in many species, those millions of sperm are necessary to ensure the fertilization of just the one egg. For example, in the domestic chicken *(Gallus domesticus)* a male has to produce one hundred million sperm per ejaculation to insure that fertilization will occur (Brillard and Antoine 1990, cited in Birkhead and Moller 1993). To this can be added the cost of sperm that are "lost" (i.e., have no chance of fertilizing an egg) because of various forms sperm competition (including mating order effects) or because the female ejects, destroys, or absorbs sperm after the male ejaculates (Birkhead and Moller 1993). Additionally, ejaculates contain more than just sperm, including costly accessory gland secretions and, in some species, spermatophores. Thus, in comparing the cost of gametes, one should compare one egg (or at least a relatively tiny number of eggs) to one ejaculate. It is not at all clear that when the comparison is adjusted in this fashion, the overall investment of males is really that much different from the overall investment of females.

Even in mammals, in which there is an added female investment because of gestation and lactation (Smuts 1992, in press), it may not be valid to assume that overall female investment in reproduction outweighs male investment (see also Hrdy 1986). Surely, the costs incurred by males that must defend territories in order to mate, that engage in active combat with other males prior to mating, or that provide protection and care to the young (admittedly a relatively rare trait in mammals), must be enormous, albeit difficult to measure.

Behavioral data also do not support the generalization that females are always sexually "coy" or that they are reluctant to mate. For example, DNA fingerprinting has shown that "extra-pair copulations" are common in many bird species that had previously been presumed to be monogamous, and that, in many cases, it is the females that initiate these sexual encounters with other males (Birkhead and Moller 1992, 1993). Females in other taxa, including primates, are also known to engage in high levels of sexual behaviors with a large number of males (reviewed in Hrdy 1986). As extreme examples, during their week-long estrus period, female lions may mate as many as 100 times per day with different males (Eaton 1976, cited in Hrdy 1986), and some primate females may change partners approximately every ten minutes and repeatedly solicit males both inside and outside their social group (Hrdy 1986).

The preponderance of the evidence at present suggests that a major tenet of modern evolutionary and sociobiological theory—namely costly eggs and cheap sperm—has been based on what appear to be invalid and unwarranted assumptions. Scientists influenced by the sexual dynamics (coy females; sexually aggressive males) of modern Euro-American societies, apparently could not imagine that females in other species (and cultures) might behave differently. They, therefore, erected a theoretical framework (costly eggs and cheap sperm) to rationalize their biases. Once this framework was created and dogmatized it became difficult to envision an alternative or to challenge it.

A second, near dogmatic assumption made by many evolutionary biologists, including most sociobiologists and many sociobiological feminists (e.g., Gowaty 1992, Smuts and Smuts 1993) is that female reproductive success is limited by a female's ability to gain access to resources controlled by males, while male reproductive success is limited by access to females. This assumption (that males control the resources needed by females) seems to be such an integral underpinning to so many sociobiological feminist formulations that it is interesting to ask if there are alternative hypotheses and how these alternatives might change the conclusions drawn about male-female relationships in humans.

For example, Wrangham (1979) has proposed a model of primate social systems that emphasizes female control of resources. In this model, females compete (or in some cases cooperate, as with their sisters) with other females for control of resources; males distribute themselves so as to have access to the groups of females that defend and control the resources. Hrdy (1981) appears to support this model and states, "Wrangham's model applies beautifully to the Hanuman langurs that I know best . . . the most persistent defenders of the troop's territories are often female relatives who inherited this feeding area from their mothers and grandmothers" (p.125). She concludes ". . . the basic outlines of primate social structure are better explained by Wrangham's approach than they have been by any previous model that I am aware of" (p. 126). The same pattern seems to hold for many other mammalian social species in which female kin clusters are the core of the social unit. Related female prairie dogs, for example, defend stable and permanent territories; males form temporary associations with these groups of females, helping to defend the territory during their tenure in the group (Halpin 1987).

Wrangham's model illustrates several interesting points about sociobiological thinking and methods. First, it demonstrates that, even on a question as critical as the control of resources, sociobiological analyses can lead to diametrically opposed conclusions. Second, it shows that sociobiologists often fail to examine or consider alternative models and hypotheses, including other sociobiological models (Alcock 1989 is an exception to this); thus, some sociobiological feminists (e.g., Gowaty 1992, Smuts and Smuts 1993) take male control of resources as a given and do not entertain the alternative model of female control of resources. Thirdly, it shows the potential danger of building an entire edifice of theory premised on an assumption that may not be true and about which there is no consensus even in the sociobiological literature.

### Cross-Cultural Comparisons

Sociobiologists sometimes use cross-cultural comparisons to argue for the universality of certain human traits. Universality is then taken as evidence that the trait probably has a genetic basis and is the result of human organic evolution. The problems with this approach include the assumption that human traits are genetic, the selection of human cultures to compare, and the handling of cultural differences.

*Genetic Bases of Human Traits.* Sociobiologists often assume that human traits are genetically based and then proceed to create elaborate evolutionary scenarios based on these assumptions. However, because their statements are usually couched as speculation, it is extremely difficult to critique them because they can always claim that they never really said what they said. Wilson (1975a), for example, frequently couches his genetic arguments in conditional terms such as: "Dahlberg . . . showed that *if* a single gene appears that is responsible for success and an upper shift in status, it can be rapidly concentrated in the upper socioeconomic classes" (Wilson 1975a, p. 554, emphasis mine), or " . . . *if* such genes (for homosexuality) really exist they are almost certainly incomplete in penetrance and variable in expressivity . . ." (Wilson 1975a, p. 555, emphasis mine). Although his scenarios clearly endorse the probable genetic basis of a variety of human behaviors and cultural institutions, Wilson can always claim that he only laid out *one* plausible scenario and that he never actually said that such genes really *do* exist (e.g., Wilson 1976).

Sociobiologists sometimes castigate their critics for saying that sociobiologists advocate a genetic basis for specific human behaviors. Wilson (1976, p. 187), for example, argues that sociobiology only presupposes a genetic basis for the "most widespread, distinctive qualities of human behavior—human nature . . . ," not for specific behaviors. Other sociobiologists speak of "genetic tendencies." However, even in a book intended to examine the interactions of genes and culture, Lumsden and Wilson (1981, p. 357) maintain that a large number of human social behaviors are the result of inflexible and selective developmental rules that limit patterns of behavior regardless of environmental variation, such that "the cultural patterns they influence will change relatively little in the course of history."

If sociobiologists really believed *only* that there are certain genetic foundations that make us human, then one could not quarrel with them. Humans demonstrably are not fish, or earthworms, or lions and certainly are genetically different from other nonhuman species. I also have no quarrel with the notion that the complexity of the human brain evolved as a result of natural selection (although environmental factors can affect brain development in individuals) and that this complexity grants enormous flexibility to human behavior. Furthermore, it also is highly unlikely that a human culture would ever develop in certain directions; I would not, for example, expect to find a human society patterned after a honeybee colony. But when sociobiologists argue (overtly or covertly by developing "plausible" genetic scenarios) in favor of a genetic basis for *particular* human behaviors, social structures, or institutions, such as male dominance, sexual coercion of females, war, social stratification, religion, or xenophobia (Alexander 1979, Wilson 1975a, 1975b, 1976, 1978) they are developing theories for which there is no credible evidence. There is no scientifically reliable, genetic evidence, whatsoever, that any of these specific traits has a genetic basis. Moreover, demonstrating the genetic basis of these and other traits in humans would be extremely difficult, if not impossible, because socialization and culture play such a major role in the development of human behavior. The appropriate quantitative genetic experiments to tease out the genetic and environmental influences on human behaviors are simply not feasible.

*Selection of Cultures.* Human cultures are at least as diverse as primate social structures (e.g. see Harris 1979, Mead 1949, Rodseth et al. 1991, Rorlich-Leavitt et al. 1975, Sahlins 1976). Consequently, any time that a culture or cultures are selected as representative of the human condition, or to argue for the universality of certain human traits, some choices, usually based on unspoken assumptions or preconceptions, must be made. Hinde (1987, p. 413), for example, states, "Since there are about two hundred different species of primates, and an even larger number of recognizably different human societies, it is not difficult to find parallels to prove whatever one wishes. In any one case the use of a different species or a different culture could produce a very different perspective."

*Universality or Diversity?* A major difficulty with the use of cross-cultural studies to infer the genetic basis of human traits is that any finding can be advanced as evidence for genetic influence. I refer to this as the "have your cake and eat it too" axiom of sociobiology. For example, if a trait is found to be universal (in itself a debatable conclusion, see Sussman 1978, 1995), the universality of the trait is assumed to be the result of selection for an ubiquitous genetic characteristic of humans. On the other hand, if a trait varies from one culture to another, two explanations can be offered. The first is that one expression of the trait represents an aberration of the normal human pattern. The second is that the diversity itself may represent genetic differences among cultures. Each of these explanations will be considered in turn.

The argument used by sociobiologists to dismiss, as deviant, societies that differ from the expected sociobiological patterns, is illustrated by the following example. Draper (1975) found that the !Kung San have a remarkably egalitartian society in which male and female children are treated the same, sex roles are varied and flexible, and women are valued and have control over the food they gather. Wilson (1978) discusses these findings and presents evidence that as the !Kung have been forced into an agricultural lifestyle (which has been extremely disruptive to their hunter-gatherer culturer), more rigid sex roles and male dominance have emerged. He concludes that the changes seen in agricultural !Kung societies "are constrained by the genetically influenced behavioral predispositions that constituted the earlier, simpler adaptations of preliterate human beings" (Wilson 1978, p. 89). Thus, he assumes that the changes observed are expressions of a genetic substrate. Moreover, a subsequent statement, "So only a single lifetime is needed to generate the familiar pattern of sexual domination in a culture" (Wilson, 1978, p. 91), suggests that he also believes that male dominance is the normal, evolved condition in human societies and that the agricultural !Kung are returning to this natural human condition. Apparently, then, the egalitartan society of hunter-gatherer !Kung was nothing more than a temporary aberration.

At the same time that sociologists rely on universality as evidence for the genetic basis of human behaviors and institutions, they also hold that cultural differences may reflect genetic differences. For example, Wilson (1975a, p. 550) states, "Although the genes have given away most of their sovereignty, they maintain a certain amount of influence in at least the behavioral qualities that *underlie variations* between cultures" (emphasis mine).

Since sociobiologists argue that both universality and cultural differences are evidence in favor of a genetic

substrate for human cultural traits, their assumptions based on cross-cultural studies cannot be falsified. Thus, no matter what their data show, the information will be considered consistent with their genetic hypotheses. This may be a win-win situation for sociobiology but it is not science.

Are there human universals? Yes, I think so. For example, all human beings die, babies need to be taken care of to survive, all women eventually undergo menopause, only women can give birth, only women lactate, humans can't breathe under water, and we all need to sleep. The issue, however, is not whether such universals exist but what they mean for male-female relationships and for other aspects of human social behaviors. In the absence of solid empirical evidence to the contrary, and particularly in view of modern technology and cultural influences, probably very little.

### Adaptive Story Telling

One of the most common and troubling methodologies used by human sociobiologists is adaptive story telling. Characteristically, a trait is identified and assumed to be adaptive, a hypothetical assumption is presented as a given, and an explanation as to why the trait is adaptive (based on the initial assumption) is constructed. As long as the explanation is plausible and consistent with evolutionary theory, it is accepted as fact. Thus, what is essentially a hypothetical postulate is accepted as evidence and elevated to the status of a conclusion.

An excellent example of sociobiological story telling is provided by two sociobiological scenarios on the evolution of human homosexuality (apparently meaning specifically male homosexuality). Wilson (1975a, p. 555) suggests that male homosexuality may have evolved through kin selection: "The homosexual members of primitive societies may have functioned as helpers, either while hunting in company with other men or in more domestic occupations at the dwelling sites ... they could have operated with special efficiency in assisting close relatives. Genes favoring homosexuality could then be sustained at a high equilibrium level by kin selection alone." So ... there we have it: the "homosexual helpers at the nest" hypothesis, or as Kitcher (1985, p. 251) says, ". . . the helpful homosexual. Every home should have one."

What evidence did Wilson have to make this claim? Although the existence of genes that predispose men towards homosexuality is currently a hotly debated topic (e.g., Hamer et al. 1993, Hubbard and Wald 1993, Radford 1993), at the time that Wilson proposed his kin selection hypothesis there was no clear evidence that "homosexual genes" exist. (He does cite evidence that there is a high concordance for homosexuality among identical twins—but then, there is probably also a high concordance for being Republicans or being Democrats!). Thus, his scenario was not based on actual knowledge of genes for homosexuality. Likewise, there is no evidence that homosexual men functioned as helpers in either primitive or modern societies. Further, Wilson presented no evidence whatsoever that the inclusive fitness of gay men is higher than, or even comparable to, that of heterosexual men. Therefore, one is forced to conclude that his kin selection hypothesis is nothing more than a figment of his imagination that allows him to conclude that homosexuality is both genetic and adaptive—a classical just-so story (after Gould 1980).

An alternative hypothesis is proposed by Alcock (1989, pp. 524–526). According to Alcock, men evolved to have an immense desire for sexual activity, a low threshold for sexual arousal, and an extreme interest in sexual variety. These genetic predispositions serve most men well by increasing their reproductive success, but some unfortunate men have these exaggerated sexual desires but are unable to attract females. Alas, apparently under the control of their raging sexual urges, these males seek inappropriate and maladaptive sexual partners—other men. Alcock (1989, p. 525) then asserts that "most homosexuals are actually bisexuals" (information that undoubtedly will come as a big surprise to most gay men!) and that "homosexuality occurs more commonly in populations of males unable to secure heterosexual partners." As evidence, he cites the fact that most gay men are unmarried (i.e., presumably because they could not find a woman to marry). He also suggests that it is possible that "the average reproductive success (direct fitness) of males that engage in some homosexual behavior during their lifetime is the same, or even higher, than that of exclusive heterosexuals." Lastly, Alcock (1989, p. 525) also argues that females have evolved to be much less sexual than males, and that while males of many species of animals engage in homosexual behavior, there is an "almost complete absence of female homosexuality in nonhuman animals . . ."

There are many interesting aspects of this scenario. First, Alcock argues that male homosexuality results from the inappropriate expression of *adaptive* tendencies, thus preserving the adaptationist paradigm. Second, he argues that homosexuality most commonly occurs among men who are not able to secure a heterosexual partner, yet these men end up having as high or higher reproductive success as compared to heterosexual men. (Exactly how men who have problems securing female mates manage to have this higher reproductive success is not made entirely clear! And does this mean that homosexuality is adaptive after all?). Third, Alcock confounds cause and effect when he alleges that the fact that most gay men are unmarried is evidence in support of his hypothesis; apparently, he never considers the possibility that most gay men are not married precisely because they are not attracted to women! Concomitantly, he violates one of the most basic principles of scientific logic: Correlation is not the same as causation. The fact that being

gay correlates with being unmarried does not allow one to logically conclude that being unmarried *causes* men to be gay. Yet this is precisely the faulty reasoning that Alcock employs. Fourth, Alcock's claim that there is little information on homosexual behavior in female animals is just plain wrong. Beach (1968), Michael et al. (1974), Fedigan and Gozoules (1978), Nishida and Hiraiwa-Hasegawa (1987), and Fedigan (1992) all report homosexual behavior among female mammals. Vasey (in press) provides an extensive review of homosexual behaviors in both male and female primates. (But see also Beach's 1978 critique of facile comparisons of homosexual behaviors in animals and humans).

For anyone with more than a superficial knowledge of human homosexuality, there are other troubling aspects of Alcock's (1989) analysis. For starters, "homosexuality," as it is understood in the United States and most western European societies, is a socially constructed concept that is not shared by many other modern and preliterate societies (see Weinrich and Williams 1991). However, Alcock (and also Wilson) reify homosexuality and "the homosexual" as if they were dealing with a universal trait. Additionally, Alcock treats homosexuality as a strictly sexual phenomenon (i.e., men who engage in sexual acts with other men are "homosexual"), rather than seeing it primarily as part of the core identity of an individual's personality. Thus, in Alcock's scenario there is no room for gay men (or lesbians) who choose to be celibate (yes, there really are celibate gay men). As a result of this equation of homosexuality with sex, Alcock is able to lump together very different instances of male-male sexual behavior as equivalent cases of "homosexuality." Thus, he equates the conditional and generally transitory male-male sexual behaviors seen in prisons, and the exploratory sexual behaviors of adolescent boys, with the permanent, and generally exclusive sexual orientation of men who identify as "gay."

In summary, Alcock presents an adaptive story, based on inaccurate information, a naive understanding of human homosexuality, and his own biases and preconceptions about what gay men are like. He makes many assertions but provides little empirical evidence in support of his hypothesis.

*Human Traits as Genetic Adaptations.* Story telling in human sociobiology assumes a priori that the traits under consideration are adaptive, or the result of adaptive behaviors, and that these adaptive traits have a genetic foundation. Alcock (1989), for example, assumes that even behavior that is apparently maladaptive must be derived from adaptive behavior. These assumptions are fallacious on two counts: (1) not all traits (in either humans or animals) are adaptive, and (2) not all human traits that are adaptive have a genetic basis.

Gould and Lewontin (1979), Gould (1980), and Futuyma (1986) critique the "traits are always adaptive" assumption. They point out that some traits may be: (1) the result of natural laws (e.g., a fish that goes back into the water after leaping out does so because of the force of gravity, not because it is adaptive (Futuyma, 1986); (2) the effects of cultural evolution (learned or culturally acquired traits are passed on from generation to generation); (3) anachronisms (they may have been adaptive at some time in the past, but no longer are, a condition that is also consistent with one of Alcock's hypotheses); (4) the result of developmental allometry, defined as fixed differences in rate of growth of different features during ontogeny; (5) the result of genetic drift (random changes in gene frequencies); or (6) by-products or consequences (epiphenomena) of other traits that did evolve under selection (another condition included in Alcock's list of hypotheses).

To conclude that a trait is adaptive, it is essential to demonstrate a correlation between the trait and appropriate measures of fitness. It is not enough to make predictions of patterns of social behaviors that are consistent with the proposed hypothesis. Rather, alternative and *mutually exclusive* hypotheses, both adaptive *and* nonadaptive should be tested and tested rigorously.

Assuming that adaptive traits must be genetically based is a second major misconception among many (although not all) sociobiologists (see critiques by Gould 1980, Smuts in press). Among humans, numerous traits arise through cultural evolution. Although many of these traits may be adaptive in the sense that they increase survival (and maybe even reproductive success), they do not have a genetic basis. For example, speaking Greek is certainly adaptive for someone who lives in a small, isolated village in Greece. However, speaking Greek is not a genetically based trait (although the capability to speak and learn human language may be) and it did not evolve through natural selection. Thus, the demonstration that a human trait is adaptive can not be taken as prima facie evidence that the trait is also under genetic control or that it evolved under natural selection.

It is not enough for sociobiological feminists to claim that the use of terms such as Darwinian selection, natural selection, and kin selection in their analyses do not imply a genetic foundation for their arguments. These terms, as routinely used in evolutionary biology, do, in fact, imply a genetic substrate. Given the social and political dangers inherent in traditional, genetically based sociobiology, sociobiological feminists should be particularly careful not to use confusing terminology that can lead to muddled interpretations.

## Our Cheating Genes and Hearts: A Case Study for the 90s

The August 15, 1994 issue of *Time* magazine featured a cover story by Robert Wright entitled, "Our Cheating Hearts." In February 1995, *Dateline,* an NBC weekly pro-

gram, presented a three-part series entitled, "Our Cheatin' Hearts." This article and program were an attempt to popularize recent ideas about infidelity and human sexual behaviors developed by "evolutionary psychology" (the newest incarnation of human sociobiology). Evolutionary psychologists (e.g., Buss 1994a, 1994b, Fisher 1992, Wright 1994a, 1994b) maintain that mating patterns among humans, and adultery and infidelity in particular, are genetically based and the result of human evolution aimed at maximizing reproductive success.

While evolutionary psychologists agree on some aspects of human sexuality, they disagree on others. For example, they all appear to agree that male reproductive success depends on access to females and that female reproductive success depends on access to resources controlled by males (but see discussion on Wrangham's model of primate sociality, above). Thus, men engage in adulterous trysts and/or leave their older wives or girlfriends for younger women, as a strategy to spread their genes by leaving more offspring with the many women they use as sexual partners. Women, on the other hand, look for a male's ability to provide resources for her and her offspring. Wright (1994b) uses the marriage of Aristotle Onassis to Jackie Kennedy as one example of this phenomenon, despite the fact that they had no children and that it is unlikely that Onassis' wealth contributed anything to Jackie's reproductive success! One area of apparent disagreement among evolutionary psychologists, however, involves the intensity of sexual drive in women. Thus, while Buss (1994a, 1994b) argues that women are much less sexually active and much more discriminating than men, Fisher (1992, pp. 90–95) believes that high levels of sexual activity and an interest in a sexual variety are characteristic of women in most cultures and societies.

Because of space limitations, I will not attempt a thorough critique of evolutionary psychology. Instead, I will only highlight some of the more obvious problems with its methodology and logic. All of the methodologies described above for human sociobiology (i.e., crossspecies comparisons; cross-cultural comparisons; adaptive story telling) are used by evolutionary psychologists, and these approaches suffer from the same problems discussed previously.

For example, Buss (1994a) analogizes human behaviors to those of many other species, including sandpipers (p. 90), roadrunners (p. 99), bullfrogs (p. 110), sunfish (p. 110), waterstriders (p. 124), and wasps (p. 153). The only apparent rationale for the choice of these species is that they exhibit behaviors that superficially resemble human behaviors (and in some cases the resemblance is so superficial indeed that only the most unrestrained flights of fancy are likely to imagine a resemblance!). Thus, Buss compares extra-pair copulations in sandpipers with the Marla Maples–Donald Trump affair (p. 90), male wasps that pollenize orchids resembling receptive female wasps with men who are deceived into taking to dinner women who later deny them sex (p. 153), and male waterstriders who ride on the back of a female with whom they have mated to men who exhibit jealousy towards their sexual partners (p. 124). No evidence is provided that these behaviors are truly similar.

The assumption that making predictions and then gathering data that are consistent with these predictions constitutes a test of one's hypothesis is one of the most important misconceptions of sociobiology, including evolutionary psychology and some aspects of sociobiological feminism. Hypotheses can only be truly tested when they are mutually exclusive in the sense that they yield alternative predictions that make it possible to falsify one hypothesis by demonstrating that the predictions of one fit, while the predictions of the other do not (Platt 1964, Popper 1959).

## Is There a Role for Sociobiological Feminism?

The preceding critique is intended to highlight the problems inherent in sociobiological assumptions, methodologies, and approaches. Insofar as sociobiological feminists use similar approaches, their work also suffers from these weaknesses.

On the other hand, it is fair to say that sociobiological feminists have made some very important contributions. Gowaty's (1982) critique of the use of value-laden, anthropomorphic terminology in sociobiology, and her recommendation that terms be operationally defined, have had an undeniably positive impact on animal behavior in general, and sociobiology in particular. Hrdy's (1986) critique of one of the most influential axiomatic assumptions of evolutionary biology and sociobiology (female coyness and male promiscuity) is excellent; unfortunately, it has not received the attention it deserves from evolutionary biologists (although many feminists are familiar with it). Her reexamination of the origins of concealed ovulation in women cautions against the selective use of data and critiques adaptive story telling not based on a solid and broad consideration of data (Hrdy, 1988). Smuts (in press) offers an instructive critique of the assumption that adaptive behaviors are always genetically based. Likewise, her conclusion that female bonding in many species of primates reduces male sexual aggression and coercion provides interesting insights (but comes as no surprise to feminists who have always advocated mutual support as an effective antidote to male dominance in human societies).

Sociobiological feminists have made their most important contributions, however, when they have used a feminist perspective to critique or re-examine some of the methods, assumptions, or misconceptions of sociobiology as a broader discipline. Additionally, the conclusions that sociobiological feminists sometimes draw about effective strategies to end sexist oppression, more often than not, are the same strategies that could have been arrived at through economic or sociological analyses. It is not clear, therefore, what it is that sociobiological feminism adds to these alternative approaches.

The main problem with sociobiological feminism is that it draws from a discipline that is not only scientifically suspect but also has been, and will continue to be, used to justify male dominance and sexist oppression. By accepting sociobiology as a valid form of inquiry despite its pseudoscientific trappings, sociobiological feminists are buying into a world-view that has not been friendly to women; they are also giving credibility to their misogynistic colleagues. Sociobiological feminists should guard against becoming so enamored of their method that they fail to realize that they are helping to legitimate a field that inherently justifies and condones male domination, western patterns of male-female gender roles, and many other forms of social inequality.

## References

Alcock, J. (1989) *Animal Behavior: An Evolutionary Approach.* Sunderland, MA: Sinauer Associates.

Alexander, R. (1979) *Darwinism and Human Affairs.* Seattle: University of Washington Press.

Ardrey, R. (1961) *African Genesis.* New York: Dell Publishing.

Barraclough, C. A.; Gorski, R. A. (1962) "Studies on mating behavior in the androgen-sterilized female rat in relation to the hypothalamic regulation of sexual behaviour." *J Endocr.,* 25:175–182.

Beach, F. A. (1968) "Factors involved in the control of mounting behavior by female mammals." In *Perspectives in Reproduction and Sexual Behavior.* M. Diamond, ed. Bloomington: Indiana University Press.

Beach, F. A. (1971) "Hormonal factors controlling the differentiation, development and display of copulatory behavior in the ramstergig and related species." In *The Biopsychology of Development.* E. Tobach, L. R. Aronson, and E. Shaw, eds. New York: Academic Press.

Beach, F. A (1978) "Sociobiology and interspecific comparisons of behavior." In *Sociobiology and Human Nature.* M. Gregory, A. Silvers, and D. Sutch, eds. San Francisco: Jossey-Bass Publishers.

Birkhead, T.; Moller, A. (1992) *Sperm Competition in Birds: Evolutionary Causes and Consequences.* San Diego: Academic Press.

Birkhead, T.; Moller, A. (1993) "Female control of paternity." *Trends Ecol. Evol.,* 8:100–104.

Buss, D. M. (1994a) *The Evolution of Desire: Strategies of Human Mating.* New York: Basic Books.

Buss, D. M. (1994b) "The strategies of human mating." *Am. Scient.,* 82:238–249.

Carpenter, C. R. (1940) "A field study in Siam of the behavior and social relations of the gibbon (*Hylobates lar*)." *Comp. Psych. Monogr.,* 16:1–212.

Daly, M.; Wilson, M. (1983). *Sex, Evolution, and Behavior.* Boston: Willard Grant Press.

Draper, P. (1975) "!Kung women: Contrasts in sexual egalitarianism in foraging and sedentary contexts." In *Towards an Anthropology of Women.* R. Reiter, ed. New York: Monthly Review Press.

Fedigan, L. M. (1992) *Primate Paradigms.* Chicago: University of Chicago Press.

Fedigan, L. M.; Gouzoules, H. (1978) "The consort relationship in a troop of Japanese monkeys." *Rec. Adv. Primat.,* 1:493–495.

Fisher, H. E. (1992) *Anatomy of Love: The Natural History of Monogamy, Adultery, and Divorce.* New York: Norton.

Futuyma, D. J. (1986) *Evolutionary Biology.* Sunderland, MA: Sinauer Associates.

Gorski, R. A.; Gordon, J. H.; Shryne, J. E.; Southam, A. M. (1978) "Evidence for a morphological sex difference within the medical preoptic area of the rat brain." *Brain Res.,* 148:333–346.

Gould, S. J. (1980) "Sociobiology and the theory of natural selection." In *Sociobiology: Beyond Nature/Nurture.* G. W. Barlow and J. Silverberg, eds. Boulder, CO: Westview Press.

Gould, S.; Lewontin, R. (1979) "The spandrels of San Marco and the Panglossian paradigm: A critique of the adaptationist programme." *Proc. Royal Soc.,* London 205B:581–98.

Gowaty, P. A. (1982) "Sexual terms in sociobiology: Emotionally evocative and, paradoxically, jargon." *Anim. Behav.,* 30:630–631.

Gowaty, P. A. (1992) "Evolutionary biology and feminism." *Hum. Nat.,* 3:217–249.

Halpin, Z. T. (1987) "Natal dispersal and the formation of new social groups in a newly established town of black-tailed prairie dogs *(Cynomys ludovicianus)*." In *Mammalian Dispersal Patterns: The Effects of Social Structure on Population Genetics.* B. D. Chepko-Sade and Z. T Halpin, eds. Chicago: University of Chicago Press.

Hamer, D.; Hu, S.; Magnuson, V.; Hu, N.; Pattatucci, A. (1993) "A linkage between DNA markers on the X chromosome and male sexual orientation." *Science,* 261:321–27.

Harris, M. (1979) *Cultural Materialism: The Struggle for a Science of Culture.* New York: Random House.

Hinde, R. A. (1987) "Can nonhuman primates help us understand human behavior?" In *Primate Societies.* B. B. Smuts, D. L. Cheney, R. M. Seyfarth, R. W. Wrangham, and T. T. Struthsaker, eds. Chicago: University of Chicago Press.

Hrdy, S. B. (1981) *The Woman That Never Evolved.* Cambridge, MA: Harvard University Press.

Hrdy, S. B. (1986) "Empathy, polyandry, and the myth of the coy female." In *Feminist Approaches to Science.* R. Bleier, ed. Elmsford, NY: Pergamon Press.

Hrdy, S. B. (1988) "The primate origins of human sexuality." In *The Evolution of Sex.* R. Bellig and G. Stevens, eds. San Francisco: Harper & Row.

Hubbard, R.; Wald, E. (1993) *Exploring the Gene Myth.* Boston: Beacon Press.

van Iersel, J. J. A.; Bol, A. C. (1958) "Preening in two tern species: A study in displacement behaviour." *Behaviour,* 13:188.

Jolly, A. (1972) *The Evolution of Primate Behavior.* New York: Macmillan.

Kitcher, P. (1985) *Vaulting Ambition: Sociobiology and the Quest for Human Nature.* Cambridge, MA: The MIT Press.

Le Vay, S. (1991) "A difference in hypothalamic structure between heterosexual and homosexual men." *Science* 253:1034–1036.

Lorenz, K. Z. (1938) "A contribution to the comparative sociology of colonial-nesting birds." *Proc. 8th Int. Orn. Congr.* Oxford: Oxford University Press.

Lumsden, C. J.; Wilson, E. O. (1981) *Genes, Mind, and Culture: The Coevolutionary Process.* Cambridge, MA: Harvard University Press.

Mead, M. (1949) *Male and Female: A Study of the Sexes in a Changing World.* New York: William Morrow.

Michael, R. P.; Wilson, M. I.; Zumpe, D. (1974) "The bisexual behavior of female rhesus monkeys." In *Sex Differences in Behavior.* R. C. Friedman, R. M. Reichart, and R. L. van de Wiele, eds. New York: Wiley.

Money, J.; Ehrhardt, A. (1972) *Man and Woman, Boy and Girl.* Baltimore: Johns Hopkins University Press.

Nishida, T.; Hiraiwa-Hasegawa, M. (1987) "Chimpanzees and bonobos: Cooperative relationships among males." In *Primate Societies.* B. B. Smuts, D. L. Cheney, R. M. Seyfarth, R. W. Wrangham, and T. T. Struthsaker, eds. Chicago: University of Chicago Press.

Orians, G. (1969) "On the evolution of mating systems in birds and mammals." *Am. Nat.,* 103:589–603.

Pfeiffer, J. E. (1969) *The Emergence of Man.* New York: Harper and Row.

Phoenix, C. H.; Goy, R. W.; Gerall, A. A.; Young, W. C. (1959) "Organizing action of prenatally administered testosterone propionate on the tissue mediating mating behavior in the female guinea pig." *Endocrinology,* 65:369–382.

Platt, J. R. (1964) "Strong inference." *Science,* 146:347–53.

Popper, K. R. (1959) *The Logic of Scientific Discovery.* New York: Harper and Row.

Purton, A. C. (1978) "Ethological categories of behaviour and some consequences of their conflation." *Anim. Behav.,* 26:653–670.

Radford, T. (1993) "Straight talk on the gay gene." *World Press Rev.* September 23–25.

Rodseth, L.; Wrangham, R. W.; Harrigan, A. M.; Smuts, B. B. (1991) "The human community as a primate society." *Current Anthro.,* 32:221–254.

Rohrlich-Leavitt, R.; Sykes, B.; Weatherford, E. (1975) "Aboriginal woman: Male and female, anthropological perspectives." In *Toward an Anthropology of Women.* R. R. Reiter, ed. New York: Monthly Review Press.

Rowell, T. (1972) *Social Behaviour of Monkeys.* Baltimore: Penguin Books.

Russel, R. J. (1993) *The Lemurs' Legacy: The Evolution of Power, Sex, and Love.* New York: Tarcher/Putnam.

Sahlins, M. D. (1976) *The Use and Abuse of Biology.* Ann Arbor: University of Michigan Press.

Shields, W.; Shields, L. (1983) "Forcible rape: An evolutionary perspective." *Ethol. Socio.,* 4:115–36.

Smith, W. J. (1963) "Vocal communication of information in birds." *Am. Nat.,* 97:117–125.

Smuts, B. (1992) "Male aggression against women: An evolutionary perspective." *Human Nat.,* 3:1–44.

Smuts, B. (in press) "The origins of patriarchy: An evolutionary perspective." In *Origins of Gender Inequality.* A. Zagarell, ed. Kalamazoo, MI: New Issues Press.

Smuts, B.; Smuts, R. W. (1993) "Male aggression and sexual coercion of females in nonhuman primates and other mammals: Evidence and theoretical implications." *Adv. Stud. Behav.,* 22:1–63.

Sussman, R. W. (1978) "We can't blame our genes." *Washington University Community Magazine,* 4:11.

Sussman, R. (1994) *The Lemurs' Legacy* (book review). *Am. J. Phys. Anthro.,* 95:365–367.

Sussman, R. (1995) "The nature of human universals (book review)." *Rev. Anthro.,* 24:35–45.

Swaab, D. F.; Fliers, E. (1985) "A sexually dimorphic nucleus in the human brain." *Science,* 228:1112–1115.

Swaab, D. F.; Hoffman, M. A. (1990) "An enlarged suprachiasmatic nucleus in homosexual men." *Brain Res.,* 537:141.

Thornhill, R.; Thornhill, N. W. (1983) "Human rape: An evolutionary analysis." *Ethol. Sociobiol.,* 4:137–173.

Tiger, L.; Fox, R. *The Imperial Animal.* New York: Holt, Rinehart and Winston.

Trivers, R. L. (1972) "Parental investment and sexual selection." In *Sexual Selection and the Descent of Man 1871–1971.* B. Campbell, ed. Chicago: Aldine.

Vasey, P. (in press) "Homosexual behaviour in primates: A review of evidence and theory." *Int. J. Primatol.*

Washburn, S. L.; DeVore, I. (1961) "Social behavior of baboons and early man." In *Social Life of Early Man.* S. L. Washburn, ed. Chicago: Aldine.

Washburn, S. L.; Lancaster, C. S. (1968) "The evolution of hunting." In *Man the Hunter.* I. B. Lee and I. DeVore, eds. Chicago: Aldine.

Weinrich, J.; Williams, W. (1991) "Strange customs, familiar lives: Homosexualities in other cultures." In *Homosexuality: Research Implications for Public Policy* (pp. 44–59). J. Gonsiorek and J. D. Weinrich, eds. Newbury Park, CA: Sage Publications.

Wilson, E. O. (1975a) *Sociobiology: The New Synthesis.* Cambridge, MA: Harvard University Press.

Wilson, E. O. (1976) "Academic vigilantism and the political significance of sociobiology." *BioScience,* 26:182–190

Wilson, E. O. (1978) *On Human Nature.* Cambridge, MA: Harvard University Press.

Wrangham, R. W. (1979) "On the evolution of ape social systems." *Soc. Sci. Information,* 18:334–368.

Wright, R. (1994a) *The Moral Animal: The New Science of Evolutionary Psychology.* New York: Pantheon Books.

Wright, R. (1994b) "Our cheating hearts." *Time,* Aug. 15: 45–52.

Zawistowski, S.; Hirsch, J. (1983) In *Comparing Behavior: Studying Man Studying Animals.* D. W. Rajecki, ed. Hillsdale, NJ: Lawrence Erlbaum Associates.

# Chapter 43

# *The Biology of Violence*

## Robert Wright

*Is inner-city violence a response to the social ravages of poverty, or a biochemical syndrome that may be remedied with drugs? Fallout from that debate derailed the Bush Administration's Violence Initiative, but a school of new Darwinians is proposing an answer that will unsettle both sides.*

Frederick Goodwin has learned a lot during a lifetime of studying human behavior, but no lesson is more memorable than the one driven home to him over the past three years: becoming known as someone who compares inner-city teen-agers to monkeys is not a ticket to smooth sailing in American public life. As of early 1992, Goodwin's career had followed a steady upward course. He had been the first scientist to demonstrate clinically the antidepressant effects of lithium, and had become known as a leading, if not the leading, expert on manic-depressive illness. He had risen to become head of the Alcohol, Drug Abuse and Mental Health Administration, the top position for a psychiatrist in the federal government, and was poised to be the point man in a policy that the Bush Administration was proudly unveiling: the Federal Violence Initiative. The idea was to treat violence as a public-health problem—to identify violently inclined youth and provide therapy early, before they had killed. The initiative held the strong support of the Secretary of Health and Human Services, Louis Sullivan, and Goodwin planned to make it his organization's main focus.

Then, in early 1992, while discussing the initiative before the National Mental Health Advisory Council, Goodwin made his fateful remarks. Speaking impromptu—and after a wholly sleepless night, he later said—he got off onto an extended riff about monkeys. In some monkey populations, he said, males kill other males and then, with the competition thus muted, proceed to copulate prolifically with females. These "hyper-aggressive" males, he said, seem to be also "hypersexual." By a train of logic that was not entirely clear, he then arrived at the suggestion that "maybe it isn't just a careless use of the word when people call certain areas of certain cities jungles." Goodwin elaborated a bit on his obscure transition from monkeys to underclass males, but no matter; these few fragments are what came to form the standard paraphrase of his remarks. As the Los Angeles *Times* put it, Goodwin "made comparisons between inner-city youths and violent, oversexed monkeys who live in the wild."

As if a few seemingly racist quotes weren't enough of a public-relations bonanza for opponents of the Violence Initiative, Goodwin also injected what some took to be Hitlerian overtones. He talked about "genetic factors" inclining human beings toward violence, and suggested that one way to spot especially troublesome kids might be to look for "biological markers" of violent disposition. Within months, the Violence Initiative was abandoned, amid charges of racism. And Goodwin, facing the same charges, was reassigned to head the National Institute of Mental Health—not a huge demotion, but a conspicuous slap on the wrist. Finally, last year, he left that job for a position in academe after intermittent coolness from the Clinton Administration. Though no Clinton official ever told him he was a political liability, Goodwin found himself no longer invited to meetings he had once attended—meetings on violence, for example.

Goodwin is a victim of a vestigial feature of the American liberal mind: its undiscerning fear of the words

From *The New Yorker*, March 13, 1995.

"genetic" and "biological," and its wholesale hostility to Darwinian explanations of behavior. It turns out, believe it or not, that comparing violent inner-city males to monkeys isn't necessarily racist, or even necessarily right wing. On the contrary, a truly state-of-the-art comprehension of a comparison yields what is in many ways an archetypally liberal view of the "root causes" of urban violence. This comprehension comes via a young, hybrid academic discipline known as evolutionary psychology. Goodwin himself actually has little familiarity with the field, and doesn't realize how far to the left one can be dragged by a modern Darwinian view of the human mind. But he's closer to realizing it than the people whose outrage has altered his career.

As it happens, the nominally dead Federal Violence Initiative isn't really dead. Indeed, one of the few things Goodwin and his critics agree on is that its "life" and "death" have always been largely a question of labeling. Goodwin, who recently broke a thirty-month silence on the controversy, makes the point while dismissing the sinister aims attributed to the program. "They've made it sound like a cohesive new program that had some uniform direction to it and was directed by one person—namely, me," he told me. "The word 'initiative,' in bureaucratese, is simply a way of pulling stuff together to argue for budgets. In effect, that's what this was—a budget-formulation document, at Sullivan's request." Goodwin's critics look at the other side of the coin: Just as the bulk of the Violence Initiative predated the name itself, the bulk of it survived the name's deletion. Thus the war against the violence initiative—lower case—must go on.

The person who was most responsible for turning Goodwin's monkey remarks into a life-changing and policy-influencing event is a psychiatrist named Peter Breggin, the founder and executive director of the Center for the Study of Psychiatry, in Bethesda, Maryland, just outside Washington. The center doubles as Breggin's home, and the center's research director, Ginger Ross Breggin, doubles as Breggin's wife. (Goodwin says of Peter Breggin, in reference to the center's lack of distinct physical existence, "People who don't know any better think he's a legitimate person.") Both Breggins take some credit for Goodwin's recent departure from government. "We've been all over the man for three years," Ginger Breggin observes.

Goodwin and Peter Breggin interned together at SUNY Upstate Medical Center in the 1960s. Both took a course taught by Thomas Szasz, the author of *The Myth of Mental Illness*, which held that much of psychiatry is merely an oppressive tool by which the powers that be label inconvenient behavior "deviant." Szasz had formed his world view back when the most common form of oppression was locking people up, and Breggin, since founding his center, in 1971, has carried this view into the age of psychopharmacology. He fought lithium,

Goodwin's initial claim to fame. He fought the monoamine-oxidase inhibitors, a somewhat crude generation of antidepressants, and now he fights a younger, less crude generation of them. *Talking Back to Prozac*, written in collaboration with his wife and published last June, is among the antipsychopharmacology books he has recently churned out. So is *The War Against Children*, published last fall, in which the Breggins attack Goodwin, the Violence Initiative, and also the drug Ritalin. In Breggin's view, giving Ritalin to "hyperactive" children is a way of regimenting spirited kids rather than according them the attention they need—just as giving "anti-aggression" drugs to inner-city kids would be an excuse for continued neglect. And Breggin is convinced that such drugs will be used in precisely this fashion if the Goodwins of the world get their way. This is the hidden agenda of the Violence Initiative, he says. And Goodwin concedes that pharmacological therapy was a likely outcome of the initiative.

Breggin's all-embracing opposition to psychopharmacology has earned him a reputation among psychiatrists as a "flat-earther." Some, indeed, go further in their disparagement, and Breggin is aware of this. "I am not a kook," he will tell a reporter whether or not the reporter has asked. People try to discredit him, Breggin says, because he is a threat to their interests—to the money made by drug companies, which insidiously bias research toward chemical therapy, and to the power of Goodwin and other "biological psychiatrists," who earn their status by "medicalizing" everything they see. "How is it that some spiritually passionate people become labeled schizophrenic and find themselves being treated as mental patients?" he asks in a 1991 book, *Toxic Psychiatry*.

Breggin says he is struck by the parallels between the Violence Initiative and Nazi Germany: "[T]he medicalization of social issues, the declaration that the victim of oppression, in this case the Jew, is in fact a genetically and biologically defective person, the mobilization of the state for eugenic purposes and biological purposes, the heavy use of psychiatry in the development of social-control programs." This is the sort of view that encouraged some members of the Congressional Black Caucus to demand that Goodwin be disciplined; it also helped to get Breggin on Black Entertainment Television, and led to such headlines in black newspapers as "PLOT TO SEDATE BLACK YOUTH."

Breggin's scenario, the question of its truth aside, did have the rhetorical virtue of simple narrative form. ("He made a nice story of it," Goodwin says, in a tone not wholly devoid of admiration.) There has lately been much interest in, and much federally funded research into, the role that the neurotransmitter serotonin plays in violence. On average, people with low serotonin levels are more inclined toward impulsive violence than people with normal levels. Since Goodwin was co-author of the first paper noting the correlation between serotonin and violence, he would seem to have a natural interest in this issue. And, since the "serotonin-reuptake inhibitors," such as Eli Lilly's Prozac, raise serotonin levels, there would seem to exist a large financial incentive to identify low serotonin as the source of urban ills. Hence, from Breggin's vantage point it all fell into place—a confluence of corporate and personal interests that helped make serotonin the most talked-about biochemical in federal violence research. But, Breggin says, we mustn't lose sight of its larger significance: Serotonin is "just a code word for biological approaches."

It was in the late seventies that Goodwin and several colleagues stumbled on the connection between serotonin and violence, while studying servicemen who were being observed for possible psychiatric discharge. Since then, low serotonin has been found in other violent populations, such as children who torture animals, children who are unusually hostile toward their mothers, and people who score high for aggression on standardized tests. Lowering people's serotonin levels in a laboratory setting made them more inclined to give a person electrical shocks (or, at least, what experimenters deceived them into thinking were electrical shocks).

It isn't clear whether serotonin influences aggression per se or simply impulse control, since low serotonin correlates also with impulsive arson and with attempted suicide. But serotonin level does seem to be a rough predictor of misbehavior—a biological marker. In a study of twenty-nine children with "disruptive behavior disorders," serotonin level helped predict future aggression. And in a National Institutes of Health study of fifty-eight violent offenders and impulsive arsonists serotonin level, together with another biochemical index, predicted with 84 percent accuracy whether they would commit crimes after leaving prison.

It doesn't take an overactive imagination to envision parole boards screening prisoners for biological markers before deciding their fate—just as Goodwin had suggested that using biological markers might help determine which children need antiviolence therapy. These are the kinds of scenarios that make Breggin worry about a world in which the government labels some people genetically deficient and treats them accordingly. In reply, Goodwin stresses that a "biological" marker needn't be a "genetic" one. Though NIH studies suggest that some people's genes are conducive to low serotonin, environmental influences can also lower serotonin, and federal researchers are studying these. Thus a "biological" marker may be an "environmental" marker, not a "genetic" one. To this Breggin replies, "It's not what they believe, it's not in a million years what they really believe." This attempt to cast biological research as research into environment "shows their desperation, because this was never their argument until they got attacked," he says. "It's a political move."

In truth, federal researchers, including Goodwin, were looking into "environmental influences" on biochemistry well before being attacked by Breggin. Still, they do often employ a narrower notion of the term's meaning than Breggin would like. When Goodwin talks about such influences, he doesn't dwell on the sort of social forces that interest Breggin, such as poverty and bad schools. He says, for example, that he has looked into "data on head injuries, victims of abuse, poor prenatal nutrition, higher levels of lead," and so on.

In other words, he is inclined to view violence as an illness, whether it is the product of aberrant genes or of pathological—deeply unnatural—circumstances, or both. This is not surprising, given his line of work: He is a psychiatrist, a doctor; his job is to cure people, and people without pathologies don't need curing. "Once I learned that 79 percent of repeated violent offenses were by 7 percent of youth, it began to look to me like a clinical population, a population that had something wrong with it that resulted in this behavior," he says. Other federal researchers on violence tend to take the same approach. After all, most of them work at one of the National Institutes of Health, whether the National Institute of Mental Health, the National Institute on Alcohol Abuse and Alcoholism, or some other affiliate. For the Violence Initiative to be successful in the pragmatic aims that Goodwin acknowledges—as a way "to argue for budgets" for the Department of Health and Human Services—it pretty much had to define violence as a pathology, characteristic of inner-city kids who have something "wrong" with them.

Breggin would rather depict violence as the not very surprising reaction of normal people to oppressive circumstances. A big problem with biological views of behavior generally, he says, is that they so often bolster the medical notions of "deviance" and "pathology"—and thus divert attention from the need to change social conditions.

But "biological" views don't have to be "medical" views. This is where the field of evolutionary psychology enters the picture, and modern Darwinian thought begins to diverge from Goodwin's sketchier and more dated ideas about human evolution. Evolutionary psychologists share Goodwin's conviction that genes, neurotransmitters such as serotonin, and biology more generally are a valid route to explaining human behavior; and they share his belief in the relevance of studying nonhuman primates. Yet they are much more open than he is to the Bregginesque view that innercity violence is a "natural" reaction to a particular social environment.

To most NIH researchers, evolutionary psychology is terra incognita. Goodwin, for one, professes only vague awareness of the field. But the field offers something that should intrigue him: a theory about what serotonin is, in the deepest sense—why natural selection designed it to do the things it does. This theory would explain, for example, the effect that Prozac has on people. More to the point, this theory would explain the link that Goodwin himself discovered between low serotonin and violence.

The two acknowledged experts on human violence within evolutionary psychology are Martin Daly and Margo Wilson, of McMaster University, in Ontario. Their 1988 book, *Homicide,* barely known outside Darwinian-social-science circles, is considered a classic within them. Listening to Margo Wilson talk about urban crime is like entering a time warp and finding yourself chatting with Huey Newton or Jane Fonda in 1969. "First of all, what's a crime?" she asks. It all depends on "who are the rule-makers, who's in power. We call it theft when somebody comes into your house and steals something, but we don't call it theft when we get ripped off by political agendas or big-business practices." And as for gang violence: "It's a coalition of males who are mutually supporting each other to serve their interests against some other coalition. How is that different from some international war?"

To hear this sort of flaming liberal rhetoric from a confirmed Darwinian should surprise not just Peter Breggin but anyone familiar with intellectual history. For much of this century, many people who took a Darwinian view of human behavior embraced the notorious ideology of social Darwinism. They emphatically did not view social deviance as some arbitrary and self-serving designation made by the ruling class; more likely, crime was a sign of "unfitness," of an innate inability to thrive legitimately. The "unfit" were best left to languish in jail, where they could not reproduce. And "unfit" would-be immigrants—those from, say, Eastern Europe, who were congenitally ill equipped to enrich American society—were best kept out of the country.

What permits Margo Wilson to sound a quite different theme is two distinguishing features of evolutionary psychology. First, evolutionary psychologists are not much interested in genetic differences, whether among individuals, or among groups. The object of study is, rather, "species-typical mental adaptations"—also known as "human nature." A basic tenet of evolutionary psychologists is that there *is* such a thing as human nature—that people everywhere have fundamentally the same minds.

A second tenet of evolutionary psychologists is respect for the power of environment. The human mind, they say, has been designed to adjust to social circumstances. The vital difference between this and earlier forms of environmental determinism is the word "designed." Evolutionary psychologists believe that the developmental programs that convert social experience into personality were created by natural selection, which is to say that those programs lie in our genes. Thus, to think clearly about the influence of environment we must think about what sorts of influences would have been favored by natural selection.

If, for example, early social rejection makes people enduringly insecure, then we should ask whether this pattern of development might have had a genetic payoff during evolution. Maybe people who faced such rejection saw their chances of survival and reproduction plummet unless they became more socially vigilant—neurotically attentive to nourishing their social ties. Thus genes that responded to rejection by instilling this neurotic vigilance, this insecurity, would have flourished. And eventually those genes could have spread through the species, becoming part of human nature.

These two themes—universal human nature and the power of environment—are related. It is belief in the power of environment—of family milieu, cultural milieu, social happenstance—that allows evolutionary psychologists to see great variation in human behavior, from person to person or from group to group, without reflexively concluding that the explanation lies in genetic variation. The explanation lies in the genes, to be sure. Where else could a program for psychological development ultimately reside? But it doesn't necessarily lie in differences among different people's genes.

This is the perspective that Martin Daly and Margo Wilson bring to the subject of violence. They think about genes in order to understand the role of environment. And one result of this outlook is agreement with Peter Breggin that inner-city violence shouldn't be labeled a "pathology." In a paper published last year Daly and Wilson wrote, "Violence is abhorrent. . . . Violence is so aversive that merely witnessing an instance can be literally sickening. . . . " There is thus "but a short leap to the metaphorical characterization of violence itself as a sort of 'sickness' or 'dysfunction.'" But, they insisted, this leap is ill advised. Violence is eminently functional—something that people are designed to do.

Especially men. From an evolutionary point of view, the leading cause of violence is maleness. "Men have evolved the morphological, physiological, and psychological means to be effective users of violence," Daly and Wilson wrote. The reason, according to modern evolutionary thought, is simple. Because a female can reproduce only once a year, whereas a male can reproduce many times a year, females are the scarcer sexual resource. During evolution, males have competed over this resource, with the winners impregnating more than their share of women and the losers impregnating few or none. As always with natural selection, we're left with the genes of the winners—in this case, genes inclining males toward fierce combat. One reflection of this history is that men are larger and stronger than women. Such "sexual dimorphism" is seen in many species, and biologists consider it a rough index of the intensity of male sexual competition.

To say that during evolution men have fought over women isn't to say that they've always fought directly over women, with the winner of a bout walking over and claiming his nubile trophy. Rather, human beings are somewhat like our nearest relatives, the chimpanzees; Males compete for status, and status brings access to females. Hence skills conducive to successful status competition would have a "selective advantage"—would be favored by natural selection. As Daly and Wilson have put it, "if status has persistently contributed to reproductive success, and a capacity for controlled violence has regularly contributed to status, then the selective advantage of violent skills cannot be gainsaid."

It's easy to find anecdotal evidence that status has indeed tended to boost the reproductive success of males. (It was Kissinger, who said that power is an aphrodisiac, and Representative Pat Schroeder who observed that a middle-aged congresswoman doesn't exert the same animal magnetism on the opposite sex that a middle-aged congressman does.) But more telling is evidence drawn from hunter-gatherer societies, the closest thing to real-life examples of the preagrarian social context for which the human mind was designed. Among the Ache of Paraguay, high-status men have more extramarital affairs and more illegitimate children than low-status men. Among the Aka Pygmies of central Africa, an informal leader known as a *kombeti* gets more wives and offspring than the average Aka. And so on. The Aka, the Ache, and Henry Kissinger all demonstrate that violence against other men is hardly the only means by which male status is sought. Being a good hunter is a primary route to status among the Ache, and being a wily social manipulator helps in all societies (even, it turns out, in chimp societies, where males climb the status ladder by forging "political" coalitions). Still, in all human societies questions of relative male status are sometimes settled through fighting. This form of settlement is, of course, more prevalent in some arenas than others—more in a bikers' bar than in the Russian Tea Room, more in the inner city than on the Upper East Side. But, as Daly and Wilson note, one theme holds true everywhere: Men compete for status through the means locally available. If men in the Russian Tea Room don't assault one another, that's because assault isn't the route to status in the Russian Tea Room.

According to Daly and Wilson, a failure to see the importance of such circumstances is what leads well-heeled people to express patronizing shock that "trivial" arguments in barrooms and ghettos escalate to murder. In *Homicide* they wrote, "An implicit contrast is drawn between the foolishness of violent men and the more rational motives that move sensible people like ourselves. The combatants are in effect denigrated as creatures of some lower order of mental functioning, evidently governed by immediate stimuli rather than by foresightful contemplation." In truth, Daly and Wilson say, such combatants are typical of our species, as it has been observed around the world: "In most social milieus, a man's reputation depends in part upon the maintenance of a credible threat of violence." This fact is "obscured in modern mass society because the state has assumed a monopoly on the legitimate use of force. But wherever that monopoly is relaxed—whether in an entire society or in a neglected underclass—then the utility of that credible threat becomes apparent." In such an environment, "a seemingly minor affront is not merely a 'stimulus' to action, isolated in time and space. It must be understood within a larger social context of reputations, face, relative social status, and enduring relationships. Men are known by their fellows as . . . people whose word means action and people who are full of hot air."

That a basic purpose of violence is display—to convince peers that you will defend your status—helps explain an otherwise puzzling fact. As Daly and Wilson note, when men kill men whom they know, there is usually an audience. This doesn't seem to make sense—why murder someone in the presence of witnesses?—except in terms of evolutionary psychology. Violence is in large part a performance.

Thus the dismay often inspired by reports that a black teenager killed because he had been "dissed" is naïve. Nothing was more vital to the reproductive success of our male ancestors than respect, so there is nothing that the male mind will more feverishly seek to neutralize than disrespect. All men spend much of their lives doing exactly this; most are just lucky enough to live in a place where guns won't help them do it. These days, well-educated men do their status maintenance the way Goodwin and Breggin do it, by verbally defending their honor and verbally assailing the honor of their enemies. But back when dueling was in vogue even the most polished of men might occasionally try to kill one another.

This view from evolutionary psychology in some ways jibes with a rarely quoted point that Goodwin made during his rambling remarks on monkeys: that inner-city violence may be caused by a "loss of structure in society"; in an environment where violence is deemed legitimate, the male inclination for violence may reassert itself. Of monkeys, Goodwin had said, "that is the natural way of it for males, to knock each other off," and the implicit comparison was supposed to be with all human males, not just black ones; his point was that many black males now live in neighborhoods where social restraints have dissolved. This is the sense in which Goodwin says he meant to compare the inner cities to jungles, and the transcript of his remarks bears him out. His poor choice imagery still haunts him. "If I had said that in the Wild West, where there was no structure, there was a hell of a lot of violence, no one would have noticed."

There is a crucial difference between this emphasis on social milieu as rendered by Goodwin and as rendered by evolutionary psychologists; namely, they don't abandon it when they start thinking about the interface between biology and environment. Whereas pondering this interface steers Goodwin's thoughts toward "pathology"—the biological effects of malnutrition, or brain damage due to child abuse—evolutionary psychologists try to figure out how normal, everyday experience affects the biochemistry of violence.

Consider serotonin. In particular, consider an extensive study of serotonin in monkeys done by Michael McGuire, an evolutionary psychologist, and his colleagues at UCLA. Vervet monkeys have a clear male social hierarchy: Low-status males defer to high-status males over access to limited resources, including females. McGuire found that the highest-ranking monkeys in the male social hierarchy have the highest serotonin levels. What's more, the lower-ranking males tend to be more impulsively violent. Other studies have linked low serotonin to violence in monkeys even more directly.

At first glance, such findings might appear to be what Peter Breggin, and many liberals, would consider their worst nightmare. If this biochemical analogy between monkeys and human beings is indeed valid, the lesson would seem to be this: Some individuals are born to be society's leaders, some are born to be its hoodlums; the chairman of IBM was born with high serotonin, the urban gang member was born with low serotonin. And what if it turns out that blacks on average have less serotonin than whites do?

There certainly is evidence that some sort of analogy between the social lives of monkeys and human beings is in order. McGuire has found that officers of college fraternities have higher serotonin levels than the average frat-house resident, and that college athletes perceived as team leaders have higher levels than their average teammate. But grasping the import of the analogy requires delving into the details of McGuire's monkey research.

When McGuire examines a dominant male monkey before he becomes a dominant—before he climbs the social hierarchy by winning some key fights with other males—serotonin level is often unexceptional. It rises during his ascent, apparently in response to sometimes inconspicuous social cues. Indeed, his serotonin may begin to creep upward before he physically challenges any higher-ranking males; the initial rise may be caused by favorable attention from females (who play a larger role in shaping the male social hierarchy than was once appreciated). When, on the other hand, a dominant male suffers a loss of status, his serotonin level drops.

What's going on here? There is no way to look inside a monkey's mind and see how serotonin makes him feel. But there is evidence that in human beings high serotonin levels bring high self-esteem. Raising self-esteem is one effect of Prozac and other serotonin boosters, such as Zoloft. And, indeed, high-ranking monkeys—or, to take a species more closely related to us, high-ranking chimpanzees—tend to behave the way people with high self-esteem behave: with calm self-assurance; assertively, yes, but seldom violently. (This subtle distinction, as Peter Kramer notes in "Listening to Prozac," is also seen in human beings. Prozac may make them more socially assertive, but less irritable, less prone to spontaneous outbursts.) To be sure, an alpha-male chimp may periodically exhibit aggression—or really, a kind of ritual mock-aggression—to remind everyone that he's the boss, but most alphas tend not to be as fidgety and perturbable as some lower-ranking apes, except when leadership is being contested.

All this suggests a hypothesis. Maybe one function of serotonin—in human and nonhuman primates—is to regulate self esteem in accordance with social feedback; and maybe one function of self-esteem is, in turn, to help primates negotiate social hierarchies, climbing as high on the ladder as circumstance permits. Self-esteem (read serotonin) keeps rising as long as one encounters social success, and each step in this elevation inclines one to raise one's social sights a little higher. Variable self-esteem, then, is evolution's way of preparing us to reach and maintain whatever level of social status is realistic, given our various attributes (social skills, talent, etc.) and our milieu. High serotonin, in this view, isn't nature's way of destining people from birth for high status; it is nature's way of equipping any of us for high status should we find ourselves possessing it. The flip side of this hypothesis is that low self-esteem (and low serotonin) is evolution's way of equipping us for low status should our situation not be conducive to elevation.

This *doesn't* mean what an earlier generation of evolutionists would have thought: that Mother Nature wants people with low status to endure their fate patiently for "the greater good." Just the opposite. A founding insight of evolutionary psychology is that natural selection rarely designs things for the "good of the group." Any psychological inclinations that offer a way to cope with low status provide just that—a way to cope, a way to make the best of a bad situation. The purpose of low self-esteem isn't to bring submission for the sake of social order; more likely, its purpose is to discourage people from conspicuously challenging higher-status people who are, by virtue of their status, in a position to punish such insolence.

And what about the antisocial tendencies, the impulsive behavior linked with low serotonin in both human beings and monkeys? How does evolutionary psychology explain them? This is where the demise of "good of the group" logic opens the way for especially intriguing theories. In particular: Primates may be designed to respond to low status by "breaking the rules" when they can get away with it. The established social order isn't working in their favor, so they circumvent its strictures at every opportunity. Similarly, inner-city thugs may be functioning as "designed": Their minds absorb environmental input reflecting their low socioeconomic standing and the absence of "legitimate" routes to social elevation, and incline their behavior in the appropriately criminal direction.

The trouble with breaking rules, of course, is the risk of getting caught and punished. But, as Daly and Wilson note by quoting Bob Dylan, "When you ain't got nothin', you got nothin' to lose." In the environment of our evolution, low status often signified that a male had had little or no reproductive success to date; for such a male, taking risks to raise status could make sense in Darwinian terms. In hunter-gatherer societies, Daly and Wilson write, "competition can sometimes be fiercest near the bottom of the scale, where the man on track for total [reproductive] failure has nothing to lose by the most dangerous competitive tactics, and may therefore throw caution to the winds." Even as low self-esteem keeps him from challenging dominant males, he may behave recklessly toward those closer to him on the social ladder. Thus may the biochemistry of low status, along with the attendant states of mind, encourage impulsive risk-taking.

This theory, at any rate, would help make sense of some long-unexplained data. Psychologists found several decades ago that artificially lowering people's self-esteem—by giving them false reports about scores on a personality test—makes them more likely to cheat in a subsequent game of cards. Such risky rule-breaking is just the sort of behavior that makes more sense for a low-status animal than for a high-status animal.

To say that serotonin level is heavily influenced by social experience isn't to say that a person's genetic idiosyncrasies aren't significant. But it is to say that they are at best half the story. There are not yet any definitive studies on the "heritability" of serotonin level—the amount of the variation among people that is explained by genetic difference. But the one study that has been done suggests that less than half the variation in the population studied came from genetic differences, and the rest from differences in environment. And even this estimate of heritability is probably misleadingly high. Presumably, self-esteem correlates with many other personal attributes, such as physique or facial attractiveness. Impressive people, after all, inspire the sort of feedback that raises self-esteem and serotonin. Since these attributes are themselves quite heritable—traceable largely to a person's distinctive genes—some of the "heritability" estimate for serotonin may reflect genes not for high serotonin per se but for good looks, great body, and so on. (The technical term for this oblique genetic effect is "reactive heritability.")

At least some of the variation in serotonin level is grounded more directly in genetic difference. NIH researchers have identified a human gene that helps convert tryptophan, an amino acid found in some grains and fruits, into serotonin, and they have found a version of the gene that yields low serotonin levels. Still, there is no reason to believe that different ethnic groups have differ-

ent genetic endowments for serotonin. Indeed, even if it turned out that American blacks on average had lower serotonin than whites, there would be no cause to implicate genes. One would expect groups that find themselves shunted toward the bottom of the socioeconomic hierarchy to have low serotonin. That may be nature's way of preparing them to take risks and to evade the rules of the powers that be.

This Darwinian theory integrating serotonin, status, and impulsive violence remains meagerly tested and is no doubt oversimplified. One complicating factor is modern life. People in contemporary America are part of various social hierarchies. An inner-city gang leader may get great, serotonin-boosting respect ("juice," as the suggestive street slang calls it) from fellow gang members while also getting serotonin-sapping signs of disrespect when he walks into a trendy jewelry store, or even when he turns on the TV and sees that wealthy, high-status males tend to bear no physical or cultural resemblance to him. The human mind was designed for a less ambiguous setting—a hunter-gatherer society, in which a young man's social reference points stay fairly constant from day to day. We don't yet know how the mind responds to a world of wildly clashing status cues.

Another hidden complexity in this Darwinian theory lies in the fact that serotonin does lots of things besides mediate self-esteem and impulsive aggression. Precisely what it does depends on the part of the brain it is affecting and the levels of other neurotransmitters. Overall serotonin level is hardly the subtlest imaginable chemical index of a human being's mental state. Still, though we don't yet fathom the entire biochemistry of things like self-esteem, impulsiveness, and violence, there is little doubt among evolutionary psychologists that the subject is fathomable—and that it will get fathomed much faster if biomedical researchers, at NIH and elsewhere, start thinking in Darwinian terms.

If evolutionary psychologists are right in even the broad contours of their outlook, then there is good news and bad news for both Frederick Goodwin and Peter Breggin. For Goodwin, the good news is that his infamous remarks were essentially on target: He was right to compare violent inner-city males—or any other violent human males—to nonhuman primates (though he exaggerated the incidence of actual murder among such primates). The bad news is that his Violence Initiative, in failing to pursue that insight, in clinging to the view of violence as pathology, was doomed to miss a large part of the picture; the bulk of inner-city violence will probably never be explained by reference to head injuries, poor nutrition, prenatal exposure to drugs, and bad genes. If violence is a public-health problem, it is so mainly in the sense that getting killed is bad for your health.

Evolutionary psychology depicts all kinds of things often thought to be "pathological" as "natural": unyielding hatred, mild depression, a tendency of men to treat women as their personal property. Some Darwinians even think that rape may in some sense be a "natural" response to certain circumstances. Of course, to call these things "natural" isn't to call them beyond self-control, or beyond the influence of punishment. And it certainly isn't to call them good. If anything, evolutionary psychology might be invoked on behalf of the doctrine of Original Sin: We are in some respects born bad, and redemption entails struggle against our nature.

Many people, including many social scientists and biomedical researchers, seem to have trouble with the idea of a conflict between nature and morality. "I think this is a source of resistance to evolutionary ways of thinking," says John Tooby, a professor at the University of California at Santa Barbara, who along with his wife, Leda Cosmides, laid down some of the founding doctrines of evolutionary psychology. "There's a strong tendency to want to return to the romantic notion that the natural is the good." Indeed, "one modern basis for establishing morals is to try to ground them in the notion of sickness. Anything people don't like, they accuse the person doing it of being sick."

Thomas Szasz couldn't have said it better. Herein lies evolutionary psychology's good news for Peter Breggin: Yes, it is indeed misleading to call most violence a pathology, a disorder. The bad news for Breggin is that, even though the causes of violence are broadly environmental, as he insists, they are nonetheless biological, because environmental forces are mediated biologically—in this case by, among other things, serotonin. Thus, a scientist can be a "biological determinist" or a "biological reductionist" without being a genetic determinist. He or she can say—as Daly and Wilson and Tooby and Cosmides do—that human behavior is driven by biological forces impinging on the brain, yet can view those forces largely as a reflection of a person's distinctive environment.

This confronts Breggin with a major rhetorical complication. Much of his success in arousing opposition to the Violence Initiative lay in conveniently conflating the terms "biological" and "genetic." He does this habitually. In suggesting that the initiative grew out of Goodwin's longstanding designs, Breggin says he has Baltimore *Evening Sun* articles from 1984 in which "Goodwin is talking about crime and violence being genetic and biological." In truth, these articles show Goodwin saying nothing about genes—only that violence has some biological correlates and might respond to pharmacological treatment. In Breggin's mind, "genetic" and "biological" are joined at the waist.

That these terms are not, in fact, inseparable—that something utterly biological, like serotonin level, may differ between two people because of environmental, not genetic, differences—poses a second problem for Breggin. The best way to illuminate the environmental forces he stresses may be to study the biological underpinnings of behavior, and that is a prospect he loathes. If serotonin is one chemical that converts poverty and disrespect into impulsiveness or aggression or low self-esteem, then it, along with other chemicals, may be a handy index of all these things—something whose level can be monitored more precisely than the things themselves. (Studies finding that blacks on average don't suffer from low self-esteem are based on asking black people and white people how they feel about themselves—a dubious approach, since expressions of humility seem to be more highly valued in white suburban culture than in black urban culture.)

That Breggin may be wrong in the way he thinks about biology and behavior doesn't mean that the unsettling scenarios he envisions are far-fetched. The government may well try to use biochemical "markers" to select violently inclined kids for therapy, or to screen prisoners for parole. (Then again, if these chemicals aren't simple "genetic markers," but rather are summaries of the way genes and environment have together molded a person's state of mind, how are they different from a standard psychological evaluation, which summarizes the same thing?) There may also be attempts to treat violently inclined teenagers with serotonin-boosting drugs, as Breggin fears. And, though some teenagers might thus be helped into the mainstream economy, these drugs could also become a palliative, a way to keep the inner city tranquil without improving it. The brave new world of biochemical diagnosis and therapy is coming; and, for all the insight evolutionary psychology brings, it won't magically answer the difficult questions that will arise.

The point to bear in mind is simply that less eerie, more traditionally liberal prescriptions for urban violence continue to make sense after we've looked at black teenagers as animals—which after all, is what human beings are. The view from evolutionary psychology suggests that one way to reduce black violence would be to make the inner cities places where young men have nonviolent routes to social status and the means and motivation to follow them. Better paying jobs and better public schools, for example, wouldn't hurt. Oddly enough, thinking about genes from a Darwinian standpoint suggests that inner-city teenagers are victims of their environment.

# Chapter 44

# *Modern Biological Determinism: The Violence Initiative, The Human Genome Project, and the New Eugenics*

Garland E. Allen

## INTRODUCTION

The cover of the November 1992 issue of *The Journal of NIH Research* shows a howling rhesus monkey clinging to a tree. However, the story inside is not about rhesus monkeys. Rather, it deals with the "Violence Initiative" of the United States Government's Department of Health and Human Services, including the National Institutes of Health.[1] The Violence Initiative is a $400,000,000 program designed to apply the tools of biology—particularly organic psychiatry and behavior genetics—to potential criminals, especially black and Latino youth in America's inner cities. Dr. Frederick Goodwin, in 1992 Head of the Alcohol, Drug Abuse and Mental Health Administration, described the Violence Initiative as "a public health approach to violence," focusing on screening out and treating preventively " violence-prone individuals."[2] According to Goodwin, various studies within the context of the Violence Initiative aim "to design and evaluate psychosocial, psychological and medical interventions for at-risk children before they become labeled as delinquent or criminal. This is the basic point of it all ... identifying at-risk kids at a very early age before they have become criminalized.[3] According to Goodwin this is a public health, or medical, approach to the recurrent problem of violence in our society. Estimated by some to comprise a population of 100,000 or more, such at-risk children come predominantly from what Goodwin calls "high impact urban areas." He also claims that targeted groups would include those in the inner city, families in which the parents (or other custodial adults) have a low income and

low educational level, or female-headed households—all synonyms, of course, for poor, urban, African American (or in some areas Hispanic American) populations.

According to Goodwin, the Violence Initiative is the federal government's highest priority for fiscal 1994. One of Goodwin's public remarks indicates the basic approach that the "public health, or medical model" would take:

> If you look at other primates in nature—male primates in nature—you find that even with our violent society we are doing very well. If you look, for example, at male monkeys, especially in the wild, roughly half of them survive to adulthood. The other half die by violence. That is the natural way of it for males, to knock each other off and in fact, there are some interesting evolutionary implications of that because the same hyperaggressive monkeys who kill each other are also hypersexual, so they populate more and reproduce more to offset the fact that half of them are dying.[4]

For his purposes it is a good thing that Goodwin did not bother to check with any primatologists, because he would have found that there is no substantiation for such a claim that in nature half of male rhesus monkeys die violently at the hands of other males.[5] There is also no evidence that those males designated as "hyperactive" necessarily reproduce more offspring (though they may copulate more frequently). Goodwin then goes on to offer the "insights" he claims to have about today's urban problems from this bit of pop ethology:

> Now one could say that if some of the loss of social structure in this society and particularly within the high impact inner city areas, has removed some of the civilizing evolutionary things [influences(?)] that we have built

From *Sociology of the Sciences Yearbook,* Vol. 19, 1996.

up . . . maybe it isn't just a careless use of the word when people call certain areas of certain cities "*jungles*" that we may have gone back to what might be more *natural* without all the social controls that we have imposed on ourselves over thousands of years in our evolution.[6]

To complete the circle of logic, Goodwin then suggested that one more part of the Violence Initiative should be an NIH-funded study of rhesus monkey behavior in nature and in the laboratory as a model for how to deal with inner city youth.[7]

In May 1992, Goodwin addressed the American Psychiatric Association, presenting further details of what research into biological factors in violent behavior would entail.[8] He suggested that elementary schools in "high impact urban areas" could be used as testing grounds for the first stage of a "triage" system to identify children that might become violent as teenagers or young adults. Elementary school teachers would be asked to identify 12 to 15 percent of the children who showed characteristics of "early irritability and uncooperativeness." That pool of suspected violence-prone children would then be involved in follow-up studies, including psychiatric screening of the family via telephone and then in-person interviews with mental health experts. Apparently thinking and planning is far enough along on the Violence Initiative to provide cost-estimates for the screening program: 7¢ per student for teacher screening and $7.00 per family for the phone and personal interviews. Once identified, the fate of violence-prone children is not clearly spelled out by Goodwin, in either of his talks, but several suggestions have an ominous ring: "day camps" for younger children from poor environments, and the possibility of using mood-controlling drugs. The latter can be inferred from Goodwin's reference in the May 1992 talk to the American Psychiatric Association where he discussed "serotonergic biochemical imbalances in the brain as useful biochemical markers . . . for potential violence.[9] Given the current widespread use of amphetamines and methylphenidate (Ritalin), which is being given to more than a million school children every year to control "hyperactivity," as well as newer drugs such as fluoxetine (prozac) suggests that one possible outcome of the Violence Initiative would be the wholesale drugging of inner city youth. That the pharmaceutical industry casts an approving eye on such proposals should be no surprise since ritalin, amphetamines, and prozac are among their most profitable and large-selling products at the present time.

Predictably, when news of the Violence Initiative and Goodwin's comments became public in mid-May 1992, it produced a vigorous response. Dr. Peter Breggin, a Bethesda-based psychiatrist, author of *Toxic Psychiatry*, and a long-standing opponent of biological psychiatry who heads his own watch-dog operation, The Center for the Study of Psychiatry, attacked the program publicly at a press conference.[10] Newspapers carried both Goodwin's original statements and Breggin's criticisms, producing a flurry of journalistic activity in the summer of 1992.[11] As a result of the controversy Goodwin was relieved of his position as head of the Alcohol, Drug Abuse and Mental Health Administration and subsequently "demoted" to become head of the National Institutions of Mental Health (NIMH). Countering the criticism that he was simply advocating old-fashioned biological determinism, Goodwin claimed that the Violence Initiative is not just raw genetics but a multidisciplinary approach to youth violence: partly biological, based on studies showing there are modest genetic and neurophysiological factors that predispose some individuals towards violence; partly behavioral, using rhesus monkeys as animal models; and partly sociological, drawing heavily on recent research in psychology and criminology.[12] But it is clear from Goodwin's remarks and other documents that biological components are given a special prominence in the research programs that make up the "Violence Initiative."

A second stage in the furore surrounding early exposure of the Violence Initiative was the canceling of a conference originally scheduled for October 1992, on "Genetic Factors in Crime: Findings, Uses, and Implications," sponsored by the University of Maryland's Institute for Philosophy in Public Policy, with a major grant from the NIH. Responding to public and congressional pressure over the possible connection between the conference and the Violence Initiative, in early September NIH Director Bernadine Healy withdrew funds for the meeting.[13] Much hue and cry from both sides attended cancellation of the conference, originally planned to bring together both the proponents and critics of biological and specifically genetic theories of criminal and violent behavior. (As it turned out the Conference was not part of the Violence Initiative per se, but had received its funds from the NIH Program on the Ethical, Legal and Social Impact of the Human Genome Project [ELSI].) Not only the Conference but also the entire Violence Initiative has been labeled racist by psychiatrists and health-care workers such as Breggin, and by politicians such as Representative John Conyers, Jr. (D, Michigan) and the membership of the American Psychological Association and the National Association of Social Workers.[14] In response to critics, officials of the Departments of Health and Human Services (HHS), including NIH, claimed that nowhere have any of their proposals mentioned either race or ethnic groups as having a greater potential for biologically determined criminality.[15] Furthermore, with the order from NIH Director Bernadine Healy to freeze funds for the University of Maryland Conference, researchers outside as well as inside the NIH felt that their academic freedom had been seriously compromised. For many, Healy's decision represented an abdication of professional responsibility on the part of NIH, a response more to political pressure from the community, especially minority groups, than to the peer review process to which the agency is supposedly committed.[16] While at the moment the status of the Violence Initiative is uncertain, given the increased awareness of violence in the United States, it is unlikely that the entire undertaking will be scrapped. (As of this writing, funds for the conference on crime have been released with the understanding that the meeting will be restructured to focus more on ethical and philosophical issues.)

What I would like to do in the following pages is to examine some aspects of the Violence Initiative. In doing so I would like to ask two major questions: (1) For what social and political reasons is an emphasis on the biological foundation of crime and violence being raised at the present time? And (2) What can the nature of the present research tell us about the role of the natural sciences in modern political discourse with respect to the Human Genome Project and the shaping of public policy about violence and crime? To help understand some of the factors that might be responsible for the resurgence of genetic-behavioral determinism, I will compare the present case to the development of what I consider to be a similar one—the eugenics movement—during the early decades of this century. The parallels that I will try to draw may be instructive in understanding something of the social forces that are bringing these issues to the surface today. Finally, I would like to ask what are the implications of the Violence Initiative in conjunction with the Human Genome Project for American society in the years ahead?

## THE VIOLENCE INITIATIVE: SCIENCE AND ITS SOCIAL CONTEXT

The Violence Initiative is not merely the brainchild of Frederick Goodwin or even of the NIH. It is an increasingly organized effort among a number of U.S. government agencies to coordinate research and propose programs in response to increasing problems of violence in the United States.[17] In November 1992, the National Research Council, acting under a directive from the National Academy of Sciences, issued a 400-page report, *Understanding and Preventing Violence.* The study was funded in part by three other federal agencies: The Centers for Disease Control (CDC) in Atlanta, the Justice Department, and the National Science Foundation (NSF). Breggin reports that one panel member who helped in writing the study said its most significant accomplishment is "the unparalleled opportunity to examine the relationship between biomedical variables and violent behavior."[18] While discussions of social science research make up the bulk of the NAS report, biological research was stressed as providing new and important methods for understanding the roots of violent behavior. In addition, the Centers for Disease Control submitted a proposal in June 1992 to coordinate the efforts of several

federal agencies into what they termed as the "Youth Violence Prevention Initiative." Again, this proposal emphasizes the new perspectives that biological research could provide in solving the age-old problem of crime.

It is no surprise that the Violence Initiative came into being just after the Rodney King riots in Los Angeles, in March 1991. However, the Violence Initiative should not be seen primarily as a response to a single event, but to a more general economic and social trend that has been developing for over a decade. For example, the Bush administration admitted that by 1992 poverty had reached its highest rate in 27 years. Wages and benefits in many job areas have been severely cut in the past decade, while true unemployment or partial unemployment has increased steadily. In the same time period drug-related crimes and associated gang violence have increased dramatically in most large American cities. According to the Bureau of Justice Statistics, the number of prisoners convicted of violent crimes has risen from less than 25,000 in 1960 to over 75,000 in 1990, while the number convicted for drug related crimes has climbed from less than 5000 in 1960 to over 100,000 in 1990. At the same time convictions for crimes of public disorder have increased from 6000 in 1976 to 25,000 in 1990, and all of these increases have differentially affected poor and particularly African American or Mexican American populations.[19] The problem, of course, is ultimately to explain the causes of these increases in violent and antisocial behavior and thus to be able to prevent them in the future. It is in this context that the line gets redrawn between the old alternatives of *nature* versus *nurture.* It is clear the Violence Initiative speaks to the nature side of the argument.

Starting in 1985, long before the Violence Initiative as such was even proposed, a theory for the genetic basis of criminality was given considerable attention in a new book, *Crime and Human Nature* by James Q. Wilson and Richard J. Herrnstein, both distinguished professors, of government and psychology, respectively, at Harvard University.[20] The news media gave the book wide publicity, and both authors were interviewed on radio and TV as well.[21] In addition, within the last five years, a whole host of other problems of human social behavior have also been claimed to have a genetic basis, including alcoholism, manic depression, schizophrenia, general personality factors, risk-taking, homosexuality, and shyness. The general reading public has thus been treated to a barrage of articles, many of them carried as cover stories by the nation's leading popular magazines (*Time, U.S. News and World Report, Newsweek, The New Republic,* as well as a large number of daily newspapers including *The New York Times* and the *Wall Street Journal*).

Rarely in these popular accounts are the difficulties in assessing the genetic component of complex behaviors ever spelled out in full, and the impression left by the vast majority of such presentations is that new and solid evidence exists for nature over nurture as the cause of violent human behavior. Indeed, in an article on the Violence Initiative in November 1992 the *New York Times* claimed that the various government proposals being put together by Goodwin and others, were based on "new findings in genetics, biology, and neurobiology."[22] As might be expected, the so-called "new findings" are neither so new nor so convincing as their promoters would like the public to believe. Virtually all of the studies purporting to find a genetic basis for complex human behaviors, have been reviewed and summarized by Gregory Carey in a paper commissioned by the National Academy of Sciences and published in the volume, *Understanding and Preventing Violence* (1992).[23] The overall conclusion of this report is that existing studies are inconclusive, and that while a significant genetic component to such behavior cannot be ruled out, it is also the case that no clear role for genes in human social behavior has yet been demonstrated.

As an example of the sort of "new" evidence that has been forthcoming about the genetics of crime, consider the following two cases both published within the last two years. In January 1992, Dr. Allen Beck, a demographer for the Bureau of Justice Statistics, a branch of the Justice Department, compiled data on incarcerated criminals and their families.[24] Beck's survey, which covered more than 2,621 criminals from across the country for the year 1987, found that more than half of all juvenile delinquents and more than one-third of adult criminals in local jails and state institutions, have immediate family members who have also been incarcerated at some time in the past. According to the *New York Times* summary of this research, some criminologists have claimed that Beck's study provides the hard data necessary to demonstrate that criminality runs in families. What is striking is the ease with which such an obvious finding is used to support a genetic argument. Indeed, Richard Herrnstein has claimed that the data are "startling proof" that a significant component of criminal behavior is genetic. It is obvious that such statistics say *nothing* about what *causes* the incarceration of significant numbers of related people: The sociological explanation is just as likely to be true as the biological. As Dr. Marvin E. Wolfgang, professor of criminal law at the University of Pennsylvania, pointed out, "most of these people [in prisons] come from low socioeconomic backgrounds, disadvantaged neighborhoods, where a high percentage of people will be sent to jail whether they are related or not."[25] At least two letters to the editor in a subsequent issue (February 14) of *The New York Times* made the same point.[26] The very fact that such a study can be put forward, and accepted in some circles as serious scientific evidence for a genetic component of behavior is a testament to the scientific illiteracy that has been engendered by our educational system.

A second example comes from a June 1993 issue of the *American Journal of Human Genetics.* It begins with an anecdotal account of a Dutch school teacher who, in the early 1960s, traced to a biological cause what he considered to be a pattern of violent behavior among males in his family.[27] A team of Dutch and American researchers examined some of the so-called violent members of the family and found that these individuals had an abnormal gene for monomine oxidase A, an enzyme that usually breaks down several neurotransmitters in the brain. Accumulation of neurotransmitters is thought to be one of the possible causes of violent behavior. To their credit the researchers issued some cautions about how to interpret their findings. They pointed out that detection of a single gene does not mean that all those who possess the gene will necessarily show the behavior: Indeed, one member of the family with the gene has not shown any violent behavior in years, while his brother, who also has the gene, has repeated aggressive outbursts. The researchers also admitted that their study does not provide any way of determining the cause-effect relationship between the defective gene and aggressive or violent behavior. Accumulation of neurotransmitters may be involved, but the study did not purport to measure those levels; moreover, in all cases documented violent or aggressive behavior occurred in response to a variety of external provocations such as a negative job evaluation or the death of a relative.

Jonathan Beckwith of Harvard Medical School has also severely criticized the Dutch study. Although the original article was filled with large numbers of measurements of monomine oxidase A and B levels and estimates of genetic marker locations, Beckwith noted there was almost no detailed information on family history, or the nature of the violent outburst exhibited by afflicted individuals. Indeed, as Beckwith put it, "there were plenty of statistics and numbers about the mapping of the gene, but there was basically no information that one could evaluate about whether the people were truly aggressive."[28] Despite the reservations on the part of both researchers and critics, however, the *Los Angeles Times* announced the work to its lay readers with the headline: "Researchers Link Gene to Aggression."

Indeed, as these examples and the more extensive survey by Gregory Carey show, the new reports of a significant genetic basis for criminal and other social behavior share all the same old conceptual and methodological problems characteristic of this type of work in the past. Some of these problems include: (1) Poorly defined phenotypes; for example, a criminal act is defined by the rules and mores of a given society at a given point in history, so that one and the same behavior can be considered criminal in one circumstance and acceptable or even laudable in another. (2) Reduction of complex processes such as behaviors to a single entity; that is, a criminal act is not a single event or process, but is made up of a complex of intellectual, emotional, and behavioral components that cannot be reduced to a single behavioral act and thus to a single unit of study as would be expected in standard genetic analysis. (3) The use of twin and adoption studies, which experience shows entail the interaction of many variables, most of which cannot be accurately assessed. (4) Reliance on the use of heritability estimates, that is the statistical analysis of variance within a population, which does not say anything directly about the genetic components involved. (5) The uncritical and selective use of information from other sciences, especially behavioral models in other animals, particularly primates, where superficially similar behaviors are many times viewed as homologs to human behavior. (6) The tendency in all such research to resort to extreme forms of genetic reductionism, including references to "*the gene* for criminality" or "*the gene* for shyness," [emphasis added] a level of simplification that geneticists know does not apply even to relatively simple morphological traits, much less to highly complex and plastic traits such as social behavior.

It is perhaps not irrelevant to note that over the past several decades, beginning with the work of Arthur Jensen on the genetics of racial differences in IQ in the late 1960s, virtually none of those investigators propounding theories of a genetic basis for human social behaviors have actually been trained geneticists. Their naiveté about making genetical analyses and corresponding claims of genetic causality is thus all the more blatant because it would not stand up to any standard genetic scrutiny. Despite this, however, the overwhelming impression gained within certain segments of the scientific, especially psychological and psychiatric communities, and in the popular media, is that new and more accurate data has been obtained indicating a genetic basis for violent and criminal (as well as other social) behavior.

In addition to the specific claims that there are genes that determine at least a strong predisposition to criminality, the whole enterprise of attributing a variety of social behaviors to genetic causes has coat-tailed on the considerable public hype given to genetics in recent years with the advent Human Genome Project (HGP). Referred to repeatedly as biology's "Manhattan Project," the Human Genome Project is unquestionably the largest organized, government-funded research project in the history of the biomedical sciences. In arguing for such large-scale public support before Congress and in the press, proponents of the HGP project such as James D. Watson, Director of the Laboratory of Genetics at Cold Spring Harbor, New York, and Daniel Koshland, Editor of *Science,* have claimed that the project will solve every conceivable sort of medical problem, from specific genetic diseases (such as diabetes or phenylketonuria, or PKU) to major social and behavioral problems (such as criminality and homelessness). As Watson has said, "We used to think our fate was in the stars. Now we know it is in our genes."[29] Even more blatantly, in the October 12, 1990 issue of *Science,* Koshland, a biochemist by training, wrote:

It is time the world recognize that the brain is an organ like any other organ . . . and that it can go wrong not only as a result of abuse, but also because of hereditary defects utterly unrelated to environmental influences. . . . The irrational output of a faulty brain is like the faulty wiring of a computer in which failure is caused not by the information fed into the computer, but by incorrect processing of that information after it enters the black box.[30]

Given the many genuine findings that have already emerged from many areas of molecular genetics, and the prospect that at least some additional evidence of importance will result from the work of the HGP, the attempt to generate widespread belief in a genetic basis of social behaviors by linking them to the HGP, is particularly important. At the level of popular public discourse, there is a synergistic interaction taking place between molecular genetics and genetic theories of human behavior that gives the latter the appearance of increased credibility.

In summary, then, the context in which the current barrage of theories of a genetic basis of social behavior are occurring includes: (1) A persistence of economic and social problems such as unemployment, wage and benefit cuts, increased urban violence along with (2) a barrage of publicity about the great medical and psychiatric benefits to come from advances in molecular genetics, particularly those associated with the HGP.

I would now like to turn to an analysis of an earlier case study that has many similarities to the present: the rise of the "science" of eugenics in the first three decades of the present century. This case study can be useful in raising questions about the social context in which genetic studies of human behavior arise, and the political consequences to which they can lead, especially when they are widely accepted in the political arena.

## DEVELOPMENT OF EUGENICS IN AMERICA, 1900–1940

Since much has been written about the history of eugenics in recent years,[31] I will present only a brief overview of the movement with respect to the United States, in order to determine in what ways its history may be instructive for understanding the development of the Violence Initiative today.

The term "eugenics" was coined in 1883 by Francis Galton, first cousin of Charles Darwin and himself a pioneer in application of statistical and quantitative measurements to biological problems.[32] For Galton, eugenics meant "purely born," referring to his aim of improving the overall hereditary quality of the human species by planned human breeding. Although Galton never developed an active eugenics program of his own, his disciples, including Karl Pearson in Great Britain and Charles B. Davenport in the United States, pursued active research programs in eugenics. In the United States Davenport established The Station for the Experimental Study of Evolution at Cold Spring Harbor, Long Island in 1904, and next door, the Eugenics Record Office in 1910. The former was funded by the Carnegie Institute of Washington, and the latter, initially by Mrs. E. H. Harriman, widow of the railroad magnate E. H. Harriman, and later (after 1917) also by the Carnegie Institution of Washington.[33]

Building on Mendel's newly rediscovered principles of heredity in 1900, Davenport and many eugenicists claimed that social traits such as pauperism, manic depression, scholastic ability, feeblemindedness, degeneracy, epilepsy, and criminality were determined by one or two pairs of Mendelian "factors," or genes. Using primarily family pedigree studies, eugenicists in the United States traced out what appeared to be hereditary patterns for many forms of "social degeneracy" through numerous generations. Training a large number of eugenic field workers through summer courses at the Eugenics Record Office, Davenport and his superintendent, Harry H. Laughlin, collected information on thousands of families, beginning usually with members who were in state mental or penal institutions. Eugenicists used these data, along with self-administered questionnaires sent to college students and other select groups to argue for a strong hereditarian basis for most social traits.

Among the many social traits thought to have a hereditary base was criminality. Significant increases in crime rate in the larger cities of the United States at the time, particularly New York and Chicago, had raised concern among social workers, police, and political figures as well as among the socially concerned middle and upper classes. For example, between 1850 and 1890, the population of the country as a whole had increased 170 percent, while the criminal population had increased by 445 percent. In Pennsylvania, between 1880 and 1890, the number of criminals incarcerated in the state's penal system doubled, increasing the cost of operating such institutions by an alarming 35 percent.[34] In addition, there was a social cost of crime in terms of lost property, tracing and apprehension of criminals, cost of court trials and of incarceration, and so on. In one paper at the annual meeting of the National Prison Association in 1900, a distinguished New York lawyer, Eugene Smith, estimated that the annual expense to the taxpayers of the nation caused by various forms of criminal activity was $600,000,000.[35] By 1910 the Massachusetts Prison Association estimated that the cost of dealing with crime was the second largest item in the state budget, behind public education.[36] Crime was not only a social and moral problem, but also an economic one that could no longer be overlooked.

Davenport himself was particularly interested in the genetic basis of criminality, a subject on which he wrote several papers.[37] Laughlin, under the auspices of the Eugenics Record Office, worked closely with Judge

Harry Olson, Chief Justice of the Municipal Court of Chicago, on the effects of alien crime in the United States. Olson, a committed eugenicist, had founded the Psychopathic Laboratory in Chicago to apply scientific methods to the field of criminology. In 1935 Laughlin and Olson published a report of their findings: data on the rate at which crime has increased in the previous decades, the race and nationality of offenders, and the biological, specifically genetic, basis for crime.[38] Lamenting that many political discussions of crime (such as those recently organized by the governors of New Jersey and New York in 1935), virtually ignored the biological basis of criminal behavior, Olson and Laughlin claimed that:

> Crime is a social defect based on mental defect, and the mental defect is typical of two great divisions of the mind—the intelligence and the emotions. Instead of being sporadic, appearing by chance, the accumulative records show that, like all physical and mental traits, it runs in family stocks and is subject to the laws of genetics like other characteristics.[39]

For Laughlin and Olson the increase in crime so apparent in the late 1920s and early 1930s was viewed as an index of poor heredity. As they state: "Behind the criminal is a problem child; behind the problem child is the inadequate home and the problem parent; and behind the problem parent is poor heredity, which indicates that the whole sequence lies usually in an environment of economic insecurity."[40] Laughlin and Olson did not discount environment altogether, but it is clearly put in a secondary place: "The causes producing crime work from within (biological) and from without (social). Hereditary impulses are primary; the influences of environment are secondary and operate chiefly through temperamental instability which makes it difficult for the individual to withstand the pressure of his environment."[41] For Laughlin and Olson, many current social and legal experts mix up cause and effect by claiming that poverty causes crime. "Do the slums make the man or does the man make the slums?" they asked. Referring to the Brock Report, a recent analysis of the rise of crime, Laughlin and Olson argue that "a considerable proportion of defectives do come from slum surroundings but inquiries into the family history of such cases show that in the majority there is evidence of morbid inheritance . . . The inefficiency of the defective tends to depress him to the lowest economic level."[42] Citing anthropologist E. A. Hooton of Harvard University, Olson and Laughlin argue, "it can be stated positively that the biological inferiority of the criminal is no less marked than his economic ineffectiveness and his general stupidity. We need a biological New Deal which will segregate and sterilize the antisocial and mentally unfit."[43]

Among criminals and the violently prone, Laughlin and Olson presented a breakdown by racial and ethnic/national origins. A 1926 study of 2000 delinquents in

Chicago, for example, showed that 75 percent had foreign-born parents, with Italians and Slavs having the highest representation. By 1932, a similar survey showed that African Americans ("native Negroes," as Laughlin and Olson called them), Mexicans, and Puerto Ricans had all been added to the list as far overrepresented among the prison population compared to the population at large. The lesson that Laughlin and Olson drew from this message was clear: All the non-Anglo Saxon groups are to varying degrees defective and supply a large percentage of society's criminals. Quoting Charles W. Burr, M.D., Professor Emeritus of Mental Diseases at the University of Pennsylvania, they summarized their findings in as clearly hereditarian a vein as possible: "Crime is not largely the product of economic stress. The criminal, as a psychiatrist defines the word, is born and not made . . . they are not the product of the slums. They are incurable because they are not suffering from external stress and strain but from an inherent defect in protoplasm."[44]

Even before publication of these results, Laughlin and Olson had been convinced that there was a significant alien component to the increase in crime experienced in most major U.S. cities, especially in the period after World War I. Through Davenport, the Eugenics Record Office had established close contacts with the Immigration Restriction League, founded in Boston in the 1890s by Robert De Courcy Ward and Leverett Saltonstall.[45] The changing pattern of immigration from the 1880s onward had been particularly disturbing to many white, Anglo-Saxon Protestants, since it had produced a dramatic increase in immigrants from Southern Europe (Italy in particular), central and eastern Europe (Poland), the Mediterranean countries (Turkey, the Balkans, and Greece) and Russia (both before, but especially after, the Bolshevik Revolution of 1917). Since many of the "new" immigrants were Jewish, the call for immigration restriction took on an increasingly anti-semitic overtone by the time of World War I. After the war the influx of immigrants increased dramatically, due in large part to economic chaos in many European countries, and also to the United States' open-door policy. Combined with the return of U.S. soldiers, post–World War I immigration had particular dramatic economic consequences: large-scale unemployment, increased union membership and, most important, increased numbers and size of union-led strikes. Foreigners were blamed for much of the agitation, while their leadership roles in many trade unions targeted them as a particular menace.[46]

To deal with the increasing problem of immigration between 1920 and 1923, the House Committee on Immigration and Naturalization, under Albert Johnson, a rabidly anti-union, anti-communist and restrictionist congressman from Washington, held a series of hearings on immigration restriction. Johnson and other nativists did not want to restrict immigration across the board, but to selectively restrict the "new" immigrants from southern and eastern Europe and the Mediterranean countries. As honorary president of the Eugenics Research Association, Johnson called on Harry Laughlin to become "Expert Eugenic Witness" to the House Committee and to testify before the Committee about the relative genetic merit of different racial and ethnic groups. Laughlin's testimony covered a period of several days during two different meetings of the Committee on April 16 and 17, 1920.[47] With charts and a variety of statistics, he drove home the point that the so-called "new" immigrants were genetically inferior to the older, Anglo-Saxon and Nordic immigrants of the nineteenth century, and were the source of many of the nation's most glaring social and economic problems.

Prominent among the genetically determined social traits were criminality and violent behavior. Although his studies with Judge Olson on immigrant crime in Chicago were not completed in time for the final series of hearings on immigration restriction in 1924, Laughlin demonstrated that in virtually all state penal institutions he has surveyed, the foreign-born were dramatically overrepresented compared to their numbers in the population at large. Partly as a result of Laughlin's "scientific" testimony restrictionist sentiment carried the day and Congress passed the Johnson Act (Immigration Restriction Act) in 1924. The Johnson Act selectively limited immigration from southern and eastern Europe, the Mediterranean countries, the Balkans, Russia, and, in general (irrespective of geography) people of Jewish descent.[48]

In addition to immigration restriction, eugenicists such as Laughlin lobbied strongly for eugenical sterilization laws that would include, among other "defectives," repeat offenders in state penal institutions. With Davenport's support, Laughlin drew up a model sterilization law that could be introduced, with modifications to meet local needs, into the various state legislatures. Although the first law for eugenical sterilization (as opposed to strictly punitive measures) had been introduced in Indiana as early as 1907, a widespread movement to legalize involuntary sterilization did not develop serious momentum until after World War I.[49] Throughout the 1920s and 1930s, Laughlin and his associates campaigned hard in a large number of state legislatures, arguing that sterilization was an efficient and "progressive" way to stop the spread of crime—at its roots.[50] By 1935 Laughlin could boast that over thirty states had adopted such legislation and that another ten were considering it seriously.[51] And, by 1941 over 33,000 people (60 percent women) had been sterilized on the basis of these laws (over 60,000 by the late 1970s, when most of the laws had been repealed).[52] When the constitutionality of eugenical sterilization laws was tested in Virginia in 1925, in the now-famous Buck *vs.* Bell case, it was Laughlin who served as one of the primary expert eugenics witnesses to the Court (the other was E. A. Estabrook, one of Laughlin's and Davenport's colleagues at Cold Spring Harbor). Without ever meeting or interviewing the plaintiff, Carrie M. Buck, Laughlin certified that she was a "low-grade moron" with a "mental age of nine" and "the potential parent of socially inadequate offspring."[53] A few years later Laughlin's influence extended even further when his model eugenical sterilization law was used as the basis for the Nazi sterilization laws of 1933.[54]

Although it is clear that the U.S. sterilization and especially the immigration laws would probably have passed whether eugenicists had been involved, the claim for a biological basis for undesirable social traits made the legislative route far smoother. In Germany, as a number of recent historians of science have shown, biological arguments helped prepare the way for the atrocities of the holocaust.[55] Wishing neither to distort history nor to indulge in hyperbole, I do want to stress, however, the importance of recognizing the role that biological, and particularly genetic arguments, even when they appear in rather innocuous technical garb, can play in the much larger social and political arenas. In most of the formulations in which it has appeared in the past and at the present, the phrase "Biology is destiny!" leads to disastrous human consequences.

## Conclusion

There are many points of similarity between the social context of the eugenics movement in the early decades of the twentieth century and the current wave of genetic determinism circulating in the 1980s and 1990s. For one thing, both share the context of economic downswing that in their respective periods seem to show no indication of improvement. For example, unemployment hit major peaks in 1914, 1921, and 1932. The early decades of the twentieth century saw much violence, especially that associated with the "labor wars," that is, the confrontation between capital and labor with regard to union organizing and collective bargaining.[56] There were numerous strikes on a massive scale from the 1870s onward, representing the much larger, ongoing labor struggle. It is slight wonder that Laughlin, Davenport, and other eugenicists in the United States, were concerned to show that those who committed violent crimes were genetically defective. Indeed, the "lawlessness" that Laughlin and Judge Olson saw sweeping the nation was indeed, in their words, a product of "our historical past (wild west), our racial mixture, and our industrial conflicts."[57]

While the external character of the economic and social contexts of the 1980s and 1990s is different from those in the teens and twenties, the core problems have much in common. Both periods involve a sense of social unpredictability, unemployment or cutbacks in pay, a sense of social dislocation and deterioration. Both periods witnessed an increase in the number of people in state-dependent institutions such as mental hospitals or prisons, an increase in concern about immigrants taking jobs from native residents, and attacks on welfare programs and the "dependent classes" (for example, see the article on immigration in the *Wall Street Journal* of July 7, 1993). In charting the course of state sterilization laws, for example, Philip Reilly suggests that one major factor in the remarkable increase in the number of states adopting such laws in the period 1927–1935, was the severe budget cuts faced by many states in the Depression years.[58] Similarly, Paul Lombardo credits a major recession in the state of Virginia in 1923–1924 with helping overcome opposition in the legislature to the passage of a eugenical sterilization law.[59] A similarly interesting parallel is the fact that in both cases the claims for genetic determinism coattailed closely on rapid and path-breaking developments in the laboratory genetics of the day: Thus the old eugenics movement developed in the wake of the rediscovery of and expansion of Mendel's Laws of heredity, while the new movement is taking advantage of rapid developments in molecular genetics, particularly those associated with the Human Genome Project.

Although the similarities are many, there are also some differences between the new and the old arguments for genetic determinism. In the past, eugenicists were concerned primarily with legislating and controlling breeding patterns, while modern advocates focus more on a medical model for dealing with deviant behavior, including treatment by drug therapy and ultimately perhaps neurosurgery. On a more technical level, today's genetic determinists base their arguments more on statistical analyses of variance between identical twins or siblings in adoption studies, while the older eugenicists based their analyses largely on family pedigrees.

If there are differences in detail, the question still remains what function, if any, do these two movements share in terms of the political economic and social context in which they are embedded? I argue that in times of economic or social crisis, theories of genetic determinism do in fact serve very similar functions. They purport to treat complex and otherwise traditionally intractable social problems by what appear to be new "scientific" methods. Especially when the scientific approach is presented in new and highly technical terms, it is much simpler to think of a complex problem such as increase in crime rate or mental illness as a result of innate biological causes that do not in any way challenge the economic or social status quo. The victim is, under these conditions, the cause of their own problems; clearly the simplest way to deal with such problems is to "fix" them by scientific means, and thus prevent their recurrence. Although tracing social problems to genetic causes appears to take the onus off the individual, the ultimate result has always been to marginalize individuals and designate them as hopeless incurables. Consequently, any argument claiming that violent or criminal behavior is due to genetics by no means leads automatically to a more humane treatment of stigmatized individuals.

More important, genetic determinist arguments provide the rationale for an economically more "efficient" (that is, less expensive way) of dealing with so-called defective individuals. As expensive as they are, behavior-control drugs of today are cheaper than long-term social or psychological therapy, job counseling, and job retraining programs (especially if there are no jobs to go to), or reducing stress in the workplace, schools, and home. The logical outcome of medicalizing behavioral or personality problems is social control of individuals and the population at large by various biological—physiological, neurobiological, or genetic—manipulations. At a time when people are under economic and social stress, genetic determinists' theories divert attention from the real causes of scarcity or cutbacks. We end up scapegoating each other—by race, ethnic origin, gender, or sexual orientation. Instead of attacking more real and accessible causes of our social problems, such as the unequal distribution of wealth, and the control of economic resources by a tiny percentage of the population, we blame the lower socioeconomic groups for what is perceived as their own biological deficiency.

Proponents of genetic determinist arguments often complain that their critics are motivated by political biases, and simply do not want to face the very real possibility that people are not created equal biologically, and that our social and political system has to take these inequalities into account. Conversely, the proponents of genetic determinism portray themselves as politically unbiased scientists, following wherever the data may lead, even if the conclusions are not fashionable. I do not deny that my skepticism about any such theories is politically motivated, but the politics is not that of simple idealized egalitarianism. Rather, my skepticism about and opposition to, such theories arises from three separate but interrelated issues: (1) the persistently inconclusive nature of the data, (2) the historical ways in which the theories have been used, and (3) the political biases that *are* embedded in genetic determinist arguments, despite claims to the contrary.

(1) The enormous difficulty involved in obtaining data that in any rigorous way can separate the effects of heredity from those of environment in understanding the causes of human behavior ought to make anyone immediately suspicious of any strong claims about "the gene for . . . ," or "a significant genetic component to . . ." any given behavior. Whether measuring cranial index, IQ scores, or serotonin levels, over the years crimes of determinists have failed to produce data that withstands close scrutiny. Being wary or skeptical does not mean rejection of new theories out of hand; but given the methodological problems involved and the un-

broken string of misfired theories in the past, skepticism rather than naive acceptance or neutrality would seem to be the more logical response.

(2) Historically, theories of genetic (biological) determinism have always been used to deny individuals, almost always the less fortunate and downtrodden of society, access to resources, to limit rather than to expand their options. There is no logical necessity to this outcome. If indeed a trait is determined to be genetic, the social policy deriving from this information does not lead inevitably to restriction. Down syndrome is known to be a genetic condition, but that knowledge has led to two different social policies over the years. Before the 1960s, Down children were largely institutionalized and accepted as having a limited, and rather uniform range of capabilities. Largely for social reasons, policy shifted in the late 1950s, and in the last thirty years most Down patients have been raised at home and educated through special schools. Genetic limitations even when known clearly to exist, do not necessarily dictate restrictive social policy. Our social policy derives from our social values, which do not in any necessary way hinge on biological data. The historical fact that genetic determinist theories have almost always been used to limit accesses to resources suggests an underlying political bias among the social and political activists, if not of the researchers themselves, that have advocated these views. This brings me, then, to the third and last issue—political bias among those who continually advocate theories of genetic determinism.

(3) I have always found it naive, if not ingenuous, that advocates of genetic determinism claim to be "disinterested scientists" while charging their critics with political bias. We all have biases of various sorts, and biases can never be totally eliminated, nor are they necessarily a bad thing. The problem comes when we pretend *not* to have biases. Bias can help provide insights as well as blind us to alternative views, so it seems to me that the best policy is to get our biases out in the open and examine them, to find out if they are helping or hindering our goals, aims and aspirations? It is now so commonplace in the history and sociology of science to recognize and even seek out and analyze social and political biases in scientific work—the so-called social constructionist views—that is difficult to believe that many practicing scientists still cling to old positivist myths about the neutrality and objectivity of science. But I would be naive, I suppose, to assume that historians of science have yet to make that large an impact on the scientific community as a whole. At any rate, I have never found proponents of genetic determinism any less biased toward their views than I or other critics have been against them. I do not fault them for having a bias—only for not admitting what their bias is. Let's get the cards on the table and at least it will be easier to see on exactly what issues the disagreements are most clearly focused. There is little to be

gained by debating details of statistics of experimental design when large issues of political and social philosophy lie unexamined.

Given the analysis in this paper, I want to conclude with the suggestion that the "Violence Initiative" is a highly simplistic approach to the complex problems of the rising tide of violence, frustration, and anger in contemporary American society. To some, my analysis itself may appear too simplistic, perhaps no more realistic than the historical theories I am so strongly criticizing. However, the understanding we have of the solutions available to us very much depends on what we think the underlying causes to be. If my analysis is correct, that the Violence Initiative is serving much the same function in today's society as eugenics did in its day, then we have every need to monitor that development of such a program, and to expose its simplistic and unsupported claims wherever they are raised.

## ENDNOTES

1. Nancy Touchette, "Cowering inferno: Clearing the smoke on violence research," *Journal of NIH Research* 4 (No. 11, November, 1992): 31–33.

2. Frederick K. Goodwin, "Conduct disorder as a precursor to adult violence and substance abuse: Can the progression be halted?" (Washington, D.C. Address to the American Psychiatric Association, May 5, 1992). Recorded by Mobile Tape Co., Inc., 25061 West Avenue, Stanford, Suite 70, Valencia, CA 91355; see also report of Goodwin's remarks in the *Washington Post* (Wednesday, July 29, 1992): Metro Section B1.

3. *Ibid.*

4. Goodwin, in speech to National Mental Health Advisory Council, February 11, 1992; see "Partial Transcript of a Draft to the National Mental Advisory Council." (Unpublished transcript).

5. For examples of current work underscoring the complexity of primate behaviors (including the rhesus monkey, *Macaca mulatta*) see Barbara B. Smuts, Dorothy L. Cheney, Robert M. Seyfarth, Richard W. Wasserman, and Thomas T. Struhsaker (eds), *Primate Societies* (Chicago, University of Chicago Press, 1987); there is an especially useful chapter on the problems of comparing primate and human behavior; Robert A. Hinde, "Can nonhuman primates help us understand human behavior?" (Chapter 33, p. 421.)

6. Goodwin, Speech to National Mental Health Advisory Council, *op. cit.*

7. *Ibid.*

8. Goodwin, "Conduct disorder . . . " *op. cit.*

9. *Ibid.*

10. Peter R. Breggin, "The 'Violence Initiative'—a racist biomedical program for social control," *The Rights Tenet* (Summer, 1992): p. 3; also, Breggin, Peter R. and Ginger Ross-Breggin, "A biomedical programme for urban violence control in the U.S.: The dangers of psychiatric social control," *Changes* (March, 1993): 59–71, especially p. 63;

11. Breggin, Peter R., *Toxic Psychiatry* (New York, St. Martin's Press, 1991).

12. See, for example; "A cure for violence?" *Los Angeles Times* (April 24, 1992): p. E1, 4; "Hunting," *San Francisco Weekly* (July 15, 1992): pp. 2–3; "Science and sensitivity: Primates, politics and the sudden debate over the origins of human violence," *Washington Post* (March 1, 1992): p. C3; "New storm brews on whether crime has roots in genes," *New York Times [Science Times]* (Sept. 15, 1992): p. C1; "U.S. hasn't given up linking genes to crime (Letters to the Editor)," *New York Times* (Sept. 18, 1992): p. A34; "Study to quell violence is racist, critics charge," *Detroit Free Press* (Monday, Nov. 2, 1992): pp. 1, 11A; "Study cites biology's role in violent behavior," *New York Times* (Nov. 13, 1992): p. A12.

12. Goodwin, as interviewed on WAMU Radio, July 22, 1992.

13. Touchette, *op. cit.:* p. 32.

14. *New York Times (National):* Sunday, March 8, 1992: p. 34.

15. Touchette, *op. cit.:* p. 31.

16. Christopher Anderson, "NIH, under fire, freezes grant for conference on genetics and crime," *Nature* 358 (July 30, 1992): p. 357; see also David Wasserman's response to the cancellation of the conference: "In defense of a conference of genetics and crime: Assessing the social impact of public debate," *Chronicle of Higher Education,* Point of View (September 23, 1991): p. A44.

17. Breggin and Breggin, "A biomedical programme . . ." (1993) *op. cit.:* pp. 59–62.

18. *Ibid.:* p. 62.

19. Statistics from *Newsweek* (June 14, 1993): p. 32.

20. James Q. Wilson and Richard Herrnstein, *Crime and Human Nature* (New York, Simon & Schuster, 1985).

21. See, for example, Richard J. Herrnstein and James Q. Wilson, "Are criminals made or born?" *New York Times Magazine* (August 4, 1985): 31; "Genetic traits predispose some to criminality: A conversation with James Q. Wilson," *U.S. News and World Report* (Feb. 10, 1986): p. 67; Wilson has interviewed extensively on National Public Radio (NPR) and other information stations during the months immediately following publication of *Crime and Human Nature*. Despite the fact that the Wilson/Herrnstein book was reviewed adversely by a number of psychologists and sociologists, [for example: Leon J. Kamin, *Scientific American* 254 (No. 2, February, 1986): 22–27; and J. P. Scott, *Social Biology* 34 (Nos. 3–4, 198): 256–265], the popular press continued to present the findings as "new" and important evidence for a significant genetic factor in crime.

22. Fox Butterfield, "Study cites biology's role in violent behavior," *New York Times* (November 13, 1992): p. A12.

23. Gregory Carey, (University of Colorado, Boulder): Survey. [I have the preprint, but not actual publication citation yet]; it is a chapter in the NRC Report *Understanding and Preventing Violence* (1992).

24. The recent studies are still unpublished, but are summarized in the *New York Times* (Jan. 31, 1992): p. A1; earlier studies by Beck have been published as reports of the Bureau of Justice Statistics.

25. *New York Times* (Jan. 31, 1992): p. A1.

26. Letters to the Editor, *New York Times* (Feb. 14, 1992).

27. H. G. Brunner, M. R. Nelen, P. van Zandvoort, N. G. G.

M. Abeling, A. H. van Gennip, E. C. Wolters, M. A. Kuiper, H. H. Ropers, and B. A. van Dost, "X-linked borderline mental retardation with prominent behavioral disturbance: Phenotype, genetic localization, and evidence for disturbed monamine metabolism," *American Journal of Human Genetics* 52 (1993): 1032–1039; see also, H. G. Brunner, M. Nelen, X. O. Breakefield, H. H. Ropers, B. A. van Dost, "Abnormal behavior associated with a point mutation in the structural gene for monamine oxidase A," *Science* 262 (OXr 22, 1993): 578–580.

28. Sheryl Strolberg, "Researchers link gene to aggression," *Los Angeles Times* (Friday, October 22, 1992): p. A36.

29. Watson quote about our fate is in our genes. *New Republic* (July 9, 16, 1990).

30. Koshland quote from *Science* (Oct. 12, 1990): Editorial.

31. Daniel J. Kevles. *In the Name of Eugenics* (New York, Random House, 1985); M. B. Adams (ed), *The Wellborn Science* (New York, Oxford University Press, 1992); Garland E. Allen, "Eugenics and American social history," *Genome* 31 (1989): 885–889.

32. Francis Galton, *Inquiries into Human Faculty and Its Development* (London, Macmillan & Co., 1883): pp. 24–25 (n).

33. Garland E. Allen. "The Eugenics Record Office at Cold Spring Harbor: An essay in institutional history, *Osiris,* New Series 5 (1986).

34. Estimates by H. M. Boies, *Prisoners and Paupers* (New York, Putnam's, 1893): p. 10; taken from Philip Reilly, *The Surgical Solution* (Baltimore, Johns Hopkins University Press, 1991): p. 17.

35. Reilly, *op. cit.:* p. 17.

36. *Ibid.*

37. See, for example, Charles B. Davenport, "Crime, heredity and environment," *Journal of Heredity* 19 (No. 7, July, 1928): 307–313.

38. See, for example, the mimeographed pamphlet, "The Biological Basis of Crime," (1929); no author given, but containing numerous quotations from Judge Olson, and written in the informal, somewhat careless style typical of Laughlin. Numerous copies of the pamphlet were found in the H. H. Laughlin Papers, Pickler Memorial Library, Northeast Missouri State University, Kirksville, MO.

39. *Ibid.,* Frontispiece.

40. *Ibid.,* p. 5.

41. *Ibid.,* p. 5.

42. *Ibid.,* p. 6.

43. *Ibid.,* p. 7.

44. *Ibid.,* p. 9.

45. On the Immigration Restriction League and the growing nativist sentiment in the United States at the end of the nineteenth and beginning of the twentieth centuries, see: Barbara Solomon, *Ancestors and Immigrants* (Chicago, University of Chicago Press, 1972); also, Oscar Handlin, *The Uprooted, the Epic Story of the Great Migrations that Made the American People* (Boston, Little Brown, 1952); John Higham, *Strangers in the Land* (New York, Athenaeum, 1966).

46. Allen Chase, *The Legacy of Malthus* (New York, Basic Books, 1977): p. 255.

47. Frances Hassencahn, *Harry H. Laughlin, Expert Eugenics Agent for the House Committee on Immigration and Naturalization. 1921 to 1931* (Cleveland, Case Western Reserve University, Ph.D. Dissertation, 1970). Also, Kenneth Ludmerer, *Genetics and American Society* (Baltimore, Johns Hopkins University Press, 1972); Garland E. Allen, "The role of experts in scientific controversy," in H. T. Engelhardt and A. L. Caplan (eds), *Scientific Controversies: Case Studies in the Resolution and Closure of Disputes in Science* (Cambridge, Cambridge University Press, 1987): p. 183.

48. Allen Chase, *Legacy of Malthus, op. cit.:* pp. 274–295.

49. Reilly, *Surgical Solution, op. cit.:* p. x.

50. Harry H. Laughlin, "Further studies on the historical and legal development of eugenical sterilization in the United States," *American Association on Mental Deficiency* 41 (1936): 96–110.

51. *Ibid.,* p. 107 (Fig. 2).

52. See summary of sterilization data in Reilly, *Surgical Solution, op. cit.:* p. 97; for the post 1941 figure, see p. 165.

53. Paul A. Lombardo. "Three generations of imbeciles is enough: New light on Buck *vs.* Bell," *New York University Law Review* 60 (1985): 30–62. Much of Laughlin's and the other "expert" witnesses; testimony is summarized in Harry H. Laughlin, *The Legal Status of Eugenical Sterilization* (Chicago, The Psychopathic Laboratory of the Municipal Court of Chicago, 1929): esp. pp. 21–29.

54. Garland E. Allen, "The Eugenics Record Office . . . ," *op. cit.:* p. 253.

55. Robert Proctor, *Medicine under the Nazis* (Cambridge, Harvard University Press, 1988); Müller-Hill, Benno, *Murderous Science* (New York, Oxford University Press, 1988); and Paul Weindling, *Health, Race and German Politics between National Unification and Nazism. 1870–1945* (New York, Cambridge University Press, 1989).

56. Sidney Lens, *The Labor Wars* (New York, Doubleday, 1973).

57. Harry Olson and Harry H. Laughlin, "The biological basis of crime," (*op. cit.,* 1929): p. 5.

58. Reilly, *Surgical Solution, op. cit.:* pp. 91, 93–94, 101.

59. Lombardo, "Three generations of imbeciles . . ." *op. cit.:* p. 97.

# Chapter 45

# *Scapegoat Biology*

Bettyann H. Kevles
and Daniel J. Kevles

---

Biological explanations of violence are much in vogue. Part of the reason is that scientists studying the seat of behavior, the brain, and its genetic underpinnings, have learned a lot in recent years. Tendencies toward violence, they tell us, may reside in our genes or be hard-wired into our brains. Some neuroscientists have mapped brain abnormalities in laboratory animals and human murderers that seem to correlate with aggressive behavior. Others have teased out apparent connections between violent behavior and brain chemistry.

Being scientists, these researchers often try to tone down and qualify the connection between violence and biology. But even a faint message seems to fall on extraordinarily receptive ears. The findings of a team of Dutch and American scientists, for example, were recently exaggerated not only by the lay media but by the technical press as well. The researchers had come across a Dutch family in which, for five generations, the men had been unusually prone to aggressive outbursts, rape, and arson. These men were also found to have a genetic defect that made them deficient in an enzyme that regulates levels of the neurotransmitter serotonin. Han Brunner, a geneticist at University Hospital in Nijmegen, the Netherlands, and a member of the team, cautioned that the results concerned only one family and could not be generalized to the population at large, but the caveat was ignored. Stories everywhere, in both the scientific journals and the general media, spoke of his finding an "aggression gene."

There are other examples. In a 464-page assessment of the state of violence research in 1992, the National Research Council devoted only 14 pages to biological explanations. Of those 14, genetics occupied less than two pages. All the same, the *New York Times* covered the report with the headline STUDY CITES ROLE OF BIO-

LOGICAL AND GENETIC FACTORS IN VIOLENCE. Indeed, the proliferation of genetic explanations for violence prompted a *Time* writer to note wryly: "Crime thus joins homosexuality, smoking, divorce, schizophrenia, alcoholism, shyness, political liberalism, intelligence, religiosity, cancer, and blue eyes among the many aspects of human life for which it is claimed that biology is destiny."

Editors, of course, usually know what's on the minds of their audience: from rapes and murders in Rwanda or Bosnia to wrong-turn drivers cut down in a Los Angeles cul-de-sac, senseless violence has seemingly become the norm. Theater and movie audiences in the 1950s were shocked by *The Bad Seed,* the tale of a prepubescent pigtailed blond girl who was revealed to be a multiple killer. Today Americans are numb to nightly news reports of assaults in once-protected middle-class neighborhoods, child and spousal abuse in outwardly respectable homes, and clean-cut teenagers or even young children killing each other. The American Academy of Pediatrics made violence the theme of its meetings in October 1996, and the American Medical Association has alerted us to the "epidemic of violence."

This morbid fascination is to some extent justified: Violence is pervasive. Homicide is the second leading cause of death among teenagers and young adults and the leading cause among African American women and men between the ages of 15 and 34. In the past few decades, the demographics of violence in the United States have taken a turn for the worse. Almost 80 percent of murders used to involve people who knew each other. That figure has fallen to less than 50 percent. These statistics suggest that your chances of being wiped out by someone you've never met, and probably for no reason at all, have risen.

The escalation in random violence, especially among adolescents, has generated a hunger for explana-

From *Discover,* October, 1997.

tions. Biological accounts of murderous behavior do as well as any, and better than most. They are easy to grasp in principle, and they are socially convenient, locating criminal tendencies in our natures, about which we can currently do little beyond incarcerating the wrongdoers, rather than in nurture, which we might be able to remedy if we chose to invest the time and money.

The long, embarrassing history of biological theories of violence suggests caution. In the mid-nineteenth century, phrenologists—who diagnosed personality traits by the location of bumps on the head—worked out a behavioral map of the human skull, determining that area number 6 (out of 35) was the seat of destructiveness. In the early twentieth century some biologists and psychologists sought to extend the newly minted science of genetics to explanations of pernicious behavioral traits. Like today's scientists, they worked in a context of mounting social problems, including the disruptions of industrial capitalism and the flooding of immigrants into the nation's cities. They convinced themselves that poverty, alcoholism, prostitution, and criminality leading to violence all arose, in the main, from a trait called feeblemindedness, an inherited condition that they claimed was transmitted from one generation to the next as regularly and surely as the color of hair or eyes. Henry Goddard, the leading authority on the subject in the United States, taught that the feebleminded were a form of undeveloped humanity, "a vigorous animal organism of low intellect but strong physique—the wild man of today."

Perhaps not surprisingly, Goddard's theories were suffused with the bigotry of his era. Feeblemindedness was held to occur with disproportionately high frequency among lower-income and minority groups—notably recent immigrants from eastern and southern Europe. The biologist Charles Davenport, director of the Carnegie Institution Station for Experimental Evolution in Cold Spring Harbor, New York, and one of the country's prominent eugenicists, predicted that the "great influx of blood from Southeastern Europe" would rapidly make the American population "darker in pigmentation, smaller in stature, more mercurial ... more given to crimes of larceny, kidnapping, assault, murder, rape, and sex-immorality."

Such explanations of violence were commonplace in their day, but of course they proved to be hogwash, of no greater merit than the phrenological theories that had preceded them. The scientists responsible for them generally ignored the role of environment in shaping human behavior. They neglected to consider that the genetic contribution to aggression might well be very limited and, to the degree it might exist, very complex, the product of multiple genes acting in concert.

All the same, blaming violence on biology never lost its appeal to the media, the public, and even some scientists. In the mid-1960s a team of British researchers reported that a disproportionate number of male in-

mates in a Scottish hospital for patients with "dangerous, violent, or criminal propensities" had an extra Y chromosome accompanying the normal male complement of one X and one Y. Eventually, further research showed the double Y to be irrelevant to violent behavior, but not before lawyers representing the notorious Chicago multiple murderer Richard Speck announced that they planned to appeal his case on the grounds that he was XYY and therefore not responsible for his criminal acts. As it turned out, Speck didn't have the double Y chromosome after all, but the publicity helped inspire others to take up the banner. *Time* and *Newsweek* spotlighted the alleged relationship between chromosomes and crime, and a series of novels such as *The XYY Man* and *The Mosley Receipt* by Kenneth Royce featured an XYY character who struggled against his compulsion to cause havoc.

Today's biological theories of violence are far more sophisticated than their forebears. Unlike the earlier theories, they are concerned with behavior in individuals rather than groups, and they tend to be sensitive to the role of environment. They are also the product of some of the most powerful tools of modern science, including the ability to identify and isolate individual genes and to obtain pictures of the living brain. Unlike the phrenologists, neurobiologists can see—and show us—what may be wrong in a criminal's head.

Brain scans in particular seem to give a dramatic view into the biological dynamics of violence. Early PET-scan studies in the 1980s revealed that the brains of convicted criminals who had been victims of child abuse had areas of inactivity relative to the brains of control subjects (probably the result of getting banged on the head while they were babies). By early 1997, a psychologist at the University of Texas Medical Branch in Galveston could conjure up red-and-blue reconstructions of the brains of violent offenders and use them to support his view that their hair-trigger tempers were the result of an impairment of the frontal and parietal lobes of their brains.

Neuroscientists have isolated and begun to study the roles of several neurotransmitters in suicidal patients, depressives, and people prone to impulsive violence. They have connected both excesses and insufficiencies of serotonin and dopamine with impulsive violent behavior and with diseases of the brain such as Parkinson's. At the same time, the mapping of the human genome is providing pictorial representations of where our genes reside in relation to one another. We can now see our genes as strings of beads, and it seems only a matter of time before the bad bead on the string will be correlated with the suspect area in the brain scan.

Among the most interesting studies in progress is a project at Brookhaven National Laboratory on Long Island linking dopamine, cocaine addiction, the rise of euphoria, and subsequent violent behavior. The research seems to indicate that people who do not produce enough dopamine—whether through a genetically encoded trait or from some environmental cause—might seek out addictive drugs to avoid feeling depressed. Whatever the cause, brain scans of recovering addicts show damage in parts of the brain that neurologists have identified as controlling acceptable interpersonal behavior. Other studies have focused on the role of serotonin in aggression. Researchers at UCLA observed a colony of vervet monkeys whose social structure they could manipulate by controlling serotonin levels in individual animals. High levels raised the status of male monkeys in the hierarchy of the colony, and high status goes with dominant behavior.

Both scientists and popularizers have predicted that the new behavioral genetics will lead to the kinds of therapies and cures that medical genetics hopes to achieve for physical disease. Yet for all its sophistication and, in some cases, caution and care, the new biology of violence is at risk for many of the difficulties that have afflicted the entire field of human behavioral biology since the early decades of this century. Researchers continue to find it difficult to eliminate or compensate for environmental influences in their studies. For instance, putting together a control group of families that have the same complicated situations as a subject group is an inexact process, to say the least. Controlling for the existence of, say, poverty is relatively straightforward, but controlling for a family's attitude toward its own poverty—and attitude will have a big impact on how well family members cope with it—is practically impossible.

Many theories also suffer from imprecise definitions of the traits they purport to explain, or they lump disparate behaviors together—such as putting all manifestations of violence under the catchall category of "aggressiveness." These call to mind Charles Davenport's efforts to find genetic explanations for "nomadism," "shiftlessness," and "thalassophilia"—a love of the sea that he discerned in (male) naval officers and concluded must be a sex-linked recessive trait. Contemporary scientists have attributed to genes the propensity to crave thrills, to have leadership qualities, to be unhappy, to divorce, and to wear a lot of rings (or "beringedness," as one psychiatrist calls it). Researchers from City of Hope, the Duarte, California, research hospital, declared that the $D_2$ dopamine receptor gene was associated with an entire constellation of destructive behaviors, including autism, drug abuse, attention-deficit hyperactivity, post-traumatic stress disorder, pathological gambling, Tourette's syndrome, and alcoholism.

The new biology of violence has often drawn excellent correlations from studies with animals, particularly mice and monkeys. But what animals have to tell us about human behavior is severely limited. It is difficult to see how the sex lives of adolescent mice, for instance, has much at all to do with our sons and daughters. When a male rodent mounts a female, and the female assumes an accepting position, they are not doing so as a result of social pressures: Both animals are acting according to biological signals alone. It doesn't take a Ph.D. to know that such is not the case with boys and girls. Monkeys, on the other hand, are certainly behaviorally closer to humans. After all, they undergo many of the same developmental stages, and anyone who has watched adolescent vervets knows that they sometimes act a lot like college students the week after exams. But monkeys are not people by any measure.

Despite all that neuroscientists have learned about brain chemistry and structure, they in fact still know very little about how the brain works, let alone how it governs action. Much confusion over research on the biology of violence occurs because the public does not always appreciate the largely correlational aspect of the research. Scientists in general cannot yet say that a specific abnormality in the brain *causes* a person to exhibit a particular violent behavior; they can say only that the two tend to occur in the same individual. Although in some cases an abnormality may indeed be said to cause a behavior, it is sometimes equally plausible that a behavior causes an abnormality. Further muddying the waters is the obvious and unenlightening fact that all behavior—even learned behavior—is in some sense biological. We initiate a biological process every time we use a finger to press a button or pull a trigger. The biological activity that scientists observe can often be the result of our experience in life or even "pre-life" in the uterine environment. Researchers are still a long way from predicting, much less preventing, most outbursts of violence.

Meanwhile, even the hope of using biology to foretell an individual's tendency to violence poses grave difficulties for a democratic society. The prospect strikes directly at conventional notions of human dignity and freedom. If we could tell that someone has a 65 percent chance of behaving violently if he consumes alcohol, how should that information be used? Should it be made public, thus stigmatizing the person? Should legislation be passed making it illegal for such people to drink? Since the advent of the XYY research, many have worried that screening children for biological propensities to violence could lead to a self-fulfilling prophecy. Telling children that they are prone to violence might just encourage them to meet those expectations.

Another difficulty arises from the not unreasonable notion that if biology is destiny, then responsibility becomes moot—a point not lost on defense lawyers. In 1982, John Hinckley, who shot Ronald Reagan and James Brady, was sent to a mental hospital instead of prison in part because a jury accepted CT scan evidence that he was suffering from "shrunken brain" and had therefore not been responsible for his actions. While brain scans have not been used successfully to exculpate murderers, they have been employed to avoid the death penalty, and in the last several years criminal defense lawyers have proposed that a deficiency in the enzyme that regulates serotonin might make a good legal defense.

We would probably all like to cure society of violent behavior with something akin to a vaccine to prevent its spread and an antibiotic to cure what we already face. But the medical analogy gives undue weight to the biological basis of the behavior. "We know what causes violence in our society: poverty, discrimination, the failure of our educational system," says Paul Billings, a clinical geneticist at Stanford. "It's not the genes that cause violence in our society. It's our social system." We need better education, nutrition, and intervention in dysfunctional homes and in the lives of abused children, perhaps to the point of removing them from the control of their incompetent parents. But such responses would be expensive and socially controversial. That we are searching, instead, for easy answers in the laboratory is a sign of the times.

# Chapter 46

# *Genetic Ties May Be Factor in Violence in Stepfamilies*

## Jane E. Brody

A woman's live-in boyfriend murders her child fathered by another man. A woman neglects her young stepsister and punishes her so viciously that she dies. A stepfather sexually abuses his wife's daughter by a former husband.

As these examples drawn from news articles over last year demonstrate, the Cinderella story is hardly a fairy tale. Researchers are finding that the incidence of violence and abuse is vastly greater in stepfamilies than in traditional families in which the children are biologically related to both parents and to one other.

Of course, most stepfamilies do well, despite potential stresses. And plenty of families in which all the children are the progeny of both parents are fraught with violence and despair.

But stepfamilies are at much higher risk than are traditional families. For example, Dr. Martin Daly and Dr. Margo Wilson, evolutionary psychologists at McMaster University in Hamilton, Ontario, found that the rate of infanticide was 60 times as high and sexual abuse was about eight times as high in stepfamilies as is in biologically related families.

"We demonstrated a very large excess risk to stepchildren, an increase of thousands of percentage points," Dr. Daly said in an interview.

The matter is especially pressing now when rates of divorce and remarriage are at an all-time high.

Traditional sociological explanations for abuse and conflict in stepfamilies have focused on issues like economic stress, low socioeconomic status and emotional instability. But evolutionists say these are only proximate, not ultimate, causes of the difficulties that sometimes arise in stepfamilies. The underlying trigger, the evolutionists believe, lies within inherently selfish genes,

From the *New York Times* Tuesday, February 10, 1997.

which are biologically driven to perpetuate themselves. Genetically speaking, stepparents have less of an investment in unrelated offspring and may even regard them as detrimental to their chances of passing along their own genes, through their own biological children.

Citing examples among animals—from birds and bees to lions and baboons—that share the human propensity to live in family groups, the evolutionists maintain that conflicts and incestuous relations are more common among stepparents and stepchildren and among children and their half-siblings and step-siblings because they are less closely related to one another than are parents and children in a traditional family. In fact, Drs. Daly and Wilson found that when degree of genetic relatedness is taken into account, the role that economic stress plays in problems common in stepfamilies becomes almost negligible.

"There's a lot of violence involving steprelatives that can't be explained in terms of poverty, maternal youth and other commonly cited factors," Dr. Daly said.

Dr. Stephen T. Emlen, an evolutionary biologist at Cornell University, maintains that a dearth of shared genes is the unconscious force that underlies many of the difficulties encountered in stepfamilies. These problems involve not only conflicts, violence, and incest but also guilt and hurt that can result when stepparents do not form a close bond with their spouses' children, with whom they share no genes. Dr. Emlen believes that over the course of several million years, the forces of evolution have selected for behaviors within families that foster the perpetuation of the family genes.

Dr. Emlen asks, for example, whether men are really so different from, say, male lions; when taking over a new family, the male will kill any offspring still present from the female's prior matings.

In a paper recently published in the journal *Social Science Information,* he wrote, "Conflicts are intensified in stepfamilies because stepparents are unrelated to offspring of the previous pairing, and extant offspring are less related to future young of the new pairing." Dr. Emlen, who has spent twenty years studying animal family systems, says this is as true of people as it is of lower animals that live in family groups, including wolves, mongooses, rodents, scrub jays, bee-eaters, wrens, ants, bees, wasps, and termites.

He theorizes that through the process of natural selection, humans' genes have provided a template for certain behaviors that foster their perpetuation through biological offspring and prompt people to invest less energy in maintaining a set of genes that is less like their own.

Sociologists tend to reject such intimations of genetic determinism, citing the fact that humans have minds that can override the forces of genetics. They also note the relatively low rates of abuse or other violence in families with adopted children, who share none of their adoptive parents' genes. The evolutionists do not dispute these arguments; rather they say that an awareness of genetic forces can help people overcome them. Dr. Emlen suggested that a society cognizant of the inherent genetic risks can find ways to capitalize on the human intellect and head off trouble before it happens. Dr. Emlen emphasized that "genes confer only a predisposition, not a destiny."

"Individuals can modify undesirable tendencies once they are aware of them," he said. Modifications of hereditary "decision rules," Dr. Emlen said, "are routinely made based on who is watching, the person's social status, kinship, past experience with the individual and the relative age and dominance of the individual."

"I'm not deterministically saying you're going to have problems because you're a stepfamily," he said in an interview. "There are tons of stepfamilies who are doing absolutely fine." Still, he said it is best to head off trouble by anticipating possible flash points, adding that "it is sometimes very hard to alter things five years down the pike."

"The greatest potential value of the evolutionary perspective is that it tells us when, where, and between whom conflict is most likely to occur," Dr. Emlen said.

Dr. Michael Kerr, a psychiatrist at the Georgetown Family Center in Washington, who specializes in family problems, praised Dr. Emlen's suggestions for defusing potential problems in stepfamilies. "That there should be an evolutionary base to the human family makes complete sense to me," he said, adding "anything that moves society toward a more accurate understanding of what the problems are in families will be helpful in the long run."

Dr. Emlen suggested, for example, that single parents considering remarriage emulate female baboons, which do not accept a new male partner unless he demonstrates parenting skills. A new partner entering an existing family "may have to go an extra mile to develop a bond with a stepchild," Dr. Emlen said.

He added, "An individual with children should realize the need to look for different traits in a future mate. Qualities such as demonstrable interest in the children, financial generosity, and willingness to become an active participant in a ready-made family come readily to mind."

A prenuptial stepfamily agreement might be signed to assure that future stepparents are aware of "the greater statistical risks of conflict, and particularly the greater challenges involved in child rearing, that are associated with reconstituted families," Dr. Emlen said. In signing such a document, they "would be acknowledging such risks and accepting their heightened responsibility for dealing with them," he said.

If stepchildren, who share at least half the genes of one parent, are at greater risk than the biological children of both parents, should not adopted children, who are genetically related to neither parent, be at even greater risk?

"Adopted children face nothing like the risk that children in stepfamilies face," Dr. Daly said. He and Dr. Emlen pointed out that unlike stepparents, both parents of an adopted child want the child and are usually screened by professionals for parental suitability.

In contrast, Dr. Daly said, "many stepparents would really prefer that their spouses' kids had not existed," adding, "What often happens in stepfamilies is that the stepparent, who is usually a man, feels exploited, pressured in a direction that his emotions and affections are not pushing him."

He suggested that stepparents "think of their investment in stepchildren as a gift, given out of love for the partner, a part of the web of reciprocity in a remarriage." He concluded that it is better to act as if you appreciate making the investment than to act as if it's your duty.

# Chapter 47

# *Infant Killing as an Evolutionary Strategy: Reality or Myth?*

Robert W. Sussman
James M. Cheverud
and Thad Q. Bartlett

*The students nodded. They had all studied animal behavior, and they knew, for example, that when a new male took over a lion pride, the first thing he did was kill all the cubs. The reason was apparently genetic: The male had evolved to disseminate his genes as widely as possible, and by killing the cubs he brought all the females into heat, so that he could impregnate them.*

(Michael Crichton, *Jurrassic Park*)

*Infanticide (as seen in lions) also occurs in the entellus langur* (Presbytis entellus). *Marauding bands of nomadic males raid a troop, drive off the resident males, kill all the juveniles, and quickly mate with the females.*

(The Oxford Companion to Animal Behavior)

Among many primate biologists, infant killing by conspecific males is thought of as an evolutionary strategy giving adaptive advantage to the infanticidal male (Hrdy 1977, Hausfater and Hrdy 1984). In fact, as can be seen from the above, the use of the sexual selection hypothesis to explain infanticide has become a widespread, almost mythological belief, even in the popular literature. The theory is as follows. An infanticidal male gains reproductive advantage by selectively killing the unweaned offspring of his male rivals. In addition to the relative gain in genetic representation, the infanticidal act terminates lactational amenorrhea, shortening the interbirth interval of the infant-deprived female. This ensures the earli-

est possible opportunity for the infanticidal male to mate with and inseminate the infant-deprived female. Theoretically, the most likely context for this to occur is during male takeover in species with one male groups.

Recently, this theory has been expanded to include seasonally breeding species, such as the ring-tailed lemur *(Lemur catta),* in which the infanticidal male cannot immediately mate with the dead infant's mother. If a male's infant is the subject of infanticide, he is unlikely to be chosen again as a mate in subsequent years (he becomes an "incompetent father") (Perreira and Weiss 1991, Kappeler 1993). Thus, females select infanticidal males to father their offspring.

There are two major problems with the sexual selection explanation for infant killing among primates. The first involves the data; the second the theory itself.

From *Evolutionary Anthropology* Vol. 3, 1995.

## THE DATA

Recently, we examined the literature to determine precisely how many cases of infant killing actually have been observed by primate researchers. Further, we examined the context of these incidences of infanticide (Bartlett et al. 1993). We found that there were only 48 cases in which the death of the infant was observed. These cases occurred in thirteen species of primate, and almost half of the killings (21) were done by Hanuman langurs. More than half of the langur deaths occurred at one Indian site, Jodhpur (Sommer 1994).

One might argue that predation also is rarely observed and yet it is an important cause of death among primates. But the numbers are not comparable. First, the database for predation is quite broad relative to that for infanticide (Anderson 1986, Hart in prep.). A review of the literature reveals a large number of observed cases (Sussman et al. in prep.), even though documenting predation is very difficult (Isbell 1994). Second, primatologists rely on studies of very small prey populations (e.g., one or two primate groups) rather than studies on predators. Field studies of predators indicate that primates are important prey items for many species (Goodman et al. 1993, Hart in prep., Rettig 1978). Finally, primates display typical antipredator defense behaviors outlined by Endler (1991). Yet no such mechanisms exist to deter infanticidal attacks by males. A fixed action pattern towards specific predators is quite different from males associating with infants, females protecting their infants from strange males, or monogamy. In fact, Sommer notes that mothers sometimes "allowed even infanticidal males to come so close to their infants that a sudden jump would have been sufficient to grasp the hopping infant from the ground or from the mother's breast" (Sommer 1987).

A second, even more serious problem with the data is the fact that the context rarely fits the pattern predicted for sexual selection. In only eight of the 48 cases was the infanticidal male observed mating with the mother. In two of these, the male was the most likely father of the infant that he killed! Only six cases involved direct attacks on independent infants, and in an additional three cases a mother-infant pair was the subject of direct repeated attacks. The majority of infant deaths occurred during general aggressive episodes. There is evidence, among Hanuman langurs in particular (Dolhinow in press), that in these situations infants often place themselves into danger by their own actions (e.g., clinging to their mothers during attacks, or being attracted to action and excitement). Thus, of the 48 cases, only 12.5 percent fit the requirements of the sexual selection hypothesis. In 87.5 percent of observed infant killings, the context is not compatible with this hypothesis.

There appears to be no underlying consistent context in which infanticide takes place, such as group takeover. The circumstances surrounding infant deaths are highly variable and the use of a single term, with all its implications, to refer to the numerous phenomena involved in infant killing misrepresents the complexity of primate social behavior.

## THE THEORY

The fundamental assumption of the sexual selection hypothesis concerns the genetic basis for infant killing behavior. Although the inheritance of the "infanticidal trait" (Hrdy 1979, 1984, Newton 1988) is crucial for the operation of the sexual selection model, there is no evidence supporting its genetic inheritance. Are the sons of infant-killing males more likely to be infant killers themselves because of genes they inherit from their fathers?

In addition to the lack of data on genetic inheritance, selection for infant killing has never been demonstrated. Selection can be measured by quantifying the covariance between the character and relative fitness in a population that includes infanticidal males (Arnold and Wade 1984, Phillips and Arnold 1989, Schluter 1988). Relative fitness is the relative intrinsic rate of increase of the individual compared to that of the population as a whole. When lifetime relative fitness is unavailable, its time-specific components can be analyzed, with the caveat that the selection measured may be counteracted at other life stages. What is the increase in relative fitness associated with infanticide behavior?

Selection for infant killing, if it exists at all, is likely to be weak. First, variance in infant killing is low because it is a rare event (Bartlett et al. 1993) and low variance limits the covariance of the trait with relative fitness. Second, the only indication of fitness differences we have are a few cases of small decreases in interbirth intervals for females who lost infants relative to those who did not (Sommer 1987). However, a large proportion of infants die within the first months of life regardless of infant-killing males (Jacquish et al. 1991, Sade et al 1976, Sussman 1991). Some of these infants would have died anyway. The shortening of the interbirth interval due to infant killing needs to be discounted by the underlying death rate so that selection is much weaker than indicated by interbirth interval differences reported in the literature. Furthermore, differences of a few months in the timing of offspring born to infant killers compared to non-killing males who take over a group will only have a slight effect on relative lifetime intrinsic rate of increase. In fact, the necessity of using year-long age intervals in primate demography makes the likely effect smaller than measurable error. It is important to remember that the fitness increase due to infant killing would only be the slightly earlier production of offspring, since the benefits of controlling a breeding group would also accrue to non-killing males.

Even given a slight increase in fitness for infant-killing males, this increase could well be due to selection on other, correlated traits (Lange and Arnold 1983). We must avoid considering individual traits as independent evolutionary entities rather than as parts of integrated character complexes. Differences in fitness associated with infant killing may actually be due to direct selection on other functionally related characters such as overall aggression (Lange and Arnold 1983, Moore 1990). If there is direct selection on aggressiveness and aggression and infant killing are correlated, infant-killing males may have the same or lower fitness than non-killers. In this instance, infant killing would increase as a correlated response to selection for increased overall aggressiveness not due to independent adaptation.

Most witnessed cases of infant killing appear to be simply genetically inconsequential epiphenomena of aggressive episodes. At this stage, there is little evidence to suggest that infant killing is anything but a rare and evolutionarily trivial phenomenon. No evidence of genetic inheritance or direct selection for the trait has been provided, just non-quantitative plausibility arguments based on anecdotes. Until more specific evidence is available, the concept that infanticide in nonhuman primates is a widespread, adaptive behavior must be approached with appropriate caution. The burden of proof remains, as it always has, with those who favor the sexual selection hypothesis.

It is both important and enjoyable to formulate scientific hypotheses, and it is not difficult to fit them into an evolutionary framework. However, this in itself is not science. Good science begins when one collects the relevant data needed to test these hypotheses. Hypotheses that are untestable or that cannot be disproved are not useful to science. As we have indicated, there are a number of ways the sexual selection hypothesis can be tested, and we urge those interested in this question to collect the necessary data. An infant killing or disappearance does not in itself support the hypothesis of selection and selection does not cause cases of infanticide. Selection is the relationship between relative fitness and a character caused by environmental factors, and these factors, fitness, and the character itself must be measured to determine whether infant killing is an evolutionary strategy.

# REFERENCES

Anderson, C. M. (1986) "Predation and primate evolution." *Primates,* 27:15–39.

Arnold, S.; Wade, M. (1984) "On the measurement of natural selection: Theory." *Evolution,* 38:709–719.

Bartlett, T. Q.; Sussman, R. W.; Cheverud, J. M. (1993) "Infant killing in primates: A review of observed cases with specific reference to the sexual selection hypothesis." *Am. Anthrolpol.* 95:958–990.

Dolhinow, P. (in press) "A mystery: Explaining behavior." In *The New Physical Anthropology.* S. C. Strum, D. G. Lindburg, D. A. Hamburg, eds.

Endler, J. A. (1991) "Interactions between predators and prey." In *Behavioural Ecology* (pp. 169–196). J. R. Krebs, N. B. Davies, eds. London: Blackwell Scientific.

Goodman, S. M.; O'Connor, S.; Langrand, O. (1993) "A review of predation on lemurs: Implications for the evolution of social behavior in small, nocturnal primates." In *Lemur Social Systems and Their Ecological Basis* (pp. 51–66). P. M. Kappeler, J. U. Ganzhorn, eds. New York: Plenum.

Hart, D. L. (in prep) *Primates as Prey: Ecological, Morphological, and Behavioral Interrelations Between Primates and Their Prey.* Ph.D. thesis, Washington University, St. Louis.

Hausfater, G.; Hrdy, S. B. (eds) (1984) *Infanticide: Comparative and Evolutionary Perspectives.* New York: Aldine.

Hrdy, S. B. (1977) "Infanticide as an evolutionary strategy." *Am. Sci.,* 65:40–49.

Hrdy, S. B. (1979) "Infanticide among animals: A review, classification, and examination of the implications for the reproductive strategies of females." *Ethol. Sociobiol.,* 1:13–40.

Hrdy, S. B. (1984) "Assumptions and evidence regarding the sexual selection hypothesis: A reply to Boggess." In *Infanticide: Comparative and Evolutionary Perspectives* (pp. 315–319). G. Hausfater, S. B. Hrdy, eds. New York: Aldine.

Isbell, L. A. (1994) "Predation on primates: Ecological patterns and evolutionary consequences." *Evol. Anthropol.,* 3:61–71.

Jacquish, C.; Gage, T.; Tardif, S. (1991) "Reproductive factors affecting survivorship in captive Callitrichidae." *Am. J. Phys. Anthropol.,* 84:291–306.

Kappeler, P. M. (1993) "Sexual selection and lemur social systems." In *Lemur Social Systems and Their Ecological Basis* (pp. 223–240). P. M. Kappeler, J. U. Ganzhorn, eds. New York: Plenum.

Lande, R.; Arnold, S. (1983) "The measurement of selection on correlated characters." *Evolution,* 37:1210–1226.

Moore, A. (1990) "The evolution of sexual dimorphism by sexual selection: The separate effects of intrasexual selection and intersexual selection." *Evolution,* 44:315–331.

Newton, P. N. (1988) "The variable social organization of Hanuman langurs (*Presbytis entellus*). Infanticide and the monopolization of females." *Int. J. Primatol.,* 9:59–77.

Pereira, M. E.; Weiss, M. L. (1991) "Female mate choice, male migration, and the threat of infanticide in ringtailed lemurs." *Behav. Biol. Sociobiol.,* 18:141–154.

Phillips, P.; Arnold, S. (1989) "Visualizing multivariate selection." *Evolution,* 43:1209–1222.

Rettig, N. L. (1978) "Breeding and behavior of the harpy eagle (*Harpia harpyja*)." *Auk,* 95:629–643.

Sade, D. S.; Cushing, K.; Cushing, P.; Dunaif, J.; Figueroa, A.; Kaplan, J.; Laner, C.; Roades, D.; Schneider, J. (1976) "Population dynamics in relation to social structure on Cayo Santiago." *Yrbk Phys. Anthropol.,* 20:253–262.

Schluter, D. (1988) "Estimating the form of natural selection on quantitative trait." *Evolution,* 45:849–861.

Sommer, V. (1987) "Infanticide among free-ranging langurs (*Presbytis entellus*) at Jodhpur (Rajasthan/India): Recent observations and a reconsideration of hypotheses." *Primates,* 28:163–197.

Sommer, V. (1994) "Infanticide among the langurs of Jodhpur: Testing the sexual selection hypothesis with a long-term record." In *Infanticide and Parental Care* (pp. 155–198). S. Parmigiani, F. vom Saal, eds. London: Harwood Academic Publishers.

Sussman, R. W. (1991) "Demography and social organization of free-ranging *Lemure catta* in the Beza Mahafaly Reserve, Madagascar." *Am. J. Phys. Anthropol.,* 84:45–53.

Sussman, R. W.; Hart, D. L.; Rehg, J. (in prep) *Predation on Primates: A Review of Observed Cases.*

# Chapter 48

# *Infanticide: Let's Not Throw out the Baby with the Bath Water*

Sarah Blaffer Hrdy
Charles Janson
and Carel van Schaik

As originally defined by Darwin (1871), sexual selection refers to a struggle between members of one sex for access to the other with the result for the unsuccessful competitor being not death, but few or no offspring. The sexual selection hypothesis for infanticide proposes that a male increases his reproductive success by killing unrelated infants if the infant's death makes the female return to receptivity sooner than would otherwise have been the case and if it does not decrease his likelihood of subsequently mating with her. Sussman et al. (1995) first dispute the observational evidence for this hypothesis. Second, they argue that no genetic basis for infanticide has been demonstrated. Last, they assert that the proposed genetic benefits to infanticidal males are not sufficient to be subject to selection. Instead, they argue that infant deaths are incidental byproducts of generalized aggression.

Before we address Sussman et al.'s objections, let's be clear on where we agree. First, we agree that the sexual selection hypothesis is perhaps too readily invoked in both the popular and scientific literature. In the first general review of infanticide in animals (1979), the first sentence of the abstract reads: "Infanticide among animals is a widespread phenomenon with no unitary explanation." Five explanatory hypotheses for infanticide, each generating a different set of predictions concerning who would kill whom when, were laid out. The possibility that infanticide would occasionally occur as an unselected by-product of inter-group aggression or other social conflict was one of those five possibilities (see Table 48-1). If Sussman et al. wish to argue that not every case

From *Evolutionary Anthropology* Vol. 3, 1995.

of infanticide in nature is due to sexual selection, or even natural selection, who disagrees?

Secondly, we concur that we need more field data, and that larger sample sizes as well as experimental data collected under controlled conditions as exist for rodents (Parmigiani and von Saal 1994) are scientifically—if not always ethically—desirable.

## THE OBSERVATIONAL EVIDENCE

Now for the disagreements. In an effort to underscore how limited the evidence for infanticide is, Sussman et al. (1995) point out that half of all 48 (their tally) published cases of observed infanticide come from just a single species, *Presbytis entellus*, and that half of these all come from a single site, Jodhpur—the implication being that infanticide is not so widespread after all, and may largely be peculiar to some langur populations. However, this representation is misleading. First, what counts are rates of infanticide. Without information on how many animals were monitored and for how long, it is meaningless to say more killings were witnessed at one study site than another. Roughly 1000 langurs were studied at Jodhpur, over 18 years (1969–1987), by more than ten full-time doctoral or post-doctoral observers working together with local assistants in the largest scale project ever undertaken for any colobine. Second, infanticide is very widespread, having now been observed in conditions predicted by the hypothesis in species of five of the six primate radiations (the exception being tarsiers), in both captive and field conditions. Infanticidal attempts can predictably be provoked by removing a group's resi-

TABLE 48–1   Predictions Generated by Five Explanatory Hypotheses for Infanticide
(From Hrdy and Hausfater 1984)

| Class of Infanticide | Killer-victim Relatedness | Age of Highest Infant Risk | Age and Sex of Killer | Nature of Gain to Killer |
|---|---|---|---|---|
| 1) Exploitation as resource | Distant | Vulnerability and size more important than age | Either sex at any age large enough to subdue victim | Nutritional gain by killer |
| 2) Competition for resources | Distant | Vulnerability more important than age | Either sex usually (but not always adults) | Increased availability of resources for killer and killer's kin |
| 3) Sexual selection | Distant | Unweaned (but specifically younger than age at which ovulation resumes or amenorrhea terminated) | Adult of sex investing least in offspring, typically male | Additional breeding opportunity |
| 4) Parental manipulation | Close (~0.5) | Just after birth (but any age posible depending on time-course of parental investment) | Either sex, but most likely an individual of the sex investing most in the offspring, typically female | Increased inclusive fitness for one or both parents |
| 5) Social pathology | Not critical for this hypothesis | Size, proximity, and vulnerability more important than age | Adult of sex most likely to respond to social disturbance with increased aggressiveness | None for killer directly, although decrease in population density may eventually result |

dent male(s). Reported differences in rates of infanticide are found at least in part because species and populations vary in how often they meet the conditions in which male infanticide is likely (Newton 1986). Indeed, this variation could be put to use in future comparative tests of the sexual selection hypothesis.

Sussman et al. (1995) compare the evidence for infanticide with that for predation, another rare behavior, for which, they argue, the evidence is much better. However, we would argue that, if one uses the same standards of evidence, infanticide is, if anything, better documented than predation on wild primates. Forty-eight observed cases of infanticide is far greater than the number of witnessed cases of predation upon primates that made it into the professional literature. Most published estimates of predation rates for primate populations are inferred (sudden disappearance of healthy animals, cries in the night, bones under a nest, monkey hairs in a scat) (Cheney and Wrangham 1987, Isbell 1990). For example, in her landmark study of relative effects of predation and resource competition on the social system of vervet monkeys, Isbell (1990) did not witness a single predation event even though the disappearance rate for females and juveniles was 65 percent, and the rate of predation was estimated at 45 percent.

Despite the paucity of direct observations, it is widely accepted (and Sussman et al. concur) that predation has been an important selection pressure on primates who have accordingly evolved anti-predator strategies that range from careful selection of sleeping locations and avoidance of dangerous habitats to vigilance, predator-specific alarm calls and sometimes cooperative defense (Cheney and Wrangham 1987). Arguing from the larger sample of observed infanticides, we note that there is a range of male, female, and even infant behaviors that only begin to make sense when we assume that infanticide, like predation, is a recurring threat, even if

the actual events are rarely witnessed. These include adult males who closely associate with the infants they have sired (van Schaik and Dunbar 1990), females with unweaned infants holding back in encounters with strange males or avoiding the boundaries of ranges altogether (Goodall 1986, van Schaik and Dunbar 1990), mothers who attempt to abandon their infants in the company of familiar ousted males rather than take infants with them back to a troop with an interloper in it, transformations of laissez-faire mothers into obsessively restrictive ones in the presence of strange males, mothers avoiding even attacking such interlopers (Hrdy 1977), female migrations into groups coinciding with lowest vulnerability to infanticide (Sterck submitted). These examples suggest to us that behavioral counterstrategies against infanticide are common and successful and help account for its infrequent occurrence in many species. Sussman et al. contest these behavioral observations by citing cases such as some langur females, who, under extreme pressure from an infanticidal male, abandon or cease to defend an infant. Instead, we view such cases as analogous with the well-documented Bruce effect in rodents, whereby a female mouse exposed to an alien male spontaneously resorbs the fetus; such females cut their losses by ceasing to invest on behalf of an infant almost certain to be killed.

## THE GENETIC BASIS

So far the criticism has focused on the quality and quantity of the evidence for infanticide in wild primates. Sussman et al. (1995) also argue that for the sexual selection hypothesis to make sense infanticidal tendencies must have some genetic basis, and that we know virtually nothing about this in primates. Indeed, the genetic basis for almost any behavioral trait in primates is unknown.

However, experimental studies on infanticidal behavior in small-bodied, short-lived, and fast-breeding rodents (Perrigo and vom Saal 1994) provide strong evidence that genes are involved.

Among rodents marked differences exist in tendencies to commit infanticide that vary between wild-caught and lab-bred strains (Jabukowski and Terkel 1982, Svare et al. 1984). Even in strains known to be highly infanticidal, researchers find pronounced intra- as well as inter-strain differences in probability that a male or female in a given test situation will kill an infant (Perrigo and vom Saal 1994, Svare et al. 1984). Hence a male mouse belonging to the highly inbred C57B1/6KJ strain in which individuals are almost genetically identical, introduced at the age of 65 days to a pup, responds infanticidally 70 percent of the time compared to 25 percent of the time in the case of males from another strain (e.g., DBA/2J). However, even in the extremely infanticidal lines, infanticidal behavior is still facultatively expressed according to circumstances. In a male mouse social status (e.g., dominant versus subordinate), reproductive status, as well as seemingly random developmental factors such as intrauterine position, can be critical (vom Saal 1984). Interestingly, exposure to testosterone in utero appears to have a sensitizing effect on the neural area mediating infanticide (vom Saal 1984), suggesting, as some of us have long suspected, that although some infant killing may well result as an incidental by-product of aggressive thrashing about as Sussman et al. argue, the kind of goal-directed infanticidal behavior being described (Hrdy 1977, Leland et al 1984, Sommer 1994) may best be understood as a separate motivational system from aggression.

As in primates, a male mouse's response towards infants is very context-specific, changing predictably from benevolent, soon after ejaculating with a given female, to infanticidal after the number of light/dark cycles needed to wean the pups has elapsed (Perrigo and vom Saal 1994). While the mechanisms may not be exactly similar in primates, the wealth of evidence from rodents underscores the presence and variability of genetic and other mechanisms underlying infanticide in a group that is more amenable to experimental manipulation. Sussman et al. (1995) ignore these experimental results, while deploring the absence of similar rigor among wild primates. Although it would be scientifically very satisfying to have similar data for primates, various constraints (time, money, and ethical concerns) will probably dictate that advances in this area will continue to come from non-primates.

## THE RESOLUTION OF SELECTION

As their final exhibit in the case against sexually selected infanticide, Sussman et al. (1995) claim that no selection on infanticide has been demonstrated, and "if it exists at all, is likely to be weak" (Bartlett et al. 1993). True, selection on the infant-killing phenotype has never been measured. The selection gradient, commonly used to predict evolutionary change in a trait, can be estimated as the regression of the relative fitness of individuals on their trait values within a population (Arnold and Wade 1984). In practice, there is a major hurdle, because its estimation requires complete behavior records over a male's adult life as well as estimated lifetime reproductive success. No primate data set even comes close to producing these data. Sussman et al. considered this demonstration important because they felt that infanticide is "but a rare and evolutionarily trivial phenomenon" (Bartlett et al. 1993). However, their assertion that selection on infanticide is rare flies in the face of abundant evidence for strong selection on rare alleles. Furthermore, for some other primate species, infanticide is neither rare nor inconsequential.

The question is, will the average adult male ever have the opportunity to commit infanticide during his lifetime? Among Jodhpur langurs, one-third of infants born are killed by males invading the breeding unit from outside it (Sommer 1994). Similarly, 14 percent of infant mountain gorillas are killed by males (Watts 1989), as are 12 percent of red howler infants (Crockett and Sekulic 1984). While the relative mortality risk due to infanticide may be lower in many other species and populations, such numbers indicate that males successful in gaining access to females will have multiple opportunities for infanticide, and that selection could therefore act on infanticidal behavior. These percentages are quite comparable to those of other mammals in which infanticide is common and in which the evidence that it is a significant selection pressure is overwhelming, such as lions (27 percent of all cub deaths in first year due to infanticide, Pusey and Packer 1994) and prairie dogs (39 percent of litters partly or totally killed, Hoogland 1994). In lions, DNA fingerprinting reveals that all cubs born in a pride are sired by the residents (Gilbert et al. 1991), so there can be little doubt that the reproductive benefits of infanticide accrue to the infanticidal males. These studies complement the primate studies and demonstrate that the perpetrators of infanticide can derive significant fitness benefits from it.

Infanticide may be a common cause of mortality, but if natural infant mortality is high or reduction in interbirth intervals is modest, benefits to infanticidal males will be diluted. However, among mammals, primates are characterized by slow life histories and relatively low infant mortality rates. Sussman et al. (1995) claim that the only indication of fitness differences we have are small decreases in interbirth intervals for females who lost infants relative to those who did not. They arrive at this conclusion largely on the basis of the Jodhpur results (Sommer 1994). However, because of provisioning, the Jodhpur langurs have the shortest interbirth interval of which the species is capable, virtually identical to captive animals fed ad lib. By contrast, in wild red howlers, females that lose their infants to observed and inferred infanticide have interbirth intervals 37 percent shorter than other adult females (Crockett and Sekulic 1984). Because of the typically short breeding tenure of males in most infanticidal primate species, even a small reduction in interbirth interval increases the likelihood that a new male will sire offspring before he is ousted, or his progeny are old enough to escape infanticide by the next male. Additional advantages may accrue, as an infanticidal male eliminates offspring sired by rivals as well as future competitors.

## Are There Plausible Alternatives?

The alternative proposed by Sussman et al. (1995) is that "most cases of infant killing appear to be simply inconsequential epiphenomena of aggressive episodes." This implies that there has been no selection for any increased tendency for males to eliminate unrelated infants. No doubt, infanticide might once have occurred as a by-product of males encountering unfamiliar females and some infanticides may still be best explained as incidental aggression. However, the deliberate targeting and stalking of infants belonging to unfamiliar females (Hrdy 1977, Leland et al. 1984, Pusey and Packer 1994, Sommer 1994), the widespread occurrence of the male takeover/infanticide pattern, as well as the experimental data on the timing of infanticide in relation to ejaculation in rodents, imply selection for specific responses. Hence, in various rodents, the act of ejaculation with a female partner (spontaneous ejaculation does not suffice) provides a male mouse with a neural fail-safe system for timing when it is safe versus possibly genetically suicidal to destroy pups that he encounters (vom Saal 1984). Such calibrations simply do not strike us as the stuff that "genetically inconsequential epiphenomena" are made of.

## Conclusion

Where infanticide is a major source of mortality, there is every reason to expect it to affect parental behavior and even social systems. Regardless of the functional significance, if infanticide is likely in certain circumstances and if a particular behavior minimizes their occurrence, we expect selection to favor the behavior. But can such selection actually shape primate social systems (van Schaik and Dunbar 1990)? The idea remains controversial for primates, but consider data for the dung beetle *Nichophorus orbicollis* (Scott 1990). After preparing a dung ball, parents deposit the eggs. Guarding by both biological parents dramatically reduces the probability that conspecifics will usurp the resource, kill the newly hatched brood and produce a replacement clutch. Such data strongly suggest that infanticide selects for biparental care in this species.

The continuing debate over infanticide among primates reflects two different world views, both of them defendable. Consider the following summation from Bartlett et al. (1993): "Clearly, proponents of the sexual selection hypothesis accept the fact that there is variation in takeover events, yet they maintain that there is an underlying consistency—infant killing follows group takeover. *Yet, while this may be true in general terms for many cases* (emphasis ours), the use of a single term to refer to the numerous phenomena described above misrepresents the complexity of primate social behavior. . . ." Precisely. While some are interested in emphasizing the uniqueness of each case—a valid position—others are driven by the need to seek for general patterns and to use theory to explain them. For the former it is an insult to the sanctity of the individual and the sacredness of context that generalizations should extend beyond the specifics of the case in hand. The latter derive their greatest pleasure from noting that so many findings could have been correctly predicted on the basis of pitifully incomplete data sets merely by relying on logic, comparisons, and extrapolations guided by evolutionary theory.

## References

Arnold, S. J.; Wade, M. J. (1984) "On the measurement of natural and sexual selection: Applications." *Evolution,* 38: 720–734.

Bartlett, T. Q.; Sussman, R. W.; Cheverud, J. M. (1993) "Infant killing in primates: A review of observed cases with specific reference to the sexual selection hypothesis." *Am. Anthrolpologist,* 95:958–990.

Cheney, D. L., Wrangham, R. W. (1987) "Predation." In *Primate Societies* (pp. 27–239). B. Smuts; D. Chaney; R. Seyfarth; R. W. Wrangham; T. T. Struhsaker, eds. Chicago: University of Chicago Press.

Crockett, C. M.; Sekulic, R. (1984) "Infanticide in red howler monkeys *(Alouatta seniculus).*" In *Infanticide: Comparative and Evolutionary Perspectives.* G. Hausfater and S. B. Hrdy, eds. New York: Aldine.

Darwin, C. (1871) *The Descent of Man, and Selection in Relation to Sex.* London: John Murray.

Gilbert, D.; Packer, C.; Pusey, A. E.; Stephens, J. C.; O'Brien, S. J. (1991) "Analytical DNA fingerprinting in lions: Parentage, genetic diversity, and kinship." *J. Hered.,* 82:378–386.

Goodall, J. (1986) *The Chimpanzees of Gombe: Patterns of Behavior.* Cambridge, MA: Harvard University Press.

Hoogland, J. L. (1994) "Nepotism and infanticide among prairie dogs." In *Infanticide and Parental Care* (pp. 321–337). S. Parmigiani and F. vom Saal, eds. London: Harwood Academic Publishers.

Hrdy, S. B. (1977) *The Langurs of Abu: Female and Male Strategies of Reproduction.* Cambridge, MA: Harvard University Press.

Hrdy, S. B. (1979) "Infanticide among animals: A review, classification, and examination of the implications for the reproductive strategies of females." *Ethol. Sociobiol.,* 1:13–40.

Hrdy, S. B.; Hausfater, G. (1984) "Comparative and evolutionary perspectives on infanticide: Introduction and overview." In *Infanticide: Comparative and Evolutionary Perspectives* (pp. xiii–xxxv). G. Hausfater and S. B. Hrdy, eds. New York: Aldine.

Isbell, L. (1994) "Sudden short-term increase in mortality of vervet monkeys *(Ceropithecus aethiops)* due to leopard predation in Amboseli National Park, Kenya." *Am. J. Primatol.,* 21:41–52.

Jabukowski, M.; Terkel, J. (1982) "Infanticide and caretaking in non-lactating *Mus musclulus:* Influence of genotype, family group and sex." *Anim. Behav.* 30:1029–1035.

Leland, L.; Struhsaker, T. T.; Butynski, T. (1984) "Infanticide by adult males in three primate species of Kibale Forest, Uganda." In *Infanticide: Comparative and Evolutionary Perspectives* (pp. 151–172). G. Hausfater and S. B. Hrdy, eds. New York: Aldine.

Newton, P. N. (1986) "Infanticide in an undisturbed forest population of Hanuman langurs, *Presbytis entellus.*" *Anim. Behav.,* 34:785–789. For effects of male replacement see Sugiyama, Y. (1965) "On the social change of Hanuman langurs *(Presbytis entellus)* in their natural conditions." *Primates,* 6:213–217. See also Washburn, S., Hamburg, D. A. (1968) "Aggressive behavior in Old World monkeys and apes." In *Primates.* P. Jay, ed. New York: Holt, Rinehart, & Winston.

Parmigiani, S., vom Saal, F. (1994) *Infanticide and Parental Care.* London: Harwood Academic Publishers.

Perrigo, G., vom Saal, F. (1994) "Behavioral cycles in the neural timing of infanticide and parental behavior in male house in mice." In *Infanticide and Parental Care* (pp. 365–396) S. Parmigiani and F. vom Saal eds. London: Harwood Academic Publishers.

Pusey, A. E.; Packer, C. (1994) "Infanticide in lions: Consequences and counterstrategies." In *Infanticide and Parental Care* (pp. 277–300). S. Parmigiani and F. vom Saal, eds. London: Harwood Academic Publishers.

Scott, M. P. (1990) "Brood guarding and the evolution of male parental care in burying beetles." *Behav. Ecol. Sociobiol.,* 26:31–39.

Sommer, V. (1994) "Infanticide among the langurs of Jodhpur. Testing the sexual selection hypothesis with a long-term record." In *Infanticide and Parental Care* (pp. 155–198). S. Parmigiani and F. vom Saal, eds. London: Harwood Academic Publishers.

Sterck, E. H. M. (submitted) *Determinants of female transfer in Thomas' langurs.*

Sussman, R. W., Cheverud, J. M., Bartlett, T. Q. (1995) "Infant killing as an evolutionary strategy." *Evol. Anthropol.* 3:149–151.

Svare, B.; Broida, J.; Kinsley, C.; Mann, M. (1984) "Psychobiological determinants underlying infanticide in mice." In *Infanticide: Comparative and Evolutionary Perspectives* (pp. 387–400). G. Hausfater and S. B. Hrdy, eds. New York: Aldine. See also Elwood, R., Kennedy, H. F. (1994) "Selective allocation of parental and infanticidal responses in rodents: a review of mechanisms." In *Infanticide and Parental Care* (pp. 397–426). S. Parmigiani and vom Saal, eds. Switzerland: Harwood.

van Schaik, C. P.; Dunbar, R. I. M. (1990) "The evolution of monogamy in large primates: A new hypothesis and some crucial tests." *Behavior,* 115:30–62.

vom Saal, F. (1984) "Proximate and ultimate causes of parental behavior in male house mice." In *Infanticide: Comparative and Evolutionary Perspectives* (pp. 491–524) G. Hausfater and S. B. Hrdy, eds. New York: Aldine.

Watts, D. P. (1989) "Infanticide in mountain gorillas. New cases and a reconsideration of the evidence." *Ethology,* 81:1–18.

# Chapter 49

# *How the Human Got Its Spots*

## Henry D. Schlinger, Jr.

*A critical analysis of the just-so stories of evolutionary psychology.*

In 1902 Rudyard Kipling published a children's book of stories and poems with the curious title, *Just So Stories.* They included such natural curiosities as "How the Elephant Got Its Trunk," "How the Rhinoceros Got Its Skin," and "How the Leopard Got Its Spots." The stories, of course, are pure fantasy, and "just-so stories" has become a critical cliche for similarly fanciful tales that attempt to explain nature. The new field of evolutionary psychology, while different in many respects from its predecessor sociobiology, is still subject to the accusation of telling just-so stories.

As a sampling from this new science, the following are headlines from recent articles or reviews of various books appealing to evolutionary explanations of human behavior:

> *Cheating Husband: Blame It on His Genes?*
> *Is There a Gene for Compassion?*
> *Is Prejudice Hereditary?*
> *A Scientist Weighs Evidence That the X Chromosome May Carry a Gene for Gayness.*
> *IQ: Is It Destiny?*

Headlines such as these are meant to capture the attention and imagination of readers, and they usually do. They suggest that the books to which they refer are going to offer serious scientific evidence for their claims of an evolutionary explanation of much human social and intellectual behavior. Do these claims reflect the results of serious science or just more "pop sociobiology," as Kitcher (1985) calls it?

Most books on sociobiology appeared in the decade between about 1975 and 1985. Barash's 1977 *So-*ciobiology and Human Behavior, Lumsden and Wilson's 1983 *Promethean Fire,* and especially E. O. Wilson's two great works, *Sociobiology: The New Synthesis* (1975) and *On Human Nature* (1978), created a new field of study of human behavior that forcefully challenged the hegemony of behavioral psychology that had reigned so long. Despite the existence of serious critical analyses of sociobiology (e.g., Bock 1980, Futuyma 1979, Gould 1981, Kitcher 1985, Sahlins 1976), in the past few years, there has been an explosion of books offering evolutionary explanations for a variety of human behaviors, including intelligence, mortality, mating, sexual preference, aggression, xenophobia, prejudice, and even our tendency to seek out various forms of nature, such as trips to zoos and visits to national parks. These books may be classified according to two distinct but related arguments about the evolution of human behavior: (1) individuals and groups that differ behaviorally in some way (e.g., IQ), do so because of underlying genetic differences; and (2) invariant, universal human traits (e.g., morality, aggression) represent fixed expressions of the human genome (Futuyma 1979).

Recent books that argue for genetic differences between groups of humans with respect to such characteristics as intelligence include *The Bell Curve: Intelligence and Class Structure in American Life* (1994) by Herrnstein and Murray, *Race, Evolution, and Behavior* (1995a) by Rushton, and *The Decline of Intelligence in America: A Strategy for National Renewal* (1994) in Itzkoff. Books that make the case that there are distinctly human behaviors—collectively called human nature—that reflect a uniquely human evolutionary history, include *Homicide* (1988) by Daly and Wilson, *The Biophilia Hypothesis* (1993) edited by Kellert and Wilson, *The Moral Animal* (1994) by Wright, *The Evolution of Desire* (1994) by Buss,

From *Skeptic,* Vol. 4, No. 1, 1996.

*Why We Get Sick: The New Science of Darwinian Medicine* (1994) by Nesse and Williams, *Eve's Rib: The Biological Roots of Sex Differences* (1994) by Poole, *The Science of Desire: The Search for the Gay Gene and the Biology of Behavior* (1994) by Hamer and Copeland, and *The Adapted Mind* (1992) by Barkow, Cosmides, and Tooby.

Both arguments on the evolution of animal behavior rely to varying degrees on a combination of three types of supporting evidence:

1. Evolutionary logic supported by casual observations or statistical data.
2. Behavioral analogies and comparisons with animals.
3. Statistical analyses of data generated by non-experimental research methods.

Each of these types of evidence, while sometimes compelling and frequently interesting, is often flawed scientifically. This does not mean that the explanations themselves are wrong, only that the supporting evidence is insufficient. In many instances, an alternative, and much more plausible approach to understanding human behavior is that rather than selecting for specialized behavioral traits, human evolutionary history has selected for behavioral plasticity, or learning capacity (Futuyma 1979). Experimental evidence from the literature on learning shows overwhelmingly the powerful influence of the environment in shaping human behavioral similarities and differences.

In the present chapter I describe the three types of evidence with supporting examples from both evolutionary positions on human behavior and then critique them according to certain methodological criteria. I argue that, in most cases, a much more cautious and scientifically defensible position on the origin of many human behaviors is that they are a function of individual environmental, and not evolutionary, history.

## Evolutionary Logic

One of the hallmarks of the scientific method is the interpretation of phenomena that have not been subjected to experimental analysis. Scientific interpretation is the use of already established principles of science to explain novel instances of the subject matter. Hence, the logical or mathematical use of Darwinian principles of selection to interpret human behavior could have a sound basis in science. The main question is whether the interpretations of human behavior as presented in recent books and articles represent an appropriate extension of Darwinian theory.

Theorists from both positions on the evolution of human behavior cite examples of evolutionary logic and supporting data that are problematic. Theorists who emphasize genetic differences between groups of humans (races) have employed evolutionary logic to explain differences in intelligence (Herrnstein and Murray 1994, Itzkoff 1994, Rushton 1995a), brain and head size and aggressiveness (Rushton 1995a), among other traits. Evolutionary psychologists have used evolutionary logic to explain, among other things, why people kill one another (Daly and Wilson 1988), why mothers who have just given birth seem to mention their neonate's resemblance to the father more than to themselves (Daly and Wilson 1982), why social rejection may produce feelings of insecurity (Wright 1995), and why people seek out zoos and parks and easily develop phobias to natural objects, like spiders (Wilson 1993). The data cited by these theorists consist of casual observation, personal reflection, and anecdote, as well as statistics derived from non-experimental studies. To illustrate, consider an example of the use of evolutionary logic from each of the two positions on the evolution of human behavior.

Rushton (1995a) uses evolutionary logic to support his claim that human racial groups evolved under conditions where different environmental pressures selected for differences in a wide range of physical and intellectual characteristics. Rushton suggests an *r-K* reproductive strategy analysis combined with information on human evolution can be used to understand important behavioral differences between Mongoloids, Caucasoids, and Negroids, as he calls them. The *r*-strategies are those with high reproductive rates, and the *K*-strategies are those with high levels of parental investment in offspring. According to Rushton (1995a), "Mongoloid people are more *K*-selected than Caucasoids, who, in turn, are more *K*-selected than Negroids" (p. xiii). In other words, Mongoloids invest relatively more in the care of their offspring than Caucasoids who invest relatively more in the care of their offspring than Negroids. Rushton appeals to evolutionary logic to explain the presence of these different *r-K* strategies in different human racial groups. Specifically, Rushton claims that the selection pressures in the hot African savanna, where Negroids evolved, were far different in terms of the required relationship between parental investment and high reproductive rates than selection pressures in the cold Arctic environment where Mongoloids evolved. Presumably, higher reproductive rates and lower rates of parental investment are more favorable in hotter climates, whereas the opposite is true in colder climates. According to Rushton, this is the evolutionary basis for the differences in *r-K* reproductive strategies supposedly observed in humans.

The first problem with Rushton's analysis concerns the reliability of the data offered to support his evolutionary logic. For example, he provides a table of the relative ranking of races on diverse variables such as physical maturation rate, including age of first sexual intercourse and pregnancy; reproductive effort, including relative frequency of two-egg twinning and of intercourse; personality, including aggressiveness and impulsivity; brain size; and intelligence (Rushton, 1995a, 1995b). The data for these rankings were generated by nonexperimental research methods where average differences between groups were often very small. Moreover, there is no scientific evidence, other than correlations, to support many of Rushton's assumptions, including his assumption that brain size is functionally related to cognitive ability.

Rushton often relies on statistical analyses of aggregated data to bolster his claim that small differences between groups are significant. Even if we assume that the data cited by Rushton were derived from well-designed and well-controlled studies—a questionable assumption—his evolutionary interpretation of the data has several attendant problems. First, there is no way to test and thereby falsify his claim that these characteristics represent evolutionary adaptations. Rushton's evolutionary logic is not too dissimilar from that used by his sociobiological predecessors, as summarized by Futuyma (1979). He has simply imagined that higher reproductive rates and lower rates of parental investment must have conferred differential fitness in different climates, compared the predicted outcome with observations from correlational studies, and then concluded that these characteristics represent adaptive genetic traits. A second problem with Rushton's hypothesis is that his extension of the *r-K* reproductive strategy analysis (usually used to compare large differences between different species) to the small variations between groups within the human species, represents a "fatal scientific error" by assuming that behavioral differences between groups within one species can be accounted for by genetic differences (Tavris 1995). It is not even clear that behavioral differences between *individuals* reflect genetic differences or, if they do, to what extent (Futuyma 1979). A third problem is that Rushton's concept of race, which reflects that of Western culture—based on a few physical features such as skin color, hair form, and the epicanthal fold—is subjective (Futuyma 1979). And finally, any reliable differences in Rushton's data are just as likely to be due to environmental variables as genetic ones. Still, Rushton (1995a) boldly contends that his book will offer "new truths about racial group differences."

Consider, now, an example of how evolutionary logic might be used to interpret some human characteristic from the perspective of evolutionary psychology. Robert Wright, a science journalist writing in *The New Yorker* (March 1995), illustrates how evolutionary psychologists would approach the explanation of some presumably universal human behavioral trait. Suppose, Wright asks, that social rejection early in a person's life results in an enduring insecurity. According to Wright, we should ask whether this pattern "might have had a genetic payoff during evolution" (p. 71). Presumably, our ancestors who faced such rejection were less likely to reproduce unless they became more socially vigilant about nourishing their social ties as a result of the insecurity. Insecurity as a response to social rejection, then, may have been reproductively advantageous for humans. The assumptions inherent in Wright's argument can be stated as follows: (1) Human evolutionary history has selected a genetic "program" that is somehow sensitive to environmental input called "social rejection," (2) this genetic program is especially sensitive to input early in an individual's life, and (3) the behavioral response called insecurity is essentially the same for all people to this input.

There are several obvious problems with this example that are relevant to many such examples cited by evolutionary psychologists. The first problem is with the validity of the behavioral data. Wright simply assumes that insecurity, which is not objectively defined, is a general human response to early social rejection, which is also not objectively defined. Wright offers no evidence that this evolutionary model is based on precise behavioral observations. Rather, his analysis is based on common sense assumptions about human nature that have no scientific basis. A second problem deals with Wright's evolutionary interpretation of the data. Even if such a reaction could be precisely measured and were observed in most humans as a result of a precisely defined set of environmental inputs, an evolutionary interpretation that it was adaptive is untestable because there is no crucial test that can falsify the hypothesis (Futuyma 1979). Finally, an evolutionary explanation of the pattern of behavior in Wright's example may not be the most parsimonious one. For example, it might be that the reaction to rejection that we refer to as "feelings of insecurity" might be a more general psychological response to the withholding or withdrawal of reinforcement following some behavior. The effect of such environmental operations is to simultaneously produce physiological responses and to alter the stimuli that define the situation such that they suppress the behavior under similar circumstances. These are the scientific principles of *operant extinction* and *punishment*. The "feeling of insecurity" may be a by-product of the withholding or withdrawal of reinforcement with no special selective advantage of its own.

## CROSS-SPECIES COMPARISONS

A second type of evidence frequently used to support evolutionary explanations of human similarities and differences consists of analogies or comparisons between nonhuman and human behavior. It is common linguistic practice among humans, including scientists, to give names to things. When two or more forms of behavior are given the same name, it may seem reasonable to assume that they are alike functionally as well. Kitcher (1985) points out that because we have such a rich vocabulary for describing human behavior, it is easy to use this vocabulary to describe nonhuman behavior that resembles it. Once described in similar ways, it becomes easier to then move freely from the nonhuman instance back to the superficially similar human instance and to assume that both result from similar processes. According to Kitcher (1985), "vulgar anthropomorphism" is the original sin of pop sociobiologists, in that they neglect to "investigate the kinship of forms of behavior that are superficially similar" (p. 185). Even if scientists discovered a genetic basis for a behavior in an animal, which is rare, this does not mean that the human behavior that appears to be similar also has a genetic basis. As evolutionary biologists know, phenotypic similarity does not necessarily imply genotypic similarity.

Social theorists, like Rushton, who emphasize genetic differences between groups of humans typically point to between-species differences that are more than likely a function of differences in genes to make the case that within-species differences in humans are also a function of differences in genes. Rushton (1995a) employs an interesting kind of cross-species analogy to make the case for the genetic basis of human racial differences. First, he points out that significant differences in learning ability *between species* are due to genetic differences. Thus, mammals with larger brains, such as chimpanzees, rhesus monkeys, and spider monkeys, learn faster than mammals with smaller brains, such as marmosets, cats, gerbils, rats, and squirrels. Rushton then uses these comparisons to argue that *within-species* differences in human brain or head size are related to differences in intelligence, at least as measured by standardized IQ tests, and are likewise related to genetic differences. Rushton's ultimate point is that blacks have statistically smaller heads (and brains) than whites and that this correlates positively with differences in intelligence between the two groups, at least as measured by standardized tests. It is interesting to note that of the 32 studies summarized by Rushton on head size and intelligence in humans, most found low correlations.

Rushton takes a reasonable between-species example and extends it to an insupportable within-species difference. Even if the measurements of brain size and intelligence can be defended as reliable, Rushton's explanation of the behavioral differences is not the most parsimonious one, especially when one considers the myriad differences in environments on average between black and white children. Before genetic explanations of differences in learning ability between individuals or groups are proffered, environmental factors, such as nutrition, prenatal care, learning, and educational opportunities, should be investigated if, for no other reason than the variables are easier to test.

Another example of questionable cross-species analogizing by Rushton (1995a) concerns the *r-K* reproductive strategies described previously. According to

Rushton, the great apes exemplify the extreme end of the *K*-strategy because they produce one infant every five or six years and provide much parental care. At the other extreme are oysters who exemplify the *r*-strategy, producing 500 million eggs a year but providing no parental care. Although this scale is generally used to compare the life histories of widely disparate species, Rushton (1995a) applies it to the much smaller variations within the human species. Although Rushton believes that all humans are *K*-selected relative to other species, he also believes that some humans may be more so than others. He cites data showing that, compared to white women, black women average a shorter period of ovulation and produce more eggs per ovulation, which is evidenced by their comparatively higher rate of two-egg twinning. His data also show that black women have comparatively lower intelligence than white women as measured by standardized tests. Rushton claims that the correlation between IQ and biological variables related to reproduction supports his view that the within-species variations in humans can be accounted for in the same way that between-species variations can. Even if the correlation can be proven to be valid, there are serious problems with Rushton's cross-species comparison. First, there is no biological justification for extending an analysis of between-species differences to within-species differences. Second, Rushton provides no evidence other than correlations that differences in IQ and certain biological variables between women represent adaptations resulting from natural selection. Third, simply demonstrating a correlation between two or more variables in no way clarifies causal relations.

Evolutionary psychologists, like their sociobiological predecessors, frequently employ cross-species analogies and comparisons to argue their case for the existence of universal human characteristics. For example, Daly and Wilson (1988) use an analogy with female ground squirrels to show how the concept of inclusive fitness may be used to understand sibling rivalry in humans. They argue that genetic relationship should be important to solidarity and social conflict. In other words, the closer the family relationship between two individuals, the more solidarity and the less conflict should exist between them. Daly and Wilson point out that such a theory has been tested in female ground squirrels who discriminate between their full sisters and half sisters when occupying adjacent territories as adults. Full sisters will apparently help each other whereas half sisters will exhibit more territorial aggression. They then suggest that the same prediction can be made with regard to human siblings; namely, that the intensity of sibling rivalry should reflect the likelihood of common paternity. In other words, full siblings should show less competition than half siblings. In their own words, "we might have evolved specialized psychological mechanisms whose function is to assess the likelihood of common paternity and to adjust the intensity of sibling competition accordingly," and some "psychologist should check it out" (1988, p. 11).

Cross-species analogies, such as the one offered by Daly and Wilson (1988), are intriguing suggesting as they do, that certain human characteristics that we seem to have in common with other species may be understood as part of our deeper human nature. There are serious problems with such analogies, however. The first problem is that the similarity between human and nonhuman behaviors is subjective and is only suggested *after* it is believed that there may be a common genetic basis for both. In other words, behavioral similarity is often in the eyes of the beholder. Who is to say that territorial aggression among ground squirrels is anything but superficially similar to disagreements or fights among human half-siblings? The causes of these similar behaviors could be completely different. A second problem is that even if the behavior of human siblings could be compared to female ground squirrels, there is no independent evidence for the existence of an evolved "psychological mechanism" or any suggestion as to how it would work to "assess the likelihood of common paternity and to adjust the intensity of sibling competition accordingly." In the absence of such a suggestion, based on some kind of objective scientific evidence rather than inferences, Daly and Wilson's explanation is simply hypothetical.

Futuyma (1979) has pointed out several other problems with cross-species analogies. For example, even if behavioral generalizations could be supported by reliable observations, we are still left with the nagging question of whether behaviors between species that are superficially similar are functionally similar; that is, whether the same processes are responsible for both. If we discover the genetic bases of territorial aggression in female ground squirrels, does this mean that behaviors we refer to as "human sibling rivalry" also have a genetic basis? A simpler approach would be to consider first whether other factors, such as environmental ones, could produce the human behaviors of interest. Such an approach might lead us to ask, for example, whether there is as much sibling rivalry between half-siblings who are raised together from birth or infancy and who are not aware of their genetic relationship to each other as there is between siblings who know they are half-siblings. Other than the interesting evolutionary theorizing that superficially similar behaviors in different species may be functionally similar, evolutionary psychologists offer no direct scientific evidence that they are.

## CORRELATIVE ANALYSIS

It should be noted that social evolutionary theorists typically do not conduct experiments, nor do they, in most instances, cite experimental data. Rather, they rely almost exclusively on a combination of anecdotal and statistical evidence to make their case that there are species-specific behaviors in humans. Moreover, in almost no case is direct genetic evidence used to support evolutionary theories of human behavior (see below). Since genes are identified as playing a causal role in important similarities and differences between humans, a true experimental test of the hypothesis would necessarily involve direct manipulation of genes as independent variables. Such manipulations are only carried out by geneticists and, for obvious reasons, they have been constrained in such endeavors to working with relatively simple organisms, such as fruit flies with extremely short gestation periods, where the focus is more on structural than behavioral characteristics. Those who write about the genetic bases of human behaviors are typically not geneticists, however. And because they cannot make their genetic case experimentally, these evolutionary theorists must rely on data generated by nonexperimental, usually correlational, research methods. There are several problems with the ways in which some evolutionary theorists use correlative analysis.

### Validity and Reliability of the Data

The first problem is that the validity and reliability of the methods used to generate the actual data are often questionable E. O. Wilson (1993) states that one mode of testing an evolutionary hypothesis "is the correlative analysis of knowledge and attitudes of peoples in diverse cultures" (p. 34). Knowledge and attitudes, poorly defined as they are, must be obtained from surveys and questionnaires. Methodological problems with such devices are well known among researchers. For instance, there are numerous ways in which research bias may affect the outcome, such as the sampling procedure used and the way in which questions on surveys and questionnaires are worded. Even when safeguards are included, inferences to larger populations (the ultimate goal of surveys or questionnaires) are questionable. Also, as most good researchers know, the reliability of verbal self reports is notoriously poor.

In addition to surveys and questionnaires, evolutionary theorists may use psychological tests to assess more general and presumably universal characteristics of populations. Rushton (1995a) provides an example of the use of such a test. His thesis of racial differences is based on the assumption that there is "a core of human nature" or character traits "around which individuals and groups consistently" differ. To wit, he cites a study conducted in the 1920s by Hartshome and May called the "Character Education Enquiry" in which 11,000 elementary and high school students were given a battery of 33 different tests of altruism, self-control, and honesty in various contexts (home, school, church, etc.). Children's reputations with teachers and classmates are also obtained and then correlated with the scores on the battery of tests. Notwithstanding the problems with questionnaires, the only behavior measured by such tests is that of answering questions on the test. The actual behaviors called "altruistic" or "honest" are not measured in the context wherein one would normally call them altruistic or honest. This is not to say that we cannot discern something of value with such tests, but only that the test may correlate poorly with the behaviors of interest, and only a direct experimental approach can potentially yield a scientific understanding of the behaviors.

Of course, the most notorious type of test cited in the literature on evolutionary theories of human behavior is the IQ test. Volumes have been written on problems with intelligence tests, and I will not repeat them here. Suffice it to say that one problem with such tests is what they purport to measure. Rather than measuring some qualitatively distinct structure or process as defenders of such tests would have us believe, intelligence tests literally measure only the correctness of a variety of learned behaviors—answers to questions on the test—in a contrived context—the test-taking situation (Schlinger 1992). Alfred Binet knew this when he developed the first modern intelligence test (although he eschewed the use of the term "intelligence" in favor of the more descriptive and neutral, "intellectual level"). The challenge for serious scientists is to ask about the variables that affect the broad range of behaviors we describe as *intelligent;* and only an experimental analysis can answer such questions.

### The Use of Statistics

A second problem with the use of correlative analyses by evolutionary theorists concerns the complex statistical tests employed to "make sense" of the data generated by surveys, questionnaires, psychological tests, and the like. The importance of correlative analyses in making the argument for genetic explanations of human behavior is underscored in the following quotation by Sir Francis Galton, which Rushton twice cited (1995a, 1995b):

> General impressions are never to be trusted. Unfortunately when they are of long standing they become fixed rules of life, and assume a prescriptive right not to be questioned. Consequently, those who are not accustomed to original inquiry entertain a hatred and a horror of statistics. They cannot endure the idea of submitting their sacred impressions to cold-blooded verification. But it is the triumph of scientific men to rise superior to such superstitions, to devise tests by which the value of beliefs may be ascertained, and to feel sufficiently masters of themselves to discard contemptuously whatever may be found untrue.

The most obvious problem with this quote and the approach to the study of individual differences that it fostered is the equation of statistics, in the absence of ex-

perimentation, with scientific practice. Although we may debate the role of inferential statistics in the natural sciences, it is true that Galton's quote predated the application of the experimental method to the behavior of organisms by psychologists (e.g., Skinner, 1938). Rushton (1995a) and Herrnstein and Murray (1994), however, consider Galton to be the intellectual and scientific father of their genetic theories of racial differences. Rushton calls Galton "the originator of *scientific* research on individual differences" (1995a, p. 10, italics added). Herrnstein and Murray, who refer to the Galtonian tradition of intelligence testing as "the classic tradition," claim: "By accepted standards of what constitutes scientific evidence and scientific proof, that classic tradition has in our view given the world a treasure of information . . . " (1994, p. 19). This is especially interesting coming from a scientist such as Herrnstein whose own scientific output consists almost exclusively of the use of within-subject experimental designs.

Authors such as Herrnstein, Murray, and Rushton point out that while individual scores on behavioral or psychological tests, for instance IQ tests, correlate poorly, the correlations become much higher when scores are aggregated. The principle of aggregation, according to Herrnstein and Murray (1994), is where the classic (Galtonian) tradition has the most to offer. The rationale for aggregating data is that "randomness in any one measure (error and specificity variance) is averaged out . . . leaving a clearer view of what a person's true behavior is like" (Rushton 1995a, p. 19). Also, relationships between individual tests or between scores on tests are more likely to emerge. Thus, aggregating data is supposed to correct for any errors in the actual measurement of the variable(s) in question. The contradiction in this line of reasoning is that the further away one gets from the behavior of the individual, the less can be said about the individual. Herrnstein and Murray acknowledge that the practice of aggregating data does not necessarily permit the prediction, much less the understanding, of individual behavior. More importantly, aggregating data from different tests, or, worse, from different studies, is fraught with so many methodological problems as to render the results meaningless. For example, aggregating data masks differences in methodology (e.g., time, place, populations, sampling procedures, control procedures, measurement tools, etc.). Aggregating data, especially from different studies, can only mean that the results of any individual study were so equivocal that no conclusions could be drawn. Pooling data from different studies is only valid if the studies are methodologically interchangeable, which, as I have implied, is a questionable assumption in the present case. Nevertheless, Rushton (1995a) describes instances where low correlations between individual tests were raised by aggregating data from many different tests as if this were sound scientific practice.

In criticizing formalized methods of research and statistics, B. F. Skinner (1972) advocated the use of the experimental method in the study of human behavior. Each approach leads to a different strategy for dealing with measurement error. In contrast to the strategy of aggregating scores from many individuals to increase the statistical reliability of the measurement device (e.g., IQ test) or the sensitivity of the statistical method (e.g., t-test), Skinner (1972) argued for refining direct experimental control over the behavior of individual subjects. In this way, the reliability of the independent variables is enhanced and sources of variability are eliminated *before* measurements are made rather than after, as is the case when researchers aggregate data. As Skinner (1972) wrote tongue-in-cheek, "No one goes to the circus to see the average dog jump through a hoop significantly oftener than untrained dogs raised under the same circumstances . . . " (p. 114).

### Interpreting the Data

A third problem with the use of correlative analyses involves the interpretation of the data. Demonstrating that a correlation exists between two or more variables does not in any way clarify causal relations, although it may hint at possible ones. There is an oft-cited dictum among researchers: "Correlation does not imply causation" (Neale and Liebert 1973). A correlation between two or more variables is often due to an unspecified process, or "third variable." Those who argue for an evolutionary explanation of human behavior appeal to a third variable—the humane genome. Although it is theoretically possible that some human social and intellectual behaviors represent fixed expressions of the human genome, a better explanation for the behaviors in question is one in which a different third variable is implicated—the environmental histories of individuals. In many of the examples cited by social evolutionary theorists, any one or more of the multitudinous environmental variables found in the individual histories of the subjects studied may produce the reported correlations. Just as behavioral similarities between individuals may reflect genotypical similarity, they may just as easily reflect environmental similarity. The correlational evidence offered by evolutionary theorists is simply insufficient to distinguish the biological from the environmental position. The challenge for scientists is to tease apart these possible determinants of behavior, and this cannot be accomplished using correlational methods. Only an experimental analysis can potentially reveal the variable of which human behavior is a function. Galton got it wrong. The "triumph of scientific men" occurs not when human behavior can be subjected to statistical correlation, but rather when it can be subjected to direct experimentation.

Whether one conducts experimental or correlational research in the first place reflects fundamental differences in the types of questions asked. And the types of questions asked reveal differences in the motivations of the researchers. Many authors who either conduct and/or cite correlational research on the relation between behavioral and genetic differences and similarities between groups of humans, do so to show what they already believe—that genetics plays a significant role in such characteristics as intelligence, aggression, and reproductive behavior. Hubbard and Wald (1994) have noted that "scientists only look for genetic components in behaviors which their society considers important and probably hereditary" (p. 93). For instance, they point out that even though European peoples read from left to right, whereas Semitic peoples read from right to left, no one has suggested that these are inherent racial differences. As Futuyma said (p. 473):

> The history of scientists' pronouncements on human genetics and behavior is, to a distressing extent, a history of the conventional societal attitudes on these subjects; science has served more as a defense of the *status quo* than as a force for change.

## GENES

I have referred to the social theorizing discussed in this paper as evolutionary, and such a conception implicitly recognizes that what has evolved due to natural selection is a particular genotype that is different from other possible genotypes. In short, evolutionary theories are genetic theories and, as such, we should expect some supporting genetic evidence. According to Kitcher (1985), physical characteristics most susceptible to rigorous genetic analysis are not those that social evolutionary theorists find most interesting. For example, it was recently reported that scientists at the University of Basel in Switzerland have discovered the master control gene responsible for eye development in fruit flies. The scientists have been able to manipulate the gene directly so as to produce eyes in unusual places, like on the legs and thorax. Human geneticists, by comparison, are relegated to studying genetic variation that produces deleterious effects, such as metabolic disorders and defects in color vision. In other words, human geneticists are unable to manipulate the actual genes and must wait for natural genetic variation to produce outcomes that they can then investigate. The genetic evidence most often cited by social evolutionary theorists comes from the field of behavior genetics. Contrary to their name, behavior geneticists do not directly study genes. Rather, they are constrained to examining correlations between poorly defined variables such as scores on intelligence or other psychological tests and family relationships. The reliability of the observations and measurements reported by behavior geneticists is questionable because of the many methodological problems inherent in such research. For example, several authors have pointed out problems with subject selection in research on separated identical twins (e.g., Horgan, 1993; Hubbard and Wald, 1994; Kamin, 1974; Lewontin et al. 1984). Moreover, the fact that conclusions about the differences in genes must be based on family resemblance introduces a well-known confound: Family members resemble each other not only because they share genes but also because they share environments. Despite the perception that behavior geneticists have made impressive gains in demonstrating the genetic bases for a wide range of human conditions, such as aggression, homosexuality, intelligence, schizophrenia, and alcoholism, there have been an equal number of serious methodological critiques which, at the very least, temper the claims by behavioral geneticists (e.g., Byne 1994, Horgan 1993, Hubbard and Wald 1994, Kamin 1974, Lewontin et al. 1984).

Some social evolutionary theorists argue their case based on a flawed interpretation of evolutionary genetic logic. For example, Itzkoff (1985), who is neither an evolutionary biologist nor a geneticist, presents a case for the evolution of human intelligence as a function of the natural selection of the human brain. Itzkoff reasons that because so many biochemical combinations are involved in the growth and patterns of brain structure, slight variations can exist between close relatives and large variations between relatively isolated groups of humans. He concludes: "The brain evolved along a wide diversity of lines" producing differences in both "the quantity and quality of intelligence" (p. 23). He presents this rationale to support his claim that different groups of humans (blacks and whites) come into the world with different genetic potentials for intelligence. There are serious flaws in Itzkoff's reasoning, the most fatal of which is that there is simply insufficient evidence to support his conclusions that normal variation in intelligence has a genetic basis. Moreover, his argument is based on the assumption that there exists genetic variation within populations of humans, and that selection has operated differently in different human groups even though "there is insufficient evidence to conclude that normal variation in human behavioral traits has a genetic basis" (Futuyma 1979). Finally, there is a broader principle of genetics that is often not fully appreciated by many social evolutionary theorists, as Futuyma notes (p. 476):

> One cannot say that a universal trait . . . is either genetic or environmental, for *it it's the expression of genes in a series of environments.* Genetics provides no means of investigating the inheritance of an invariant trait. Thus to postulate that it's genetic is to pose an untestable and meaningless hypothesis. The only question one can legitimately ask is, Is the trait highly canalized, or does it vary greatly under different environmental conditions, compared to other traits?

If certain behavioral traits, such as aggression, sibling rivalry, sex-role behavior, or intelligence were highly canalized, then, according to Futuyma, we would not expect them to be modifiable by environmental factors.

## ENVIRONMENT

Contrary to most traditional conceptions of the environment, scientists who study the functional relationship between the behavior of organisms and environmental variables—behavior analysts—define *environment* functionally as all of the stimuli that enter into functional relationships with an organism's behavior at any one time (Schlinger 1995). Behavior analysts view the environment as consisting of energy changes (stimuli) of various sorts that not only affect the sensory receptors of organisms but, more importantly, affect their behavior. Thus, the environment is not defined necessarily by its structure prior to the study of behavior, but rather after functional relations have been established by experimentation. In other words, behavior analysts define environment by how it functions to control behavior. The environmental history of an individual represents one category of ultimate behavioral causation; the other being the evolutionary history of the species to which the individual belongs.

Over the last 50 years, scientists who study learning have amassed volumes of testable, repeatable, experimental data demonstrating the powerful influence of environmental manipulations on a wide range of behaviors. Several scientific journals are devoted almost exclusively to direct experimentation on the effects of the environment. The *Journal of the Experimental Analysis of Behavior,* for example, has produced almost 40 years of data, including direct and systematic replication experiments. In none of these instances are data aggregated in order to achieve criteria of significance. In fact, in many experiments, little, if any, statistical analysis is needed to verify the reliability of the results. Internal validity is demonstrated time and time again by direct within-experiment refinement and control of objective independent variables. External validity of these findings has been consistently shown over the same 40-year period by successfully applying the scientific principles discovered in the experimental laboratory to problem human behavior. For example, the *Journal of Applied Behavior Analysis* has produced almost 30 years of experimental research on human behavioral problems, including compliance, crying, social interaction, cooperation, aggression, walking, reading, and writing. Perhaps more convincing, numerous experiments have shown that behaviors previously thought to be impervious to environmental manipulation could be dramatically altered via operant conditioning, including psychotic behavior (Ayllon 1963), mutism (Isaacs et al. 1960), coma (Boyle & Greer 1983, Fuller 1949), and a wide range of physiological functions such as diastolic and systolic blood pressure, galvanic skin response, cardiac function, and asthma (Shapiro and Surwit 1976), to mention a few. Moreover, the neurophysiological bases of basic learning processes have recently been uncovered, thus strengthening their status as scientific laws. For example, experimental evidence now shows that individual neurons can be operantly conditioned (Stein and Belluzzi 1988, Stein et al. 1994). Such experiments demonstrate that the laws of operant conditioning discovered at the level of behavior-environment have their basis in neurophysiology.

Although volumes could be written summarizing the findings of the experimental science of behavior, suffice it to say that this is the only "cold-blooded verification" of theory that one should accept. Although not every human behavior that we find interesting can be subjected to experimental verification, a large corpus of experimental findings on basic learning processes is valuable in part because scientists can extrapolate from that foundation to novel behaviors. This is the essence of scientific interpretation (Palmer 1991, Schlinger 1995).

Some psychologists who espouse evolutionary theories of human behavior, however, cite nonexperimental, and even nonquantitative approaches to the understanding of certain human behaviors as evidence against a behavior analytic interpretation. For example, Cosmides and Tooby (1987, 1992) cite Chomsky extensively to make their argument that behaviorist approaches to language have been falsified and, therefore, cannot account for the acquisition of human language. Their conclusion is that evolutionarily adapted cognitive learning mechanisms constitute the only adequate explanation of human language acquisition. It is interesting that these citations consist solely of rationalist argument and not scientific experimentation and yet they are presented as if they are scientifically conclusive. Behavior analysts, in contrast, have not only provided substantive rebukes of Chomsky's critique of behaviorist interpretations of language (MacCorquodale 1970), but they also have argued persuasively that Chomsky's own evolutionary account of language is untenable when held to Darwinian standards (Dennett 1995, Palmer 1986).

The susceptibility of human language to operant conditioning is no longer a debatable issue. During the past 50 years the operant control of verbal behavior has been demonstrated numerous times, including experiments on the operant conditioning of infant vocalizations (Poulson 1983, Whitehurst 1972), the context of conversation (Azrin et al. 1961), fluent requests (Rosenfeld and Baer 1970), and grammatical forms, such as propositional phrases (Lee 1981) and plural morphemes (Guess 1969). Experiments have also verified Skinner's (1957) hypothesized functional verbal operants (see Oah and Dickinson, 1989 for a review). Moreover, behavior analytic principles have been used fruitfully to interpret a diverse group of studies on language development in infancy (Schlinger 1995). The critical question regarding

human language, or any complex human behavior for that matter, is whether plausible mechanisms or processes have been postulated. Operant learning principles constitute a plausible process both for verbal and nonverbal behavior, if for no other reason than they have already been shown experimentally to affect a wide range of human behaviors. Cognitive learning mechanisms, however, are not plausible in part because they are almost wholly inferred from the very behavior they are invoked to explain. Cognitive theorists cannot tell us what cognitive mechanisms look like or how they actually affect behavior.

## NATURE–NURTURE

Perhaps it would be appropriate to conclude with a word about nature–nurture, the phrase first coined by Galton. The issue of the nature or nurture of behavior is not as meaningless as some might suppose, as Dobzhansky asked (1964, p. 55): "To what extent are *differences* observed among people conditioned by the differences of their genotypes and by the differences between the environments in which people were born, grew, and were brought up?"

The question about the genesis of a given behavior is an empirical question. The only truly scientific approach is to conduct experiments in an attempt to uncover functional relations between behavior and its determinants. The amount of data demonstrating the overwhelming effects of environment on behavior establishes the plausibility of environmental interpretations not only of behavioral similarities but also of behavioral differences between humans. Evolution has obviously played an important part in human behavior. But rather than selecting for behavioral rigidity, it has selected for behavioral plasticity (Dobzhansky et al. 1977). As Futuyma concluded (1979, p. 491):

> On balance, the evidence for the modifiability of human behavior is so great that genetic constraints on our behavior hardly seem to exist. The dominant factor in recent human evolution has been the evolution of behavioral flexibility, the ability to learn and transmit culture.

## CONCLUSION

The problem with evolutionary explanations of behavior is that the evidence proffered to support them is so fraught with methodological problems that it is simply insufficient to warrant any conclusions about the role of genes and, thus, evolution. In contrast, there is already a wealth of experimental evidence establishing the plausibility of an environmental/learning account of much human behavior. This is not to say that genes play no role in human behavioral differences or similarities, only that the jury is still out on the verdict regarding the extent and nature of that role. The only way to truly make a case for genetic influence on behavior is to control for environmental variables and manipulate genetic variables, which, at present, is simply not possible with humans. Finally, from a practical point of view, environmental explanations are more valuable than evolutionary ones because they suggest immediate ways in which behavior can be changed.

Evolutionary theorists certainly succeed in making an interesting and often compelling case that perhaps there is some deeper core of human nature that ties us all together and around which we as individuals, and maybe even as groups, differ. It is a case that appeals to many people, including the media, all of whom are hungry for some evidence that sheds light on our nature. Unfortunately, the case is replete with evidential problems, and will have to be retried if and when more substantial evidence can be obtained. Until then, we should rely on what we know scientifically about human behavior.

## References

Allyon, T. (1963) "Intensive treatment of psychotic behaviour by stimulus satiation and food reinforcement." *Behaviour Research and Therapy,* 1:53–61.

Azrin, N. H.; Holz, W.; Ulrich, R.; Goldiamond, I. (1961) "The control of the content of conversation through reinforcement." *Journal of the Experimental Analysis of Behavior,* 4:25–30.

Barash, D. (1977) *Sociobiology and Human Behavior.* New York: Elsevier.

Barkow, J. H.; Cosmides, L.; Tooby, J. (1992) *The Adapted Mind: Evolutionary Psychology and the Generation of Culture.* London: Oxford University Press.

Bock, K. (1980) *Human Nature and History.* New York: Columbia University Press.

Boyle, M. E.; Greer, R. D. (1983) "Operant procedures and the comatose patient." *J. of Applied Behavior Analysis,* 16:3–12.

Buss, D. M. (1994) *The Evolution of Desire: Strategies of Human Mating.* New York: Basic Books.

Byne, W. (1994) "The biological evidence challenged." *Scientific American,* 270:50–55.

Cosmides, L.; Tooby, J. (1987) "From evolution to behavior: Evolutionary psychology as the missing link." In *The Latest on the Best Essays on Evolution and Optimality.* J. Dupre, Cambridge, MA: The MIT Press.

Daly, M.; Wilson, M. (1982) "Whom are newborn babies said to resemble?" *Ethnology and Sociobiology,* 3:69–78.

Daly, M.; Wilson, M. (1988) *Homicide.* New York: Aldine De Gruyter.

Dennett, D. C. (1995) *Darwin's Dangerous Idea: Evolution and the Meanings of Life.* New York: Simon & Schuster.

Dobzhansky, T. (1964). *Heredity and the Nature of Man.* New York: Harcourt, Brace & World.

Dobzhansky, T.; Ayala, F. J.; Stebbins, G. L.; Valentine, J. W. (1977) *Evolution.* San Francisco: Freeman.

Fuller, P. F. (1949) "Operant conditioning of a vegetative human organism." *American Journal of Psychology,* 69:587–590.

Futuyma, D. J. (1979) *Evolutionary Biology.* Sunderland, MA: Sinauer.

Gould, S. J. (1981) *The Mismeasure of Man.* New York: Norton.

Guess, D. (1969) "A functional analysis of receptive language and productive speech: Acquisition of the plural morpheme." *J. of Applied Behavior Analysis,* 2:55–64.

Hamer, D.; Copeland, P. (1994) *The Science of Desire: The Search for the Gay Gene and the Biology of Behavior.* New York: Simon & Schuster.

Herrnstein, R. J.; Murray, C. (1994) *The Bell Curve: Intelligence and Class Structure in American Life.* New York: The Free Press.

Horgan, J. (1993) "Eugenics revisited." (1993) *Scientific American,* 268:123–131.

Hubbard, R.; Wald, E. (1994) *Exploding the Gene Myth.* Boston: Beacon Press.

Isaacs, W.; Thomas, J.; Goldiamond, I. (1960) "Application of operant conditioning to reinstate verbal behavior in psychotics." *J. of Speech and Hearing Disorders,* 25, 8–12.

Itzkoff, S. W. (1985) *Triumph of the Intelligent: The Creation of Homo Sapiens.* Ashfield, MA: Paideia.

Itzkoff, S. W. (1994) *The Decline of Intelligence in America: A Strategy for National Renewal.* Westport, CT; Praeger.

Kamin, L. (1974) *The Science of Politics of IQ.* Potomac, MD: Erlbaum.

Kellert, S. R.; Wilson, E. O. (1993) *The Biophilia Hypothesis.* Washington DC: Island Press.

Kitcher, P. (1985) *Vaulting Ambition: Sociobiology and the Quest for Human Nature.* Cambridge, MA: The MIT Press.

Lee, V. L. (1981) "Prepositional phrases spoken and heard." *J. of the Experimental Analysis of Behavior,* 35:227–242.

Lewontin, R. C.; Rose, S.; Kamin, L. J. (1984) *Not in Our Genes.* New York: Pantheon Books.

Lumsden, C.; Wilson, E. O. (1983) *Promethean Fire.* Cambridge, MA: Harvard University Press.

MacCorquodale, K. (1970) "On Chomsky's review of Skinner's verbal behavior." *J. of the Experimental Analysis of Behavior,* 13:83–89.

Neale, J. M.; Liebert, R. M. (1973) *Science and Behavior: An Introduction to Methods of Research.* Englewood Cliffs, NJ: Prentice Hall.

Nesse, R. M.; Williams, G. C. (1994) *Why We Get Sick: The New Science of Darwinian Medicine.* New York: Times Books.

Oah, S.; Dickinson, A. M. (1989) "A review of empirical studies of verbal behavior." *The Analysis of Verbal Behavior,* 7:53–68.

Palmer, D. C. (1986) "Chomsky nativism: A critical review." In *Dialogues on Verbal Behavior.* L. J. Hayes and P. N. Chase, eds. Springfield, IL: Thomas.

Palmer, D. C. (1991) "A behavioral interpretation of memory." In *Dialogues on Verbal Behavior.* L. J. Hayes and P. N. Chase, eds. Reno, NV: Context Press.

Poole, R. (1994) *Eve's Rib: The Biological Roots of Sex Differences.* New York: Crown.

Poulson, C. L. (1983) "Differential reinforcement of other-than-vocalization as a control procedure in the conditioning of infant vocalization rate." *J. of Experimental Child Psychology*, 36:471–489.

Rosenfeld, H. M.; Baer, D. M. (1970) "Unbiased and unnoticed verbal conditioning: The double agent robot procedure." *J. of the Experimental Analysis of Behavior*, 14:99–107.

Rushton, J. P. (1995a) *Race, Evolution, and Behavior: A Life History Perspective.* New Brunswick, NJ: Transaction Publishers.

Rushton, J. P. (1995b) "J. Philippe Rushton responds." *Skeptic*, 3:22–25.

Sahlins, M. (1976) *The Use and Abuse of Biology.* Ann Arbor: University of Michigan Press.

Schlinger, H. D. (1992) "Intelligence: Real or artificial?" *The Analysis of Verbal Behavior*, 10:125–133.

Schlinger, H. D. (1995) *A Behavior Analytic View of Child Development.* New York: Plenum.

Shapiro, D.; Surwit, R. S. (1976) "Learned control of physiological function and disease." In *Handbook of Behavior Modification and Behavior Therapy.* H. Leitenberg, ed. Englewood Cliffs, NJ: Prentice Hall.

Skinner, B. F. (1938) *The Behavior of Organisms.* Englewood Cliffs, NJ: Prentice Hall.

Skinner, B. F. (1972) "A case history in scientific method." In *Cumulative Record.* (3rd ed.) New York: Meredith.

Stein, L.; Belluzzi, J. D. (1988) "Operant conditioning of individual neurons." In *Quantitative Analysis of Behavior:* *Vol. 7.* M. L. Commons, R. M. Church, J. R. Stellar, and A. R. Wagner, eds. Hillsdale, NJ: Erlbaum.

Stein, L.; Xue, B. G.; Belluzzi, J. D. (1994) "In vitro reinforcement of hippocampal bursting: A search for Skinner's atoms of behavior." *J. of the Experimental Analysis of Behavior*, 61:155–168.

Tavris, C. (1995) "A place in the sun." *Skeptic*, 3:62–63.

Tooby, J.; Cosmides, L. (1992) "The psychological foundations of culture." In *The Adapted Mind.* J. Barkow, L. Cosmides, and J. Tooby, eds. New York: Oxford University Press.

Whitehurst, G. J. (1972) "Production of novel and grammatical utterances by young children." *J. of Experimental Child Psychology*, 13, 502–515.

Wilson, E. O. (1993) "Biophilia and the conservation ethic." In *The Biophilia Hypothesis.* S. R. Kellert and E. O. Wilson, eds. Washington, DC: Island Press.

Wilson, E. O. (1975) *Sociobiology: The New Synthesis.* Cambridge, MA: Harvard University Press.

Wilson, E. O. (1978) *On Human Nature.* Cambridge, MA: Harvard University Press.

Wright, R. (1994) *The Moral Animal: The New Science of Evolutionary Psychology.* New York: Pantheon.

Wright, R. (1995) "The biology of violence." *The New Yorker*, March, 69–77.

# Part V

# THE BRAIN, HORMONES, AND HUMAN BEHAVIOR

In reading the chapters in this section, it becomes apparent that, as has been discovered many times before, biology, the environment, and behavior are intricately related. As we learn more about these interrelationships, we find they are extremely complicated and it is this complexity that intrigues us. For example, as pointed out by Begley in the first chapter of this section, there are sex differences in the brain, and these differences are mediated by many factors. Hormonal fluctuations at an early age can affect neural development and these changes can affect behavior and the environment. Furthermore, there is a great deal of overlap between men and women in test scores in almost all psychological tests and in structures of the brain. Environmental changes and complexity affect the structure and complexity of neuronal connections, and it seems that sex differences found in adult brains might not be found in newborns. To what extent sex differences in adult brains result from "living, feeling, and thinking" remains a question.

In Chapter 51, Sapolsky also stresses the fact that environment and past experience interact with hormonal levels to determine how a particular context will affect the behavior of an individual. It is still wrongly thought by many that the hormone testosterone *causes* aggression. However, Sapolsky states: "Testosterone levels predict nothing about who is going to be aggressive. The subsequent behavioral differences drive the hormonal changes, rather than the other way around." Why is it so hard to convince many scientists of the importance of environment and previous experience as determinants of hormonal levels rather than vice versa? Sapolsky believes this is related to a phenomena called "physics envy," where high-tech and more reductive explanations are accepted as more scientific and powerful. Another misconception about testosterone that Sapolsky addresses is what he calls the "permissive effect." You need some testosterone around for normal aggressive behavior to occur. However, the brain cannot detect differences from 20 percent of normal to twice normal levels. Castration and massive doses of testosterone do affect behavior, but even these effects are mediated by the environment and past experience. Again we see that "behavioral biology is usually meaningless outside the context of the social factors and environment in which it occurs."

Just as behavior causes endocrine levels to change, Barinaga (Chapter 52) reports on research that illustrates that behavior can cause physical changes in neurons of crayfish. Furthermore, the environmental context can lead to reversals of these changes, and the neuronal reactions in individual crayfish are related to prior experiences. As stated in the article, these animals seem to have a "different brain for different circumstances." In the report by Morell (Chapter 53), the sociobiological tenet of high reward and high reproductive success to dominant animals is called into question. In some of the earliest studies of hormonal levels in free-ranging mammals, researchers are finding the highest levels of stress-related hormones in the most dominant individuals. These levels can be related to higher miscarriage rates, shorter life spans, and a number of other stress-related symptoms—the most important point again being that there is a complex relationship between behavior, social structure, environmental context, and physiology. Perhaps we *have* jumped to generalities before obtaining adequate data about particulars, as Jeanne Altmann suggests in this chapter.

The next two articles in this section (Chapters 54 and 55) summarize physiological reward systems and imply complex interactions with environmental stimuli. Blakelee describes how the neurotransmitter dopamine transmits signals that might moderate how the brain of an individual interacts in the environment to moderate rewards and punishments from outside stimuli. However, it appears that each individual's past experiences modify his or her own reward system. In the paper by Angier, the hormone oxytocin is evaluated as a possible neurobiological substrate for affiliative behavior. It appears to play some role in mediating bonds between individuals and may have played a role in the evolution of social behavior. Although the physiology and hormones involved in aggression have been the focus of a great deal of study, noticeably less research has been conducted on the biological basis of sociality. Since all primates are highly social, and essentially all diurnal primates live in social groups, this research should prove to be quite enlightening.

In order to understand how hormones relate to genes, neurons, and ultimately to behavior, it is necessary to trace complex connections. As Donald Pfaff of Rockefeller University informs us in Chapter 56, the mechanisms involved are extremely subtle, even for simple instinctive systems. As Greenspan stated in Chapter 4, one gene–one trait doesn't hack it, even in *Drosophila*. Pfaff reiterates that: "Interactions between genes and environment as well as among gene products ensure that gene/behavior relations will be neither linear nor modular."

In Chapter 57, Tooby and Cosmides write about human universal mechanisms in the brain that have become fixed during our past "evolutionary adaptive environment"—at a time when our ancestors were supposedly hunters and gatherers. They hypothesize, for example, that the human mind contains "specialized information-processing adaptations designed to guide individuals successfully through social exchange . . . humans have specialized cognitive devices for this purpose."

These design features are seen as species typical and all that is left to do is identify the neural basis and to elucidate the genetic bases and developmental biology of these adaptations. Unlike the other articles in this section, Tooby and Cosmides do not detail very specific hormones, neuronal connections and pathways, genetically influenced proteins, and so on. Nor do they emphasize the complex interactions between current behavioral, social, and environmental contexts. Rather, these authors deal in vague generalities (e.g., design features, special design "theory of mind" module, social exchange circuits, precaution circuits), and maximize the use of jargon (e.g., event populations, social contact algorithms, complex adaptive computational designs, antientropic process). They also relate current "cognitive adaptations" to a mythical, untestable, and unlikely hunting past.

The article by Berkowitz (Chapter 58) provides an interesting contrast to that of Tooby and Cosmides. Berkowitz again examines the complex relationships between behavioral traits and genetic traits. He emphasizes the difficulty in relating a complex set of behaviors to single gene traits. "Instead," Berkowitz states, "each gene is a single player in a wonderfully intricate story, involving nonadditive interactions of genes, proteins, hormones, food, and life experiences, and leading to effects on a variety of cognitive and behavioral functions." He warns that many get around the complexities by claiming that a behavioral trait is caused by a combination of several genes, each with a small effect that interacts in a non-additive way. Thus, these behaviors are due to genes alone, but the complexity of the genetic mechanisms precludes a definitive finding with current techniques. However, as Berkowitz warns, this often leaves us simply with a number of unfalsifiable hypotheses. "There may be no way of disproving it even if it is false." He ends his article with a warning:

> A real understanding of complex characteristics may require us to come to terms with the emergent properties of multiple interactions. In the meantime, pronouncements of simple genetic causation should be met with a critical eye and with questions about exactly what has and has not been demonstrated.

In the last chapter, Sapolsky reiterates much of what Berkowitz says and gives us more reasons to believe that there is more to behavior than just genes.

# Chapter 50

# *Gray Matters*

## Sharon Begley

---

*Science: New technologies that catch the mind in the very act of thinking show how men and women use their brains differently.*

Of course men and women are different. *Boy,* are they different. In every sphere of life, it seems, the sexes act, react or perform differently. Toys? A little girl daintily sets up her dolls, plastic cups and saucers, while her brother assembles his Legos into a gun—and ambushes the tea party. Navigating? The female tourist turns her map every which way but right, trying to find the way back to that charming bistro, while her boyfriend charges ahead, remembering every tricky turn without fail. Relationships? With spooky intuition, women's acute senses pick up subtle tones of voice and facial expressions; men are insensitive clods who can't tell a sad face until it drenches them in tears. Cognition? Females excel at language, like finding just the right words to make their husbands feel like worms; males can't verbalize even one good excuse for stumbling home at 2 A.M.

Stereotypes? Maybe—but as generalizations they have a large enough kernel of truth that scientists, like everyone else, suspect there's *something* going on here. As Simon LeVay, the Salk Institute neuroscientist who in 1991 discovered structural differences between the brains of gay and straight men, put it recently, "There are differences in the mental lives of men and women."

The mind, of course, is just what the brain does for a living. So if LeVay is right, those mental differences must arise from differences in that glutinous three-pound blob. For a decade neuroscientists have been discovering evidence of differences. Although the findings are tentative and ambiguous, at the end of the day, relaxing over beers at a neuroscience conclave, most specialists agree that women's and men's brains differ slightly in structure. But the studies have been frustratingly silent

From *Newsweek,* March 27, 1995.

on whether the anatomical differences in their brains make men and women think differently. But now—drumroll, please—thanks to an array of new imaging machines that are revolutionizing neuroscience, researchers are beginning to glimpse differences in how men's and women's brains actually function.

With new technologies like functional magnetic resonance imaging (FMRI) and positron emission tomography (PET), researchers catch brains in the very act of cogitating, feeling, or remembering. Already this year researchers have reported that men and women use different clumps of neurons when they take a first step toward reading and when their brains are "idling." And, coming soon to a research journal near you, provocative studies will report that women engage more of their brains than men when they think sad thoughts—but, possibly, less of their brains when they solve SAT math problems. "Now that we actually have functional brain data, we're getting lots of new insights," says Richard Haier, professor of pediatrics and neurology at the University of California, Irvine, and leader of the SAT study. "Even at this early point we have data to support the idea that men and women in general have brains that work differently." The latest studies:

MAKE YOUR MIND A BLANK . . .

To compare male and female brains at work, subjects were instructed to think of . . . nothing. In January 1995 scientists led by Ruben Gur of the University of Pennsylvania reported a PET study of 37 men and 24 women, mostly recruited by ads in local papers. Each volunteer got an injection of radioactive glucose. Glucose is brain food; active

333

regions of the brain use more glucose than quiescent areas and so emit radioactivity, which PET detects. For 30 minutes a volunteer lay in a quiet, dimly lit room with eyes open and head in a tunnel with detectors embedded in the walls. Each volunteer was told to relax, without "exerting mental effort"—while PET read his or her mind.

In men's idling brains, the action was in the temporal–limbic system (diagram). This primitive region controls highly unsubtle expressions of emotion, such as fighting. It is often dubbed the "reptilian" brain. In most of the women's supposedly idling brains, the neurons were buzzing in the posterior cingulate gyrus, an evolutionarily newer addition to mammals' brains. Not even the researchers are sure what all of this shows. For one thing, thirteen men and four women showed activity more like the other sex's. But the real problem is that "thinking of nothing" is nearly impossible. Volunteer (and co-researcher) Lyn Mozley admits that "some of the time I was probably thinking, 'When is this going to be over?'" What the PET scans may actually be showing is that, when told to think of nothing, men fixate on sex and football, while women weave together strings of words. But if, in men, the pilot light is always on in neurons that control aggression and action, it may explain why they're more violence-prone than women.

## I Say Tomahto . . .

Last month researchers announced that men and women use different parts of their brains to figure out rhymes. Sally Shaywitz, her husband, Bennett Shaywitz, and colleagues at Yale University weren't looking for the brain's poetry center; rather, sounding out is the first step in reading, so rhyming was meant as a proxy for that skill. The 19 men and 19 women volunteers had to determine whether pairs of nonsense words (lete and jete, loke and jote), when flashed on a screen, rhymed. A volunteer lay in an FMRI machine, which is a four-foot-long tube containing a detector that pinpoints active brain regions.

In all 19 men, one region in the left inferior or frontal gyrus (that's behind the left eyebrow) lit up like Las Vegas. So far, so good: For more than a century scientists have known that the left brain controls language. But in 11 of the 19 women, that area *plus* one behind the right eyebrow lit up. The right side of the brain is the seat of emotion. Perhaps women are more felicitous with language because they draw on feelings (right brain) as well as reason (left brain) when they use words. The Yale team made one more intriguing find. In eight of the women—42 percent—the brain worked like the men's. "That some of the women's brains looked like the men's is true of all these sex studies," says neuropsychologist Melissa Hines of UCLA. "Girls play with boys' toys more than boys play with girls', for instance. Males for whatever reason are more exclusively channeled into one way of behaving"—and, possibly, thinking.

## Let X Be an Integer . . .

At Irvine, Haier PET-scanned 22 male and 22 female student volunteers while they did SAT math problems. Half the men and half the women had SAT math scores above

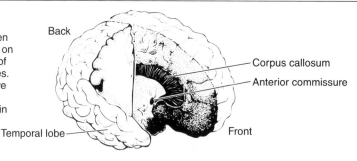

**Mapping the Neural Scene**

With all the differences in how men and women feel, act and perform on cognitive tests, you'd expect lots of differences in their brain structures. But although neuro-scientists have found fifteen such differences in rats, they've identified only a few in humans.

| | Men | Women |
|---|---|---|
| **Temporal lobe:**<br>This region of the cerebral cortex helps control hearing, memory, and a person's sense of self and time. | In cognitively normal men, a tiny region of the temporal lobe behind the eye has about 10 percent fewer neurons than it does in women. | Women have more neurons in this region, which understands language as well as melodies and speech tones. |
| **Corpus callosum:**<br>This bundle of neurons is the main bridge between the left brain and the right, carrying messages between them. | A man's corpus callosum takes up less volume in his brain than a woman's does, suggesting the two hemispheres communicate less. | In women, the back part of the callosum is bigger than in men. That may explain why women use both sides of their brain for language. |
| **Anterior commissure:**<br>This collection of nerve cells also connects the brain's two hemispheres. It is smaller and appeared earlier in evolution than callosum. | In men, the commissure is smaller than it is in women, even though men's brains are, on average, larger than women's. | The larger commissure in women may be another reason their two cerebral hemispheres seem to work in partnership on tasks from language to emotional responses. |

700; the other half scored 540 or so. According to his unpublished results, which he previewed at a science meeting last summer, in gifted men the temporal lobes were on overdrive compared with the average men. (The temporal lobes are behind the ears.) Ability seemed to correlate with effort. But in the 700-club women, the temporal lobes showed little activity, and there was a hint that the women didn't use their brain any more intensely than the average women. "There was a suggestion that women who did better [in math] might be using their brain more efficiently than women who did average," says Haier. "The men and women performed equally well. They just seemed to use the brain differently to do it." "Different," in other words, does not mean "better."

## No Hard Feelings

Last year Penn's Ruben Gur and his wife, neuroscientist Raquel Gur, enlisted PET in the aid of an old stereotype: that men can't read emotions on people's faces. (The pair got into the field of sex differences when they were struck by their own temperamental differences. He is more intrigued by numbers and details, she likes to work with people; he reacts to a setback by taking a deep breath and moving on, she analyzes it.) They and their colleagues asked volunteers to judge whether male and female faces showed happiness or sadness. Both sexes were almost infallible at recognizing happiness. But sadness was a different story. Women picked out a sad face 90 percent of the time, on men and women, but men had more trouble. They recognized sadness on men's faces 90 percent of the time—that is, they did as well as the women—but were right only 70 percent of the time when judging sadness on women's faces.

Well, of course. Evolutionarily speaking, it makes sense that a man would have to be hypervigilant about men's faces; otherwise he might miss the first hint that another guy is going to punch him. Being oblivious to a woman's emotions won't get him much worse than a night on the sofa. The Gurs may even have stumbled on why women can't understand why men find it so hard to be sensitive to emotions. According to the PET scans, women's brains didn't have to work as hard to excel at judging emotion. Women's limbic system, the part of the brain that controls emotion, was *less* active than the limbic system of men doing worse. That is, the men's brains were working overtime to figure out the faces. But the extra effort didn't do them much good.

## Sad, So Sad

The little boy in black standing at his father's funeral, the happily married woman hearing her husband demand a divorce . . . 10 women and 10 men called up these and other sad memories while psychiatrist Mark George of the National Institute of Mental Health and colleagues PET-scanned them. In both sexes, the front of the limbic system glowed with activity. But in women, the active area was eight times as big as it was in the men. That difference in intensity might explain why women are twice as likely as men to suffer major depression, say the scientists. In depression, the limbic system is unresponsive and almost lethargic; "perhaps hyperactivity during normal bouts of sadness" made these circuits unresponsive, George speculates.

The brain-imaging studies are the latest, and the highest-tech, periscope into sex differences in the brain. Yet no matter how "scientific" it gets, this research serves as ammunition in society's endless gender wars. When Raquel Gur gave a talk to M.D.-Ph.D. students in Illinois about sex differences in brains, a group of women asked her to stop publicizing the work: They were afraid women would lose 20 years of gains if word got out that the sexes aren't the same. They had good reason to worry. Among the choicier passages from recent pop-science books: Male brains "are not so easily distracted by superfluous information." "A woman may be less able to separate emotion from reason." And "the male brain is a tidier affair," as Anne Moir and David Jessel write in their 1991 book "Brain Sex." The subject of sex differences in the brain attracts almost as much inflammatory rhetoric as the "science" of racial differences in IQ.

Even before scientists caught images of the brain thinking or emoting, there were hints that men's brains and women's differed. As long ago as 1880, English surgeon James Crichton-Browne reported slight differences in the brain anatomy of men and women—a slightly larger gaggle of neurons *here* in one sex, and *there* in the other. But by far the most frequent finding through the years has been that the bundle of nerve cells through which the left side of the brain talks and listens to the right—it's called the corpus callosum—is larger in women than in men. In perhaps the best study of this kind, in 1991 UCLA neuroendocrinologists Roger Gorski and Laura Allen examined 146 brains from cadavers and found that the back part of women's callosum is up to 23 percent bigger than men's.

This brought neuroscientists as close as they ever got to jumping up and down in public. It fit their cherished idea that, in male brains, the right and the left side barely know what the other is doing, while in women there's practically nonstop left-right neural chitchat. If women's brains are paragons of holism, while men's are a house divided, it could explain findings both serious and curious. Women's language ability better survives a left-brain stroke—perhaps because they tap the language capacity of the right brain. Women tend to have better language skills—perhaps because the emotional right brain enriches their left-brain vocabulary. And women have better intuition—perhaps because they are in touch with the left brain's rationality and the right's emotions simultaneously.

There is just one problem with these tidy explanations. A bigger corpus callosum matters only if it has more neurons, the cells that carry communications. After all, fat phone cables carry more conversations only if they contain more wires. But despite years of searching, scientists cannot say for sure that women's corpus callosum has more neurons.

The quest for other anatomical differences has been only a little more successful. In rats, biologists have found fifteen regions that differ in size between males and females. Finding such differences in humans has been much tougher. But in November, at the annual meeting of the Society for Neuroscience, Sandra Witelson of McMaster University in Ontario reported results from a study of nine autopsied brains. (She gets them from people with terminal cancer who bequeath their brains to science.) Woman, despite having smaller brains (on average) than men because their whole bodies are smaller, have more neurons. The extra 11 percent are all crammed into two layers of the cerebral cortex whose job is to understand language and recognize melodies and tone of voice.

Neuroscientists know of only one force that can prune and stimulate, kill and nourish the brain's gaggles of neurons: sex hormones. Before birth, a fetus's brain is bathed in sex hormones—different ones, in different amounts, depending on whether the fetus is male or female. Ethics prevents scientists from experimenting to see how a fetus's brain would change if its hormone exposure changed. But nature has no such compunctions. Girls with a rare birth defect called CAH, which made them churn out high levels of the male hormone testosterone as fetuses, score better than the average female on spatial tests. (The extra testosterone exposure also masculinizes their genitals.) As girls, they prefer cars and trucks and other toys that boys usually grab. Other girls were exposed to male-like levels of testosterone before birth when their mothers took the hormone DES to prevent miscarriages. As children, the DES girls did better than their normal sisters on rotating a figure in space and other tasks at which boys outdo girls. Finally, boys with a syndrome that makes them insensitive to testosterone are better at language than their unaffected brothers. But they are less adept at spatial tasks—the typical female intellectual pattern. Hormonal effects, wrote psychologist Doreen Kimura of the University of Western Ontario in 1992, "appear to extend to all known behaviors in which males and females differ . . . [such as] problem solving, aggression and the tendency to engage in rough-and-tumble play."

Are these hormonal effects present at birth, or do they result from how a child is raised? The feminized boys (whose cognitive abilities resemble women's) and the CAH girls (minds like boys) are not physically normal. Their parents know they are different, and likely treat them differently from their sisters and brothers. Perhaps even more crucial, the hormonally abnormal girls might identify, psychologically, not with girls but with boys, aping their behavior and preferences. Similarly, the feminized boys might identify with girls. So if the girls play like tomboys and do better in math than normal girls, and the boys have superior language tasks compared with their normal brothers, it is impossible to tell whether the reason is hormones alone or life's experiences, too. Only Hines's DES girls are pure products of prebirth hormones: They looked like ordinary little girls, so people treated them as girls and they saw themselves as female. Their male-like cognitive function is the only one ever found that cannot be easily explained away as the result of nurture.

Hines's work has been seized as proof that biology is destiny, but other research undermines that dogma. For one thing, the overlap between men's and women's scores on just about every psychological test is huge. Any randomly chosen woman might do better at a "male" skill than a man, and vice versa. "This [overlap] is also true of brain structures," says UCLA's Gorski. More important, the nature–nurture dichotomy is simplistic. Nurture affects nature; experience, that is, affects biology. The brain is so malleable that rats raised in a cage filled with toys and mazes grow more connections between their neurons than rats raised in a bare cage. Also in rats, mothers sense their sons' testosterone and lick them more than daughters; that causes more nerve cells at the base of the tail to grow. The human brain is malleable, too: in people whose hands were amputated, scientists reported last year, the part of the brain that once registered feelings from the missing hand vanishes.

Is it farfetched to wonder whether parts of girls' brains grow or shrink, while different parts of boys' expand or shrivel, because they were told not to worry their pretty heads about math, or because they started amassing Legos from birth, or because . . . well, because of the vastly different experiences boys and girls have? "Surely the more complex social interactions among humans also sculpt the developing nervous system," argues psychologist Marc Breedlove of UC, Berkeley. "The studies provide no evidence favoring either nature or nurture." But, he adds, "there's one thing I know that testosterone does to masculinize [men's] brains. It causes them to be born with a penis. And everybody treats the baby differently [than they do a girl]. I'm sure that affects the development of the brain. Is that a biological effect or a social effect? It's both."

The recent PET scans and FMRIs are silent "on *how* the brains of men and women get to be different," says Irvine's Richard Haier. The scans probe adults, whose brains are the products of years of living, feeling, thinking, and experiencing. Children have not yet been scanned in the service of science. But in studies of fetal brains (from miscarriages) and newborns' (from still-births), "none of the sex differences in [the brain] have been reliably detected," says Breedlove.

The powerful new techniques of brain imaging are just beginning to be trained on the age-old question of what makes the sexes different. As the answers trickle in, they will surely challenge our cherished notions of what makes us think, act, and feel as we do—and as members of the opposite sex do not. But if the first tantalizing findings are any clues, the research will show that our identities as men and women are creations of both nature and nurture. And that no matter what nature deals us, it is we—our choices, our sense of identity, our experiences in life—who make ourselves what we are.

---

# IT'S TIME TO RETHINK NATURE AND NURTURE

*Ideas: Biology and free will aren't at odds. They're inseparable.*

GEOFFREY COWLEY

Every day science seems to chip away at our autonomy. When researchers aren't uncovering physical differences in the way men and women use their brains, they're asserting genetic influences on intelligence, sexual orientation, obesity, or alcoholism. Or they're suggesting that the level of some brain chemical affects one's chances of committing violent crimes. Each new finding leaves the impression that nature is winning out over nurture—that biology is destiny and free will an illusion. But the nature–nurture dichotomy is itself an illusion. As many scholars are now realizing, everything we associate with "nurture" is at some level a product of our biology—and every aspect of our biology, from brain development to food preference, has been shaped by an environment. Asking whether nature or nurture is more important is like asking whether length or width is a better gauge of size.

Darwin recognized more than 100 years ago that *Homo sapiens* evolved by the same process as every other species on earth. And philosophers such as William James were eager to apply Darwin's insights to human psychology. But during the first part of this century, the rise of Social Darwinism (a non-Darwinian sink-or-swim political philosophy) and later Nazi eugenics spawned a deep suspicion of biologically inspired social science. By 1954, anthropologist Ashley Montagu was declaring that mankind has "no instincts because everything he is and has become he has learned, acquired, from his culture."

The distinction between innate and acquired seems razor sharp until you try slicing life with it. Consider the development of the brain. While gestating in the womb, a child develops some 50 trillion neurons. But those cells become functional only as they respond to outside stimuli. During the first year of life, the most frequently stimulated neurons form elaborate networks for processing information, while the others wither and die. You could say that our brains determine the structure of our experience—or that experience determined the structure of our brains.

Social behavior follows the same principle. From the old nature-versus-nurture perspective, a tendency that isn't uniformly expressed in every part of the world must be "cultural" rather than "natural." But there is no reason to assume that a universal impulse would always find the same expression. As the revolutionists John Tooby and Leda Cosmides have observed, biology can't indicate what language a child will speak, what games she'll play, what rites she'll observe or what she'll feel guilty or jealous about. But it virtually guarantees that she'll do all of those things, whether she grows up in New Jersey or New Guinea.

Biology, in short, doesn't determine exactly what we'll do in life. It determines how different environments will affect us. And our biology is itself a record of the environments our ancestors encountered. Consider the sexes' different perceptual styles. Men tend to excel at spatial reasoning, women at spotting stationary objects and remembering their locations. Such discrepancies may have a biological basis, but researchers have traced the biology back to specific environmental pressures. Archeological findings suggest that men hunted, and women foraged, through vast stretches of evolutionary time. And psychologists Irwin Silverman and Marion Eals have noted that "tracking and killing animals entail different kinds of spatial problems than does foraging for edible plants."

## FAST FOOD

Unfortunately, a trait shaped by one environment can become deadly in another. Craving fat, and storing it efficiently, would promote survival in a setting where food sources were scarce and unpredictable. But the same tendencies cause mass heart failure when expressed in a fast-food paradise. Alcoholism wasn't even possible in the environments where humankind evolved, yet it has plagued the world since the advent of brewer's yeast. In a preagricultural setting, the evolutionists Randolph Nesse and George Williams speculate in their new book, *Why We Get Sick,* the biological traits that now foster compulsive drinking might have had "positive effects—for instance, a tendency to [pursue] sources of reward despite difficulties."

Violent crime, like overeating and drunkenness, has clear biological roots, but that doesn't mean it's inherent in anyone's nature. Males come outfitted for aggression in many sexually reproducing species, and some human males seem constitutionally more volatile than others. Since the 1970s, numerous studies have linked criminal violence to low levels of the brain chemical serotonin. That association has led some experts, including former National Institute of Mental Health director Frederick Goodwin, to view criminality as a medical disorder that might be predicted through blood testing and prevented through chemical treatment. But the biology of crime isn't that simple. As social critic Robert Wright noted in a recent *New Yorker* article, low sero-

*(continued)*

tonin may leave people more prone to violence—but poor social conditions seem to lower serotonin levels. Perhaps the best way to counter the biological causes of urban crime, he concludes, is to create better schools and higher-paying jobs—to turn the inner cities into "places where young men have nonviolent routes to social status."

## BEYOND DETERMINISM

The talk of a pharmaceutical war on crime can only feed the suspicion of liberals like Harvard geneticist Richard Lewontin, who warned in 1984 that "if human social organization . . . is a direct consequence of our biologies, then, except for some gigantic program of genetic engineering, no practice can make a significant alteration of social structure." But there is nothing inherently determinist about a biological perspective—and nothing to be gained by pretending that we live outside of nature. Biology shapes our impulses and aptitudes, but it doesn't act alone. There is always a context, and always room for resistance. "It's biologically implausible to have a gene for something like crime," Sir Michael Rutter, the British child psychiatrist, observed recently. "It's like saying there's a gene for Roman Catholicism." When that precise a gene is found, we'll have to give up on free will. For now, its status seems safe.

# Chapter 51

# *The Trouble with Testosterone*

## Robert M. Sapolsky

Face it, we all do it. We all believe in certain stereotypes about certain minorities. The stereotypes are typically pejorative and usually false. But every now and then, they are true. I write apologetically as a member of a minority about which the stereotypes are indeed true. I am male. We males account for less than 50 percent of the population, yet we generate an incredibly disproportionate percentage of the violence. Whether it is something as primal as having an ax fight in an Amazonian clearing or as detached as using computer-guided aircraft to strafe a village, something as condemned as assaulting a cripple or as glorified as killing someone wearing the wrong uniform, if it is violent, males excel at it.

Why should that be? We all think we know the answer. A dozen millennia ago or so, an adventurous soul managed to lop off a surly bull's testicles and thus invented behavioral endocrinology. It is unclear from the historical records whether this individual received either a grant or tenure as a result of this experiment, but it certainly generated an influential finding—something or other comes out of the testes that helps make males such aggressive pains in the ass.

That something or other is testosterone.* The hormone binds to specialized receptors in muscles and causes those cells to enlarge. It binds to similar receptors in laryngeal cells and gives rise to operatic basses. It causes other secondary sexual characteristics, makes for relatively unhealthy blood vessels, alters biochemical events in the liver too dizzying to even contemplate, has

a profound impact, no doubt, on the workings of cells in big toes. And it seeps into the brain, where it binds to those same "androgen" receptors and influences behavior in a way highly relevant to understanding aggression.

What evidence links testosterone with aggression? Some pretty obvious stuff. Males tend to have higher testosterone levels in their circulation than do females (one wild exception to that will be discussed later) and to be more aggressive. Times of life when males are swimming in testosterone (for example, after reaching puberty) correspond to when aggression peaks. Among numerous species, testes are mothballed most of the year, kicking into action and pouring out testosterone only during a very circumscribed mating season—precisely the time when male-male aggression soars.

Impressive, but these are only correlative data, testosterone repeatedly being on the scene with no alibi when some aggression has occurred. The proof comes with the knife, the performance of what is euphemistically known as a "subtraction" experiment. Remove the source of testosterone in species after species and levels of aggression typically plummet. Reinstate normal testosterone levels afterward with injections of synthetic testosterone, and aggression returns.

To an endocrinologist, the subtraction and replacement paradigm represents pretty damning proof: This hormone is involved. "Normal testosterone levels appear to be a prerequisite for normative levels of aggressive behavior" is the sort of catchy, hummable phrase that the textbooks would use. That probably explains why you shouldn't mess with a bull moose during rutting season. But that's not why a lot of people want to understand this sliver of science. Does the action of this hormone tell us anything about *individual* differences in levels of aggression, anything about why some males, some human males, are exceptionally violent? Among an array of males—human or otherwise—are the highest testosterone levels found in the most aggressive individuals?

---

*Testosterone is one of a family of related hormones, collectively known as "androgens" or "anabolic steroids." They all are secreted from the testes or are the result of a modification of testosterone, they all have a similar chemical structure, and they all do roughly similar things. Nonetheless, androgen mavens spend entire careers studying the important differences in the actions of different androgens. I am going to throw that subtlety to the wind and, for the sake of simplification that will horrify many, will refer throughout to all of these related hormones as "testosterone."

From *The Trouble with Testosterone and Other Essays on the Biology of the Human Predicament.* Scribner, N.Y.

Generate some extreme differences and that is precisely what you see. Castrate some of the well-paid study subjects, inject others with enough testosterone to quadruple the normal human levels, and the high-testosterone males are overwhelmingly likely to be the more aggressive ones. However, that doesn't tell us much about the real world. Now do something more subtle by studying the normative variability in testosterone—in other words, don't manipulate anything, just see what everyone's natural levels are like—and high levels of testosterone and high levels of aggression still tend to go together. This would seem to seal the case—interindividual differences in levels of aggression among normal individuals are probably driven by differences in levels of testosterone. But this turns out to be wrong.

Okay, suppose you note a correlation between levels of aggression and levels of testosterone among these normal males. This could be because (1) testosterone elevates aggression; (2) aggression elevates testosterone secretion; (3) neither causes the other. There's a huge bias to assume option1, while 2 is the answer. Study after study has shown that when you examine testosterone levels when males are first placed together in the social group, testosterone levels predict nothing about who is going to be aggressive. The subsequent behavioral differences drive the hormonal changes, rather than the other way around.

Because of a strong bias among certain scientists, it has taken forever to convince them of this point. Behavioral endocrinologists study what behavior and hormones have to do with each other. How do you study behavior? You get yourself a notebook and a stopwatch and a pair of binoculars. How do you measure the hormones? You need a gazillion-dollar machine, you muck around with radiation and chemicals, wear a lab coat, maybe even goggles—the whole nine yards. Which toys would you rather get for Christmas? Which facet of science are you going to believe in more? Because the endocrine aspects of the business are more high-tech, more reductive, there is the bias to think that it is somehow more scientific, more powerful. This is a classic case of what is often called physics envy, the disease among scientists where the behavioral biologists fear their discipline lacks the rigor of physiology, the physiologists wish for the techniques of the biochemists, the biochemists covet the clarity of the answers revealed by the molecular biologists, all the way down until you get to the physicists, who confer only with God.* Hormones seem to

many to be more real, more substantive, than the ephemera of behavior, so when a correlation occurs, it must be because hormones regulate behavior, not the other way around.

As I said, it takes a lot of work to cure people of that physics envy, and to see that interindividual differences in testosterone levels don't predict subsequent differences in aggressive behavior among individuals. Similarly, fluctuations in testosterone levels within one individual over time do not predict subsequent changes in the levels of aggression in that one individual—get a hiccup in testosterone secretion one afternoon and that's not when the guy goes postal.

Look at our confusing state: Normal levels of testosterone are a prerequisite for normal levels of aggression, yet changing the amount of testosterone in someone's bloodstream within the normal range doesn't alter his subsequent levels of aggressive behavior. This is where, like clockwork, the students suddenly start coming to office hours in a panic, asking whether they missed something in their lecture notes.

Yes, it's going to be on the final, and it's one of the more subtle points in endocrinology—what is referred to as a hormone having a "permissive effect." Remove someone's testes and, as noted, the frequency of aggressive behavior is likely to plummet. Reinstate precastration levels of testosterone by injecting that hormone, and precastration levels of aggression typically return. Fair enough. Now this time, castrate an individual and restore testosterone levels to only 20 percent of normal and . . . amazingly, normal precastration levels of aggression come back. Castrate and now generate twice the testosterone levels from before castration—and the same level of aggressive behavior returns. You need some testosterone around for normal aggressive behavior—zero levels after castration, and down it usually goes; quadruple it (the sort of range generated in weight lifters abusing anabolic steroids), and aggression typically increases. But anywhere from roughly 20 percent of normal to twice normal and it's all the same; the brain can't distinguish among this wide range of basically normal values.

We seem to have figured out a couple of things by now. First, knowing the differences in the levels of testosterone in the circulation of a bunch of males will not help you much in figuring out who is going to be aggressive. Second, the subtraction and reinstatement data seem to indicate that, nevertheless, in a broad sort of way, testosterone causes aggressive behavior. But that turns out not to be true either, and the implications of this are lost on most people the first thirty times you tell them about it. Which is why you'd better tell them about it thirty-one times, because it is the most important point of this piece.

Round up some male monkeys. Put them in a group together, and give them plenty of time to sort out where

---

*An example of physics envy in action. Recently, a zoologist friend had obtained blood samples from the carnivores that he studies and wanted some hormones in the sample assays in my lab. Although inexperienced with the technique, he offered to help in any way possible. I felt hesitant asking him to do anything tedious but, so long as he had offered, tentatively said, "Well, if you don't mind some unspeakable drudgery, you could number about a thousand assay vials." And this scientist, whose superb work has graced the most prestigious science journals in the world, cheerfully answered, "That's okay, how often do I get to do *real* science, working with test tubes?"

they stand with each other—affiliative friendships, grudges, and dislikes. Give them enough time to form a dominance hierarchy, a linear ranking system of numbers 1 through 5. This is the hierarchical sort of system where number 3, for example, can pass his day throwing around his weight with numbers 4 and 5, ripping off their monkey chow, forcing them to relinquish the best spots to sit in, but, at the same time, remembering to deal with numbers 1 and 2 with shit-eating obsequiousness.

Hierarchy in place, it's time to do your experiment. Take that third-ranking monkey and give him some testosterone. None of this within-the-normal-range stuff. Inject a ton of it into him, way higher than what you normally see in a rhesus monkey; give him enough testosterone to grow antlers and a beard on every neuron in his brain. And, no surprise, when you then check the behavioral data, it turns out that he will probably be participating in more aggressive interactions than before.

So even though small fluctuations in the levels of the hormone don't seem to matter much, testosterone still causes aggression. But that would be wrong. Check out number 3 more closely. Is he now raining aggressive terror on any and all in the group, frothing in an androgenic glaze of indiscriminate violence? Not at all. He's still judiciously kowtowing to numbers 1 and 2, but has simply become a total bastard to numbers 4 and 5. This is critical: testosterone isn't *causing* aggression, it's *exaggerating* the aggression that's already there.

Another example just to show we're serious. There's a part of your brain that probably has lots to do with aggression, a region called the amygdala.* Sitting right near it is the Grand Central Station of emotion-related activity in your brain, the hypothalamus. The amygdala communicates with the hypothalamus by way of a cable of neuronal connections called the stria terminalis. No more jargon, I promise. The amygdala has its influence on aggression via that pathway, with bursts of electrical excitation called action potentials that ripple down the stria terminalis, putting the hypothalamus in a pissy mood.

Once again, do your hormonal intervention; flood the area with testosterone. You can do that by injecting the hormone into the bloodstream, where it eventually makes its way to this part of the brain. Or you can be elegant and surgically microinject the stuff directly into this brain region. Six of one, half a dozen of the other. The key thing is what doesn't happen next. Does testosterone now cause there to be action potentials surging down the stria terminalis? Does it turn on that pathway? Not at all. If and only if the amygdala is *already* sending an aggres-

sion-provoking volley of action potentials down the stria terminalis, testosterone increases the rate of such action potentials by shortening the resting time between them. It's not turning on the pathway, it's increasing the volume of signaling if it is already turned on. It's not causing aggression, it's exaggerating the preexisting pattern of it, exaggerating the response to environmental triggers of aggression.

This transcends issues of testosterone and aggression. In every generation, it is the duty of behavioral biologists to try to teach this critical point, one that seems a maddening cliché once you get it. You take that hoary old dichotomy between nature and nurture, between biological influences and environmental influences, between intrinsic factors and extrinsic ones, and, the vast majority of the time, regardless of which behavior you are thinking about and what underlying biology you are studying, the dichotomy is a sham. No biology. No environment. Just the interaction between the two.

Do you want to know how important environment and experience are in understanding testosterone and aggression? Look back at how the effects of castration were discussed earlier. There were statements like "Remove the source of testosterone in species after species and levels of aggression typically plummet." Not "Remove the source . . . and aggression always goes to zero." On the average it declines, but rarely to zero, and not at all in some individuals. And the more social experience an individual had being aggressive prior to castration, the more likely that behavior persists sans *cojones*. Social conditioning can more than make up for the hormone.

Another example, one from one of the stranger corners of the animal kingdom: If you want your assumptions about the nature of boy beasts and girl beasts challenged, check out the spotted hyena. These animals are fast becoming the darlings of endocrinologists, sociobiologists, gynecologists, and tabloid writers. Why? Because they have a wild sex-reversal system—females are more muscular and more aggressive than males and are socially dominant over them, rare traits in the mammalian world. And get this: Females secrete more of certain testosterone-related hormones than the males do, producing the muscles, the aggression (and, as a reason for much of the gawking interest in these animals, wildly masculinized private parts that make it supremely difficult to tell the sex of a hyena). So this appears to be a strong vote for the causative powers of high androgen levels in aggression and social dominance. But that's not the whole answer. High up in the hills above the University of California at Berkeley is the world's largest colony of spotted hyenas, massive bone-crunching beasts who fight with each other for the chance to have their ears scratched by Laurence Frank; the zoologist who brought them over as infants from Kenya. Various scientists are studying their sex-reversal system. The female hyenas are bigger and more muscular than the males and have the

---

*And no one has shown that differences in the size or shape of the amygdala, or differences in the numbers of neurons in it, can begin to predict differences in normal levels of aggression. Same punch line as with testosterone.

same weirdo genitals and elevated androgen levels than their female cousins do back in the savannah. Everything is in place except . . . the social system is completely different from that in the wild. Despite being stoked on androgens, there is a very significant delay in the time it takes for the females to begin socially dominating the males—they're growing up without the established social system to learn from.

When people first grasp the extent to which biology has something to do with behavior, even subtle, complex, human behavior, there is often an initial evangelical enthusiasm of the convert, a massive placing of faith in the biological components of the story. And this enthusiasm is typically of a fairly reductive type—because of physics envy, because reductionism is so impressive, because it would be so nice if there were a single gene or hormone or neurotransmitter or part of the brain that was *it,* the cause, the explanation of everything. And the trouble with testosterone is that people tend to think this way in an arena that really matters.

This is no mere academic concern. We are a fine species with some potential. Yet we are racked by sickening amounts of violence. Unless we are hermits, we feel the threat of it, often as a daily shadow. And regardless of where we hide, should our leaders push the button, we will all be lost in a final global violence. But as we try to understand and wrestle with this feature of our sociality, it is critical to remember the limits of the biology. Testosterone is never going to tell us much about the suburban teenager who, in his after-school chess club, has developed a particularly aggressive style with his bishops. And it certainly isn't going to tell us much about the teenager in some inner-city hellhole who has taken to mugging people. "Testosterone equals aggression" is inadequate for those who would offer a simple solution to the violent male—just decrease levels of those pesky steroids. And "testosterone equals aggression" is certainly inadequate for those who would offer a simple excuse: Boys will be boys and certain things in nature are inevitable. Violence is more complex than a single hormone. This is endocrinology for the bleeding heart liberal—our behavioral biology is usually meaningless outside the context of the social factors and environments in which it occurs.

## FURTHER READING

For a good general review of the subject, see E. Monaghan and S. Glickman, "Hormones and Aggressive Behavior," in J. Becker, M. Breedlove, and D. Crews, eds., *Behavioral Endocrinology* (Cambridge, MA: MIT Press, 1992), 261. This also has an overview of the hyena social system, as Glickman heads the study of the Berkeley hyenas. For technical papers on the acquisition of the female dominance in hyenas, see S. Jenks, M. Weldele, L. Frank, and S. Glickman, "Acquisition of matrilineal rank in captive spotted hyenas: Emergence of a natural social system in peer-reared animals and their offspring," *Animal Behavior* 50 (1995): 893; and L. Frank, S. Glickman, and C. Zabel, "Ontogeny of female dominance in the spotted hyaena: Perspectives from nature and captivity," in P. Jewell and G. Maloiy, eds., "The biology of large African mammals in their environment," *Symposium of the Zoological Society of London,* 61 (1989): 127.

I have emphasized that while testosterone levels in the normal range do not have much to do with aggression, a massive elevation of exposure, as would be seen in anabolic steroid abusers, does usually increase aggression. For a recent study in which even elevating into that range (approximately five times normal level) still had no effect on mood or behavior, see S. Bhasin, T. Storer, N. Berman, and colleagues, "The effects of supraphysiologic doses of testosterone on muscle size and strength in normal men," *New England Journal of Medicine,* 335 (1996): 1.

The study showing that raising testosterone levels in the middle-ranking monkey exaggerates preexisting patterns of aggression can be found in A. Dixson and J. Herbert, "Testosterone, aggressive behavior and dominance rank in captive adult male talapoin monkeys (*Miopithecus talapoin*)," *Physiology and Behavior,* 18 (1977): 539. For the demonstration that testosterone shortens the resting period between action potentials in neurons, see K. Kendrick and R. Drewett, "Testosterone reduces refractory period of stria terminalis neurons in the rat brain," *Science,* 204 (1979): 877.

# Chapter 52

# *Social Status Sculpts Activity of Crayfish Neurons*

## Marcia Barinaga

Like rival gunslingers in the Old West, two male crayfish living in the same territory are compelled to fight it out to determine who's the boss. First they circle and size each other up. Then their well-choreographed skirmish escalates into violent combat as they try to tear each other limb from limb. The winner of that clash becomes dominant, strutting his stuff confidently through the territory, while the loser skulks about, trying to stay out of his rival's way.

Once those social lines have been drawn, the behavior of the two crayfish is so different that researchers suspected that the animals' experience must somehow change their nervous systems. Now, neurobiologist Donald Edwards of Georgia State University and his colleagues Shih-Rung Yeh and Russell Fricke provide the first direct evidence for that idea. They report that they have found a neuron in crayfish whose response to the neurotransmitter serotonin differs dramatically depending on the animal's social status. In dominant animals, serotonin makes the neuron more likely to fire, while in subordinate animals serotonin suppresses firing.

The finding's implications go beyond crayfish. For example, it complements work from Stanford University neurobiologist Russ Fernald and his colleagues, who showed several years ago that a change to dominant social status alters the brains of male cichlid fish, causing the enlargement of neurons that release hormones that stimulate the sexual organs. But the Edwards group's finding is "the first time that one has been able to link a social phenomenon to a change in a particular identified synapse," says neuroscientist Allen Selverston of the University of California, San Diego. And that is something researchers have suspected might occur throughout higher animals, but have never seen. "Even though you are seeing something that in a sense you always knew had

to be there," says Brandeis University neuroscientist Eve Marder, "it is incredibly powerful to actually see it."

What's more, the activity change that the Edwards team has linked to social status takes place in a very well-studied neural circuit—a set of nerve cells that controls the escape reflex called the tail-flip. As a result, the team is in an ideal position to unravel the molecular and cellular events by which the change occurs, as well as to ask how changes in this neuron and others combine to alter the animal's behavior. "There are going to be a constellation of [nervous system] changes that go along with this change in social status, each of which will endow the animal with different new abilities and serve it in some situation," says Fernald. "One way to think about it is that the animal in some sense has a different brain for different circumstances."

The present work grew out of a set of findings made 15 years ago by Harvard University neuroscientist Edward Kravitz and his then-student Margaret Livingstone. They found that serotonin injections caused lobsters and crayfish to assume the aggressive postures characteristic of dominant animals. That finding spurred researchers in several labs to study serotonin's effects on behaviors like the tail-flip reflex, which the animals use in both fighting and escaping.

In 1985, one of those researchers, Russell Fricke, then an assistant professor at Emory University, got a perplexing result. When he injected serotonin into young crayfish, it inhibited the tail-flip reflex in some animals, while enhancing it in others. As he tried to make sense of this, Fricke realized that the crayfish in which the reflex was enhanced had either been raised alone or were the biggest in their cage. That suggested the animals' social status might have been influencing his results.

Before going further in the work, however, Fricke left Emory to become a physician, and his observation "lay there for a long time," says Edwards. Then, in 1994, Yeh, a

From *Science* Vol. 271, January 19, 1996.

graduate student with Edwards, decided to pursue it. Yeh paired crayfish in cages, allowing them to fight and settle who was dominant. He then dissected the animals, and, in a culture dish, tested the effect of serotonin on the lateral giant neuron, which triggers the tail-flip reflex. He found that serotonin enhanced the excitability of the giant neurons from dominant animals, while it suppressed the activity of the neurons from subordinate animals.

Edwards and Yeh wondered what might be happening inside the lateral giant neuron to switch its response so dramatically. One possibility was that there was some sort of change in the receptors through which serotonin exerts its effects. There are three known types of serotonin receptors in crustaceans, which can exert different effects even within an individual cell.

The researchers' hunch proved correct. By using different compounds that activate different classes of serotonin receptors, Yeh and Edwards found that activation of one type of serotonin receptor makes the lateral giant neuron less excitable, while a second receptor type boosts its excitability. Neurons from subordinate and dominant crayfish respond differently to serotonin, says Edwards, because the subordinates seem to have "more, or more effective," receptors of the former type while in dominants, the latter type prevails.

That state of affairs isn't permanent, however. Just as social status can change in the course of an animal's lifetime, the responsiveness of the lateral giant neuron can change as well. When Yeh placed two previously subordinate crayfish together, one would become dominant. Two weeks later when he tested the dominant animals' lateral giant neurons, the neurons' responsiveness was enhanced rather than inhibited by serotonin.

Dominant animals, in contrast, let go of their dominant physiology much more slowly, perhaps because of the advantages that dominant animals enjoy in access to food and mates. When Yeh paired dominant crayfish with each other, forcing one of each pair to become subordinate, the new subordinates continued to be truculent, provoking fights and getting themselves killed by their rivals at an unusually high rate. When he tested their lateral giant neurons more than a month after the new pairing, serotonin still enhanced their firing, as if "the animals are reluctant to go from being dominant to being subordinate," Edwards says. Fernald's group sees similar results with their male cichlid fish. Dominant males, even when forced to become subordinate, are very slow to give up their dominant physiology.

One question that's still unanswered is how the change in the lateral giant neuron might help explain the aggressive behavior of dominant males. Harvard's Kravitz offers a possible explanation. In lobsters, his group has found that the lateral giant neuron not only triggers the tail-flip reflex, but also activates other neurons that squirt out a burst of serotonin. And serotonin is the substance Kravitz and Livingstone had linked to aggressive behavior in lobsters and crayfish 15 years ago.

Edwards' group doesn't know yet whether the neuron also triggers a serotonin burst in crayfish, but they suspect that it might. If it does, then a "feed-forward loop" would operate in dominant animals, says Kravitz, in which triggering the lateral giant neuron would cause a burst of serotonin, which would make the neuron even more likely to be triggered again, causing more serotonin to be released. All that serotonin would pump up the animals' aggressive behavior. In contrast, subordinate crayfish are better served by not acting truculent and inviting a fight they are likely to lose, so it is adaptive for them to put the brakes on that cycle, which is what happens when the burst of serotonin caused by the lateral giant's firing makes the neuron less likely to fire again and trigger the release of more serotonin.

Despite the appeal of that explanation, Kravitz and others point out that the lateral giant neuron alone is unlikely to be the full explanation for the behavioral changes. "You can't say this particular [neuron] . . . is causally responsible for any behavioral changes," says Brandeis's Marder. "It is probably only a piece of the story."

To fill out the remaining pieces of that story, Edwards and others are eager to learn what other neurons may be influenced by the switch in social status, and whether some of those neurons show a change in serotonin receptors, or in receptors for other molecules. One target for study is the neurotransmitter octopamine, which Kravitz's group has shown to have the opposite effect to serotonin, producing submissive rather than aggressive behavior.

In addition, the researchers plan to take a closer look at the lateral giant neuron itself, focusing on the specific pathways through which social position gets translated into cellular and molecular changes in the neuron. With all these possibilities for future work, says Kravitz, the Edwards group has opened "a potentially incredibly exciting area of investigation."

# Chapter 53

# *Life at the Top: Animals Pay the High Price of Dominance*

## Virginia Morell

Bar-Dot, the dominant female in a pack of dwarf mongooses in Tanzania's Serengeti National Park, has been keeping subordinate animals in line for at least five years, carefully watched by behavioral ecologists Scott and Nancy Creel. Day after day, Bar-Dot rushes over to other females who are acting up, bares her teeth, and threatens the others into deferring to her. It's a tough job, but there are perks: She's first in line for any food and has the sole right to reproduce. And her subordinates should be the ones who get stressed out—at least that's what the textbooks say.

Yet according to the Creels, of Rockefeller University, those textbooks are wrong. In this week's issue of *Nature,* the scientists, with Steven L. Monfort, an endocrinologist at the Smithsonian Institution's Conservation Research center, report that Bar-Dot and the other dominant female mongooses in fourteen packs had the highest levels of cortisol, a stress-related hormone, of all pack members. And they've found precisely the same effect among both male and female wild dogs in Tanzania's Selous National Park. These results, along with recent studies of female baboons by other researchers, show that dominance can exact a high price. In the baboons, the cost seems to be a higher miscarriage rate; in the dogs and mongooses, chronic stress is thought to lead to a shorter lifespan for the alpha animals.

Biologists are getting this glimpse of the costs of dominance because for the first time, they are studying hormone levels in several free-ranging rather than captive species of mammals by analyzing urine and fecal samples. "For a long time the dogma has been that the subordinates are the ones that are most stressed," explains John C. Wingfield, a comparative endocrinologist at the University of Washington, Seattle, who has studied

pecking orders in wild birds and found patterns similar to those seen by the Creels. "But much of that has been based on captive studies of rats, mice, and primates; whereas the beauty of these [the Creels'] data is that they're from the field—and all of a sudden, things start to be very different." Some scientists do, however, have a few reservations about the accuracy of the testing methods.

The older idea that subordinates are the ones who suffer from chronically high stress grew out of the research of J. J. Christian and Seymour Levine, who worked with captive colonies of rodents and primates beginning in the 1950s and 1960s. They found that subordinates, with higher levels of cortisol, suffered from ill health and reproductive failure. Cortisol and other glucocorticoids, secreted as part of an animal's "flight or fight" response, cause severe health problems if pumped out over the long haul, says Stanford University neurobiologist Robert Sapolsky, who has observed stress effects in subordinate wild male baboons. "They put all of the body's long-term processes—tissue repair, immunity, digestion, reproduction—on hold," Sapolsky explains.

The finding of high stress levels in subordinates provided an explanation for the evolution of dominance, because it meant that the more aggressive animals stood a better chance of reproducing. And that was the pattern the Creels expected to find in their wild dog and mongoose populations as well, because fertile, subordinate individuals (who receive most of the aggression) in these groups rarely reproduce. "We thought that stress could be a factor" in suppressing the subordinates' reproduction, says Nancy Creel.

From long-term observations, the Creels could identify the dominant and subordinate animals. In studying the dogs, the researchers followed individuals around and collected their fresh droppings for later hor-

From *Science* Vol. 271, January 19, 1996.

monal analysis. For the dwarf mongooses, the Creels trained the animals to urinate on a rubber sandal at a specific time each day. Both methods allowed them to collect the large number of samples (740 for the mongooses; 216 for the wild dogs) needed to establish basal stress hormone levels for each species, and to observe how individual animals deviated from the norm.

Contrary to their expectations, the Creels found higher glucocorticoid levels in the alpha males and females. "Their high glucocorticoid levels are probably the result of their aggressive behavior," Scott Creel notes. Top dogs and mongooses have to assert their rank daily. And birds do it, too. Wingfield has shown that in territorial birds such as the red-winged blackbird, dominant males with large areas to guard have higher levels of corticosterone and testosterone than the males lacking territories.

Just what this means for the dominant animals' health, however, is not clear. Alpha female baboons do have higher miscarriage rates, according to studies by behavioral ecologist Sam Wasser of the University of Washington and Center for Wildlife Conservation, but he hasn't measured their stress hormone levels. But in the birds, dogs, and mongooses, high stress hormones don't keep dominant animals from having babies. "All we can say right now is that, contrary to expectation, the higher glucocorticoid levels are not affecting the dominant animals' reproduction. So they must be paying the price in another way—perhaps in a shorter life span," says Scott Creel. That might still allow the dominants to leave behind more young in their short lives than the subordinates do in their longer ones—an area the Creels now plan to investigate.

Some researchers do worry about the methodology—that hormonal levels drawn from feces and urine will never be as precise as those taken directly from an animal's blood. "There are so many difficulties in putting together an accurate measure. Were the samples collected at the same time every day? Do the animals pool the same amount of steroids in their urine in the same way?" says Sapolsky. "These can all confound the picture." But Wingfield and others say that given the large sample size, most of this "background noise" should be filtered out.

Most importantly, he and other researchers suspect that field biologists will now see a variety of relationships between hormones and behavior in mammals—dependent not only on the individual's place in a hierarchy, but on particular populations and species. "We're realizing that hormonal levels are more and more situation-dependent," says Jeanne Altmann, a behavioral ecologist at the University of Chicago, who is studying stress hormones in free-ranging baboons with Sapolsky. "It may be that we have to examine a lot of particularities before we reach the generalities."

# Chapter 54

# *How Brain Uses a Simple Dopamine System*

## Sandra Blakeslee

In the ever-increasing cascade of new information on brain chemistry and behavior, one substance seems to pop up whenever pleasure is involved. It is even called dopamine, a name that has no connection to the slang "dope" for drugs, but might just as well, considering that dopamine plays a critical role in the way animals and people respond to cocaine, amphetamines, heroin, alcohol, and nicotine.

Dopamine has been shown to be a key modulator in an astonishing array of human behaviors. Get too much dopamine in the brain and you hear voices, hallucinate, and wrestle with twisted thoughts. Get too little of it and you cannot move. Like Parkinson's patients, you are locked in your body, depressed and joyless.

Dopamine's broad influence is an irresistible lure to scientists. And based on a few new experiments, some researchers think they have the first glimpses of a simple reward system, mediated by specialized dopamine neurons active in all vertebrates, indeed in insects and crustaceans as well. Their ideas are still more hypothesis than theory and have yet to be integrated with the exceedingly complex waxing and waning of other neurotransmitters in the human brain, but the work has drawn the attention and excitement of other prominent researchers.

The dopamine story begins deep in the brain stem with several tiny clumps of cells, together no bigger than a grain of sand. These 100 million or so cells, the only producers of dopamine, form long nerve fibers called axons that reach out to billions of cells in almost every other part of the brain.

Like other neurotransmitters, dopamine allows neurons to "talk" to each other, facilitating the transmission of signals from one brain cell to another.

This is only one small system in an incredibly sophisticated brain. But its size seems to belie its influence. And the reason may be that the brains of humans and other creatures operate on some deceptively simple rules, said Dr. Terrence J. Sejnowksi, a neuroscientist at the Howard Hughes Medical Institute and the Salk Institute in LaJolla, Calif.

An idea recently proposed by Dr. Sejnowski and others is that the dopamine system evaluates rewards—both those that flow from the environment and those conjured up by the mind. When something good happens, the system releases dopamine, which, in essence, makes the owner of the brain take some action. This account is vastly oversimplified, of course, but Dr. Sejnowski does suggest that the dopamine system works unconsciously and globally, providing guidance for making decisions, when there is not time to think things through.

Recent experiments on bees, monkeys, and humans provide the basis of these ideas about the dopamine system, which are by no means proved. They are more in the realm of well grounded speculation, Dr. Sejnowski said.

Dr. P. Read Montague, a researcher at the Center for Theoretical Neuroscience in the Baylor College of Medicine in Houston, has collaborated with Dr. Sejnowski and others in modeling the way a dopamine-like system works in bees. The bee brain has only one dopamine neuron. (It actually releases octopamine, a close cousin to dopamine that serves the same purpose.) As in other creatures, this neuron sends projections to every part of the bee brain.

Bees can find nectar-containing flowers under highly variable lighting conditions, from numerous angles and distances and during different seasons. There could be dozens of yellow flowers, of similar shape and size in a given field, yet only one or two might contain nectar. Bees can very quickly figure out which ones to sample and give the information to other bees.

How do bees do this? At the University of Illinois, Dr. Leslie Real, an experimental psychologist, has built

From the *New York Times*, March 19, 1996.

enclosures with artificial flowers spread over the floor. Bees fly around, sampling various amounts of sugar placed in each flower by Dr. Real.

In one experiment, Dr. Real put out blue and yellow flowers. A third of the blues contained high amounts of sugar; the other blues were empty. Among yellow flowers, two-thirds contained a small amount of sugar; the other yellows were empty. The experiment was rigged so that the total amount of sugar in the blue and yellow flowers were identical.

But which foraging strategy would the bee prefer? Would it go for high payoff blues? It would get the most sugar for the least amount of work but it would have to tolerate hitting more "empty" flowers. Or would the bee go the "safer" route and sample the yellows, making more work for itself?

In papers published in 1991, Dr. Real reported that bees went to the yellow flowers 85 percent of the time. In seeking reward, they were averse to taking risks.

Fascinated by this finding, Dr. Montague, in collaboration with Dr. Sejnowski and Dr. Peter Dayan of the Massachusetts Institute of Technology's department of brain and cognition, wondered how the bees computed rewards. And so he built a virtual bee inside a computer, with a model of the dopamine system that might explain genuine bee behavior.

"We made a fake bee and let it fly over the blue and yellow flowers" with variable amounts of sugar, Dr. Montague said. Each time a virtual bee landed on a flower, its dopamine neuron was alerted. As in most animals, the dopamine neuron at rest fires signals at a steady, base-line rate. When it is excited, it fires more rapidly. When it is depressed, it ceases firing.

The virtual bee's neuron was designed to give three simple responses. If the amount of sugar was more than expected (based on what the bee knows about similar-looking flowers), the neuron would fire vigorously. Lots of dopamine meant lots of reward and instant learning. If the amount of sugar was less than predicted, the neuron would stop firing. Sudden lack of dopamine, going to other parts of the brain, told the bee to avoid what had just happened. If the amount of sugar was the same, as predicted, the neuron would not increase or decrease its activity. The bee learned nothing new.

This simple prediction model—the dopamine neuron "knows" what has just happened and is waiting to see if the next reward is greater or smaller or the same—offers one explanation for how the bee behavior might arise, Dr. Sejnowski said. When the dopamine neuron encounters an empty flower, it throws the bee brain into an unhappy state. The bee, in fact, cannot stand hitting so many empties. It would rather play it safe and get more numerous, smaller rewards—or no rewards at all—by sticking to the yellow flowers. A paper describing this work was published on Feb. 1, 1996 in the journal *Nature*.

This model is also consistent with what is known about human behavior and the human brain, Dr. Sejnowski said.

Here is how Dr. Sejnowski theorizes that the system works. Sensory information flows into the brain from the outside world and from internal representations. What you see, touch, feel, smell, taste, hear, and imagine all combine to produce sensory states. These change from moment to moment.

The brain also contains memories and prior experiences about these states. Some are good; you want more. Others are to be avoided.

Both representations—what is happening now and what you know about it from past experience—are funneled to the dopamine system, Dr. Sejnowski said. Then a simple rule is followed. The dopamine system compares the brain's expectation of the reward (gee, this was pretty good the last time I experienced it) with what is actually happening at the moment.

If the reward is higher than predicted, dopamine is sent to many parts of the brain, giving a green light to action to get more rewards. If the reward is less than predicted, the dopamine signal is not broadcast and other systems involving avoidance are activated. In both instances, action does not take place until the dopamine system has evaluated the sensory state you are in and detected an error in your prediction about it, Dr. Sejnowski said.

The researchers described this model on March 1, 1996 in *The Journal of Neuroscience*.

Both these papers involve theoretical arguments and computer models. Recent experiments carried out by Dr. Wolfram Schultz and his colleagues at University of Fribourg in Switzerland have shown that dopamine cells in monkeys do indeed behave in just the way theorized. Electrodes were placed in monkey dopamine cells and the animals were given squirts of apple juice paired with a flashing yellow light. At first, the dopamine cells would fire when the animals got the juice or saw the light, since the reward was not expected.

But when they were no longer surprised by the reward, their dopamine cells no longer fired, Dr. Schultz said. Dopamine cells only fire when the prediction is wrong, he said. And they only fire when the stimulus carries a reward.

Dr. Montague supervised an experiment by his graduate student, David Egelman, to test 40 people in an experiment similar to the one done on bees.

People sit in front of a computer screen with two buttons, labeled A and B. Whenever they press one of the buttons, a vertical bar appears on the screen, Dr. Montague said. It represents one dollar. If the whole bar is colored, it means they earn a dollar. If 60 percent of the bar is colored, they earn 60 cents. If 30 percent is colored, they get 30 cents and so forth.

The task is to push either button and to maximize the amount of money you earn over 250 trials, Dr. Montague said.

But, like the blue and yellow flowers shown to the bee, the game is rigged. Button A gives smaller rewards, but more of them. Button B gives much larger rewards, but they occur infrequently.

Most people behaved just like the bees, Dr. Montague said. They might start by choosing A, which would give them a good return for several tries. But then A might fall to ten cents or five cents. Their dopamine systems could not tolerate this, he said, so they would switch to button B. But B, as rigged, gives many more low than high payoffs, so the player would quickly switch back to A, he said.

Those who keep switching earn far less than those who have more patience in exploring the potential payoffs in button B, Dr. Montague said.

# Chapter 55

# *Illuminating How Bodies Are Built for Sociability*

## Natalie Angier

The most vicious and mulish winter in memory finally behind us, let us now praise gentleness, in temperature and temperament alike. For as much as people must compete for status or global markets, they need sociability, affection, love. These are not options in life, or sentimental trimmings; they are part of the species survival kit.

Children who are not held or given love when young may grow up into disturbed, scared, and sometimes dangerous people. Adults who isolate themselves from the world, refusing to so much as own a pet, are likelier to die at a comparatively young age than those who cultivate companionship. This unshakable dependence on others is not confined to humans, but extends to any creature designed for group living. Carnivores need meat, migratory animals need motion, and social animals must socialize.

The importance among a wide variety of species of comity and friendship, grooming sessions and peace-making gestures, and what one researcher wryly dubbed nature's original "family values," received its celebratory due at an unusual conference held here recently at Georgetown University. The meeting, called "The Integrative Neurobiology of Affiliation," was organized by the New York Academy of Sciences to address a subject long neglected and even scorned in scientific circles: the biology of benevolence.

In the thematically broad embrace of the conference, scientists discussed the rituals of reconciliation and solace that chimpanzees and other nonhuman primates engage in after a nasty fight that threatens social ties: gestures like holding out a hand to shake and make up, or hugging and grooming, or mouth-to-mouth kissing. The researchers considered the neural and hormonal differences between the rodent species that form inseparable pairs and those that prefer to go it alone. They explored instances of humans who are unable to love or connect with others, the sorrowful outcome of neuropsychiatric disorders like autism and schizophrenia.

From the *New York Times*, April 30, 1996.

Throughout the meeting, scientists made clear what may at first seem counterintuitive, that the capacity to be pleasant toward a fellow creature is in a sense hard work. It is not the default mode. Instead, affiliative behavior requires a hormonal and neural substrate, an activation of circuitry every bit as intricate as the mechanisms controlling the body's ability to fight an opponent or flee from danger.

Dr. Kerstin Uvnäs-Moberg, of the Karolinska Institute division of physiology and pharmacology in Stockholm, made the point graphically by displaying opposing slides, one of a fierce, snarling battle-ready man, fists cocked, and the other of a nursing Virgin Mary, she of the exposed breast and benignant mien. The warrior's so-called stress circuitry is indicated and labeled. The levels of fight-or-flight hormones like cortisol and epinephrine are surging, his heart rate has accelerated, his blood pressure and blood sugar are soaring, and any gastrointestinal activity that could divert energy from his muscles has ceased. All in all, he is in a state of physiological catabolism, a mobilization and breaking down of the body's energy stores for the business of attacking an enemy.

Of the calm Madonna circuitry—the physical condition that defines a woman who is nurturing her baby—comparatively less is known, Dr. Uvnäs-Moberg said, but researchers are beginning to flesh out the details. In a lactating woman, anabolism replaces catabolism: The emphasis is on building up rather than tearing apart. Insulin levels mount, the better to pull sugar from the blood and store it in cells; so, too, do the concentrations of gastric acids and hormones like gastrin and cholecystokinin, all of which aid in efficient digestion and the transfer of energy from food to the body and to breast milk.

Within minutes after beginning a bout of nursing, the mother's cortisol levels subside and her blood pressure drops, fostering a sense of relaxation that keeps her willingly quiescent for as long as it takes to sate her child; at the same time, the blood vessels of her chest dilate, which turns her into a living space heater to warm the suckling infant.

If the fight-or-flight response is seen as a strengthening of the distinction between self and the other—a tightening of the body's response mechanisms, like springs compressed into a box—then the affiliative, nurturing circuitry suggests an opening up, an expansion of self toward others, and a trading of anxiety for at least a momentary state of quiet joy.

Orchestrating this broad suite of maternal responses, Dr. Uvnäs-Moberg said, is the hormone called oxytocin. A small yet gorgeously powerful peptide hormone originating in the hypothalamus deep within the brain, oxytocin is the hormone that acts as a muscle contractor and gets milk flowing from the breast in the first place. But, beyond simply releasing breast milk, it modulates the many accompanying changes in body and behavior.

Oxytocin was in fact the hormonal luminary of the conference, coming up repeatedly in discussions of nearly every type of animal bonding: parental, fraternal, sexual, and even the capacity to soothe one's self. Dr. C. Sue Carter of the University of Maryland in College Park, one of the organizers of the conference, is renowned in the field of oxytocin research. She suggested in her talk that oxytocin might have played an essential role in the evolution of social behavior, particularly for mammals.

"The neuroendocrinology of lactation may be important to the wiring of the mammalian brain," she said. "Its development was revolutionary."

Oxytocin's first and strongest role may have been in helping to forge the mother-infant bond. But its ability to influence brain circuitry may have been co-opted to serve other affiliative purposes that allowed the formation of alliances and partnerships, thus hastening the evolution of advanced cognitive skills.

Dr. Carter also emphasized that the capacity to affiliate with others increases, not just the quality of life, but its length as well; animals that live in groups enhance each other's chances of survival, not to mention the survival of each other's offspring. "Social behavior contributes to both individual survival and reproductive fitness," she said. "You can have it all."

Dr. Cort A. Pedersen, an oxytocin researcher from the University of North Carolina at Chapel Hill, chimed in with a paean to maternal behavior as the source of the world's brilliance. "Sustained maternal production and nurturing of offspring until they are able to fend for themselves allowed a much higher rate of survival," he said. "Mothering also permitted a much longer period of brain development and was therefore a prerequisite for the evolution of higher intelligence. Species that mother their offspring have come to dominate every ecological niche in which they dwell."

In his studies, Dr. Pedersen has demonstrated that oxytocin is essential for the initiation of maternal behavior in a rat after giving birth but that other cues, like the sensation of the pups suckling the mother's nipples or the taste of the pups as the mother licks them, eventually replace the hormone as a sustainer of motherly affections. Consequently, oxytocin levels subside.

Yet if the mother and her pups are kept physically separated in the cage, unable to interact in any way other than visually, the mother's oxytocin concentrations remain elevated. Once reunited with the pups, no matter how many days later, she immediately resumes all her mothering duties. But the willingness to nurture anew is dependent on the sustained oxytocin pulses during the semi-separation; if given a drug that blocks the effects of the hormone, she appears to forget that she ever gave birth at all.

Other scientists at the conference argued that the root of affiliative behavior lies not in motherhood, but in the act preceding it: sex. The need for one organism to meld its genes with another drives the need for one organism to overcome temporarily any innate antipathy it may feel toward strangers and cooperate—affiliate—long enough to court.

"Reproduction is the single most important event in an animal's life," said Dr. David Crews of the University of Texas at Austin. "I believe that social and affiliative behaviors evolved from reproductive behaviors." And once such anti-antipathy mechanisms had been established—for example, in the limbic areas of the brain, which control emotion and sex drive—such mechanisms could be put to use for entirely new purposes, like promoting the formation of monogamous pairs to rear offspring or teams of creatures to fend off predators.

Dr. Crews and others pointed out that even blue-green algae, which reproduce asexually by cloning themselves, must for unknown reasons come together en masse before any one of them can beget new buds. Somehow the stimulation of group life—perhaps chemical, perhaps physical—stimulates their individual photocopying effort.

In other words, the forces that impel a living creature to seek succor from others of its kind are knit into the very principle of life; even DNA, for that matter, is a double-stranded molecule, pair-bonded with its complementary mate.

To speak of algal affiliation, though, strikes most researchers in the field as stretching the concept of sociality beyond recognition. Dr. Stephen W. Porges of the University of Maryland in College Park sees the ability to affiliate in any meaningful way as a largely mammalian and avian privilege, and he views it as the by-product of mammals' comparatively efficient metabolism. In a novel theory with the faintly mystical name of "the polyvagal theory of emotion," Dr. Porges proposes that the capacity for emotion, and its consequent role in social behavior, is dependent on the advanced nature of the mammalian autonomic nervous system, the part of the nervous system that is essentially automatic, controlling vital functions like heart rate and digestion.

Through phylogenetic comparisons across the evolutionary spectrum, Dr. Porges has identified the vagal

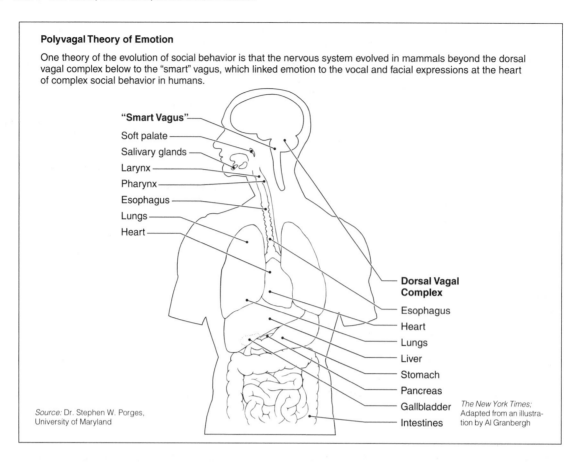

**Polyvagal Theory of Emotion**

One theory of the evolution of social behavior is that the nervous system evolved in mammals beyond the dorsal vagal complex below to the "smart" vagus, which linked emotion to the vocal and facial expressions at the heart of complex social behavior in humans.

"Smart Vagus"
Soft palate
Salivary glands
Larynx
Pharynx
Esophagus
Lungs
Heart

**Dorsal Vagal Complex**
Esophagus
Heart
Lungs
Liver
Stomach
Pancreas
Gallbladder
Intestines

*Source:* Dr. Stephen W. Porges, University of Maryland

*The New York Times;* Adapted from an illustration by Al Granbergh

nerve complex, a cardinal component of the autonomic nervous system, as a possible key to the development of mammalian emotions and hence sociality. This complex has ancient origins in vertebrate evolution, beginning as a simple connection between the brainstem and the gut, heart, and other organs of the body. Its original purpose was to conserve energy. When a fish encounters a reduction of oxygen in its watery world, for example, its primitive vagus nerve slows its heartbeat and digestion and thus cuts back on the fish's oxygen needs.

As life became more complicated and new threats arose, Dr. Porges said, the vagal system of nerve fibers likewise became elaborated. It split into two divisions: the original, oxygen-thrifty circuitry—the dorsal vagal complex—and a newer component that communicates with the sympathetic nervous system. Each element of the vagal nerve complex links up to a different region of the brainstem. Rather than slowing things down, the sympathetic nervous system speeds things up; it allows an animal to use more than the usual amount of oxygen and thus makes possible the famed fight-or-flight response.

With the arrival of mammals came yet a third element of the vagal system, what Dr. Porges calls the "smart" vagus. This vagal nerve complex controls the facial muscles and the larynx, and therefore allows facial expressiveness and vocalizations, the kindred souls of emotionality. It is also coupled with the regulation of the heart, breathing, and digestion, keeping the heart beating and digestion running smoothly; at the same time, it inhibits the sympathetic nervous system—the fight-or-flight response—to prevent a state of hyperstimulation that would needlessly burn oxygen and calories. The new vagus allows one to make all sorts of facial expressions—a smile, a frown, an artful widening of the eyes—and any number of calls, or, in the case of people, words, with little effect on breathing or metabolism.

"This enables us to signal other organisms and to be fully engaged in our surroundings, without major metabolic demands or challenges," Dr. Porges said. Yet even with the sophisticated new vagus, the older vagal systems remain, Dr. Porges said, and are called upon should the higher vagal reactions fail. If we try to talk our way out of danger, for instance, and find that the threat remains, the fight-or-flight response kicks in. If we cannot escape no matter how fast our heart beats and muscles throb, and our attacker moves in for the kill, the primitive dorsal-vagal response assumes command as a final attempt to save all life-support systems. It dramatically slows breathing and heart rate, sending one into a state of terrified shock. Alas, the last-ditch effort may prove fatal, Dr. Porges said, for a mammal cannot live long without oxygen coming in and with a heart rate slowed to nearly zero.

In a sense, then, when we lose our capacity to affiliate, we may be on our way to dying of fright.

# Chapter 56

# *Hormones, Genes, and Behavior*

## Donald W. Pfaff

In several papers published recently in *Cell, Nature,* or *Science,* biologists working with *Drosophila* have reported their discoveries that targeted expression of particular genes or deletion of certain genes can markedly alter *Drosophila* behavior. The very success of these interesting analyses has heightened the danger of some readers who are not in biological or medical fields getting the impression that "genes will organize our thinking" about brain mechanisms for behavior. This is not likely to happen.

More generally, I fear that oversimplified public reactions to discoveries in *Drosophila* sometimes will anticipate a preponderance of straightforward genetic programming in higher animals. Like most scientists, I cannot believe that "one gene–one behavior" formulations will work for mammals. Even in *Drosophila* it is rare to see a single gene underlying a behavioral polymorphism. And, clearly, opportunities for sophisticated physiological integration are simply very limited in invertebrates compared with mammals (Figure 56–1).

The best studied examples of mammalian brain–behavior mechanisms show that genes do indeed influence behavior through both direct and indirect routes in higher animals and humans. But the chains of causation from genes to behavior are multiple and complex, defying simple description and demanding, for the systematic unraveling of behavioral mechanisms, some very fine physiology. That is, the most orderly summaries of behavioral mechanisms will be based not in genetics but in physiology.

Therefore, for biomedical scientists who lack the research background of *Drosophila* geneticists and for others who think mainly about humans, clear examples of reasoning from gene to mammalian behavior are given. Well analyzed mechanisms of hormone/brain/behavior relations illustrate how subtle the reasoning can be, even for simple instinctive behaviors.

From *Proceedings of the National Academy of Science,* Vol. 94, December, 1997.

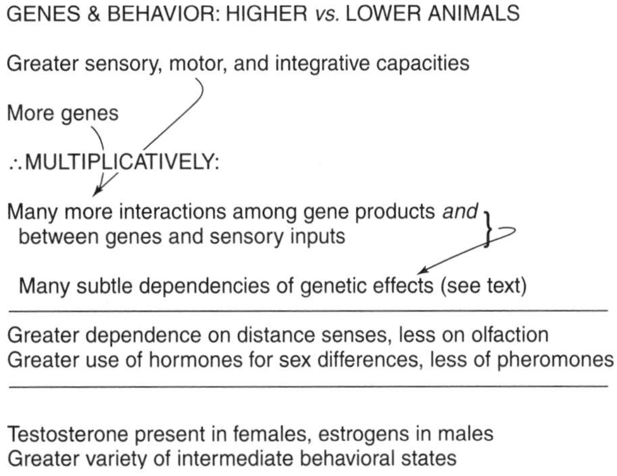

GENES & BEHAVIOR: HIGHER *vs.* LOWER ANIMALS

Greater sensory, motor, and integrative capacities

More genes

∴MULTIPLICATIVELY:

Many more interactions among gene products *and* between genes and sensory inputs

Many subtle dependencies of genetic effects (see text)

Greater dependence on distance senses, less on olfaction
Greater use of hormones for sex differences, less of pheromones

Testosterone present in females, estrogens in males
Greater variety of intermediate behavioral states

**Figure 56–1** Causal relationships of genes to behaviors pose a greater analytic challenge in mammals than in *Drosophila* because of the multiplicative nature of sensory, motor, and interneuron combinations and because of the greater variety of intermediate behavioral states.

## ATTEMPTS TO SYSTEMATIZE

Despite a long history of brilliant work on genetically amenable organisms such as *Drosophila,* we still cannot easily trace the causal routes and mechanisms by which genes could influence behavior. There are at least four reasons for this state of affairs. First, the pleiotropy of genetic actions (Hall 1994) dictates that any one gene may have many effects, relations among which may be difficult to discern. Second, overlap among functions of different genes precludes a simple demonstration that a given gene contributes to a given behavior. Third, incomplete and variable penetrance of a dominant allele render the statistical analysis of behavioral results harder to explain. Fourth, and most important, any map of possible mechanistic routes, direct and indirect, from genes to behavior must be as complex as the physiology of the organs contributing to the behavior. Because these routes will always include the central nervous system, the complexity of the mammalian brain guarantees that the task of discerning gene/neuron/behavior relations will not be finished quickly.

## EXAMPLES FROM GENES FOR NUCLEAR RECEPTORS

*Direct effects* of genes on behavior during adulthood are clearly illustrated by estrogens and progestins working through nuclear estrogen and progesterone receptors to control female reproductive behaviors (Pfaff 1999). Early work indicated that the estrogen receptor (ER) drives lordosis behavior, a component of female reproductive behavior in many higher organisms (Pfaff et al. 1994), and this was confirmed with ER antagonists (Howard et al. 1984). Recently, the ER knockout (ERKO) mouse has proven that classical ER gene expression is indeed required for estrogenic effects on lordosis (Figure 56–2) (Ogawa et al. 1996). Indeed, ERKO yields a female mouse that is more *masculinized,* behaving less like a genetic female and actually treated as a male by other mice (Ogawa et al. 1996).

Likewise, the progesterone receptor (PR) gene is required for progestin effects on female reproductive behavior (Lydon et al. 1995). Fluctuations of PR mRNA and PR binding levels in the hypothalamus are well correlated with lordosis behavior, and in fact the ability to reduce female reproductive behavior hypothalamic PR antisense DNA administration (Ogawa et al. 1994) perfectly anticipated the behavior of PR knockout mice (Figure 56–3).

### Males

The plot thickens when one looks at the genetic male with an ER knockout. Surprisingly, ERKO males show virtually no intromissions or ejaculations even though several indices of their sexual motivation appear normal (Ogawa et al. 1997). Overall, such estrogen-deficient males show marked decreases in a subset of their masculine-typical be-

| | Incidence of female reproductive behavior | Incidence of female-female aggression |
|---|---|---|
| Wild type | normal | 2/21 mice |
| Estrogen Receptor Knockout | none | 10/25 mice* |

**Figure 56–2** Behaviors of wild-type and ERKO female mice. ERKO females would not show lordosis behavior. Summarized from data in Ogawa et al. (1996)*, Aggression exhibited by ERKO females mainly offensive attacks typical of intermale aggression.

haviors and a trend toward a more *feminine-type* behavioral profile. That is, ERKO males achieved fewer intromissions and virtually no ejaculations. Their aggressive behaviors were dramatically reduced, and in particular they showed absolutely no male-typical offensive attacks. Their emotional responses to the open-field test were demasculinized. Thus, we are left with the situation in which the ERKO gene alteration renders genetic female mice more masculine (see above), yet renders genetic male mice more feminine. *The lesson: As far as a gene like that for the ER is concerned, its effect on the development of behavior depends on the sex of the animal in which it is expressed.*

Finally, analyses of hormone-dependent behaviors also show how the effect of a gene on a specific behavior depends on exactly where and exactly when that gene is expressed. Even as the ERKO female (above) is more *masculinized* in its behavior (Ogawa et al. 1996), temporary antisense DNA interruption specifically of hypothalamic ER mRNA during neonatal testosterone administration to females actually *prevents* full masculinization of the rat brain (McCarthy et al. 1993). That is, McCarthy et al. (1993) showed that ER gene product disruption limited to the hypothalamus and applied only on one neonatal day actually reduced the masculinization of forebrain and behavior due to experimentally administered testosterone. In contrast, the ER gene disruption in ERKO females is limited neither in time nor in space, and this genetic maneuver allowed more masculinized behavior (Ogawa et al. 1996). *The lesson: The effect of a genetic alteration is a function of exactly where and for how long it is applied.*

### Additional Cautions

Even slight increases in the complexity of the behavior analyzed can lead to corresponding complexity of interpretation, as illustrated by maternal behaviors, whose susceptibility to oxytocin *depends exquisitely on the precise conditions of assay* (Fahrbach et al. 1986). Female rats were not sensitive to oxytocin when they were unstressed or severely stressed, but at intermediate levels of mild stress oxytocin facilitated their maternal behavior (Fahrbach et al. 1986).

More generally, few would expect mammalian behaviors to depend only on a small number of genes—they are the perfect examples of multigenic traits. Thus, we should expect to see, for any given knockout mouse, influences of genetic background on the magnitude of the effect of any given gene (Gerlai 1996).

In summary, the gene product for the nuclear hormone receptor for estradiol has both direct and indirect (developmental) effects on reproductive behaviors. Further, even though masculinization and feminization typically are viewed as naming "opposite ends" of a continuum in reproductive biology, normal expression of the gene for the ER is necessary both for a full pattern of masculine behavior and for a full pattern of feminine behavior.

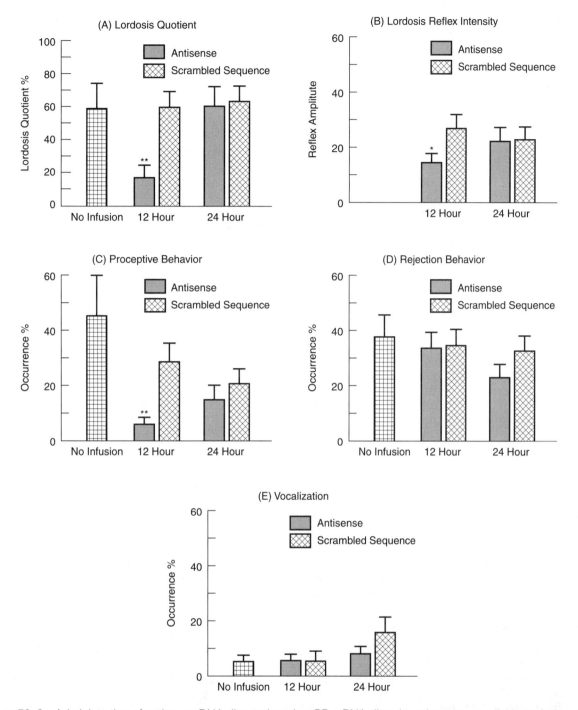

**Figure 56–3** Administration of antisense DNA directed against PR mRNA directly to the ventromedial hypothalamus significantly reduced lordotic behavior in female rats (*A* and *B*). The effect was even larger on courtship ("proceptive") behaviors, which are known to depend heavily on progesterone (*C*). In contrast, rejection behaviors were not affected (*D*), nor were vocalizations (*E*). Adapted from Ogawa et al. (1994).

## KALLMANN SYNDROME

A human syndrome provides an example of how subtle and indirect the relationships between genes and social behavior can be. Kallmann syndrome, hypogonadotropic hypogonadism, afflicts men with a striking behavioral change: absence of libido as part of a disinterest in the opposite sex. Causation of X-linked Kallmann syndrome

is now understood in light of the surprising findings that neurons producing gonadotropin-releasing hormone (GnRH) are not born as expected near brain ventricular surfaces, but instead are born in the olfactory epithelium. That is, they must migrate from the nose to the brain. In fact, X-linked Kallmann syndrome caused by genetic damage at Xp-22.3 has been correlated with a failure of migration of GnRH neurons—they were dammed up in the olfactory apparatus and never reached the brain (Schwankel-Fukuda and Pfaff 1989, Schwankel-Fukuda et al. 1989). In turn, this neuron migration disorder is rationalized by the fact that damage at Xp-22.3 disrupts a specific gene (Franco et al. 1991, Legouis et al. 1991) whose damage causes X-linked Kallmann syndrome, and this gene codes for a cell surface protein present during migration of GnRH neurons into the brain.

Putting these and related facts in a logical order leads to a clear example of complex participation by an individual gene in human behavior through its actions during neural development. That is, in males suffering from X-linked Kallmann syndrome, behavioral libido is reduced *because* of low testosterone levels, in turn *because* of reduced gonadotropins, luteinizing hormone (LH), and follicle-stimulating hormone (FSH), which in turn are low *because* there is no GnRH coming from the brain to enter the pituitary, *because* there are no GnRH cells in the brain, *because* GnRH neuronal migration has failed, *because* of the absence of the protein produced by a gene at Xp-22.3.

Thus, these data prove a genetic influence on an important human social behavior but also illustrate the complicated and indirect nature of that effect. Simplistic extrapolations from lower animals would be as unjustified here as they would be for the mammalian behaviors described above.

## IMPLICATIONS

In summary, specific genes clearly contribute to the causation of specific mammalian social behaviors and in the case of certain hormone-dependent behaviors, neurochemical mechanisms operating in known neural circuits can be specified (reviewed in Pfaff et al. 1994, Pfaff 1999). Nevertheless, the multiple determinants of the sizes and directions of these genetic effects and the many indirect routes of causation make it seem virtually impossible that simple charts of gene/behavior relationships can be drawn. Interactions between genes and environment as well as among gene products ensure that gene/behavior relations will be neither linear nor modular.

Under these circumstances, the safest theoretical approach is to flip the problem upside down. After all, biological systems are organized according to physiological function, not gene by gene. Therefore, instead of looking for elegant, systematic thinking "starting with the gene" and moving out, modern neurobiologists will do better to start with each obviously essential, "axiomatic" biological function and, in a "geometric" fashion, deduce how neural and, ultimately, molecular mechanisms satisfy that biological function. As part of that effort, illustrated for hormone-dependent behaviors above, genetic contributions both during development and in adulthood to each clearly defined biological func-

tion can be woven into the fabric of neurophysiological and neurochemical mechanisms as data accumulate.

## REFERENCES

Fahrbach, S. E.; Morrell, J. I.; Pfaff, D.W. (1986) Effect of varying the duration of pre-test cage habituation on oxytocin induction of short-latency maternal behavior. *Physiol. Behav.,* 37: 135–139.

Franco, B.; Guioli, S.; Pragliola, A.; Incerti, B.; Bardoni, B.; et al. (1991) A gene deleted in Kallman's Syndrome shares homology with neural cell adhesion and axonal path-finding molecules. *Nature (London),* 353: 529–533.

Gerlai, R. (1996) Gene targeting studies of mammalian behavior: Is it the mutation of the background genotype? *Trends in Neuroscience,* 19:177–181.

Hall J. C. (1994) Pleiotropy of behavioral genes. In *Flexibility and Constraint in Behavioral Systems,* pp. 347–359. R. J. Greenspan and C. P. Kyriacou, eds. New York: Wiley.

Howard, S. B.; Etgen, A. M.; Barfield, R. J. (1984) Antagonism of central estrogen action by intracerebral implants of tamoxifen. *Hormones and Behavior,* 18: 256–266.

Legouis, R.; Hardelin, J. P.; Levilliers, J.; Claverie, J. M.; Compain, S.; et al. (1991) The candidate gene for the x-linked Kallmann's Syndrome encodes a protein related to adhesion molecules. *Cell,* 67: 423–432.

Lydon, J. P.; DeMayo, F. J.; Funk, C. R.; Mani, S. K.; Hughes, A. R.; Montgomery, C. A. Jr.; Shyamala, G.; Conneely, O. M; O'Malley, B. W. (1995) Mice lacking progesterone receptor exhibit pleiotropic reproductive abnormalities. *Genes and Development,* 9: 2266–2278.

McCarthy, M. M.; Schlenker, E.; Pfaff, D. W. (1993) Enduring consequences of neonatal treatment antisense oligodeoxynucleotides to estrogen receptor messenger ribonucleic acid on sexual differentiation of rat brain. *Endocrinology,* 133:433–443.

Ogawa, S.; Lubahn, D. B.; Korach, K. S.; Pfaff, D. W. (1997) Behavioral effects of estrogen receptor disruption in male mice. *Proc. Nat. Acad. Sci., USA* 94:1476–1481.

Ogawa, S.; Olazabal, U. E.; Parhar, I. S.; Pfaff, D. W. (1997) Effects of intrathalamic administration of antisense DNA for progesterone receptor mRNA on reproductive behavior and progesterone receptor immunoreactivity in female rats. *Journal of Neuroscience* 14:1766–1774.

Ogawa, S.; Taylor, J.; Lubahn, D. B.; Korach, K. S.; Pfaff, D. W. (1996) Reversal of sex roles in female mice by disruption of estrogen receptor gene. *Neuroendocrinology* 64:467–470.

Pfaff, D. W.; *Drive.* Cambridge: MIT Press, 1999.

Pfaff, D. W.; Schwartz-Giblin, S.; McCarthy, M. M.; Kow, L.-M. (1994) Neural and molecular mechanisms of female reproductive behavior. In *The Physiology of Reproduction* (pp. 107–220) (2nd ed.). E. Knobil and J. Neill, eds. New York: Raven.

Schwanzel-Fukuda, M.; Bick, D.; Pfaff, D. W. (1989) Leuteinizing hormone-releasing hormone (LHRH)-expressing cells do not migrate normally in an inherited hypogonadal (Kallmann's) syndrome. *Mol. Brain Res.,* 6: 311–326.

Schwanzel-Fukuda, M.; Pfaff, D. W. (1989) Origin of leuteinizing hormone-releasing hormone neurons. *Nature (London).* 338: 161–164.

# Chapter 57

# *Think Again*

John Tooby
Leda Cosmides

As part of an effort to introduce an evolutionarily rigorous research framework into psychology and the other behavioral sciences (and to strengthen it within biology itself, where it is surprisingly rarely understood), we and a few others have introduced and used the term *evolutionary psychology*. Despite a widespread traditional conviction in many fields that behavior, social relations, culture, or mental phenomena are somehow outside of the scope of Darwinian analysis (see, for discussion, Tooby and Cosmides 1992), the principles of core Darwinism constitute an organism design theory whose engineering principles apply with as much force to the computational and neural machinery that produces behavior as to any other set of organs or tissues in the body (Cosmides and Tooby 1987). Indeed, increasingly accurate characterizations of the designs of these computational devices must eventually form the centerpiece of any meaningful theory of behavior, for any species, in any discipline (e.g., economics; see Cosmides and Tooby 1994).

In this sense, theories of behavior and theories of the structure of psychological mechanisms are simply two sides of the same coin. Observing patterns in behavior is one source of information that helps to reverse engineer the computational designs of the mechanisms that generate those patterns. Reciprocally, accurate knowledge of these designs yields precise theories of the behaviors that these designs generate. Evolution is logically linked to behavior only through its engineering impact on the psychological mechanisms that regulate behavior, and so evolutionary theories of behavior are, inevitably, psychological theories, whether their proponents explicitly recognize it or not. This is why behavioral measures and field studies are a regular part of evolutionary psy-

chological research, along with a broad array of other methods, such as the study of focal brain damage, electromyography, hormone assays, psychophysics, cross-cultural comparison, experimental economic studies, neuroimaging, cognitive experimentation, psychopharmacological dissociations, the analysis of incidence rates from archive-derived data, and so on. Indeed, this is why evolutionary psychology and behavioral ecology are, in reality, essentially the same discipline. The only difference is that the term *evolutionary psychology* was adopted to identify a research program within modem evolutionary biology and behavioral ecology that adheres strictly to the logical structure of Darwinism and that is committed to characterizing the phenotypic designs of mechanisms, which are (usually complex) adaptations. Many researchers who identify themselves as behavioral ecologists share this program, but many do not.

By adaptations we mean inherited arrangements of elements in organisms that have been brought into their specific mutual relationship because that configuration, over evolutionary time, promoted the frequency of that inherited arrangement. In other words, adaptations are systems of functional machinery that assumed their improbably well-ordered functional relationships because, in the ancestral lineage's environment of evolutionary adaptedness, these relationships successfully accomplished tasks that increased the frequency of the alleles coding for those traits. Most phenotypic design consists of adaptations that are complex, that is, consisting of many components that depend for their existence on alleles at multiple loci. Because of sexual recombination and the combinatorics of alleles, most complex adaptations in humans and similar species will necessarily be species-typical and will depend on alleles at many loci being at or near fixation (for analysis, and appropriate qualifications, see Tooby and Cosmides 1990a).

From *Human Nature* Laura Betzig, (ed.), 1997.

With the foregoing as background, one can define the *environment of evolutionary adaptedness* for an adaptation as that set of selection pressures (i.e., properties of the ancestral world) that endured long enough to push each allele underlying the adaptation from its initial appearance to near fixation, and to maintain them there while other necessary alleles at related loci were similarly brought approximately to fixation. Because moving mutations from low initial frequencies to fixation takes substantial time, and sequential fixations must usually have been necessary to construct complex adaptations, almost all complex functional design in organisms owes its detailed organization to the complex and enduring structure of each species' past. Each design feature present in a modern organism is there because of a large and structured population of events in the past, and these event populations must be characterized if the design features are to be understood. It is a surprising lapse in many excellent evolutionary researchers' thought (see, e.g., Reeve and Sherman 1993) that they are not adaptationists in this strict Darwinian sense but focus instead on the present fitness consequences of a trait, which cannot logically play any role in explaining its existence (Symons 1992; Tooby and Cosmides 1990b).

Because selection is an antientropic process that operates across generations to build functional order into an organism's design, pushing upstream against entropy, the standards required to establish that a set of traits as an adaptation are probabilistic in nature (as they are in any good science). More specifically, one can use a knowledge of selection pressures, ancestral conditions, and computational principles to formulate hypotheses about the likely existence of various cognitive adaptations. To evaluate whether there is evidence for a particular adaptation, the question to be asked is: How improbably well ordered are the elements of the proposed adaptation, if one assumes its function was to reliably solve an adaptive problem or achieve an adaptive outcome in the organism's EEA? The metric is not optimality but rather, how much better than random is the adaptation at achieving biologically functional outcomes? In Williams's language, what is the evidence of special design (Williams 1966)? That is, what is the evidence that the problem is solved with efficiency, reliability, economy, precision, and so on?

As one part of our research, we have been investigating the hypothesis that the human mind contains specialized information-processing adaptations designed to guide individuals successfully through social exchange. To provide a prototype of what an adaptationist psychological research paper might look like, we wrote "Cognitive Adaptations for Social Exchange," discussing selection pressures, ancestral conditions, predicted design features, and experimental evidence of special design, as well as the by-product counterhypotheses that had been eliminated experimentally. Since this paper, we and others have now produced a much larger body of evidence supporting the hypothesis that humans have specialized cognitive devices for this purpose (e.g., Cosmides and Tooby, in prep.; Fiddick et al. in prep; Gigerenzer and Hug 1995; Hoffman et al. 1996). One task is to show that any proposed complex psychological adaptation is effectively human universal, and not limited to some cultures but not others. Toward that end, these results have been replicated not only in a number of literate populations around the world but also using nonliterate subjects drawn from the Achuar, a hunter-horticulturalist population in the Amazonian region of Ecuador (Sugiyama et al. in prep.).

A second approach is to demonstrate that this specialized reasoning ability is a discrete, independent computational ability distinct from other abilities to reason, with its own unique properties and principles of activation. Toward this end, we have also accumulated a significant body of evidence supporting the existence of, and allowing us to separately characterize, three other reasoning adaptations (out of what we expect to be hundreds) with sharply differentiated functions and properties. These three include one for detecting lapses in taking precautions to avoid danger; one for detecting bluffs when one is threatened; and one for detecting double crosses when one is threatened. The most common counterhypothesis is that human reasoning is general purpose and does not contain multiple reasoning specializations that operate according to domain-specific principles. If this were true, and there was only one psychological mechanism involved, then neither neurological impairments nor experimental manipulations should lead to dissociations in performance on tasks that differ only in whether they concern social contracts or precautions. To the human mind, these would all be instances of the same task, solved by the same mechanism, embodied in the same neural circuitry. However, subjects do experience experimentally induced dissociations that break down along the predicted lines—indicating that social exchange mechanisms and precaution mechanisms are cognitively real and separate mechanisms in humans (Fiddick et al. in prep.). We are presently collaborating on a study to identify the neural basis of these mechanisms by identifying individuals who suffer selective impairments to one or another of these mechanisms as the result of neurological damage. Indeed, Maljkovic (1987) has found that the ability to detect cheaters is maintained in schizophrenics, while other, more general deliberative reasoning abilities are impaired. This dissociation between social contract algorithms and general problem-solving ability constitutes another line of evidence suggesting that the social exchange mechanisms are a distinct and specialized competence. We are also collaborating on another study into the precaution and social exchange competences of individuals with autism. Autism is now believed to be a disorder caused by damage to part of an evolved faculty of social cognition—specifically, to the "theory of mind" module, a mechanism that causes people to infer that the actions of others are caused by unobservable mental attributes, such as beliefs and desires. Social exchange circuits are a part of social cognition, while precaution circuits need involve no social dimension. One intriguing possibility is that individuals with autism will be able to reason correctly about precautions, since they are nonsocial, but not about social exchanges. Another facet of this research program involves expanding the theoretical analysis from dyadic cooperation or social exchange to *n*-person cooperation, and mapping the set of computational devices that allow humans to form, participate in, manipulate, and abandon coalitions. The existence of a set of specialized cognitive devices that make sophisticated coalitional action possible is one central way in which human sociality differs from that of virtually all other species. Preliminary evidence suggests that at least some of the predicted coalitional mechanisms do exist.

In summary, a number of researchers have gone a long way toward establishing the existence of complex adaptive computational designs in the mind, designed to reason about social exchange. The weight of evidence now indicates that such mechanisms are species-typical. We anticipate that in the foreseeable future, we will be able to identify the neural basis of these mechanisms and their relationship to other related subsystems in human social cognition. What remains distant is the elucidation of the genetic bases and developmental biology of these adaptations.

# REFERENCES

Cosmides, L.; Tooby, J. (1987) "From evolution to behavior: Evolutionary psychology as the missing link." In *The Latest on the Best: Essays on Evolution and Optimality* (pp. 277–306). J. Dupré, ed. Cambridge, MA: MIT Press.

Cosmides, L.; Tooby, J. (1994) "Evolutionary psychology and the invisible hand." *American Economic Review,* 84:327–332.

Cosmides, L; Tooby J. (in prep.) "Social contracts, precaution rules, and threats: How to tell one schema from another."

Fiddick, L.; Cosmides, L.; Tooby, J. (in prep.) "Dissociations between reasoning modules: Evidence from priming studies."

Gigerenzer G.; Hug, H. (1995) "Rationality: Why social context matters." In *Interactive Minds: Life-Span Perspectives on the Social Foundations of Cognition.* P. Baltes and U. Staudinger, eds. Cambridge, UK: Cambridge University Press.

Hoffman, E.; McCabe, K.; Smith, V. (1996) *Behavior Foundations of Reciprocity: Experimental Economics and Evolutionary Psychology.* Unpublished manuscript.

Maljkovic, V. 1987. *Reasoning in Evolutionarily Important Domains and Schizophrenia: Dissociation between Content-Dependent and Content-Independent Reasoning.* Unpublished graduate honors thesis, Dept. Psych., Harvard University.

Reeve, H. K.; Sherman, P. W. (1993) "Adaptation and the goals of evolutionary research." *Quarterly Review of Biology,* 68:1–32.

Sugiyama, J.; Tooby, J.; Cosmides, L. (in prep.) Cheater-detection in a Yanomamo population.

Symons, D. (1992) "On the use and misuse of Darwinism in the study of human behavior." In *The Adapted Mind: Evolutionary Psychology and the Generation of Culture* (pp. 137–159). J. Barkow et al., eds. New York: Oxford University Press.

Tooby, J.; Cosmides, L. (1990a) "On the universality of human nature and the uniqueness of the individual: The role of genetics and adaptation." *Jounal of Personality,* 58:17–67.

Tooby, J.; Cosmides, L. (1990b) "The past explains the present: Emotional adaptations and the structure of ancestral environments." *Ethology and Sociobiology,* 11:375–424.

Tooby, J.; Cosmides, L. (1992) "The psychological foundations of culture." In *The Adapted Mind: Evolutionary Psychology and the Generation of Culture* (pp. 19–136). J. Barkow et al., eds. New York: Oxford University Press.

Williams, G. C. (1966) *Adaptation and Natural Selection: A Critique of Some Current Evolutionary Thought.* Princeton, NJ: Princeton University Press.

# Chapter 58

# *Our Genes, Ourselves?*

## Ari Berkowitz

"Now we know, in large measure, our fate is in our genes." So said James Watson (Jaroff 1989), Nobel laureate, co-discoverer of the structure of DNA, and first leader of the Human Genome Project.

Is he right? We in the United States seem to be of two minds. Most of us have an intuition that, although our genes provide advantages and constraints, we retain great control over our lives. But we are developing a second, competing intuition that, like it or not, our genes determine our abilities, our preferences, and our emotions. Perhaps this second intuition is what induced Rutgers University President Francis Lawrence, a man who has spent years trying to increase opportunities for minorities, to say that blacks do not have "the genetic, hereditary background, to do as well as whites on college admissions tests," a statement that caused an uproar across the country (Olen 1995). We would like to think we are much more than the sum of our genes, but scientists have apparently demonstrated that our genes determine some of our most complex behavioral and cognitive characteristics.

Science is not an unblemished source of objectivity. Science is done by scientists. Scientists both influence contemporary culture and are influenced by the culture. Research questions are chosen and framed partly in response to current medical, social, and political concerns. The process of obtaining research funding requires scientists to write proposals to compete for grants and encourages them to present flashy results on issues of immediate public interest. The development of powerful new methods for studying DNA in the past three decades has led to a proliferation of explanations of all sorts of human characteristics in terms of genes.

The focus on genes as the primary mode of biological explanation has been especially clear in the marketing of the Human Genome Project. In support of this project, some respected biologists have expressed views that are surprisingly similar to those once held by the leaders of the American eugenics movement, which brought us racially based immigration quotas and laws for forced sterilization of the "feeble-minded."

Charles B. Davenport, the biologist who led the American eugenics movement as founder and director of the Eugenics Record Office at Cold Spring Harbor, New York, wrote in 1928:

> [T]he widespread existence of crime enforces the lessons of eugenics. We are breeding too many people with feeble inhibitions and without proper social instincts; persons who have a tendency toward periodic outbreaks of temper and to assaults; persons who are liable to periodic bad behavior, including the kind that is associated with the epileptic state; persons who are introverts, selfish and non-social. Satisfactory progress will be made only when we understand how those with congenital criminalistic make-up are bred and try to prevent such breeding. If we permit them to be born, then we must apply such special treatment as will prevent their behavior from disorganizing society.

Daniel E. Koshland, Jr., a contemporary molecular biologist and then Editor-in-Chief of the journal *Science*, wrote in *Science* in 1990:

> Last week a crazed gunman terrorized hostages in a bar in Berkeley, killing one and wounding many others.... Schizophrenia (the disease from which the Berkeley gunman is thought to have suffered) and other major mental illnesses can have a multigenic origin. A sequenced human genome will be a very important tool for understanding this precise category of diseases.... The combination of new tools may not only let us help in reducing crime, but also aid some of our most disadvantaged citizens, the mentally ill. Although increased funding of mental health centers, stricter gun control, increased supervision of the mentally unbalanced, or higher standards for probation officers may be desirable, they are

From *BioScience* Vol. 46, No.1, 1996.

Band-Aid remedies. In the long run, the solution will be found in the knowledge required to produce accurate diagnoses and cures. The research to provide that knowledge will be far cheaper, and the results much fairer, than Draconian law enforcement.

Robert L. Sinsheimer, biologist and former chancellor at the University of California, Santa Cruz and an architect of the Human Genome Project, wrote in 1969:

> The new genetics would permit in principle the conversion of all of the unfit to the highest genetic level.... I know there are those who find this concept and this prospect repugnant.... They are not among the losers in that chromosomal lottery that so firmly channels our human destinies.... [such as] the 50,000,000 "normal" Americans with an IQ of less than 90.... Equality of opportunity is a noble aim given the currently inescapable genetic diversity of man. But what does equality of opportunity mean to the child born with an IQ of 50?

In 1991, in support of the Human Genome Project, Sinsheimer affirmed, "[i]n the deepest sense we are who we are because of our genes."

Does the available scientific evidence actually tell us that our genes determine our behavioral, emotional, and cognitive characteristics? Do single genes specify particular behavioral traits? To answer these questions, most nonspecialists depend upon the cursory reports of new research findings that appear regularly in the lay press. These reports are often oversimplified and may be shaped by the desire of both journalists and scientists to create an exciting story. Sober-minded assessments with broader perspectives seldom attract as much interest, either in the lay press or in scientific journals. As a result, our perceptions of the scientific evidence may be skewed by a few dramatic findings, some of which may be wrong.

Nowhere has this been more clear than in the representation of the roles of genes in determining uniquely human characteristics, involving our thoughts, emotions, and behaviors. Within the past decade, there have been highly visible reports localizing genes for schizophrenia (Sherrington et al. 1988), manic-depression (Baron et al. 1987, Egeland et al. 1987), alcoholism (Blum et al. 1990), and homosexuality (Hamer et al. 1993). Recently, there was even a report of a "gene site for bed-wetting" (Goleman 1995). Other groups of scientists have generally been unable to reproduce the findings for schizophrenia (Kennedy et al. 1988), manic-depression (Detera-Wadleigh et al. 1987, Hodgkinson et al. 1987), and alcoholism (Gelernter et al. 1991, 1993). Authors of two studies claiming to have found a gene for manic-depression (in two different places), have both published retractions of their conclusions (Baron et al. 1993, Kelsoe et al. 1989), unusual and embarrassing events among scientists. These reversals have led to much methodological soul-searching within the pages of scientific journals and books, but have been described cursorily in newspapers and less, if at all, on television. Research linking genes to complex human mental and behavioral characteristics has been tremendously successful in molding public opinion, in the absence of much lasting scientific evidence.

There is only one antidote for the effects of skewed research reporting: Nonspecialists must learn more about experiments and interpretations used in this branch of science. Examining the types of methods and experiments that are used to support simple genetic explanations of human behavior allows one to see how ambiguities and biases can lead to misinterpretations. The relationship between a gene and a human behavior is rarely, if ever, a one-to-one correspondence, even though disruption of a single gene occasionally has a dramatic effect on behavior. Nor can one quantify the contribution of genes as a whole to any particular behavior or cognitive ability. Instead, each gene is a single player in a wonderfully intricate story, involving nonadditive interactions of genes, proteins, hormones, food, and life experiences, and leading to effects on a variety of cognitive and behavioral functions. Our thoughts, emotions, and behaviors certainly have biological mechanisms, but this does not mean we can separate and quantify the genetic contributions to these processes.

## LINKAGE STUDIES

It has long been observed that certain human behavioral characteristics tend to "run in families," but these characteristics might be caused by either genes or environments, or some combinations of the two. For much of this century, some investigators have attempted to demonstrate and quantify genetic contributions to human cognition and behavior, most notably IQ, by examining identical twins and applying questionable interpretations (see Kamin 1974, Lewontin et al. 1984, and below). More recently, some researchers have taken advantage of new techniques for manipulation of DNA to attempt to locate individual genes that either determine or convey a propensity to behavioral characteristics. Such studies are much easier to conduct with nonhuman animals, in laboratory settings where environmental effects and mating pairs can be controlled, than with human beings, but it is eventually necessary to examine human DNA if one wishes to find genes that cause, for example, human psychiatric conditions.

Experiments linking a gene to a complex human characteristic can be informative, but they also can produce misconceptions if they are not interpreted with care. Such experiments generally rely on a statistical argument that a segment of DNA and a complex characteristic tend to co-occur in individuals more often than one would expect at random. In particular, the statistical argument relies on the natural process of "crossing over," in which the matching chromosomes of each parent pair up and sometimes exchange pieces of DNA. Thus, two genes that had begun on the same chromosome can end up on different chromosomes. The probability that two stretches of DNA will end up in the same gamete (and thus the same person), despite crossing over, is related to their proximity on the chromosome: the closer together they are, the more likely they are to remain on the same chromosome.

When scientists begin searching for a gene that may be related to a complex human characteristic, they usually know nothing about the likely location of the gene, the protein that it specifies, or the function of that protein. Instead of directly examining whether a particular gene causes a particular characteristic, they use easily traceable pieces of DNA, called genetic markers, to narrow down the possible location of such a gene. If a marker is consistently found in individuals who have a particular characteristic, and not found in other individuals, then it is inferred that there is a gene near the marker that is "linked" to the characteristic. The gene need not include the marker; if they are sufficiently close together, they will tend to remain together despite crossing over. Thus, linkage between a marker and a trait does not indicate that a relevant gene bas been identified, but may indicate that a relevant locale has been found. In some cases, investigators begin with an educated guess: rather than using random genetic markers, they look for linkage to particular genes that have already been identified, called candidate genes, which they believe might function in the behavior under study. Experiments on nonhuman animals sometimes suggest candidate genes, but this by no means guarantees that a similar gene in human beings will be linked to the behavior of interest.

This type of research has been very successful in locating genes that cause a disease in an all-or-none manner. Huntington's disease, for example, is a complex behavioral disorder that is known to be caused by a single gene. Proponents of genetic determination can point to this example and suggest that many other complex behavioral disorders are probably determined by single genes. But the inheritance pattern for Huntington's disease is very different from inheritance patterns for conditions like manic-depression, schizophrenia, and alcoholism.

For more than a century, Huntington's disease was known to be caused by a single gene on the basis of its strikingly reliable pattern of inheritance: Half the offspring (on average) of each victim of Huntington's disease develop the disease. This means that the disease is caused by a single gene that only needs to be present in one copy; it was just a matter of finding the gene.

In contrast, patterns of occurrence within families are very irregular and unpredictable for manic-depression, schizophrenia, and alcoholism. These patterns of occurrence are not consistent with there being a single gene that determines whether one develops the condi-

tion (Risch 1994). Instead, if indeed there are genes that can have important effects on these conditions, there are likely to be several genes, each of which has only a small effect on its own, that may interact in a nonadditive manner with one another and with environmental factors to generate each condition. An assumption of single-gene causation can lead to an unwarranted conclusion that linkage has been demonstrated, in addition to over-interpretation of genuine linkage.

A closer examination of one example will illustrate some of the difficulties of genetic linkage studies of complex human characteristics. In 1987, Janice A. Egeland and colleagues reported in the journal *Nature* that they had localized "a dominant gene conferring a strong predisposition to manic-depressive disease" on human chromosome 11, and demonstrated "by a linkage strategy that a simple genetic mechanism can account for the transmission" of manic-depression in the family they studied. *Nature* highlighted this report, saying, "[t]he use of DNA markers has shown that manic-depressive illness can be caused by a signal gene" (Robertson 1987). In the same journal issue, *Nature* published two related studies (Detera-Wadleigh et al. 1987, Hodgkinson et al. 1987); each reported that they had found no linkage between the same genetic markers used by Egeland and manic-depression in other families. These negative findings received relatively little attention.

There were at least three possible reasons for the discrepancies in linkage results. First, either Egeland's study or both of the other studies could have been in error; in the former case, the apparent linkage might have occurred purely by chance. Second, manic-depression might have been caused largely by a single gene in the family Egeland studied, but caused by nongenetic factors and/or the interaction of several genes, each having a small effect, in the other families. Third, manic-depression might have been caused largely by a single gene in each of the families studied, but by a different gene, in a different location, in the families with no linkage to the chromosome 11 markers, a situation known as heterogeneity. Surprisingly, only the third possibility was considered. Hodgkinson and colleagues concluded "that there is genetic heterogeneity of linkage in manic depression," despite the fact that Hodgkinson's study had found no evidence at all for a gene linked to manic depression. *Nature* said, "[t]his means there are at least two different genes predisposing to affective disorder."

There was apparently great eagerness to support a hypothesis of simple genetic causation for manic-depression. Meanwhile, another group of researchers published a report of linkage between manic-depression and a different region of DNA, on a different chromosome, also in *Nature* (Baron et al. 1987). They concluded that their results "provide confirmation that a major psychiatric disorder can be caused by a single genetic defect."

In 1989, Egeland's group published a "reevaluation" of their own findings (Kelsoe et al. 1989), also in *Nature*, based on a change in diagnosis for two family members, as well as new data from additional family members. The updated analysis demolished the statistical argument; they now "excluded" their proposed linkage. In discussing this reversal, they introduced the possibilities that the original linkage was "due merely to chance," that a single gene might not have a major effect on manic depression, and "that nongenetic factors may contribute." They suggested that the reevaluation had highlighted "problems that can be anticipated in genetic linkage studies of common and complex neuropsychiatric disorders."

In 1993, Baron et al. also published what amounts to a retraction of their linkage claims, based on a similar reevaluation. Despite these retractions, a recent human genetics textbook (Lewis 1994) informs students that manic-depression "can be inherited as a sex-linked recessive trait or as an autosomal recessive trait," without citing evidence. In 1994, there were two more reports of genetic links to manic-depression, each pointing to yet another chromosome (Berrettini et al. 1994, Straub et al. 1994). Similar events have already undermined the reported genetic linkages to schizophrenia (Kennedy et al. 1988) and alcoholism (Gelernter et al. 1991, 1993).

Why did the genetic linkage studies of manic-depression go astray? Joseph S. Alper and Marvin R. Natowicz (1993) have argued that a "preconceived belief that the primary cause of these illnesses is in fact genetic" can lead to "erroneous conclusions." Ambiguity and bias can potentially creep into at least two important phases of genetic linkage studies of complex human characteristics: the diagnosis or categorization of the characteristic and the statistical evaluation of linkage.

Given the variety and complexity of human behavior, it may be difficult, or even impossible, to assign each person unambiguously to a category such as "normal" or "manic-depressive." Is there exactly one condition that goes by the name "manic-depression"? Can the diagnosis be shaped partly by the currently available methods and categories for diagnosis or by the objectives of the study?

Analogous questions need to be asked regarding diagnoses or assignments for many other complex human characteristics, including schizophrenia, alcoholism, homosexuality, and intelligence. For example, following the 1990 report of a gene linked to alcoholism, authored by Kenneth Blum, Ernest P. Noble, and colleagues, several other scientists expressed skepticism (Peele 1990) and later reported that they were unable to replicate this finding (Gelernter et al. 1991, 1993). Noble initially countered that the gene they studied was not linked to alcoholism per se, but to "pleasure-seeking behaviors" (Peele 1990). Later, Blum and Noble amended this to "addictive-compulsive behaviors" (Blum and Noble 1994). Their claim thus became a moving target.

The appropriate statistical methods for concluding that there is genuine linkage to a complex human characteristic are a matter of considerable debate within the field. In order to calculate the probability of linkage to a complex human trait, researchers have usually proposed a "model" for genetic transmission of the trait that includes values of several parameters that cannot be measured independently. These parameters include the frequency of occurrence of each form of the gene of interest and the probability that a person carrying the gene will in fact exhibit the trait (this probability is often less than 100%, even when a single gene is linked to the trait). Researchers estimated or assumed values for these parameters in the families they studied. The calculated probability of linkage, as well as its interpretation, depend importantly on the validity of these assumptions.

Many human behavioral geneticists now believe that each of these more complex behavioral disorders is caused by a combination of several disrupted or altered genes (see Gershon and Cloninger 1994). Each of these genes may have only a small effect, they may interact in nonadditive ways, and different abnormal forms may occur in different families. So each of these disorders might be due to genes alone, but the complexity of the genetic mechanisms might preclude a definitive finding with current techniques.

This suggestion is theoretically possible and may in itself lead to useful experiments in which additional relevant genes are identified. However, it also may be an "unfalsifiable hypothesis." That is, there may be no way of disproving it even if it is false; a proponent of genetic causation could always argue that there has been no reliable demonstration of the effect of particular disease gene because there are additional unknown disease genes or gene interactions that cloud the picture.

In essence, this view retains the mind-set that applies for a single-gene disorder, while recognizing that several genes may be involved. As will be argued below, if interactions between a gene and other genes or environmental factors are acknowledged to influence a condition, it becomes difficult to describe or quantify the effect of one gene, or all genes, on the condition.

In the absence of definitive evidence, the language of human behavioral genetics may create a bias in favor of simple genetic explanations. For example, by defining any mental condition or characteristic as a "trait," one suggests that the characteristic is somehow like Mendel's traits of wrinkled or smooth peas and thus may show a regular pattern of inheritance. Similarly, "disease" suggests a biological process that is relatively independent of psychological influences. Attaching a name like "schizophrenia" or "intelligence" to a set of behaviors or functions suggests that the named category corresponds to a physiologically well-defined entity or state, which it may not. Even if a gene has a real effect on a cognitive or behavioral characteristic, such categorization may create a distorted view of what the gene's effect really is (Cloninger 1994).

Sometimes, researchers find that a characteristic (or "phenotype") can be caused entirely by nongenetic factors; these nongenetic cases are termed "phenocopies" (i.e., copies of the phenotype), as if they are facsimiles of the condition rather than the real thing. For example, fruit flies develop with four wings instead of two if they have a mutation in the bithorax gene or if they are exposed to heat or chemical stress at a critical phase of embryonic development (Capdevila and Garcia-Bellido 1978). The environmentally induced effects are termed phenocopies of bithorax, but one might just as well term the bithorax mutation a "genocopy," following Steven Rose (1995).

The less we know about the chain of events linking a gene to a behavior, the greater the likelihood that a correlation is established that does not indicate causation. Even if a correlation between a stretch of DNA and a well-defined, complex human characteristic can be firmly established, what does this tell us? We would like to know what causative role a gene plays in the chain of events leading to a behavioral outcome. This chain of events should include which gene is involved, which protein it codes for, what the function(s) of this protein is, and how this protein could produce changes in the nervous system that could underlie the mental characteristic. This is obviously a daunting task, but it is a necessary one. Research addressing such questions, mainly using nonhuman animals, in fact constitutes a major part of current biological research. But such causal schemes can be elucidated only gradually, while new linkages between genes and human behaviors can appear at any time.

To see how misleading linkage studies might be in the absence of a plausible causal scheme, consider genes that we already know something about. If I have one of the genes that contributes to pale skin, and I sit in the sun for several hours without sunscreen, I will probably get a bad sunburn. If I do it enough, I may stand a higher risk of getting skin cancer. If we knew only that there was linkage between that segment of DNA and occurrences of sunburn or skin cancer, we might conclude that it was a gene for sunburn or even a gene for skin cancer. Consider a gene that contributes to extraordinary growth. Suppose that researchers found linkage between this segment of DNA and the tendency to play NBA basketball; would we say that this is a gene for basketball playing?

## TWIN STUDIES

When human genetic linkage studies are unable to provide definitive evidence for a gene's role in causing a complex condition, proponents of genetic causation often fall back on twin studies to demonstrate that genes are crucially involved in the condition. For example, following retraction of Egeland's reported genetic linkage to manic-depression in 1989, *Nature* stated, "this leaves us with no persuasive evidence linking any psychiatric disease to a single [genetic] locus." Nonetheless, *Nature* argued on the basis of twin studies that readers "should

have no reason to doubt the existence of genetic predisposition to psychiatric disease, nor the ability of molecular geneticists eventually to identify the genes responsible" (Robertson 1989). In 1993, following the retraction of the Baron et al. reported genetic linkage to manic-depression, with no substantiated evidence remaining for genetic linkage to either manic-depression or schizophrenia, David L. Pauls, one of Egeland's coauthors, nonetheless asserted that "there is overwhelming evidence that genetic factors play an important role in the manifestation of all major neuropsychiatric conditions" (Pauls 1993).

Twin studies are also used as evidence that genes play a large role in determining normal mental characteristics, such as those labeled "personality type" or "general intelligence." Such categories of normal cognitive function are not generally expected to derive from a single gene, even if some complex disorders are due to alteration of a single gene. As an analogy, one can break a transistor radio by removing one component, but no one would seriously argue that the missing component alone normally causes the radio to play a particular radio station. (In support of this argument, no one has yet claimed to have located a gene for intelligence.) But twin studies are used to estimate the net effect of all genes on a characteristic.

Twin studies are often based on the premise that one can estimate the percentage "heritability" for complex human traits. Heritability here is a technical term, indicating the proportion of variation (or variance) in a measurable trait (or phenotype) that is statistically associated with genetic variation.

There are several major problems with the use of this measure in human studies (Hartl and Clark 1989, Kempthorne 1978, Lewontin 1974). The first is that heritability can only be estimated accurately if one can compare the effects of different sets of genes (or genotypes) in organisms that face controlled environments throughout development. This requires that individuals mate randomly with respect to their environments, to eliminate gene-environment covariance, a situation that cannot be achieved in studies of human beings. Then one can estimate how much variance is associated with the genotype, provided that one can first estimate the variance associated with the environment and the variance associated with gene-environment interactions, because the effects of genes and environments are not generally additive. This is also not possible in human studies. In the absence of such controlled experiments, researchers have attempted to estimate the variation associated with different genotypes by comparing individuals that are categorized by the researchers as having faced similar environments.

Even in breeding studies of plants or nonhuman animals, where heritability can often be estimated accurately, heritability only indicates the proportion of variance associated with genotypic variation for the particular population of genotypes and the particular range of environments tested. Even if a trait has a high heritability within each of two groups of genotypes (for example, African Americans and Caucasian Americans), this says nothing about the source of any differences between these groups. Even if a trait has a high heritability in the environments tested, a major change in the environment (which might include improving education or health care in human cases) may dramatically alter not only the phenotypes but the heritability as well. In short, heritability cannot be measured accurately in human studies and would not indicate the relative importance of genes and environments anyway. Proponents of genetic causation have probably gotten a lot of mileage out of human heritability estimates (especially of IQ) by confusion of the statistical term "heritability" with the ordinary use of the word "heritable."

In human twin studies, heritability is estimated by comparing phenotypic variance in identical twins, who share 100 percent of their genes, and fraternal twins or other siblings, who share 50 percent of their genes (on average). This estimate also assumes that the similarity in environment for identical twins is no greater than for fraternal twins. However, there are many reasons for thinking that identical twins share an unusually similar environment. For example, parents often dress them identically and involve them in the same activities; in addition, identical twins often have an extraordinarily close relationship with one another.

The heritability estimates produced by these studies have generally ranged between 40 percent and 70 percent for general intelligence or personality type (Bouchard et al. 1990, Plomin et al. 1994). Billings and colleagues (1992) have pointed out that for complex characteristics influenced by combinations of genes, these numbers are likely to be overestimates for the general population, because identical twins share all their genes, whereas even a small change in the combination of genes, such as is likely to occur for fraternal twins, can have a large effect on the characteristic.

Because studies of twins raised together are ambiguous, much of the weight of genetic causation of complex human mental characteristics sits on the shoulders of the relatively few studies of identical twins raised apart; about 300 pairs of such twins have now been studied (Powledge 1993). These cases appear to provide well-controlled accidental experiments that demonstrate the role of genes alone. However, there are subtle reasons why this may not be so. Twins in such studies often were raised by relatives or close family friends; in some cases, the twins came into contact with each other and became close friends, as has been documented by psychologist Leon J. Kamin (Kamin 1974, Lewontin et al. 1984). These kinds of events confound the effect of identical genes with the effects of similar environments; more-

over, information on potentially correlated environments is often not available for reexamination.

Another factor now recognized to be important is the different responses (and hence different environments) elicited by children who have different characteristics early on (including race, sex, size, attractiveness, and activity level). That is, children partly create their own environments, and children who are initially similar (due mainly to their genes) will tend to create similar environments, which in turn lead to additional similarities.

Thomas J. Bouchard, Jr. and colleagues, the authors of some of the most influential twin studies, have argued that identical twins "tend to elicit, select, seek out, or create very similar effective environments and, to that extent, the impact of these experiences is counted as a genetic influence" (Bouchard et al. 1990). Richard Dawkins, an ethologist and popular author of *The Selfish Gene,* claims that "[i]f a genetic sex difference makes itself felt through the medium of a sex-biased education system, it is still a genetic difference" (Dawkins 1982). These comments underscore the fact that even the simple term, "genetic," can be used in a manner that misleads the unwary reader into believing in a simple scheme of genetic causation.

A common-sense view of this situation is that interactions between genes and environment in human child-rearing may be too complex to disentangle by examining such cases. In fact, one might argue that any comparisons of identical twins are rigorously useful only for measuring nongenetic factors; any differences in individuals who have identical genes must be due to nongenetic factors.

In addition to the methodological drawbacks of twin studies, there is a fundamental difficulty with heritability estimates: They supply a number in place of an explanation. A satisfying explanation of the cause of a human mental characteristic would describe a chain of causal events (including activation of genes), rather than just arithmetic. If we knew everything we would want to know about a single gene whose protein interacts with the environment to produce additional effects, we might end up with a progression like, "A caused B, which combined with C to produce D, which was modified by E," and so on. How does one then quantify the role of A or C? It is a bit like asking what percentage contribution George Washington made to the establishment of the United States. Any sensible answer would not be a percentage; it would be a story.

## GENE REGULATION

An indication of the kind of story that is likely to emerge for complex human mental characteristics can be gained by examining recent findings in the areas of gene regulation and the neurobiological mechanisms of behavior. It has become clear in recent years that the story of how a particular gene leads to production of a particular protein at the right time and place, and in the right amount, is often much richer than was previously believed.

Our current understanding is based on a large number of careful studies by molecular biologists working with nonhuman animals or with generations of cells grown outside the body. For many genes, there is a sophisticated network of regulatory mechanisms that fine tunes the production of the protein. This regulatory network includes pieces of DNA adjacent to the gene and other pieces of DNA quite distant from the gene, both of which strongly influence the amount of protein produced. These regions of DNA can have their effects modified by interactions with multiple proteins produced by other genes and with substances acquired from the diet. Interactions with intermediary RNA molecules are also common. Each interaction can either increase or decrease the amount of protein produced; these interactions are not necessarily additive. The net effect of all these interactions is that the amount of protein produced from a particular gene in a particular cell can depend on its history of cell division, its location in the body, its hormonal environment, and the amount and existence of substances from the diet found in the bloodstream. The picture is one of an immensely complex regulatory system, something like the federal bureaucracy, but one that runs smoothly and efficiently in most circumstances.

Many gene regulatory systems probably include important environmental contributions at the molecular level. Such influences are still difficult to study in human beings, but some have been studied in detail in microorganisms. For example, when the bacteria *E. coli* is grown in the presence of two sugars, glucose and lactose, it uses all of the glucose first, then switches to lactose. To do so, it activates several genes for lactose metabolism only when lactose is present and glucose is absent, via interactions among several types of sugar and protein molecules.

If such complex interactions with food molecules occur in single-celled organisms, which are often thought of as being entirely programmed by their genes, interactions with the environment are likely to be very extensive in human beings, leading to a variety of changes in metabolism and physiological functions. Most genetic and environmental effects on behavior are mediated by the nervous system. Environmental conditions have been shown to affect the growth of individual nerve cells (neurons) and the number and strength of connections amongst neurons, both during development and in adults (Greenough and Bailey 1988).

For example, adult rats develop more structural elaborations in neurons if they live in a complex environment full of toys, than if they live in a blank cage. More dramatic changes can occur in early development. For example, if a cat or monkey is reared with one eye closed during the first several weeks of life, the organization of inputs to a visual portion of the cerebral cortex is permanently altered, and neurons that would normally respond to an object seen by either eye now respond only via the eve that has remained open throughout (Purves and Lichtman 1985).

In embryonic stages, when the numbers, types, and locations of all cells are determined, genes specify players and rules for an extraordinarily complex game, which must be played out to create the body design. The conditions of the playing field can play a critical roll. Imagine that the Los Angeles Raiders are playing football against the Chicago Bears; it could make a great difference whether the game is played on a warm, sunny day in Los Angeles or in Chicago in a snowstorm.

For example, a human fetus is normally exposed to sex hormones that have diverse effects on gene regulation, leading to changes in the brain and laying the groundwork for all external sex differences (Breedlove 1994). Most, but not all, of the hormones are produced by the fetus itself. However, if for some reason the fetus or the mother produces too little or too much of a specific hormone (for example, testosterone or another androgen), or if the fetus lacks appropriate receptor molecules for the hormone, the results can be dramatically different. In cases of androgen-insensitivity syndrome, for example, a genetically male human being can become a completely normal female, except that her internal reproductive organs are inadequately formed; in these cases, the fetus has a defective gene for the androgen receptor protein. In other cases, the amount of circulating androgen can be too great and cause prenatal masculinization of genetic females, transforming the clitoris partly or completely into a penis; this condition can be caused either by a genetic defect (producing adrenal hyperplasia) or by treatment of pregnant women with the hormone progestin (a practice that occurred in the 1950s, before the effects were realized; Money and Erhardt 1972).

For most genes, it is difficult to predict what will happen if you delete or alter one gene. The effects are not likely to be limited to the amount of the protein coded for by that gene. Instead, there may be positive or negative effects on several other proteins, because each gene may interact with other DNA, RNA, proteins, hormones, and substances from the diet to mediate gene regulation. An analogy can be drawn between these interactions and the interactions amongst neurons that mediate behavior. The concept that each neuron can affect many other neurons in a complex interactive network has received considerable attention in neurobiological research. Findings from neurobiological research may thus be useful for understanding gene regulation.

## What Can We Learn from Neurobiology?

Since the nineteenth century, neurobiologists have debated whether particular functions can be identified with particular regions of the brain. It is now recognized that particular sets of neurons and connections amongst neurons do serve particular functions. However, the functions they serve do not necessarily correspond to categories of behavioral function that we have names for. Also, within a given small region of the nervous system, one may find neurons that are involved in quite different functions. If one region of the brain is damaged, particularly in children, functions formerly subserved by that region may not be disrupted seriously or permanently; remaining neurons may continue to mediate the function reasonably well and other regions may gradually take over the functions of the damaged region. These insights have led to the concept of a "distributed network" to describe the nervous system. I suggest that the regulation of protein production from genes, and thus genetic effects on behavior, may also be mediated by a distributed network.

Some of the most popular targets for research on genes affecting mental characteristics are genes that code for neurotransmitter receptors. Neurotransmitters are the substances that mediate communication between neurons; they produce an electrical signal in a recipient neuron by altering the structure of neurotransmitter receptors, which in turn prevent or allow positively or negatively charged molecules to enter or leave the neuron. Drugs that affect cognition or behavior, including drugs that are used to treat depression and schizophrenia, produce their effects by attaching to specific neurotransmitter receptors.

The reported genetic linkage to alcoholism, by Blum, Noble, and colleagues in 1990, claimed linkage to a candidate gene, which was a form of the gene for a particular receptor of the neurotransmitter dopamine. It would not be surprising if alterations in a neurotransmitter receptor had widespread effects on the nervous system, but how likely is it that a particular neurotransmitter or neurotransmitter receptor can be identified with one of our categories of human mental and behavioral characteristics?

Each neurotransmitter is used by a very large number of neurons that are distributed over much of the nervous system. Neurons that communicate using one neurotransmitter are often interspersed with neurons that use others instead. There are generally several types of neurotransmitter receptors for a given neurotransmitter; each type can confer distinct electrical properties on the neurons that house them.

Even just a single type of receptor for a single neurotransmitter is generally distributed over much of the nervous system, in a complex but reliable pattern. Such patterns do not appear to delimit the set of neurons that participate in any single function that we can name. Instead, it now appears likely that each neurotransmitter receptor is like a component of an electrical circuit. Different types of components are useful for different electrical purposes. For example, one neurotransmitter receptor, called the NMDA receptor, has special properties that produce an electrical signal only when multiple, associated events occur simultaneously: In this case, the electrical signal lasts for an especially long time. Each cognitive or behavioral process probably involves a variety of such specific components deployed as needed in different portions of its "circuit."

Neurobiologists have tried to understand the roles played by particular neurons or connections among neurons in distributed networks. They have found that even after a network of interactions has been almost completely described, it is difficult to define the role of any single element. Such detailed knowledge of a network is currently available only for very small neural systems, such as one responsible for swimming in a marine mollusk named Tritonia and another responsible for digestion in lobsters and crabs. Researchers have drawn "circuit diagrams" of these systems, but examination of these diagrams, in which each neuron is connected to several other neurons, has not revealed what each neuron does during operation of the circuit.

Even these relatively simple systems involve interactions that are too complex for human understanding to assimilate directly. Instead, researchers have found it useful to create computer-based models of these networks, in which they can easily alter just one neuron or one interaction and see what outcome the network then produces, which can be surprising.

For example, physiological experiments revealed a set of neurons that are active during swimming in Tritonia, but it was not clear how their interaction could produce swimming, nor whether these neurons alone are sufficient to generate swimming. Some of the connections among these neurons are very complex, involving both inhibition and excitation of each recipient neuron, each with a distinct time course. A computer simulation of this network showed that this set of neurons could produce an output very similar to swimming and that the network created swimming by effectively alternating between two patterns of neuronal connectivity on each cycle of swimming (Getting 1983). Computer experiments like these gradually increase our understanding of the role of each neuron and each interaction.

This line of research may provide a lesson for the study of gene regulation. Understanding the full behavioral effect of altering a particular gene may require knowledge of all the interactions that involve that gene and their functional consequences. Even then, the effects of a gene may not correspond to a particular category of function.

We may find that a network of interactions, rather than a gene, can be more accurately identified with a particular function. In other words, there may be "emergent" properties of the network that are not evident in the effects of most single genes or single proteins on their own. In such cases, the same gene may have quite different effects on a behavior depending on the context, which may include important environmental influences.

In addition, the same gene may have effects on multiple types of behavior or cognitive function. Thus, even if a genuine genetic link to manic-depression, for example, is someday found, it might turn out that the gene can exacerbate certain symptoms of manic-depression, but only if combined with other factors, and that the gene also can have effects on individuals who are not categorized as manic-depressive. In such a situation, the notion that the gene's effect is to cause manic-depression could be quite misleading.

## THE ALLURE OF SIMPLE GENETIC EXPLANATIONS

Given the complex interactions that appear to mediate the development and operation of human cognitive and behavioral functions, why do some scientists and journalists apparently search for simple genetic explanations? The search for a gene for each category of experience and behavior may partly be a result of the culture of modern science. Scientists generally seek to reduce complex phenomena to simple descriptions. Such simplification has proven to be extremely useful in devising experiments that will give clear and informative results. Scientists often choose an object for study (such as a particular function in a particular organism) because it is simple and thus more tractable. Such choices have facilitated remarkable progress in understanding principles of function. However, in the desire to extrapolate findings from simple systems to the most sophisticated functions of human beings, it is sometimes forgotten that different or additional principles may apply to the most complex systems.

Some simplification is also key to any understanding of a phenomenon. In providing any scientific explanation, scientists define the essential factors at work, extracting them from a morass of detail, much of which is unimportant for the questions at hand. But the type of explanation that provides us with the most understanding is not necessarily the simplest. The reductionism that most scientists espouse leads to descriptions in terms of progressively simpler and usually smaller elements. But many phenomena have emergent properties that cannot be observed or appreciated in descriptions of the smallest components.

Instead, explanations that describe processes at a level of organization not too distant from the phenomenon itself often provide the most understanding. For example, an explanation of human behavior that includes a description of how certain networks of neurons are active during the behavior may provide greater understanding of how the behavior is produced than an explanation solely at the level of genes or smaller components. If we had a complete description of alcoholism in terms of subatomic particles alone, would you feel that you now understood alcoholism?

There is also a danger of oversimplification by omission or inaccurate portrayal of factors that are crucial to research objectives. Scientists are often schooled to provide the most parsimonious explanations of phenomena, on the grounds that a complicated explanation should not be put forward if the evidence supports a simple scheme just as well. The problem is that the desire for parsimony can sometimes lead researchers to choose a simple explanation even when the evidence actually points to a more complicated scheme. For example, it has been known for some time that concordances (the odds that two individuals will either both have or both not have a given trait) for schizophrenia are much higher for identical twins (39–46%) and for children of two schizophrenic parents (34–43%) than for first-degree relatives (4–12%). This situation is incompatible with single-gene causation of schizophrenia independent of the environment, yet that is exactly what many investigators looked for (Cloninger 1994).

An additional misinterpretation of studies claiming linkage between a gene and a human behavior is the notion that the behavior is therefore destined. There is a widespread and yet completely false notion that if something has a genetic cause, it is unalterable, but if it has an environmental cause, it is alterable. Some people respond to new claims of linkage between a gene and a certain characteristic—for example, alcoholism or homosexuality—by arguing that this proves that the characteristic was fixed from birth.

Such an explanation may seem attractive if one wishes to deny that either personal choice or societal conditions contribute to the characteristic. For example, in a recent report on the mouse obese gene (Monmaney 1995, p. 21), the *Los Angeles Times* stated: "An important social implication of the obesity gene research, researchers say, is that it shows that obesity is not a weakness or a failure of willpower. In that sense, this high-tech lab work may help erase some of the stigma of being fat."

In fact, some conditions known to be caused by genes alone can be prevented or reversed by nongenetic means, such as providing a phenylalanine-free diet to children who have the genetic disorder phenylketonuria (PKU). On the other hand, some environmental events, such as alcohol abuse by pregnant women, can often have permanent effects (Spohr et al. 1993).

The idea that our genes make us who we are has been so successful that even scientists occasionally mistake evidence of a biological correlate of a mental or emotional characteristic for evidence that the characteristic is determined genetically. For example, when a group of researchers reported in 1994 that they had isolated the mouse "obese" gene, they introduced their work by stating, "[a]lthough obesity is often considered to be a psychological problem, there is evidence that body weight is physiologically regulated" (Zhang et al.

1994). In fact, psychological influences are necessarily mediated by physiological mechanisms.

A discovery of a biological correlate addresses neither the role of genes nor the role of nongenetic factors. The notion that "biological" implies "genetic" seems to assume that nongenetic events affect us without affecting our bodies, and in particular our brains. Within a scientific world view, at least, such a view is untenable. One expects all effects on cognition or behavior to be mediated by changes in the body, usually in the nervous system. This says nothing about the original cause of the change, nor our responsibility for it.

Research into gene regulation and neurobiology has revealed intricate interactions among genes, proteins, hormones, food, and life experiences. These findings suggest that lasting explanations of most human mental and behavioral characteristics will not be simple and will arise only gradually. A real understanding of the causation of complex characteristics may require us to come to terms with the emergent properties of multiple interactions. In the meantime, pronouncements of simple genetic causation should be met with a critical eye and with questions about exactly what has and has not been demonstrated.

## References

Alper, J. S.; Natowicz, M. R. (1993) "On establishing the genetic basis of mental disease." *Trends in Neuroscience,* 16:387–389.

Baron, M.; Risch, N.; Hamburger, R.; Mandel, B.; Kushner, S.; Newman, M.; Drumer, D.; Belmaker, R. H. (1987) "Genetic linkage between X-chromosome markers and bipolar affective illness." *Nature,* 326:289–292.

Baron, M.; Freimer, N. F.; Risch, N.; Lerer, B.; Alexander, J. R.; Straub, R. E.; Asokan, S.; Das, K.; Peterson, A.; Amos, J.; Endicott, J.; Ott, J.; Gilliam, T. C. (1993) "Diminished support for linkage between manic depressive illness and X-chromosome markers in three Israeli pedigrees." *Nature Genetics,* 3:49–55.

Berrettini, W. H.; Ferraro, T. N.; Goldin, L. R.; Weeks, D. E.; Detera-Wadleigh, S.; Nurnberger, J. I. Jr.; Gershon, E. S. (1994) "Chromosome 18 DNA markers and manic-depressive illness: Evidence for a susceptibility gene." *Proc. Natl. Acad. Sci.,* 91:5918–5921.

Billings, P. R.; Beckwith, J.; Alper, J. S. (1992) "The genetic analysis of human behavior: A new era?" *Social Science and Medicine,* 35:227–238.

Blum, K.; Noble, E. P.; Sheridan, P. J.; Montgomery, A.; Ritchie, T.; Jagadeeswaran, P.; Nogami, H.; Brigg, A. H.; Cohn, J. B. (1990) "Allelic association of human dopamine D2 receptor gene in alcoholism." *JAMA,* 263:2055–2060.

Blum. K.; Noble, E. P. (1994) "The Sobering D2 Story." *Science,* 265:1346–1347.

Bouchard, T. J. Jr.; Lykken, D. T.; McGue, M.; Segal, N. L.; Tellegen, A. (1990) "Sources of human psychological differences: The Minnesota study of twins reared apart." *Science,* 250:223–228.

Breedlove, S. M. (1994) "Sexual differentiation of the human nervous system." *Annu. Rev. Psychol.,* 45:389–418.

Capdevila, M. P.; Garcia-Bellido, A. (1978) "Phenocopies of bithorax mutants: Genetic and developmental analyses." *Wilhelm Roux's Archives,* 185:105–126.

Cloninger, C. R. (1994) "Turning point in the design of linkage studies of schizophrenia." *Am. J. Med. Genet.,* 54:83–92.

Davenport, C. B. (1928) "Crime, heredity and environment." *Journal of Heredity,* 19: 307–313, p. 313.

Dawkins, R. (1982) *The Extended Phenotype.* Oxford, UK: W. H. Freeman and Co.

Detera-Wadleigh, S. D.; Berrettini, W. H.; Goldin, L. R.; Boorman, D.; Anderson, S.; Gershon, E. S. (1987) "Close linkage of c-Harvey-ras-1 and the insulin gene to affective disorder is ruled out in three North American pedigrees. *Nature,* 325:806–808.

Egeland, J. A.; Gerhard, D. S.; Pauls, D. L.; Sussex, J. N.; Kidd, K. K.; Allen, C. R.; Hostetter, A. M.; Housma, D. E. (1987) "Bipolar affective disorders linked to DNA markers on chromosome 11." *Nature,* 325:783–787.

Gelernter, J.; O'Malley, S.; Risch, N.; Kranzler, H. R.; Krystal, J.; Merikangas, K.; Kennedy, J. L.; Kidd, K. K. (1991) "No association between an allele at the D2 dopamine receptor gene (DRD2) and alcoholism." *JAMA,* 266: 1801–1807.

Gelernter, J.; Goldman, D.; Risch, N. (1993) "The A1 allele at the D2 dopamine receptor gene and alcoholism: A reappraisal." *JAMA,* 269:1673–1677.

Gershon, E. S.; Cloninger, C. R. (1994) "Genetic approaches to mental disorders." Washington, DC: American Psychiatric Press.

Getting, P. A. (1983) "Mechanisms of pattern generation underlying swimming in tritonia. II. Network reconstruction." *J. Neurophysiol.,* 49:1017–1035.

Goleman, D. (1995) "Gene link found to bed-wetting, proving problem isn't emotional." *New York Times,* 1 July: 1.

Greenough, W. T.; Bailey, C. H. (1988) "The anatomy of memory: Convergence of results across a diversity of tests." *Trends Neurosci.,* 11:142–147.

Hamer, D. H.; Hu, S.; Magnuson, V. L.; Hu, N.; Pattatucci, A. M. L. (1993) "A linkage between DNA markers on the X-chromosome and mate sexual orientation." *Science,* 261:321–327.

Hartl, D. L.; Clark, A. G. (1989) *Principles of Population Genetics.* (2nd ed.) Sunderland, MA: Sinauer Associates.

Hodgkinson, S.; Sherrington, R.; Gurling, H.; Marchbanks, R.; Reeders, S.; Mallet, J.; McInnis, M.; Petursson, H.; Brynjolfsson, J. (1987) "Molecular genetic evidence for heterogeneity in manic depression." *Nature,* 325:805–806.

Jaroff, L. (1989) "The gene hunt." *Time,* 20 March: 62–67.

Kamin, L. J. (1974) *The Science and Politics of IQ.* Potomac, MD: Lawrence Erlbaum Associates.

Kelsoe, J. R.; Ginns, E. I.; Egeland, J. A.; Gerhard, D. S.; Goldstein, A. M.; Bale, S. J.; Pauls, D. L.; Long, R. T.; Kidd, K. K.; Conte, G.; Housman, D. E.; Paul, S. M. (1989) "Reevaluation of the linkage relationship between chromosome 11p loci and the gene for bipolar affective disorder in the old order Amish." *Nature,* 342:238–243.

Kempthorne, O. (1978) "Logical, epistemological and statistical aspects of nature-nurture data interpretation." *Biometrics* 34:1–23.

Kennedy, J. L.; Guiffra, L. A.; Moises, H. W.; Cavalli-Sforza, L. L.; Pakstis, A. L.; Kidd, J. R.; Castiglione, C. M.; Sjogren, B.; Wetterberg, L.; Kidd, K. K.; (1988) "Evidence against linkage of schizophrenia to markers on chromosome 5 in a northern Swedish pedigree." *Nature*, 336:167–170.

Koshland, D. E. (1990) "The rational approach to the irrational." *Science*, 250:189.

Lewis, R. (1994) *Case Workbook in Human Genetics.* Dubuque, IA: Wm. C. Brown Publishers, p. E17.

Lewontin, R. C. (1974) "The analysis of variance and the analysis of causes." *Am. J. Hum. Genet.,* 26:400–411.

Lewontin, R. C.; Rose, S.; Kamin, L. J. (1984) *Not in Our Genes.* New York: Pantheon Books.

Money, J.; Erhardt, A. A. (1972) *Man & Woman, Boy & Girl.* Baltimore, MD: The Johns Hopkins University Press.

Olen, H. (1995) "Rutgers remains embroiled over power of a few words." *Los Angeles Times,* 20 Feb.:EA5

Pauls, D. L. (1993) "Behavioural disorders: Lessons in linkage." *Nature Genetics,* 3:4–5.

Peele, S. (1990) "Second thoughts about a gene for alcoholism." *The Atlantic Monthly,* August:52–58.

Plomin, R.; Owen, M. J.; McGuffin, P. (1994) "The genetic basis of complex human behaviors." *Science,* 264:1733–1739.

Powledge, T. M. (1993) "The inheritance of behavior in twins." *BioScience,* 43:420–424.

Purves, D.; Lichtman, J. W. (1985) *Principles of Neural Development.* Sunderland, MA: Sinauer Associates.

Risch, N. J. (1994) "Mapping genes for psychiatric disorders." In *Genetic Approaches to Mental Disorders.* E. S. Gershon and C. R. Cloninger, eds. Washington, DC: American Psychiatric Press.

Robertson, M. (1987) "Molecular genetics of the mind." *Nature,* 325–755.

Robertson, M. (1989) "False start on manic depression." *Nature,* 342:222.

Rose, S. (1995) "The rise of neurogenetic determinism." *Nature,* 373:380–382.

Sherrington, R.; Brynjolfsson, J.; Petursson, H.; Potter, M.; Dudleston, K.; Barraclough, B.; Wasmuth, J.; Dobbs, M.; Gurling, H. (1988) "Localization of susceptibility locus for schizophrenia on chromosome 5." *Nature,* 336: 164–167.

Sinsheimer, R. L. (1969) "The prospect of designed genetic change." *Engineering and Science,* 32:8–13.

Sinsheimer, R. L. (1991) "The human genome initiative." *FASEB Journal,* 5:2885.

Spohr, H. L.; Wilms, J.; Steinhausen, H. C. (1993) "Prenatal alcohol exposure and long-term development of consequences." *Lancet* 341:907–910.

Straub, R. E.; Lehner, T.; Luo, Y.; Loth, J. E.; Shao, W.; Sharpe, L.; Alexander, J. R.; Das, K.; Simon, R.; Fieve, R. R.; Lerer, B.; Endicott, J.; Ott, J.; Gilliam, T. C.; Baron, M. (1994) "A possible vulnerability locus for bipolar affective disorder on chromosome 21q22.3." *Nature Genetics,* 8:291–296.

Zhang, Y.; Proenca, R.; Maffel, M.; Barone, M.; Leopold, L.; Friedman, J. M. (1994) "Positional cloning of the mouse obese gene and its human homologue." *Nature,* 372:425–432.

# Chapter 59

# *A Gene for Nothing*

## Robert Sapolsky

Well, these last six months have been an exciting time for the sheep named Dolly, ever since it was revealed that she was the first mammal cloned from adult cells. There was the night she spent in the Lincoln bedroom and the photo op with Al Gore; the triumphant ticker-tape parade down Broadway, the billboard ads for Guess Genes. Throughout the media circus, Dolly has been poised, patient, cordial, and even-tempered—the epitome of what we look for in a celebrity and role model. But despite her charm, people keep saying mean things about Dolly. Heads of state, religious leaders, and editorialists fall over themselves in calling her an aberration of nature and an insult to the sacred biological wonder of reproduction. They thunder about the anathema of even considering applying to humans the technology that spawned her.

What's everyone so upset about? Why is cloning so disturbing? Clearly, it's not the potential for droves of clones running around with the exact same renal filtration rate that has everyone up in arms. It's probably not even the threat of winding up with a bunch of clones who look identical, creepy though that would be. No, the read horror is the prospect of having multiple copies of a single brain, with the same neurons and the same genes directing those neurons, one multibodied consciousness among the clones, an army of photocopies of the same soul, all thinking, feeling, and acting identically.

Fortunately, that can't happen, as people have known ever since scientists discovered identical twins. Such individuals constitute genetic clones, just like Dolly and her "mother"—the sheep from which the original cell was taken. Despite all those breathless stories about identical twins separated at birth who flush the toilet before using it, twins are not melded in mind, do not behave identically. For example, if an identical twin is schizophrenic, the sibling, with the identical "schizo-phrenia gene(s)," has only about a 50 percent chance of having the disease.

A similar finding comes from a fascinating experiment by Dan Weinberger of the National Institute of Mental Health. Give identical twins a puzzle to solve and they might come up with closer answers than one would expect from a pair of strangers. While they're working on the puzzle, however, hook the twins up to a PET scanner, a brain-imaging instrument that visualizes metabolic demands in different regions of the brain. You'll find the pattern of activation in the pair differing considerably, despite the similarity of their solutions. Or use an MRI to get some detailed pictures of the brains of identical twins and start measuring stuff obsessively—the length of this part, the width of that, the volume of another region, and the surface area of the cortex—and those identical twins with their identical genes never have identical brains. Every measure differs.

The careful editorialists have made this point. Nonetheless, that business about identical genes producing identical brains, tugs at a lot of people. Gene-behavior stories are constantly getting propelled to the front pages of newspapers. One popped up shortly before Dolly, when a team of researchers reported that a single gene, called fru, determines the sexual behavior of male fruit flies. Courtship, opening lines, foreplay, who they come on to—the works. Mutate that gene and—get this—you can even change the sexual orientation of the fly. What made the story front-page news, of course, wasn't our insatiable fly voyeurism. "Could our sexual behaviors be determined by a single gene as well?" every article asked. And a bit earlier, there was the hubbub about the isolation of a gene related to anxiety in humans, and shortly before that, a gene related to novelty-seeking behavior, and a while before that, a gene whose mutation in one family was associated with violent antisocial behavior, and before that . . .

Why do these stories command attention? For many, genes and the DNA they contain represent the

From *Discover*, October, 1997.

holy grail of biology, the code of codes (two phrases often used in lay discussions of genetics). The worship at the altar of the gene rests on two assumptions. The first concerns the autonomy of genetic regulation: It is the notion that biological information begins with genes—DNA is the commander, the epicenter from which biology emanates. Nobody tells a gene what to do; it's always the other way around. The second assumption is that when genes give a command, biological systems listen. Genes, the story goes, instruct your cells as to their structure and function. And when those cells are neurons, their functions include thought, feelings, and behavior. Thus, the gene worshipers believe, we are finally identifying the biological factors that make us do what we do.

A typical example of the code-of-codes view recently appeared in a lead *New Yorker* article by Louis Menand, an English professor at the City University of New York. Menand ruminates on anxiety genes, when "one little gene is firing off a signal to bite your fingernails" (there's that first assumption—autonomous genes firing off whenever some notion pops into their heads). He asks himself how we can reconcile societal, economic, and psychological explanations of behavior with those ironclad genes. "The view that behavior is determined by an inherited genetic package" (there's the second assumption—genes as irresistible commanders) "is not easily reconciled with the view that behavior is determined by the kinds of movies a person watches." And what is the solution? "It is like having the Greek gods and the Inca gods occupying the same pantheon. Somebody's got to go."

In other words, if you buy into the notion of genes firing off and determining our behaviors, such modern scientific findings are simply incompatible with the environment having an influence. Something's gotta go.

Now, I'm not sure what sort of genetics they teach in Menand's English department, but the something's-gotta-go loggerhead is what most behavioral biologists have been trying to unteach for decades, apparently with limited success. Which is why it's worth another try.

Okay. You've got nature—neurons, brain chemicals, hormones, and of course, at the bottom of the cereal box, genes. And then there's nurture, all those environmental breezes gusting about. Again and again, behavioral biologists insist that you can't talk meaningfully about nature or nurture, only about their interaction. But somehow people can't seem to keep that thought in their heads. Instead, whenever a new gene is trotted out that "determines" a behavior by "firing off," they see environmental influences as the irrelevant something that has to go. Soon poor, sweet Dolly is a menace to our autonomy as individuals, and genes are understood to control who you go to bed with and whether you feel anxious about it.

Let's try to undo the notion of genes as neurobiological and behavioral destiny by examining those two

assumptions, beginning with the second one—that cells, including those in our heads, obey genetic commands. What exactly do genes do? A gene, a stretch of DNA, does not produce a behavior. A gene does not produce an emotion, or even a fleeting thought. It produces a protein. Each gene is a specific DNA sequence that codes for a specific protein. Some of these proteins certainly have lots to do with behavior and feelings and thoughts; proteins include some hormones (which carry messages between cells) and neurotransmitters (which carry messages between nerve cells); they also include receptors that receive hormonal and neurotransmitter messages, the enzymes that synthesize and degrade those messengers, many of the intracellular messengers triggered by those hormones, and so on. All those proteins are vital for a brain to do its business. But only very rarely do things like hormones and neurotransmitters cause a behavior to happen. Instead they produce tendencies to respond to the environment in certain ways.

To illustrate this critical point, let's consider anxiety. When an organism is confronted with a threat, it typically becomes vigilant, searches for information about the nature of the threat, and struggles to find an effective coping response. Once it receives a signal indicating safety—the lion has been evaded, the traffic cop buys the explanation and doesn't issue a ticket—the organism can relax. But that's not what happens with an anxious individual. Instead this person will skitter frantically among coping responses, abruptly shifting from one to another without checking whether anything has worked. He may have a hard time detecting the safety signal and knowing when to stop his restless vigilance. Moreover, the world presents a lot of triggers that not everyone reacts to. For the anxious individual, the threshold is lower, so that the mere sight of a police car in the rearview mirror can provoke the same storm of uneasiness as actually being stopped. By definition, anxiety makes little sense outside the context of what the environment is doing to an individual. In that framework, the brain chemicals and genes relevant to anxiety don't make you anxious. They make you more responsive to anxiety-provoking situations, make it harder to detect safety signals.

The same theme continues in other behaviors as well. The exciting (made-of-protein) receptor that apparently has to do with novelty-seeking behavior doesn't actually make you seek novelty. It makes you more pleasurably excited than folks without that receptor variant get when you happen to encounter a novel environment. And those (genetically influenced) neurochemical abnormalities of depression don't make you depressed. They make you more vulnerable to stressors in the environment, to deciding that you are helpless even when you're not.

One might retort that in the long run we are all exposed to anxiety-provoking circumstances, all exposed to the depressing world around us. If we are all exposed to those same environmental factors but only the people who are genetically prone to depression get depressed, that is a pretty powerful vote for genes. In that scenario, the "genes don't cause things; they just make you more sensitive to the environment" argument becomes empty and semantic.

The problems here, however, are twofold. First, a substantial minority of people with a genetic legacy of depression do not get depressed, and not everyone who has a major depression has a genetic legacy for it. Genetic status is not all that predictive by itself. Second, we share the same environments only on a very superficial level. For example, the incidence of depression (and its probable biological underpinnings) seem to be roughly equal throughout the world. However, geriatric depression is epidemic in our society and far less prevalent in traditional societies in the developing world. Why? Different societies produce remarkably different social environments, in which old age can mean being a powerful village elder or an infantilized has-been put out to a shuffleboard pasture.

The environmental differences can be more subtle. Periods of psychological stress involving loss of control and predictability during childhood may well predispose one toward adult depression. Two children may have had similar childhood lessons in "there's bad things out there that I can't control"—both may have seen their parents divorce, lost a grandparent, tearfully buried a pet in the backyard, faced the endless menacing of a bully. Yet the temporal pattern of their experience is unlikely to be identical, and the child who experiences all those stressors over a one-year period instead of over six years is far more likely to come with the cognitive distortion, "There's bad things out there that I can't control and, in fact, I can't control anything," that sets you up for depression. The biological factors that genes code for in the nervous system typically don't determine behavior. Instead they affect how you respond to often very subtle influences in the environment. There are genetic vulnerabilities, tendencies, predispositions—but rarely genetic inevitabilities.

Now let's go back to that first assumption about behavioral genetics—that genes always have minds of their own. It takes just two startling facts about the structure of genes to blow this one out of the water.

A chromosome is made of DNA, a vastly long string of it, a long sequence of letters coding for genetic information. People used to think that Gene 1 would comprise the first eleventy letters of the DNA message. A special letter sequence would signal the end of that gene, the next eleventy and a half letters would code for Gene 2, and so on, through tens of thousands of genes. Gene 1 might specify the construction of insulin in your pancreas; Gene 2 might specify protein pigments that give eyes their color; and Gene 3, active in neurons, might make you aggressive. Ah, caught you: might make you more sensitive to aggression-provoking stimuli in the environment. Different people have different versions of Genes 1, 2, and 3, some of which work better than others. An army of biochemicals do the scut work, transcribing the genes, reading the DNA sequences, and following the instructions they contain for constructing the appropriate proteins.

As it turns out, that's not really how things work. Instead of one gene coming immediately after another, with the entire string of DNA devoted to coding for different proteins, there are long stretches of DNA that don't get transcribed. Sometimes those stretches even split up a gene into subsections. Some of the nontranscribed, noncoding DNA doesn't seem to do anything. It may have some function that we don't yet understand, or it may have none at all. But some of the noncoding DNA does something very interesting indeed. It's the instruction manual for how and when to activate genes. These stretches have many names—regulatory elements, promoters, responsive elements. Various biochemical messengers may bind to each of them, altering the activity of the gene immediately "downstream"—immediately following it in the string of DNA.

Far from being autonomous sources of information, then, genes must obey other factors that regulate when and how they function. Very often, those factors are environmental. For example, suppose something stressful happens to a primate. A drought, say, forces it to forage miles each day for food. As a result, the animal secretes a stress hormone, cortisol, from its adrenals. Cortisol molecules enter fat cells and bind to cortisol receptors. These hormone-receptor complexes find their way to the DNA and bind to a regulatory stretch of DNA. Whereupon a gene downstream is activated, which produces a protein, which indirectly inhibits that fat cell from storing fat. It's a logical thing to do—while starving and walking the grasslands in search of a meal, the primate needs fat to fuel muscles, not to laze around in fat cells.

In effect, regulatory elements introduce the possibility of environmentally modulated if-then clauses. If the environment is tough and you're working hard to find food, then make use of your genes to divert energy to exercising muscles. The environment, of course, doesn't mean just the weather. The biology is essentially the same if a human refugee travels miles from home with insufficient food because of civil strife. The behavior of one human can change the pattern of gene activity in another.

Let's look at a fancier example of how environmental factors control the regulatory elements of DNA. Suppose that Gene 4037 (not its real name—it has one, but I'll spare you the jargon), when left to its own devices, is transcriptionally active, generating its protein. However, as long as a particular messenger binds to a regulatory element that comes just before 4037 in the DNA string, Gene 4037 shuts down. Fine. Now suppose that inhibitory messenger happens to be very sensitive to temperature. In fact, if the cell gets hot, the messenger goes to pieces and comes floating off the regulatory element. Freed from the inhibitory regulation, Gene 4037 will suddenly become active. Maybe it's a gene that works in the kidney and codes for a protein relevant to water retention. Boring—another metabolic story, this one having to do with how a warm environment triggers metabolic adaptations that stave off dehydration. But suppose, instead, Gene 4037 codes for an array of proteins that have something to do with sexual behavior. What have you just invented? Seasonal mating. Winter is waning, each day gets a little warmer, and in relevant cells in the brain, pituitary, or gonads, genes like 4037 are gradually becoming active. Finally some threshold is passed and, *wham,* everyone starts rutting and ovulating, snorting and pawing at the ground, and generally carrying on. (Actually, in most seasonal matters, the environmental signal for mating is the amount of daily light exposure, or the days are getting longer, rather than temperature, or the days are getting warmer. But the principle is the same.)

Here's a final, elegant example. Every cell in your body has a distinctive protein signature that marks it as yours. These "major histocompatability" proteins allow your immune system to tell the difference between you and some invading bacterium—that's why your body will reject a transplanted organ with a very different signature. When those signature proteins get into a mouse's urine, they help make its odor distinct. For a rodent, that's important stuff. Design receptors in olfactory cells in a rodent's nose that can distinguish signature odorant proteins similar to its own from totally novel ones. The greater the similarity, the tighter the protein will fit into the receptor. What have you just invented? A way to distinguish between the smells of relatives and strangers—something rodents do effortlessly.

Keep tinkering with this science project. Now couple those olfactory receptors to a cascade of chemical messengers inside the cell, one messenger triggering the next until you get to the DNA's regulatory elements. What might you want to construct? How about: *If* an olfactory receptor binds an odorant indicating the presence of a relative, *then* trigger a cascade that ultimately inhibits the activity of genes related to reproduction. You've just invented a mechanism by which animals could avoid mating with close relatives. Or you can construct a different cascade: If an olfactory receptor binds an odorant indicating a relative, then inhibit genes that are normally active and that regulate the synthesis of testosterone. There you have a means by which rodents get bristly and aggressive when a strange male stinks up their burrow but not when the scent belongs to their kid brother.

In each of these examples you can begin to see the logic, an elegance that teams of engineers couldn't do much to improve. And now for the two facts about this regulation of genes that will dramatically change your view of them. First, when it comes to mammals, by the best estimates available, more than 95 percent of DNA is noncoding. Ninety-five percent. Sure, a lot of it may have no function, but your average gene comes with a huge instruction manual for how to operate it, and the operator is very often environmental. With a percentage like that, if you think about genes and behavior, you have to think about how the environment regulates genes and behavior.

The second fact involves genetic variation between individuals. A gene's DNA sequence often varies from person to person, which often translates into proteins that differ in how well they do their job. This is the grist for natural selection: Which is the most adaptive version of some (genetically influenced) trait? Given that evolutionary change occurs at the level of DNA, "survival of the fittest" really means "reproduction of individuals whose DNA sequences make for the most adaptive collection of proteins." But—here's that startling second fact—when you examine variability in DNA sequences among individuals, the noncoding regions of DNA are considerably more variable than are the regions that code for genes. Okay, a lot of that variability is attributable to DNA that doesn't do much and so is free to drift genetically over time without consequence. But there seems to be a considerable amount of variability in regulatory regions as well.

What does this mean? By now, I hope, we've gotten past "genes determine behavior" to "genes modulate how one responds to the environment." The business about 95 percent of DNA being non-coding should send us even further, to "genes can be convenient tools used by environmental factors to influence behavior." And that second fact about variability in noncoding regions means that it's less accurate to think "evolution is about natural selection for different assemblages of genes" than it is to think "evolution is about natural selection for different sensitivities and responses to environmental influences."

Sure, some behaviors are overwhelming under genetic control. Just consider all those mutant flies hopping into the sack with insects their parents disapprove of. And some mammalian behaviors, even human ones, are probably pretty heavily under genetic regulation as well. These are likely to code for behaviors that must be performed by everyone in much the same way for genes to be passed on. For example, all male primates have to go about the genetically based behavior of pelvic thrusting in fairly similar ways if they plan to reproduce successfully. But by the time you get to courtship, or emotions, or creativity, or mental illness, or any complex aspect of our lives, the intertwining of biological and environmental components utterly defeats any attempt to place them into separate categories, let alone to then decide that one of them has got to go.

I'm a bit hesitant to reveal the most telling example of how individuals with identical genes can nonetheless come up with very different behaviors, as I have it third-hand through the science grapevine, and I'll probably get some of the details wrong. But what the hell, it's such an interesting finding. It concerns the very extensive opinion poll that was carried out among sheep throughout the British Isles. Apparently, the researchers managed to get data from both Dolly and her gene-donor mother. So get a load of this bombshell: Dolly's mother voted Tory, listed the Queen Mum as her favorite royal, worried about mad cow disease ("Is it good or bad for the sheep?"), enjoyed Gilbert and Sullivan, and endorsed the statement, "Behavior? It's all nature." And Dolly? Votes Green Party, thinks Harry and William are the cutest, worries about "the environment," listens to the Spice Girls, and endorsed the statement, "Behavior? Nature. Or nurture. Whatever." You see, there's more to behavior than just genes.

# Index